Contributing Authors

Harold M. Anderson, University of Colorado
Vernon E. Anderson, University of Maryland
David C. Bartelma, University of Colorado
Frederick W. Bierhaus, University of Colorado
Nelson L. Bossing, Southern Illinois University
William G. Brink, Northwestern University
G. Robert Carlsen, State University of Iowa
Edwin R. Carr, Orange State College
Richard B. Dierenfield, Macalester College
Harl R. Douglass, University of Colorado
Edgar M. Draper, University of Washington
T. Bentley Edwards, University of California, Berkeley
Cloy S. Hobson, Fairbanks Public Schools, Alaska
Paul B. Jacobson, University of Oregon
Ann E. Jones, University of Colorado
Walter V. Kaulfers, University of Illinois
Lucien B. Kinney, Stanford University
Frances F. Kline, Fordham University
Dora S. Lewis, Hunter College of The City University of New York
John D. McNeil, University of California at Los Angeles
David Mallery, National Association of Independent Schools and West-
    ern Personnel Institute
Delmas Miller, West Virginia University
Hubert H. Mills, University of Colorado
Ira I. Nelson, The University of Texas
Albert I. Oliver, University of Pennsylvania
Ella J. Rose, formerly University of Minnesota
Clarence D. Samford, Southern Illinois University
Myllan Smyers, Southern Illinois University
Edwin A. Swanson, San Jose State College
L. A. Van Dyke, State University of Iowa
Gordon F. Vars, Cornell University
Ralph K. Watkins, University of Missouri
Bob G. Woods, University of Missouri

THE HIGH SCHOOL CURRICULUM

Edited by

HARL R. DOUGLASS

University of Colorado

38839

THIRD EDITION

THE RONALD PRESS COMPANY • NEW YORK

Library of Congress Catalog Card Number: 64–13941

PRINTED IN THE UNITED STATES OF AMERICA

Preface

This volume is intended as a textbook for courses in the high school curriculum and as a reference for teachers concerned about curriculum improvement. The Third Edition, like its authoritative predecessors, is the work of a group of recognized specialists whose years of training and experience in education have been employed in improving and constructing theories and practices in their respective fields.

The student using this book will gain an understanding of current curriculum problems as well as an insight into how basic theories of curriculum are analyzed and put to use. In-service teachers and other professionals in the field of education will find herein discussions of problems existing not only in their specific area but in other curriculum areas as well. Each chapter concludes with a selection of questions, problems, and topics for discussion that can be used at the discretion of the instructor. Some of this material will also prove very useful as a stimulus and guide to practicing teachers. The references at the end of each chapter were chosen, for the most part, with a view to supplementing the discussion in the chapter and to introduce new ideas, considerations, and facts.

The editor is greatly indebted to the various contributing authors, without whose sincere and painstaking cooperation this volume could not have been prepared. For them it was a labor of love and a desire to make a professional contribution in this area. The editor and the contributing authors are especially indebted to the writers and publishers of other publications from which quotations were made. Specific acknowledgment to each is indicated in footnotes throughout the book.

HARL R. DOUGLASS

Boulder, Colorado
January, 1964

Contents

THE HIGH SCHOOL
CURRICULUM

The Current Curriculum Problem

SOCIETAL NEEDS

The secondary school curriculum is usually a reflection of the society it serves. Provision for societal needs is likely to be listed as one of the basic objectives in curriculum development. It is true that discussion often centers around the question as to whether the curriculum should point the way to a better society or reflect the present needs. Even a cursory examination, however, of the secondary school curriculum will reveal that it is planned principally to help the pupil solve his daily problems rather than reshape society.

International Relations. There is a complexity of factors shaping societal needs. These factors must be recognized by secondary school curriculum planners, if the curriculum is to reflect the turbulent social order. Great challenges are posed on both the international and the domestic scene. International relations are increasingly complex: On the one hand is the fierce conflict between the two dominating ideologies of democracy and communism, posing the challenge of peaceful coexistence with economic and cultural parity; on the other is the exceedingly difficult task of coping with the social, economic, and cultural problems existing within the orbit of the free world itself. International understanding is no longer a lofty cliché, it is an absolute necessity for survival. The diminishing distances between peoples of the world and the increasing cultural exchanges of diverse extractions make necessary a fluid system of communication. Language barriers must be surmounted, and appreciation for the dignity of all cultures must be expedited.

1

Growth of Labor and Industry. The growth of materialism resulting from an industrialized society poses other complex challenges. Industry, by both necessity and design, has formed huge, dominating corporate organizations. Various industrial processes are completely controlled by single or interlocking corporate concerns. The forces of labor too, by either necessity or design, have organized into a limited number of powerful groups with tactical agreements for mutual cooperation.

In the field of mass communication, the trend is toward a limited number of powerful monopolistic media. Newspapers, television, and radio are dominated by merging, powerful corporate bodies marking the demise of the strong independent voice so necessary in a democratic order. People, themselves, are being affected by bigness and mass formations. The rapid urbanization of community living is marked by many problems such as increased crime and juvenile delinquency. The struggle for status symbols is evidence of the individual's effort to keep from being immersed in the anonymity of mass existence.

Government—a Big Business. Materialistic objectives dominate the industrialized social order, creating both gratifying benefits and grave problems. The area of government is illustrative of this situation. The tendency is for bigness and centralization. Multimillion dollar defense contracts are awarded; vast amounts of money are collected for social security and old-age benefits; and large areas of the nation are reclaimed for crop production through gigantic irrigation projects. The hugeness and complexity of government shrink the importance of the individual citizen. His identity suffers the possibility of being lost in a labyrinth of directives. All of these and other myriad social problems are important factors that must be considered by secondary school curriculum planners.

Population Changes. The second school curriculum for the sixties will be influenced tremendously by the population explosion and the continuing concentration of people in metropolitan areas. Both factors are associated with the mechanization and automation of the present age, and they greatly augment the complexity of educational and vocational needs. The occupational and social needs of space-age society are marked by extremes: On the one hand, automation places workers in sprawling factories, huge office buildings, and large mercantile establishments where they stand or sit all day and push buttons, a repetitious operation requiring little thought or ingenuity; while, on the other hand, the same automation and mechanization pave the way for swiftly advancing science and technology that may make the next fifty years the most significant in human history.

In 1930, farms and villages of less than 2,500 people were inhabited by 44 per cent of the population. By 1950, this figure was reduced to

36 per cent; by 1960, to 29 per cent; and it has continued to drop since. To conclude that the dulness of farm life and the glamor of the city are the basic causes of this migration is erroneous. The simple fact is that the development of scientific farming and the mechanization of processes have greatly reduced the need for manpower. Outside of periods of seasonable harvests, many workers must leave the rural area to seek employment. Further, it is estimated that one-half of the rural population must migrate, since the number of farm boys eighteen years of age is double that of older farmers who pass out of the picture.

The urbanization of people has been a change not merely in type of dwelling but also in mode of earning a living, relationship with other people, manner of recreation, home responsibilities, and many other aspects of daily living. Most of these changes are directly associated with problems of the youth, his home, and his school life. Work is largely divorced from family and home. The son is not needed to help his father, and the daughter is not needed to help her mother. Apartment dwellers have no lawns to mow, no snow to shovel, and no vegetable gardens to tend. Nor do factories, offices, or stores have apprenticeship openings for teen-agers. Youths often are deprived of the chance to work and are faced with the alternatives of going to school or roaming the streets. This leaves the secondary school curriculum planner with the unenviable task of meeting the needs of the total adolescent population.

Changes in Work Situations. Associated with the problem of meeting societal needs of the total youth population is the ever increasing complexity of skills needed for a wide variety of educational pursuits. White-collar workers have more than doubled in number since 1950 and now represent almost half of the labor force. It is predicted that, by 1975, 25 per cent of the working group will be classified as professional, technical, and managerial. The demand for non-trained or non-skilled labor will be reduced to almost none at all. This means that growing needs in the service fields will necessitate some type of preparatory training. The increased employment in the service fields is another impact of technological change. The nation now has more people engaged in industries that produce services than in industries that produce tangible goods. There are 33 million workers engaged in such areas as transportation, trade, finance, and government.

Expanding Technology. Educational needs as well as vocational needs are greatly increased by the expanding population and the advancing technology. The nation has rapidly passed through the atomic age and is now well into the space age. The demand for education beyond secondary school has increased correspondingly. There are hundreds of technical and subprofessional specialities that require from one to four years beyond high school. It is easy to foresee the time when more than half, perhaps three-fourths, of all young people of college age will be getting some kind of formal education above the high school level. It can be reasonably assumed that the program of education beyond the high school necessarily will be much broader and more diversified. This has far-reaching implications for the curriculum needs of the preparatory stages of education that remain the responsibility of the secondary school.

Increased Complexity of Life as a Citizen. Society has always looked to its schools for broadly comprehensive training in citizenship. The schools have responded with such declarations of purpose as the "Seven Cardinal Principles" and the "Ten Imperative Needs of Youth." The comprehensive secondary school is emblematic of the unique ideal that causes the secondary school curriculum not only to provide for the educational and vocational needs of all youth but also to ensure general education experiences that prepare for civic and social responsibility inherent in a democracy. The citizen of today is faced with many problems that require both accurate information and discerning judgment. The changing complexity of his government requires not only intelligent choice at the ballot box but also numerous decisions as to what is expedient in the legislative halls. The federal government has undertaken to assist both individuals and society in meeting the economic needs of present-day living. This is reflected in myriad acts of social legislation that cause concern as to the relative position of government in the life of an individual.

Need for Intelligent Consumers. The role of the consumer in an abundant economy requires critical judgment of values and integrity. The wide variety of material goods, easy credit arrangements, and high-pressure advertising exploit the naïveté and gullibility of the buying public. Bloated appetites and overstimulated desires cause unwise decisions in the marketplace. The "hidden persuaders" are most successful when the consumer does not maintain stable values. The growth of mass media of communication brings to the average citizen a wealth of material including topical information, entertainment, advertising, and various kinds of propaganda. Radio, television, films, and other audio-visual devices, as well as a multiplicity of printed forms, are transmitting a wide variety of materials to vast audiences. Here again, new techniques of evaluation are needed by all ages of society. The art of intelligent listening is an ever increasing necessity.

Maintaining the Importance of the Individual. A basic societal need in a democracy is to emphasize the importance of the individual. As society becomes more and more complex, the struggle to maintain this individuality becomes more and more difficult. It requires the development of strong ethical character on the part of each citizen. It necessitates the maintenance of close personal relations between individuals in the various social and economic processes that provide deterrents for unethical practices. As these processes become more and more complex, there is danger of the individual losing his importance in the mass struggle for existence. Governments other than the democracies openly declare the individual subservient to the state, and use education as a means of inculcating the philosophy of their police state. It is axiomatic that the democracies should use the great potential of education to perpetuate basic ideals of democratic living. It is a task of education to help the individual to be better fortified for the maintenance of personal integrity.

Increased School Enrolments. The decade 1960–1970 will be marked by greatly increased enrolments all along the line. According to the Research Division of the National Education Association, the entire national population of income-producing people, ages twenty-two to sixty-four, will increase by 12 per cent during the decade. At the same time, those of elementary school age, five through thirteen, will increase by 17 per cent, and those of high school age, fourteen through seventeen, will increase 43 per cent. Those of college age, eighteen through twenty-one, will advance 57 per cent. Population increases create problems for those in charge of curriculum development. Some of the problems are administrative, such as housing the pupils and securing competent teachers, but an ever increasing school population means increasing numbers of divergent abilities, and the greatest increase is likely to be among those of lesser ability. Thus the holding power of the curriculum becomes pivotal. Curriculum planners must be cognizant of the needs of a school population almost double in size with the concomitant factors of an increased college population and the increased complexities of terminal employment.

Changes in Home Life. No discussion of societal problems would be complete without consideration of the so-called breakdown of the home. Many of the ills of modern society are assigned to the collapse of stable home life. Educators claim it causes a major share of pupil adjustment problems. The church and the community are wont to use it as a scapegoat for their many shortcomings. Social workers pile high the statistics to substantiate a picture of general alarm. The question might be raised as to whether the home should continue to be evaluated in the light of its former function. It is probably more realistic to recognize the home as a changing social institution that is not necessarily breaking down but that may be only adjusting to the complex demands placed on it by all areas of society. It is of little value to recall with nostalgia the open fireplace with a patriarchal father reading the Bible and conducting family prayers. This is only a memory in a space age where economic necessity takes both the father and mother out of the home to become wage earners, and where well-meaning social and educational agencies place such heavy demands on the time of youths that the latter become "visitors" in the home rather than functioning members of a closely knit family unit for work, leisure, cooperation, and the passing on of important aspects of the social heritage. The working mother is a part of the national scene whether her baby is fourteen days or fourteen years old. She is an economic necessity for supplementing her husband's income to maintain a standard of living that society has made appear desirable. The adjustment of the home as a social institution and ever increasing numbers of females entering the working world outside the home require both diversity and complexity in planning for societal needs through the school curriculum. Education in a changing society is a developmental process that calls for creative and meaningful curriculums wherein obsolescence is viewed realistically and bold new programs are planned with confidence and foresight.

THE WORLD OF YOUTH

There is a temptation to take an extreme position in describing the problems youth will be facing in the world of tomorrow. The amazing scientific developments of the present age lend credence to the prediction of almost unlimited technological wonders for the future. The pessimist contends atomic discoveries may lead ultimately to man's annihilation, and this could be true, if the moral integrity of society does not keep abreast of its technological development.

It may be prosaic, but probably realistic, to suggest that the contrasts and conflicts youth faces in the social order are more perplexing than the multiple uses of the electronic tube. Values and ideals present a blurred image because of the multiplicity of possible answers to every social problem. There is the contention of widespread social progress contrasted with the doubt of any net gains. Frugality is praised as a virtue, yet lavish spending is rampant. Social injustice and bigotry are recognized as prevalent throughout the social order, yet there is a reluctance to "stand up and be counted" with the determined opposition.

Sophistication of Youth. Youths of the present era have been described as aimless, frivolous, apathetic, and lacking in purpose. The use of such generalities exhibits a lack of understanding of the underlying nature of young people, and it does great injustice to the millions of youths who show unusual stability in a world of uncertainty. What tendency there might be among young people to be confused or lacking in purpose is probably a reflection of the adult society surrounding them. Two world wars, a devastating depression, and the frustration of a prolonged cold war have created a generation of confused elders. Fortunately, youth prides itself in its independence and does not like to take its cue from the inequities of the past.

There is no reason to believe the world of the future will be any less trying than the world of the past. Indications point, in fact, to increased complexities. The structure of education needed to prepare young people for such a world must be at best a calculated guess. It is obvious, however, that the coming generation will have to be more sophisticated about its problems than its evaluators predict. It will have to build on the assumption that the results of science can be either greatly beneficial or vastly destructive. Its task will be to redefine social values in terms appropriate to the nation's changing stature as a world symbol for freedom. Youth must be prepared to accept the responsibility of carrying the nation to new levels of greatness.

The Probable Dropouts. Curriculum activities tend to run in cycles. Stress is first on the subject-centered curriculum and then on the child-centered curriculum. Presently, the academically talented and the college-bound are in the spotlight. Overemphasis on one phase of the school program usually results in lack of emphasis elsewhere. The fact that many pupils are not intellectually gifted and are not going to college is reason for re-emphasizing the necessity of a more balanced curriculum to meet the needs of all pupils. A perennial problem, regardless of what the curricular emphasis may be, is the fact some pupils drop out of school before the completion of their program. The discovery of an alarming number of unemployed dropouts in urban centers led Dr. Conant to label them "social dynamite."

Secondary education is an established link in the program of continuous training and development that is so necessary in the life of any individual. One out of every three pupils entering the ninth grade fails to finish high school. Persons without a high school diploma are the first to be without jobs in periods of excessive unemployment. A predicted increase of 13.5 million in the labor force in the 1960's points to a continued struggle for jobs. The competitive position of the dropout is very precarious. Added to this is the fact that juvenile delinquency is ten times greater among dropouts than among high school graduates.

Generally, pupils likely to leave school before graduation are not difficult to identify. Typically, they are around sixteen years of age; their relations with their teachers and fellow students are marked by tension, suspicion, and strain; their attendance is poor; they are usually retarded by as much as two years; their parents are not interested in education and heap scorn on anything erudite; their families usually need financial assistance; and these pupils do not participate in extrasubject activities and show general apathy or frustration in regard to classwork. To keep them in school, attention must be focused on a meaningful curriculum and greatly increased guidance efforts.

If the dropout problem is to be solved, an attack must be waged on a number of fronts. That all pupils do not want the same things from school is unequivocal. A permanent goal must be to provide each pupil with the type of training and education best suited for him as an individual and for his expected needs as an adult. The school must succeed in showing the pupil the concrete value of what is being taught and its relationship to real life situations.

Effective guidance programs have much to offer in retaining youth in school. Potential dropouts can be identified, administered proper tests of interest, and aided in seeing the worthwhileness of an education. The dropout is characteristically a youth who has not found the curriculum adjusted to his needs as he envisages them. Neither does he desire to participate in extrasubject activities. Here he feels he does not "belong." It is possible that, if he decided to join in an extrasubject activity, he might discover a lasting interest. In cases of financial hardship, guidance counselors can assist worthy pupils in finding part-time work or other financial assistance.

Education's response to the challenge of the dropout is not a lagging one. Programs are under way throughout the nation. The schools will continue to struggle with this enigma. The dropout problem is largely a curriculum problem as far as the schools are concerned, but it extends beyond the confines of formal education, and part of the solution will come from extensive social and economic realignments.

Impoverished Homes. The culturally impoverished youth and the home he represents form serious problems for social and educational planners. The mobility of large segments of the population has created a cultural incompatibility and has caused educational inadequacies. Urban slum districts are locales of many perplexing problems. The homes in these areas are characterized by poverty, disease, instability, and conflict. Pupils from these homes are often hungry or ill. They are accustomed to physical punishment and violence, and they tend to be emotionally unstable. It is difficult to organize school programs for youths of this background, particularly since the districts in which they live are financially impoverished and cannot support the clinical and therapeutical type of education they need. Frequently, the school compounds the problems of these disadvantaged youths by adding to their personal insignificance and inadequacy through an unending succession of failures. If the school is to familiarize its pupils with the best things in a democratic culture, it must provide them with alternatives to the self-defeating experiences of their families and neighbors. The school alone, however, cannot carry the responsibility for solving the problems of impoverished youth. The communities that spawn cultural degradation must be modified. This places a responsibility on the social order itself. While the school program can be modified extensively, it can serve well only those pupils who are physically, mentally, and emotionally capable of responding to it.

CURRICULUM PLANNING

Curriculum Identity. It is important for curriculum workers in secondary school education to establish the identity of the curriculum. A survey of definitions of the secondary school curriculum will reveal a wide range of educational activities from the narrow conception of mere courses of study to the inclusion of all experiences of a pupil during his waking hours. A summary of areas thought of as curricular by most secondary school curriculum workers shows three divisions: direct learning experiences, written documents, and certain auxiliary activities.

The direct learning experiences involve the actual learning situation in the classroom. Here the teacher and the pupil share experiences and information that result in expected growth on the part of the pupil. According to accepted psychological principles, both the pupil and the teacher bring to the learning situation the sum total of their environmental experiences. For the teacher, this involves subject matter and teaching techniques. For the pupil, it involves an integration of previous learning activities, preparation of new experiences, and a reasonable desire for assimilation of learning. These learning experiences in the classroom form the end product of the total secondary school curriculum enterprise.

The written-document area of the school curriculum is easy to define. It is here that the curriculum is identified according to plan, structure, purpose, and patterns of procedure. It includes the courses of study, the curriculum guides, the subject-matter specialization material, the instructional units, the textbooks, the listing of psychological concepts, and the listing of principles, practices, purposes, and goals. This is a necessary and vital phase of secondary school curriculum work. It is exceedingly important, however, that it be kept in proper perspective. It is a means to an end and never should become an end in itself. Too often, elaborate effort in time and money is put into this phase of curriculum work and its implementation is sadly neglected. The dust-gathering properties of the written curriculum document are perplexing.

The most promising practice in present educational procedures for implementing curriculum materials is in the involvement processes used. It is time-consuming and often wasteful to involve large numbers of classroom teachers, administrators, supervisors, and curriculum consultants in the formation and writing of courses of studies, curriculum guides, and other such material, but it appears to be the most promising procedure for ensuring that these materials will be part of the learning process in the classroom.

The degree of specialization often determines the relationship of certain auxiliary educational activities to the secondary school curriculum. The field of guidance is a good example. In its formative years, guidance was largely a classroom function and as such was an integrated part of the classroom learning process. Specialization of the guidance function now takes it outside the classroom and gives it auxiliary standing. To a degree this also has been true in the extrasubject field, though some of the more important extrasubject activities have been moved into the regular schedule of the school. For purposes of identification, however, both guidance and extrasubject learning activities qualify as parts of the secondary school curriculum, whether they be integral parts of the program, supplementary activities, or functions of an auxiliary activity.

Levels of Responsibility. Curriculum planning and development are complex activities involving time and effort on the part of many people. There is no established pattern to follow and no authority to say how and when they shall be done. Legally, education is a state function, and it could be assumed that curriculums might be established by state authority, but this is true only to a limited degree, and practices differ greatly among the states. There are differences of opinion as to what constitutes effective planning and how to implement such planning. A decision must be made as to whether the curriculum is to be conceived by experts on a high level and handed down to the teacher or whether it is to originate with the teacher. The one consistency today lies in the involvement of classroom teachers regardless of the level of activity. There are those who argue that the exclusive use of teacher committees for curriculum planning often results in the pooling of prejudices, since such committees do not have access to the scholars and scientists who can bring expert knowledge to bear on the development of curriculum materials. Others are equally vehement in their contentions that the expert often lacks practical experience and does not understand the problems of the classroom.

The following question might be asked: If the state does not exercise its authority for planning and developing the curriculum, where shall it be done—on the local level or on the national level? The bulk of this responsibility has been accepted at the local level, although there is quite a bit of activity on the part of professional organizations at the national level. Indeed, some believe that a national curriculum design should be established that would expose all pupils to a common set of values and a common fund of knowledge. It is reasoned that education should prepare pupils to hold a common belief in democratic ideals. It is suggested that curriculums locally concerned and developed by individual teachers cannot adequately do the job.

In a period of national peril and of great scientific, technological, and social change there is a need for redefinition of national objectives and reappraisal of ways of achieving them. In a nation committed to the principle of state and local control of education, however, the task of formulating curriculums is essentially the responsibility of policy makers at state and local levels.

Ultimately, of course, the most effective curriculum work is done at the local level. State and national curriculum study may provide the superstructure, but in order to reach the real curriculum objective—the pupil in the classroom—local educators must reshape, adjust, and often originate ideas and concepts that ensure the process a reasonable chance of success. The local task is to set up objectives for giving direction to curriculum study. Establishing guidelines for determining these objectives and implementing the curriculum action to follow are local procedures.

Creativity in Curriculum Planning. The center of action in curriculum study should be in the area of creativity. New research tools are needed for identifying innovations in educational practices that will afford solutions to problems quite different from those of any previous era. It is inconceivable that the urgency in the situation would permit the procrastinating acceptance of an allegedly inevitable "curriculum lag" or allow time to be wasted in justifying present inadequacies. This does not mean, of course, that the solid foundations of the past will be abandoned or that reliable research efforts and procedures will be junked; rather, it inherently dictates that these be the basis for creating solutions to problems in today's highly complex society.

Leadership in Curriculum Planning. Curriculum development is dependent upon dynamic, intelligent leadership. This leadership must necessarily come from the administrative area of the educational structure. Regardless of organization, the pivotal responsibility will fall on the superintendent or principal, and, in the case of secondary school education, this most likely will be the principal. The success of leadership on the part of the school principal will depend on how effective he is in involving alert, intelligent teachers in a full partnership for curriculum-development action. The nurturing of ingenuity and creativity on the part of the classroom teacher offers great potential for educational progress. Implementation of curriculum action is inherent in the process.

The space age has created the necessity for intense activity in the curriculum field. This is equally true in the elementary and the secondary school. The focus of attention on the activities in the secondary school field probably is greater owing to the preparatory aspects of secondary school education. This is a natural consequence, since the secondary school is charged with the responsibility of preparing youth for academic and vocational pursuits. In times of stress and trouble, the critics quickly assign any blame to faulty preparation. It is not the thesis here to condone or defend this charge, but rather to identify the position of the secondary school curriculum in the present decade. Further identification also reveals that part of secondary school curriculum activity is associated with instructional materials. Criticism in this realm also appears to be a natural concomitant during periods of stress and uncertainty.

Lines of communication are vitally important to successful curriculum development. All involved in the educational process must be reliably and consistently informed of curriculum problems and issues. It is a mistake to assume that involvement by representatives from various groups will be sufficient here. There must be a planned program of complete coverage, using the many forms of modern communication media. Both educational and lay people need to be given updated information at all times. This process will reveal divergent points of view and provide for better understanding. Articulate leadership will synthesize points of view into constructive thinking. Uninformed opinions are often precursors of disaster.

The Challenge to the Comprehensive School. The comprehensive secondary school is a unique educational institution. It represents the fulfilment of a national ideal that calls for adequate educational opportunities for all youths. It is organized on the fundamental principle of general basic education for all secondary school youths, plus specialized education for each according to ability and interest. It places an obligation on the school community for providing an adequate education for all pupils in order to fortify them with ability to meet the changing needs of society.

The comprehensive school represents a culmination and a combination of several factors in curriculum development. It provides instruction for all levels of ability, as well as assuming a dual responsibility for developing each pupil according to his capacity and for preparing him to contribute to the society that supports him. Balance and flexibility are fundamental ingredients of the comprehensive school curriculum. It provides a general basic education for all and gives equal dignity to the various subject-matter areas. It makes possible flexibility of experiences for meeting special interests resulting from well-developed guidance programs.

The comprehensive secondary school represents an evolving process in curriculum planning and development. A tendency has existed in the secondary school to specialize in strictly academic areas or to make the school partly a vocational training institution. The recent trend toward comprehensiveness reveals an effort to integrate these two areas of specialization. The size of the school can be a troublesome factor in building a good comprehensive school. Since approximately one-third of the high schools enrol less than 100 pupils, lack of necessary programs greatly reduces the comprehensive features of these schools. It is difficult to maintain a teaching force sufficiently large in number to provide the necessary offerings. While extremely large high schools can offer almost unlimited curriculum offerings, such schools violate many other desirable principles of a good institution. Faculty size should not exceed 35, if the group is going to meet and plan together. Some of these schools have over 200 teachers. Various plans have been tried to subdivide large schools within the framework of the same administration, but usually with a sacrifice in comprehensiveness.

To achieve its purpose, the secondary school must truly represent a cross-section of society in its pupil population. It must affect positively the behavior of its pupils as adolescents, and later as adults—not only as wage earners, citizens, and family members, but as unique human beings as well. This requires a curriculum arranged to challenge all pupils in basic academic subject fields and to provide elective subjects consistent with interests, needs, and abilities.

RESEARCH, STAFF UTILIZATION, AND THE CURRICULUM

Innovations in educational practices are usually ways of helping the pupil develop at his own rate of speed and toward his own goals. Some of the newer innovations seek to aid the pupil in assuming increased responsibility for his own learning. Provisions for independent study, problem solving, and research within the framework of the regular school curriculum are notable examples. The continuing quest for methods and procedures leading to maximum growth on the part of each individual pupil is of highest priority.

Controlled Experimentation. Experimentation and research form the cornerstones of educational progress. Functional, effective curriculums will result from extensive testing of theoretical patterns representing the best creative thinking in the educational laboratories. Theory is a necessary ingredient for growth, but it can be confused with prejudice and can foster ideas of maintaining the status quo. Only controlled research and experimentation will provide the validity of good educational theory. Current analyses of ungraded school curriculums may establish better methods for grouping pupils. Pseudo-informed adversaries are prejudging the merits of this fundamental curriculum issue, but the valuable answers will come from careful experimentation.

Action Research. Action research holds significant promise for curriculum development. Vital curriculum changes are likely to result from the involvement in research of curriculum workers responsible for making changes. This means that administrators, supervisors, teachers, pupils, and parents must examine the processes in which they are involved, evaluate these processes, and decide on changes necessary for improvement. If this procedure is used in a systematic fashion and changes follow a planned design, noteworthy results may be expected. Action research calls for the creative and constructive use of imagination in identifying practices that should be modified to meet changing educational needs. This calls for courage in trying out more promising practices and gathering evidence to prove their worth.

There are those who contend that action research, when properly developed, is a necessary supplement to the more sophisticated research forms. Action research follows a specific design. It calls for the identification of a problem by an individual or a group moved to action by an educational concern. Establishment of desirable goals calls for a hypothesis and the accumulation of evidence necessary for action. After the goals are accomplished, certain generalizations will result. From the continuous retesting of these generalizations, desirable curriculum patterns will emerge.

The Team-teaching Investigation. One of the most significant contributions of research has been made by the Commission on Staff Utilization Studies, sponsored by the Curriculum Committee of the National Association of Secondary School Principals and financed by funds from the Ford Foundation. This commission, created during a period of acute teacher shortages, was searching for ways and means of stretching the use of the available good teachers through experimentation and research in more than 100 junior and senior high schools.

The work of the Commission on Staff Utilization Studies had not progressed very far when the original intent of finding ways of relieving the teacher shortage was relegated to the background and the center of interest was shifted to the improvement of curriculum patterns and methods of learning. This was an interesting development in the search for better utilization of good teachers. In fact, some of the evolving curriculum patterns required more rather than less teachers. These were teachers with lower qualifications to be used in conserving the time and energy of the more qualified. In some instances, they were cadet teachers; in others, they were lay citizens with college backgrounds.

Because of their impact on the secondary curriculum, it is pertinent that an analysis be made of two of these organizational innovations—

team teaching and flexible scheduling. Team teaching is the pooling of knowledge and talent by a group of teachers to provide improved instruction to a larger number of pupils. The basic pattern in team teaching provides opportunities for teams of teachers to present large-group lectures, small-group seminars, and individual instruction when necessary. The composition of teams is varied. Numerically, a team may be composed of as few as two teachers scheduled to teach the same subject simultaneously, or several teachers responsible for large blocks of time and the integration of several subject-matter areas. A common procedure is to have all members of the team participate in planning the total operation including material to be covered, team personnel responsibilities, and evaluation of learning criteria. Team members are selected for large-group instruction according to their field of specialization and mastery of presentation. Two English teachers, for example, may hold identical degrees and have the same number of years of training, but one may be an expert in poetry and the other in grammar. Usually the only limitation on the size of the group is the availability of space. Large-group instruction is followed by small-group seminars to ensure individual participation in the discussions. These small-group seminars may provide for analytical study of the major presentation, or they may probe new areas and problems leading to individual study.

Team teaching is a worthy innovation in curriculum planning because of the possibilities it offers for improvement of instruction through better use of teaching talent and through the regrouping of subject-matter material according to modern psychological concepts of learning. The so-called master teacher is available for areas of specialization, whether it be in making a highly motivating presentation to a large assemblage or piquing the curiosity of imaginative minds in small-group discussions. In team teaching, paramount emphasis is placed on planning learning activities. Superior teachers teach larger number of pupils in fewer repetitious sessions, thus giving ample time for planning. There is opportunity to organize learning material into meaningful units for presentations. Subject-matter lines can be broken through in the search for concepts, understandings, and relationships. Teachers can associate themselves with the environment of the students through planned experiences.

Flexibility in Time Allotments. A major curriculum problem is created by the rapidly increasing accumulation of knowledge. Even after discriminating selection of subject-matter areas and of content within the areas, time is still not available within the secondary school years to teach all that is worth knowing. This suggests, of course, a general pruning of the curriculum to ensure a strong basic education and adequate specialization, rather than a continued proliferation of courses. But it especially suggests careful analysis of values in relation to time that can be devoted to various areas of learning. The traditional pattern of an hour a day, five days a week, is reaching a stage of questionable justifiability. It is becoming increasingly necessary to vary the frequency and spacing of time allotments to the multiplicity of subjects in the secondary school curriculum according to the nature of the subjects, the ability and interest of the pupils, the talents of the teachers, and the type of instruction. Flexibility of curriculum patterns is in evidence when the time allotted to classes expands and contracts according to knowledge requirements and learning capacities, when greatly increased opportunities for independent study and research are provided for capable pupils, and when small-group instruction is adjusted to requirements of learning and reinforcement of learning.

Space here does not permit an extensive review of the Staff Utilization Studies, but it is cogent to call attention to the many interesting experiments in the use of equipment and material aids to instruction. Seeking the most effective ways of motivating learning, capable teachers construct, collect, and use a large amount of excellent audio-visual material. The most extensively used equipment includes television, the overhead projector, and the tape recorder. This identity does not exclude the use of many types of audio-visual equipment and materials that, having proved useful in the past, continue to be an integral part of good learning situations.

INTENSIFIED REPORTS TO SELECT NEW SUBJECT-MATTER MATERIALS

The pattern of present-day curriculum planning is a most promising one in that it involves large numbers of professional people from kindergarten to graduate school, giving the process both theoretical and practical aspects. It ensures a great degree of implementation, because the participants feel a responsibility for causing their ideas to work. There is a democratic involvement of the skilled practitioner in the classroom, the careful research and experimentation of the curriculum specialist, the experience and tempered judgment of the school administrator, and the scientific thinking of the college theorist.

Science and Mathematics. The fields of science and mathematics are good examples of the unification of educational forces in the production of exciting new curriculum materials. Such programs as the School Mathematics Study Group; the Beberman Program, at Illinois; the Biological Sciences Curriculum Study; the Chem Study and Chem Bond formulations; and the Physical Sciences Study have been developed and tested experimentally through coordinated efforts of high school teachers and college subject-matter specialists. This has never occurred before on such a grand scale, nor have college personnel participated in the comfortable position of partnership rather than as dominating advisers. College professors have contributed from their knowledge of an unparalleled development of content materials, and classroom teachers have drawn on their practical experience to give the material functional structure. This cooperative contact between the secondary school and college classrooms gives both groups a better awareness of the need for articulated learning conditions on each level. It presupposes a fortunate union of theory and practice for some time to come.

Another significant development in curriculum planning is the great amount of time and effort going directly into different phases of instruction. Subject-matter fields are very much in the center of the picture, and the treatment of instructional material is most significant. Emphasis is on the adjustment of material to psychological concepts of learning rather than on scope and sequence. Terms such as *problem solving, critical analysis,* and *scientific thinking* are part of the subject-matter discussions on all levels. Curriculum development in the fields of science and mathematics is a good example. Emphasis there is on problem solving and integration of related information. Stress on major concepts and principles give pupils firsthand practice in mathematical and scientific thinking. Pupils are given a means of controlling factual detail rather than relying on frantic memorization. College participants in these curriculum studies are discovering the possibilities of learning integration that secondary school people have been trying to effect for some time. While the college professors seek to extricate principles from the mass of available information, they are finding a great many interconnections among the sciences, as well as among the divisions of mathematics, that can serve to reinforce the learning of pupils in the classroom.

Foreign Languages, Industrial Arts, and Business Education. The functional aspects of subject matter in the lives of pupils are being given due consideration. A functional emphasis in such fields as modern languages, industrial arts, and business education is one way of infusing content into the learning of pupils, for efficiency of use in a rapidly changing society. The audio-lingual approach to modern foreign-language teaching is gaining momentum. The procedure calls for increased experiences in listening to oral expression. Research shows this approach enables the pupil to communicate quickly in the language and does not detract from ability to read and write effectively. This will lead to the enjoyment of the literature, an understanding of culture, and creation of a permanent interest in another of the world's civilizations. A worthy objective for the next decade would be to have every high school graduate bilingual.

Industrial-arts objectives, as presented by curriculum leaders in the field, shows a definite trend toward meeting the needs of youth in an industrialized society. Whereas earlier objectives emphasized the manipulative skills in the use of hand tools and the execution of simple basic operations, newer objectives include emphasis on problem solving, design, and experimentation as facets of a more wholesome approach to learning through intelligently organized experiences that help orient the pupil in the realm of industrial and technological subject matter. The "take-home project" is rapidly giving way to objectives more consistent with understanding of the real industrial processes.

A most pressing demand in the field of business education is the determination of what constitutes adequate preparation for the new types of positions available in business as a result of the rapid technological shifts. There is ample evidence that more and more people will need higher-level skills than were formerly required for many business positions. The exact nature of these skills is yet to be ascertained. The dilemma in business education is how to satisfy objectives of general education and at the same time prepare pupils for positions in a world of automation.

Physical Education and the Fine Arts. Searching re-examination is going on in the arts and in physical education. It may appear paradoxical to group these subjects in the same paragraph, but their function in a society with ever increasing leisure, on the one hand, and a complexity of living, on the other, gives credence to a similarity of purposes in meeting general-education objectives. The arts are subject disciplines that emphasize the use of the intellect as well as the development of sensitivity, creativity, and the capacity to make reasoned, aesthetic decisions in extending the range of human experience. The arts include experiences for those who create, those who perform, and those who consume. The ability to make intelligent decisions in all three areas is a worthy curriculum objective. The arts have much to offer in a functional way for the enjoyment of leisure and relief from the monotony of industrial automation. Physical education carries the responsibility for helping pupils gain knowledge of how to care for their physical well-being, and shares with the arts the responsibility for improvement of mental well-being. Concepts of how to keep physically fit in a sedentary society and how to engage in wholesome, invigorating recreational activities are top priorities among functional physical-education objectives.

The English Language Arts and the Social Studies. Increased interest in the English language arts and the social studies is evidence of an effort to maintain balance in curriculum planning. Financial subsidies given for curriculum emphasis in mathematics, physical sciences, and foreign languages have created what might be termed a condition of neglect in the fields of English and the social studies. There is a tendency for pupils to score lower in these fields on national testing programs than they do in other basic subjects. Criticism is being leveled at pupil deficiency in the use of English and in understanding of the cultural heritage. Both fields are in the midst of intensive study.

There can be no question of the need for functional objectives in the teaching of the English language arts, but there continues to be a divergence of opinion as how to achieve these objectives. It is a debate between those who contend that accepted usage by large numbers of people determines what is good writing and speaking, and the opposing forces who say that, although usage is a powerful factor in linguistic change, it is not an adequate criterion for acceptance or rejection. The former suggest that language be viewed as a psychological, historical, and sociological phenomenon, rather than a corrupt descendant of a more perfect parent. The latter hold that, for the sake of logical consistency, certain rules must be maintained. It is debatable, however, whether the resolution of this dichotomy will solve the enigma of continued pupil deficiencies, notwithstanding the great amount of time given to instruction in the English language arts.

Elements of soul searching are apparent in the field of social studies. Citizenship goals, eclectic nature of content, and value emphasis make social studies peculiarly sensitive to pressures. The vulnerability of curriculum decisions is apparent in many places where the choice of textbooks, the inclusion or elimination of certain units of study, and even methods of instruction are being dictated outside professional ranks. At least one state legislature has decreed that a unit on communism must be taught in all high schools. Fortunately, this dictatorial approach is the exception rather than the rule in social studies curriculum development. In an increasing number of schools, units or courses are being offered in world culture, history of non-Western civilization, and comparative government, as well as an increased emphasis upon economics. One of the functional objectives being emphasized involves the effort to give pupils experiences in the actual practice of the tenets of democracy. Critical thinking and problem solving are in the forefront, as well as the development of discriminating powers and ability in decision making.

Selection and Arrangement of Materials for Special Groups of Students. Closely allied with the emphasis being given subject-matter materials is the attention centered on the grouping of pupils for instruction. The pros and cons of grouping constitute one of the continuing debates in educational circles. The protagonists of grouping are increasing numerically. Many new approaches to groupings are being advocated. They include grouping on the basis of physical and mental maturity, grouping according to subject-matter proficiency, and grouping related to various citizenship experiences.

Two types of grouping are emerging that give promise of being consistent with good curriculum objectives. One plan calls for variability and flexibility of pupils' schedule assignments during the school day. In subject-matter areas where high-level abstract thinking is required, grouping of the most capable is practiced. In areas of general education, these highly capable pupils are heterogeneously regrouped. This arrangement permits the capable from being harnessed to the learning pace of the less capable and at the same time provides for a leavening process in subject-matter areas where general life activities are being experienced. A second grouping plan is based mainly on the pupil's intensity of purpose and level of achievement. This might be identified as grouping according to special talents. In this grouping assignment, the emphasis is also on providing the capable with the opportunity to learn at a pace commensurate with ability. Talent grouping may be made according to aesthetic and artistic capabilities, manipulative skills, or physical accomplishments. These pupils, too, would return to heterogeneous groups for other phases of their daily program. It is evident that pupils should be grouped in various ways in different phases of their high school experience. It suggests basic-content grouping for all pupils and depth-content grouping for pupils of special interests and abilities.

The Challenges—Present and Future. The changing social order poses many problems for secondary school curriculum planners. Secondary school youths, in the midst of a rapidly changing technological society and the nation's struggle to symbolize freedom in a cold war, are hard pressed to determine realistic values. The curriculum of the comprehensive secondary school appears to offer satisfactory solutions to many of the bewildering curriculum problems. It places an obligation on the school for providing an adequate education for all pupils in order to fortify them with ability to meet the changing needs of society.

New approaches to curriculum structure, increased emphasis on flexible schedules for meeting individual needs, and the reshaping of subject-matter materials are all part of present and future curriculum developments. The approach to subject matter calls for the arrangement of content according to modern psychological concepts of learning. Problem solving, interrelations, understandings, and practical applications are being stressed. Scope and sequence are of lesser importance. The next decade will bring many new and interesting subject-matter patterns. The entire field of curriculum planning and development shows promise of exciting educational achievement.

QUESTIONS, PROBLEMS AND ISSUES FOR FURTHER THOUGHT

1. Certain educational leaders are proposing a national secondary school curriculum for all pupils. What is your reaction to this proposal?
2. Evaluate the decision of a board of education to build a new school building for the exclusive use of team teaching.
3. How can effective curriculum revision help solve the dropout problem?
4. Is it the function of the secondary school curriculum to interpret social needs or train pupils to build a better society?
5. What would be the feasibility of having most of the factual learning material programed for machine teaching and freeing the master teachers for creative learning activities?
6. To what extent do you agree with the critics of electronic instructional devices who apply the label "gadgetry"?
7. Why is the comprehensive secondary school advocated by so many curriculum leaders?
8. What is "new" about the new mathematics?
9. What is the function of research in curriculum planning and development?
10. Why did the Commission on Staff Utilization Studies shift its emphasis?
11. What should be the relation between general education and specialized education in the secondary school curriculum?

SUPPLEMENTARY MATERIALS

SELECTED READINGS

AMERICAN ASSOCIATION OF SCHOOL ADMINISTRATORS. *The High School in a Changing World.* 36th Yearbook. Washington, D.C.: The Association, 1958. Pp. 4–62. A survey is made of the current problems facing secondary education. The American high school as a unique instrument for democratic education is stressed. It is suggested that the way to progress lies in doing more of the good things already under way.

GILCHRIST, ROBERT S. "What Is a Comprehensive High School," *Journal of the National Education Association,* LI (November, 1962), 32–33. Definition is given of a comprehensive high school, and four essential features for a truly comprehensive school are suggested. Better balance in the curriculum is urged.

GROSS, NEAL. *Who Runs Our Schools?* New York: John Wiley & Sons, Inc., 1958. Chapter 12, "What Can Be done?" draws conclusions based on responses of Massachusetts superintendents and school board members to a questionnaire. A number of forces acting on the curriculum are assessed.

KRUG, EDWARD A. *The Secondary School Curriculum.* New York: Harper & Row, 1960. Pp. 195–510. Extensive attention is given to the content and organization of the high school curriculum involving both the classroom studies and the non-classroom services and activities. The philosophical and content foundations of the secondary school curriculum are evaluated.

Position Papers, Committee on Curriculum Planning and Development, National Association of Secondary-School Principals. 1958–1962. (One issued each year in a subject-matter field.) This is a series of position papers developed by the N.A.S.S.P. Curriculum Committee, in the fields of sci-

ence, mathematics, modern foreign languages, English language arts, social
studies, and the arts. It could serve as good material for in-service curriculum study by a secondary school faculty.

PRITZKAU, PHILO T. *Dynamics of Curriculum Development*. Englewood Cliffs,
N.J.: Prentice-Hall, Inc., 1959. Pp. 337–49. Curriculum Improvement is
equated with teaching. Questions and problems relative to the provision for
a wide range of ideas and meanings in the learning environment are considered in detail.

RUBIN, L. J. "Curricular Senility," *California Journal of Secondary Education*,
XXXIV (November, 1959), 426–28. In this short article, the force of tradition upon the curriculum of the high school is strikingly set forth. According
to the author, the lag between what we do and the best we know is now
twenty years instead of fifty years as formerly.

SCHREIBER, DANIEL. "School Dropouts," *Journal of the National Education
Association*, LI (May, 1962), 51–59. Identity of the dropout is established,
and attention is called to the need for curriculum adjustment. There is a
review of several state and local plans for dealing with the dropout.

STEEVES, FRANK L. *Fundamentals of Teaching in Secondary Schools*. New York:
Odyssey Press, Inc., 1962. Pp. 259–332. The role of the teacher in curriculum study is identified. A survey is made of the program of studies in the
secondary school. The part played by guidance and special services is
explained, and an adequate analysis of the extrasubject field is made.

WILSON, ALAN B. "Residential Segregation of Social Classes and Aspirations
of High School Boys," *American Sociological Review*, XXIV (December,
1959), 836–45. A number of schools in a large urban area were divided
into three groups. The educational and vocational aspirations of boys attending these schools were compared between social classes within individual
schools and between schools within social classes. Fewer sons of professionals attending working-class schools desired a college education than
sons of professionals attending middle-class schools.

AUDIO-VISUAL MATERIALS

Film

How Good Are Our Schools? Dr. Conant Reports. National Education Assn.,
Public Relations. Washington, D.C. 28 minutes, 16 mm., black and white
or color, sound.

2

The Function and Nature
of the Curriculum

THE RELATION OF THE CURRICULUM TO THE
OBJECTIVES OF EDUCATION

The final evaluation of the school's curriculum is based on the effectiveness with which it promotes the achievement of the school's objectives. Any description of the nature and function of the curriculum must reckon with its relation to the objectives of education.

Concepts of Curriculum. The curriculum from the school's point of view is the environment for learning that it provides for its pupils. The curriculum from the pupil's point of view is the experiences he has in response to his perception of the environment provided. Since experience resides only in the organism itself, and since only experience educates, the pupil's curriculum—his interaction with his environment—determines what he learns. The school, then, attempts to provide the environment that will in face occasion in the pupil reactions appropriate to the learnings that the school desires.

This concept of the curriculum is fundamentally opposed to the belief of many teachers, if their practice is indicative of their beliefs, that the mastery of school subjects will per se produce the desired learnings. The school subjects are indeed an important element in the pupil's educative environment, but their mastery alone is not necessarily educative.

A commonly used definition of this curriculum—all of the pupil's experiences under the direction of the school that contribute to his growth —is technically correct. Since, however, the school cannot control the pupil's experiences, except as it stimulates them through the environment it provides, the emphasis in this chapter will be on the nature of the schools' provisions for stimulating experiences appropriate to the desired learnings.

The Nature of the Objectives of Education. Just what, then, are the desired learnings? Hundreds of notable statements have been made about what individuals or groups of individuals have believed were the aims of education. These statements have been in terms of knowledge of school subjects—commonly called "acquisition of the culture of the race" —competences persons should possess, and appropriate behavior patterns in a democratic society. It seems reasonable to assume that behavior in a democratic society—the performance of the functions of living—is the end goal of education, that the individual competences are the means of perfecting this behavior, and that knowledge of school subjects is instrumental in gaining the needed competences. Edwards and Richey state, "The purpose of educational institutions is to prepare the learner to participate intelligently and helpfully in the social order of which he is a part."[1]

The Relationship of Ultimate and Intermediate Objectives. The ultimate purpose of education is to stimulate and guide the development of the individual so that, as he progresses from immaturity to maturity and from dependence to independence, he will participate with increasing competence in our society, with satisfaction to himself and with benefit to society. With participation or behavior the goal and with continuing individual development the route, the intermediate goals are seen as the instruments of individual development. The school curriculum is these intermediate goals.

The School Subjects and the Objectives of Education. The analysis of society as a whole, as represented by the organized experiences of the race recorded for the large part in the school subjects, is the most valuable content that the school may use to stimulate in pupils the appropriate experiences for the achievement of the desired educational goals. Merely passing on the cultural heritage as it is entombed in textbooks does not alone achieve these goals. Many schools, however, regard the school subjects as their total curriculum and take little or no responsibility for aiding the pupil in relating what he learns to his daily living, much less employing it.

Good teachers, as they teach, keep in mind both *what* they teach and what they teach *with*. They teach what the pupil will become. If they do not teach what the pupil will become, they are not good teachers and

---

[1] Newton Edwards and Herman G. Richey, *The School in the American Social Order* (Boston: Houghton Mifflin Co., 1947), p. xi.

do not teach; for a teacher has not taught until a pupil has learned. They teach with the educational environment with which they surround the pupil. This includes the school subjects along with all the other environmental influences, in school and out, that the teacher uses in promoting the development of the pupil. Thus, the place of the school subjects in the curriculum and their relation to the objectives of education are defined. They are an intermediate goal, a useful instrument, in the teaching-learning process, but not the end product of education.

The Hierarchy of Goals. An illustration of the relative intermediacy of goals may help to clarify the concept of teaching *what* and teaching *with*. An English teacher teaches verbal communication not as an end product but as an instrument of social intercourse. Communication is an intermediate goal that the pupil must achieve before he can be an effective participant in our society. The teacher assigns theme writing as a method of learning written communication. Theme writing becomes an intermediate goal to communication. To write themes effectively, the pupil achieves numerous subordinate intermediate goals such as sentence structure, spelling, punctuation, capitalization, paragraphing, and handwriting and possibly typewriting. These are all useful tools or instruments necessary to make possible the achievement of the ultimate purpose. The intermediate goals are not the end products of education; they are not *what* the teacher teaches but are what the teacher teaches *with*.

Thus, a detailed course of study or curriculum guide must be organized and administered with all levels of goals in their proper perspective. For illustration: The ultimate goals of secondary education, the goals of the language-arts department, the goals for a particular year or semester, the goals for a particular unit of instruction, and the goals for one day must all be given a proper place in the planning and execution of the school curriculum. The over-all purposes are achieved through the instrumentality of the subordinate purposes.

Does the pupil always see—indeed, does the teacher always see—the interdependences of the several levels of intermediate goals? Do the teacher and the pupil think he has learned his school lesson when he has achieved an intermediate goal? What the teacher thinks is usually apparent in the kinds of questions he asks the pupil in his tests and examinations. Too often the intermediate goals are the only goals tested and, in the mind of the pupil, the only learning deemed important by the teacher.

Direct teaching of the elements within the school subjects must occupy a place in the teaching-learning process. A pupil must be taught both spelling and grammar, if he is to use these tools in effective communication. He must possess the tool in order to use it. A large part of the teaching-learning process, however, is helping the pupil to use the tool—the school subjects, or the intermediate goals—in achieving the ultimate goals.

THE RELATION OF CURRICULUM TO GROWTH

One of the foundations of the curriculum is the body of principles describing how the human organism grows and develops. In order to make, modify, or, indeed, use a curriculum effectively in the teaching-learning process, the teacher needs a functional understanding of these principles. Revisions of these principles occur as research and experimentation in the area of human development refute old and produce new findings. Continuous study of educational psychology is necessary to keep the teacher alert to the best available answers to the many questions related to the learning process.

Growth as a Continuous, Persistent Process. Every living organism, plant or animal, is constantly undergoing change. The most rapid period of growth of most organisms is in the first 5 to 25 per cent of their normal life-span. It is also in the early period of the organism's life that its growth is most positive and integrative as contrasted with the tendency toward degeneration in the last period. For instance, the normal life-span for cats is approximately fifteen to eighteen years; for dogs, from ten to twelve years; it is within the first year of life that cats and dogs undergo the large part of their growth physically and mentally, though they may continue to grow both physically and mentally and persist, until death, in undergoing (at a decreased rate) changes which may be called learning.

Since growth is so rapid in the first portion of the life of the organism, those organisms for whom this period is relatively long have greater chance to be influenced in their growth by environment—in other words, to be educated. Having a longer period of infancy than all other animals, the human species is indeed favored by nature, for it has the greatest opportunity of profiting from experience. Hence the long period devoted to formal schooling. In earlier times this period ended at the time of physical maturity, pubescence. Currently it extends, in many cases, well beyond physical maturity through high school, college, graduate school, and even beyond. Informal education for most individuals extends throughout life.

The organism, whether among the lower forms or human, has an innate tendency to grow. The repeated question of the small child. "Why?" indicates his persistence in wanting to know. The desire for learning continues throughout life. The learning of the individual in the human family, like the growth of the lower forms, is on a selective and a permissive basis—he selects the environmental elements he can use and he permits them to influence his development. The school and the teacher, like the person who has the culture of plants and animals in his charge, succeed only when they accommodate this persistent seeking by providing in the environment the elements that the organism will select and can use.

Growth as a Result of Heredity. All change in an organism is attributable to two sources. The first of these is heredity. When a seed is planted in the ground, it may be fairly reliably predicted even at that time what will be the shape, size, color, and, in general, the patterns of its life performance as a plant. To be sure, some influence may be exerted over these matters by control of heat, light, moisture, and other factors in its environment, but the influence of these environmental factors is limited. A carrot seed, for example, may not be developed so as to produce tomatoes or large round leaves.

Likewise, the pattern of growth of an animal is determined in advance by the genes transmitted from the ancestors of the individual animal. The offspring of a stud and a mare will always be a colt, never a calf or a lamb, and will possess or come to possess the appearance and behavior typical of a horse. Whether it will be a bay or a gray horse, a large or a small horse, will depend upon its particular ancestry.

Environment has little influence upon the color of eyes, shape of ears, and length of legs and arms of a human being. These and many other physical characteristics are strictly a matter of heredity—whether species heredity, race heredity, family heredity, or a combination of these factors. The color of one's eyes, the shape of one's nose, and the length of one's fingers and ears are not matters of environmental control. The normal color of one's skin is also a matter of heredity, though a light skin may be modified by environment.

Growth as a Result of Contact with Environment. Certain aspects of growth, then, are matters of heredity; other aspects are matters of environment. The sounds a child in the cradle can make are conditioned by inherited physical mechanisms; the verbal language he later uses in communication is acquired from his environment. A child who hears English understands and speaks English. If his environment were French, he would speak French. The culture he acquires—knowledge, skills, habits, attitudes, and ideals—is a product of his interaction with his environment.

In all directions, however, limits to growth are set by heredity—by the nature of the species and by the heredity of the individual—apparently by the character of the tissues of its cortex and nervous system for the most part, but also by all of its physical structure. For example, the

capacity of a bird to acquire a language is indeed very limited as compared to the capacity of a normal human being. The capacity of the
human for growth is an individual as well as a racial matter. Racial
differences in capacity for growth, according to anthropologists, are much
less significant than those among individuals of the same race.

Differences among individuals in capacity to learn are both qualitative
and quantitative. Rate, direction, and ultimate level of development are
individual. True, the route of development in any area such as language
or mathematics is, in general, the same for all pupils. Each one must take
approximately the steps each other one must take in sequential order in
progressing toward maturity in that area. The time required for moving
from one step to the next and the difficulty encountered and the help
they must have in taking the step differs widely with individuals as do
the upper limits of attainable progress. For example, some pupils in the
sixth grade will read on a twelfth-grade level, whereas some in the
twelfth grade will read on the sixth-grade level, indicating a wide range
in the rate at which they are able to master the steps in this area of
language development. Some individuals may never achieve more than
sixth-grade reading competence. These differences in achievement will
occur even when the pupils concerned have had identical schooling.

The Criterion of Value in Curriculum. The first section of this chapter
described the curriculum as the educative environment provided by the
school for the purpose of stimulating desirable learning experiences in
pupils. The environment cannot make the pupil learn; it can only afford
him the opportunity to learn. If the opportunity is to be utilized by the
pupil, the environment provided must have relationships, which the
pupil actually recognizes, to his needs, interests, and current life situation. The basic criterion of the value of the curriculum is its influence
on the lives of boys and girls—its ability to stimulate the optimum direction and rate of growth and development that result ultimately in desirable behavior patterns. Failure to understand these concepts allows
employment of curriculum materials and instructional methods that do
not contribute to the growth of the pupil.

This basic criterion also holds in judging the educational validity of
all types of curriculum materials and activities: pictures, excursions,
assembly programs, discussions, laboratory and shop activities, conferences, community participation, and participation in debate, dramatics,
and sports, as well as reading material, recitations, pupil writings, and
teacher talks. Anything in or out of school, in or out of books, in or out
of subjects that gives pupils educative experience—that is, experience
resulting in desirable growth—has a legitimate place in the "curriculum"
in proportion to its influence upon desirable growth. Even exhibition of

traits of character and personality by the teacher influences growth. Hence, it is clear not only that the curriculum, or educational environment, of the school includes all extracurricular activities, but also that all such activities and services should be planned, carried on, and evaluated on the basis of the same fundamental philosophy as the rest of the curriculum.

Curriculum Fallacies. This concept of what constitutes education is in clear-cut opposition to the viewpoint which seems to be held by many secondary school teachers and those who have prepared them for the job of teaching. According to the growth concept of education, education from the standpoint of the pupil is growth as influenced by environment while, from the standpoint of the teacher, education is the guidance and stimulation of growth by partial control of the pupil's environment. This concept is fundamentally opposed to the theory that education is merely the mastery of school subjects, as such. It is, further, opposed to the assertion of certain well-publicized college presidents and professors that education is no more than acquaintance with great books.

The differences may well be illustrated by the difference between two ways in which the sentence "The teacher taught John Latin" may be construed. If the sentence were written in Latin, the endings of the words for "Latin" and for "John" would indicate clearly whether "John" was in the accusative or in the dative case. But in English, that inflectional index is lacking. Hence, we may arrive at either of the following two conclusions:

1. "Latin" is the direct object of "taught," and "John" is the indirect object, i.e., the teacher taught Latin to John.
2. "John" is the direct object, and "Latin" is the ablative of instrument, i.e., the teacher taught John with Latin.

Many teachers are inclined to hold the former interpretation. Their instructional practice, both the content and the method used, is based on an outmoded psychology, sometimes called the reservoir, or storage, theory, which considers the mind a receptacle into which learning can be poured. Their nearly exclusive use of textbook content and authoritarian lecturing are illustrations of this pouring-in practice. They are teaching subjects rather than helping pupils to learn. Their practice rejects the fact that learning is an interactive process, the interaction of the learner with his environment.

The public, including parents, seems to subscribe to a like fallacy. The attention given to "quiz kid" television shows is indicative of a widespread belief that education is principally the acquisition of subject matter facts.

Another fallacy held to by some parents is a belief in the magic of going to school. The diploma is a significant symbol; what the pupil did to get it is unimportant. Hutchins, commenting on the contribution parents expect the school to make toward the success in life of their children, said, "You could get ahead a little better if you went to school a little longer. The more expensive and famous the school, the greater the advantage it conferred. It followed, of course, that what went on in the school was of little importance to anybody. What was important was not what went on in the school, but the fact that the pupil had been there."[2]

A third fallacy held to by some parents ins buttressed by a form of vanity that causes them to exaggerate both the value and the difficulty of the subjects they studied in school, the degree to which they mastered them, and the values their schooling had in daily living. They want school to be like it was when they went to school. Many persons of academic repute would like to see schools revert to the subject-matter learning of the earlier part of this century.

It is in part the fallacious attitudes of the public, in part the failure of administration and supervision to help teachers break with tradition, and in part the lethargy of teachers that contributes to the continuation of a non-functional curriculum. An institution that fails to perform the function its clientele demands of it has three choices: (1) It may change its materials and procedures until the function is performed; (2) it may secure a change of function in keeping with its materials and procedures; or (3) it may ignore its function, fall into obsolescence, and see its function performed by other agencies. The second choice is unlikely in that our society probably will demand more, not less, relationship between school curriculums and real-life situations. The third choice has at times been rejected by secondary school principals and teachers. The attitude of secondary school principals and teachers toward CCC and NYA is one evidence of this rejection. The first choice, then, is the only one remaining. When will it be implemented?

THE RELATION OF CURRICULUM TO BEHAVIOR

What the individual is at any one time and what he finally becomes can be most accurately described by his behavior. The basic function of the school is to aid the individual in his progress toward maturity and independence, toward becoming a self-sufficient, fully functioning individual. The becoming is never finished, for the progress of the individual

[2] Robert M. Hutchins, "The Issues in Education: 1946," *The Educational Record,* Part V, Vol. 27, No. 3 (Washington, D.C.: American Council on Education, 1946), p. 367.

does not end with formal schooling but is continuous throughout life. At any time, the level attained will be indicated by his behavior pattern.

A committee of college and university examiners stated, "Nevertheless, it was the view of the group that educational objectives stated in behavioral form have their counterparts in the behavior of individuals. Such behavior can be observed and described, and these descriptive statements can be classified."[3]

Various classifications of educational objectives have been proposed. A set of three categories, slightly modified from the set proposed by Bloom and his group, appears useful here. The categories with some illustrations under each are given below.

1. Knowledge and understandings
   a. America was discovered by Columbus in 1492.
   b. A foot is equal to twelve inches.
   c. Carbon dioxide is commonly used in fire extinguishers.
   d. Water is made of two parts hydrogen and one part oxygen.
   e. London is the capital of England.
   f. The square of a binomial is the sum of the squares of the two terms of the binomial plus or minus twice their product, the sign of the cross-product term being that of the second term of the binomial.
   g. The understanding of the meaning of democracy, the concept of evolution, orientation in a new community or school, the meaning of cartels, the significance of endocrine glands for physiological processes
2. Attitudes, ideals, and appreciations
   a. The ideal of being courteous, the ideal of being honest, the desire to be well thought of, the desire to be like a certain person, the desire to be respected as a good worker, the desire to be of service to one's fellow men
   b. Interests in national public affairs, interest in flowers, interest in airplanes, interest in skilful speech, interest in improving one's social graces, interest in the advancement of the field of medicine
   c. Liking for good literature, dislike for ostentatious dress, liking for exercise, liking for company of intelligent people, dislike for cheap literature and low-grade movies
   d. Open-mindedness in matters of religion, appreciation of the good qualities of the Chinese, fair opinion of people of low economic status, favorable opinion of democracy, and unfavorable opinion of unfair practices

[3] Benjamin S. Bloom (ed.), *Taxonomy of Educational Objectives* (New York: Longmans, Green & Co., Inc., 1956), p. 5.

3. Skills, habits, and behavior patterns
    a. Ability to add, subtract, multiply, etc., ability to think logically, ability to outline or abstract printed materials, ability to translate French
    b. Riding a bicycle, dancing, operating a machine, skating
    c. Various habits of courtesy, various habits of neatness, various habits of healthful and sanitary living, various habits of thought (such as withholding judgment until all, or practically all, pertinent data have been considered), various habits of personal appearance
    d. Self-control, effective communication, efficient work habits, competence in manipulation of quantities
    e. Competent family membership, general sociability, fairness and consideration in dealings
    f. Efficiency in recreational and vocational pursuits, responsibility in economic affairs
    g. Intelligence and helpfulness in civic participation, responsibility in supporting community decisions

The above listing is not comprehensive. It is merely illustrative of the types of expectations the teacher should envisage for his pupils. It is apparent that behavior is made up of the three general categories and that the possessions in the first and second determine the competence with which the individual will be able to perform the third, that is, behavioral goals such as those listed in the third category may be achieved only through the psychological possession of the goals listed in categories one and two. The curriculum is the instrument by which the school stimulates the individual experiences necessary for the pupil to gain such a possession of the contributory goals that he will, in fact, achieve the behavioral goals.

The determination of what should be included in the curriculum may best be made by following a procedure similar to the following:

1. Determine the objectives of education in terms of the kind of end product desired, e.g., good citizenship, vocational competence, etc.
2. Determine for each of the characteristics of the kind of person desired the necessary or contributory information, attitudes, interests, skills, habits, tastes, concepts, principles, and understandings.
3. Select and arrange according to the pupil's interests, abilities, and previous growth curricular materials that will result in the development of the necessary information, skills, attitudes, etc.

Upon first thought, this procedure seems quite logical and practical. If these determinations and selections could be made objectively and accurately, we would, indeed, be well on our way toward a science of education. Needless to say, however, the matter is not as simple as that. Too many factors are involved, and too much information is needed, particularly relative to step 3, that is not available. Curricular materials result in different experiences in different individuals, and experiences apparently alike result in different influences upon growth, to say nothing of the fact that the school is only one, if indeed a most important one, of the sources of environmental influences upon growth.

Components of Behavior in the Curriculum. Nevertheless, it is a useful procedure, almost indispensable to clear curriculum thinking, for each of these principal areas or objectives of education to be broken down into smaller units. There is no one item of behavior that we can call good citizenship. The components of good citizenship behavior exist in great number and variety, and each of these components is a phase of growth that requires guidance and stimulation. To enumerate even the majority of these would involve more space and time than are available here. However, they tend to fall into categories, and the good curriculum provides stimuli for experiences in all categories.

The teacher and anyone else who participates effectively in constructing a course of study must think through what information, concepts, habits, skills, interests, ideals, attitudes, tastes, and appreciations are required for good citizenship, health, vocational efficiency, recreation and leisure, or home leadership and efficiency. This is an important intermediate step that can be eliminated or scamped only at the peril of constructing inferior curriculum guides. Only from such a determination can one safely proceed to plan a learning environment that will result in achievement of the objectives of secondary education. Only on the basis of such a determination can one help pupils to use the content of the curriculum, school subjects or otherwise, as the instrument of individual development in these great experiential areas.

Behavior Components and Instruction. Each of the objectives of education is achieved only to the extent that appropriate behavior components have been acquired. Vocational competence consists of appropriate skills, habits, information, attitudes, and interests. Some of these are general, or universal, in that they apply to all or a large number of specific occupations. Some are quite specialized for a given occupation. Some behavior components such as attitudes toward industry and skills in reading are involved in several, if not all, objectives of education.

The function of the curriculum is to stimulate experience that will result in desirable growth, that is, the acquisition, to an optimum degree in view of the limitations of time and the capacity and maturity of the students, of as many behavior components involved in the various objectives of education as possible. These experiences must be considered in proportion to the importance of the particular behavior component to the achievement of objectives and to the number and significance of such objectives. It becomes increasingly clear how complicated the matter of adapting curriculum to objectives really is, when one bears in mind also that, with the passage of time, there is certain to be an increase or decrease in the relative contribution of some of the more specific components such as certain items of information and specific skills to a given objective of education.

Concomitant Behavior Outcomes. The process of curriculum construction is further complicated by the fact that, in the attempt to develop desired behavior components, there are always by-products—sometimes quite important, sometimes quite undesirable. Such outcomes of instruction and learning Kilpatrick aptly termed concomitant outcomes. They are the result of not only the content but also the methods of instruction and, indeed, a combination of the two.

A child's attitudes toward school, toward authority, toward learning in general, toward himself, toward his parents, and toward his classmates are usually influenced by how interesting and useful the curriculum appears to him and how capable he is of mastering it. His interests in various fields of learning or vocations are undoubtedly affected by his experiences with school subjects as they are taught.

Those who are familiar with guidance, with mental hygiene, and with the problems of boys and girls are well aware of this phenomenon and can cite impressive instances in which teachers have caused the development of most powerful growths in personality—some of them malignant and systemic, some of them, fortunately, healthful as well as pervasive. Very often the concomitant, or by-product, outcome is much more important than the growth intended by the teacher as a direct result of the learning activities. A popular lecturer some years ago, commenting on the influence his teachers had on him, said, "That eighth-grade teacher taught me to love democracy through hatred of autocracy. She was the most unbearably autocratic individual I have ever known."

The fact is particularly important in the use of incentives in the curriculum. Curriculum activities that appeal to the child as pleasant, or for some other reason worth performing for their own sakes, result in favorable attitudes toward everything associated with them, including the subject, the school, and the teacher. To a much smaller degree, curriculum activities will result in these favorable attitudes if they are not pleasurable in themselves but appeal to the student as worthwhile anyway for the sake of the resulting learning. For some individuals, the desire to learn is so strong that they will persist in learning even though the situation is unpleasant. This type of learning is most likely to occur if the individual is convinced not only that the learning likely to result is worthwhile to him but also that it will bring him returns not too far in the future.

Also very important with respect to concomitant learning is the degree to which the pupil succeeds in mastering the tasks involved in the learning activities. If he fails consistently or frequently, he is likely to develop unfavorable attitudes toward the materials, the subject, the school, the teacher, and possibly toward himself; he is quite likely to develop a lack of confidence in himself, at least with respect to the particular field of learning.

COORDINATION OF THE CURRICULUM WITH OTHER INFLUENCES ON GROWTH

Curriculum makers—which, of course, includes teachers—should bear in mind at all times that the pupil is influenced in his learning by the elements in his total environment with which he interacts. He brings with him into the classroom the influences of his experiences at home, on the street, at play, at work, and in meeting and mingling in the corridors. These influences combine with the school curriculum in stimulating and directing his learning experiences. The resultant learning is the product of many component forces, only one of which is the school curriculum. The reader will recall the distinction made earlier in this chapter between the school curriculum and the pupil's curriculum.

Among these other component forces that combine with the school curriculum to make up the pupil's curriculum are the following:

1. Previous acquisitions of the pupil
   a. Communication skills of listening, reading, speaking, and writing
   b. Interests, ambitions, and expectations
   c. Background of information and understanding
   d. Attainments in the various school subjects
   e. Attitudes toward life, toward school, and toward other social institutions
   f. Standards of achievement that he has set for himself, somewhere between the best he can do and merely getting by
   g. Habits of work
   h. Specific skills
   i. Attitudes toward himself, such as self-esteem, self-confidence, and his estimate of his own competence
2. Influences of other persons
   a. Interests, attitudes, and socioeconomic status of parents and family friends
   b. Peer associations and his position in the peer group

     c. Confidence in, and respect for, teachers

     d. Hero worship

  3. The outside environment

     a. Opportunities in the home for learning through books, period-
icals, radio, television, family work and play together including
trips

     b. Opportunities in the community for learning through libraries,
museums, theater, youth clubs, and organizations including
religious organizations

     c. Recreational opportunities

     d. Business and industry influences through work opportunities
and the images they cast

In view of the vast array of educational opportunities for youth outside
of the school, some curriculum planners have said that the school must
recognize and implement both the residual and the normative functions.
By *residual* is meant the provision for the pupil of those learning opportunities, within the accepted educational objectives, that are not adequately provided by outside agencies. By *normative* is meant the re-
education of the pupil in those areas in which outside-agency influences
are inconsistent with the accepted educational objectives.

The Complementary Nature of the Curriculum. Thus, in school curriculum and the outside influences on learning are complementary. The
pupil's curriculum is a composite of both. The adjustment the school must
make to discharge its part of the obligation in this complementary relationship may be governed by such principles as the following:

1. The specifications for the desired product of the schools must be
drawn in the light of the conditions and demands of society as the
student will find it, including conditions that call for compensation or corrective education.

2. When some other social institution or area of the student's environment no longer influences growth toward the objective of education as it did formerly, the school must follow one of these
alternatives:

     a. Re-educate the particular social institution or some other
agency to take over and serve as a replacement.

     b. Allow the particular educational service to go unperformed.

     c. Adapt the school program so as to assume the particular func-
tion no longer operative.

3. When the educative influences of out-of-school experiences duplicate those of the school, the school should

     a. Determine the degree to which certain instructional materials
and activities are no longer necessary, and

     b. Adapt the curriculum by excluding unnecessary materials or
activities.

In another chapter will be found a discussion of the more important changes in American society pertinent to the provision of formal education appropriate to that society. It should be said here, however, that

1. Curriculum makers should have a functional understanding of American society: the conditions of living, the agencies and institutions through which people secure their wants and needs, the adequacy of these institutions, the forces operative for and against change, the relative strengths and weaknesses of these forces, and the probable direction of change.
2. They should evaluate these social elements in terms of human welfare and estimate the influence they will and should have on the provisions of educational opportunities in the schools.
3. They should visualize accurately the elements within American society outside the schools which have potential for the education of pupils, the contribution these elements can make, and how the school curriculum can best be organized and administered to provide its complementary contribution, both residual and normative.

Significant Variation of Individual Responses. It has been noted that education is an individual matter. The growth of a group of individuals may be stimulated or guided by a common stimulus—a book, a lecture, or pictures. But is it not the group that grows; it is the individuals. There are as many separate and different growth results as there are individuals within the group. From reading a passage from *Julius Caesar,* one individual may develop an interest in Shakespeare and a confidence in school and the teacher; while another pupil may develop a prejudice against Shakespeare, an increased dislike for school, and an increased lack of confidence in the teacher; and still another may develop an awe for Shakespeare, a fear of the teacher, and a lack of confidence in himself.

One is reminded of an experiment in chemistry with a rack of test tubes containing different liquids and a beaker with still another liquid. Upon being mixed with some of the fluid in the beaker, the liquid in one test tube turns brown, another green, another black. What transpires in a child's mind, and, indeed, in his nervous system, is a matter both of the outside stimulus and the inside apperceptive mass. Pupils must be allowed great flexibility in election not only of school subjects but also of content within the subjects. Each pupil is unique. The teacher must develop the methods and resources for teaching individuals in class groups. The pupil must be helped to do, read, say, think, and feel—in short to experience and, hence, to learn—those things that are appropriate for him as an individual.

Until recently, the principal tendencies in the matter of adapting to the variations among individuals have been toward multiplying subjects and toward differentiation of pupil groups according to differences in needs, interests, abilities, and industry. Today the tendency is in another direction—that of adaptation to the individual within the class.

Such adaptation is necessary, if teaching effort is to attain its potential, in all subject areas—in vocational-education classes as well as in both required and elective academic subjects. School people have become aware of the fact that, in the vocations employing the majority of the population, all the specific vocational training required may be obtained on the job in a few weeks or months. It has become apparent that, whether or not sections for instruction are formed on the basis of general mental ability, on probable need, or on any other basis, there will always remain a wide variety among the abilities, capacities, interests, present needs, future needs, and experiential backgrounds of the individuals who compose the section.

Responsibilities of the Teacher for Adjustment. Because of these significant variations among students, curriculum guides must have as their major characteristic flexibility. It is well to have these guides as well as textbooks and reference books. They cannot, however, be followed slavishly; they do not teach themselves. They must be adapted by the teacher to the particular class and to the individuals within the class. The essential element in the teaching act is such a selection and adaptation of content and method that each pupil will learn. What does this requirement demand of the teacher?

Effective selection and adaptation of content and method require the teacher to have a detailed and functional understanding of (1) the nature of the pupil and (2) the nature of the educative environment. To make these understandings operational, the teacher must select and present the environmental elements that will in fact help each pupil use his unique possessions to move toward the educational goals appropriate for him.

A file of information about each pupil, that is, a case study, should be under development and should be available to the teacher. Each teacher may be expected to contribute to the continually accumulating data for the file. The information in the file may include data on mental ability, aptitudes, likes and dislikes, physical competence, emotional nature, past experience, and present circumstances that afford opportunities for, or handicaps to, learning. Many cumulative school records include some but not all of the useful data that may be collected. Teachers need to distinguish between fact and opinion recorded in the file and to study diligently to acquire a picture of the pupil that is as nearly true and complete as possible. They should also be sensitive to the fact that the picture is constantly changing. Their estimate of the pupil at any one time is only tentative and may need to be reviewed as new evidence is added to the file.

The teacher needs to evaluate the elements in the learning environment as to their potential for stimulating in pupils of various descriptions the learning experiences necessary for the achievement of accepted educational objectives. What contribution can a school subject and the various phases of that subject be expected to make to the growth and development of pupils? What methods of instruction are most likely to elicit the optimum contribution? What stimulation can be expected from out-of-school activities, and how can they best be utilized in connection with school subjects to exploit their greatest usefulness for learning? These questions and many others may be analyzed into their details and answered by teachers. Only then will teachers be able to employ to the full the opportunities for learning available to the pupil.

Knowledge of the pupil and understanding of the educative environment ready the teacher for bringing the two together in an interactive relationship for optimum pupil development. Doubtless, many teachers do not have this concept of curriculum or do not know how to implement it. It does require reorganization of traditional curriculum and methods. Such reorganization may be effected on paper in curriculum guides as they are developed by modern curriculum makers. To be effective in the lives of pupils, such reorganization must reach into classroom practice, into what teachers·do while they teach.

Sharp, in his book *Curriculum Development as Re-education of the Teacher*,[4] makes it clear that actual change in the curriculum occurs only with actual change in the teacher. The profession cannot expect the reorganization of the curriculum in the classroom, necessary to implement the concept of pupil interaction with his environment, until teachers do, in fact, educate themselves away from traditional practices toward modern practices.

Pupils Help Teachers in Curriculum Planning. How can the teacher bring the pupil and his total environment into contact favorable for learning? Probably the surest method is to secure the aid of the pupil in planning. The teacher may well permit and encourage the pupil to help set up for himself available educational activities appropriate to his capacities, interests, and needs. The degree of freedom of choice granted the pupil must always be related to his capacity for making relatively wise choices. The pupil will need constructive guidance from the teacher in developing capacity for making choices of the what and how of his learning. Pupils need to learn to bring into closer relationship their wants

4 George Sharp, *Curriculum Development as Re-education of the Teacher* (New York: Teachers College, Bureau of Publications, Columbia University, 1951).

and needs. They need to learn to visualize distant goals and to see the value of the necessary intermediate goals. Teacher suggestion is necessary to supplement the limited understanding of immature minds as to what curricular activities will provide best for specific needs. Under wise guidance in how to choose, the pupil may be granted ever wider freedom of choice. The teacher, at the same time, will gain deeper understanding of the nature of both the pupil and the environment through the pooling of pupil and teacher insights.

Pupil participation in curriculum making is necessary in such a society as ours for many reasons. Among them are

1. Teachers need help from pupils in interpreting the pupils' natures including their interests and needs.
2. Teachers need help from pupils in discovering the learning activities in school and out that will in fact stimulate learning experience.
3. Pupils are likely to become lifelong learners—an essential in a society characterized by rapid, continuous change—if they learn how to identify learning needs and how to select from the environment those elements that help them to achieve that learning.

The course of study, then, is to be regarded, on the one hand, as guideposts and available materials and, on the other, as something yet to be adapted and adjusted to the individuals—perhaps not tailor-made, but susceptible to alterations to meet the requirements of the individual. This is an important characteristic of the curriculum and one with implications for classroom teachers that probably go far beyond the concepts and practices of the majority of teachers today.

It should not require pointing out that the curriculum should be in harmony with what is known about learning, its psychology and economy. In the following chapters will be found a more complete discussion of those principles of learning, of motivation, and of mental hygiene that are most important for good curriculum construction.

The Curriculum and Methods. It may be serviceable for purposes of discussion to differentiate between curriculum and method.[5] It should be recognized, however, that they are inseparably interrelated and are associated parts of the educational environment of students in school. Methods are usually thought of as the procedure for bringing the student into contact with the curricular content. They may indeed serve also as stimuli for learning experiences. Some writers have contended that method is often more influential than content in producing the desired stimuli.

It should be clear that the resulting growth is partially determined in both nature and amount by the method of bringing students into contact

[5] See Chapter 30.

with subject matter or other learning materials. What happens educationally to the student is determined in part, and often in large part, by such aspects of methods as the following:

1. The adequacy of adaptation of assignments to the time, interests, and background of the student and the objectives of the unit and subject of instruction
2. The nature of questions and questioning evaluated in the light of their adaptation to the interests, abilities, and backgrounds of the student and the objectives and sequence of the unit and subject of instruction
3. The opportunity provided for initiative, planning, and responsibility of the student
4. The efforts of the instructor to emphasize ideals, attitudes, interests, judgments, and understanding as compared to factual knowledge and subject skills
5. The measuring programs of the teacher and the consequent relative emphasis upon such things as those just mentioned
6. The opportunities provided for such experiences as applying principles of life, projects and other "doing" activities, group cooperation, discussion, and community participation
7. The manner of speech and other phases of personality of the teacher
8. The use of auditory and visual aids including field trips and other community resources
9. The "self-discovery" method whereby the pupil discovers for himself rather than learns from authority

While the opportunities for writing method into textbooks and courses of study are limited, the last determiner of what the "curriculum" really is for the student is the teacher. Teachers should not fail to recognize the educational significance of method and to teach so as to provide the best possible educational environment for growth toward the objectives of education.

THE CURRICULUM, A CURRICULUM, OR MANY CURRICULUMS

In what sense can there be *the* curriculum? In what sense can there be *a* curriculum? In any school and in any classroom there may be—indeed, there must be—a broad framework with significant details developed for the purpose of directing the general course of the teaching and learning previous to the classroom contacts of the teachers and pupils. Such a framework must be consistent with the ultimate objectives accepted by the American people as the obligations of the school. It must also be consistent with the foundations of American education, such as those described by Rugg in his book *Foundations for American Education*.[6] But the predeveloped framework with details should not govern completely the activities of the teacher, and it cannot govern completely the interactions of the pupils. The preplanned framework may be called *the* curriculum. What goes on in the classroom, however, is *a* curriculum, for it cannot be anticipated and it cannot be repeated.

Laura Zirbes tells of a teacher who apologized to a visitor for the poor progress of her class. She said, "I don't know why these pupils aren't learning. I am teaching them just the way I taught my class last year." Possibly she *was* repeating as nearly as possible her practices of the previous year. The pupils, however, were reacting differently, for they were different pupils.

New Interpretations of the National Ethic Direct Curriculum Change. Flexibility must be the chief characteristic of a modern curriculum because of the constant change in the foundations of education in a democratic society. Our national ethic, which may be designated as the *democratic idiology,* must, of course, be the first foundation. The American concept of democracy and how it functions as a control of human behavior is not a fixed entity. It changes with the experience of the population in attempting to promote increasingly satisfactory human welfare. The founding fathers, when they wrote the Constitution, had no expectation that the concepts of equality of opportunity and responsibility would be applied to as wide a segment of the population as today. These concepts may never be fully implemented, but, as greater and more nearly universal equality is realized, the ways in which behavior is affected will change in both kind and degree.

Many illustrations of cultural changes resulting from changes in the interpretation of the American ethic are at hand. Three important ones may be cited:

1. The extension of suffrage to women and to various minority groups has been effected.
2. The rights of the laboring man to a more adequate wage and to better conditions of employment are becoming more and more widely accepted and implemented.
3. A vast array of constitutional amendments and of statutes and common law has tended to protect the many from exploitation by the few.

These three areas of change, along with many others, will undoubtedly continue to be affected by advancing interpretations of the ethic. Na-

[6] Harold Rugg, *Foundations for American Education* (New York: Harcourt, Brace & World, Inc., 1947).

tional changes in ideals, whatever they may be, have significant effects on educational practice including particularly an ever changing curriculum to meet new beliefs.

Social Changes Direct Curriculum Change. Closely related to the first is a second foundation that impels curriculum change. It may be designated the *dynamics of social change*. Numerous forces, other than a changing ethic, occasion social change. Natural conditions, science and invention, and contention among social groups are among the factors that operate with great force and persistence. The school, as the servant of society commanded to preserve that society and at the same time to improve its practices, must change as society changes. In the first place, the pattern of responsibility of the school changes from time to time. With changes in the home, in modes of amusement, in national and international problems, in vocational life, and in numerous other areas, the responsibility of the school for education for vocation, for intelligent citizenship, for home membership, for mental and physical health, for recreation, and for other things not only increases or decreases but the nature of the education required changes. Changes in recent decades and contemporary trends are so marked and of such great importance for education in general and the curriculum in particular that it has seemed wise to devote a whole later chapter of this volume to them and their implications for the curriculum.

It follows naturally that, if the curriculum is to remain in anything like adequate relation to the needs and conditions of American society and to the students' needs and responsibilities, teachers as well as textbook writers and other curriculum makers must be in touch with American society—its institutions, its problems, its trends, and the implication of all these for the curriculum. It is also a logical corollary that the curriculum should be regarded as a growing, living thing that, in all probability, is at best a few steps behind social changes. As a matter of fact, the lag of the curriculum is in many respects a matter of decades rather than of years.

Better Understanding of How Pupils Learn Directs Curriculum Change. It has already been said that, because of the wide range of individual differences, the school cannot provide one curriculum that is suitable for all but must provide curriculums accommodated to the needs of each pupil. There should be actually as many school curriculums as there are pupils. Fortunately, a number of pupils in any one class may not differ widely one from another, and often all members of the class may have a common need. Thus, the several curriculums in the class may have some common material; each one will also have differentiated material suited to the needs of the pupil for whom it is planned.

Another consideration, however, already mentioned in this chapter and related to the fact of individual differences, leads us to the third foundation, which, like the others, dictates continuous curriculum change. The curriculum is affected materially by how pupils learn, by how the human organism grows and develops. The third foundation is psychological and may be designated the *principles of human growth and development*. These principles and their use as a foundation of curriculum are detailed in another chapter, but it is pertinent to say here that they are not static. They may change in two ways: (1) actual change as human nature is affected by social change and (2) apparent change as the profession discovers more and more nearly accurate estimates of how the human organism interacts, in its efforts toward growth and development, with the educational environment.

The sciences of physiology and psychology, through research and experimentation, develop new findings on how the body and the mind function. These findings bring to the teacher ever changing interpretations of how the organism develops. These the teacher must translate into ever changing content and method that will stimulate more effectively the experiences necessary to occasion the desired learnings.

Two psychological theories, one old, the other new, may be cited to illustrate how learning theory changes. The "reservoir" theory held that the pupil learned through a pouring-in process, a filling of the "reservoir" of the mind. The "interaction" theory holds that the individual interacts with his environment and learns through active participation. Just as the one was found to be an inadequate explanation, so the other, although possibly more nearly accurate, is today not wholly satisfactory. Research and experimentation will continue the attempt to discover a complete and accurate explanation of how the human organism develops and how stimuli may be applied to aid that development. The ultimate explanation is illusive and may never be found. But as the findings approach nearer and nearer to the true explanation, curriculums must continue to change, making use of the newest reputable findings to improve the teaching-learning act.

Is it *the* curriculum, *a* curriculum, or many curriculums? The answer, in view of the foregoing, is obvious. The fact of individual differences requires the provision of individualized curriculums, except for a relatively small common core. The constant changing of the foundations will not permit a static curriculum. To be consistent with the continuously changing foundations, curriculums must be fluid, must be in a continuous state of change. The effective school, therefore, will have not *the* curriculum but curriculums. Curriculum workers, all members of the school staff concerned with instruction of pupils, have a continuing task, which is never finished, of developing the curriculums needed to provide appropriate educative opportunities for each pupil, consistent with the foundations of American education.

QUESTIONS, PROBLEMS, AND ISSUES FOR FURTHER THOUGHT

1. Discuss the psychological validity of the distinction made in this chapter between the school's curriculum and the pupil's curriculum.
2. List five to ten competences a person must possess in order "to participate intelligently and helpfully in the social order of which he is a part." What can each of the subject-matter disciplines contribute to the achievement of each of these competences, and how may they be taught to assure optimum contribution?
3. Develop hierarchies of goals in outline form, beginning with the basic functions of living (such as using leisure time wisely) for the main headings and supplying the contributing intermediate goals in descending rank until the lowest level is stated in terms of an appropriate classroom exercise.
4. Speculate, for each of several items of subject-matter content (such as Components of Vectors in Physics), on how the human race discovered this bit of knowledge, and describe how the teacher may direct the pupil in its rediscovery.
5. Identify and describe in general several of the kinds of growth the individual achieves in his development toward maturity (such as physical, language, quantitative relationships, social). Which of these are promoted largely by hereditary influences; which, by educational ones?
6. State clearly what is meant by the statement, "How one acts, feels, or thinks is determined by how one has acted, felt, or thought previously." Comment on the validity of the statement and its relation to the concept that "education changes behavior."
7. Describe five important recent changes in American society. Detail for each change appropriate changes in curriculum, both additions and subtractions or increases and decreases in emphasis.
8. Discuss the advantages and disadvantages of participation in curriculum making by pupils, by inexperienced teachers, by experienced teachers, and by parents and other lay persons. What functions can each participating group perform? Who determines finally what is included in the school's curriculum?
9. List some types of out-of-school educative experiences of pupils. Describe some specific classroom uses that can be made of these out-of-school experiences.

SUPPLEMENTARY MATERIALS

SELECTED READINGS

ANDERSON, VERNON E., and WILLIAM T. GRUHN. *Principles and Practices of Secondary Education* (2d ed.). New York: The Ronald Press Co., 1962. Chapter 1, "Bases for Judging Secondary Education."

ASSOCIATION FOR SUPERVISION AND CURRICULUM DEVELOPMENT. *New Insights and the Curriculum.* Washington, D.C.: The Association, 1963. Outstanding scholars describe new insights, and some outstanding educators describe the implications for education of this new knowledge.

BLOOM, BENJAMIN S. (ed.). *Taxonomy of Educational Objectives*. New York: Longmans, Green & Co., Inc., 1956. An analytical listing of substantive objectives of education.

DOUGLASS, HARL R. "The Growth Theory in Modern Secondary Education," *Educational Theory*, Part II, April, 1952, 108–15. A statement of the growth theory of education and the function of the curriculum in the light of that theory.

————. *Secondary Education in the United States* (2d ed.). New York: The Ronald Press Co., 1964. Chapter 2, "Secondary Education and Our Democratic Society"; Chapter 10, "The Subjects in the Curriculum"; Chapter 11, "The Subjects in the Curriculum (Continued)."

EDUCATIONAL POLICIES COMMISSION. *The Central Purpose of American Education*. Washington, D.C.: National Education Association of the United States, 1961. An emphasis on the responsibility of education in a free society for teaching reflective thinking.

EDWARDS, NEWTON, and HERMAN G. RICHEY. *The School in the American Social Order*. Boston: Houghton Mifflin Co., 1947. Chapter 17, "The Quest for a Content of Education"; Chapter 20, "Charting the Future Course."

FRENCH, WILL, et al. *Behavioral Goals for General Education in High School*. New York: Russell Sage Foundation, 1957. Part III—"Organization of Proposed Behavioral Outcomes."

HUTCHINS, ROBERT M. "The Issues in Education: 1946," *The Educational Record*, XXVII, No. 3, pp. 365–75. The need for a change in public expectations of education.

KRUG, EDWARD A. *Curriculum Planning*. New York: Harper & Row, 1957. Chapter 2, "Preparing Statements of Educational Objectives"; Chapter 3, "The Bases of Educational Objectives"; Chapter 6, "Teaching and Learning."

RUGG, HAROLD. *Foundations for American Education*. New York: Harcourt, Brace & World, Inc., 1947. A description of biopsychology, sociology, aesthetics, and ethics as the foundations of curriculum.

WILHELMS, FRED T. "Curriculum Sources," *What Are the Sources of the Curriculum: A Symposium*. Washington, D.C.: Association for Supervision and Curriculum Development, National Education Association of the United States, 1962. The bases of selection of curriculum content.

3

The Adolescent and the Curriculum

FUNDAMENTAL RELATIONSHIPS AND POSTULATES

It is obvious that, to be effective and practical, a curriculum must be developed in view of, and adapted to, the characteristics of the pupils with whom it is to be used. It must be built with a view to the interests, learning capabilities, educational status, ages, and needs of adolescents, as well as their present and future educational needs—both those that are recognized by the adolescent and those that are not. Adolescents differ greatly from each other with respect to these things. This is true not only of adolescents in general but also of adolescents in any given school and, indeed, in any given class.

While heterogeneity with respect to some of the more important types of variation may be reduced materially by grouping students into sections, particularly if it is carefully done, there will still be very important variations from student to student. This is without question one of the reasons why curriculum builders in the past have more or less neglected attempting to build curriculums for individuals as individuals but have built instead a curriculum in terms of subject-matter mastery, with appropriate standards. It also explains why concentration was on what were believed to be appropriate standards in the attempt to turn out something like a standard product of excellence, permitting those who could not or would not achieve the standards accepted to withdraw and to go to work.

The situation is further complicated by the facts that interest and educational needs change significantly with age. The interests of adolescents today are quite different in certain very important respects from those of adolescents of a generation ago or, for that matter, of ten or twelve years ago. This is obviously true with respect to musical tastes and with respect to interest in making sufficiently good grades to graduate from high school and possibly enter college. Nevertheless, we can, with some safety, generalize with respect to the interests, capabilities, educational status, and educational needs of adolescents. Through the years, knowledge concerning these things has increased, and later in this chapter an attempt will be made to list and describe briefly the more important characteristics of adolescents of today.

Junior High School Adolescents. It should be remembered that in the junior high school there are many boys and girls who are not yet adolescents but who are approaching adolescence. Their bodies have not yet begun to undergo the physiological changes that differentiate men and women from boys and girls. Nevertheless, they have begun to be like adolescents in their interests, in their social life, in their current educational needs, and in their opinions relative to what constitute their own educational needs and interests.

There is a very great amount of variation from youngster to youngster in the age at which they enter adolescence and, in addition, girls mature, on the average, about eighteen months earlier than boys. In general, however, it may be said that the very large majority, probably 80 to 90 per cent, of all girls are in the period of adolescence from the ages of twelve to sixteen, while about the same proportion of boys are at this stage between the ages of thirteen and a half and eighteen. In the seventh grade, the great majority of girls are at least in the early stages of adolescence—being, with few exceptions, twelve years of age or older—while the majority of boys in the seventh grade and a goodly percentage of those in the eighth grade are still preadolescents.

Adolescents Stay in School Longer. Until well into the present century, the boy or girl who stayed in school beyond the ninth grade was exceptional in a number of ways. In 1900 less than 5 per cent of the adolescents in the United States remained in school until graduation from high school. In every subsequent decade until 1920, the number of students attending grades nine through twelve approximately doubled. Although the population increased somewhat at this time, the increase in enrolments was even greater and the increase in the proportion of students attending grades ten through twelve was doubled.

In 1900 a little more than 10 per cent of the youngsters of appropriate age were attending grades nine through twelve. By 1930 this had increased to approximately 50 per cent, and by 1960 to approximately 80 per cent. It is safe to predict that by 1970 nearly 90 per cent of the young people of appropriate age will be enrolled in secondary schools.

As was previously indicated, in 1900 less than 5 per cent of the adolescents remained in school long enough to graduate from high school. By 1930 this proportion had almost reached 50 per cent, and by 1960 it had slightly exceeded 60 per cent. It is safe to predict that by 1970 more than two-thirds of all young people will be graduating from high school and that by 1980 approximately three-fourths will be doing so. Consequently, the high school student body is approximately a random sample of young people of high school age and is becoming more nearly so.

PERTINENT CHARACTERISTICS OF ADOLESCENTS

A Period of Transition and Inner Development. Two fundamental characteristics of adolescents are very important for the thinking of educators: (1) Boys and girls of this age are in a period that is obviously one of transition from childhood to manhood and womanhood, and (2) very great changes are taking place in their bodies, in their attitudes, in their interests, and in their capabilities. In planning the program of the schools including planning the daily work, there must be kept in mind the facts that these young people are undergoing these important changes and that the school must work with them and guide them accordingly.

Secondly, curriculum planners should bear in mind that individual boys and girls in any given class or grade differ greatly with respect to the rapidity with which these important changes are taking place and that their interests differ greatly with respect to the degree of advancement that they have obtained in their transition from children to adults.

Many investigators of adolescence have set forth what they believe to be the characteristics of adolescents that are important for education. While there is rather common agreement among these investigators, they differ in their conclusions. In the following pages of this chapter, an attempt is made to set forth what seems to be a consensus of the opinions of those whom the author thinks are the most outstanding authorities on adolescence.

A careful examination of these characteristics reveals that they all seem to be expressions of self, of a changing and growing ego, and of consciousness of self. With the onset of adolescence, boys and girls tend to think more about themselves—their bodies, their social relations, the degree of acceptance they receive, and their vocational, educational, and marital futures.

They also are prone to carry on in their minds an examination of the degree to which they are "normal," and in what respects they may be abnormal, particularly where they are likely to be handicapped in achieving their desires for recognition, admiration, and acceptance by their peers.

The Desire for Recognition. Characteristic of all human beings from shortly after birth until death is the desire to be recognized, respected, envied, feared, and loved by other human beings. People not only attempt to discover and develop qualities that will bring about favorable recognition, but they also spend effort and develop techniques for attracting attention that will, they hope, result in favorable recognition. For adolescents, satisfaction may take many forms: It may involve recognition by adults in their family of the fact that they are now larger and more mature—that they are no longer children. It almost always takes the form of independence from adults, particularly their parents. It may take the form of acceptance by age peers of both sexes. It usually involves admiration for increased strength, attractive personality, material possessions such as clothes and automobiles, and the degree to which they have achieved independence from adults and adult standards.

It is exceedingly important for all those who plan for, and work with, adolescents to recognize the critical importance of the increased and increasing desire of young people to operate under their own command and to receive greater recognition. Among other things, it is exceedingly painful to adolescents to undergo types of embarrassment that in their minds tend to detract from favorable recognition and acceptance. For example, the use of satire, ridicule, or open and sharp criticism before others; being given educational tasks they cannot perform well; and constant inability to satisfy their desire for independence, recognition, and approval are unusually unfavorable for the development of sound personalities and good attitudes toward themselves, adults, school, teachers, and learning. It should likewise be borne in mind by curriculum makers, counselors, teachers, and school administrators as well as parents, that young people must be given responsibilities that interest them at least to some extent—tasks that challenge them by not being too easy and too simple but that offer them hope of achieving at least some satisfying degree of success.

Unfortunate Effects of Frustration and Failure. The writer of this chapter has visited four penal institutions for young people, three for boys and one for girls. He has discussed youth problems with the educational directors and counselors and has examined carefully records in two of these institutions—one the federal penitentiary for young people in Denver, Colorado, and the other the youth school at Tracy, California, established and operated by the California Youth Authority. It was very revealing to discover the extent to which these youngsters have suffered frustration and failure in school and had been humiliated, scolded, and punished in various way by teachers and parents for their inferior educational achievements and unsocial behavior at school. Only a small percentage had remained in school to graduate. It seemed, also, that their aggressive misbehavior had had important roots in frustrations associated with school—its curriculum and methods employed in efforts to motivate or enforce them to perform tasks in which they were not interested or which they were unable to understand and accomplish.

It also has been noticed by psychologists, counselors, and others who have studied youth and its problems that, in the period of adolescence —indeed, in any period of life—frustration and failure, whatever slight contributions such experiences make to development of character, constitute a very great hazard, usually diminishing confidence in oneself, in others, and in the fairness of life and life situations and causing a tendency to withdraw from reality. Indeed, the great majority of cases of mental illness among young people, which has become much more common in recent years, is some form of neurosis, if not schizophrenia, that has resulted from a retreat from real situations into daydreaming and an imaginary world in which they are able to satisfy their very strong instinctive desires and appetites. In many others, there is no serious mental illness but there is a tendency to withdraw to some extent from reality and to find expression by identification with heroes and heroines in literature, movies, popular music, and television and, indeed, with their friends, particularly those who are attractive in appearance and those who are leaders in revolt against adults and adult standards.

The Desire for Security. Among the characteristics of adolescents is the increased desire for security not only for the present but also for the future. This may express itself in many ways and may be seen in many areas of adolescents' behavior. They wish to feel secure in their homes and obviously loved by their parents. They wish to feel secure in school, to have the good will and respect of their teachers, and to be well established among, and well liked and admired by, their peers. Indeed, it might well be said that the desire to be admired and accepted by their peers is perhaps the strongest wish of typical adolescents, though there are those who believe that this wish is not as imperative in the 1960's as it was in several previous decades.

The Dependence and Independence Duality. It is interesting to note an apparent inconsistency of the typical adolescent though at times craving to be independent, to operate under his own will, and to "stand on his own feet," he evidences almost, if not actually, at the same time a very keen desire for protection and for security. Marriage counselors report that one of the major reasons for early marriage is the desire of young people to be associated closely with another young person, frequently of the opposite sex, and to enjoy the security that comes from living together and from consciousness of common goals. By marriage, such young people escape from the dread loneliness and from the sense of insecurity that loneliness brings.

The Desire for Novelty and Excitement. Another characteristic of adolescents is the increased desire for excitement and novelty. They wish to have new experiences. With the development of their bodies and minds, they seem to want to do many things that create excitement out of which they will get a "bang" or a "kick." At this period, too, they have an increased amount of curiosity about the world around them, which is characteristic of children, but which goes farther than their immediate environment. Idealism and curiosity operate together to cause adolescents to intensify their search for a scale of values, for personal and social ideals, and, indeed, for a philosophy of life, usually including religion, that will give them some standards for behavior and may involve recognition by a supernatural power and a possibility of immortality.

A Period of Conflicts. Adolescence is also a period of conflicts, some of which are extremely important for young people, for example, the conflict between the new knowledge of science and religion, the conflict between the new knowledge of ethics and the behavior of adults about them, the conflict between the urge for satisfaction of sex appetites and the restraints of convention and the ethics of the great majority of other human beings, and the conflict between a great amount of selfishness and a growing desire for recognition and approval of others as well as for the satisfaction of one's conscience by altruism and fairness. Young people, for example, who are very much concerned with discrimination against Mexicans in Denver, Negroes in the South, and Puerto Ricans and Negroes in New York City are not immune to temptation to be quite unsportsmanlike at basketball games, attempting to disconcert opponents and expressing excitement by throwing pop bottles and other waste materials on the basketball floor, endangering players and officials.

Because these traits vary greatly with individuals, it is very desirable for teachers who are planning course-of-study materials from day to day and, indeed, for curriculum makers in general to acquire much information about the individual students with whom the curriculum is to be used, by means of questionnaires, check lists, observations of teachers, statements from parents and counselors, and as many sources as are available in a particular school. Even if the basic desires of young people had been very much the same at birth, each individual has been conditioned by his previous experience at home, at school, and with his peers, as well as by television and by reading so that these basic desires and propensities have been strengthened, weakened, or given direction in a variety of ways, producing much variation among individuals.

The Need for Direction. It should be recognized by all having to do with planning and working with youth that, in general, human nature among adolescents cannot be changed. One can only work with it, attempting to direct it into more useful, at least less harmful, channels, realizing that, all along, compromises must be made. Nothing can be done, nor should it be done even if it could be, to suppress or to frustrate the desires of young people for independence, recognition, security, power, and success. Indeed, to a relative extent, the same may be said of the sex drive, which develops greatly in adolescence.

RECENT DEVELOPMENTS AFFECTING ADOLESCENT LIFE

It has been recognized by many recent students of adolescence that some patterns of expression of these characteristics, particularly the more important ones, may be attributed to certain definite causes including the following:

1. There is a greatly decreased opportunity for companionship between young people and their parents; young people work much less alongside their parents in the home, in the field, in the shop, in the store. Hence, there is much less opportunity for young people to absorb adult ways of thinking and for adults to pass on to their children the knowledge, insight, and wisdom that come through many years of life experience.

2. There is a greatly increased amount of materialism. They witness all about them a greatly increased absorption of adults including their parents with desires for material things such as cars, household appliances, jewelry, cosmetics, improvement of appearance, consumption of alcohol, sex, television programs, and movies.

3. There is apparently a significant increase in the physical and psychological energy of young people that seems to go along with a marked increase in weight and height of both male and female adolescents. The reasons for this are not clear, although it is thought likely that better foods rich in vitamins have made substantial contributions.

The trend toward urbanization involves, as city life does, important additional hazards. The mere fact of relative anonymity tends to release one from the behavior-restricting bonds of ethics. The lack of playgrounds and of play opportunities, the great opportunities for amusement of borderline if not vicious and immoral types, and the lack of close friends and acquaintances in the neighborhood all contribute to the possibility of unsocial behavior and to the development during adolescence of attitudes that are opposed to the standards and ideals of adults.

Adolescents from Substandard Environments. As a result of the development of slums in American cities and of the increased problems of juvenile delinquency in substandard homes in such areas, problems of providing appropriate educational counseling and guidance programs for adolescents who come from these substandard homes have developed to a greater extent than formerly.

In some of the larger cities, notably, Chicago, Milwaukee and New York, special attention is being given to this problem and special programs are being developed. It has been found that, for these programs to be effective, they definitely must draw in the parents as well as the students. Parents are called upon and urged strongly to visit the school at times when it is not in session and at times when entertainment programs likely to be of interest to parents of the community are provided. Breaking down the barriers of suspicion, bitterness, and inferiority complexes that these people erect between themselves and the schools and many other social agencies is not easy, and unusual efforts are being put forth in an increasing number of cities to bring them into the school, where contacts may be established that can be exploited for the benefit of the adolescents in school. It has been noted in several of these cities that, where appropriate contacts have been made, particularly where a considerable proportion of the parents have been brought into the schools several times, not only do the interest of the affected students in school subjects increase and their grades improve, but juvenile delinquency declines among those groups.

In some districts, plans are being made to erect a community school building that is useful not only for the regular program of the school but also as a community center open Saturdays, evenings, and in the summer, for recreation and appropriate social events and for adult education.

NOTABLE STATEMENTS OF THE NEEDS OF ADOLESCENTS

Imperative Needs as Set Forth by the Educational Policies Commission of the National Education Association.

1. All youth need to develop salable skills and those understandings and attitudes that make the worker an intelligent and productive participant in economic life. To this end, most youth need supervised work experience as well as education in the skills and knowledges of their occupations.
2. All youth need to develop and maintain good health and physical fitness.

3. All youth need to understand the rights and duties of the citizen of a democratic society and be diligent and competent in the performance of their obligations as members of the community and citizens of the state and nation.
4. All youth need to understand the significance of the family for the individual and for society, and the conditions conducive to successful family life.
5. All youth need to know how to purchase and use goods and services intelligently, understanding both the values received by consumers and the economic consequences of their acts.
6. All youth need to understand the methods of science, the influence of science on human life, and the main scientific facts concerning the nature of the world and of man.
7. All youth need opportunities to develop their capacities to appreciate beauty—in literature, art, music, and nature.
8. All youth need to be able to use their leisure time well and to budget it wisely, balancing activities that yield satisfactions to the individual with those that are socially useful.
9. All youth need to develop respect for other persons, to grow in their insight into ethical values and principles, and be able to live and work cooperatively with others.
10. All youth need to grow in ability to think rationally, to express their thoughts clearly, and to listen with understanding.[1]

Needs of Junior High School Students. A group of junior high school administrators revised the list and set forth the following statement as especially applicable to the junior high school level:

1. All junior high school youth need to explore their own aptitudes and to have experiences basic to occupational proficiency.
2. All junior high school youth need to develop and maintain abundant physical and mental health.
3. All junior high school youth need to be participating citizens of their school and community, with increasing orientation to adult citizenship.
4. All junior high school youth need experiences and understandings, appropriate to their age and development, which are the foundation of successful home and family life.
5. All junior high school youth need to develop a sense of values of material things and of the rights of ownership.
6. All junior high school youth need to learn about the natural and physical environment and its effects on life, and to have opportunities for using the scientific approach in the solution of problems.
7. All junior high school youth need the enriched living which comes from appreciation of and expression in the arts and from experiencing the beauty and wonder of the world around them.
8. All junior high school youth need to have a variety of socially accept-able and personally satisfying leisure-time experiences which con-

[1] National Education Association of the United States, Educational Policies Commission, *Education for All American Youth* (Washington, D.C.: National Education Association of the United States, 1944), pp. 225–226.

tribute either to their personal growth or to their development in wholesome group relations, or to both.

9. All junior high school youth need experiences in group living which contribute to personality and character development. They need to develop respect for other persons and their rights [and] to grow in ethical insights.

10. All junior high school youth need to grow in their ability to observe, listen, read, think, speak, and write with purpose and appreciation.[2]

Under the rather ambiguous heading of "developmental tasks" of adolescents, Professor Havighurst, of the University of Chicago, and others have listed types of goals for adolescents that constitute real needs and needs usually recognized by adolescents. The following are most often listed:

1. Accepting one's physique and accepting a masculine or a feminine sex role.
2. New relations with age mates of both sexes.
3. Emotional independence of parents and other adults.
4. Achieving assurance of economic independence.
5. Selecting and preparing for an occupation.
6. Developing intellectual skills and concepts necessary for civic competence.
7. Desiring and achieving socially responsible behavior.
8. Preparing for marriage and family life.
9. Building conscious values in harmony with an adequate scientific world picture.[3]

Interests of the Adolescent. While interests vary greatly from individual to individual and somewhat between the sexes, and, indeed, with the passage of time, nevertheless, in general, they seem to have more or less common and permanent characteristics. It is necessary, however, for the curriculum maker, the teacher, and the counselor to become acquainted with the differing interests of adolescents of the age level with which they are working and the individual interests of the particular boy or girl, or boys and girls, with whom they are working.

Students of adolescents have always pointed out the tendency of young people to be associated with groups, to form gangs of one kind or another for various purposes, good or bad. That tendency, of course, has taken many forms in the past few years, including a very well developed and somewhat sophisticated social life, much group competition, expansion of activity programs in the school, development of group learning activities in the classroom and out, and, of course, the unfor-

[2] California State Department of Education, *Handbook for California Junior High Schools,* Bulletin 18 (Sacramento: California State Department of Education, 1949), pp. 6–11.

[3] Robert J. Havighurst, *Developmental Tasks and Education* (New York: Longmans, Green & Co., Inc., 1950), p. 2.

tunate banding together of young people who, wishing to please their leaders and being, in many instances, embittered or disgruntled and certainly aggressive and defiant, to commit various serious crimes, particularly vandalism, arson, sex crimes, and attacks upon the person of parents and other adults who restrict their freedom.

It is natural that adolescents become more and more interested in cars as cars become both faster and more available. Cars also play a part in adolescent social life, for instance, as a locale for courtship.

The interests of both boys and girls, particularly boys, in space travel have greatly increased, although this interest has always characterized preadolescents and adolescents.

Young people have become more interested in clothing in the present generation than in the previous ones. They have also become more interested in cosmetics and hair styling including the "bushy head" and other extreme types of hairdos for girls, the beards and mustaches of the "beatniks," and the sideburns of the "greasy-haired kids."

No discussion of interests would be complete without emphasizing the greatly increased interest in security that adolescents have developed in recent years. Oddly enough, most of them do not try to keep the lines of communication open with their parents but look elsewhere for security, particularly to leaders among their peers and to daydreaming. The lack of opportunities for employment and the necessity for military service have put a new complexion on this need and have contributed to the increase of fears that the adolescent usually attempts to conceal but that, nevertheless, one observes to be very permanent in the typical adolescent. The increased difficulty of becoming acceptable vocationally and socially merely by completion of school and, if possible, one or more years of college has generated further fears on the part of a good many young people.

There may be seen running through the above interests a very strong and deep-seated desire for recognition. To be sure, this is a characteristic of practically all individuals, but it has been noted to blossom out to become stronger with the onset of adolescence, and today its manifestations are even more obvious than heretofore.

COURSE-OF-STUDY PLANNING FOR THE LESS CAPABLE AND FOR THE MORE CAPABLE

Characteristics of the Dull Pupil. Following is a statement of the more important characteristics of the less capable adolescent:

1. He learns in shorter steps or units.
2. He needs more frequent checkups on his progress and more remedial work.

3. His vocabulary is more limited and less precise.
4. He needs to have many new words made very clear in meaning.
5. He does not see relative generalizations or meaning as readily.
6. He has less creative ability and less ability to plan for himself.
7. He is more interested in individuals and in practical topics.
8. He is slightly slower in acquiring mechanical and motor skills, particularly complicated ones.
9. In proportion to his dulness, he tires less quickly of mechanical routine tasks and he tires more quickly of difficult reading or abstract discussion.
10. He is quick to generalize crudely, is lacking in self-criticism, and is easily satisfied with superficial answers.
11. He is less envious.
12. He has had unhappy experiences with previous schoolwork and is, hence, more likely to be irritable in class, lacking in self-confidence, and more interested in non-school life.
13. He is more susceptible to the suggestions of other persons.
14. His difficulties in learning are cumulative.
15. He has a narrow range of interests.
16. He possesses a slow reaction time.
17. He tends to engage in overcompensating activities.
18. He is less able to see the end results of his actions. Remote, long-range goals are not impelling to him.
19. He fails to detect identical elements in different types of situations.
20. His attention span is short and must be reinforced by engaging appeal.
21. He especially needs evidence of his progress.

Characteristics of the Abler Pupil. Following are characteristics of the bright student that must be kept in mind when planning for him:

1. The bright student possesses greater energy and more curiosity.
2. He is usually more sociable and works better with others.
3. He is especially good in furnishing leadership in learning situations.
4. He is much more capable in dealing with abstractions and needs much less concrete learning material such as audio-visual aids, although they are very effective with him.
5. He requires much less repetition in drill work, although even with the brightest some drill work is necessary.
6. He perceives relationships much more clearly and quickly.
7. He usually prefers to work under his own planning and initiative and can do so more profitably.
8. He is much more interested in exploring new and advanced areas of learning, particularly book learning.

9. He becomes bored more quickly with simple routine tasks, particularly those the meaning of which he does not understand.

10. He learns mechanical processes much more quickly than the average pupil.

11. He dislikes tasks he does not understand and memorization, although he is superior at the latter.

12. He has confidence in his own abilities and is much less sensitive to criticism and suggestions.

13. He is very likely to appear lazy if given uninteresting things to do, and is likely to seek short cuts unless he possesses a rather wide range of worthy interests.

IMPORTANT FACTORS IN ADOLESCENT LEARNING

Curriculum builders must, of course, keep in mind the way in which young people learn and the factors or conditions that are favorable to effective learning activity.

The Factor of Activity, Use, Repetition, and Review. It has been said by many that one learns only by doing. Of course, accurately interpreted, this means one learns only by means of experience and, therefore, what is to be learned must be read, performed, felt, seen, or heard—experienced in some fashion so that a sufficient impression, or modification of the cortex and neural system, has been achieved that will enable the individual to recall facts or experiences, to perform skills, to behave to some extent along the lines of desirable habits, and to acquire ideals, interests, appreciations, and attitudes. Naturally, the selection and arrangement of curriculum materials involves deciding upon ways in which these appropriate learning experiences may be developed, the amount of repetition, the amount of practice, and the provisions for review.

The Factor of Associated Satisfaction. It has long been observed that there is a tendency to repeat an experience that is pleasurable—one that satisfies interest or desire or contributes to the achievement of goals. This was, for many years, referred to as the "law of effect." It has also been observed that one tends to avoid unpleasant experiences in school, as well as elsewhere, although unpleasant experiences may be recalled for many years.

As an illustration of this law, we may point out the favorable effect upon learning of knowledge of success in learning activities or in performed activities that have an indirect influence upon learning. Manufacturers of teaching machines have exploited this idea not only in their advertising but to a considerable extent in the construction and operation of the machines.

It has also been noted that learning activities that are planned and conducted by groups of students as peers seem to set up conditions that give pleasure and, consequently, to facilitate learning. Likewise, materials for learning and learning activities that tend to minister to the needs and desires such as curiosity, the desire to construct something, or the desire to get into college are pleasurable and favorable to learning.

The Factor of Application and Association. Learning that has been associated in mind, muscles, and nerves with other learning tends to be recalled more readily and more accurately than learning not so associated. Because of this factor, there is much to be said for having subject materials organized in broad categories rather than in small segments, in core and fusion integrated plans of curriculum, as well as arranging items of curriculum materials and learning activities in such a way as to be associated with uses and applications in life and with other items of knowledge and experience.

The Factor of Apperception and Readiness. What one learns is definitely conditioned by the nature and quantity of what one has already learned, and by the ease with which earlier learning has been achieved. One can interpret new experiences only in the light of previous experiences. This factor makes it necessary in curriculum construction for development of continuity, for the use of preparatory materials that may have relatively little value in themselves but that pave the way for important associated learnings to come later.

Particularly important in the preparation of young people in the primary grades for learning to read and for the study of arithmetic, there operates throughout elementary and secondary schools the principle of readiness, in other words, the principle that holds that individuals may be best introduced to learning activities if they have had experiences from which the new materials may normally develop. Various facets of this principle have been set forth for many years, such as (1) from the simple to the complex, (2) from the concrete to the abstract, (3) from the near to the remote, (4) from the present to the past and the future, and (5) from the psychological to the logical.

The Factor of Intensity of Experience. Not only is learning conditioned by the degree of pleasurable effect of the learning experience, it is also conditioned by the intensity of the experience. Usually, for example, experiences that come from real things rather than from symbols, such as observed pictures, objects, and human beings rather than words only, are more effective with respect to both the permanence and accuracy of learning. This argues for the use of audio-visual materials, demonstrations, field trips, and other learning materials and situations that possess a much greater degree of reality than words. To be sure, many verbal curriculum materials can be employed in much less time than audio-visual materials, and the compromise must be made, but the most successful curriculum maker will be alert to the opportunities to use non-verbal materials where they are obviously superior to verbal ones.

Interest and Intensity of Experience. The intensity of any learning experience depends very much upon the attitude and the interest of the student. In other words, the keenness of the experience depends upon the desire of the student to learn a particular item or items, and his interest in them for other reasons.

The following principles of relative interest are observed by the more effective curriculum maker: Direct, or intrinsic, interest is more effective than an indirect interest. In other words, something that is done or read because it is in itself sufficiently interesting to attract, regardless of what learning may result, is the preferred type of curriculum material or learning activity. Learning for the purpose of obtaining good grades, passing a test, or satisfying a teacher is, of course, associated with an indirect interest that is not as powerful or as profound as direct interest. Years ago, an attempt was made to determine the attention spans of children in various grades. It was discovered that attention spans were very short for materials and activities not directly interesting, and that they were much longer for learning activities that were in themselves interesting than had been stated in articles and textbooks treating the subject.

To materials and activities definitely of direct interest to students is given what is called spontaneous attention, and, with those in which they have only indirect, or extrinsic, interest, reliance must be made upon forced attention that grows out of a feeling of a need to satisfy standards of others or to obtain money or some distinction toward which the learning appears to contribute.

Generic vs. Specific Needs. Needs may be generic or specific. For example, a youngster may need to know a specific fact, to construct a specific object, or to obtain something that he wishes to have, that is, the answer to his specific need. On the other hand, he may participate in learning activities for the purpose of obtaining a grade; that, of course, is a generic need, because it applies to many types of learning materials and activities.

Immediate vs. Deferred Needs. Immediate needs are much more likely to result in motivation and an intense experience than deferred needs. It is typical of all human beings including adolescents to discover that interest in performing a task for which one is responsible is often inversely proportional to the amount of time before the material must be learned or the responsibility discharged.

Negative and Positive Needs or Incentives. While teachers very commonly appeal to negative needs, that is, to the desirability of avoiding punishment or other unpleasant experiences, it has been demonstrated over and over again that better learning is obtained by ministering to positive needs, in other words, assisting a student to acquire something he desires rather than to avoid an experience he feels he will not like.

There has been a tendency, in recent years, for good teachers to rely less and less upon artificial incentives that are of the nature of reward or punishment for learning effort or achievement rather than natural outcomes of learning. While the use of artificial incentives may seem to be necessary at specific times when all else fails, it is quite clear, from the points of view of developing permanent interests and of effects upon personality growth, pupil-teacher relationships, and other concomitant outcomes, that very extensive use of artificial incentives is almost certain to be harmful and should be resorted to only in the absence of natural incentives, specific needs, and intrinsic interest.

QUESTIONS, PROBLEMS, AND ISSUES FOR FURTHER THOUGHT

1. Review the statement of the characteristics of adolescents, with a view to assessing the importance of each in determining the curriculum. Can you think of other traits that you believe to be also important to those concerned with the curriculum?

2. What do you think is the relative importance of attempting to develop a curriculum adapted to the interests, capabilities, educational status, and recognized needs of adolescents, as compared to orientation toward the needs of society, in preparing them to take their place and meet their responsibilities in life as they will find it?

3. What do you believe to be the relative importance of current needs, recognized or not, of adolescents, as compared to their future needs, in the matter of curriculum construction?

4. Do you agree with the author's statement that the expanding ego of the adolescent is the basis for the types of behavior indicated in the chapter?

5. What do you believe to be the relative importance of the desire of adolescents for excitement and adventure as a criterion for the selection and organization of curriculum materials and learning experiences? Can you give a good example of how learning materials might be selected and employed that will tend to satisfy this yearning?

6. To what extent do you believe that the desire of young people to finish high school and perhaps go on to college may be used as motivation for learning curriculum materials not in themselves of direct interest to adolescents?

7. In what ways do you think that boys and girls in the early stages of adolescence differ from those in the later stages?

8. To what extent do you believe that the power of the desire for independence should be taken into consideration in the selection, organization, and utilization of curriculum materials?

9. Do you believe that interests and similar traits of adolescent boys differ from those of adolescent girls? Do such differences as you may think of suggest anything to those responsible for curriculum?
10. In what ways, in connection with curriculum construction, do you think that the keen desire of adolescents for recognition may be utilized as a criterion? Do you believe that desires for recognition and for experiences that tend to bring recognition are of service? Do you believe that there is any illustration of this in our experience with the Peace Corps?
11. To what extent do you consider the apparent desire for association with other adolescents a useful criterion in the selection and organization of curriculum materials and learning experiences?
12. Give some illustrations of how curriculum materials as they exist in some subjects in some schools tend to be oppressive or frustrating to adolescents.
13. Evaluate the relative importance of the factors in adolescent life set forth on pages 49 to 54 of this chapter.
14. Can you think of any ways in which the curriculum may be developed so as to cultivate and put to use the ideals and idealism of adolescents?
15. In what ways can the curriculum be improved with a view to having the youngsters experience success and have immediate knowledge of success?

SUPPLEMENTARY MATERIALS

Selected Readings

Alberty, Harold B., and Elsie J. Alberty. *Reorganizing the High School Curriculum* (3d ed.). New York: The Macmillan Co., 1962. Chapter 4, "The Adolescent in American Society."

Barnes, Melvin W. "The Nature and Nurture of Early Adolescents," *Teachers College Record,* LVII (May, 1956), 513–21.

Christensen, Harold I. "Adolescence: Madness, Mystery, or Milestone?" *The Education Digest,* XXVII (November, 1961), 29–31.

Faunce, Roland C., and Morrel J. Clute, *Teaching and Learning in the Junior High School.* San Francisco: Wadsworth Publishing Co., Inc., 1961. Chapter 2, "Characteristics and Needs of the Early Adolescent."

Gallup, George, and Evan Hill. "Youth: The Cool Generation," *Saturday Evening Post,* CCXXXIV (December 23, 1961), 63–83.

Harvey, C. C. "Most Serious Problems of Seniors," *Bulletin of the N.A.S.S.P.,* XL (September, 1956), 52–57.

"Junior-High Girls," *The Education Digest,* XXVII (September, 1961), 38–40.

Klausmeier, Herbert J. *Teaching in the Secondary School.* New York: Harper & Row, 1958. Chapter 2, "Adolescents Today: Their Nature and Needs."

McNassor, Donald. "The Changing Character of Adolescents," *California Journal of Secondary Education,* XXXI (March, 1956), 128–33.

Noar, Gertrude. *The Junior High School—Today and Tomorrow.* Englewood Cliffs, N.J.: Prentice-Hall, Inc., 1961. Chapter 2, "Meeting the Needs of Youth," 30–53.

Patterson, Franklin. "The Adolescent Citizen and the Junior High School," *Bulletin of the N.A.S.S.P.,* No. 274 (May, 1962), 68–79.

Rivlin, Harry S. *Teaching Adolescents.* Appleton-Century-Crofts, Inc., 1961. Chapter 14, "Contribution to Adolescents' Personal and Social Adjustment."

VAN TIL, WILLIAM, GORDON F. VARS, and JOHN H. LOUNSBURY. *Modern Education for the Junior High School Years.* Indianapolis: The Bobbs-Merrill Co., Inc., 1961. Chapter 7, "The Personal-Social Needs of Early Adolescents."

WATTENBERG, W. W. "Preadolescents in the Junior High," *Educational Leadership,* XIV (May, 1957), 473–77.

AUDIO-VISUAL MATERIALS

Films

Age of Turmoil. McGraw-Hill. 20 minutes.
Appointment with Youth. McGraw-Hill Text-Films. 26 minutes.
Emotional Maturity. McGraw-Hill Text-Films. 20 minutes.
Meaning of Adolescence. McGraw-Hill. 16 minutes.
Meeting the Needs of Adolescents. McGraw-Hill. 19 minutes.
Meeting the Needs of Adolescents. McGraw-Hill Text-Films. 19 minutes.
Physical Aspects of Puberty. McGraw-Hill Text-Films. 19 minutes.
Social-Sex Attitudes in Adolescence. McGraw-Hill Text-Films. 22 minutes.
The Changing Voice. International Film Bureau Inc. Educational Films. 45 minutes.

Filmstrip

Adolescent Development Series. McGraw-Hill, 1953. 34 frames, black and white.

4

Community and the Curriculum

To understand the community as it relates to the curriculum and its purposes necessitates a consideration of the meaning and importance given to past relationships and an interest in, and concern for, improved community-school relationships as they affect the curriculum today. That these relationships exist and are to be perpetuated is important; however, an analysis of these relationships as they affected the curriculum in the past and will affect it in the future should help to define not only the role of the professional educator but also the place of significance to be enjoyed by those who cooperate in making education meaningful for youth today.

It is necessary, to facilitate an understanding of these relationships, to consider the several meanings given to them, to reveal how individuals from several communities were active in their concern for the curriculum, to indicate the tendency on the part of communities today to be very directly involved in curricular matters, and to show how the local school and community today integrate these experiences through the leadership they are now permitted to exert. Without such an analysis of these factors, it would be difficult to understand the true value of the community and its impact on the curriculum.

MEANING GIVEN TO PAST RELATIONSHIPS

Several interpretations are made of the relationships existing between the curriculum and the community. Of interest here are those that consider the definition of the community and the impact of that definition on the curriculum, reveal the student as the result of the community, consider the community as a resource for curricular experiences, view the curriculum in terms of the needs of the community, and view the relationships as involving personal relationships.

Nature of the Community and the Curriculum. To some, the role of the community as it relates to the curriculum entails a consideration of each of the "communities" of which the student is a member. At that level, it incorporates such communities—if the community is defined as a geographical area that concerns itself with its own problems and needs, has some feeling of unity, has something of a power structure, and creates a feeling of belongingness for the individual within it—as the world, the nation, and the local community. At the local level, however, the family, the neighborhood, and the school are also communities; in fact, they are the communities in which youths take an active part. What happens in each of these communities affects not only the content of the curriculum but also the changes in its objectives, the selection of learning experiences, the means to arrive at the fulfilment of the objectives, and whatever techniques are utilized to determine whether or not the objectives have been attained. Thus, how the community is defined determines the direction of the learning experience.

Youths, to another group, are the results of the communities of which they are a part; thus, what happens in the curriculum will have meaning only to the extent that the impact of the several communities on youth are recognized, known, and considered in the teaching-learning process. Thus, the experiences to which youths are exposed in the classroom must be considered in the light of the background from which they came.

Community Resources and the Curriculum. To many, the relationship between the curriculum and the community is most real at the *community-resources* level. People, places, and things in the community have been of concern in every field included in the curriculum. In fact, there is ample evidence in the literature of the use of community resources in the development of the intellectual, social, physical, recreational, and aesthetic interests of youth. Thus, stores, museums, libraries, government agencies, field trips, national monuments, etc., have commonly been used by teachers to make the child conscious of what words mean, sensitive to the need for intelligent observation, and responsive to the value of community itself. That the school has utilized community resources on both planned and unplanned bases is well known to community leaders and educators alike.

Community Needs and the Curriculum. In some communities, educators have attempted to build the curriculum around the community, narrowly defined, and have considered their mission to be the development of the curriculum through the development of the community. While not as common in this country today, this approach still exists in a few places.

Personal Relationships with Community Members and the Curriculum. At another professional level, educators themselves were to consider it their obligation to become personally involved in the community—to know its people, its problems, and its desires. Thus, it was hoped that, through the involvement of those engaged in the teaching process, the teachers would learn of the human resources, appreciate the desires of the community, and consider them in the learning experience. The relationship between the community administration and the local board of education was considered the most significant; together they acted on matters relating to the curriculum.

Thus, any consideration of the community and the curriculum must first include a definition of the relationship between them, for the type of relationship in existence in each community reveals the philosophy of learning and teaching—the very meaning of the curriculum for those engaged in education. Care must be exercised lest the definition limit the significance of the community in today's schools. To arrive at the true picture of the community could mean combining some of the meanings so as to create what would, in most cases, be a more realistic view of the impact of the community on the curriculum.

COMMUNITY CONCERN WITH THE CURRICULUM

Historically, each generation in every community has transmitted certain principles, practices, and values that it had found significant in the resolution of the challenges and problems of that generation. Each has indicated what it considered traditionally and culturally sound and necessary and how, through the mastery of certain facts, skills, attitudes, and appreciations, it had intended to educate the succeeding generation in such a manner as to ensure not only its survival but the survival of its culture as well. While much of this was handed down from generation to generation by word of mouth only, it did, nevertheless, constitute what was to be learned.

In fact, each generation reacted to its heritage. A given community could maintain the status quo and consider that contribution to be its duty to society; it could ignore the status quo in whole or in part and degenerate; it could, conditions permitting, seemingly and on occasions actually, so modify the past heritage through the incorporation of others as to produce another. Aspects of all three of these reactions to the heritage could, at times, in certain cultures, and with due regard to factors affecting the acceleration or retardation of the process, operate simultaneously. Thus it is possible to see how this process was continuous and to observe in every community those principles, practices, and values that remained significant. Certain of them remained constant from the very beginnings of American society in colonial life, while others came to include much more from the European cultures from which they were borrowed, and others were modified to fit the demands of the day. Even the retention of the constant values did not just happen, for, throughout the history of America, values were fought for—verbally and otherwise.

There were other communities within the local community that also affected not only the quantity but also the quality of the educational experiences to which the youths were exposed. At the local level, there was the family, the neighborhood, the school, and organizations that made their influences on the curriculum felt. Simultaneously, governments at the national, state, and local levels made their influence on the curriculum apparent.

Family Influences on the Curriculum. Foremost among the communities that affected the child was the family, for it was in the family that the child received his first education. What he learned there, how much he learned, what education he was to get, why, and where: all were felt in time by the schools to which families related their desires and aspirations or failed to do so. In fact, the family could decide what kind of education its children should have. The influences of the home as they were reflected by the youth in schools were well known, for, in the teaching that took place, the instructors had to consider the reserve of experiences students had gained before entering upon the more formal aspects of education in the classroom. These experiences were the stepping stones to the curriculums with which the teachers and students were concerned.

Nature of the Local Neighborhood and the Curriculum. Such was also the case of the influences that the neighborhood exerted on the curriculum, for the neighborhood, as another of the communities in which youth took a more active part and in a more intimate frame of reference, was felt to affect the progress of youth in the school. It was up to the teacher to relate these experiences to the curriculum or vice versa, in some instances to detour around them. A school located in a neighborhood interested in the best for its children presented a challenge of another sort. Thus, the type of neighborhood in which the school was located affected the work of the student and the teachers.

School Life and the Curriculum. The school is the most formally organized of the communities of which youths are a part. They approach the school with preconceived, but nevertheless real to them, attitudes toward the home, the neighborhood, the school, and the community— broadly and narrowly defined. From each, they may have experienced feelings of acceptance or rejection, recognition or lack of it, frustration or satisfaction, anxieties or releases from tension. They bring their experiences with them. These experiences may be responsible for their successes and their failures in the school. In the school, they find another power structure, another set of traditions, customs and mores, and values that may or may not be in agreement with what they had previously encountered. For, in the school, youths are obliged to adjust to the adult population there, to their peers, and to the well-developed pattern of living that is innate in the organization of the school as a community. To be equal to reconciling the frequently conflicting values that result from this adjustment or lack of it is one of the greatest challenges faced by youth. Needless to say, the school must consider, too frequently, values that are not of its making.

Special-Interest Groups and the Curriculum. Organizations, associations, and institutions given to special interests have, almost from the inception of American education, made their influence on the curriculum felt. Regarded as part of an evolving way of life, these groups are frequently influential in determining not only what is to be taught but what means are used in the teaching.

Thus, members of these several communities work individually and concurrently on matters relating to the educational experiences of youth. Being established within the legal framework of a Constitution, the American way of life is further clarified: Man himself is important and, with time, becomes even more important. He does not exist for the state. He is an active participant in society and in the government that is a part of it. Democracy, founded almost as an experiment, has come to be the pattern for living in the United States. Yet, a review of the early history of American education reveals that it had always been concerned with all youths or with curriculums that take into consideration either individual differences or the desires of society—narrowly or broadly defined.

Federal and State Government and the Curriculum. Although the education of youth was early left to the local community with the guidance that it was to need coming in time from the state government, the federal government has by no means ignored what was going on or was to go on in the nation's schools. Thus, any attempt to appreciate the value of the community without considering these governmental interests would be incomplete.

Federal-Government Assistance to Education. At the national level, directly and indirectly, the federal government, from the latter part of the eighteenth century on, has had a definite interest in education. While much of this interest was not directed to the curriculum itself, certain federal grants-in-aid affected the financial status of the schools. Those after 1862, which were special-purpose grants, made definite provision for curriculums in agriculture, homemaking, trades, and industry. These grants admitted the necessity for making education functional and for considering education as including more than it had before. In fact, they extended education beyond the school and into the community by providing money for the extension of services, for specialists, and for the training of teachers for these areas.

An act of Congress in 1866 provided for the establishment of schools for military personnel in which the men could receive instruction in the common branches of English and in the history of the United States. The armed services themselves conducted or sponsored other types of educational programs that had the potential for serving military personnel at the time of service and later when they returned to civilian life. West Point, Annapolis, and, eventually, the Air Force Academy, whose curricular offerings, while unique in purpose, were not necessarily narrow in scope, were established by the federal government. Since 1917, when the Smith-Hughes bill was passed by Congress, providing federal aid for vocational education, the federal government has influenced the curriculum of secondary school.

State-Government Influences on the Curriculum. Since the federal Constitution had delegated the responsibility for the establishment of schools to the state, matters of immediate import relating to the curriculum depended on leadership from the state. With time, much deliberation, and very active leadership, the several states were able to stabilize practices relating to the possible content of the curriculum, to suggest means of accomplishing the purposes of the particular studies, to indicate the resources—broadly and narrowly defined—that could put life into learning, and to recommend possible techniques for measurement and evaluation that were related to student needs.

Considered also have been the lengths of the school period, the school day, and the school year, as well as methods of reporting to parents. Procedures related to the administration of the curriculum became part of standard practice. All of this and more was but to one end—the development of the kind of individual that it was hoped would be produced. Again, this did not just happen, for educators at every level became involved, and together they resolved difficulties and considered directions to take in the development of youth. Thus, the state as a community served as the coordinating force in the education of its youth.

Local Factors. Historically, an interest in education existed at the local level long before any of the colonies were even part of the union. In fact, the curriculum as it existed early in American history was not considered equal to the needs of the times, with the result that, by the time of Benjamin Franklin, the immediately functional was considered necessary for consideration in the curriculum of the day, so the interests of those in navigation, engineering, and commerce came to be felt. The arguments presented then were not too much different from some presented today, but the interests of the local community were heard, and their requests were considered in formulating curriculums that became a part of American education. Thus, early in American history and ever since then, the goal of having everyone educated was being realized for reasons other than those given by people of other countries.

The actual formal education of youth then and now has taken place at the local level. While the other communities were instrumental in suggesting and determining policies considered important in producing the educational product—the educated American—the success of American education depended largely on how successful the local system was in accomplishing its purposes. It was at the local level that educators visibly practiced their faith in a democracy as they referred it to the education of youth. On these educators depended the application of those psychological principles that were known to affect learning. The meaning they gave to guidance affected how they regarded and dealt with children.

At the local level, curriculums have taken form, objectives have become realities, and experiences have been selected in terms of the ends to be met. Together with representatives of the local community, the local superintendents of schools, considered experts in school affairs, worked out problems relating to what was to be taught and why it was to be taught. The history of this relationship would, by and large, reveal considerable understanding of the role of both parties and willingness on the part of each to work together.

COMMUNITIES IN THE TWENTIETH CENTURY

This century of life in the United States might well be considered as one of the most dynamic in American history. Within this past score of years, the complexion of the entire economy changed from one largely agricultural in nature and geared to peacetime production at the national level to one modified to fit the needs of a war economy. With the speed and ingenuity needed, America adjusted to a wartime economy so rapidly that it was able to provide what was needed at home and for much of the rest of the world. Then came the return to a peacetime economy that could not be a mere reversion to the past, as the world was not the same and neither was the nation. A transition period has brought America where it is today. Now is the time in which the knowledge, skills, attitudes, and dreams of a generation are intent upon creating

an even greater nation by the advances it can make. The impact of all
this on every community makes it difficult to call a community rural
anymore, just as it makes it difficult to say that all this happened at just
one time.

Social Mobility and Community Life. This transfer from the rural to
the urban was responsible not only for a social mobility that took place
and is still taking place but also for a change in what was of value.
Value, once considered in terms of ownership of land and homes, now
came to mean something else. People moved from the farm to the town,
from the town to the city, from one city to another, and from one region
to another not like so many nomads but for purposes that had hitherto
not existed. This mobility occurred in another way: Millions moved from
one house to another within a year, and other millions from one neighborhood to another and from the city proper to suburbia. To many, the
nation became small; communities were both similar and dissimilar; and
adjustments to neighborhoods and changing patterns of living were to be
anticipated.

Differences Among Communities. Today, communities more than 300
years old are but minutes away from communities less than a generation
old. Communities wealthy in economic resources that have made them
great are also but minutes away from communities whose resources are
no longer needed. Within each are neighborhoods where every privilege
may be enjoyed, and in each are neighborhoods where there is want,
degradation, and suffering. There are communities in which man, no
matter what his creed, color, or ethnic background is respected because
he is man; and there are others that question his form of worship, consider but certain ethnic groups, often their own only, as desirable, or
regard the color of a man's skin as the criterion for acceptance. Yet,
none of these communities can live alone, for successful living cannot
long endure at the expense of others.

Americans have prided themselves on their regional differences and
on their individuality; yet communities throughout the country bear
marks of distinction peculiar in part to their location, as well as to the
aspirations of their leaders—and their ability to envision the future and
prepare for it. Aware, too, of problems emanating from these differences,
these leaders saw that individuality, though desirable, existed in a frame
of reference that was not constant.

Similarity of Communities. While each community is unique and,
through its own individuality, has given much to the richness of national
life, communities do not differ so much as to eliminate their similarities.
Each is responsible for considering the needs of its members; each
attempts to satisfy the purposes that account for its existence; each estab-

lishes agencies responsible for the effective administration of the community. Thus, each establishes schools and other needed youth-serving institutions. Every community makes its demands on these institutions known and, through its selected representatives, takes the intiative in making known the desires of the community. It is, indeed, the prerogative of the community to indicate what it wants done.

New Patterns for Living Emerge. The parents of today's boys and girls look at the world differently. Many of them have been in, lived—possibly fought in—areas around the globe, and the world wars have made places that had been but names on a map very real to them. They know that modern means of transportation and communication have welded together, for a common cause, a conglomeration of individuals not only from their own local, state, or national community but also from other nations, areas, and regions. No longer was the world small to them. The parents of today's youth bring a different background of experiences to their families; they introduce new concepts which were not necessarily new, to their families.

Changes in the Role of Women. The war effort of World War II utilized the energies and the abilities of women. Since then, so much has their status changed that no longer is a working mother considered in financial need. Instead, society has established agencies to assist her with her work. That woman's place is only in the home was being questioned. Now she has broken the barriers of every profession. Women constitute a significant part of the labor force. Many are interested in becoming part of the labor market after their child-rearing years and make preparations to fit into possible positions. This is part of today's living, a part to which youths are becoming accustomed.

Challenges to the School. That many of these challenges became the concern of the schools is well known; perhaps the schools constituted the one community that did the most to consider them in their proper perspective. For many years, most educators have endeavored to produce the active citizen, the participant in community affairs, the man who wants value equal to, or even beyond, his expenditures, the person interested in improvement, the man who is alive to the events of the day on every scene, the man who has ideals, the man who is sensitive to the necessity for disturbing the status quo if the status quo is no longer equal to modern expectations. If educators had one fear, it was the fear of producing a man who merely copies the past and lives in the smugness of self-satisfaction. It could well be that the work of the schools has been very effective in relation to these general goals of education. In fact, one could conclude that American education has finally produced a generation that takes its birthright seriously.

Community Criticism. Thus, those who would ascribe to Sputnik, or to some of the critics of American education shortly thereafter, the responsibility for community interest in education seem to fail to take into consideration the fact that everything was moving forward at the time and that the community, broadly and narrowly defined, seemed to be in a state of readiness to do more to make education functional. Those who are aware of what is happening in the world at large and in every community know that not only American schools but a way of life would have been in jeopardy had the criticisms been honest. Actually, they did not reflect what was really happening in American education seen in its totality. Had the schools failed or been remiss in their duty, the nation could hardly have enjoyed the world leadership it did or been able to meet the challenges it faced.

However, while these criticisms were, by and large, unjustified, they came at what might have been a very opportune time. It is doubtful whether the present wholesome condition would have come into existence if what the schools were doing had been discussed in a positive way. While some educators had difficulty in recovering from the shock of these criticisms, others felt that the time was ripe for an evaluation of what was being done and of what could be done.

Every administrator knows that how far he may go in a school is defined in large part by the community in which the school is located. He knows that, while he must exert his leadership in the resolution of problems with the designated body from the community, there are factors within the community itself that often prevent the complete fulfilment of his plans. He and his staff react by making the adjustments to the situation as the community has defined it. It could well be that, in questioning what the school is doing, the community is criticizing itself both positively and negatively. In any event, the situation is presently one in which the several communities are assisting the schools to do what they are supposed to be doing.

Continued Federal-Government Interest. Continuing its interest, directly and indirectly, in the experiences to which children in the schools react, the federal government considered measures relating to education insofar as they concerned either the national defense or the general welfare of the nation. The act most directly related to the curriculum was the National Defense Education Act (NDEA). Its impact was so great as to modify not only what went on in science, mathematics, and foreign languages but how it went on. Of concern were the materials and resources for instruction, research of significance, and guidance, which were to be equal to the task of assisting American youth. This act revolutionized the teaching of selected disciplines and placed a value on

the student of ability. It was responsible for a consideration of the importance of the remaining disciplines as they referred to the kind of individual American that education intended to produce.

From the departments of the Interior, Commerce, and Health, Education, and Welfare, especially, have come materials that indicated trends
bearing on curriculum practices. Of particular interest are those relating
to occupational information, which, projected into the future, indicate to
the school the directions it may take. Of recent significance to health
education has been the present physical-fitness program. Suggestions
emanating from the White House Conferences and pronouncements from
the United States Office of Education made materials of significance
available. The results of the research furthered by the Cooperative
Research Program are well known. Agencies less directly concerned with
education but still closely aligned to the government make their contributions to education readily available.

Continued State Influences. At the state level, where, in some instances,
special legislation had to be passed to permit the use of NDEA funds,
leadership bearing on the curriculum comes from state departments of
education and from institutions of higher learning. Together they have
worked and are working to improve practices, suggest newer practices,
and encourage experimentation. This is, indeed, an age of experimentation.

Growth of Special-Interest Groups. American society has been so frac-
tured by groups interested and organized by special interests that it is
frequently characterized as being a segmentalized society. Each has its
purpose for being; each satisfies particular interests. It is not surprising
that many of them make their interest and concern for education known.
While their concern is primarily with furthering their particular interest,
familiarizing the schools with their existence, or making their influence
felt, they do, by the very nature of American life, have a right to exist.
Thus, the educator, while open-minded to the needs and interests of
these groups, is objective in his selection and use of the vast amount of
material they make available to him. His is the duty, as well as the privilege, of evaluating what is of interest and of using what is appropriate
to the learning experience. The school, then, in educating all the children
of all the people for purposeful living must by intent consider the interests of all groups and be responsible to the total community.

THE LOCAL COMMUNITY AND THE CURRICULUM TODAY

School-community relations as they exist in the American scene do
not present the insurmountable challenge that some would make of them.
It is not a matter of the school's fearing it is losing its significance as

the agency responsible for the education of the young, but rather of insisting that, while it is so designated, it is not the only community responsible for, or participating in, education. That does not mean that any of the educators will in any way lose their significance in the power structure of any community; instead, every teacher, supervisor, and administrator will reveal his potential for leadership to bring about the best in effective school-community relations.

What this means, then, is not only an awareness on the part of school men and women that the school belongs to the community but an awareness also on the part of the community that it must, in a way not hitherto practiced, indicate just what it wants and what it will do to bring about a further realization of what education, both curricular and cocurricular, can really be. Any consideration of what the curriculum and the community can be must be in terms of what is presently being done.

Non-school Agencies. Furthermore, it means that the school will not permit itself to be considered the only agency responsible for the education of youth. Each local community is responsible for encouraging, and aiding in, the development of such other youth-serving agencies as relate to recreation, employment, counselling, the family, the courts, and church-related activities. To be effective, these agencies must cooperate with whichever other agencies are affected, for conflicts necessitating the services of a particular agency are reflected in others. Unemployment, family dissension, unhappy encounters with the law, parental disinterest, unhealthy forms of recreation, and other similar phenomena relate directly to the success or failure of a child in school. Very frequently, what happens in the classroom is incidental to the problems most concerning the child.

Museums, Planetaria, Libraries, etc. Local museums, planetaria and libraries participate in the curriculum, and many now have educational directors and guides who consider their function to be teaching as they, on an organized basis, do that only. In addition, these institutions offer courses of instruction to youths and adults, and their published material, which is also geared to the young and to the adult, gives to each of the institutions an educational status it never had before. Programs of a similar nature are offered by zoos and botanical gardens. Those actively engaged in the opera and the symphony orchestra provide educational services through a variety of media.

Business and Industry Work with Schools. That the interest of business and industry in education is not exactly recent may be noted from the character of their cooperation in vocational education. The success of work-experience programs has been dependent on the quality of the work done in the school and the quality of the experience on the job, neither of which would have meaning without the cooperation of the school, its coordinators, and the businesses themselves. Vocational schools, interested in the automotive trades, food preparation and meat processing, and the textile industries, for a few examples, have profited from the interest of related business and industry. That the AFL-CIO has offered suggestions relating to vocational education is a matter of history and immediate concern. That it offers scholarships and in other ways assists students is also well known.

Intended for youths who have experienced extreme difficulty with the school's curriculum because of their lower potential for academic success are programs designed by some communities to combine work and study. Old enough to have working papers, and of the type having the potential of becoming truants because of their failure to do passing work or to adjust to school life, certain students obtain jobs in the neighborhood through the school, which they retain only so long as they go to school on a basis defined by the type of job. Some alternate employment and attendance at school, each for a week at a time; others, much more highly screened, obtain training in other areas. The nurse's aides' and practical nurses' programs alternate work in hospitals with attendance in schools for longer periods of time. Thus, youths can gain on-the-job experience and accumulate academic credit at the same time. The teachers in charge of such programs work with smaller numbers of students, since they serve as teachers, supervisors, and coordinators.

The success of these programs depends on the cooperation and faith of the educators and of the businesses and industries involved. To date, such programs are new in certain areas and older in others. In some instances, they may be limited to the locality that can afford them; in others, they are part of a state's concern. Many, because of this community-school cooperation, have finished high school, and thus it has reduced the dropout problem. Geared to its success is the belief that many more youths may be served, for, while these programs are expensive, the youths so served generally become contributing members of society and not burdens to it.

The Business-Industry Section of the National Science Teachers Association is concerned with opening avenues of communication between schools and business, utilizing the resources of each, and producing a better end product from the use of resources peculiar to their individual purposes. Thus, educational advisers are now a recognized part of the largest American businesses and industries. Together with educators, they share experiences and resources in a most constructive manner. These experiences vary from the production of materials for teachers as they relate directly and indirectly to the businesses themselves, to the use of consultants from and to both education and industry, to cooperative agreements between business and education that include on-the-job upgrading through added academic educational experiences, to a mutual concern for, and engagement in, experimentation in methodology. It is a well-known fact that the use of programed instruction is more effective in business and industry than it has been to date in education.

Work done in economic education at the local, state, and national levels has assumed its present significance owing to the need felt by educators who questioned the quality and the quanity of knowledge youths had, not only about economics as such, but also about how economics affected their lives. Representatives from every school level and representatives from business, industry, labor, and government at all levels have worked together to update a curriculum and assist teachers in as many ways as possible.

Parent Groups. The schools themselves have engaged in a variety of experiences at the level of parent participation. Such organizations as the Parent-Teacher Association, the more recent Parent, Teacher, Student Association, mothers' clubs, fathers' clubs, and parent clubs have done remarkable work in resolving problems related to the curriculum and in furthering understanding of what the schools are doing. Many of the teacher aides and teacher assistants who have relieved teachers of much of the clerical and routine tasks related to teaching have come from these groups. Chaperones from these groups have made field trips possible, for no teacher alone could be responsible for the numbers frequently taking trips considered worthwhile for the understanding of a discipline or any of the goals of education.

The Teacher's Use of Community Resources. In an ordinary learning situation, the student's understanding of what is to be learned is in terms largely of his experiences and his ability to understand the written and the spoken word. Thus, what he grasps from the learning-teaching situation could be limited. For that reason, the use of audio-visual aides became necessary and will continue to be necessary, as much of learning can best be accomplished by their use. However, they are not actually part of the students' lives. In addition, students learn, not from seeing and hearing alone, but also from feeling, tasting, and smelling. Therefore, direct contact with the senses, the avenues for learning, must be taken, when feasible, from life. Resources from the life of the community present sensory appeals in a lifelike situation that are not found in other resources.

The most common use of community resources is for the purpose of making the content of any subject real. At this level, a word, an object, a fact is seen as it is in life. Understandings, concepts, attitudes, and appreciations are seen as the result of the operation of several circumstances or conditions in life, rather than just taken for granted because "the book said so."

The teacher may use these resources to develop any of the general goals of education. For example, field trips to the laboratory of a nuclear physicist, a pharmaceutical firm, a courtroom, a meat-processing plant, a demonstration classroom, or a newspaper plant could have a vocational value. Studies of what the local community offered as wholesome recreation at either the active or passive level could affect the students' awareness of what constituted wholesome recreation and what actually existed. Perhaps negative in approach, but nevertheless stimulating, could be field trips to family courts, family-welfare agencies, foundling hospitals, which might affect students' concepts of wholesome living.

The teachers' purposes for using community resources could vary from using a person, place, or thing from in or out of the classroom as a resource for an introductory experience in a unit of study, as a motivational device, or as part of the developmental sequence, the medial summary, or the culminating experience.

While the teacher's interest in, and use of, community resources is significant for the reasons already intimated, nevertheless, teacher involvement geared to be *using* a community without any sincerity could well negate values to be accrued from pleasant relationships and actual living in a community. Thus, knowing the citizenry, enjoying its life, becoming acquainted with its values and aspirations, and joining its organized groups affect the understanding the teacher has of his students, what he is to consider in teaching them, and what he must do. Simultaneously, these associations may well make life more pleasant, for teaching is a social process, teachers are human beings, and the socially adjusted teacher could make life and learning pleasant and worthwhile for himself and his students.

Educators View the Present and the Future. The administrator is aware of the necessity of his considering his role in view of present and future needs of society as he sees it and as others see it. He knows that he must relate to the community at more than the written level, which has value, but which is no longer equal to the times. His duty is to relate directly to the people. He knows too that his role differs from that of a lawyer, doctor, dentist, or engineer, since his community is the people to whom he is responsible. Yet, his is a profession in which his leadership must always be apparent, for he is the expert in advisement.

He is skilled in human relations and expert in the use of democratic processes. He is aware of his responsibility to keep the public, through its board of education, parents, and school youth, informed of the best in curricular practice as it refers to the education of each child. He assists in resolving problems relating to teacher and student effectiveness and to incorporation of their concerns within the framework of effective administration. He makes what occurs in the school intelligible. He is active in community life, for delegation of that responsibility automatically removes from him the leadership he must have to direct the learning in today's schools as it relates to the activities of tomorrow.

He is better placed for leadership today than he has ever been: He has more resources made available to him than he ever had before; he has an interested and active citizenry willing to work with him. He knows, too, that failure and misunderstanding develop when improper human and public relations are allowed to develop.

QUESTIONS, PROBLEMS, AND ISSUES FOR FURTHER THOUGHT

Given are descriptions of conditions existing in three hypothetical situations. Much more could be given, but, with these data, proceed to determine what you would do if you were there.

1. Assume that you teach in a neighborhood in a metropolitan area that is culturally deprived, changing from one that was predominantly white to one that no longer is, in need of a school plant, and in a larger community composed of older retired citizens. Most of the teachers have a minimum of fifteen years of teaching experience. The principal, who has been in the system for two years, believes that every child should receive an education equal to his potential. Three-quarters of the children are of seemingly average or below-average ability. Less than 1 per cent intend or want to go to college. The neighborhood believes that everything that is educational is the job of the school. What would you do to help the principal? The youth?

2. Now assume that you are teaching in a high school with an enrolment of 500 students. Its community is fifty miles from the nearest metropolitan area. The school population is composed of the sons and daughters of third-generation Americans. The community itself, at the last census, numbered 5,000 individuals. The principal is interested in the potential of every child. The community has but moderate wealth and, at best, can retain but 5 per cent of its graduates, so most of the students must look elsewhere for employment. Seven-eighths of the staff have less than five years of teaching experience. The community is very much interested in producing well-rounded individuals, the school itself has won a reputation for success in its various programs that has exceeded even its own expectations. With what problems would you be concerned? What use would you make of the various communities? Of what resources would you avail yourself?

3. Now assume that you are teaching in one of the "best" high schools, in a very wealthy neighborhood of a large metropolitan city. The school has an enrolment of 3,000 students, who have few, if any, economic problems. Ninety per cent of them intend to go to college, yet 45 per cent have academic difficulties, and 10 per cent seem to be misfits who are academically lost. The principal and staff encourage academic accomplishment, but theirs is a losing battle. Most of the parents are college graduates, and

the staff is composed of teachers having at least a master's degree. The salary scale and promotional policies are among the best in the state. The teachers are obliged to live away from the community. The principal has been in this school for six years, and there is a very low teacher turnover. There are limitless resources in the community. Would you encounter any conflicts here? Is there a necessity for multiple curriculums? Could the use of community resources help? How?

SUPPLEMENTARY MATERIALS

Selected Readings

ADLER, IRVING. *What We Want of Our Schools.* New York: John Day Co., Inc., 1957. Chapter 7, "Progressive Education: Boon or Bane?"; Chapter 8, "The Critics of Progressive Education."

ALBERTY, HAROLD. *Reorganizing the High School* (rev. ed.). New York: The Macmillan Co., 1962. Chapter 2, "American High School: Its Philosophy and Goals."

ALPREN, MORTON. "What Curriculum Developments Are Finding Their Way into Practice?" *Bulletin of the N.A.S.S.P.*, No. 272 (March, 1962), 13–17.

ASSOCIATION FOR SUPERVISION AND CURRICULUM DEVELOPMENT 1963 YEARBOOK COMMITTEE. *New Insights and the Curriculum.* Washington, D.C.: National Education Association of the United States, 1963.

DOUGLASS, HARL R. *Secondary Education in the United States* (2d ed.). New York: The Ronald Press Co., 1964. Chapter 2, "Secondary Education and Our Democratic Society."

EHLERS, HENRY, and GORDON C. LEE. *Crucial Issues in Education.* New York: Holt, Rinehart & Winston, Inc., 1959. Part IV—"Issues Pertaining to the Direction and Design of the Curriculum."

ELICKER, P. E. "The Next 25 Years in Secondary Education," *Bulletin of the N.A.S.S.P.*, No. 237 (December, 1957), 1–6.

GWYNN, J. MINOR. *Curriculum Principles and Social Trends.* New York: The Macmillan Co., 1960. Chapter 1, "An Overview of the Evolution of the Curriculum"; Chapter 2, "Conflicting Educational Theories."

LEE, GORDON C. *Education in Modern America.* New York: Holt, Rinehart & Winston, Inc., 1957. Part II—Chapter 7, "The Challenge of the Philosophical Controversy."

LEONARD, J. PAUL. *Developing the Secondary School Curriculum* (rev. ed.). New York: Holt, Rinehart & Winston, Inc., 1953. Chapter 9, "Theories of Secondary School Education, Position 1: Intellectual Subject Matter"; Chapter 11, "Recent Curriculum Concepts."

RAYWID, M. A. *The Ax-Grinders: Critics of Our Public Schools.* New York: The Macmillan Co., 1962.

RINKER, FLOYD, WALTER AUFFENBERG, GALEN JONES, and JOHN E. DOBBIN. "New Developments in Secondary-School Program and Services," *Bulletin of the N.A.S.S.P.*, No. 264 (April, 1961), 189–95.

SAND, OLE, et al. *The Principals Look at the Schools: A Status Study of Selected Instruction Procedures.* Washington, D.C.: National Education Association of the United States, 1962.

SMITH, MORTIMER. "Basic Education: What Is It? What Should the Curriculum Include?" *A Citizens Manual for Public Schools. The Education Digest,* XXV (March, 1960), 10.

5

The Curriculum and Changing American Life

The curriculum in the secondary schools of all countries is highly conditioned by the setting in which it occurs. The United States offers no exception. In fact, our uniqueness goes far in explaining what we have in this area. Geographical location, mushrooming population and its distribution, scientific achievement, and the approach of new eras such as that of aerospace are illustrative of the factors that condition our life and, in turn, the curriculum of our secondary schools.

THE CONTINUOUS NATURE OF CHANGE IN AMERICAN LIFE

Rapid and accelerating change has been the most characteristic thing about American life from the beginning of our nation and remains so today. Each generation has felt that the changes taking place at its respective time were the most profound that had ever occurred. The conclusion was regularly a correct one. Probably each generation also felt that it was going through the most perilous period that had ever existed. Maybe that conclusion was also true.

Change as Related by the Elders After 1900. The elder people of the first quarter of this century related achievements of preceding years to the youth. They told about the development of alternating electrical currents, the incandescent light bulb, and of a practical internal combustion engine. In addition, they related details about the discovery of X-rays, radioactivity, and the electron. This same period saw Einstein's formulation of the theory of relativity, the development of an almost practical horseless carriage, and the first flight of a heavier-than-air machine. The number of additional inventions and discoveries was considerable. They included the transmission of wireless signals, the evolution of a workable telephone system, and immunization against several of the infectious diseases. The foregoing naturally caused Americans at the time to feel that a changed world had arrived and that it was important to make proper adjustments including necessary changes in the secondary school curriculum.

Change as Related by the Elders in 1960. Senior citizens of 1960 enlightened the youth of that year with a story of the factors that helped to produce change. Mass-production techniques, radio and television broadcasting, the discovery of antibiotics, and the development of radar were obviously eligible for mentioning. To these could be added changes brought about by the perfection of nuclear weapons, nuclear power for the production of electrical energy and the propulsion of ships, and the wide use of commercial aircraft for civilian purposes.

When the elders referred to above concentrated on the more recent period of 1945 to 1960, they stressed the rapid speed of jet planes, the surge of Americans into suburbia, shopping centers, and the use of tranquilizers, antibiotics, and a multitude of other miracle drugs. They emphasized that the American families of this era were spending on the average nearly forty hours a week viewing television. Many predicted that many young married couples, starting in the next decade, would buy air-conditioned houses, wear clothing made from newly created materials, and eat foods that were first frozen, dehydrated, precooked, and enriched—which they do.

While those responsible for curriculum in the secondary school have made some changes as a result of the advances that took place in American life, there remains a great lag. Change is always with us. Those living today, and at any time in the future, will never return to conditions of a previous period. Some have yearned to regain so-called normalcy. This cannot occur. Curriculum construction must take into account the fact of this changing nature of America, not only through constant study of the current changes that are apparent but also through attempts to foresee trends that lie ahead.

Supplementary Nature of School and Curriculum. It should be borne in mind, in all thinking relative to the content and nature of instruction, that the school is only a part of the educational environment of the student. Important educational influences are wielded by the home, the church, business, industry, play and social activities, and various other institutions and activities that, with or without conscious educational direction or purpose, determine in part the experiences of human beings and consequently their growth and future thinking, feeling, and acting. It would, therefore, seem impractical and unwise to plan the curriculum of the school without careful inventory of the nature and power of these other determinants of experience and growth.

It is a unique characteristic of the school that, theoretically at least, it is flexible and controllable. Consequently, as is pointed out in Chapter 2, it follows that the curriculum of the school should supplement the educational experiences of the learner outside the school. Unnecessary or unwise duplication should not exist. When types of growth are adequately stimulated and conditioned by experience undergone as a result of typical home life, the school should eliminate or reduce materially the time and emphasis given to curriculum experience, whose major purpose contributes to the same educational objective. Conversely, when valuable educational experiences are no longer assured in the out-of-school life of young people, the school should consider favorably the possibility and desirability of providing curriculum stimulation for experiences contributing to those objectives.

It should of course be borne in mind that an alternative exists to the policy or practice of the school's assuming educational functions no longer served by other institutions or activities. It may exert its influence to get some non-school institution such as youth-serving organization, the home, business, or industry to assume appropriate responsibility, or it may so educate those in school now and adults that they are willing and able to carry out the particular educational functions effectively.

This alternative to the assumption of direct responsibilities for the ever increasing complex of problems calling for solutions requires alerting the community to difficulties as they arise, and a confidence that it can examine the proposals espoused by advocates of various hypotheses.

Only to a small degree can we foresee the specific obstacles and opportunities that must be assessed and dealt with even in the near future, but we can project inquiring minds and resolute hearts into that future—minds and hearts that will face each problem as it may arise.

CHANGES IN POPULATION, WORK, AND HOUSING

Increasing Population and Redistribution of Age Groups. Recognizing that profound changes will again occur in the years ahead and that the school and extraschool agencies provide the educational opportunities for youth, it becomes desirable to identify certain characteristics of American life today. It is even more important that implications for curriculum be suggested.

Let us turn first to population and related problems. The population of the United States may exceed 230 million by 1975. Similar spectacular increases are also expected in other lands around the globe. Julian Huxley once remarked that it is in human numbers that man is facing his greatest challenge. This is no less true today. During the period of classical Roman civilization, life expectancy at birth was, at best, about thirty years. We know that with us today the figure has increased to seventy years. Numbers read like magic in relation to population trends. *Newsweek* is quoted as follows:

Three times every second, somewhere in the world, the torment ends, and a baby is born. Nearly 2,000,000 babies were born last week, enough to double the population of Minnesota. This sheer growth of humanity is called the "population explosion." . . . The current rate of growth continued for 600 years, would leave every inhabitant of the world with only one square yard to live on. By the year 3500 the weight of human bodies on the earth's surface would equal the weight of the world itself. By the year 6000, the solid mass of humanity would be expanding outward into space at the speed of light.[1]

Let us return to the here and now in American life. Our country is really what our people are. We must be concerned with the age distribution of the 230 million expected by 1975. It is estimated that approximately 27.8 per cent will be under fifteen years of age; 21.7 per cent, between fifteen and twenty-five; 23.4 per cent, between twenty-five and forty-five; 19.1 per cent, between forty-five and sixty-five; and 9.5 per cent over sixty-five.[2] An examination of these data suggests that we are to have relatively more younger and also more older people; naturally, the percentage of those in the prime of their lives will be smaller. The nation will be taxing its ingenuity and resources to care for the two dependent groups. The vigorous group in the middle will be responsible for most of the production needs, a task not too difficult to meet, as will be pointed out below.

The facts have many implications for the secondary school curriculum. Among them are the following:

1. Increased attention must be given to child care and development. Infant mortality will remain an area in need of study and improvement. Dietary, medical, and recreational needs of young people will be studied and met better than they are today.

2. Health, safety, and sanitation are topics that must receive increased emphasis. The needs, and even dangers, cumulate as the number of people increases. Effort will be made to increase life expectancy through these efforts in the immediate future just as has been done in the past.

[1] "How Many Babies Is Too Many?" *Newsweek*, Vol. 60 (July 23, 1962), p. 27.
[2] *Changing Times: The Kiplinger Magazine*, Vol. 15 (January, 1961), pp. 20–21, discusses this phase of population composition in detail.

3. Teaching people how to get along well with each other will become even more crucial. The matter of proximity is pertinent. We have always attempted to relate tolerance, respect, good will, and other such personal traits to the curriculum. These are a bit easier to apply to those living somewhat removed from us geographically than to those who are literally as close as our right and left arms.

4. Importance of the individual will necessarily be stressed even more through the curriculum of the immediate future than it has been in the past. Otherwise, his identity could be lost among the masses. This emphasis will not be overlooked for another reason. Reference is made to the fact that we shall be vigilant to keep the competition among world ideologies from shifting our historic concern for individual welfare to a less desirable goal.

5. Finally, population facts will lead to more emphasis on geriatrics as a topic of study. Its presence as an American problem will warrant its inclusion along with such other population problems as housing, race relations, law enforcement, education, production and consumption of economic goods and conservation.

Shifting Nature of Work and Job Opportunities. These new and ever increasing millions of Americans will earn their livings by performing a changed type of labor. Unskilled labor is not needed in American life today to the degree that it once was. A smaller percentage of the population produces the food needed by today's Americans than was the case in earlier decades. An increasing number of professional and personal service helpers are needed, because the population itself is larger. A vastly increased number of technicians are needed because of still other changes to be presented below.

Even a brief description of the nature of work activities in American life must include references to computers and automation. To ensure clarity, a two-part definition follows:

One class, usually referred to when one speaks of "automation," is made up of devices that automatically perform sensing and motor tasks, replacing or improving on human capacities for performing these functions. The second class, usually referred to when one speaks of "computers," is composed of devices that perform, very rapidly, routine or complex logical and decision-making tasks, replacing or improving on human capacities for performing these functions.[3]

Casual observation reveals many additional examples everywhere that illustrate the application of computer and automation discoveries to American life. In manufacturing, the executive can quickly secure precise

[3] Donald N. Michael, *Cybernation: The Silent Conquest* (Santa Barbara, Calif.: Center for the Study of Democratic Institutions, 1962), p. 5.

information about his product in production stages, information that is accurate and typed out in numbers and words. In banking, the story of a check could once have been told quickly and simply to a child. Today, one cannot keep up with the speed that accompanies the automatic reading, sorting, and bookkeeping related to it. A single trained operator can do in a few hours what was formerly done by a few hundred operators in an entire working day. In other record keeping, hours of man labor and volumes of paper are eliminated. The armed services, for example, can know quickly and accurately the location and amount of total inventories. Many bookkeeping operations, regarded as routine in both government and industry, are so huge that they just could not have been performed by methods used only a few years ago.[4]

New Housing and Physical Facilities. These more numerous people are likely to live in houses that are generally different from those of today. Outside appearances may not present changes as startling as will be found inside. Manufacturers of aluminum feel that their product will eliminate structural framework. Such walls can also be connected with an electrical current and serve as a medium of heating. Plastic producers foresee that their products will be used for floors, walls, the exterior, and often the roof. The steel industry predicts popularity for the all-steel "prefab" house, which may even have interior walls that are mounted on rollers for variable types of arrangement.

Inside, there are plans for mechanical units composed of a freezer and an electronic oven that will produce a full meal in less than fifteen minutes. Along with this are ovens, cabinets, refrigerators, and dishwashers that can be automatically raised or lowered. Automatic plastic-dish makers and ultrasonic dishwashers are also planned. Variations may include refrigerated cabinets and drawers placed at various places around the kitchen. Some further innovations may include stoves with solid electric surface units, refrigerators that open from front and rear, and stoves that can be turned on and off by dialing "instructions" over the telephone.

There will be all sorts of appliance equipment, possibly vacuum cleaners that propel themselves, power mowers that do the same, closed-circuit television that can be used to keep an "eye" on other rooms in the house, and cooled air piped into many rooms or homes from a common source.

The implications for the secondary school curriculum from this area include obvious ones. Two will be suggested: (1) The units taught in homemaking courses will become increasingly important. Placement of

---

[4] A further discussion of the changed opportunities for, and the nature of, jobs is given in Chapter 10.

materials and equipment in the home, most efficient use of the same, and maintenance of attractiveness are topics about which homemakers need to know. (2) The "man of the family" will need to know a bit more about equipment maintenance and care. This does not suggest at all that he will be a technician to the extent of providing complete servicing. However, he must know, even better than did his forefathers, the complete story of buying household items on the instalment plan. This includes knowing the actual percentage of interest being paid.

CHANGES IN NATIONAL ECONOMICS AND CARE FOR THE INDIVIDUAL

New Concepts and Practices in Economic Activities. Those of our citizens who think critically are much aware of the importance of economics in our daily lives, in our national affairs, and even in cold-war strategy. The ordinary mastery of the laws of supply and demand, selling price, and bimetallism still has its place. To this has been added the study of a complicated national economy. What shall be the incidence of taxation? How shall tax money be distributed? What is the relation of our system of taxation to a healthy and growing economy? How can we cooperate and/or compete with a European Common Market? These are, as the typical adolescent is prone to say, "good" questions.

An American in the common chore of going shopping may quickly sense that he is in a changed setting so far as economics is concerned. A description of a design for such purchasing of goods and services follows:

Now look at 1975. You ride into the cylindrical building from the parking lot on a covered moving sidewalk. An attendant gives you a special marker bearing a code number. You step onto a continuously moving elevator, ride to the top of the building, step onto another moving sidewalk. As you ride past shelves of groceries, you spot what you want, step off the sidewalk, stamp it with your marker, and deposit it in a receiving station. The moving sidewalk takes you down the spiral ramp of the supermarket past every item on display, until you finally reach an automated check-out counter. Every item you selected is ready on the counter before you. A computer adds up what you owe and lists everything you bought by weight and price. You put your money into an automated cash register, get your change, go to your car, pick up your order all wrapped at a parcel station. Time consumed: about ten minutes.[5]

Our people live exciting lives in the economic realm. More sober reflection could tell us that always around the corner lies the possibility of a severe economic depression. Less discernment would be needed to

[5] Arnold B. Barach, *1975 and Changes to Come* (New York: Harper & Row, 1962).

observe the strained relations between labor and employer that so often result in crippling strikes, or the existence of great business organizations wielding tremendous power.

Curriculum implications include the following: (1) There is need for increased attention to consumer economics. The ease with which goods can be had tempts people to purchase even beyond their ability to pay. The school must teach students how to spend wisely and, also, to remember that when a dollar has been expended on a particular selection it is gone forever. (2) Students must also be taught how to make quality judgments as they buy goods. There will be fewer and fewer human salesmen to answer questions and to furnish information.

Increased Medical Care and Improved Health. It was stated above that life expectancy has increased, and the prediction is that this trend will continue. Even so, many problems of health and physical well being remain. There has been an increase in the number of cases of venereal diseases in recent years. Likewise, the number of patients seeking help with mental-health problems has risen markedly. The far greater number of emotionally disturbed individuals who do not seek professional help is of concern to all. Improvement has been dependent upon progress in medical care and improved health habits. Specific advances have recently been made or are approaching in such areas as heart disease, cancer, polio, high blood pressure, diabetes, measles, tuberculosis, the common cold, and tooth decay. This progress is publicized from day to day. It extends dramatically to others of man's maladies. Not only are Americans living longer, they are also, on the average, living more pleasurable lives in terms of health.

Among the more important implications for the curriculum are the following: (1) Continued attention must be given to a rigorous program of physical fitness. The last two presidents have called for such emphasis. Evidence at hand indicates that "softness" does not contribute to longevity. (2) Attention has been given, and must continue to be accorded, matters of mental health and hygiene. The prominence of the work of the psychiatrist substantiates this point. (3) Basic courses must be planned for, and offered in, the secondary school for those anticipating later study of medicine, dentistry, nursing, psychiatry, and all of the technical fields related to these areas of work and service. (4) Finally, there should be studies of the proper role of government in providing information about health and physical fitness, and also of the obligations of government in providing medical care and hospitalization for all or certain identified groups in the population.

Broadened Concern of the Government for the Individual. Government concern for individual welfare is a feature of American life that is thought about too little and by too few. It is something that is taken too much for granted. Today's role of government in relation to its citizens approaches the opposite of the "rugged individualism" known during the early part of this century. Let us proceed with examples:

Social security represents a systematic plan to provide for the financial needs of millions of our people, especially in their later years. This was virtually undreamed of only a few decades ago.

Public-works programs are often initiated as much or more for their help in furnishing employment as for the need of the finished projects involved. Unemployment benefits are available in many situations and are often enlarged or extended. Federal support of many phases of our educational program has been consistently provided and tends to be extended to more areas. Retraining programs, as was mentioned above, are common for those whose jobs are no longer essential owing to scientific advancement and automation.

The national government regularly helps individuals by helping selected groups. Entire states and/or regions may be the recipients of various kinds of aids if they qualify as distressed or depressed areas. Those in a type of work such as agriculture may receive price supports and other kinds of direct or indirect helps. Members of the armed forces, upon re-entering civilian life, have often been assisted with such financial benefits as separation pay, pensions, hospitalization, eligibility for loans, etc.

The concern of the government for, and its direct aid to, the individual have been increasing. There is no indication of a trend in the opposite direction.

Pertinent curricular implications for the secondary school suggest that, in addition to learning well the mechanics of government, students should approach many questions through the problem approach. Among them are the following: (1) What is the real nature and function of government? (2) Upon what basis should the government provide financial assistance? (3) Does the interest of today's government in the individual tend to threaten individual initiative? (4) What constitutes balance in designing a national budget? (5) What are some urgently needed reforms in local, state, and national government?

THE SHRINKING WORLD AND UNIVERSE

American Life and the Aerospace Age. American life, like that of all mankind, now has as its setting a new space age (aerospace). This fact in itself is making all phases of activity different. The situation is comparable to that produced by the coming of the age of bronze or, later, the Industrial Revolution. The principal difference is that the acceleration of current revolutionary changes is greater than has existed previously.

No effort is made here to outline all of the events commonly associated with aerospace development. The major ones are well known to most people. In fact, it would be impractical to attempt to do this, since each few weeks brings to pass other major events.

However, it does seem apt to mention a very few of the peacetime uses that are resulting from this new aerospace age. The medical profession has gained new information and initiated novel practices. Pathological symptoms, drug effects, nutrition, the value of rest, and preventive medicine are areas that have received increased attention. In bioastronautics, the number of scientists, engineers, and technicians has increased rapidly. New information is cumulating in relation to (1) the reaction of the body to physical stress, temperature, and pressure changes, (2) the effect of radiation and chemical dosages on bodily functions, (3) dietary tolerances, (4) vision assurance, and (5) reactions of the nervous system to modified conditions.

Developments in Science and Technology. Psychologists are engaged in new research and are gaining new insights in this new age. These relate to human motivation, psychomotor performance, and the relationship between behavioral and physiological reactions to various kinds of stress. Related to this is progress in the field of human engineering. Emphasis is placed upon how man receives and processes the various forms of information that come to him. True, investigations in these areas are carried on primarily to advance aerospace technology. Even so, the contributions to information about learning theories, decision-making analysis, human relations, and industrial psychology will be tremendous.

Engineering is naturally a specialization that is essential as part of aerospace technology. Peacetime uses of knowledge gained from developing substances that combine lightness, resistance to radiation and to re-entering temperatures, and adjustment to acceleration and deceleration will be extensive. Energy conversion is an area of engineering that receives much attention from aerospace technicians and that will have peacetime usefulness. For example, the knowledge gained from the use of solar batteries may result in electric power being provided in places far removed from hydroelectric sources. Electronic engineering will likewise meet and accept numerous challenges which will indirectly result in greater comforts and services.

Geodesy and geography are subjects of intensive study in this aerospace age. To these may be added law and international politics. In these

fields, more accurate information is being attained along with a phe-
nomenal expansion of principles and procedures.

Developments in Transportation. In commercial aviation, great strides
are being made. A glance at selected current descriptions of regular
passenger-carrying planes reveals the following capacities: 21–24 passengers with speed of 190–207 miles per hour, 36–40 passengers with
speed of 286 miles per hour, 60–95 passengers with speed of 365 miles
per hour, 74–85 passengers with speed of 405 miles per hour, and 88–
110 passengers with speed of 615 miles per hour. The aerospace age has
accelerated greatly this peacetime phase of transportation. Let us remember that we have had the airplane only about six decades. It was not until
the third of these decades that a passenger could buy a ticket on a
regularly scheduled airline. In a recent year, the American scheduled
airlines operated 1,800 planes and carried more than 60 million passengers. In the same year, foreign and domestic airlines alone employed
more than 300,000 people. Obviously, not all of these people were flying
planes. Among them were dieticians, meteorologists, salesmen, luggage
handlers, electronic engineers, and navigators. For each airplane crew
that ascends, there are some hundreds of people working on the ground
to service the plane, assist passengers, and provide flight facilities.

It is predicted that there will be further changes in relation to the
use of commercial planes. Speeds of 2,000 miles per hour may be reached.
Helicopters will surely be more widely used. Convertiplanes (planes that
rise vertically from the ground and then convert to horizontal flight) will
most likely have wider usage in commercial aviation.

Developments in Communications. Closely related to the changes just
enumerated for transportation are those taking place in mass communications—newspapers and periodicals, radio, television, and communications satellites. The first favorable reaction is that we have herein a
powerful force for potential good. Statistics giving daily circulation of
the publications and the number of receiving sets show clearly that our
people are almost universally reached by these media. It should be
possible to use them to do many things all the way from removing
illiteracy, at one end of the scale, to providing cultural programs that
appeal to those with considerable background in the fine arts.

All have by now heard of Telstar. Its first successful performance has
been ranked in importance with the invention of printing, the first transmission of Morse's telegraph, the laying of the first Atlantic cable, and
the sending of the first radio signal across the Atlantic. This is saying a
great deal for a 170-pound sphere three feet in diameter. When it was
first launched, Telstar's most spectacular achievement lay in its radio
and TV relay system, which made it a communications satellite. The

prospects of seeing the Olympics, the coronation of a new monarch, and history-making events became immediately inviting to contemplate.

Various ideas as to implications followed the launching of Telstar in 1962. Some felt that the success was a testimony to the virtue of the economic system of free enterprise. Others saw it as an indication of the willingness of our nation to emphasize the peaceful uses of scientific progress rather than the military ones. In any event, American life has experienced a revolution in communications.

There is one factor common to most of these mass-communications media: They are supported by sponsors and advertisers who are likely to hold specific points of view. This must be taken into consideration in the total study of this aspect of American life.

Changes in Our International Relations. When one understands the complex nature of our relations with others, he properly concludes that this is almost a new area of concern. Isolation, brought about by oceans deep and wide, is no longer effective. Even the desire that some might have to live apart is impossible. We are only a few hours removed from the most distant spot on the globe. Our people visit annually everywhere to be, in turn, visited by those living beyond our borders.

We have, at the top governmental level, attempted to meet this problem well. Leadership was given to forming a League of Nations. A former presidential candidate, after due observation and reflection, wrote *One World*. The birth of the United Nations and the successes which it has enjoyed have been made possible, to a great extent, because of American concern and leadership.

Being a member of the "One World," and, especially, occupying a position of leadership, imposes a high price to pay for the privilege. Our motives in efforts to extend economic aid are always examined and seriously questioned by the well-established nations. Newly formed governments naturally look to us for leadership in efforts to secure the blessings of liberty but often feel that they fail to find proper kinship. Ideological differences arise. These bring about such terms as *coexistence* and *cold war*.

Indeed, it is not possible to describe or understand the nature of American life without considering our international setting. Many curricular implications are clear. We must teach courses or units dealing with (1) international relations, (2) the recent history of Asia and Africa, (3) economics as related to the international setting, (4) world geography, and (5) tolerance and respect for all people, regardless of race, or creed. Other curricular implications for secondary education are numerous, of great importance, and not all, yet identified. Among them are the following: (1) Every effort must be made to provide comprehensive education. There is danger that, in an age that seems to be based so greatly upon science, the deeper insights and appreciations may be neglected. (2) Even so, basic science and mathematics must be provided for and required of all. In addition, specialized courses must be available in each field for academically talented students. (3) There must be a process of curricular revision that condenses and/or discards much content that we have previously taught; in its place, there should be substituted the new learnings that have come as part of this aerospace era.

THE CHANGING AMERICAN EDUCATION

Changes in the Nature of the Clientele. A clearly observable feature of current American life is the interest in, and place of, education at all age levels. An examination of enrolment data reveals an ever increasing number of enrollees. In secondary education, we have so often seen the figures given by decades, starting with 1890. These are indicative of the constantly greater desire on the part of our people for more education. This is even clearer when it is observed that the percentage growth of high school attendance has exceeded the growth of the general population. The high school quickly became the "common school" or "poor man's college."

Changes in Program. Not only have parents come to desire more and better education for their children; young people have found that they must be educated reasonably well just to get along—to have the ability to compete and deal with their fellow men. This means more knowledge is required today to perform the ordinary tasks of enjoyable living.

Secondary education now, as in the past, is featuring many curricular changes. Foundation courses in science, mathematics, English, and social studies are looked upon as basic for all. Language study has been, and is being, extended to include Russian, Chinese, Japanese, and selected languages from other parts of Asia and from Africa. Content within courses, in mathematics, for example, is being re-examined and revised to meet today's needs.

Changing Higher Education. The rise and growth of community-oriented junior colleges is regarded by many as the greatest revolution that is taking place in education. More than one-fourth of the post-high school enrollees are found in junior colleges. The proportion is steadily increasing. Our nation is looking with favor upon this institution for at least four reasons: (1) Many worthy students who could not afford the cost of education away from home can arrange to continue in school if they can live an additional two years with their family. (2) Certain students are judged by their counselors as more likely to succeed if they enrol in a school smaller than most universities. Such students may need remedial work, guidance related to study techniques, or help in solving personal problems. Another group of such students has been termed "late achievers." They need a special type of school such as a typical junior college. (3) A large number of high school graduates desire, and would be successful with, some education beyond high school but do not prefer the pursuit of a full four-year degree program. They are being well served by two-year terminal curriculums on programs of even less duration. (4) Many students who seek admission to degree-granting institutions are rejected through selective processes. Rarely has a public junior college failed to admit any who have graduated from high school.

Technical schools, either as part of junior-college programs or in specially planned programs, are increasing in popularity. This phenomenon is explained largely by the description of occupational shifts described previously. The prestige of these schools has increased greatly. Their graduates are regarded as individuals who are highly intelligent, whose services are needed, and whose wages and salaries should be commensurate with the educational experiences they have gained.

The interest in, and need for, higher education is recognized as part of American life today. The demand has exceeded the availability of space, classroom and laboratory facilities, and teaching personnel. Parents and their college-age children have developed natural anxieties about the high cost of higher education and about the difficulty of gaining admission to schools of their choice. We are concerned today not only with who should go to college but also with who are the best-qualified students and who are most able to profit from a college education.

The implications for secondary school curriculums are many and varied. Among them are the following: (1) There must be extreme diversity in the offerings. Slow learners, so-called normal pupils, and those academically talented must be taken into account. (2) This same heterogeneity of population dictates that guidance and counseling must continue to receive increased attention. Problems of personal and group adjustment are so many and so real that a considerable number of young people need help. (3) Vocational and technical portions of the curriculum will need revision frequently enough to keep pace with science, invention, and practices found in the age of automation and technology. (4) The strictly college-preparatory parts of the curriculum will need to be better planned as part of an articulated total program of education extending into the universities. Advanced placement and honors programs are of special plans. (5) Continuous experimentation must be deliberately planned in relation to methods of teaching, use of resource materials, and staff utilization.

OTHER SIGNIFICANT CHANGES

The Changed American Home. It is not suggested that the changes in American life outlined above are all-inclusive. A case could be made for the American home as an institution that has changed markedly. All are aware that, some years ago, the home was a more closely knit unit than is the case today. In earlier years, the son often learned a trade by working with his father and observing him at work. The son's benefit from learning a trade was augmented by a feeling of close comradeship with his father. Similarly, the daughter learned the skills and art of home-making by working with her mother and observing her as a full-time homemaker. All of this has changed. American fathers race to offices and shifts far from home. Their sons know little about the nature of the work done. The percentage of mothers employed outside the home has constantly increased. Therefore, there is little time left to teach daughters how to perform well domestic duties. The role of the family as an effective teacher of vocational skills, moral and spiritual values, and the meaning of democracy in action has regrettably decreased.

The Trend Toward Urbanization. The trend toward urbanization is another topic that suggests changes in American life. Recent census data make the point abundantly clear that, whereas we were once predominantly a nation of rural people, the reverse has come to pass. Urbanization has brought slums and suburbs. On the one hand, there has come about a rise of suburbia. Beyond the former narrow city limits has arisen new housing for the executives of business and industry as well as for other higher-paid individuals. Shopping centers, making available all of the merchandise formerly found only in the restricted business area have become common. Community churches have been built to meet the religious needs of the new and rapidly growing suburbs. New schools have been needed and constructed as part of a rapid growth of educational facilities. Each morning witnesses the feverish exodus of suburban workers on their way to work in the city. Naturally, suburbia has experienced growing pains. Laying out of subdivisions, paving of new streets, construction of sewer lines, and provision of community services are expensive. Adequate sources of taxation have frequently been hard to find.

The growth of the suburban area has had a counterpart, namely, the slum. This is not a new factor, but it is one that has recently become greatly accentuated. Housing in slum areas is typically substandard. Unemployment rates are very high. The youth too often does not have access to an educational program that meets its needs for citizenship training and the making of a living at an early age. Juvenile delinquency flourishes. Conant[6] has well pointed out the potential dangers to our welfare that must be met by improving the lot of our people in many of these areas across the nation.

Metropolitan centers and even cities of lesser size have attracted a growing percentage of our population. This has been caused partially by the fact that there has been increased productivity in agriculture; many farm laborers, relatively untrained and no longer needed in agriculture, have sought employment in the cities. This phenomenon has crowded the slums and, consequently, increased juvenile delinquency. It has also fostered the development of powerful political machines and increased unemployment.

There is a brighter side. Urbanization has produced centers of culture and modern comforts of living hitherto unknown.

The rural community today is much less "rural" than its predecessors. The movies, radio, television, telephones, automobiles, good roads, rural mail delivery, and other recent developments tend to break down the lines of distinction between rural and urban people. There is much more homogeneity than formerly in appearance, speech, interests and tastes, leisure pursuits, knowledge, and attitudes. This elevation of standards for rural people adds to the task of their education.

With the development of efficiency in farm production, and of national and international interdependence, the problems of farm people have shifted from production to marketing. The nature of education for successful farming has, therefore, changed from concentration upon animal husbandry and crops to include—in fact, to emphasize—training in economics and political science, particularly in current developments.

The transfer of wealth from rural to urban centers has created problems in the support of education in the less wealthy states and communities. The development of highways and automobiles has increased the possibilities of abandoning inferior small schools in favor of larger ones capable of every superior educational service, far faster than advantage has been taken of these opportunities.

Changes in Religious Attitudes and Spiritual Values. The nature of religion and the church and their influence upon the daily lives of people also differ from what they were a few decades ago. More people than ever before attend church. However, the percentage of the total population that represents those affiliated with the churches is not increasing. There is less emphasis upon the necessity to respond to the church because of fear of eternal punishment. Also, many Americans have less interest in the finer shades of denominational differences than was once

[6] James B. Conant, *Slums and Suburbs* (New York: McGraw-Hill Book Co., Inc., 1961).

the case. Along with these changes is the diminished emphasis upon religious training and family worship in the home. Even though change has taken place, it should be emphasized that religion and the church offer many educational experiences, provide solid comfort to those attempting to establish a sound set of values by which to live, and hold forth eternal hope as a reward for temporal labors.

Further changes throwing much light on our educational problems are those that have taken place in our predominant ideals and typical American philosophy. In the pioneer epoch of the economic development of our country, it was natural for unusual importance to be attached to those virtues most necessary in a pioneer period. In a day of the exploration and settlement of new lands, of the building of new enterprises in new regions, individual strength was paramount. Cooperation was not only necessarily limited to small and more or less isolated groups, but, comparatively, it was unnecessary and impossible. Independence, self-reliance, and initiative were the mainstays of the pioneer.

However much the characteristics that gave us modern America may be enshrined in our hearts, we are now entering an epoch in which it seems that these virtues are of somewhat less relative importance. They must be so developed as to operate within the bounds set by the dependence upon cooperation for continued progress. Education today must develop other and less primitive and natural virtues. In order to carry on the magnificent work of their fathers and grandfathers, youths of today must possess another set of virtues, based upon the cooperative character of their age as differentiated from the more individualistic epoch which preceded it.

It was almost inevitable that, in an age of exploration and pioneering marked by the astounding technical and commercial developments that have taken place within a single lifetime, materialism would be emphasized out of all logical proportion. Possession of material goods and power has come to be universally sought with an intensiveness that cannot be justified on the basis of the guaranties of happiness these acquisitions can give. As a result, the American people have failed to utilize other types of opportunities for enjoyment of life to the fullest extent. The schools have the opportunity to develop perspective, a scale of values, and appropriate tastes, skills, and knowledge that will open many avenues to happiness not now being employed.

QUESTIONS, PROBLEMS, AND ISSUES FOR FURTHER THOUGHT

1. State the arguments for the thesis "The primary responsibility of the public schools is to society and for the common welfare." What is the opposite thesis? To what extent does the individual benefit by improving the common welfare?

2. Read carefully the statement of basic trends in society today and add at least five more.
3. List thirty important trends of change in American life, and classify them according to the area in which the change has taken place, for example, increasing population, shifting nature of work and jobs, housing, methods of producing and distributing goods, travel, communication, medical care and improved health, concerns of the government for the individual, and the aerospace age.
4. What changes in the curriculum are called for by changes that have taken place owing to population increases and redistribution?
5. What changes in the curriculum are called for by changes that have taken place in the nature of job opportunities?
6. What changes in the curriculum are called for because of modern housing and physical facilities?
7. What changes in the curriculum are called for because of new concepts and practices in economics?
8. What changes in the curriculum are called for because of increased medical care and improved health?
9. What changes in the curriculum are called for because of the broadening concern of the government for the individual?
10. What changes in the curriculum are needed because Americans live in an aerospace age?
11. How has the pattern of education changed with changing America?
12. How should the curriculum change because of the new problems associated with international relations?
13. Select one subject, for example, mathematics, and list all the suggestions from the chapter for the curriculum and courses of study in that field.

SUPPLEMENTARY MATERIALS

SELECTED READINGS

ANDERSON, VERNON E., and WILLIAM T. GRUHN. *Principles and Practices of Secondary Education* (2d ed.). New York: The Ronald Press Co., 1962. Chapter 3 covers briefly the fundamental principles involved in planning and designing a secondary school curriculum and is helpful for those desiring a quick overview.

"Automation," *Scholastic*, LXXI (November 7, 1962), 13. The impact of automation today and its probable effect upon the future.

CONANT, JAMES B. *Slums and Suburbs*. New York: McGraw-Hill Book Co., Inc., 1961.

FURNAS, C. C. "Changing World—Changing Curricula," *The Educational Forum*, XXII (January, 1958), 209–14. This and the preceding entry describes two areas of the cultural environment that are too little understood, and call for quick and intelligent action.

HAUSER, PHILIP M. "America's Population Crisis," *Look*, XXV (November 21, 1961), 23–28.

O'BRIEN, ROBERT. "The U.S.A. in 1970: A Forecast of Things to Come," *Reader's Digest*, XL (January, 1961), 25–29. Another preview of the years that lie ahead. Well-organized brief presentation.

AUDIO-VISUAL MATERIALS

Films

City in Trouble. Finley Films, 1958. 20 minutes. Sound, black and white or color.

Look at Mid-century America. Neubacher Productions, Los Angeles 4, 1958. 16 minutes. Sound, color.

Science and Human Responsibility, Number 14, Population, Resources, and Fulfillment, N.E.T. Film Service, Indiana University, A. V. Center, Bloomington, 1956. 30 minutes. Sound.

6

Progressive and Conservative Influences on the Curriculum

THE REVOLT AGAINST THE LATIN GRAMMAR SCHOOL

Nature of the Curriculum in the Latin Grammar School. The first secondary schools in the United States were Latin grammar schools patterned after secondary schools existing in England and on the continent of Europe in the middle of the seventeenth century. These all had as their prototype the *Gymnasium* at Strasbourg, the curriculum there having been developed by Johann Sturm, formerly professor of classical languages at the University of Paris.

The purpose of the Latin grammar school in the United States was to prepare the abler boys for the ministry and other learned pursuits. It was intended to prepare them for admission to Harvard and other colleges that had been established in the early days. A typical curriculum of a Latin grammar school is that of the Boston Latin Grammar School in 1789:

First Class   Cheever's Accidence. Corderius's Colloquies—Latin and English. Nomenclator, Aesop's Fables—Latin and English. Ward's Latin Grammar, or Eutropius.

Second Class   Clarke's Introduction—Latin and English. Ward's Latin Grammar, Eutropius, continued. Selectae e Veteri Testamento Historiae, or, Castilio's Dialogues. The making of Latin, from Garretson's Exercises.

Third Class   Caesar's Commentaries. Tully's Epistles, or Offices. Ovid's Metamorphoses. Virgil. Greek Grammar, The making of Latin from King's History of the Heathen Gods.

101

Fourth Class   Virgil, continued.—Tully's Orations. Greek Testament. Horace. Homer.—Gradus ad Parnassum. The making of Latin continued.[1]

Later, more modern and practical subjects were added, especially as the academy movement began to get under way—arithmetic, trigonometry, algebra, geometry, English history, government, and, after 1800 in many schools, commercial subjects, navigation, surveying, and accounting. The course of study of the Latin grammar school, at first only four or five years in length, gradually extended to six and seven.

Teaching methods consisted largely of assignment of lessons and lesson learning motivated chiefly by rewards and punishments including corporal punishments. The schools began as early as 7:30 or 8:00 A.M. and lasted until 4:00 or 5:00 P.M., with a noon intermission, usually of about two hours. The schools were supported not by taxes but by funds from a variety of sources. Latin grammar schools were established in various parts of the colonies, but not in large numbers except in New England.

Limitations of the Latin Grammar School. The Latin grammar school had the following limitations:

1. The curriculum, transplanted from European secondary schools, was not suited to the life of pioneers.
2. The school did not provide for girls.
3. The quality of the teachers and that of the teaching were not well standardized and, in many instances, were mediocre or worse.
4. The school was not publicly supported.
5. The methods of teaching were unpsychological and cruel and had many bad results on the personality of students.

The Realism Movement and the Academy. Because of the limitations just mentioned, it was inevitable that the Latin grammar school would not continue to be the principal type of secondary school in this country. It gave way to a more practical type of school, the academy, as various types of realism in Europe began to have an impact on secondary education there and to spread to the thinking of the intellectual leaders of the United States.

Three major types of realism developed in the thinking of educational philosophies in the sixteenth and seventeenth centuries. The major characteristics of the advocates of these approaches will be reviewed briefly in the following paragraphs.

1. *The humanistic realists* included such persons as Erasmus, the great scholar of Holland, and Rabelais the French writer, who were influential

---

[1] Alexander Inglis, *Principles of Secondary Education*, pp. 164–165. Copyright 1918, by Houghton Mifflin Co. (Boston), and quoted with its permission.

in the first part of the fifteenth century, and John Milton the English poet of the seventeenth century. These men protested against the mistake of substituting the form for the spirit—linguistics for literature, grammar for content. They protested, for example, against the emphasis upon training in Ciceronian style to the neglect of the content and messages of Cicero's writings; some also protested for additional subjects. They argued for a complete and generous education of youth. In Milton's book *The Academy*, he suggested the addition to the curriculum of arithmetic, geometry, some agriculture and geography, physiology, engineering, architecture, and history. He also proposed that the academy's curriculum should include a modern language (preferably Italian), what we would call social studies today, logic, exercise, and play. This, we can see, marks a great step forward from concentration upon Latin and Greek and emphasis upon linguistics rather than the content of the Latin and Greek books, but it was more than a century before his ideas were put into practice in any considerable number of schools.

2. *The sense realists* including the great Francis Bacon, of England, had a great deal of influence not only upon curriculum but also upon method. Ratichius, in Germany, and Comenius of Moravia, for example, set forth such principles as "memorize only what is understood" and "study things before words." To Latin and Greek and other subjects that had been taught for centuries, they proposed adding a great deal of new subject matter in the fields of science and the social studies, in fact replacing a large part of the classical material with writings in the vernacular. They believed in physical education for health, not for sports alone. They believed in replacing coercion to a considerable extent by the development of pupil interest. They advocated more understanding and use of visual aids. They believed in the use of the native language, rather than Latin and Greek, as the language of instruction. They believed in the use of the scientific instructive method and teaching by developing the student's own conclusions.

3. *The social realists* including John Locke, in England, and Montaigne, in France, were concerned with the education of youths of the upper social class and, hence, argued for training that would result in well-bred gentlemen acceptable in the higher social circles. They advocated travel and training in manners, in riding, and in social conventions. John Locke seemed to believe that the study of foreign languages would result in a discipline of the mental powers appropriate to a gentleman. While the social realists had a very questionable constructive program, they served a valuable purpose by attracting attention to the wisdom of proceeding to plan educational programs in the light of what kind of persons they were intended to produce through the educational materials and procedures.

The Academy. Without doubt stimulated by the influence of the realists were the *Ritter Academien,* in Germany, which were secondary schools with a more modern and practical curriculum than the *Gymnasium—* then the prevailing type of secondary school in Germany and in Scandinavian countries. Further results of the same type of thinking were reforms in more conventional German secondary schools. The *Realgymnasium* was developed, with more emphasis upon modern languages and mathematics, and the *Realschule* and the *Oberrealschule,* with more emphasis upon science, mathematics, and modern languages and much less upon Greek and Latin. The secondary schools of other countries as well were influenced, including particularly those in the United States.

Dissatisfactions, Revolts, and Reforms. Parents as well as students were not satisfied with what was taught in the Latin grammar schools. It seemed ill fitted to prepare young people for life in the American colonies as it existed at that time. While reforms were made in many Latin schools in the way of introducing new subjects in the field of history, literature, and, indeed, in some schools, navigation and surveying, the Latin grammar school disappeared from the scene and was replaced in the latter half of the eighteenth century and the early half of the nineteenth century by non-public academies.

The Nature of the Academy. Many academies, some of which still exist, were established in the latter half of the eighteenth century. It was estimated by E. G. Dexter[2] that, by 1860, more than 3,000 academies had been established in the United States.

The academy was usually small, with one, two, or three teachers and twenty to seventy-five pupils. The curriculums of the different academies included hundreds of subjects, since no two academies apparently taught the same subjects. In the earlier period of the academies, the curriculum was much more varied and modern and placed much less emphasis on languages and classical materials than was true of the Latin grammar schools.

The following list of the offerings of Wesleyan Seminary in 1856 is typical of the programs of students in an academy in the middle of the nineteenth century:

First Term: Mental Arithmetic; Elocution; Rhetoric; Geometry; Geography of the Heavens; Bookkeeping; Botany; Political Economy; Astronomy; Governmental Instructor [probably a civics manual].

[2] *A History of Education in the United States* (New York: The Macmillan Co., 1904), p. 173.

Second Term: English Composition; Analysis of Words; Ancient Geography; Universal History; Geometry, completed; Trigonometry; Mental Philosophy; Elements of Criticism; Evidences of Christianity; Natural Theology.

Third Term: Modern Geography; History of the United States; Surveying and Navigation; Mental Philosophy; Logic; Agricultural Chemistry; Animal Chemistry; Analogy and Religion; Geology; Mineralogy.

Every Term: English Grammar; Analysis of Language; Written Arithmetic; High Arithmetic; Elementary Algebra; Higher Algebra; Anatomy and Physiology; Natural Philosophy; Chemistry; Drawing; Painting; Music; Greek; Latin; French; and German.[3]

According to W. J. Gifford, the 167 academies that by 1853 had been established in New York State offered the following almost bewildering array of subjects; the tendency to make secondary education more practical is evidenced by the addition of so many new applied subjects:

Arithmetic; geography 162
Spelling
Reading; pronunciation
Grammar
Writing
Declamation
Composition
Rhetoric; elements of criticism 107
General history 119
Mythology 16
Astronomy 152
Analytic geometry 19
Mensuration 58
Calculus 12
Descriptive geometry 6
Conic sections 24
Civic engineering 12
Natural philosophy 161
Logic 31
Electricity 50
Hydrostatics 3
Magnetism 42
Natural theology 22
Evidences of Christianity 26
Moral philosophy 83
Intellectual philosophy 97
Political economy 21
Bookkeeping 146

French 152
Spanish 12; Italian 12
Greek 136
Latin 162
U. S. History 95
Drawing 24
Drafting 1
Algebra 165; logarithms 44
Plane geometry 157
Trigonometry 102
Surveying 103; leveling 20
Navigation 25
Technology 7
Optics 34
Mechanics 43
Chemistry 141; agricultural chemistry 14
Anatomy 66; hygiene 41
Botany 119; natural history 35
Greek antiquities 34; Roman antiquities 26
Law and government 95
German 69
Hebrew 3
Principles of teaching 33
Geology 56; meteorology 17; mineralogy 16[4]

[3] I. L. Kandel, *History of Secondary Education*, p. 415. Copyright, 1930, by Houghton Mifflin Co., and quoted with its permission.

[4] Numbers following subjects indicate in how many of the 167 academies Gifford found that the subject was offered. W. J. Gifford, *Historical Development of the New York State High School System* (Albany, N.Y.: Williams Press, Inc., 1922), p. 81.

Many academies were established for girls, and, in later years, there was a considerable number of coeducational academies. The curriculum was much the same for girls as it was for boys. But it substituted courses in music, the fine arts, and, in many such academies, what was called "manners" for such subjects as navigation and surveying.

The pupils in the academies of the eighteenth century were usually between the ages of twelve and sixteen, and the course of study was three or four years in length. After about 1860, the academies were based upon eight years of elementary school, and the youngsters were correspondingly a year or two older.

A larger percentage of the pupils were boys, who came primarily from middle-class and upper-class families. In the academies, athletics and other extracurricular activities developed in the nineteenth century, including cricket, basketball, literary societies, debating, and declamation activities.

With the development of colleges and universities throughout the country, more and more attention was given to preparation for college, and the curriculum and methods of the academies began to revert materially to those of the Latin grammar schools. More emphasis was placed upon foreign languages, particularly Latin, because, in the colleges of the nineteenth century, proficiency in Latin was almost universally required for entrance. As time went on, more attention was given to the teaching of precollege mathematics, algebra, geometry, and trigonometry and to college-preparatory science and history, until the academies were, by 1850, no longer serving the function for which they were brought into existence, but had become very largely college-preparatory schools.

The Philadelphia Academy and Benjamin Franklin. The early academies as well as Latin grammar schools did not offer what seemed to many the functional and practical curriculum ministering to the needs of young people in this country in those days. The conservatives opposed the introduction of new subjects and were inclined to be contemptuous of it and to stimulate fear and lack of appreciation on the part of parents of students. This is well illustrated by developments at the Philadelphia Academy.

At a meeting of the American Philosophical Society, in Philadelphia, in 1748, Benjamin Franklin read a paper in which he outlined what he thought were needed reforms in the philosophy and curriculum of a school for American youth. His colleagues in the society became interested and urged him to draw up a more specific plan, which he did. It was then agreed that they should establish an academy in Philadelphia that would implement this philosophy and these ideas. Instead of establishing a completely separate academy, the mistake was made of attempting in 1751 to set up, alongside of the practical course in the Philadelphia Academy, what was called the "English course."

Benjamin Franklin believed that in this "English course" much of what was to be taught would be useful rather than merely ornamental. He would have included such subjects as health, writing, drawing, arithmetic, accounts, geometry, astronomy, written and oral English, literature, history, and government. He also expected training in geography, natural history, commerce, invention, the rise of manufacture, and the progress of trade—what we might call economics today. In the next few years, Franklin was engrossed in international affairs and spent some time in Europe. Several years later, upon returning to Philadelphia and visiting the Academy, he was astounded to find the great extent to which his ideas had been sabotaged. How indignant he was is indicated by the following quotation from a review by William McAndrew, formerly editor of *School and Society,* of a book written by Thomas Woody and entitled *The Educational Views of Benjamin Franklin:*

Versatile and lovable old Ben, so Dr. Woody reminds us, held a life-long contempt for the system of higher education which wastes upon Latin and unapplied mathematics the time that could have been devoted to preparing youth to serve the public. Among the Franklin experiences, assembled in this volume of the McGraw-Hill education classics, the academy adventure reads like educational fiascoes of here and now. Franklin was the father of the project. He drew the prospectus and gathered the money. Here was to be an institution released from tradition and conditioned by public need. Life was too short and obligations too pressing to permit youth to devote precious time to dead languages and unapplied science. However, trustees of wealth and position must be got on the board. They are for the good old curriculum suitable for a gentleman and a scholar. Franklin, according to his life-long principle, takes half a loaf as better than no bread. He compromises on a school with two courses—a classical, and English. Then follows the oftplayed educational game of putting the prospectus in the cupboard and throwing away the key. Like Ezra Cornell's or Jacob Tome's educational purpose, Franklin's, in the hands of educators, gets more and more moulded into the traditional pattern until it is hardly recognizable.

Absent in Europe and busied with the affairs of the Revolution, Poor Richard scarcely knows what the old-timers are doing to this project. But old, sick and within a year of his death, the philosopher wrote one of the most scathing reports ever submitted to a school board. It consists of a series of minutes from the board records, exposing a startling contrast of resolutions with performances. "From the beginning, the contempt of your employees for the new, the English, course has been allowed to damage it. They get you to give the Latin master a title. You gave none to the English principal. To the Latin head you gave 200 pounds: to the English, one half as much money and twice as many boys. You voted 100 pounds to buy Greek and Latin books, nothing for English. I flatter myself, gentlemen, that from the board minutes it appears that the original plan has been departed from; that the subscribers have been deceived and disappointed, that good masters have been driven out of the school and that the trustees have not kept faith."[5]

Franklin's disappointment with the academy, left to the management of traditional educators, has a strikingly similar parallel in the departure of the high school between 1850 and 1925 from the ideas and the plans of the men who persuaded the state legislatures to tax the people for the schools. This instance is quite typical of the tendency to preserve the educational status quo and, when it has been departed from, to regress toward it. To this tendency may be attributed in large part the slow progress of public education toward a more functional program.

In addition to the fact that the academies were not free schools, the conservative influences as well as the financial conditions operated to prevent the curriculum reform desired by many parents, educators, and men of public affairs. As a consequence, throughout the middle half of the nineteenth century, the academies were replaced by public high schools, beginning with the one in Boston in 1821. A Massachusetts law of 1827 required every village or town of 500 or more families to maintain a high school in which were taught United States history, geometry, algebra, bookkeeping, and science. If the population were 4,000 or more, Latin, Greek, and logic and rhetoric were added to the required curriculum. The public high school spread rapidly through New England, the northern part of what was then the United States.

In the English department of the Boston public secondary school the following curriculum was offered, which gave expression to the demand for more practical instruction of secondary school students:

First Year: English Grammar including exercises in Reading, in Parsing, and Analysing, in the correction of bad English; Punctuation and Prosody; Arithmetic; Geography, and Algebra through Simple Equations.

Second Year: English Grammar continued; Geometry; Plane Trigonometry and its application to heights and distances; Mensuration of surfaces and solids; Elements of Ancient History; Logic; Rhetoric; English Composition; Declamation and exercises of the forensic kind.

Third Year: Surveying; Navigation; Elements of Chemistry and Natural Philosophy with experiments; Elements of Modern History, particularly of the United States; Moral and Political Philosophy, with English Composition, Forensics, and Declamation continued.

By 1837, the following subjects were offered in a secondary school in New York State: arithmetic, algebra, architecture, astronomy, botany, bookkeeping, Biblical antiquities, biography, chemistry, composition,

[5] From *The Educational Views of Benjamin Franklin* by Thomas Woody. Copyright, 1931, by the McGraw-Hill Book Co., Inc., and quoted with their permission.

conic sections, Constitution of the United States, Constitution of New York, elements of criticism, declamation, drawing, dialing, English grammar, evidences of Christianity, embroidery, civil engineering, extemporaneous speaking, French, geography, physical geography, geology, plane geometry, analytic geometry, Greek, Grecian antiquities, German, general history, history of the United States, history of New York, Hebrew, Italian, Latin, law (constitutional, selected revised statutes, criminal, mercantile, Blackstone's Commentaries), logic, leveling, logarithms, vocal music, instrumental music, mapping, mensuration, mineralogy, mythology, natural history, navigation, nautical astronomy, natural theology, orthography, natural philosophy, moral philosophy, intellectual philosophy, penmanship, political economy, painting, perspective, physiology, English pronunciation, reading, rhetoric, Roman antiquities, stenography, statistics, surveying, Spanish, trigonometry, topography, technology, principles of teaching.

Nevertheless, as time went on, conservative elements, as has always been the case in the history of secondary education, became active and aggressive and few of the public high schools offered little more than a conventional academic curriculum stressing classical languages and mathematics.

THE RENEWED BATTLE TO INCREASE THE BREADTH OF THE HIGH SCHOOL CURRICULUM

Developments Calling for a More Comprehensive Curriculum. In the latter part of the nineteenth century, beginning in the 1880's, the enrolment of both boys and girls in public high schools began to increase greatly. Indeed, from 1880 to 1930, the number of students attending public secondary schools doubled every decade. Naturally, many of these students came from families of limited incomes and had little chance of attending a college. There was, naturally, a growing demand on the part of the students, their parents, and others for the curriculum to become more practical to prepare boys and girls for life situations outside of college life.

New Subjects. Particularly after 1890, new subjects were introduced, here and there at first and then rather generally, in the curriculum of the public high schools. Among the earlier additions were courses for girls in the field of home economics and shop courses for boys. Beginning in the late 1890's and spreading rapidly thereafter, business-education courses were added to the curriculum of secondary schools everywhere, particularly courses relating to bookkeeping, typewriting, and, a little later, secretarial work and shorthand.

Early in the twentieth century, courses in the social studies, particularly civics and then, a little later, economics and sociology, were added. Also fairly early in the twentieth century, a course in general science was added in most schools, replacing what was then called physical geography—which, by the way, in most schools had a content that could ill afford to be dropped.

Opposition by Conservatives. It was an uphill struggle to modify and improve the high school curriculum. Aristocrats and conservative educational philosophers were active and, indeed, were disproportionately represented on local boards of education. Furthermore, the majority of the teachers themselves had vested interests, being specialists in the older subjects that they feared would be replaced by the newer ones—a fear never realized, because the increased enrolments in secondary schools meant increased enrolments in the older subjects as well as the newer ones.

Whether knowingly or not, the conservatives did not hesitate to employ specious and unsound arguments, among those receiving most widespread acceptance at that time being what came to be known as the doctrine of formal discipline or transfer of training. As many of them said, it was not the subject matter that really counted; it mattered not so much what was taught as how it was taught, the demands it made upon young people, and its consequent contribution to the development of qualities of character. "Discipline," of a somewhat mystic character, and prestige values were invoked. Similarly, the students and lay people rather generally were told that education consisted of the older, more respectable academic subjects. Even though such subjects may have had no direct practical value, they served to give cultural and social status to those who had at least a superficial acquaintance with them.

A third approach was the argument that the academic subjects, particularly mathematics and foreign languages, had unique and unusual values as preparation for college. Since the great masses of the population had never been in college and had little knowledge of it, they were not in a position to do other than to accept the statements of "educators" in the secondary schools and colleges who represented vested interests.

Reaction of the Progressives—the Eight-Year Study. Beginning in the 1920's, investigations were made that revealed that the superior or unique values of certain subjects as preparation for college existed largely in the imagination or propaganda of those who wished to encourage enrolment in those subjects. Investigations carried on in a score of universities and colleges revealed that, with the intelligence of the student held constant, there was negligible correlation among (1) the grades made in college, (2) the number of years of study of any subject in high school, and (3) the following of a conservative curriculum instead of a progressive experimental program.

Most prominent of these investigations was one carried on by progressive education for eight years, the conclusions of which were most encouraging for reforms in the curriculum and methods, though they were pooh-poohed and discarded by conservatives and, indeed, fairly soon forgotten by many progressives. In the report made in 1938 by the Committee on the Eight-Year Study, the following conclusions of the Study were set forth:

1,475 graduates from the thirty experimental schools were matched with 1,475 graduates of conventional high schools. Comparison of the two groups on matched criteria of college success established conclusively that no particular plan of college preparation, so far as subjects in high school are concerned, is superior to any other plan. Specifically, the comparison of the matched pairs revealed that the graduates of the thirty experimental schools

1. earned a slightly higher total grade average;
2. earned higher grade averages in all subject fields except foreign languages;
3. specialized in the same academic fields as did the comparison students;
4. did not differ from the comparison group in the number of times they were placed on probation;
5. received slightly more academic honors each year;
6. were more often judged to possess a high degree of intellectual curiosity and drive;
7. were more often judged to be precise, systematic, and objective in their thinking;
8. were more often judged to have developed clear or well-formulated ideas concerning the meaning of education—especially in the first two years in college;
9. more often demonstrated a high degree of resourcefulness in meeting new situations;
10. did not differ from the comparison group in ability to plan their time effectively;
11. had about the same problems of adjustment as the comparison group, but approached their solution with greater effectiveness;
12. participated somewhat more frequently, and more often enjoyed appreciative experiences, in the arts;
13. participated more in all organized student groups except religious and "service" activities;
14. earned in each college year a higher percentage of nonacademic honors (officership in organizations, election to managerial societies, athletic insignia, leading roles in dramatic and musical presentations);
15. did not differ from the comparison group in the quality of adjustment to their contemporaries;
16. differed only slightly from the comparison group in kinds of judgments about their schooling;

17. had a somewhat better orientation toward the choice of vocation;
18. demonstrated a more active concern for what was going on in the world.[6]

Opposition of the Intellectuals. The conclusions of this study did not materially discourage the critics of reform of the curriculum, particularly those who might be classified as intellectuals, would-be intellectuals, or pseudo-intellectuals. They made many criticisms of the modern changes in the high school curriculum, and among the more commonly voiced were the following:

1. *Students in secondary schools in other countries, for example, Russia, Switzerland, France, England, and Germany, are further along in the sciences and mathematics and foreign languages than students at a comparable stage in secondary schools in the United States.* Since it seems quite certain that some, if not all, of these critics knew that students graduating from secondary schools in most European countries are much more a select fragment of adolescents and are at least older on the average than those graduating from secondary schools in the United States and attend schools more weeks in the year and more hours in the week, it is not logical or ethical to compare the achievement of this select percentage of the students in foreign secondary schools with the general rank and file of young people that were attending American secondary schools. As a matter of fact, secondary schools in England, Germany, France, Japan, China, Russia, and elsewhere are becoming more like those in the United States.[7]

2. *Secondary schools are largely concerned with "life adjustment" courses, which have little to do with developing the intellect or scientific or cultural knowledge.* None of these critics defined what was meant by "life adjustment" courses, although a few suggested that most vocational courses were "life adjustment" courses, as were courses in home economics and in "coed cooking." Much was made of the fact that the "Prosser" resolution,[8] which really started the education for life adjustment movement in American secondary education, was introduced and passed at a meeting of the American Vocational Association, in St. Louis, in 1946. This was a rather wild and gratuitously hazardous inference that education for life adjustment as proposed by the regional and national committees and as practiced by the schools was closely associated with vocational education. The attention of some of the critics who were

[6] Wilford M. Aikin, *The Story of the Eight-Year Study*, pp. 111–112. Copyright, 1942, by Harper & Row and quoted with their permission.

[7] "French Industry Urges Education Changes," *France Actuelle*, Vol. 11 (April 15, 1962), pp. 1–5, reviewed in the *Reader's Digest* (October, 1962).

[8] Introduced by Dr. C. A. Prosser, then headmaster of Demwoody in the Institute of Minneapolis.

profuse in the use of epithets such as *"Educational Wastelands," "Diminished Minds,"* etc., was called to more important publications on the subject of education for life adjustment and to the fact that in these publications there were chapters on English literature, English grammar, science, mathematics, history, and the social studies, but this did not seem to deter them in their fanatical frenzy of abuse and misrepresentation.[9]

3. *Many high schools offer "snap" courses.* As far as this criticism was applied, and its application was indeed limited, it was a useful criticism. Critics were often embarrassed by being unable to name many specific "snap" courses, and there was disagreement among the critics as to just what were "snap" courses. A common answer was "life adjustment" courses without naming of specific ones.

4. *The requirements for graduation do not ensure an adequate introduction to culture or a well-rounded education.* There was little question but that in many schools this unfortunate situation has developed. The elective system has been carried beyond its original intentions and, indeed, beyond any sound educational philosophy. Students have been graduated from high school with great gaps in their general education, some not having had more than one or two years of instruction in science beyond the sixth grade, some not having had any mathematics beyond the eighth grade, some not having had more than two or three years of history and the social studies (perhaps none except in American history) above the eighth grade, and a very large percentage not having had any instruction in foreign languages, music, or art. This situation has been corrected in a very large proportion of the schools where it once existed.

5. *Inadequate provision is made in the curriculum for bright children.* This criticism was also justified to a considerable extent, but, in recent years, there have existed in the typical school several different types of courses for special sections of bright children.

6. *The schools do not provide appropriate curriculum materials for the less able students.* This criticism was also to a considerable extent justified, and, likewise, to a considerable extent the situation has been remedied by the organization of courses of study in various academic fields of a nature to be appropriate for the interests, for the intellectual capacity, and to meet the needs of the slow and less able students.

7. *The curriculum of most schools contributes to physical as well as intellectual flabbiness.*

However, even the critics generally acknowledged that the curriculum did include adequate provision for character and citizenship education, for moral and spiritual education, and for sex and parenthood education.

[9] Harl R. Douglass *et al. Education for Life Adjustment: Its Meaning and Implementation* (New York: The Ronald Press Co., 1950).

In spite of the fact that it now appears clear that many of the criticisms made by the conservatives were unjust, constituting cries of "wolf," and were sensationalism for ulterior purposes and to attract attention, the public generally has come to believe that it was badly deceived and misled.

Despite the unfairness of much of the criticism and the ultimate exposure of such critics, the Progressive Education Association became a casualty and gave up the ghost in the middle 1950's. To some extent, this demise was the result of attacks upon progressive education for political rather than for educational reasons by individuals and organizations intent upon destroying the public confidence in John Dewey, the outstanding leader of the progressives, especially since he was a political liberal considered by many of the politically conservative individuals and organizations to be a radical exponent of socially progressive philosophy and governmental measures and to be friendly to the working man.

Recent Compromises and Continued Progress. The recent compromises to some extent giving hope of improving the curriculum have been the work of various national committees on curriculum in mathematics, in science, and in English, and of national organizations such as the National Association of Secondary School Principals and the Association for Supervision and Curriculum Development. Much more attention has been given to curriculum provisions for the bright child through advanced placement, seminars, honors courses, etc., and special curriculum provisions have been introduced for the creative student, as well as for the potential dropouts and for less able students. Teaching machines and programed materials owe part of their splurge of initial popularity to the desire of educators and others to improve upon the curriculum and to the readiness of such people to accept innovations with any promise of accomplishing that. These and other progressive developments will be described in later chapters in this volume. Progress is, as always, slow and irregular, but it is, nevertheless, constantly going on in spite of vigorous efforts to impede it by those with limited backgrounds and vested interests.

QUESTIONS, PROBLEMS, AND ISSUES FOR FURTHER THOUGHT

1. Why did our forefathers in New England, within a few years after settling there in the early part of the seventeenth century, set up Latin grammar schools for their youth?
2. Why, through centuries, have conservatives been so successful in slowing down, postponing, and, in some instances, defeating progressive and forward-looking movements in curriculum planning?

3. How do you account for the fact that the academies, established in protest against the narrow curriculum of the Latin grammar schools, gravitated toward a similar narrow type of curriculum as the years went by?

4. What were the forces developing in the latter half of the nineteenth century that contributed to the spread of the public high school in the United States and to the broadening of the curriculum in the last quarter of the nineteenth century?

5. What are the principal implications of the conclusions of the Eight-Year Study by the Progressive Education Association for curriculum improvements?

6. What are the fundamental principles of progressive education, and what implications do they have for the curriculum?

7. What movements are being carried on now by progressive forces in England, France, and other European countries to modernize secondary school curriculums?

8. What is "basic education" organization, and what part does it play in opposition to progressive ideas?

9. In what way did examination of draftees and enrollees for the armed forces in World War I and World War II stimulate the addition of courses in physical education to the curriculum?

10. What do you think are some of the more important progressive ideas of recent years intended to improve the high school curriculum?

SUPPLEMENTARY MATERIALS

Selected Readings

Anderson, Vernon E., and William T. Gruhn. *Principles and Practices of Secondary Education* (2d ed.). New York: The Ronald Press Co., 1962. Chapter 6, "The Teacher's Role in Curriculum Development."

Krug, Edward P., Chester D. Babcock, and John Guy Fowlkes. *Administering Curriculum Planning.* New York: Harper & Row, 1956. Chapter 5, "Teachers and Students in Curriculum Planning"; Chapter 6, "Public Participation."

Lee, Gordon C. *Education in Modern America.* New York: Holt, Rinehart & Winston, Inc., 1957. Part VII—Chapter 27, "Freedom To Teach and To Learn: Academic Freedom and Academic Responsibility."

Leese, Joseph, Kenneth Frasine, and Meuritz Johnson. *The Teacher in Curriculum Making.* New York: Harper & Row, 1961.

Miller, Delmas F., *et al.* "The Principal's Role in Improving the Curriculum," *Bulletin of the N.A.S.S.P.,* No. 244 (February, 1959), 1–119.

Seyfert, Warren C. "Do Colleges Determine What the High Schools Teach?" *The Clearing House,* XXXIV (May, 1960), 515–20.

Spalding, Howard G. "Role of the Principal in Curriculum Work," *Teachers College Record,* LVIII (December, 1956), 153–58.

Van Til, William, Marvin D. Alcorn, and James M. Linley, *Issues in Curriculum Development.* New York: Harcourt, Brace & World, Inc., 1959. "Participants in Curriculum Construction," pp. 304–25.

7

Participants in Curriculum Determination

Many individuals and groups operate and influence, cooperatively and independently, often through opposition, to determine what learning materials and activities shall constitute the curriculum. In the following pages the more important of these will be reviewed.

TEXTBOOK WRITERS

Through the long gloom of the Middle Ages, only brief shafts of enlightenment were seen and these were largely from the church. The cultural events of the period were recorded in a spoken literature and handed down from one generation to the next by word of mouth. Variation, rather than change, occurred, depending upon the skill and imagination of the teller and the accuracy of the listener's memory rather than upon the influence of social change.

Even after the invention of printing, in the middle of the fifteenth century, by which time the Renaissance was well started, few students at Heidelburg, Aix, Caen, Oxford, or Cambridge could afford to buy a text for themselves, and so we find the professor lecturing, expounding, and even shamelessly reading to his students. Only the best of prose can withstand such punishment, and the earliest translations of old Greek into the new Latin must have required a great thirst for knowledge on the part of the student. Most of the vigor of the program in the early universities derived from the disputation—a class in which the student was required to demonstrate possession of the knowledge and understanding he had supposedly received.

The reading of Socrates, Plato, and Aristotle, of the Bible and Thomas Aquinas, of Hippocrates and Galen, and of Cicero was soon facilitated by the demand that scholars be able to read and write Latin and Greek before admission to the University. Schools for adolescent boys appeared as if by magic. There were the *Gymnasien,* the British public schools, and, in 1620, the first Latin grammar school in Boston. Hence the textbooks; hence the classical curriculum.

Most teachers still depend largely upon textbooks, and, consequently, modern schools make use of many texts, so many that the production of them has become a vast economic as well as intellectual enterprise. Because the texts must appeal to many teachers, and because they are costly to produce, their influence is still conservative.[1]

Since 1959, there has been a flurry of interest in mechanical teaching devices. Ginther,[2] after examining this movement, has reached the conclusion that programed materials are at the heart of the discussion. If his analysis proves true, we can look forward to attempts to write textbooks that accord, if this is possible, with the diverse views of learning held by both Skinner and Pressey. The insights of Skinner will be used to smooth a path that is too difficult; where the going should be easier, the student will be encouraged to work out his own understandings. A proper balance between attention to the line, on the one hand, and the completed figure, on the other, should do much to increase pupil interest in the text.

OTHER PROFESSIONALS

Curriculum Specialists. Ideas concerning the curriculum are now so numerous and complex that a separate specialty has developed to look after them. Curriculum specialists are found in departments and schools of education in nearly all our universities and in the administrative and supervisory offices of school districts. From colleges and universities, they conduct research to assess both the efficiency and the effectiveness of a variety of curricular modifications, and they also write books and articles describing the results of their experiments. Just as importantly, they are constantly going over the existing ideas concerning the curriculum and modifying them in the light of fresh knowledge. Summaries of these ideas are then included in curriculum books which are used to increase the understanding of teachers and administrators.

Presumably, classroom practices are affected by what the teachers learn before they begin to teach, though most professors of education would

[1] See Chapter 10, for more detailed discussion of textbooks as curriculum materials.
[2] John R. Ginther, "A Model for Analyzing Programed Materials," *Administrator's Notebook,* Vol. 10, No. 1 (January, 1962).

be surprised to learn that their influence is as great as some of the more outspoken critics of the schools have claimed. There seems no doubt that classroom practices are strongly affected by in-service membership on curriculum committees. Many of the ideas used by such committees derive, of course, from the thinking and writing of curriculum specialists in the colleges and universities.

Most curriculum specialists belong to the Association for Supervision and Curriculum Development (ASCD), which sponsors a yearbook as well as several periodicals and is a department of the National Education Association of the United States (NEA). Another department of the NEA is the National Society for the Study of Education, which also publishes a yearbook. Many of these organizations are directly or indirectly concerned with the curriculum of the secondary schools. Still a third department of the NEA is the National Association of Secondary School Principals. In recent years, especially, their monthly bulletin has shown primary concern for the curriculum of the secondary schools.

Subject-Matter Specialists. There has, in recent years, been an increased participation by individuals who have always shown concern for the high-school curriculum, the faculties of colleges and universities, who teach subject matter to prospective teachers.

Several new courses in mathematics and science have been worked out in close cooperation with groups of teachers. These courses, all with unmanageable names, are often referred to by their initials. The Physical Science Study Committee[3] beginning with Zacharias at Massachusetts Institute of Technology (M.I.T.) is known as PSSC. In its high school physics, an agglutination of mechanics, molecular physics, heat, light, sound, electricity, and nucleonics are given at least a semblance of rational cohesion. The authors of the course are by no means unwilling to draw upon material from other sciences than physics to round out the structure and to make it more appealing. The Chem Study Materials,[4] beginning with Seaborg, then chancellor of the University of California at Berkeley, centralized laboratory work. Pupils are given a minimum of directions, and the text is aimed at leading them to discover the generalizations of chemistry for themselves. The Chemical Bond Approach Committee[5] (CBAC) has provided a set of instructional materials in which the generalizations are deduced from theories of atomic and molecular structure. Several new mathematics courses have been worked out in detail, using such fundamental generalizations as the commutative law and set theory.

[3] Physical Science Study Committee, *Physics* (Boston: D. C. Heath & Co., 1960).
[4] Chemical Education Materials Study, *Chemistry: An Experimental Science* (Berkeley: The Regents of the University of California, 1960).
[5] Chemical Bond Approach Committee, *Chemistry: Trial Edition* (Portland, Ore.: The Reed Institute, 1960).

The ones that seem to be most popular at present are those emanating from the School Mathematics Study Group[6] (SMSG). Finally, the American Institute of Biological Sciences[7] (AIBS) has produced three sets of materials for the high school biology course, based on three different approaches to the study of life science. The most difficult emphasizes modern theories of genetics and demands an understanding of the most advanced research into the chemistry of hereditary transmission. In these BSCS (Biological Sciences Curriculum Study) materials, the key substance is known by a name, deoxyribonucleic acid, that is so long that it, too, must be familiarized to DNA.[8]

In addition, the National Science Foundation[9] has established a great many summer and year-long institutes across the country where teachers not only can learn to use the new materials, they also receive funds while attending, so that they can continue to support themselves and their families. Hence, although these programs have stimulated both modernization and rationalization of high school courses in science and mathematics, they have been costly to produce, and the money has been supplied largely by the federal government.[10]

As soon as the members of academic faculties left the sidelines where some of them, unfortunately, had used their energies only to jeer at the plight of the high schools, they found that writing a course was one thing and teaching the ideas in it to children something quite different. Hence, the special talents of curriculum workers and other educationists have been increasingly called upon as the work has proceeded.

Perhaps the best-known instance of extensive cooperation between scientists, mathematicians, historians, linguists, psychologists, and educationists was that reported by Bruner.[11] His position, introduced but not exhaustively analyzed, is that the various disciplines have separate structures that distinguish each from the other and that it is this lasting framework or order that the high school student must get hold of, if he is to use the ideas of the discipline in his daily living, enjoy his study of the subject, and continue adding throughout life to his knowledge and understanding.

Scholars in fields other than mathematics and science have made tentative beginnings of a similar nature, and so we have Project English, sup-

[6] School Mathematics Study Group, *Mathematics for High School Geometry*, Part I (for example) (New Haven: Yale University Press, 1959).

[7] American Institute of Biological Sciences, *High School Biology* (Boulder, Colo.: Director, Biological Sciences Curriculum Study, University of Colorado, 1960).

[8] See Chapter 24, for more detailed discussion of these projects.

[9] See Chapter 24, for more detailed discussion.

[10] Dorothy M. Fraser, *Current Curriculum Studies in Academic Subjects* (Washington, D.C.: National Education Association of the United States, 1962).

[11] Jerome S. Bruner, *The Process of Education* (Cambridge, Mass.: Harvard University Press, 1961).

ported to the tune of several million dollars by the federal government, and demonstration centers in other areas of the curriculum, at least in the planning stage.

Advances in the teaching of foreign languages have not stressed the scholarly approach, which is largely critical, grammatical, and historical. Instead, the emphasis has been upon the acquisition of spoken fluency, and, to this end, the methods and, indeed, the machinery of the armed services has been the pattern. The federal government, through the various titles of the National Defense Education Act (NDEA) has supplied the necessary funds.

Administration of the various teacher institutes for mathematics and science has been left to universities and colleges chosen by a national advisory committee from among those applying for such an institute. The expenditures under NDEA[12] have been administered through state departments of education.

GOVERNMENT CONTROL

Local. Although the volume of written criticism of American public high schools has subsided from its frenetic post-Sputnik peak, the advance toward sanity in the discussion being led by Conant,[13] the fallacy that curricular problems can be settled simply has seduced a large section of the American public. What is far worse is that parents are provided with phrases, sentences, and even paragraphs with which to bombard local administrators. It is important that the harassed administrators be provided with counterarguments. A carefully documented statement of this kind has been provided by Parker.[14] Unfortunately, defense that entails rushing to the aid of a straw man is hardly worth the time of a man of intelligence, and the complicated answers to education problems that men of good will and intelligence must seek cannot be communicated by catchwords. The best administrative defense is first to screen the arguments to see if they have anything to offer other than the tired old clichés and then to engage in an educational offensive that will show the public just what it is that the schools are doing. The administrator must be ready for genuine difference of opinion that derives from the philosophical conflict referred to earlier. Hook[15] has been careful

[12] See, for example, Colorado Senate Bill No. 234, Chapter 219, SL '59.
[13] James Bryant Conant, *The American High School Today* (New York: McGraw-Hill Book Co., Inc., 1959).
[14] J. Cecil Parker, T. Bentley Edwards, and William H. Stegeman, *Curriculum in America* (New York: Thomas Y. Crowell Co., 1962), pp. 475–492.
[15] Sidney Hook, "Modern Education and Its Critics, *Seventh Yearbook of the American Association of Colleges for Teacher Education* (Washington, D.C.: American Association of Colleges For Teacher Education, 1954).

to point out the basis of this quarrel, and his article on the subject should be read and reread by the administrator who wishes to argue the point.

Not all segments of the American public are equally vocal. Unfortunately, the personality characteristics associated with a willingness to talk loudly but not necessarily with intelligence are also those of people who are down on the public schools. Like the rest of us, they care less for the accuracy of the pattern than for its availability. To ensure that all segments of public opinion are provided with an opportunity to influence school procedures, more and more school boards are appointing committees of lay citizens to advise them. These committees are large, sometimes with thirty members, and they are representative of all socioeconomic classes and all sections of the community. When they are provided with the time needed to make a careful study of school procedures and so become able to base their deliberations and opinions firmly on fact, their advice can be most helpful to governing boards.

State. Local school boards can only make use of authority delegated to them by the various state governments. Before the wave of criticism began, legislation at the state level was largely confined to the control of policy in only certain well-defined areas, and was adopted after consultation with various groups of professional educators. Since the criticism has developed, a few state legislatures have tried to take back, at least partially, control from local school boards by the passage of laws that specifically affect the high school curriculum, and the advice of teachers has been largely ignored. On the other hand, the effect of the criticism on national legislation has been just the opposite. In opposition to federal aid to education, the cry of "federal control" has been sounding loud and clear, even against the National Defense Education Act. To understand these two apparently contrasting effects, one must conclude that the critics are aiming at a reduction in school costs rather than an increase in national safety and that the alleged Russian superiority in mathematics and science is merely a screen to hide the campaign to cut down school costs. The wild talk about the need to streamline the teaching of reading, writing, and arithmetic has all been aimed toward simplification of school procedures, with corresponding reduction in financial support. Statewide examinations would measure the gross educational product; schools would be converted to assembly lines, with machines for teachers; and the taxpayer, especially the large industrial taxpayer, would save money. The legislated efficiency would derive from the state rather than the federal government, for the latter is such a ponderous vehicle as to be not only autonomous and free from control by the taxpayer but also easily capable of "eating up the profits."

State legislative codes have long included laws concerning school curriculums. Such legislation may relate to health, the Constitution, teacher certification, the influence of narcotics, fire prevention, manners and morals, or patriotic instruction including the teaching of American history. One state, at least, calls for reference to Frances Willard in American-history courses. A number of people have thought that reference to Emma Willard would be more appropriate. It is obvious that several of these laws have been made in response to pleas from certain groups of citizens. To the extent that they do so, they probably represent poor legislation.

Recently, the legislature of the state of California has enacted two highly specific laws into the California Education Code—one providing for details concerned with the preparation of teachers,[16] and the other calling for the teaching of foreign languages in elementary schools.[17] In the administration of these two laws, the State Department of Education, though sympathetic to the sense of the laws, is experiencing enormous difficulty. The law concerning teacher certification requires teachers to hold a major in an academic subject. Definition of this significant phrase is proving most elusive. The teaching of foreign languages may possibly be highly desirable, but the necessary teachers are not available to do the job, and there is no money to engage their services if they were. Members of academic departments in colleges and universities are said to have given their support to this legislation.[18] If this is so, their activities along this line have been far less helpful than in the preparation of new courses and they have been needlessly disruptive of general progress in teacher preparation.

National. New courses in mathematics and science have been provided with financial support by several agencies of the federal government, and these have been already described. Historically, the federal government has had a continuing interest in vocational education. In 1914, Congress appointed a Commission on National Aid to Vocational Education, and from the Commission report grew the first federal aid to secondary education, the Smith-Hughes Act of 1917. Other acts authorizing grants to the several states for vocational education have followed.

In December, 1962, the U.S. Office of Education presented to President Kennedy a voluminous report of a searching and exhaustive inquiry by

[16] Roy E. Simpson, "The Development of New Credential Requirements," *California Schools*, Vol. 33, No. 8 (August, 1962), pp. 1–24.

[17] Roy E. Simpson, "Principles, Policies, and Recommendations for Foreign Language Instruction in California Schools," *California Schools*, Vol. 33, No. 2 (February, 1962), pp. 37–47; see also California Education Code, 1961, Section 7604(c).

[18] James C. Stone, *California's Commitment to Public Education* (New York: Thomas Y. Crowell Co., 1961), p. 48.

an impressive panel of consultants into vocational education. This report was made at the request of President Kennedy, and there seems little or no doubt that modifications in the series of laws relating to federal support for vocational education will occur. At present, these laws benefit 4 million students, half of whom are adults, in two-thirds of American high schools as well as in many colleges. A $250 million local-state-federal program is in effect throughout the Union.

Use, by the President, of the U.S. Office of Education, has drawn attention to the need for a reassessment of the duties and responsibilities of this office, which was left for four months in the last half of 1962 without a commissioner to run it. There are those who feel that, because of the recently acknowledged importance of the effects of secondary education upon national and international relationships, a Secretary of Education is needed in the President's cabinet. Others are in favor of supporting a Commissioner of Education by a National School Committee.

Despite the recent failure of legislation authorizing direct federal aid to education, there is not the slightest doubt that expenditures of federal funds for education will increase, that the concern of national leaders for education will deepen, and that, eventually, the appropriate national machinery will be established for translating this concern into action.

ACCREDITATION AGENCIES

Accreditation is the device used by the various associations of schools and colleges throughout the country to ensure that the high schols from which they accept students offer college-preparatory courses and have at least average educational programs, housing, and equipment, and well-prepared teachers.

In two states, California and Michigan, responsibility for accreditation is given by law to the state university. In the former, this has been rapidly turned over to the newly formed Western Association of Schools and Colleges, which makes use of accreditation procedures worked out by the California Association of Secondary School Administrators.[19] Instruments developed by this association derive from the famous Evaluative Criteria[20] used by what was called the Cooperative Study of Secondary School Standards, which is now called the National Study of Secondary

[19] National Study of Secondary School Evaluation, *Evaluate Criteria* (3d ed.) (Washington, D.C.: California Association of Secondary School Administrators, 1960).

[20] Accrediting Commission for Secondary Schools, *Visiting Committee Handbook, WASC Accreditation Program, Public Secondary Schools* (Mimeo.) (Burlingame, Calif.: Accrediting Commission for Secondary Schools).

School Evaluation. Although this change in name was made in compliance with a Washington law prohibiting the use of the word "cooperative" in the title of a non-profit organization, it also draws attention to a shift that has been taking place over the years from a checking system to see that the school reaches certain minimum standards to a full-scale evaluation aimed at finding out the extent to which the school achieves excellence in a variety of endeavors.

When a school wishes to be evaluated and accredited by one of the large associations of schools and colleges, it is provided with a number of instruments. Central in importance among these instruments is one that stimulates the school, through its own local committees, to make explicit its philosophy of education. This instrument has recently been revised to remove, as far as possible, all questions that would lead a given school to believe that the association places greatest value on a particular philosophic system. Other instruments lead various local committees to examine in depth the curricular offerings, the guidance system, the administrative organization, the capabilities of the faculty, the nature and function of the secretaries and custodians, the quality of the buildings and of the library, and, especially, the characteristics of the students and the community in which they live. All of this self-searching and filling of forms occupies at least a semester and sometimes more.

Almost as soon as a school applies for accreditation, a visiting committee is appointed *ad hoc*. Members of these committees may be administrators and teachers from other districts, college and university professors, or state and county education officers. Teachers from other districts are not as heavily represented as they might be or perhaps should be for the simple reason that their services are less easily dispensed with. However, more and more governing boards are recognizing the need to engage the services of substitutes so that teachers, the ones most likely to benefit, can receive the experience of examining another school in detail.

The visiting committee spends two or three days in the school, visiting classes freely, going over all parts of the buildings and grounds, and meeting with the committees responsible for completing the instruments. The chief purpose here is to see that the reports are accurate and not colored with administrative perceptions exclusively or biased in any other way.

Reports of visiting committees are brief, and a first draft, at least, is usually completed during the visit. The committee does not itself accredit, but its recommendations are usually followed by the regional board. A number of private institutions apply for accreditation each year, as well as many public high schools. The plan, which can be characterized as a system of self-evaluation followed by a careful check by an outside committee, has now been in operation for nearly thirty years.

Numerous doctoral dissertations in departments of education in Pennsylvania and Oregon have documented the effectiveness of the system.

Accreditation of teacher-preparation institutions is common, but the system lacks many of the self-evaluative procedures and a number of the safeguards that have been evolved to produce the high standards of the accreditation of high schools.

When the two systems of accreditation are considered together, and especially if allowance is made for improvements that could be made in the evaluation of programs of teacher education in colleges and universities, specific legislation with respect to curriculums and standards to be reached seems wholly unnecessary.

STUDENTS

Adaptation to the Student. The entire point of the self-evaluative procedures just described would be lost unless it is recognized that curriculums must be made suitable for the boys and girls who are to take part. Wide variations among students are therefore implied with respect to all those dimensions of personality that interact with the curriculum procedures. Generalizations with respect to students must, therefore, be provided for the teachers by psychologists and guidance workers with the help of these dimensions.

The complete list of dimensions of personality so far identified is not to be the starting point for curricular plans. One reason is that knowledge of them is incomplete and is likely to remain so. Because the knowledge is incomplete, the assumption that additional dimensions are significant in the educational process is probably safe. Another reason is that highly specific modifications by the teacher in the light of student differences are not possible—the teacher is too busy. Even if each teacher had a computer into which the constantly changing measures could be fed, he would spend most of his time testing and "computerizing." But, knowing the range of attributes of his pupils, the teacher can plan ahead, keeping this range in mind. He can also introduce a variety into his curricular plans that can be expected to capitalize upon the variety of attributes that his pupils will display. The definitive reason that curricular plans cannot start with the students is that other participants in the determination of the curriculum are much more powerful.

Student Participation. The teacher must check his curricular plans against the known dimensions of his students. Many teachers accomplish this by permitting the students to review proposed classroom and laboratory procedures. To do so is to require that the pupils be able to assess themselves normatively. Most of them are lacking in the needed insights. However, there are other reasons for teacher-pupil planning, and these are chiefly motivational. If it is not entirely appropriate to ask students to judge curricular proposals, it is even less appropriate to ask them for original suggestions.

Ways in which curricular plans might be suitably modified to accord with known variations in student characteristics will be illustrated with reference to facts about potential for learning, socioeconomic status, and interests including educational and vocational aspirations. Although these three attributes overlap to some extent, they provide the teacher with a variety of manageable information about the student which is known to affect academic success.

Potential for Learning. Only two sets of facts will be used here. The first is that, in a study made by Dillon, 86 per cent of seventh graders with an I.Q. about 115 remained to graduate, whereas only 54 per cent in the I.Q. range 85–94 remained that long.[21] The second is that a study by Harmon showed one out of thirty Ph.D.'s had recorded an I.Q. below 100 when in high school.[22]

The responses to these facts and to others like them range all the way from nonchalance to serious concern. Those who are impressed with the efficiency of the intelligence test as a screening device to prevent teachers in high school and college from wasting their efforts will regard the facts as support for their view. They may even go so far as to claim that the one in thirty should never have been awarded the Ph.D.! Those who believe that the task of the high school should be to educate each to the greatest extent possible and who see the intelligence test as but a summary of past achievement will take the facts as a serious indictment of the high school curriculum, or even of the elementary school curriculum. Durkin, for example, points to the need for the child showing a low I.Q. in the primary grades to be taught to read early.[23] If he is doing poorly in high school, he needs a program that will unite his present concrete interests to an interest in ideas and that will then provide him with insights into the number system and increase his facility with words. Admittedly, pedagogical technique is as important here as curriculum, but, though these two may be separated for purposes of analysis and discussion, they can never be separated in practice. Bruner, who emphasizes the structure and process of a discipline to arouse the interest of the child, says that all we can conclude at present is that "any subject can

[21] H. J. Dillon, *Early School Leavers: A Major Educational Problem* (New York: National Child Labor Committee, 1949).

[22] Lindsey R. Harmon, "High School Backgrounds of Science Doctorates," *Science,* Vol. 133 (1961), pp. 679–688.

[23] Dolores Durkin, "Children Who Learned To Read at Home," *Elementary School Journal,* Vol. 62 (October, 1961), pp. 14–18; Dolores Durkin, "Kindergarten and Reading," *Elementary English,* Vol. 39 (March, 1962), pp. 274–276.

be taught effectively in some intellectually honest form to any child at any stage of development."[24]

Socioeconomic Status. Study after study has indicated the correlation of the success of the child in school with the success of his father at making a living.[25] Again, the finding is regarded in one way by some and another way by others. If convincing evidence were available to show that teaching of children from lower socioeconomic groups is inherently difficult, those who ignore the rejection of lower-class children by the schools might be excused. The only evidence available shows that different methods and curriculums must be used.

Interests. Coleman has shown that high school students, collectively, do not demonstrate high esteem for academic achievement, a finding that may or may not prove helpful to the curriculum worker.[26] Edwards and Wilson have been able to show that intrinsic interest in school subjects is almost equally common among children from various socioeconomic classes.[27] But, because the I.Q. correlates with socioeconomic status and because the I.Q., or tests that correlate highly with it, is used to select children for further education, a child with strong academic interests but with parents of very limited income has very much less chance of being selected than a rich child with equally strong interests and with well-to-do parents.

THE TEACHER

Although the debate over the purposes and practices of education in America is far from complete, the position that the high school curriculum is fixed and that only those capable of profiting from it should be allowed to stay is losing its relatively few adherents. Essentially, the view is simple as well as traditional. According to the viewpoint of the fixed curriculum, the textbook is the final authority, though the teacher is afforded respect for his ability to interpret the text and because he prepares and grades the examinations.

[24] Jerome S. Bruner, *The Process of Education* (Cambridge, Mass.: Harvard University Press, 1961), p. 33.

[25] Cyril Burt, "Ability and Income," *British Journal of Educational Psychology,* Vol. 13 (1943), pp. 83–98; R. J. Havighurst and L. L. Janke, "Relation Between Ability and Social Status in a Mid-western Community: I. Ten-Year-old Children," *Journal of Educational Psychology,* Vol. 35 (1944), pp. 357–368.

[26] J. S. Coleman, "Social Climates in High Schools," *Cooperative Research Monograph No. 4* (Washington, D.C.: U.S. Office of Education, 1961); J. S. Coleman, *The Adolescent Subculture* (New York: The Free Press of Glencoe, 1961).

[27] T. Bentley Edwards and Alan B. Wilson, "A Study of Some Social and Psychological Factors Influencing Educational Achievement," *Final Report to U.S. Office of Education* (June, 1961) (Mimeographed).

The Teacher as Curriculum Determiner. When the teacher is expert in his field and also able to communicate his knowledge and understanding, splendid accomplishments sometimes result with a comparatively few students. All of us have been privileged at one time or another to listen to a really first-class lecturer. One of the arguments for team teaching is that only the better lecturers among the faculty will address the large groups of 100 or more.

To broaden the appeal of the textbook-and-lecture approach to those with low educational and vocational aspirations, popularization seems generally to have been the method employed. Textbooks with an easier vocabulary have been written, or at least produced—plenty of pictures have been inserted—and an abundance of contemporary, immediate, and concrete references has been provided. The teacher has often made use of fairly broad humor. Engaging in classroom practices calculated to appeal more than to instruct, he has permitted more talking and playing around and he has emphasized greater student freedom in the classroom. To those who complained about a "watered-down" course, he has retorted that the opposite, a "dried-up" course, is scarcely better.

The education of children with a low I.Q., or from homes where fewer of the cultural advantages are enjoyed, has sometimes been successful with a quite different approach. In fact, we seem to be in the middle of a pedagogical upheaval from which improved curriculums and teaching methods for all children can be expected. Among these will be an emphasis upon the structure or process of a school subject, an emphasis that can be expected to attract the interest of the student at the same time as he grasps important insights. With it, the student may be led to engage in learning for its own sake and not only as a troublesome step toward some distant educational or vocational goal. Linear programed learning has taught us the importance of the psychological development of the subject; and branched programed learning, that different children demand different sequences.[28] Growth of intrinsic interest may accompany the increase in skill and understanding, or a separate sequence to provide for it may be needed. Discovery by the student of at least a part of the structure of the subject, and practice by him with the process or mode of inquiry of it, is calculated to increase his natural propensity to be creative.

Problem solving by individuals and by groups of students seems to be the method par excellence by which the foregoing is to be best accomplished. The greatest hindrances to the general adoption of problem solving as a pedagogical method are the needs for, first, lists of problems

[28] A. A. Lumsdaine and Robert Glaser, *Teaching Machines and Programmed Learning: A Source Book* (Washington, D.C.: Department of Audio-Visual Instruction, National Education Association of the United States, 1960).

carefully graded as to difficulty of solution and degree of interest demanded, second, reading and reference material and equipment with which to solve the problems, third, schools to be specially arranged for problem-solving activities, and, finally, teachers who know how to use this demanding technique. The variety of instructional materials, as well as the variety of problem-solving demands that are introduced in a single classroom, can match the range of ability of the students. When problem solving and team teaching are combined, a far wider range of resources can be brought to bear upon a range of differences that is only slightly increased.[29]

Importance of Teachers. Despite the vigor of the present conflict over the curriculum, most of the conflicting groups and individuals seem willing to assign the central role in curriculum decision making to the teachers. Those who see education exclusively as a vast bureaucracy with the teachers operating within it solely as completely interchangeable functionaries might at first glance seem to assign negligible influence to the teachers. A second glance will reveal the importance that even this group attaches to teacher *training*.

Even those who at one time put their faith in written courses of study were careful to bring groups of teachers together to write these courses. What the leaders hoped was that other teachers would identify easily with the few who put their ideas on paper. What the leaders found was that teacher opinions concerning the best classroom behaviors did not converge.

Curriculum Development. After the failure of written courses of study to alter markedly classroom practices, cooperative curriculum development was attempted in a number of places. The Illinois Curriculum Program, the focus of the earliest and bitterest attacks by some of the most extreme intellectuals, was the prototype.[30] Individual teachers were asked to define their own problems, and, once a sufficient number had come forward, all the resources of a vast state system of education were marshaled for their support. The device caught on among curriculum workers, but the expected wave of improvement in classroom practices failed to materialize.

Teacher morale generally does not seem capable of supporting the uncertainty that accompanies the generation of completely new ideas. The proper balance between ritual and adventure must be achieved. It is

[29] J. Lloyd Trump and Dorsey Baynham, *Focus on Change: Guide to Better Schools* (Chicago: Rand McNally and Co., 1961).

[30] Charles W. Sanford, "The Story in Nineteen Schools," *Illinois Secondary School Curriculum Program Bulletin No. 10,* Circular Series A., No. 51, Office of the State Superintendent of Public Instruction, Springfield, Ill. (September, 1950).

of unusual interest and importance that curriculum workers have sometimes found teachers either running ahead of the developments of the last six or seven years or bypassing them completely. Several unexpected rapprochements have resulted with certain of the large foundations as well as with academicians.

To some extent, the success, or at least the acclaim, of nationally sponsored programs in science and mathematics derives from the money and prestige that have been lavished on them. But the fact that all include sharp, authoritative patterns must not be overlooked. Difficult though it may be, educators with more complicated views of the purposes of education in American democracy must strive to be equally definite. Actually such programs will be shaped by, and their effectiveness conditioned by the teachers who undertake to implement them.

Behavioral Science. In attempts to achieve such clarity, a number of professional educators have sought help from behavioral sciences other than their traditional source, psychology. The writings of anthropologists, political scientists, and social scientists generally—all have been combed for helpful insights and for unifying concepts. A number of social scientists have come forward on their own to help or to meddle, depending upon the view that is taken of the value of their assistance.

As a result, educational writing is bristling with references to partially digested concepts that may or may not prove helpful. One writer, for example, sees strength in the position of "realists" and refers to others as only "nominalists."[31] Here is an alleged break in the ranks of educators at the most fundamental level, without so much as a hint as to how a basis of communication is to be provided.

Attempts by curriculum workers to make use of concepts from the social sciences are a good deal like the attempts of teachers to make direct use of learning theory. Successful application, far more difficult and complicated than the application of the science of chemistry to the practice of medicine, calls for long and highly specialized research.

DETERMINING "POWER"

To summarize this chapter on the determinants of the curriculum, references will be made to the political concept of "power." Many educators find this expression distasteful, to say the least. To them, it raises thoughts of either elbowing or intrigue, both in contrast to the homely ideal most of them cherish that the good man in education as elsewhere

[31] Philip H. Phenix, "The Disciplines as Curriculum Content," *Curriculum Crossroads,* A. Harry Passow (ed.) (New York: Teachers College, Bureau of Publications, Columbia University, 1962).

needs only to be right. A more realistic view accepts the need for conflict, at least of opinion, in a vigorous society and agrees that to unite one's efforts with those of people with similar views is a moral as well as a sensible procedure. The concept of power, properly applied, can rescue the curriculum from the dangers of unrestrained anarchy, on the one hand, and unrelieved bureaucracy, on the other.

Teachers in isolation from each other are nearly helpless against the weight of tradition. Left to himself, as an individual, a teacher will probably choose a textbook according to its fame rather than its merits. In a period of rapid change, he would be forced to choose only among books that are out of date. Only when teachers organize can a few of their number be provided with the time needed to search for a book that is not only good but also reasonably new.

Theory, by its very nature, bristles with oddities that only practice can remove. Theory also contains the seed of improved practices. Educators at all levels could recover this seed more easily if their organization were improved. The individual practitioner is told something by an individual theorist (in a college or university classroom, by means of a book or article, or by direct consultation). Machinery by which the power of educational theorists generally can be used to censor the suggestion immediately is almost totally lacking—the idea may not even appear in the journals for a year. Although machinery may be available by which the body of teachers can consider this suggestion through conventions of teachers and meetings of teachers generally, either this machinery is tied up in other ways or there is reluctance to deal with the issue for some other reason. Although two teachers can sometimes be found who are willing to discuss frankly the secrets of the classroom, most teachers associate a degree of intimacy with classroom events that prevents them from doing so. A strong argument for team teaching is that the secrets are revealed.

Until recently, the various state organizations of teachers have been able to lobby successfully for or against the passage of bills concerning education. Now, as a result of the barrage of criticism, they find their old weapons of "Johnny" and "the flag" torn from their grasp and actually used against them. One educational writer has gone so far as to suggest that this loss of power was invited when teachers and administrators called upon citizens' committees to help them make curriculum decisions.

Curriculum workers realize the loss of power they sustained when successful new courses in mathematics and science were written by mathematicians and scientists almost without their help. They themselves ought to have seen the need for such courses long ago. The fact that no such courses have been produced by scholars in English and history leaves the path open for curriculum workers to recover some of this lost influence by describing general outlines for new courses in these two areas, for getting financial support from the federal government, and for paying teachers and scholars to help them produce and implement these plans.

The manner in which the various associations of schools and colleges throughout the country have proceeded with accreditation of high schools is a splendid example of the use of power in school politics. So long as one group, the universities, was so much more powerful than any other in the evaluation of a high school, just so long were the requirements of the general or vocational student slighted.

Students in high school display more political power than is sometimes admitted. Some of them derive this power from their parents. Perhaps it is inevitable that the child of a wealthy and powerful parent will be afforded more consideration in the school milieu than an equally deserving child of weaker parents. Other students derive power from a sheer weight of numbers, especially if the student organization in a school is fairly tightly knit. Faculties and administrators display varying degrees of talent for enlisting this power on the side of education, or for organizing opposing forces when such enlistment is not feasible.

At present, there are two major organizations of teachers in America, the American Federation of Teachers and the National Education Association. The former is closely allied with labor and seems to be committed to a conservative view of the curriculum. The other is a loose federation of state organizations most of which, if they consider the curriculum at all, seem to display a typically charismatic leadership that almost fails to affect classroom procedures except in formal and stylistic fashion.

According to Huebner,[32] a struggle for control of the curriculum of the American secondary school is probably necessary and is satisfactory where conflicting ideologies exist side by side, each with its contending elite. It is most appropriate that highly selected groups of teachers and curriculum workers remain in the struggle.

QUESTIONS, PROBLEMS AND ISSUES FOR FURTHER THOUGHT

1. Organizations such as banks, societies of veterans, women's groups, and service clubs exert influence upon the school curriculum. Choose one such organization, describe what it does concerning schools, and try to estimate its effect.
2. Try to formulate a research proposal that would study the total effect upon the schools of the National Defense Education Act.

[32] Dwayne Huebner, "Politics and the Curriculum," *Curriculum Crossroads,* A. Harry Passow (ed.) (New York: Teachers College, Bureau of Publications, Columbia University, 1962), pp. 87–95.

3. Bills in Congress to provide direct aid to the schools of the country have not been successful. What arguments can be made pro and con. Suggest reasons for the failure.
4. Choose one of the new courses in mathematics or science. Describe how it was written and who wrote it. What steps were taken to introduce it into the schools?
5. Choose a subject in which you are interested and compare the way it is taught now with the way it was taught fifty years ago. Include both method and content.
6. Bruner is unable to make clear any distinct "process" or "structure" that is peculiar to the social studies. Account for his lack of success.
7. Visit a local high school, and find out firsthand how the school is accredited and what the principal and faculty think of the procedure used.
8. Describe certain teaching skills that you possess and that are not possessed by everyone. What additional skills and abilities would you like to have?
9. Try to estimate the influence of a particular body of research on the curriculum of the high school.
10. What political activity are you prepared to engage in that can be expected to help the high school education in your community prove more effective?

SUPPLEMENTARY MATERIALS

SELECTED READINGS

BRESLOW, ALICE, et al. "Forces Influencing Curriculum," *Review of Educational Research*, XXX (June, 1960), 199–225. In this article, seven authors write fluently on the topic and provide 157 references. The final paragraph is a wistful apology for the chaos of the field.

BURTON, WILLIAM H. "Power Politics and the Teacher," *The Teacher's Role in American Society*. 14th yearbook, John Dewey Society. New York: Harper & Row, 1956. Chapter 16, pp. 216–31. There are two sections in this chapter. The first summarizes the forces acting upon teachers and curriculum. The second discusses the activities of teachers as "power politicians" in their own right. Teachers are said to seek benefits to education for the sake of the pupils.

CLARK, BURTON R. *Educating the Expert Society*. San Francisco: Chandler Publishing Co., 1962. Chapter 4, pp. 121–62. Although control of college curriculums is included in this chapter, there is much that is relevant to the secondary school. The clear distinction between centralized and decentralized control of education in a democratically organized country is especially interesting.

CONANT, JAMES B. *Slums and Suburbs*. New York: McGraw-Hill Book Co., Inc., 1962. All of the books by Conant have been influential. In this, the author delves more deeply than in the past and permits himself to use more emotional language. He speaks of the children of overambitious parents in suburban schools and those of apathetic parents in slum schools. He refers to slum adolescents as "social dynamite."

FRENCH, WILL, et al. *Behavioral Goals of General Education in High School*. New York: Russell Sage Foundation, 1957. Part I—"General Education in High School," pp. 21–46. Few will wish to quarrel with the outcome set forth in this chapter. The author seems to imply that the way to build a curriculum is to elucidate these goals in a detailed fashion and to build a curriculum calculated to achieve them. Those interested in this rational but complex procedure would do well to read the second and third parts of the book.

GREEN, EDWARD J. *The Learning Process and Programmed Instruction.* New York: Holt, Rinehart & Winston, Inc., 1962. Presents an analysis of the learning process as it relates to programed instruction and teaching machines.

GROSS, NEAL. *Who Runs Our Schools?* New York: John Wiley & Sons, Inc., 1958. Chapter 12, "What Can Be done?" Draws conclusions based on responses of Massachusetts superintendents and school-board members to a questionnaire. A number of forces acting on the curriculum are assessed.

LYDA, W. L. "A Suggested Conceptual System for Decision-making in Curriculum Development," *Educational Record,* XLI (January, 1960), 74–83. An involved system purporting to be an answer to Goodlad's plea. It is interesting, but it assumes goals of education that not all can be expected to accept.

"New Aids—New Opportunities," *Educational Leadership,* XX (April, 1963), 423–90. Treats many aspects of instructional technology by devoting the entire issue to this subject. Places emphasis upon the challenge new aids create for the curriculum worker.

"Programed Instruction," *Phi Delta Kappan,* XLIV (March, 1963), 241–304. Analyzes programed instruction from many points of view by focusing the entire publication on articles on programed instruction, some of which are written by practitioners, and others by theorists.

RUBIN, L. J. "Curricular Senility," *California Journal of Secondary Education,* XXXIV (November, 1959), 426–28. In this short article, the effect of tradition upon the curriculum of the high school is strikingly set forth. According to the author, the lag between what we do and the best we know is now twenty years instead of fifty years as formerly.

WILSON, ALAN B. "Residential Segregation of Social Classes and Aspirations of High School Boys," *American Sociological Review,* XXIV (December, 1959), 836–45. A number of schools in a large urban area were divided into three groups. The educational and vocational aspirations of boys attending these schools were compared among social classes within individual schools and among schools within social classes. Fewer sons of professionals attending working-class schools desired a college education than sons of professionals attending middle-class schools.

AUDIO-VISUAL MATERIALS

Films

Learning and Behavior. Carousel Films, Inc., New York. 26 minutes. Sound. Black and white. Drs. B. F. Skinner and R. J. Herrnstein show the relationship of reinforcement to learning and how this is implemented by the teaching machine in the learning process.

Teaching Machines and Programed Learning. Division of Audio-Visual Instructional Service of the National Educational Association of the United States. Washington, D.C. 26 minutes. Sound. Black and white. Takes up both linear and branch programed materials and their use with teaching machines. Questions pertaining to teaching machines and programed learning

are discussed by Dr. Skinner, of Harvard University; Dr. Lumsdaine, of
the University of California; and Dr. Glaser, of the University of Pittsburg.

The Second Classroom. Division of Audio-Visual Instructional Service of the
National Educational Association of the United States. Washington, D.C.
25 minutes. Sound. Black and white. Shows the proper use of instructional
television as a teaching tool, with illustrations in music, language, and
science classes.

Unique Contribution. Encyclopedia Britannica Films, Inc., Wilmette, Ill. 36
minutes. Sound. Color. Presents ways in which motion pictures can make
a unique contribution to effective classroom instruction.

Filmstrips

Effectiveness of Audio-Visual Materials. Basic Skill Films, Pasadena, Calif. 45
frames. Color. Presents information on the tested effectiveness of all types
of audio-visual materials, answering the questions: Why are these materials
effective? How well do they teach facts, develop motor skills, and change
attitudes? What factors are important in increasing their effectiveness?

Instructional Materials. Bel-Mort Films, Portland, Ore. Depicts the proper
utilization of the textbook, blackboard, models, graphs, opaque projector,
filmstrips, recordings, radio, motion pictures, television, and teaching machines in modern classroom instruction.

Teaching by Television. Basic Skill Films, Pasadena, Calif. 51 frames. Color.
Summarizes the research on what is known about teaching by television,
in relation to what television teaching can do, how to use television in the
classroom, and how to teach over television.

Teaching Machines. Basic Skill Films, Pasadena, Calif. 62 frames. Color.
Describes what teaching machines are, the types of teaching machines,
what a teaching machine "program" is like, and the educational role of
teaching machines.

Recent Developments and Current Trends[1]

8

As was described in the previous chapter, changes have appeared in the political, social, economic, and industrial conditions in our society owing primarily to the Industrial Revolution and scientific research. At the same time, high school enrolments have increased from year to year, and approximately 10 million pupils of varying abilities and interests presently are attending public secondary schools for one or more years. Both changes in society and increased enrolments have necessitated modifications in the program of studies of the secondary school.

Enrolments have increased greatly in recent years owing to the population explosion during and immediately following World War II. The public high schools, with the assistance of the federal government, through NDEA funds, have attempted to meet this challenge with curricular changes together with increased and improved guidance services. At the present time, nevertheless, approximately 1 million pupils drop out of high school each year, because they cannot adjust to developments in the academic fields and in the extraclass program of activities. Failure to adjust also appears to be related to the interests, abilities, economic status, and family background of pupils. As a result, development of an educational program for youth has continued to challenge educators to reconsider curriculum theories and practices and to reorient housing, equipment, facilities, and services, as well as methods of instruction and classroom materials and resources, to the needs of all pupils.

[1] This overview of the more recent developments and current trends in curriculum will be followed in subsequent chapters by more detailed descriptions and discussions.

For example, the sequence of secondary education has been extended from four to eight years and the scope of the program of studies has been modified from time to time to meet the needs and interests of superior, average, and below-average pupils in the junior high school, senior high school, and junior college. At the present time, there is great interest in new developments in the curriculum of the secondary school. This is due to a number of factors:

1. An extension of academic, general, and vocational education to realize the American way of life through meeting the needs and interests of all pupils has taken place.

2. In recent years, curricular offerings have been changed for superior pupils, to permit such pupils to prepare for advanced-placement examinations in institutions of higher education.

3. The failure to provide experiences in depth, particularly in mathematics and science, was criticized by professional and lay members of society after the first Russian satellite and during the ensuing race for space control and superiority in the military use of nuclear energy. The implication that a gap existed between scientific achievement in Russia and the United States, owing to different goals in curriculum planning, was of great concern to the American people.

4. There have developed organized groups that support either a program of *basic education*[2] or a plan for life-adjustment education.[3] Wide publicity has been given to these points of view through the publication of books, magazine articles, newspaper editorials, and brochures, as well as presentations on radio and television. Educators generally support the position that excellent high schools can be maintained for the gifted, the average, and the low achievers, if sufficient funds are made available for a comprehensive program. Recent reports from England indicate that the English people also support this position and that funds have been allocated for the development of the comprehensive secondary school in that country.

The continuing controversy in this country has developed considerable heat and it is apparent that many of the statements made concerning American, European, or Russian education should be accepted only as additional information becomes available relative to present programs and proposed changes in secondary education. Supporters of the Amer-

[2] See James D. Koerner (ed.), *The Case for Basic Education* (Boston: Little Brown & Co., 1957). Chapter 5, by Clifton Fadiman, presents the position of this group.

[3] See publications of the American Youth Commission of the American Council on Education. Also see Florence B. Stutemyer *et al.*, *Developing a Curriculum for Modern Living* (New York: Teachers College, Bureau of Publications, Columbia University), Chapters 5, 6, and 7.

ican secondary school have recognized the validity of some of the critical statements, and changes have been made in the curriculum. Usually, they have emphasized, however, that the consolidation of school districts, providing more funds for high schools, will implement the expansion of the program and provide enriched offerings in depth and advanced-placement programs for secondary pupils.

BASIC CONSIDERATIONS IN PLANNING THE HIGH SCHOOL PROGRAM OF STUDIES

The following changes have appeared recently in the program of studies and have influenced the educational opportunities provided for adolescents:

1. Addition of new subject-matter fields and new courses of study in traditional fields, and acceptance of academic credit for curricularized extracurricular activities.
2. Fusing of courses of study in a subject-matter field, as well as the relating of subject-matter fields such as language arts and social studies.

The addition of subject-matter fields has been considered constantly by educators, but the fusing of courses of study and the relating of subject-matter fields constitute recent developments at the secondary school level. At the present time, however, both of these developments are in evidence to some extent in representative high schools and are affecting curriculum improvment programs throughout the United States.

Educators generally subscribe to the thesis that pupils who participate effectively in the learning experiences and activities of the high school will appreciate our heritage and the basic values in our way of life and will be challenged to continue as participating citizens after being graduated. Consequently, they have studied relationships inherent in subject-matter fields and courses of study, as a means of enriching the experiences of pupils. Often, learning experiences in one subject-matter field may be theoretical unless they become functional in the lives of pupils through related experiences in another field.

The contributions of certain subject-matter fields should be studied in relationship in order to approximate normal life activities. For example, science and mathematics do not represent specialized interests for all pupils or adults, but limited learning experiences in these areas are significant for everyone, since they are related to living in general and often are basic to effective participation in the activities of the average citizen. Many experiences in social living would be unproductive in developing understanding and desirable attitudes if certain scientific facts and basic scientific procedures were not interrelated with the developments in the various subjects included in the social studies field. It is important for educators to realize that the knowledge of science, as well as its application to living in society, has greatly increased in every century since 1550. Furthermore, they should be challenged by the fact that 90 per cent of all trained scientists in the history of the world are experimenting in the field of science at this time.

An Integrative Curriculum. As school people have attempted to gear education to contemporary life, many relationships between subject-matter fields have been indicated at once. If any of the current activities of people in conservation, education, communication, transportation, production, consumption, health, or safety are considered, it is apparent that a compartmentalized approach in curriculum planning will not suffice as a vehicle for inducting young people into an understanding and appreciation of the scientific, economic, social, and political world in which they are living. Too often, the emphasis in curriculum improvement in high school centers on modifying a particular subject-matter field such as English and little or no consideration is given to relating experiences in that one field to other subjects so that (1) the evolving new course of study will provide integrating experiences from current social, economic, scientific, and political problems and (2) the broader implications of citizenship in a democracy can be inculcated into pupil-teacher relationships and become effective in helping pupils to study their needs, improve their academic work, and reorient their activities and interests.

A pupil's activities, unless they are purposeful, continuous, and related to patterns of conduct, have little effect on his judgment, growth in understanding, and ability to postulate ongoing, significant goals or to select ways and means of realizing these goals. It appears that there is a definite relationship between the foresight of the teacher and the insight of the pupil. Thus, the development of a philosophy of education and the formulation of educational goals based on consideration of subject matter, pupils, and society often result in an interrelated approach to the organization of learning experiences, teaching procedures, and guidance programs. The diversity of plans initiated in various schools, however, indicates that experiments are in progress and that evaluative studies are being made of the results.

Emphasis on the Needs and Interests of Pupils. The emphasis on the growth and development of youths, and their interests and needs, has been exerting great influence in placing the adjustment of pupils at the center of the curriculum-improvement program. The integration of pupils is realized, in part, through the relating of courses of study, which reinforces learning experiences, because both the objectives and the suggested learning experiences have much in common. In the past, studies of the needs and interests of pupils and analyses of the contributions of subject matter to their integration as members of society have been considered incidentally, if at all, in the development of learning experiences in the classroom.

Emphasis on the Social Adjustment of Pupils. The social adjustment of pupils to all aspects of their environment also has been stressed in recent years. A democratic society is not static, with its goals predetermined, but is an evolving experience for all of its members. Effective citizenship requires training in essential techniques, in the development of realistic attitudes, and in the ability to make intelligent interpretations of facts and information concerning the place of governmental agencies and other groups in the economic, political, and social spheres of life. It is a function of the high schools to provide general and specific training so that the pupils will be able to participate intelligently in adult society with appreciation and understanding of its evolutionary nature in a democracy.

Educators interested in this area have been concerned that the schools lagged behind social, economic, and political developments and that the materials and procedures utilized in developing significant learning experiences of pupils in high schools were not related specifically to observable and changing conditions in society. Others felt that the program of the schools not only should be related to current social changes but also should indicate goals and procedures in developing a better society.

While many educators, interested in the social adjustment of pupils, do not advocate this telic function of the secondary schools, there is general agreement that learning experiences should be related closely to life activities and that the transition from school activities to life activities should not be abrupt or present problems of adjustment to the individual. If the high school is sensitive to the progressive development of the basic social functions of living, it will be possible for the pupil leaving the school to adjust to current social patterns and to participate effectively in the further evolution of society.

Emphasis on the Personality Development of Pupils. The interrelationship of curricular experiences and group guidance experiences in the classroom is of paramount importance in developing the personalities of the pupils. In the first place, pupils need to achieve and to have their success or improvement noted by their peers; second, pupils need assistance in adjusting to all phases of their environment, including school activities, and developing integrated personalities. In order for pupils to have a sense of accomplishment and to experience a feeling of encouragement arising out of doing an assignment successfully, it is necessary for teachers to organize learning experiences for individual pupils rather than attempt to fit all pupils with a course of study.

A pupil inherits a personality, but he may modify his personality through learning to live with himself and to cooperate effectively with other people. A person who learns to adjust to his environment becomes more and more a socialized individual and able to avoid unsatisfactory social situations and human relationships. A classroom situation that stimulates both individual initiative and cooperative group or committee work can be instrumental in developing status for the pupil in the group, in promoting a feeling of security in a social situation because there is friendliness and warmth in the personal relationships, and in showing appreciation of the achievements of students who have improved their powers to discern, to evaluate, and to discriminate in learning situations. In selecting promising and rewarding practices and procedures, in working and planning with others, a pupil is becoming more integrated and is developing a more pleasing personality.

School-Community Cooperation in the Improvement of the Community and of the Educational Program. People in the community who support the schools, the children who constitute the clientele of the schools, and professional teachers and administrators are more than ever uniting their efforts in programs of community betterment and curriculum improvement. Their efforts are evidenced in many ways and are effective in promoting plans for improving all phases of community life—recreation, libraries, water supply, sewage disposal, park, playing fields—and in understanding new developments in education in the fields of curriculum, guidance, and special services.

As leaders in the community become conscious of the needs in many areas of living in the immediate neighborhood, they comprehend the necessity for teachers and parents to be associated in studying educational problems, gathering data bearing on the solution of these problems, and evaluating tentative innovations that have been made as a result of cooperative research. In the field of education, community study committees suggest the following initiatory plans and procedures:

1. A citizens' council should be organized to represent the community in planning with the educational leaders. This body would be non-legal and would not include any of the members of the board of education. All educational problems of vital interest to educators and of concern to members of the community would usually be referred to this planning council for study and recommendation. Studies at the community level often include the educational needs of the school district, based on data concerning annual increases in school enrolment, taxation, occupations of people in and out of the community, industrial development, and the

characteristics of nearby urban and rural areas as presenting opportunities for consolidation of school districts.

2. Cooperative studies by school and community committees should consider the effectiveness of the school curriculum in realizing educational objectives acceptable to educators and citizens. The holding power of the high school should be determined, and valuable data concerning the curriculum should appear in reports from dropouts and graduates. Through cooperative effort and study, the curriculum improvement program usually becomes a matter of general interest, receiving wide publicity, and the community as a whole would be educated by understanding and informed members of the community—not by teachers and administrators. Nevertheless, educators have a truly significant responsibility of providing data to the community concerning the development of a program for improving the learning experiences of the pupils.

RECENT DEVELOPMENTS IN SUBJECT-MATTER FIELDS

Beginning with the junior high school and extending through the senior high school, an increasing emphasis is being placed upon appropriate up-to-date subject matter. It is being stressed particularly in the senior high school because of tradition, the influence of college entrance requirements, and the demands by both lay people and educators that superior pupils be given opportunities for advanced study and that the learning experiences of all pupils be related to their vocational and professional ambitions.

The comprehensive high school provides a program of studies to meet the needs of all pupils. It is probable that superior pupils in high school who are preparing for definite life goals have their most integrating experiences in working intensively in one or more highly organized subject-matter fields such as mathematics, science, art, music, history, or literature. The average and the below average have needs and interests that cannot be served except through a reorganization of curriculum materials to provide learning experiences at their level of achievement.

Extracurricular activities have been developed extensively in secondary schools in order to relate the activities of pupils with real-life situations often denied them in the academic curriculum. Recently, a number of the extraclass activities, especially music, speech, dramatics, and journalism, have been curricularized and these new courses have been added to existing subject-matter fields or developed as new fields. Learning experiences primarily developed through journalistic, dramatic, and speech and debate activities are now included in the English department as courses of study in journalism, drama, and speech and debate or as functional aspects of a language-arts curriculum. The impact of the extraclass experiences of pupils on the administration of the school has been evidenced also in the provision of student participation in government through regularly scheduled activities in classrooms, homerooms, and activity periods, culminating in the presentation of plans and suggestions to the student council.

Dr. Conant supported this concept of the comprehensive high school in the following statement:

No one who realized the wide range of academic ability among the pupils in the type of high school I was talking about will advocate making the study of trigonometry or physics or foreign languages a requirement for all. *There must be elective courses in the senior comprehensive high school which will occupy about half the pupil's time.* And since we are living in a free country, the decision regarding what subject high-school children study is, in the last analysis, a decision of the child and parent. But good guidance and good counselors can influence this decision, and should. In the satisfactory schools I have visited there was almost invariably a good guidance program. . . .

It seems presumptuous in a free society for anyone to say what a boy or girl ought to study (unless it be the parent); yet this philosophy of individual freedom could well be tempered by two considerations; the welfare of the individual, and the welfare of the nation. Clearly, a balance is required. The first constraint upon the complete education development of the future citizen of our free society, certain studies must be pursued by all for a period of years. Beyond that, the rest of the program of studies should be, if possible, related to the pupil's ambitions beyond high school. He or she should have a vocational goal in mind. And for certain pupils this goal should be a professional one, requiring as the next step a college education, and here both individual and national interest come into consideration.[4]

Scientific developments in the United States and Russia have stimulated great interest in subject matter, and educators have responded by organizing advanced courses for brilliant and talented youngsters. As a result, improvements have been noted in the subject-matter fields of mathematics, science, the social studies, and foreign languages, as well as in the development of guidance programs. The most significant of these include (1) the complete reorganization of a subject-matter field such as mathematics, (2) the enrichment of present courses of study in language arts and social studies, (3) the reorganization of a subject-matter field such as science to offer greater depth for honors pupils, (4) the addition of subject-matter courses previously reserved for the college level, in order to qualify pupils for advanced-placement examinations, and (5) the improvement of guidance and counseling services for all pupils as an inherent phase of curriculum improvement. Parents and pupils have indorsed the new programs to such an extent that institu-

[4] James Bryant Conant, speech, "The American High School Today: A First Report to Interested Citizens" (Seattle, Wash., 1959).

tions of higher education are being challenged to provide classrooms and staff to accommodate those accepted for work upon entrance.

Recent innovations in the curriculum of the secondary school have been due, in large measure, to factors on the international, national, state, and local levels. These have been mentioned throughout the text, and it is appropriate here merely to summarize some of these.

Interest in Educational Systems of Foreign Countries. People in the United States have been impressed with the claims made of the ability of curriculums of foreign secondary schools, particularly Russian schools, to meet the needs of superior pupils and to prepare them for advanced work in college in the fields of science and mathematics. As a result, educators in this country have been considering changes in curriculum and in methods of presenting subject matter to our superior and talented young people.

The National Defense Education Act of 1958. Public Law 85-864 contained two titles that have been of great importance in promoting developments in curriculum improvement: Title III provided financial assistance for strengthening science, mathematics, and modern-foreign-language instruction. Funds have been allocated to local school districts, through the state departments of education, to provide half of the cost of additional equipment including audio-visual materials and equipment, printed materials other than textbooks, and remodeling of laboratory or other space used for materials or equipment. Title V-A provided financial assistance, on the same basis as Title III, to local school districts for approved projects in guidance counseling and testing and in identification and encouragement of able students.

Institutes have been developed in institutions of higher education for periods of approximately six months, for the purpose of providing further intensified training of counselors. Loans and fellowships have been provided for in order that outstanding young teachers might develop their mental resources and technical skills.

Contributions of Foundations, Commissions, Associations, National Councils, and Other Groups in Subject-Matter Fields. Studies by professional groups in each of the subject-matter fields have indicated the need for a restatement of goals, a reorganization of teaching materials, and a revision of methods of instruction. As a result of suggestions and recommendations, significant changes are being made as rapidly as (1) new textbooks and experimental teaching materials can be developed, evaluated, and published and (2) teachers can be trained to use the modern materials and new methods of instruction in working with pupils.

The upsurge of interest in curriculum improvement for the American high school has been reflected in the attitude of large foundations. For example, (1) the Carnegie Corporation has sponsored studies by Dr. James Conant (formerly President of Harvard University) of the senior high school, the junior high school, and the teacher-training program in this country, and, in addition, the same corporation has made a grant of $2.5 million to the Modern Foreign Language Association for the development of a modern-foreign-language curriculum; (2) the Ford Foundation has financed several experimental programs in American education such as (a) the provision of airplane-borne transmitters to cover schools in six states with educational television and (b) the establishment of a Learning Resources Institute to tape educational television programs and to prepare accompanying text and resource materials; and (3) the Rockefeller Fund provided a grant for the panel that developed a significant statement on the "Pursuit of Excellence."

The recommendations for curriculum improvement in the following subject-matter fields[5] have been challenging to educators because of the emphasis on significant changes in instructional materials and methods of instruction:

Mathematics. Studies have been developed by the Commission on Mathematics, College Entrance Examinations Board; the School Mathematics Study Group Project; The National Council of Teachers of Mathematics, Secondary School Curricular Project; the "Madison Project," at Syracuse University; The University of Illinois Committee on School Mathematics Project; the University of Maryland Mathematics Project; and the National Science Foundation. A publication by the National Council of Teachers of Mathematics entitled *The Revolution in Mathematics* presents a clear statement of the reasons behind the changes in the field, a brief description of the nature of these changes, and a discussion of how to realize these changes in classrooms.

The training or retraining of mathematics teachers is basic to the development of the new program. These objectives in teacher training are being realized through institutes on college campuses during summer sessions, in-service teacher training programs in public school systems, and in-service programs on college campuses arranged for teachers in one or more school systems. In some instances, funds are available to pay fellowships to teachers as well as the expenses of teachers and their families while in attendance.

Science. The National Science Foundation is concerned primarily with the improvement of the quality of science and mathematics education and encourages research in educational materials and methods of instruction in these fields. The objectives of the program are to improve mathematics and science teaching through presenting to teachers complete and

---

[5] See Chapters 16–25 for detailed discussions of each of the subject fields.

up-to-date knowledge of new developments in curriculum, as well as training in new methods of instruction in chemistry, earth sciences, mathematics, physics, or some combination of these subjects. The Physical Science Study Committee has developed a new program in physics, while the School Mathematics Study Group has planned and developed an experimental program for senior and junior high school mathematics.

Significant changes are being stressed, such as (1) problem solving by pupils, with emphasis on understanding and application of principles, (2) pupil experimentation rather than the "laboratory cookbook" program, (3) introduction of new units of work in radiation biology and nuclear energy, and (4) homogeneous grouping of pupils in science courses. Instructional programs for teachers generally have been conducted on the campuses of colleges and universities, and, except in the summer fellowship program, the candidates have been selected by the institutions of higher education themselves. These are full-time programs extending over the school year, and teachers can apply the credits earned toward an advanced degree.

Economic Education. The National Task Force on Economic Education issued a report entitled *Economic Education in the Schools,* which defined goals and stressed the need to replace unreasoned and emotional judgments by objective, rational analysis. The National Materials Evaluation Committee issued a report on *Study Materials for Economic Education.* A special committee is now preparing tests, following recommendations of the Task Force, and these will measure basic economic understanding for effective citizenship. Efforts have been made by state and local groups to upgrade teacher training in this area by (1) emphasizing economic education as important in the social studies field and (2) developing summer workshops, in-service courses in public schools, and state and regional conferences.

Modern Foreign Languages. Many high schools are increasing their offerings in modern foreign languages by expanding the number of languages offered and adding one or two years of advanced courses in each language. The Modern Foreign Language Association has received grants enabling the Association to initiate studies in such areas as that of the audio-lingual approach through the use of electronic equipment in the language laboratory.

Social Studies. The important developments in this field have focused the attention of teachers on world geography, crucial problems in the modern era, and the Eastern Hemisphere. As a result, the significance of the geography, civilization, cultural patterns, and political theories of the countries of the Far East, the Middle East, the Near East, and Africa are being included in the sequence of social studies in both junior and senior high school. Crucial problems facing the United States, as our country attempts to provide world leadership in a nuclear age, also are being emphasized particularly in the tenth, eleventh and twelfth grades.

Language Arts. The National Conference on Research in English and the Research Committee of the National Council of Teachers of English have indicated areas of research in this field. The more important include vocabulary, linguistics, reading and corrective reading, writing, grammar and usage, spelling, speaking and speech correction, listening, and semantics. Conferences, institutes, and workshops have been developed (1) to acquaint teachers with progress in language study and (2) to qualify them to participate in the further developments in the scope and sequence of language arts and with modifications in teaching materials and methods of instruction.

The above examples are typical of the efforts being made in various subject-matter fields to provide high school staffs with new curriculum materials, as well as suggestions regarding classroom methodology. If space had permitted, worthwhile study and research, as well as stimulating recommendations, by national associations in the fields of art, music, industrial arts, home economics, physical education, and health could have been included in this summary of recent developments in subject-matter fields.

ADJUSTING PUPILS TO NEW DEVELOPMENTS IN SUBJECT-MATTER FIELDS

Identifying, and Providing for, Exceptional Pupils. Reorganization of subject-matter fields has been stimulated, in part, by a desire to provide a rich and challenging educational program for the superior and talented pupils. Approximately 10 to 15 per cent of present enrolments in secondary schools are in these categories, and gifted and superior pupils are being identified on the basis of the following characteristics:

1. Reading rate and comprehension
2. Vocabulary
3. Originality and creative ability
4. Perseverance in attaining objectives
5. Physical and mental maturity
6. Acceptance of opportunities to engage in research-type activities and in independent study
7. Profit from learning experiences in advanced educational programs and from opportunities to demonstrate leadership qualities in extraclass activities such as participation in school government and in club programs in speech interest areas, both academic and non-academic, and in fields such as music and art requiring special talents

Teacher evaluation of talented pupils in class and in extracurricular activities is important, but there is always the danger of misjudging the actions or appearance of pupils and making incorrect decisions. While observation is highly regarded in interpretation, superior pupils often are difficult to recognize because of (1) differences in skill subjects such as reading, (2) emotional and personal problems that are frustrating them in their home and school life, (3) lazy, inattentive habits resulting from being bored by the level of school work assigned, and (4) lack of cultural advantages that is embarrassing to them and blocks their communication and participation. For these reasons, it is imperative that teacher observation be supplemented by (1) studies of intelligence through group tests and individual tests, (2) analysis of accomplishment in academic subjects and of talents in fields such as music and art, (3) analysis of home conditions and the reports of parents, (4) studies of cumulative records, and (5) use of sociometric procedures.

Advanced Placement of High School Pupils. In the past, superior pupils have been offered the opportunity to register in extra subjects and, thus, to complete high school in less time (acceleration) or to enrol in classes providing for learning experiences in depth (enrichment) and maintain a regular schedule. Both of these plans have been successful, in part, but have not provided the answer for a curriculum for talented young people. In 1953, The School and College Study of Advanced Placement was instituted and centered its attention upon both acceleration and enrichment for the superior high school pupil. Thus, the brilliant pupil may qualify for courses offered at the college level or may take examinations on graduation that are supervised by the Educational Testing Service and be admitted to advanced placement and, indeed, in an increasing number of cases receive college credit, in one or more academic areas.

High schools large enough to include faculties competent to develop and offer courses at the college level and to prepare and offer materials and resources essential in such courses have accepted the challenge to program and schedule advanced-placement classes, and curriculum planning in this area has been developing rapidly in recent years. In many high schools, college-level classes are being provided in science, mathematics, English, foreign languages, and specific areas of the social studies. In science, for example, the superior pupil in a four-year high school enrols in biology as a freshman, in chemistry as a sophomore, in physics as a junior, and in college-level courses in biology, chemistry, and physics in his senior year.

Colleges and universities generally have increased entrance requirements for high school graduates, but they have introduced greater flexibility at the same time in order that superior pupils may qualify for advanced placement or college credit. Institutions of higher education are also cooperating with high school staffs in curriculum planning for the college-level courses, and many have appointed directors of the Advanced Placement Program who work directly with high schools. It is their function to relate the efforts of the high school staff and the faculty of the department, school, or college in planning college-level courses for the high school.

Many school systems not affiliated with the Advanced Placement Program have organized honors courses or advanced-placement courses in mathematics, language arts, and other academic fields. Pupils enrolled in these courses may apply to take the advanced-placement examinations of the College Entrance Examination Board and present the results to the higher institutions of their choice. Also, it is possible for pupils with ability to take advanced-placement examinations even though they have not been registered in any organized placement program.

Better Provision for Average and Basic Pupils. Any program for identifying superior pupils will also classify other pupils as average or below average. It is imperative in planning curriculum-improvement programs in the comprehensive high school that all pupils receive consideration and that nothing be done in planning or scheduling that will impare the status of the less able. Flexibility should be maintained so that pupils can be transferred from one level to another in particular fields as interests and attitudes are more adequately assessed. In identifying superior pupils and developing advanced academic curricular programs as well as problem-solving approaches to teaching, high school staffs also have found rewarding experiences in determining appropriate content and methodology for those with limited abilities.

Providing for Ability Levels. Ability grouping is provided in larger schools through the organization of programs for academic and non-academic high schools so that only academic subjects will be offered in some while others will emphasize a core of general education and training courses leading to technical and trade careers. Generally, however, ability groups are established to provide for individual differences in the same building and to meet the needs and interests of pupils scheduled in so-called homogeneous classes. The superior pupils are not grouped in all classes and activities and do associate with other pupils in extracurricular activities and in some of the academic subjects and special fields. It is important to offer a program suited to the needs of each level, but one which does not lessen the opportunities for any one group and does not sacrifice any of the values associated with the American way of life.

Planning Curriculum Materials for Potential Dropouts. The pupils who will drop out of high school constitute a major concern for educators. As a result, programs are being developed across the nation to study the characteristics of dropouts and the ways and means of increasing the holding power of the high schools through improvement of the guidance services and the curricular offerings. The results to date appear to indicate the following facts:

1. Potential dropouts cannot be identified as a type or as a group. In general, however, the dropout will be retarded two years in reading, will have failed in three times as many courses as those who stay in high school and graduate, and will have been retarded in one or more grades during his school experience.

2. Intellectually, the average dropout appears to have the ability to do work at the high school level. Studies have indicated that 70 per cent of those in commerce and industry have I.Q.'s above 90 and that 13 per cent have scores above 110.

3. The market for unskilled labor is declining, and the dropout faces a situation in which jobs are hard to secure, employment is irregular, and opportunities to advance are limited.

4. High school staffs are endeavoring to improve both curricular offerings and guidance services. Teachers, counselors, pupils, and members of communities are being placed on committees (1) to study the curricular needs of pupils, (2) to investigate home conditions as well as the environment of the pupil outside of the school, and (3) to serve community cooperation both in placing dropouts in jobs and in following their progress.

Planning Curriculum Materials for Underachievers and Low Achievers. Low achievers may be classified as (1) unwilling learners who have ability but do not attain results, because of lack of interest or failure to respond to a challenge, or (2) pupils of low ability who cannot make satisfactory progress in an academic program. Prior to attempting to motivate academic interest and achievement, it is important to determine if the unwilling learner has any academic weaknesses, for instance, in reading rate; emotional instability; or simply a poor attitude toward school. The basic or below-average pupils will be citizens tomorrow and will help determine policies affecting our way of life, even though they do not possess the potential to complete academic courses.

To serve these youth, a "core," or "basic," curriculum consisting of learning experiences and activities in social studies and language arts, supplemented by activities in music, art, industrial arts, and home economics, has been developed in some high schools. Parents and pupils have indicated great interest in such basic programs because opportunities are presented to achieve in a regularly organized program and the pupils have status in the high school. Results to date appear to indicate that an increasing number of youth of very limited capacity for learning at school are being retained in high school with their classmates and are being recognized at the commencement with the graduating class. There is a growing feeling, however, that some of the low achievers who cannot or will not learn should be permitted to drop out, keeping contact with the school through its counseling or extension services, while the local community shoulders more responsibility for its youth.

CURRENT TRENDS IN RELATIVE COURSES OF STUDY IN A SUBJECT-MATTER FIELD

Fusion of Courses of Study in Subject-Matter Fields. Fusion was developed to counteract the tendency to increase high school offerings as a panacea for meeting the challenge of increasing enrolments. Generally, it is employed in fields such as English, social studies, science, and mathematics. For example, the field of English usually includes courses in composition, literature, journalism, public speaking, creative writing, dramatics, and oral expression, in addtiion to special courses such as remedial reading. The fused course of study in language arts offers opportunities to read, write, speak, listen, and dramatize, while honors courses offer opportunities to those with unusual talents and abilities to engage in research and patricipate in activities for advanced placement in institutions of higher education. Fusion of courses of study in a subject-matter field enables pupils to participate in the learning experiences of the field as a whole rather than in those assigned to a particular course. Thus the fused, or unified, course of study in a subject-matter field emphasizes subject-matter goals that will meet the needs of pupils and motivate their interests because of the wide range of activities.

The Broad-Fields Curriculum. The broad-fields curriculum is an excellent illustration of the principle of fusion. First, the high school program of studies is reorganized so that all academic subjects are included in a limited number of required subject-matter fields such as social studies, science, language arts, physical education and health, and guidance. These constitute the scope of the program of studies, and the course of study for each field includes essential learning experiences for the grades in the secondary school, together with suggested materials, resources, and teaching procedures.

RECENT TRENDS IN RELATING SUBJECT-MATTER FIELDS

The establishment of relationships between subject-matter fields is referred to as *correlation* and normally follows the fusing of learning experiences in each of the fields. If two fields such as social studies and language arts have not been fused, attempts at correlating learning experiences often are limited to relating two courses of study such as American literature and history of the United States. Correlation of courses of study in two subject-matter departments may involve only two teachers in the initial stages, but this limited experiment ultimately may challenge other teachers to participate in correlation programs or in team teaching. The following examples of correlation of subject-matter fields will serve to focus attention on some of the current procedures in secondary schools.

Back-to-Back Correlation. An English teacher and a social studies teacher may arrange to have a class scheduled for two successive periods and assigned to them in order to relate their class activities and learning experiences in American history and American literature. The class may meet with the English teacher for an hour and with the social studies teacher for the following period, or with both teachers for a combined period of two hours. The extended class period provides adequate time for visitations or excursions, for study, and for development of investigations and research activities by individuals or groups.

The Common Problem. Two or more subject-matter fields may be correlated through the utilization of the common-problem approach. An example of this procedure can be found in the science and social studies courses of study, since many of the major problems in society have both scientific and social implications. The faculties of the two departments may study and analyze these problems so that they may be presented concurrently or sequentially in realizing objectives of each department and in making the problem more meaningful to the pupils. In many instances, it will be found desirable, in furthering the psychological integration of pupils, to present the work relating to the course problem either prior to or following the presentation of the problem in the other class. The purposes of concurrent or sequential presentations are to motivate the interest of the pupils and to enrich their learning experiences in both classrooms.

Basic Social Functions and Crucial Problems in American Life. When subject-matter fields have been fused and experimental studies are being initiated by a school staff to relate learning experiences of pupils in two broad fields such as language arts and social studies, it is necessary to consider either basic social functions or crucial problems as guidelines in developing significant relationships. As pupils study the social functions in the American way of life, they will utilize all aspects of the social studies—geography, history, economics, sociology, anthropology, and political science—and all phases of language arts including reading, outlining, developing reports, and making critical appraisals of their ability to do research and to plan and organize reports of their work.

Numerous statements of social functions have been developed for the guidance of secondary teachers in determining the curriculum. The following usually are included:

1. Conservation and wise use of our natural resources
2. Production and distribution of goods and services
3. Communication and transportation
4. Recreational activities
5. Expression of aesthetic interests
6. Organization and government in the American way of life
7. Performing as citizens in a republic
8. Understanding our educational system

The crucial-problem approach in determining guidelines utilizes the problem areas in American life rather than social functions. The following usually are included: race relations, integration of schools, big business, labor and management, education, conservation of natural and human resources, urbanization, federal support of education, federal or public power development, etc. In comprehensive secondary schools, curriculum improvement is concerned not only with developing learning experiences in each crucial problem area but also with analyzing each problem area so that significant materials and procedures can be organized for below-average, average, and superior groups of pupils.

Effective use of social functions or crucial problems in developing learning experiences depends upon the cooperative efforts of the staff. For this reason, a number of schools are including a free period for the teachers participating in the program so that they can meet daily (1) to discuss the scope and sequence of the learning experiences, (2) to organize projects for the immediate future, (3) to analyze the interests and needs of their pupils, (4) to determine effective classroom procedures, and (5) to analyze carefully techniques of evaluation. If language arts and social studies are being correlated, and music and art are being related to the correlated program to a limited extent, the teachers of language arts and social studies should have a free period and a conference room where they can meet daily to exchange experiences and consider new materials, resources, and teaching procedures. Also, the teachers of music and art should be scheduled so that they may have an occasional free period at this time in order to confer concerning the over-all correlation of the four fields. It is important for all of these teachers to confer with the pupils in their classes, parents, administrators, and counselors in order that the learning experiences proposed may be considered in relation to the abilities, interests, needs, and special adjustment problems of individual pupils.

RELATING HIGH SCHOOL COURSES OF STUDY AND WORK EXPERIENCE

Work experiences are being provided in more communities, but the high school usually is responsible for the supervision, coordination, and evaluation of the programs. Teachers and counselors are closely associated with the pupils in planning their course work in high school in relationship to their work experiences on the job. It is important to schedule all required courses at times convenient for the work-experience pupils.

In Russia, work experiences are being required of brilliant students as well as those who do not complete the secondary school curriculum. As a result, Russian school systems have been extended from ten-year schools to eleven-year schools. At present, educators in the United States are inclined to organize work-experience programs for pupils with good records in commercial work and distributive education as a significant aspect of their preparation for employment in offices or industrial plants or as salesmen of goods and services. On the other hand, educators and teachers are concerned to a great extent with keeping pupils in high school who otherwise might drop out and seek full-time employment in the community.

In some respects, work-experience activities compare with early experiences in the extracurricular field in that they are being developed without adequate supervision and are not being related to an academic program. Generally, pupils are working in diversified occupations, and it is difficult to relate their activities to either vocational or educational training in the high school. It is evident also that training in communication, citizenship, health, worthy home membership, and recreational activities are significant responsibilities of the high school for all pupils.

At present, many high schools are engaged in research studies in this area to determine if boys can be held in high school through more carefully prepared curriculum materials in the school, greater emphasis on good work habits and attitudes in all phases of the program, and better scheduling and planning of school and work experiences.

The objectives of a high school directed program of work experiences are generally recognized as

1. To retain pupils in high school
2. To supervise and improve employment conditions for all pupils who are working part time
3. To relate learning experiences in the school with learning experiences on the job
4. To assist pupils in becoming efficient in making applications for jobs and in making satisfactory adjustments on the job
5. To provide opportunities in the school program for pupils to make personal and social adjustments

In general, high schools have distinguished between various types of work experiences that have developed in recent years:

1. Exploratory experiences in which pupils observe, and participate in, a number of situations in order that they determine if they have any interest in any of them or if they are attracted by the activities engaged in by the workers
2. In a more advanced program, work experiences on real jobs, to enable pupils to develop proficiency and become adjusted to working conditions
3. Vocational experiences, related to the courses they are taking in high school, provided for pupils through part-time employment in the community

In programs of work experiences, pupils usually are granted credits by the school and are paid by their employer. Teachers, pupils, and members of the communities participating in the program are in general agreement that it provides excellent training for those who participate and establishes a pattern of good school-community relationships.

RELATING CURRICULAR ACTIVITIES AND GROUP-GUIDANCE ACTIVITIES

Guidance activities may be divided into group guidance by the teacher in the classroom and counseling by specially trained staff members that is usually developed as an interview or conference with an individual pupil. Attempts were made in the past to organize group guidance through homeroom programs, but this separation of academic work and group guidance generally was unsuccessful, and the homeroom has generally become a brief period for reading announcements and checking attendance.

The development of correlated academic fields and core curriculums has necessitated an extended period of two or three periods for general education. In many instances, group guidance has been included in the block of time and the teacher has assumed responsibility for teaching language arts and social studies and for relating group-guidance activities to the academic work.

The key person in developing related curricular and group-guidance experiences is the teacher, since subject-matter competence is essential in two major academic fields, an understanding of adolescents, as well as a personal interest in each of the pupils, is very important, a familiarity with basic guidance techniques such as interviews and case studies is imperative, and the ability to develop problem-solving situations in the classroom, where pupils plan and work as groups and as individuals, affords many opportunities to observe pupils as they develop in personal responsibilities and in social activities.

In organizing resource units for classes in an extended block of time, it is necessary to develop a scope and sequence for guidance activities as well as for the academic activities. For example, teachers and pupils should be concerned with such group-guidance activities in the seventh grade of the junior high school as orientation to the school, planning of an academic program for the junior high school, and planning of participation in the extracurricular program. These group-guidance activities, and many more, can be effectively related to their planning of problem-solving activities in the academic fields.

PROBABLE DEVELOPMENTS IN THE FUTURE

Significant changes in organization and presentation of instructional materials are evident in various high schools. Some are truly experimental in character, and evaluations have been difficult because of differences in the attitudes and competences of teachers, inadequate facilities, lack of space, and failure to provide flexibility in the scheduling of classes. As a result, the research to date has not indicated that the goals proposed for these new approaches have been achieved. Nevertheless, attention should be directed briefly to some of the new developments in curriculum and method.

Team Teaching. Planning of instruction by a team of two or more teachers involves both curriculum reorganization and revisions in methodology. In its simplest form, two teachers in social studies and language arts may relate their efforts in teaching, for example, the history of the United States and American literature to the same pupils in sequential periods. They may meet the class separately, or they may cooperate in relating their subject-matter fields in a two-hour period. In more advanced plans, pupils are being organized in large groups for general presentation or in small groups for discussions and for planning investigations in problem areas and are being encouraged to work individually on studies and research of interest to them in laboratories, libraries, study carrels, or study halls. In general, about 40 per cent of the pupil's time is spent in large groups (100 to 150) where teachers lecture and present demonstrations through slides, filmstrips, films, television, recordings and overhead projectors; 20 per cent of the school day is devoted to small groups of 15 pupils where a teacher or an assistant becomes really acquainted with pupils through observing and studying them as they engage in discussions centering on the lectures and demonstrations in the large-group meetings; and 40 per cent of the time is devoted to individual study and research, if the pupil is capable of doing independent work.

Recently, team teaching has been developed in many secondary schools as a result of the efforts of the Commission on Staff Utilization of the National Association of Secondary School Principals. Professor Lloyd Trump, Associate Secretary of the National Association, developed a basic plan for team teaching that was adopted by the Commission on Staff Utilization and publicized extensively in national meetings and in the official publications. Since 1958, the *Bulletin* of the Association has devoted one issue each year to experimentation in team teaching, in order to improve teaching and learning at the secondary level.

While lack of large classrooms has handicapped the development of team teaching, such limitations can be overcome through remodeling old buildings and providing for flexibility in new schools. It has been evident, also, that adequate time and space must be provided for professional meetings of the staff members in order to plan the program effectively. If the large- and small-group meetings with pupils achieve these goals, the classwork must be carefully programed in advance by the teaching team.

Teaching Machines and Programed Materials. It is becoming quite evident that programed-material use in a teaching machine will not be employed as many teachers and administrators were lead at first to think that they would be, namely, as a course in the curriculum. They will be employed instead as an adjunct to regular instruction, because they are susceptible to very serious limitations including the following:

1. By their nature, they tend to emphasize the learning of facts and skills or, perhaps, to put it this way, to underemphasize and neglect the development of interests, attitudes, social and discussion skills, and spiritual values.

2. There must be some substitute for (1) professional contact and inspiration of the teacher and (2) the contact with, and learning from, participation with, cooperation with, and competition with one's fellow students.

3. In a situation where each student goes on at his own pace, within a brief period of time the youngsters are scattered throughout the course, some of them completing it before Christmas and others perhaps completing only two-thirds or three-fourths of it at the close of school, around June 1.

4. The most valuable teaching machines are very expensive to supply individually for students, and those less expensive are less valuable and useful and permit "fudging" by youngsters.

5. They do not provide adequately for the bright child who needs not so much to do faster the programed work developed for average youngsters as he needs learning activities and learning materials that are appropriate for his unusual ability and that will develop his unusual talents.

6. The same sort of reasoning leads one to the conclusion that unless appropriately supplemented, they are not well adapted for the slow youngster, the emotionally disturbed youngster, the potential dropout, and the youngster from an underprivileged home or area.

7. The program materials for the teaching machines and for use without them must be greatly improved before they will be on a par with the textbooks already available. The textbooks have been in the process of improvement for over a century, are far superior to textbooks of a few decades ago, and, of course, are generally recognized as being very much superior to those employed in many other countries. Programed materials have as yet a long way to go to be as well organized and developed as teaching materials and teaching aids as textbooks are today for use with the average youngster.

In view of the foregoing, the use of teaching machines and programed materials will need to undergo changes and improvements and teachers will need to discover what is the best use that may be made of them.

1. It seems clear that programed materials should be broken up into units, that, at the conclusion of a unit of two or three weeks of work, the bright student should be given extra materials of a type appropriate to his abilities, capacities, potentialities, and probable future needs, and that the slow youngster should be given special help and assistance and permission to omit certain of the more difficult but non-sequential materials in that unit.

2. The teaching machine will be most useful in situations where individuals enter upon a unit of learning at various times throughout the year. This type of situation exists in industry and in the armed forces, and the future of teaching machines in these situations is indeed attractive.

3. The teaching machine may be employed to advantage in homes, and, indeed, there is already a big scale of them for that purpose. It is probable, however, that they will be employed by parents in ways that are not conducive to the best development of the child either in the subject matter or emotionally in his attitude toward his parents. The parents will need much instruction along these lines, particularly of a kind that will lead them not to drive the youngster too hard and develop negativistic emotional reactions that will tend to diminish communication between the parents and the child. •

4. There is without question a place for teaching machines and programed materials in reviews. This will have to be worked, however, somewhat carefully. Apparently it was not contemplated in the beginning that this would be a major use of teaching machines.

It is apparent that there must be supplementary teaching by the classroom teacher for the purposes mentioned above, particularly for work on individual projects and work as members of a group either on projects or in discussion.

It is doubtful if good teaching will result from the use of programed materials if the teacher has never organized a planned sequence of learning experiences and does not understand the process involved in using programs and machines. It is basic in utilizing any new developments in curriculum that teachers have experience in organizing new materials and resources and are being upgraded continually through in-service teacher-training programs.

At present, careful preparation and editing are lacking in some of the available programed materials. Since the effectiveness of teaching machines in presently programed materials is dependent upon editing, educators generally are awaiting further developments in this field.

It is probable that the most successful use of programed materials has been in the audio-lingual approach in modern-foreign-language laboratories utilizing electronic devices. This calls for increased emphasis on speaking the language and listening to correct pronunciation of the spoken word. In mathematics and science, carefully organized materials have been prepared for presentation to classes through the use of programed materials and machines, as well as by means of ordinary or closed-circuit television.

Programed instructional materials are being used by about 4,000 schools this year, according to a report of the Center for Programed Instruction, prepared for the U.S. Office of Education.[6] This estimate is based on a 20 per cent return of questionnaires sent to 15,000 school superintendents.

[6] From "Programed Instruction in Use in 4000 Schools," *Nation's Schools* (February, 1963) p. 106.

Twelve per cent of the schools use devices with the programs. The eighty-three-page report will be available soon from the U.S. Government Printing Office.

Television. In recent years, television programs from national networks, regionally organized networks for schools, and locally operated stations have become a part of the curriculum for all high schools except those that are very small or do not have a local signal. It is possible to tape programs and present them at convenient periods for various classes. An example of improving instruction through open- or closed-circuit television can be observed in modern-foreign-language classes where outstanding instructors prepare lectures and discussions and present them to classes in various schools, using the audio-lingual approach.

Developments in the use of television are concerned primarily with (1) the closed circuit and (2) the two-way closed circuit, for the improvement of classroom instruction. In the closed-circuit program, two or more classes can remain in their own rooms and be taught by one instructor using an overhead camera and controls, together with a number of television sets and resources in each of the classrooms. Lessons must be carefully programed and presented by an outstanding teacher. The instructor cannot see all of the pupils, but communication between the instructor and the various classes can be maintained by telephone. The two-way closed circuit provides an opportunity for the teacher to observe the pupils in all of the classrooms and to communicate directly with them during the lecture and demonstrations.

There appear to be developments in this area that will affect curriculum programs in secondary schools dramatically in the near future. For example, large rooms, in which 100 to 150 puipls can be assembled in team-teaching situations, will not be required in this flexible arrangement.

The Block of Time. The extended period is not new in secondary education, but, as it is used by more schools, especially junior high schools, significant changes are occurring in planning curricular and guidance experiences for pupils. Too often, the block of time has been a scheduling device and teachers have not been provided with resource units to help them relate subject-matter fields and group-guidance activities. Two recent developments should stimulate the professional preparation of teachers in both curricular and guidance activities for the block: (1) the reorganization of teacher-training programs to include professional preparation for block-of-time teaching, as well as the development of in-service teacher-training programs to provide training on the job, and (2) the recognition by administrators and supervisors that only adequately prepared teachers in social studies, language arts, and guidance should be assigned to these extended periods, unless experienced teachers and supervisors are available to assist and direct the efforts of inexperienced and untrained staff members.

Flexibility in Scheduling Classes. In order to accomplish many of the innovations discussed in this chapter, it will be helpful to modify the

TABLE 8–1

FUTURE BASIC SECONDARY SCHOOL PROGRAM

(For schools with periods of at least 55 minutes for grades 10, 11, and 12, and 50 minutes for grades 7, 8, and 9, and with term of at least 190 days.)

Required:[a]	7[b]	8	9	10	11	12
English[b]	5	5	5	4	4	4
Hist. & Soc. St.[c]	5	5	5	4	4	4
Math. & Science[d]	5	5	5	4	4	4
Phys. & Health Ed.[e]	4	4	4	4	4	4
Electives:						
Art[e]	4	4	4	4	4	4
Music[e]	4	4	4	4	4	4
Typing (Personal)[e]			4	4		4
Shop[e]	4	4	4	4	4	4
Home Econ.[e]	4	4	4	4	4	4
For. Lang. 1	4	4	4	4	4	4
For. Lang. 2				4	4	4
Voc. Courses: (2 units credit each year) Trades & Industries, Business Agriculture, Home Economics Diversified Occupations						
College Prep. Math.			4	4	4	4
College Prep. Sci. (incl. lab.)				5	5	5
Speech[e]				3	3	3
Dramatics[e]				3	3	3
Journalism[e]				3	3	3

[a] Required for graduation from senior high school: 13 units toward which 1 unit for algebra in the ninth grade and 2 units for three years of foreign language in the grades 7, 8, and 9 may be counted, thus permitting industrious bright students to graduate in five years from junior and senior high school.

[b] English courses should include English literature, American literature, language and grammar, speech, and written composition. In some grades at least, in most high schools, they will be combined with social studies in a core curriculum or other large block-of-time program.

[c] Would include, in the junior high school, one year of geography, one year of American history, and a year of civics and social problems; in the senior high school, a year of world history, one semester each of economics, American history since 1890, study of peoples of other countries, and comparative government.

[d] Mathematics and General Science may be omitted by those taking college-preparatory mathematics and science in any year in senior high school.

[e] One half unit of credit each year in senior high school toward graduation.

[f] In grades 7, 8, and 9, students should be in class at least 27 to 30 periods. Bright students only should be in class more than 30 periods. In grades 10, 11, and 12, students should be in class 22 to 25 periods. Bright students only should be in class more than 25 periods.

scheduling of certain classes. In some high schools, classes are continuing to meet five days each week, but the periods vary from day to day; while other classes are meeting five days each week but are scheduled for one period on certain days and for double periods on other days. Superior students often are scheduled for extended periods in libraries, laboratories, or offices for study and research. Increasingly, classes are scheduled for only four periods a week, usually periods of not less than 56 minutes net.

The advantages of flexible scheduling are obvious in science classes where the double period is used for laboratory work; in social studies and language arts where visual aids, outside speakers, literary work, excursions, class reports, or tests can be planned for the double period; in shop classes where pupils can work more effectively on projects. Investigations indicate that pupils profit from the flexible scheduling of classes because of the opportunity to do intensive work, while teachers benefit because of additional preparation periods. If present trends continue, the future basis of the secondary school program most commonly found most likely will closely resemble that shown in Table 8–1 (page 161).

QUESTIONS, PROBLEMS, AND ISSUES FOR FURTHER THOUGHT

1. Prepare a form that can be used effectively in making a community survey preparatory to initiating a curriculum-improvement program.
2. Can you justify including extracurricular activities and guidance in the curriculum?
3. Discuss the advantages and disadvantages of (1) adding subject-matter fields to the program of studies and (2) relating courses of study or subject-matter fields already included in the program of modern courses of study in secondary schools.
4. Select any curriculum-improvement program being developed on a national, state, or local level, and indicated (1) objectives, (2) procedures utilized, (3) tentative results, and (4) plans for evaluating the various phases of the experiment.
5. Define *integrative curriculum* as a factor in promoting the integration of the individual pupil.
6. Compare the scope of a curriculum-improvement program based on fusion of courses of study with that of one based on correlation of subject-matter fields. (Indicate both likenesses and differences.)
7. Define and discuss (1) *programed learning*, (2) *flexible scheduling*, (3) *machine teaching*, (4) *two-way closed-circuit television*, (5) *one-way closed-circuit television*.
8. Distinguish between *enrichment* and *acceleration* in curriculum planning.
9. Discuss cooperation planning by institutions of higher education and secondary schools in developing advanced-placement programs.
10. Define *action research*. Develop a design for an action-research project.

SUPPLEMENTARY MATERIALS

SELECTED READINGS

ALPREN, MORTON. "What Curriculum Developments Are Finding Their Way into Practice?" *Bulletin of the N.A.S.S.P.*, 272 (March, 1962), 13–17.

ANDERSON, VERNON E., and WILLIAM T. GRUHN. *Principles and Practices of Secondary Education* (2d ed.). New York: The Ronald Press Co., 1962. Chapter 3, "American Culture and the Secondary School."

ASSOCIATION FOR SUPERVISION AND CURRICULUM DEVELOPMENT. *Guidance in the Curriculum.* 1955 yearbook. Washington, D.C.: National Education Association of the United States. Chapter 1, on the relationship of guidance to instruction, and Chapter 11, emphasizing the integration of guidance with instruction, will be very helpful to the student.

———. *What Shall the High Schools Teach?* 1956 yearbook. Washington, D.C.: National Education Association of the United States. The following chapters are recommended: Chapter 4, on the selection and organization of curriculum content, and Chapter 5, on the foundations of general education in the high school.

———. *Balance in the Curriculum.* 1961 yearbook. Washington, D.C.: National Education Association of the United States. Four important areas of curriculum improvement are discussed: values in curriculum decision making, balance and the problem of purpose in education, balance in teaching methods and learning processes, and balance and the selection of content.

CRONBACH, LEE J. "Programmed Instruction," *N.E.A. Journal*, LI (December, 1962), 45–47. An excellent analysis of programed instruction at the present time.

DOUGLASS, HARL R. *Trends and Issues in Secondary Education.* Washington, D.C.: The Center for Applied Research in Education, 1962. Chapter 3, "Curriculum Offerings, Organization, and Administration." Students will find this concise book an excellent source for further details concerning content of subject-matter fields, team teaching, teaching machines, programed learning, and the adaptation of instruction to the individual.

GILCHRIST, ROBERT S. "Promising Practices in Education," *Phi Delta Kappan*, XLI (February, 1960), pp. 208–11; XLI (March, 1960), 269–74. These articles are based on studies and observations of promising practices such as individualization of instruction, homerooms for pupils, team teaching, electronic aids, and challenging programs in curriculum improvement in various subject-matter fields.

SCHRUBER, DANIEL. *School Dropouts. N.E.A. Journal*, LI (May, 1962), 51–59. An excellent presentation of the national problem, together with discussions of various state and local plans.

TRUMP, J. LLOYD. *A Better High School Program. N.E.A. Journal*, XLIX (April, 1950), 41–43. A brief statement of six methods to improve instruction, including team teaching, small groups, and independent study by pupils.

———, and DORSEY BAYNHAN. *Focus on Change: Guide to Better Schools.* Chicago: Rand McNally & Co., 1961. This volume was produced by the Commission on the Experimental Study of the Utilization of the Staff in the Secondary School, appointed by the National Association of Secondary

School Principals. While the entire volume is challenging to those interested in developments in curriculum, the following sections deserve special attention: "Small Classes," "Independent Study," "Large Classes," "Flexible Schedules," "Individual Differences in Pupils and Teachers," and "Team Teaching."

WILES, KIMBALL. *The Changing Curriculum of the American High School.* Englewood Cliffs, N.J.: Prentice-Hall, Inc., 1963. Students will profit from reading Chapter 11, on individual and group roles in curriculum change, and Chapter 4, which discusses organization for curriculum improvement.

WILLIAMS, PERCY V. *School Dropouts. N.E.A. Journal,* LII (February, 1963), 10–12. A concise report of the Maryland study on dropouts, conducted by the State Department of Education, the county systems of education, and the Baltimore City Department of Education. Every high school in the state participated in a study of 13,715 pupils who had withdrawn from secondary education.

AUDIO-VISUAL MATERIALS

Films

Broader Concepts of Curriculum. McGraw-Hill. 20 minutes. Sound.

Challenge of the Gifted. McGraw-Hill. 11 minutes. Sound. Color.

Focus on Change. National Education Association of the United States. 23 minutes. Color.

How Good Are Our Schools? (*Dr. Conant Reports*). National Education Association of the United States. 31 minutes.

Teaching Machines. Parts I and II. Washington University. 66 minutes.

9

Curriculum Goals for Social and Individual Growth

ESSENTIAL RELATIONSHIPS

Necessity for Objectives. Human beings, to the degree to which they are intelligent, have and keep in mind objectives to guide them in planning their activities. While much may be reduced to habit and retained in activities of our everyday life, and, indeed, to some extent in vocational pursuits, rational human beings engage daily in problem-solving activities oriented with respect to attainment of goals of which the individual is conscious. This is true of activities in all areas of life, including activities of skilled trades and semiskilled and unskilled labor in civilized society, but it is true to a much greater extent in professions. Indeed, to the extent that teachers, supervisors, and administrators have in mind worthwhile goals and develop a worthwhile system of values and keep these in mind as criteria by which they select, organize, and utilize educational materials and activities, they render a more valuable service. To do otherwise—and some teachers do otherwise very frequently, while almost all teachers and administrators do otherwise to some extent at least occasionally—suggests characteristics of a fanatic as defined by George Bernard Shaw: "one who having lost sight of his objectives redoubles his efforts."

As was pointed out in Chapter 2, it is the function of the curriculum of the schools to provide the means for students to have experiences that will influence their physical, social, and emotional growth in desirable ways and toward desirable ends. The curriculum is not an end in itself;

it is a means to an end. This applies to the extrasubject aspects of the curriculum as well as to the subjects.

The School an Agent of Society. Education, through its agent, the school, has been an instrument of every society not only for the purpose of preparing young people to take their places in that society but also for the purpose of informing, shaping, and directing their minds, emotions, and bodies in a way that will ensure that they will pass on the cultural heritage and the particular philosophy of that society. While this is obviously easy to note in the case of totalitarian societies such as Germany, Italy, and Japan in World War I and in World War II, it is also an obvious special function of education in China, Russia, Yugoslavia, the Communist satellites, and, indeed, every country in which totalitarian regimes exist, apparently since they can be maintained only by misinformation and indoctrination of the people.

Not quite so obvious, but nevertheless not difficult to see and to accept, is the fundamental principle that schools in a democracy have equal if not more important responsibilities of educating its general population for intelligent participation and cooperation in solving the problems of national society and of the preparation of leaders for the national and general welfare. This relationship and the fact that the principal function of a public school is to contribute to the general welfare are particularly true of any democracy, in which all the people are subject to taxes for the schools in proportion to wealth and income, whether or not they have children in public schools or in school at all, out of proportion to the degree to which they benefit directly from public schools.

Passing on the social and cultural heritage of any people, particularly in the United States, may not be done entirely by books, regardless of what certain well-known individuals have claimed as the great value of the Great Books. It includes passing on also the individual skills and habits of behavior—ideals, mores, and customs—that have been found useful and that contribute to the general welfare of the people. It also involves skills of interpersonal and group relationships that are important not only for the individuals concerned but also for the groups as a whole and for the nation. Because this is true, student participation in extrasubject activities largely managed by the students has excellent possibilities for contribution to education and to the nation—a contribution greater than many people realize and, indeed, potentially a much greater contribution than that realized in schools today.

The Individual and the School. Nothing in the reasoning in the foregoing paragraphs should be interpreted as meaning that the school does not have a great responsibility for bringing about education and growth of individuals for the benefit of the individuals themselves. Indeed, the welfare of a democratic society, particularly one depending as much as the United States today upon the contributions and cooperation of individuals, is achieved by preparing individuals in schools to make contributions that yield great values to the individual as well as to society. Vocational education, for example, while usually thought of as having the purpose of enabling the individual to earn a living, is a definite necessity for the welfare of the economic and, indeed, the political life of a nation. This involves workers of all sorts—agricultural, industrial, trade, professional, etc.

For example, it is becoming apparent today that we need many more well-trained doctors, teachers, engineers, and scientists, with better vocational training. It has also become apparent that the lack of appropriate vocational education on the part of several million would-be workers contributes to the millions of unemployed—and also to the greatly increasing number of people on relief, involving great expense to local, state, and federal governments for the maintenance of the needy.

General, or Common, Needs and Individual, or Special, Needs. Many educators have thought of education for vocational competence and education for leisure as specialized and individual needs only. Upon careful study of the matter it should become clear that there are general needs common to very large numbers of people in different vocations and engaging in different leisure pursuits, as well as individual or specialized needs. For example, in many occupations, if not the great majority of them, there is a common need for skills in reading, listening, thinking, and writing. Likewise, there is of necessity a common need for understanding of quantitative concepts and processes and for skill in arithmetical and algebraic computation and manipulation of fundamental geometrical concepts.

Similarly, development of common skills and interests in reading and development of skill and vigor in the uses of the major body muscles open the doors to satisfactory participation in a great many physical sports and, indirectly, to interest as a fan in a great many competitive sports. Still another example, applicable to vocational and leisure needs as well as common family and health needs, is the knowledge of many aspects of biological and physical sciences that have widespread applications to the large majority of human activities.

THE KINDS AND SOURCES OF CURRICULUM GOALS

Types of Approaches to the Determination of Goals. Educators for many generations have differed with respect to the type of approach to be employed to determine what should be the goals of education, particularly with respect to the secondary schools. In the lives of primitive people, even, apparently, in the lives of prehistoric peoples, as judged by artifacts that have been discovered, the goals centered largely around the fundamental function of the school to prepare young people to perform well the activities performed by their elders, including the arts of warfare, the killing of game, the preparation of food, the building of shelter, the construction of canoes, and the use of animals.

Primitive education involved passing on ideals and ways of thinking, especially those that contributed to the morale of the tribe or group of people, including of course those implied in the tales of great heroes in battle. It also taught arts of various types with respect to pottery, weaving, and decoration of the body, as well as passing on from the older men of the tribe, particularly those who had established themselves as medicine men or "philosophers," superstitions and explanations of the various natural phenomena of the weather, the stars, the sun, the moon, and the means of propitiating the powers that lay behind the natural phenomena relevant to success in war and in the production of food.

As civilization developed, there came to be a body of subject matter committed first to manuscripts and then to printing in which there was set down the knowledge of the race in various fields. These libraries were convenient vehicles for passing on to young people knowledge possessed by their elders and previous generations. It was perfectly natural that eventually schools would start with such a body of knowledge and plan a way of using it for the education of young people, particularly at the secondary school level, where only the select minority continued to study. Quite naturally, the relative emphasis upon ultimate goals was shifted from the preparation of young people for specific types of participation in adult life activities to the mastery of the subject matter.

Either consciously or unconsciously, the latter approach is still employed by a great many educators, partly as a matter of convenience and expedience and partly because of the feeling on the part of some leaders, and many in the rank and file of teachers, that they dare not trust themselves to think through what educational experiences and materials are most useful for preparation of young people for life. It was in order to bolster up the philosophy behind this type of approach that there were formulated conceptions of the phenomenon of the transfer of education acquired in one field to other fields, to justify teaching subject matter of little obvious utilitarian value that served to give status to those who became at least superficially familiar with it.[1]

Indeed, quite a large portion of the subject matter was originally placed in the curriculum because of very definite contributions to very practical ends of education and of society. But, as the conditions of life

[1] Pointed out by Harold R. Benjamin in his *Sabre Tooth Curriculum* (New York: McGraw-Hill Book Co., Inc., 1938).

changed and the needs for some of this subject matter diminished, appropriate pruning, re-adaptation, and replacement of certain bodies of the subject matter were never done. A good illustration of this is, of course, in the continuation of the requirement of Latin long after Latin was no longer used as the international language—the language of the church attended by the great majority of people, and the language in which all scholars wrote.

The Life-Activities Approach to Ultimate Goals of Education. It was only natural that rational human beings more and more questioned, and more critically, the place of materials in the curriculum, particularly since social change became accelerated and people no longer clung to cherished positions but were forced to adapt to changing conditions and ways of life. These people were largely those who thought of education as preparation for life and insisted upon adopting the educational materials and activities that would best prepare boys and girls for their life activities, responsibilities, needs, and desires, not only in their adolescent years but in their adulthood as well.

This approach involved, of course, analysis of the principal responsibilities, activities, and needs of people in life today and of what can be done in the public schools to stimulate, condition, and direct young people so that they will best fit into life situations and take advantage of them for their own benefit, for the welfare of society, and for the advancement of knowledge of civilization. In 1900, Herbert Spencer, an eminent English philosopher and educator, set forth in his *Education*[2] the classification of the activities of life that he insisted must be kept in the foreground of the consciousness of educators in planning, if the schools were to prepare the young people for "complete living" as he insisted that they should.

1. Of most importance are those activities that contribute to self-preservation. These include passing on of information and development of habits, skills, and understandings that would enable human beings to protect themselves from disease, accidents, and death.
2. Next most important are activities related to obtaining the necessaries of life, which contribute to self-preservation.
3. Next in importance are activities that have as their purpose the disciplining and education of offspring.
4. Activities involved in the maintenance of proper and effective social and political relations are next in order of importance.
5. Of least importance, but nevertheless important, are those activities that make up the leisure part of life and that are devoted to the gratifications of tastes and feelings.

[2] Herbert Spencer, *Education* (New York: Appleon-Century-Crofts, Inc., 1900).

One might infer from Spencer's treatment that the first four of his groups of activities were the essentials, but they were actually largely means to an end, the end being the satisfaction that one got in life. Spencer was very critical of the curriculums in the English secondary schools at that time, insisting, as they did, largely of ancient Latin and Greek, modern languages, mathematics, and English literature. In his book on education, one finds him saying the following:

If by some strange chance not a vestige of us descended to the remote future save a pile of our school books or some examination papers we may imagine how puzzled an antiquary of that period would be on finding in them no indication that the learners were ever likely to be parents. This must have been the curriculum for their celibates. I perceive here an elaborate preparation for many things especially for reading the books of extinct nations and of other co-existing nations (from which indeed it seems clear that the people had little worth reading in their own tongue); but I find no reference whatever to family life or the bringing up of children. They could not have been so absurd as to omit all training for this greatest of all responsibilities. Evidently then, this was the school course of one of the monastic orders.

In both England and the United States, what may be thought of as a "cart before the horse" approach to determining what should be the goals of education continued throughout the nineteenth century with slight modifications. Courses in bookkeeping, surveying, and navigation introduced for the boys, and courses in music, cooking, drawing-room manners, and etiquette, for girls, enjoyed very little respectability.

Instructors in these subjects were looked down upon by those who had learned enough of foreign languages, mathematics, ancient and medieval history, and what passed for science to be able to interpret the textbooks in those fields to the boys and girls in their classes and to insist that the students learn enough to be able to pass a written examination.

Psychological-Growth-Achievement Approach. Many educators concentrated upon certain types of changes which they felt should be brought about in the development of young people, changes that may not be the same as the subject-matter-mastery achievements, such as development of certain intellectual skills, understandings, ideals, aspirations, and moral values. While this no doubt constituted a valuable contribution to thinking about the goals and the curriculum and methods of education, it did not start from scratch. No great amount of time or effort was spent upon consideration of the analysis of activities of life for which young people should be prepared; rather, they set up, with considerable validity, their own versions of what types of growths should be developed. Among these might be mentioned as examples the development of skill in clear thinking, of habits of reflected judgment, of skill in reading, of skill in numerical computations, of respect for the rights of others, of interest in good music and in good literature and good art, of understanding of the theory of evolution, etc. There is much to be said for this approach to determining what should be the goals in education, yet it is evident that it is only part of a complete philosophy of what should be "learned."

The Effective Approach. More recently, an increasing number of leaders in thinking about secondary education, particularly in the United States, have pointed out the desirability of thinking first like Herbert Spencer of the areas of life and the types of responsibilities that would eventually devolve upon young people, including those in which they already were engaged, and then addressing oneself to the task of determining what types of educational growth would enable young people to be best prepared in those areas of life. In other words, they would break down such areas as citizenship into items of knowledge, concepts and understandings; social, physical, and intellectual skills; social, physical, and intellectual habits; interests; attitudes; ideals; and appreciations—which would be very desirable if not necessary to prepare well for citizenship. Indeed, this eclectic philosophy of the purposes of education has been growing steadily for a half-century and in great probability will be the approach employed by the great majority of people with adequate professional background.

THE CARDINAL PRINCIPLES OF SECONDARY EDUCATION

Prior to 1917, the documents of all the great national committees appointed to recommend ways to improve education contained recommendations in terms of what subject matter should be taught and, largely, what should be mastered and what should be learned from the study of the prevailing subject matter. Improvements were to be made largely within the broad framework of the existing curriculum. Indeed, Charles W. Eliot, when president of Harvard, insisted upon the retention of the prevailing academic curriculum with modifications and improvements and better methods of teaching, saying that a good preparation for college would constitute an excellent preparation for life. Among such committees were the following: The Committee of Ten on Secondary School Studies of the National Education Association, under Charles W. Eliot (1894); The Committee on the Economy of Time, appointed by the National Education Association (1895); The Committee of Fifteen (1895); The Committee on the Comprehensive High School (1905); The National Committee on Mathematical Requirements (1920–1923); The Classical Investigation (1921–1925); and The Committee on Modern Foreign Language Study (1924–1927).

In 1912, there was appointed a committee that was to exert great influence on thinking about the goals and other aspects of secondary education; this was called The Commission on the Reorganization of Secondary Schools. While the report of this committee, commonly known under the title Cardinal Principles of Secondary Education, and published in 1918 by the Bureau of Education in Washington, D.C., was a compromise and contained many conclusions that have since been modified or eliminated, this group of educators, for the first time in the history of American education, started with an analysis of the types of activities of life somewhat after Herbert Spencer's approach. The objectives set forth by this epoch-making commission have come to be very widely but erroneously known as "The Seven Cardinal Principles." The seven areas of life designated were as follows: (1) wealth, (2) command of the fundamental processes, (3) worthy home membership, (4) vocation, (5) civic education, (6) worthy use of leisure, and (7) ethical character. This statement of objectives has been modified and published by a number of authors; one version, which seems to be gaining the widest acceptance, and which was set forth by the author of this chapter in 1937 in a publication of the American Youth Commission, *Secondary Education in Modern America,* is as follows:

(1) Activities, responsibilities, and opportunities of citizenship in local, state, national, and international groups;
(2) Mental and physical health and sturdiness;
(3) Earning a living—vocational competence;
(4) Home living—involving marital relationships, consumer education, rearing of children, etc.;
(5) Leisure activities of a nature pleasant to the individual, in harmony with ethical standards, and conducive to the best interest of people in general.

An evaluation of this statement of goals is made up of not a single system of categories but a dual system. For example, some of the objectives have to do with the activities of life and some have to do with certain aspects of development of the individual. Mentioned among the former are homemaking, work, world citizenship, occupational information, and among the latter are such types of growth as involve health habits, reading the mother tongue efficiently and writing it effectively, habits of courtesy, and powers of judgment. It should also be noted that there is a great amount of overlapping between some of the major objectives. For example, the objectives of human relationships are valuable and important parts of objectives of civic responsibility and self-realization.

In attempting to make major contributions to many of these psychological developments and types of growth that contribute to effectiveness in various areas and responsibilities on life, the restricted subject fields taken separately are limited and handicapped. For that reason, there is much merit in plans that involve material for more than one field, such as the core plan, the fusion plan, the correlated plan, the unified study plan, and the common learnings approach. There have been those who have held that, for at least a part of the learning activities of students in school, the approach should be through the problems of life, particularly the problems that the young people feel that they need to deal with at the time, employing materials and activities from any field or fields that may contribute to the solution of the problem or developing the students' effectiveness in the particular area, which also involves units of the extrasubject activities.

It seems that, for some time in the future, the approach will involve a compromise. Existing in many and an increasing number of schools, particularly junior high schools, is the problem core approach involving some subjects and, in most schools, at least with most teachers, following the broad-fields approach, adapting materials, and using methods of learning and teaching that will emphasize the applications and the use of materials for the type of psychological development that will enable the students better to participate and profit from various types of life activities.

ULTIMATE LIFE OBJECTIVES AND NEEDED GROWTH OBJECTIVES—THE ECLECTIC APPROACH

Objectives Cut Across Subjects. In order to achieve ultimate life objectives—good citizenship or vocational competence, for example—a student must grow in a variety of ways involving principally the following types of growth acquisitions as a result of his experiences in contact with his environment:

1. Factual information, understandings, meanings, vocabulary, principles, and laws
2. Intellectual, physical, and social habits of behavior as associated with types of situations that he is likely to find himself facing many times
3. Intellectual, physical, and social skills that may be employed, for example, in home living, in maintaining mental and physical health, in vocational life, in citizenship, and in leisure activities
4. Interests in appropriate activities and important areas of life, of knowledge, and of leisure
5. Attitudes that make for character, worthy home living, vocational success, mental and physical health, and effective good citizenship
6. Ideals that provide inspiration for an individual to think and act in ways that will contribute to good citizenship, good health,

vocational success, effective home living, and socially accepted leisure pursuits

Many of these types of psychological outcomes, for example, skills, habits, and ideals, are not developed in one subject field alone but are outcomes from learning activities and materials in a number of subject fields, for example, the ideal of service, the attitude of open-mindedness, skill in problem solving, and the habit of courteous and thoughtful social behavior.

Because these things are so, the curriculum materials and learning activities must be selected and planned with a view to providing experiences that will result in students' acquisition, as far as possible, of psychological growth outcomes of the types mentioned above, which are necessary or at least desirable for effective participation in various areas of life activities.

Growth Goals for Citizenship Education. One may take, for example, the goal of becoming good and effective citizens in local, state, and national groups of human beings. Upon analysis, it will become clear that, among other things, being a good citizen involves the following:

1. The good citizen knows what is right and effective in his society. This knowledge consists of some habits and ideals that must have been learned during the period of childhood and youth, some that the citizen will acquire incidentally from living in his society, and some that he will no doubt have to acquire as the specific needs arise. These last are extremely important in a society such as ours, which is characterized by rapid changes.

The good citizen also possesses a working collection of useful concepts and basic general ideas that enables him to understand and evaluate human experience and proposed lines of social action. He knows, for example, what elements constitute democracy, communism, fascism, and socialism. He is not satisfied with cheap substitutes for sound concepts of democracy and is neither stampeded into high-sounding, fallacious doctrines nor deceived by the application of terms like *communism* or *facism* to practices that are really democratic in nature, or of the term *democracy* to communistic practices.

2. The good citizen is willing to behave in a way that is right and effective. This may be in part a matter of heredity, but it is probably in larger part a matter of learning. To ensure right and effective behavior, the individual must gain through educative experiences appropriate ideals and attitudes and must avoid developing ideals and attitudes likely to lead to unacceptable behavior, for example, ideals of excessive personal power or gain, of racial bias, or of national or racial supremacy over others; attitudes of ill will or contempt toward other groups or classes

of society; or attitudes of indifference to matters of honesty and to the welfare of others.

Being willing and able to behave in a right and effective manner also involves having interests that will lead one to read and investigate and to become informed about matters upon which intelligent decision must be made by the citizens of the society in which he lives, such as problems of labor and management, international relations, and various types of social welfare measures.

3. The good citizen has developed skills in getting on with others, in self-expression, in thinking clearly, and in evaluating what he reads or hears on questions of public policy, and he practices the use of these skills in all appropriate situations.

4. The good citizen possesses a wealth of appropriate habits, for right and effective behavior among adults is in large part a matter of habit rather than a matter of decision.

The foregoing brief analysis might well be expanded into a more detailed analysis that would occupy a sizable volume in itself. No teacher will be capable of bearing in mind all the possible skills, attitudes, information, etc., that we may call behavior components, even though he may be able to identify all of them. Nevertheless, he must become so oriented in such matters that, in daily service, he recalls the appropriate ones.

Growth Goals for Vocational Competence. Similarly, a great many items of knowledge; understandings; principles; intellectual, physical, and social skills; intellectual, physical, and social habits; interests; ideals; attitudes; and appreciations contribute to vocational competency. Hence, the curriculum materials and related activities must be selected, and the student must be brought into contact with them in a way that will be calculated to contribute to the development of the desirable psychological outcomes of these types.

It is important to realize and bear in mind that certain specific psychological outcomes or types of growth, such as a very specific type of skill, may be developed in a course in vocational education, for example, auto mechanics, salesmanship, or vocational cooking, and that, likewise, some skills, habits, attitudes, etc., that contribute materially to vocational success are those toward which contributions may be made in each of most of the subjects taught in secondary schools, as well as in extra-subject student activities. Indeed, the teacher of any subject in secondary school, in any grade, and the sponsor and coach of any non-subject student activity must realize this truth and look for, and capitalize upon, the opportunity for seeing that students have experiences that will contribute to growth toward these desirable specific outcomes, which contribute to vocational efficiency. A further discussion of different aspects of this will be found in Chapter 16 in this volume.

Growth Goals for Effective and Pleasant Home Living. Very much the same may be said with respect to the selection, arrangement, and utilization of materials and student activities for the purpose of making important contributions to the ultimate life goal of effective and satisfying family life. Some specific outcomes are best developed in courses in the field of household arts. These include, for example, knowledge about food and diet; skill in sewing; habits of neatness and cleanliness about the home; interest in family life and family activities; favorable attitudes toward one's companions in the home and toward children in general; interest in various aspects of home life, including, of course, home furnishings and home social activities; ideals of being an effective father, mother, son, daughter or other member of a family group; and appreciation of the importance of home life.

Nevertheless, there are many specific outcomes that add materially to effective and satisfying home life to which contributions can be made in almost any subject, for example, the attitude of thoughtfulness for others, ideals of fairness, skill in working and playing with other individuals, habits of courtesy and thoughtfulness, and information, understandings, and principles of health. Likewise, special outcomes may be developed that are more or less peculiar to certain subjects other than home economics and that contribute to effective and satisfying home living. These include, for example, skills in arithmetic; knowledge, understanding, and principles of physiology and sanitation; desirable attitudes toward one's competitors in sports and games; interests in good reading, good plays, and good television programs; and appreciations related to good taste in art and music.

Growth Goals for Effective Use of Leisure Time. To ensure that youths will spend a greatly increased amount of leisure time in activities that are satisfying and pleasant as well as acceptable to society and free from unfortunate social, moral, and physical side effects, much care needs to be taken in the selection, organization, and utilization of curriculum materials and learning activities so as to develop a number of growth outcomes of each of the major types—understandings; factual information; knowledge; principles; physical, intellectual, and social skills; intellectual, physical, and social habits; ideals; attitudes; appreciations; and tastes. While major contributions may be made to education for leisure, along various specific lines in connection with certain subject fields and in extrasubject student activities, for example, in classes in English, art, music, physical education, social studies, and science, nevertheless, there are valuable opportunities for development of specific items of growth as the outcome of contact with mathematics, foreign languages, business subjects, shop work, and other less closely associated subject fields.

In the selection, organization, and utilization of subject materials and learning activities in order to make material contributions to education for leisure, certain principles have come to be seen as sound and effective. Some of these call for changes in learning materials and learning activities from the practice in the past. Among these changes may be mentioned the following:

1. The development of taste and appreciation cannot be forced. Tastes and appreciation are long-term developments growing out of contacts and activities carried on under conditions of voluntary participation, without compulsion.

2. Materials must be adapted to the present status of tastes and interests and must not be presented prematurely. Much of the distaste for, and indifference to, the better things in English and American literature is directly attributable to the misguided enthusiasms of teachers who "pressed." "Pressing" in developing the tastes of people, young people especially, is as ineffective as "pressing" in golf, or "fighting one's cards" in bridge. One must let nature take its course under favorable conditions, realizing its course will leave much to be desired, at least for the present, in the cases of many pupils. Many persons have learned later in life to enjoy things they formerly despised when presented prematurely by teachers. The author of this discussion recalls clearly his negative reaction to Bryant's "Thanatopsis" when it was forced upon him by an "eager beaver" sixth-grade teacher who insisted upon memorization of the entire poem at a time when her students could understand but little of its real meaning. Later, with increased maturity and broader experience, the beauty of the inspiring thoughts became evident so that the poem became one of the writers' favorites:

3. Allowance and provision must be made for differences among individuals with respect to

   a. present status of taste or interest in any given field or activity
   b. rate of development of tastes and interests
   c. capacity for development of tastes and interests in each field

4. It is usually conductive to the development of tastes to provide for, and encourage subtly, but not too quickly, expression of reactions, either verbal or in some other form. It is natural for young people to want to "do something about" things that are beginning to interest them —to talk about them, to imitate others, to engage in appropriate physical activity, to play, to sing, and to dramatize, for example.

5. In directing the development of young people's tastes in music, literature, or art, it has proved wise not to overemphasize technical

analysis, particularly in the earlier stages. That must come gradually. At first, in literature, content is the thing; in music, it is pleasure in listening, playing, or singing, and not merely looking for technical merit.

Growth Goals for Physical and Mental Health and Safety. Much more attention has been given recently in educational thinking to improving the contributions of the schools to mental health, as well as to physical health and safety. Increased attention and improved thinking have been directed toward the matter of physical well-being. Not only have we been able to identify a much larger percentage of cases of people who are suffering from some type or types of mental or emotional disturbances and disorders, but there is very convincing evidence to justify the conclusion that, from whatever causes may have been operating, a much larger percentage of people are so affected. Indeed, more than half of the hospital beds in the United States are now occupied by people whose major illness is mental or emotional, in spite of the fact that an increasing proportion of patients of psychiatrists and hospitals for the mentally ill are dealing with their people on an outpatient basis, in the neighborhood or indeed in the home, at some distance in a great many cases. Here again, the selection, organization, and utilization of curriculum materials and learning activities should contribute to the development of appropriate growth outcomes of the types mentioned in the foregoing pages—information, skills, habits, ideals, etc.

Even more so than in education for most other areas of living, classroom practice has placed an exaggerated emphasis on, and attached a disproportionately large amount of importance to, the acquisition of information relative to mental and physical health. However valuable in itself, it is primarily a means to an end. Even more effective in contributing to the ensurance of physical and mental health and sturdiness are habits, skills, attitudes, ideals, and interests, as well as understanding of oneself.

Furthermore, school activities and goals must be of such a nature as to contribute to the development of favorable growth outcomes rather than to the development of unfavorable ones. It has become clear to most students of mental hygiene and psychiatry that, from the standpoint of mental hygiene and healthy emotional development, life in school and life at home as it relates to schools are, in a very large percentage of cases, at least somewhat unhealthy, often involving frustrating, depressing, and destructive experiences and relationships with teachers. This is particularly true with respect to domination by teachers and the failure to experience success in the attempt to do well in school subjects and in attaining standards set by teachers and parents. Also, even more unhealthy are the disappointments, frustrations, and failures in developing satisfying social relations with one's peers of both sexes.

In this area, perhaps even more than in the education for life areas and general growth goals, the teacher or other curriculum maker must be constantly concerned with opportunities to contribute to the development of healthy personality and emotional balances, as well as with carefully avoiding undue stresses and the extremely unhappy situations that contribute heavily to the deterioration of the personality and mental health. This especially important to those who have to do with determining the experiences of young poeple in connection with the extra-subject activities including guidance.

It should definitely be borne in mind by educators not only that boys and girls must learn how to live in the future in order to have healthy bodies and minds but also that they must actually live in the present according to the knowledge that is now available relative to the development and maintenance of good physical and mental health. It should go without saying that opportunities should be taken in all subjects to contribute to the development of information, fundamental concepts, ways of thinking, ideals, attitudes, habits, and interests that are favorable to developing and maintaining physical and mental health.

GENERAL EDUCATION FOR ALL STUDENTS

Programs of *general* education should result in individuals who

1. Are skilled in communicating with others, which implies an ability to obtain another person's ideas through reading, listening, and seeing, and to express one's own thoughts effectively through speaking and writing
2. Are in possession of useful work habits, study skills, methods of thinking, and mathematical tools
3. Have a guiding set of democratic values that are used in making choices and judgments involving both personal and social affairs.
4. Maintain good physical health through proper habits of rest, exercise, eating, and routine, and the wise use of medical and dental care
5. Maintain a balanced emotional adjustment, in both personal and social activities, on a basis of understanding of human behavior
6. Enjoy living and working cooperatively with others
7. Are skilled in leisure-time activities that are personally satisfying and socially desirable.
8. Are effective participants in a family group, understand the major problems of family living, and have the skills and attitudes likely to lead to future worthy home membership.

9. Actively and intelligently participate in the consideration and solution of local, state, national, and international problems involving the community health and social, economic, political, and personal welfare

10. Utilize the scientific method wherever it is applicable, understand the basic discoveries of science and their influence on thought and ways of living, understand the basic maladjustments resulting from the discrepancies between scientific progress and existing social arrangements, and recognize the dangers in the control of science by any special-interest group

11. Enjoy and appreciate beauty wherever it is found—be it in literature, music, art, or nature—and understand the arts as expressions of individuals and the culture

12. Have at least a minimum level of understanding and skill in the use of the principal materials, processes, and appliances that characterize modern life

13. Are well-oriented vocationally and are able to choose a satisfying and socially desirable occupation that will utilize fully their capabilities

14. Operate effectively as economic units, purchasing wisely and otherwise handling economic affairs appropriately and intelligently

QUESTIONS, PROBLEMS, AND ISSUES FOR FURTHER THOUGHT

1. Which do you think is more important in planning a curriculum—the welfare of the society that supports the schools or the welfare of the individual students who invest their time and efforts in education?

2. Do you think it is possible for the teacher or other curriculum maker to bear in mind the five great life areas of objectives for secondary education and at the same time think of possibilities for developing contributory growth outcomes such as information; understanding; knowledge; principles; social, physical, and intellectual skills; social, physical, and intellectual habits; attitudes; ideals; interests; and appreciation?

3. If you were to set up a list of the life areas of goals of secondary education, would you use Spencer's list, the list given in the "Cardinal Principles of Secondary Education," the list presented in this book, or some other list? How would you list the major areas of life activities for which young people must be prepared?

4. Examine carefully and evaluate the statement in this chapter of the "eclectic" approach to the goals of secondary education.

5. How different from the goals of public secondary schools would you say are the legitimate goals of (1) independent but non-religious schools and (2) parochial and other religious non-public schools?

6. If you were to make a list of twenty-five of the most important types of growth outcomes contributing to education for citizenship (for example, skill in propaganda analysis), into what category of growth outcomes—factual information; understanding, social, physical, and intellectual skills;

social, physical, and intellectual habits; interests; ideals; attitudes; or appreciations—would the largest number of your twenty-five outcomes fall?

7. Do the same for education earning a living, for education for leisure, for education for home living, and for education for mental and physical health.

8. Do you think that mastery of the fundamentals for continued learning is a life-area goal or an immediate-psychological-outcome goal or group of goals?

9. Do you think that preparation for college is a life-area goal, an immediate-psychological-outcome goal, or a group of goals?

10. Distinguish between the common needs and the individual needs for vocational competence, and between the common and individual needs in education for leisure.

11. Locate somewhere at least one printed statement of the goals of education, and evaluate it, pointing out specifically its major shortcomings, if you believe it has any.

12. Take one particular subject field, for example, mathematics or a business subject, and discuss briefly what opportunities you think it offers for contributing to education for each of the five life areas dealt with in this chapter.

SUPPLEMENTARY MATERIALS

SELECTED READINGS

HORTON, ROBERT C. "Ten Important Obligations of Youth," *Phi Delta Kappan*, XLI (December, 1959), 100–101.

LEE, GORDON C. *Education In Modern America*. New York: Holt, Rinehart & Winston, Inc., 1957. Part VII—Chapter 24, "The Scope of the Educational Task."

MILLS, HUBERT H., and HARL R. DOUGLASS. *Teaching in High School* (2d ed.). New York: The Ronald Press Co., 1957. Chapter 7, "Different Kinds of Growth."

RICHEY, R. W. *Planning for Teaching*. New York: McGraw-Hill Book Co., Inc., 1959. Chapter 5, "Broader Concepts of Education, subdivision 7, "Objectives of Education in American Democracy."

ROMINE, STEPHEN A. *Building the High School Curriculum*. Chapter 6, "The Nature of Learning as a Basis for Curriculum Building"; Chapter 7, "The Purposes of the Secondary School Curriculum."

AUDIO-VISUAL MATERIALS

Films

Importance of Goals. McGraw-Hill Text-Films. 19 minutes.
Social Acceptability. McGraw-Hill Text-Films. 20 minutes.

Filmstrip

Your Educational Philosophy—Does It Matter? Audio-Visual Materials Consultation Bureau. Wayne State University, Detroit. 40 frames. Black and white.

Recordings

Personality Development in the Classroom, #217. Louis P. Thorpe. Educational Growth Series. Educational Recording Services. Los Angeles. 36-44-minute discussion. 33⅓ rpm.

Some National and International Educational Problems, #238. Earl J. McGrath. Educational Growth Series. Educational Recording Services. Los Angeles. 36-44-minute discussion. 33⅓ rpm.

The Citizen Child: His Needs in a Free World, #234. Mrs. John E. Hayes. Education Growth Series. Educational Recording Services. Los Angeles. 36-44-minute discussion. 33⅓ rpm.

The High School Curriculum for Life Adjustment, #216. Harl R. Douglass. Educational Growth Series. Educational Recording Services. Los Angeles. 36-44-minute discussion. 33⅓ rpm.

10

Types and Sources of
Instructional Materials

Revolutionary changes have occurred in the field of instructional materials and technology during the past decade, and, according to all indications, we have only reached the threshold of the advancements that are to come in the years ahead. These changes have given the teacher new tools, new materials, and new responsibilities, and, in general, have contributed to the improvement of the secondary school curriculum. Educational television continues to improve and to expand; programed instructional materials and teaching machines are catching the fancy of psychologists and educators; the content of the new textbooks in certain subject fields has brought about the obsolescence of those published only a few years ago; and the language laboratory and instructional-materials center have become standard components of the modern secondary school plant. In fact, owing to the nature of the changes that have occurred and that are presently under way in the field of educational materials and equipment, this chapter could as well have been named "Instructional Technology and Materials."

Although space does not permit an analysis of the various factors that have contributed to the revolutionary advancements in instructional materials and technology, a few of them are worthy of mention here. Basic to all others perhaps have been the intensification of the cold war and the concern of the American public for the continuation of our leadership role among the nations of the world. This concern brought about the allocation of funds from the federal government for the improvement of education and gave impetus to the granting of greater

sums of money by large foundations for educational research. The availability of financial backing revived the interest of scholars of the various
disciplines, of experimental psychologists, and of professional educators
in seeking ways to improve education at all levels. Thus, we are witness-
ing drastic changes in instructional materials and equipment, many of
which offer great promise for the improvement of the secondary school
curriculum.

SELECTING INSTRUCTIONAL MATERIALS

A notable attribute of education in this country for many years has
been the availability of a vast quantity of instructional materials. This
fact is often little appreciated by the typical American teacher until he
has an opportunity to learn of the dearth of materials available to his
counterpart in other countries of the world. The resourceful teacher in
this country, even in a school having very limited financial support, can
obtain through the state educational agency, public libraries, and business
firms and organizations a multitude of excellent instructional materials
for an expenditure of only a small amount for postage. The crucial problem is that of making proper selections.

The problem of selecting curriculum materials grows more difficult
from year to year because of the increasing number of sources and types
that are available. A clear understanding of the role of instructional
materials in the teaching-learning situation will enable the educator to
make more discriminating selections. Basic to the process of selection is
the formulation of the teaching objectives. With the clarification of goals
appropriate for the course, stated in terms of behavioral outcomes, the
teacher has a guide to follow in selecting subject-matter content along
with the instructional materials and teaching methodology to employ in
the given situation. The instructional materials, together with the way
in which they are employed (the instructional activities), become the
vehicles through which the student assimilates the subject content in the
attainment of the educational objectives. The proper selection of the instructional materials is of fundamental importance to the effectiveness of
the teaching-learning situation. Improper or poorly chosen materials may
result in ineffective teaching and even failure on the part of the pupil,
whereas appropriate materials will bring about the successful attainment
of the desired outcomes in an efficient and expedient manner.

The selection of the various types of instructional materials and
resources involves the consideration of several different factors. The purposes the materials are to serve and the manner in which they are to be
employed have an important bearing on the process of selection. Selecting
a textbook that is to become the basic guide in a given course for a period

of five years, for example, calls for greater prudence than the selection
of a picture for a bulletin-board display. Nevertheless, certain guiding
principles, or criteria, are useful to the teacher in the selection and use
of all types of instructional materials. A list of criteria having general
applicability is as follows:

1. *The instructional materials should be appropriate for, and contribute
to, the attainment of the teaching objectives.* Instructional materials
should not be utilized because they are convenient or interesting or
because the teacher is not prepared and wants to occupy the time of the
students. Unless a teaching aid contributes to the attainment of the cog-
nitive, psychomotor, or affective goals of the course or of the core curriculum, as the case may be, they have no place in the instructional
program.

2. *The difficulty of the instructional materials should be commensurate
with the readiness level of the students for whom they are selected.* If the
instructional materials are beyond the comprehension of the student,
learning will be very inefficient, or, if the materials are beneath the student's educational level, boredom will result. This principle also implies
that there is a need for providing materials that are appropriate for the
varying degrees of readiness existing among the members of the class.

3. *An attempt should be made to select materials that will interest and
motivate the students.* Instructional materials vary greatly in the qualities
that attract the attention of the adolescent. The teacher needs to be
cognizant of these qualities and to utilize them when making a selection.
In general, the materials that most closely simulate actual experiences
are to be preferred.

4. *The instructional materials should be objective, accurate, and un-
biased.* Many of the materials readily available to teachers are poorly
prepared and edited. Research studies have produced evidence to show
that errors in textbooks and other types of printed materials are common.
Certain organizations and groups develop materials especially for use in
secondary schools. It is not uncommon to find such materials that present
only one side of a controversial issue and thus are not suited for classroom
use except when the analysis of propaganda devices is the objective.

5. *The time required for the proper utilization of a given teaching aid
should be reasonable in terms of the purposes it is to serve.* Time must be
spent wisely in the classroom. If the use of a filmstrip or a simple demonstration will accomplish a given purpose equally as well as the use of a
film, in considerably less time than the film, the latter should not be used.

6. *Careful planning in the use of all instructional materials is required
on the part of the teacher in order to ensure the attainment of the teaching
objectives.* The professional teacher studies the materials in advance,

decides how they can be utilized best in the instructional activities to contribute to the teaching objectives, and evaluates their effectiveness. Inadequate planning on the part of teachers in the use of instructional materials results in educational waste.

7. *The cost of a given teaching aid or type of instructional material should not place an unjustifiable burden on the materials budget.* This principle becomes increasingly important as more and more fancy and elaborate instructional materials and equipment, many of which have not been thoroughly tested, are placed on the market. Few schools are financially able to budget for all the instructional materials that teachers would like to have at their disposal. Careful planning of the expenditure of available funds is, therefore, necessary in order to obtain the most needed types of materials for bringing about the desired educational outcomes.

Many school systems have established policies for the selection and use of all types of instructional materials. A teacher in a school system having such policies must work within the existing framework. Most professional educators believe that the teacher should have complete freedom to select the materials he uses in teaching his classes, subject only to budgetary limitations. Teachers in systems that grant this privilege are obligated to use great care in the selection and use of all types of instructional materials and teaching aids.

Before the discussion of the various types and sources of instructional materials is presented, one other point concerning materials selection and use needs to be made. While instructional materials play a major role in successful teaching, effectiveness cannot be assured through materials alone. The research evidence shows that differences in teachers are more significant than differences in materials, when pupil learning is used as the evaluating criterion. A teacher may have a wealth of excellent instructional materials at his disposal and yet be very ineffective in his teaching. Successful teaching requires careful selection of instructional materials in both kind and number, together with skilful use of those selected.

PRINTED MATERIALS

Although much attention is being devoted to all types of teaching materials and devices, many of which were unheard of a decade ago, printed materials are still the most basic vehicle of educational communication. Printed materials take on many forms, ranging in length from pamphlets of a few pages to multivolume encyclopedia sets containing thousands of pages. The quality of printed materials is no less variable than their scope. In the interest of space, this discussion of printed materials has been limited to the following six major classifications: (1) instructional guides, (2) textbooks, (3) workbooks, (4) supplementary reference materials, (5) paperback books, and (6) current reading materials.

Instructional Guides. In order to clarify the scope of the curriculum and to ensure some semblance of continuity from one grade level to the next, the need for some type of instructional guide for the teachers of the various subject fields has long been recognized. During the first half of the present century, many states developed courses of study under the supervision of the state educational agency, which usually solicited the aid of practicing teachers and administrators. During the years when teacher-certification standards were lax, courses of study tended to be lengthy documents that spelled out the requirements for the various courses in the secondary school curriculum in considerable detail. Many of these courses of study included course objectives, extensive outlines of subject content, suggested instructional activities, lists of instructional materials, tests, and, in some cases, a time schedule for the teacher to follow.

Since teachers are now better prepared than they were two or three decades ago, the trend has been toward the development of instructional guides of a less prescriptive nature than were the traditional courses of study. This newer type of instructional aid is commonly referred to as a "curriculum guide." The development of such materials by city and county school systems, as well as by state departments of education, is a widespread practice. Although curriculum guides for the secondary school level vary greatly in format and content, most of them indicate the scope and sequence of the various courses within a given subject field, in grades seven through twelve, through the presentation of course objectives and other relevant information. A section of the curriculum guide is frequently devoted to clarifying the relationship of each subject field to the over-all philosophy of the school and to the curriculum as a whole. In addition to the objectives for each of the courses, curriculum guides often include a topical outline or unit breakdown of the course, a limited number of suggested instructional activities, and lists of instructional materials such as reference books, motion-picture films, and records.

Curriculum guides are sometimes developed for special phases of the instructional program that are not specifically related to a given subject field. Such curricular areas as citizenship education, international understanding, homeroom, and vocational guidance are strengthened through the development and use of such guides. Curriculum guides for core-curriculum courses have been found to be most beneficial to teachers in schools having this type of program.

Curriculum guides are usually developed by committees of teachers under the direction of the curriculum supervisor. Such a committee is provided with an array of materials including textbooks and guides from other school systems. The outright adoption of a curriuculum guide from another system is rarely a good practice. Neither is it a recommended procedure to develop a guide to conform to a given textbook. In its final form, the guide should be compatible with the characteristics and needs of the local school and community. Before being printed in final form, they are often duplicated and subjected to a try-out period of a year's duration. Final revision is then made in the light of the discovered weaknesses. Some school systems have found it expedient to bind their curriculum guides in a loose-leaf fashion in order that changes can be made conveniently.

Instructional guides, whether they be in the form of the traditional courses of study or the more recent version of curriculum guides, are valuable aids to curriculum improvement. They provide a means of vertical and horizontal coordination of the curriculum, both within a given school and among all the schools of a school system. Curriculum guides are valuable aids to teachers in planning their courses and preparing resource units, since objectives are clarified and specific suggestions are often made for course organization and instructional activities. Beginning teachers and teachers new to a system find them to be especially helpful. Other types of instructional guides such as resource bulletins, containing illustrative resource units, and scope and sequence charts are also used by some school systems to achieve better continuity of the instructional program.

Regardless of the type of instructional guides used by a school system, they should be under the continuous scrutiny of the teachers and the supervisory staff for needed changes. The rapidity with which new developments are occurring in the various disciplines, in the psychology of learning, and in instructional methodology soon renders an instructional guide obsolescent.

Textbooks. The most widely used and still the most indispensable of all instructional materials is the textbook. Traditionally, teachers have, more often than not, utilized the adopted textbook as the instructional guide, and there is little evidence to indicate a significant change in this practice in the near future. While there are many excellent textbooks available for virtually all subject fields at the secondary school level, very rarely should the textbook become the course of study. Occasionally, this practice might be acceptable in a course in mathematics or science, if the text is a recent publication containing up-to-date material. However, the text should be more often regarded as a basic resource or common reference for use by the pupils and teacher. Because of the peculiar characteristics and needs of the local school and community, most textbooks need to be supplemented with other materials, and in some cases parts of the adopted textbook need to be treated very lightly or even ignored.

Today's textbooks are of higher quality in both format and content than they were a decade ago. Modern printing techniques have made it possible to illustrate them better through the use of multicolored photographs and drawings, even on the covers. As for the content, the latest textbooks in some subject fields make those that were published no more than three or four years earlier completely obsolete. This has been especially true in mathematics and, to a lesser extent, science. Radical changes will be forthcoming in the near future in the textbooks for English, social studies, and other areas of the secondary school curriculum.

Perhaps the most important present-day trend in the writing of secondary school textbooks has been the participation of scholars of the academic disciplines in their authorship. In some cases the academicians, as individuals, have undertaken the writing of textbooks, and in other cases they have participated as members of sponsored or unsponsored committees. An excellent example of the committee approach to textbook preparation is that of the School Mathematics Study Group (SMSG), which has received its support from the National Science Foundation. This group has been primarily interested in developing improved textbooks for college-capable students, grades seven through twelve, although they have also devoted attention to the development of textbook materials for the less able secondary school students and for the elementary grades. College professors of mathematics, specialists in the teaching of mathematics, and classroom teachers have participated in this project. A very commendable aspect of the SMSG program has been the field-testing of the preliminary versions of the textbooks, followed by revision and refinement of the materials before publishing the texts for general use.

The content of the textbooks prepared by the various study groups such as SMSG, the Physical Science Study Committee (PSSC), the Biological Sciences Curriculum Study (BSCS), and the Chemical Bond Approach Project (CBA) is based upon the new concepts of learning advocated by Bruner and other leading psychologists.[1] Much of the nonfunctional and less essential subject matter, which comprised a large portion of traditional textbooks in these fields, has been deleted. Emphasis has been placed on the structure of the subject, that is, the fundamental concepts and relationships basic to advanced study in the field. The newer concept of readiness, advocating the introduction of certain mate-

[1] Jerome S. Bruner, *The Process of Education* (Cambridge, Mass.: Harvard University Press, 1960).

rial at a much earlier age than was once believed possible, and subject-matter presentation designed to produce intuitive thinking and discovery have also been incorporated into these new textbooks. The teacher's manuals and the supplementary materials that accompany these books are designed to help the teacher put these ideas into effect. In all probability, the textbooks of the future in virtually all secondary school subjects will follow these examples.

The process of textbook selection varies among the states and from one school system to another. Only two of the states follow the single-textbook adoption plan. The trend is toward the "open" plan, which permits the local school system complete freedom to select all textbooks. A number of states take a middle-of-the-road position in that an adoption list of several textbooks for each course is approved. The local school system is permitted to choose any of the textbooks on the adoption list. Most educators are of the belief that the teachers should have the privilege of making the selections for their courses. In school systems having many teachers in each subject field, the committee approach in which teacher representatives from the various schools work together in making textbook selections is most often used. Regardless of whether the selection is done at the state or the local level, the teachers who are to use the textbooks should be adequately represented in the process.

The selection of a textbook is often facilitated by the formulation of criteria to follow in evaluating the textbooks under consideration. Ready-made scorecards are also useful in comparing one textbook with another. There is considerable literature available dealing with the criteria and processes for making a textbook selection.[2]

Another issue in textbook selection hinges on the question of whether a single-textbook or a multiple-textbook adoption should be employed in teaching a given class. There are advantages and disadvantages to each plan, and these vary from one subject to another. Some of the advantages of single-textbook adoption are (1) all pupils have ready access to the same basic material; (2) parents expect their child to have the same text as all other students; (3) the student feels more secure when he knows he is responsible for the material in one basic text; and (4) less planning and preparation are needed by the teacher. The advantages of the adoption of multiple textbooks for a given course are (1) textbooks can be assigned to pupils according to their individual differences in reading ability and academic aptitude; (2) the student's possible belief in the infallibility of textbooks is altered; (3) the cultivation of critical

[2] Ralph and Marian Brown, "How To Select a Social Studies Textbook," *Social Education,* Vol. 25 (December, 1961), pp. 391–397; Pershing Vartanian, "Criteria and Techniques for Textbook Evaluation," *The Social Studies,* Vol. 53 (April, 1962), pp. 123–127.

thinking results from the student having to compare, analyze, and evaluate the viewpoints of several authors; (4) a more comprehensive coverage of the subject matter is available to the student; and (5) rote memorization of textbook phraseology is discouraged.

Although the advantages of multiple-textbook adoption appear to outweigh the advantages of the single-textbook plan, many schools have returned to the latter after a brief tryout of the multiple-textbook approach. The superiority of the multiple-textbook method has not been borne out by research, although the evidence indicates that it results in better study skills. The preferred procedure in most schools is to adopt a single textbook for each course and to supplement this with a variety of other types of instructional materials. One of the major reasons why the multiple-textbook plan has been abandoned in many schools is because it gained the disfavor of the teachers, most of whom were poorly prepared for using this approach.

Textbooks are presently, and probably will long remain, a basic teaching tool at all levels of education—primary grades through graduate school. The pertinent question is not whether they should or should not be used, but how they can be improved, and how they can be used more effectively.

Workbooks. The value of the use of workbooks in teaching has been debated by educators for years. Those who oppose the use of workbooks state that teachers use them as a crutch and thus avoid the necessity of having to plan carefully and prepare for their classroom teaching. The proponents of workbooks say that they are helpful in providing drill and study for pupils who are deficient because of absences from school and for other reasons. They are also helpful in providing for bright students, who can proceed at their own rates. There is nothing inherent in workbooks to make them either beneficial or detrimental as instructional devices. Like other instructional aids, the workbook is a teaching tool that can make a valuable contribution to learning, depending upon the quality of the workbook itself and the skill with which it is used by the teacher. No significant research on the use of workbooks at the secondary school level has been reported in the literature.

Supplementary Reference Materials. In order to develop problem-solving ability on the part of the student and to foster a program of independent study, many types of reference materials must be made readily available in the school. The amount of information contained in the adopted textbook is necessarily limited and must be supplemented if students are to engage in problem solving and study in depth. The general types of reference sources to which secondary school pupils should have access are encyclopedias, dictionaries, atlases, almanacs, thesauri, and an assortment of textbooks in the various fields, ranging from fifth- or sixth-grade through college level.

Teachers have found classroom libraries to supplement the central library to be of great value in teaching students techniques of problem solving and the proper use of reference materials. Multiple copies of textbooks other than the adopted one, dictionaries, a set of encyclopedias, and books on special topics related to the subject field are considered adequate for classroom references. However, reference materials of these types in every classroom of the school become very costly. A satisfactory substitute is to make these materials as mobile as possible by placing them on book carts which can be moved from room to room.

According to Thomas and Swartout,[3] the following encyclopedia sets are most useful at the junior high school level: *Book of Knowledge, Compton's, Our Wonderful World, World Book, Lincoln Library, Volume Library,* and *American Peoples Encyclopedia.* For the senior high school level, they recommend all of the above except *Book of Knowledge* and add the following: *Encyclopedia Americana, Encyclopedia Britannica,* and *Collier's Encyclopedia.*

Paperback Books. Advocates of the use of paperback books in secondary schools are growing in number, and, according to all indications, this development will continue in the years ahead. Sauer, an authority in the teaching of English, recommends widespread use of paperback books in the teaching of literature.[4] Paperbacks are an excellent means of supplementing or even replacing the traditional anthologies, which some English teachers find too restrictive for the course of study they wish to pursue. Paperback books also provide an economical means of expanding the resources of the library in the sciences, social studies, and virtually all other fields of the curriculum.

The Jefferson County, Colorado, Public Schools found that paperback books not only saved money but also resulted in improved learning.[5] After eighteen months of experience in the extensive use of paperbacks, which included several experimental studies, the following advantages were also revealed: Paperbacks encourage student reading; they have an amazing drawing power for youngsters who have experienced reading difficulties; students purchase them for their own libraries; the low cost of paperbacks makes it possible for the school to buy multiple copies of classics and high-circulation books; and *paperback books do not lessen*

[3] R. Murray Thomas and Sherwin G. Swartout, *Integrated Teaching Materials* (New York: Longmans, Green & Co., Inc., 1960), pp. 90–92.

[4] Edwin H. Sauer, *English in the Secondary School* (New York: Holt, Rinehart & Winston, Inc., 1961), p. 5.

[5] J. William Rioux, "Nine Tested Reasons for Using Paperback Books," *Nation's Schools,* Vol. 70 (November, 1962), pp. 74–76.

the use of hardbound books. In the Jefferson County schools, reading is encouraged by making the paperbacks readily accessible through the use of rotating, wire display racks. The paperback books can be circulated about fifteen times before needing to be replaced.

Current Reading Materials. Newspapers, popular magazines, and professional journals are extensively used as instructional resources by many classroom teachers. Newspapers and magazines provide excellent supplementary reading materials for students because of the high interest appeal and the different levels of readability of the contents of these media. Professional journals are invaluable aids to the alert educator who is continually seeking ways to improve his instruction.

Newspapers and Popular Magazines. A large portion of the adult population does little reading beyond the daily newspaper and popular magazines, and study and use of these materials in the classroom are valuable educational endeavors. Among the most important purposes of classroom use of these materials are the following: (1) to contribute to the development of reading skills and broader reading interests, (2) to aid in developing the student's ability to read critically, (3) to enrich the instructional program of the school with the reports of the latest developments within the various disciplines, and (4) to develop the desire to keep abreast of current sociological, political, and economic occurrences.

In addition to the newspapers and magazines published for the general adult market, periodicals published especially for classroom use are available to schools at nominal costs. Besides the current-events publications designed primarily for use in the social studies, periodicals are available for the fields of English, homemaking, and science. Classroom periodicals are accompanied by teacher editions that contain pertinent suggestions for using these materials.

In selecting adult newspapers and popular magazines for the classroom, several factors must be taken into consideration by the teacher. Care must be taken to choose publications having a level of readability that is comprehensible to the students for whom they are intended. The use of several different newspapers and magazines representing different political and social views and having different editorial policies is also desirable in order to stimulate discussion and critical thinking. A newspaper of national significance, such as the *Christian Science Monitor* or *The New York Times,* can make a valuable contribution to the subject fields of science, social studies, and literature. There are many excellent magazines available, which, if used properly, can be valuable assets to the secondary school curriculum. Among these are *National Geographic Magazine, Holiday, Harper's, Good Housekeeping, Time, Newsweek, McCalls, U. S. News and World Report, New Republic,* and others.

Newspapers and magazines are also valuable to teachers for the collection of articles, pictures, and other illustrative materials in the building of resource files. These materials can be mounted on heavy paper to facilitate their later use with an opaque projector, in bulletin-board displays, and for general classroom use.

Professional Journals. One of the most valuable ways for teachers to learn about new developments in education is through the professional education journals. Some professional journals publish articles and research reports that pertain to a variety of curricular topics and subject fields; others are devoted to a single subject. Teachers who are desirous of improving their instruction subscribe to one or more of the publications specifically related to their teaching field. Some schools also receive a selection of professional journals made available to teachers through the instructional-materials center. The types of articles vary from reports of how a specific instructional activity can be executed to proposals of extensive curricular changes involving the scope and sequence of content within a subject field throughout all levels of the school system. Professional-minded teachers find the research reports of experimental studies that evaluate new practices to be of special interest and value. The extent to which these publications are used depends to a large degree upon the climate of professionalism in the school that is established by the leadership of the principal.

Other types of professional literature of value to curriculum study and improvement are yearbooks, special bulletins, and pamphlets. The yearbooks published by the National Society for the Study of Education and the various departments of the National Education Association are prepared by committees made up of outstanding educators who are specialists in the field under study. In many cases, the yearbooks are based upon research conducted by the committees or they are devoted to a summarization of the best literature in the field. Some of these yearbooks have proved to be real landmarks in the improvement of American education. The special bulletins and pamphlets that are published from time to time proposing curricular changes or clarifying issues have also made significant contributions to curriculum development. Examples of these are *Cardinal Principles of Secondary Education,*[6] *Learning the Ways of Democracy,*[7] and *Education for All American Youth.*[8]

[6] Commission on the Reorganization of Secondary Education (Washington, D.C.: Government Printing Office, 1918).

[7] Educational Policies Commission (Washington, D.C.: National Education Association of the United States, 1940).

[8] Educational Policies Commission (Washington, D.C.: National Education Association of the United States, 1944).

AUDIO-VISUAL MATERIALS

Good teaching is good communication, and the alert teacher is constantly searching for ways of communicating more effectively with his students. Teachers need to develop proficiency in all modes of classroom communication and to make optimum use of them. While some students learn quite well through their sense of hearing, to most individuals seeing is a far more impression-producing and profitable type of learning experience. This fact is borne out by research. In one study, it was found that learning through the five senses is distributed as follows: 1 per cent through taste; 1½ per cent, touch; 3½ per cent, smell; 11 per cent, hearing; and 83 per cent, sight.[9] There is also research evidence to show that instructional activities involving a multisensory approach are superior to those directed toward a single sense. The realization of this fact has caused teachers to become keenly interested in audio-visual instruction.

What is "audio-visual instruction"? This question has been answered by Cross and Cypher as follows:

"Audio-visual instruction" has become a collective term which refers to basic and symbolic aids both audio and visual. "Audio-visual instruction" and "audio-visual education" are two terms used to label what individual teachers and others engaged in instruction and training programs are doing to make optimum use of known facts about how audio and visual aids help people learn. They are terms which label the efforts of these individuals to promote basic experience-getting activities, with sight and sound media, which will "give meaning" to words and symbols. At the same time, the term "audio-visual aids" has been commonly applied to all special categories of these controlled experiences. Motion pictures, filmstrips, printed pictures, maps, models, sound recordings, radio broadcasts, telecasts, and the like are called audio-visual aids or audio-visual aids to learning.[10]

The great influx in the number of pupils in our schools, along with the teacher shortage and the increasing cost of education, has given impetus to audio-visual instruction. This movement is a part of the constant search for ways of improving education within the limits of the available financial and professionally qualified human resources.

Audio-visual aids or materials can be classified in several ways, varying from simple to complex, for purposes of study and discussion. One of the more intricate classifications is that used by Dale[11] which is illustrated

[9] Socony-Vacuum Oil Co. Studies.
[10] A. J. Foy Cross and Irene F. Cypher, *Audio-Visual Education* (New York: Thomas Y. Crowell Co., 1961), p. 8.
[11] Edgar Dale, *Audio-Visual Methods in Teaching* (Rev. ed.) (New York: Holt, Rinehart & Winston, Inc., 1954), pp. 42–56.

by his "cone of experience." The base of the cone is made up of direct, purposeful experiences and ranges upward, layer by layer, each one representing a progressively more indirect or abstract experience until the pinnacle of the cone is reached—learning through verbal symbols. The intervening layers, eleven in all, consist of experiences provided through such audio-visual aids as television, motion pictures, and recordings. In the interest of space, a commonly used classification that groups audio-visual aids into four major classifications—three-dimensional, pictorial, graphic, and auditory—is followed in this presentation.

Three-dimensional Materials. The "concrete" audio-visual aids are three-dimensional and consist of such materials as objects, specimens, models, mock-ups, and cutaways. Concrete audio-visual materials may be thought of as consisting of two types—simulated, or artificial, and authentic, sometimes referred to as "realia." Collections of insects, rocks, stamps, tools, and pottery are examples of realia used by teachers in classroom instruction. Teachers of art, home economics, agriculture, science, or shop courses utilize to good advantage many types of realia in their instruction. Teachers of social studies or foreign languages more often have to resort to models, dioramas, and mock-ups, which are excellent concrete audio-visual aids, though not authentic. Examples of simulated concrete instructional materials are globes, puppets, costumed dolls, and scale models of famous ships and objects of historical importance.

The use of realia in the classroom or laboratory provides the student with direct, purposeful experience, which, from the standpoint of learning, is highly effective. Field trips are also means of utilizing realia in providing direct experience to students through the actual visitation of places being studied. However, it is not always possible, nor desirable even if it were possible, to provide direct experience through the use of realia. For example, the operation of a gasoline engine can be learned more efficiently by observing the moving parts in a cutaway model than by actually observing a real engine operating.

Although teachers often prefer to have their students construct dioramas and models, many excellent simulated three-dimensional instructional articles are available from commercial sources. They are made of various materials such as wood, metal, plastic, rubber, clay, and papier-mâché and range in scale from miniature planetaria to life-sized cutaway models of the human body and exploded models of a molecule.

Pictorial Materials. Pictorial visual materials are those that present a two-dimensional representation or visual likeness of their subjects. Of the four major classifications of audio-visual materials discussed here, this classification comprises the most versatile and the most widely used. Pictorial teaching aids are made up of non-projected pictures and projected pictures, the latter category of which may be still or moving. For many years, teachers have used flat pictures from varied sources to improve communication with their students. Seeing the form, size, color, and certain details in a picture conveys meaning to the student that often cannot be attained through any number of words. Resource files containing many types of flat pictures—photographs, postcards, pictures from magazines, cartoons, and sketches—are often developed by teachers to facilitate classroom instruction.

There are various ways of projecting pictures on a screen or wall, which permits the entire class to view the picture at once and contributes to study in much more detail because of the blown-up size. Non-transparent pictures of all types (not exceeding $10'' \times 12''$) can be projected by an opaque projector. Since pictures do not have to be specially prepared for use with the opaque projector, this type is one of the most versatile and useful visual aids. Pictures found in books, including printed pages, can be projected by this means.

Still pictures projected through the use of transparencies are also excellent teaching aids. Filmstrips, slides ($2'' \times 2''$; $3\frac{1}{4}'' \times 4''$), and large transparencies for use with overhead projectors have a significant advantage over motion pictures as teaching tools in that they permit sustained viewing. Filmstrips and slides have become particularly popular with teachers, because they are relatively inexpensive, easily stored, and simple to use. More and more teachers are making their own filmstrips and $2'' \times 2''$ slides with the use of 35-mm cameras.

Filmstrips are available from commercial suppliers and are accompanied by disc or tape recordings, which are usually narrations explaining the subject material as it is depicted by the filmstrip. If a special sound filmstrip projector is not available, a regular filmstrip projector can be used with a phonograph or tape recorder. The various sources of filmstrips including sound filmstrips may be obtained from the *Filmstrip Guide.*[12] Another useful list of filmstrip sources is the *Educators Guide to Free Slidefilms.*[13]

The sound motion-picture film is a favorite audio-visual aid of teachers at all levels of instruction. Combination of pictures, motion, sound, and color, provides students with classroom experiences in areas of learning that are difficult to present through any other instructional media. Important historical events can be recreated years later in the classroom. The miracles of nature that escape the human eye, such as the growth of a plant or the life processes of a one-celled animal, can be observed by the student through special motion-picture film techniques.

[12] Published periodically by the H. W. Wilson Co., New York, N.Y. Paperbound supplements are issued between the major revisions.
[13] Published annually by Educators Progress Service, Randolph, Wis.

The adaptability of the motion picture adds to its potency as a teaching device. Unlike television, which requires the school's schedule and the pacing of the curriculum to be adjusted to it, timing presents no problem with motion pictures. Assuming that the films are readily available, they can be synchronized with the instructional program. It is also possible to preview them and to repeat them as needed.

Motion pictures, both silent and sound, have had their widest application as occasional supplementary instructional aids; however, extended series of films, designed to be used as more or less self-contained instructional programs, are gaining in use. Examples of these are the 162 films making up the introductory physics course produced by Encyclopedia Britannica Films, Inc., and the series of 160 films on economic education entitled "The American Economy," sponsored jointly by the Learning Resources Institute, the American Economic Association, and the Joint Council on Economic Education. One of the most promising uses of these "canned" courses is in the small schools that cannot obtain fully qualified teachers and thus find it difficult to provide adequate instruction in any other manner. The results of several experimental studies using the physics films have shown that the students who studied physics by the film method have attained a level of achievement not significantly different from that attained by students taught by the conventional method.[14]

Two useful publications that list available motion pictures are the *Educational Film Guide*[15] and the *Education Guide to Free Films*.[16] Many films other than those produced primarily for classroom use have curricular value. Teachers should be aware of the educational possibilities of entertainment films, as well as travelogs, newsreels, documentaries, and other types of films.

Television is also a type of pictorial audio-visual aid, but, owing to its great potential as an instructional medium, it is discussed in a separate section.

Graphic Materials. Instructional materials such as blackboards, graphs, maps, charts, cartoons, and flannel boards, which communicate to the student through the use of visual symbols, are versatile teaching aids. Because of the limited experiential background of the student, relationships and comparisons are sometimes difficult to teach through a strictly

[14] Kenneth E. Anderson and Fred S. Montgomery, "An Evaluation of the Introductory Physics Course on Film," *Science Education*, Vol. 43 (December, 1959), pp. 386–394.

[15] Published by The H. W. Wilson Co., New York, N.Y. Supplements are published periodically.

[16] Published annually by Educators Progress Service, Randolph, Wis.

verbal method, whereas a graph, diagram, or chart quickly conveys the message. Graphics differ from pictorial visual aids in that they explain rather than represent. For example, a diagram showing the relationships between the three branches of the federal government or the structure of the United Nations explains or illustrates the formal organization of each.

Some types of graphic visual aids, such as maps of many varieties and diagrams of the human body used in teaching physiology, are available through commercial sources. However, the majority of graphics used in classroom instruction are made by teachers and their students. Students not only acquire knowledge and understanding through constructing graphics but also develop valuable study skills.

Auditory Aids. Teaching aids that stimulate learning through the sense of hearing are used to advantage by many teachers, particularly teachers of social studies, language arts, and music. The principal types of auditory aids are the radio and recordings. The radio has been regarded as a useful instructional tool by teachers for years. Broadcasts by commercial as well as by educational stations are sources of valuable educational programs. The non-commercial educational stations, usually operated under the auspices of colleges or universities, in addition to their educational programs for the lay public, often broadcast programs designed to tie in with the curriculum of secondary schools in the broadcast areas. Supplementary printed materials are frequently provided to teachers in order for them to make optimum use of the programs.

The potential value of the radio as an educational tool is illustrated by a true story of a high school boy who was being scolded for not having prepared his written report on Admiral Byrd for history class: When asked by the teacher what he did the night before to prevent his preparing the report, the lad replied, "I was talking with Admiral Byrd at the North Pole." The irate teacher, who dismissed the boy from class for his impudence, was astonished to learn later that the boy's story was true! He was a ham radio operator.

Magnetic tape and disc recordings have made significant inroads into curriculums as instructional media. Depending upon their nature and the manner in which they are used, recordings contribute to the acquisition of knowledge and to the development of attitudes and appreciations as well as to the improvement of listening and speaking skills. The tape recorder offers great versatility as a teaching device, because it permits both recording and playback, is easy to operate, and is relatively inexpensive. The recorder serves as a motivating device for the student by permitting him to record his performance and to evaluate it immediately afterward through the playback. Tape recorders are also used to record musical programs, speeches, and radio broadcasts in making a collection of tapes for the school's instructional-materials center.

Disc and tape recordings of educational value are available on a free-loan or rental basis from state departments of education, audio-visual departments of universities, agencies of the federal government, and certain non-profit organizations. Publications of value to teachers in obtaining recordings are *Suggested Sources of Recordings for Educational Use,*[17] *National Tape Recording Catalog,*[18] and *Educators Guide to Free Tapes, Scripts, and Transcriptions.*[19]

Although both are valuable instructional sources, teachers prefer recordings to radio for classroom use. Lack of opportunity to preview or to reuse and difficulty in timing are disadvantages of radio that present no problem with the use of recordings. Adkins reported that approximately 75 per cent of all difficulties incurred in classroom use of radio stemmed from the medium rather than the content or nature of the programs.[20]

The various types of language laboratories, which are essentially auditory instructional aids, are discussed in a separate section because of their growing importance to the curriculum of the secondary school.

INSTRUCTIONAL TELEVISION

Since the Federal Communications Commission set aside a portion of the television channels for educational use in 1955, instructional television has spread rapidly. The shortage of teachers, together with the desire of educators to discover ways of bringing about educational improvement, has contributed to the growth of classroom use of both open- and closed-circuit television. Although instructional television has proved an effective instructional medium in all subject fields and for all grade levels, the evidence shows that it has been used with greater success at the junior than at the senior high school level. It has also proved more successful in science and mathematics than in the humanities, history, and literature.[21]

[17] Published by the Office of Education, U.S. Department of Health, Education, and Welfare, Washington, D.C.

[18] Published by the Department of Audio-Visual Instruction, National Education Association of the United States, Washington, D.C.

[19] Published annually by Educators Progress Service, Randolph, Wis.

[20] Gale R. Adkins, "A Study of Certain Factors That Influence the Use of Radio Broadcasts and Recordings in Public School Classrooms" (Abstract) *AV Communication Review,* Vol. 9 (March-April, 1961), p. 158

[21] Wilbur Schramm, "Learning from Instructional Television," *Review of Educational Research,* Vol. 32 (April, 1962), p. 158.

Like other teaching tools, television has its unique advantages as well as certain disadvantages. It affords a means of extending the services of outstanding teachers to large numbers of students. As a teaching device, it is most effective with large-group instructional methods such as lectures, demonstrations, and panel discussions. No other teaching tool provides students with the opportunity both to see and to hear important events as they occur. In instructional situations where student response is desirable, television has an obvious weakness, although immediate feedback is possible when the classroom is equipped with a direct-line telephone to the studio. Perhaps the major disadvantage of instructional television is its inflexibility. The school's schedule must be adapted to the timing of the telecasts. The pacing of the students in the course of study must also be made to conform with that of the televised instruction, thus making it more difficult to make adjustments for the slow and the rapid learners. Using kinescopes, which reproduce TV programs on motion-picture film, solves the problem of timing or having to see the program when it is live. The cost of this process, however, is prohibitive for many schools.

Several large-scale projects in the use of instructional television have attracted the attention of educators throughout the nation. The Hagerstown project, in Washington County, Maryland, involves extensive use of closed-circuit television. Approximately 90 per cent of the pupils in the county school system receive at least one period of televised instruction daily. The Midwest Council on Airborne Television Instruction, which was begun in 1961, telecasts instruction to thousands of pupils by means of a video-tape-equipped plane circling at a high altitude over northern Indiana. The potential range of this project is 5 million students in thousands of schools over a six-state area.

On the basis of a survey of 393 research studies comparing the relative effectiveness of instructional television and conventional classroom teaching, Schramm makes the following evaluation: "The conclusion is that the average student is likely to learn about as much from a TV class as from ordinary classroom methods; in some cases he will learn more and in some less, but the over-all verdict has been, 'no significant difference.' "[22]

Curriculum workers should view instructional television not as a medium possessed of magic but as a tool offering unique advantages and having distinct disadvantages. Its effectiveness is not inherent in the nature of the medium but depends upon the teacher and the manner in which it is employed. Although there is much to be learned about its use, instructional television's greatest potential appears to be in extending the effectiveness of outstanding teachers to large numbers of students in an economical manner.

[22] *Ibid.*, p. 156.

LANGUAGE LABORATORIES

Language laboratories had their beginning during World War II, when the military was confronted with the need of men possessing oral proficiency in certain foreign languages. It was at this time that educators became interested in the development of conversational ability as a major objective of foreign-language instruction and began to realize the inadequacy of the traditional grammar-translation approach in achieving this goal. Another factor contributing to renewed interest in modern foreign languages have been the recognition of the value of languages in developing international understanding and improved human relations. Through the provisions of the National Defense Education Act of 1958, which provided matching funds for equipping language laboratories and underwrote the cost of summer institutes for teacher training, language laboratories have become standard equipment in the modern secondary school.

The present trend in the teaching of modern foreign languages places emphasis upon listening and speaking in the early stages, followed by increasing attention to reading and writing in the more advanced courses. Various types of language laboratories are in use that facilitate drill for the attainment of listening comprehension and speaking ability. Language laboratories vary in design and may be classified according to how the student studies. The three major types are as follows:

1. *Audio-passive*—The student listens to a master record or tape recording through the use of headphones. There is no provision for recording the student's voice.
2. *Audio-active*—In addition to listening to the master recording, the student responds into the microphone and immediately hears the playback of his own voice through headphones.
3. *Audio-active-comparative*—The student, in addition to listening to, responding to, and playing back the recording of his own voice, may record the master voice as well as his own and play back the tape for comparative purposes.

Other dimensions permitting greater versatility may be added to language laboratories. For example, it is possible to provide each student with a recording commensurate with his own level of achievement and learning needs rather than to require all students to listen to the same recording. In some systems, visual aids are coordinated with the auditory devices for the purpose of developing an understanding and appreciation of the culture of the nation in which the language is spoken. Some electronics companies have developed automatic language laboratories operated by remote control from a teacher's console, permitting an electromechanical selection of the proper recording for each student. One system permits the student to select the appropriate lesson, listen, record, play back, or talk to the teacher. In order to make optimum use of such language-laboratory systems, the teacher must, indeed, be an educational technician.

Linguistic specialists maintain that the language laboratory is not self-sufficient for teaching a language but is another teaching tool. The teacher must keep the proper relationship between the classroom and the laboratory clearly in mind for efficient attainment of the desired objectives. There is need for much more research on the effectiveness and proper utilization of language laboratories.

PROGRAMED INSTRUCTION

Another rapidly growing facet of the widespread movement in educational technology is programed instruction. Attesting to the mushrooming growth of programed instruction is the fact that, whereas the two-year volume of the *Education Index* for the period ending June 30, 1959, omitted the topics of "programed teaching" and "teaching machines," the volume for the two-year period ending June 30, 1961, includes over a hundred different articles under these topics.

While instructional television, radio, motion pictures, and other audio-visual aids are media for instructing large groups, programed instruction is designed to individualize the teaching process. It is based upon printed materials that divide the subject matter to be learned into small, discrete, logical steps or frames. Each frame consists of the stimulus, the response, and the confirmation or correction. The stimulus presents some information, varying in amount and complexity according to the desires of the programer, followed by a question or a problem. After studying the information, the student responds to the question or problem and then compares his answer with that supplied in the confirmation section of the frame.

Programed materials may or may not be designed for use with a teaching machine. The types of teaching machines that are available through commercial outlets vary from simple, manually operated devices to intricate electromechanical machines. If teaching machines are used, their main functions are (1) to prevent the student from looking ahead to the correct answer before supplying a response of his own, (2) to record the student's response for later analysis, and (3) to provide immediate feedback that confirms or assists in correcting the student's response.

Linear and branch programing are the two major methods utilized in preparing programed materials. Linear programing utilizes constructed-response frames that require the student to supply his own answer to the stimulus. Branch programing utilizes selected-response or multiple-choice answers. If the student selects an incorrect answer, he is directed to a branch route or "detour" that is designed to correct his deficiency before he is permitted to go ahead with more advanced material. Dr. B. F. Skinner, the major advocate of linear programing, contends that the need for branching can and should be avoided by carefully constructing the frames in a manner that will minimize student errors. This can be accomplished by constructing the frames to cover a relatively small bit of the subject matter and by using contextual and semantic prompts and other types of coaching cues. Dr. N. A. Crowder, the leading proponent of branch programing, contends that branching enables the programer to provide for individual differences by permitting the capable student to bypass several small steps and by providing extra material for the slow learner, or to correct misconceptions on the part of the students. Since many programers feel that student interest is enhanced by mixing the two methods of programing, the linear-branching dichotomy is evidently disappearing.

The advantages claimed for programed instruction (with or without the aid of teaching machines) are as follows:

1. The student may proceed to learn the subject matter at a rate commensurate with his own ability, thus making programed instruction an excellent means of providing for independent study.
2. The teacher is freed from the presentation of certain parts of the subject matter, thus permitting him to devote more time to providing for the pupils' individual needs.
3. The immediate confirmation or correction tends to motivate the student, reinforces learning, and contributes to the retention of what is learned.
4. Self-instruction programs can make a valuable contribution to the attainment of all types of teaching objectives—knowledge, understanding, skills, attitudes, and appreciations.
5. The student can master certain types of complex materials in much less time through the use of programed materials than is needed with conventional methods.

As is true of any type of instructional materials, programed instruction has certain shortcomings and limitations. In the first place, the student's level of reading comprehension is basic to his successful use of programed materials. A non-reader or poor reader is definitely handicapped in profiting from this medium of instruction. Another significant limitation is that it does not contribute to the development of socialization skills and other concomitant educational outcomes that are important to democratic living.

Although much more research is needed on the use of programed instruction including teaching machines, the existing evidence indicates that it is effective for a variety of different subjects and for students of all levels of ability.[23] Just how and where programed instruction can make its greatest contribution to the secondary school curriculum are questions that curriculum workers have yet to answer.

FREE OR INEXPENSIVE INSTRUCTIONAL MATERIALS

Any discussion of materials sources would be incomplete without the inclusion of free and inexpensive instructional materials. This category does not comprise a unique *type* of instructional materials, since it is made up of printed materials, graphics, recordings, motion pictures, and other types previously mentioned, but, instead, it represents a *source* of materials of value to virtually all teachers. Rarely can teachers justifiably blame the scarcity of instructional materials as the cause of inferior teaching, when there is such a wealth of all types of materials to be had for the expenditure of a small amount for postage. Free and inexpensive materials are especially useful to teachers having limited access to audiovisual and library materials.

The teacher's first step in selecting free and inexpensive materials is to learn the policies of the local school board with regard to the use of this category of teaching aids. Some school boards permit the use of materials made available by government agencies—federal, state, or local —and prohibit the use of any sponsored materials whether they be made available by profit or non-profit business groups or other types of organizations. In some schools, a selection committee is assigned the responsibility of screening sponsored materials for classroom use and of issuing lists of approved materials. In other schools, no regulations are made concerning the use of sponsored materials, thus leaving the matter entirely to the discretion of the administrative and instructional personnel.

In school systems that grant the instructional staff complete freedom in selecting free and inexpensive materials, it would be well for the teachers to be cognizant of at least one selection criterion in addition to those presented in the early part of this chapter. *Materials containing excessive or obtrusive advertising should not be used.* The sponsoring firm's name on the material is normally acceptable. However, when the commercial aspects of the materials outweigh their educational value, they should be rejected. Guidelines for the solution of this problem are presented in a pamphlet by the American Association of School Ad-

---

[23] Lawrence M. Stolurow, *Teaching by Machine* (Washington, D.C.: Government Printing Office, 1961), p. 103.

ministrators.[24] As was previously mentioned, the study of slanted or highly commercialized materials is a justifiable classroom activity only when the teaching objective is concerned with propaganda analysis.

Although a vast amount of free and inexpensive instructional materials is designed and distributed for the specific purpose of selling a product or expounding a particular point of view, some materials are produced with the forthright objective of making an educational contribution. Toward this end, many business and professional organizations have employed highly competent, professionally-trained curriculum specialists to produce educational materials. When properly used, these materials make a significant contribution to the school's curriculum.

Since free and inexpensive materials such as pamphlets and bulletins can be produced and distributed in a relatively short time, they often have the important advantage of being more up-to-date than textbooks. Some of the materials sponsored by business organizations contain elaborate pictorial and graphic illustrations that, because of the cost involved, would not be available to most classroom teachers if it were necessary to purchase them. Another possible advantage of sponsored materials is that they often present a definite point of view on controversial issues, which authors of textbooks usually avoid.

Bibliographies of free and inexpensive materials are available from various sources. Some of the bibliographies consist of items that have been screened according to certain predetermined criteria, thus providing the teacher with additional assurance of the acceptability of the materials. Among the selected bibliographies are *Educators Index to Free Materials*,[25] *Sources of Free and Inexpensive Educational Materials*,[26] *Vertical File Index*,[27] *Free and Inexpensive Learning Materials*,[28] and lists published periodically in professional education journals. Teachers should also be familiar with the excellent federal-government sources. The U.S. Government Printing Office, the world's largest publisher, issues, on a biweekly basis, a list of inexpensive materials covering many subjects, which is made available to teachers upon request.[29]

Teachers need to know where to obtain and how to select useful free and inexpensive instructional materials. The use of such materials is justifiable on the basis of their providing the student with valuable

[24] *Choosing Free Materials for Use in the Schools* (Washington, D.C.: National Education Association of the United States, 1955), p. 9.

[25] Published annually by Educators Progress Service, Randolph, Wis.

[26] Published annually by Field Enterprises Educational Corp., Chicago, Ill.

[27] Monthly publication listing inexpensive materials, with an annual cumulative publication, published by The H. W. Wilson Co., New York, N.Y.

[28] Published annually by George Peabody College for Teachers, Division of Surveys and Field Services, Nashville, Tenn.

[29] "Selected United States Government Publications" (Washington, D.C.: U.S. Government Printing Office, Division of Public Documents).

educational experiences that cannot be obtained through the regular classroom materials, and not merely on the basis of the materials being free or inexpensive.

COMMUNITY RESOURCES

Every community, whether urban, suburban, or rural, affords many excellent sources of valuable learning activities. These range from government agencies, factories, museums, libraries, mines, farms, ranches, fields, and streams to resource people of all types. Surveys of such resources have been made by many school systems, and files making the information available to teachers have been placed in the library or instructional materials center. Alert teachers make use of these real-life materials to vitalize their instruction. See Chapter 28, for further information on this topic.

INSTRUCTIONAL-MATERIALS CENTERS

Adequate procedures for making instructional materials available to the teacher and the pupils at the time they are needed in the instructional program is tantamount to their success as teaching aids. The expanding use of teaching aids for both mass instruction and individual or independent study requires efficient methods of procuring, storing, and distributing instructional materials and equipment of all types. To facilitate this task, some schools have established instructional-materials centers designed to serve teachers and pupils by making all types of teaching aids readily available.

The instructional-materials center represents an expanded concept of the school library. It catalogs and makes available, in addition to books and other types of printed materials, all types of graphics, tape and disc recordings, films, filmstrips, models, specimens, and other varied types of materials, as well as the equipment needed for their use. There is no better place or agency within the school than the library to coordinate the handling of such materials. Having a central coordinating agency is more important than locating the materials together, although the latter is also desirable. The instructional-materials center is a place for teachers and pupils, collectively and individually, to plan and develop new materials as well as to evaluate and select the most desirable of the existing materials for classroom use.

In school systems having many school buildings, a system-wide center is often established, headed by a director of instructional materials, who coordinates the procurement and distribution of the materials for the entire system. Under the supervision of the director is a coordinator for the instructional-materials center in each building. The efficient coordinator is a materials specialist with an understanding of the importance to the school's curriculum of all types of instructional materials—printed materials as well as the various audio-visual aids. He is qualified to assist the teachers in developing teaching aids and in planning how the various types of materials can make their maximum contribution to the instructional program.

In 1960, the American Association of School Librarians issued a revision of its standards for school libraries.[30] The revised standards are based upon the premise that the school library should serve as an instructional-materials center—a concept that was adopted by the Association in 1956. The standards state that there is no conflict between printed and audio-visual materials and emphasize that a major objective is to assist young people in becoming intelligent users of all types of instructional materials.[31]

The 1960 edition of the *Evaluative Criteria*[32] contains a special set of criteria with which to appraise the effectiveness of the instructional-materials services of a high school. The criteria pertain to the numerical adequacy, preparation, and status of the instructional-materials staff; to their responsibilities and the services they offer; and to the selection of materials and equipment, along with the financial provisions.

An instructional-materials center that provides adequate printed materials, audio-visual aids, and services to the teachers and the pupils makes a valuable contribution to the curriculum of the modern secondary school. The proper use of such materials provides an experiential background for the students, motivates learning, and contributes to the attainment of educational objectives.

QUESTIONS, PROBLEMS, AND ISSUES FOR FURTHER THOUGHT

1. What are the more important criteria for the selection of instructional materials?
2. Is it desirable to have administrative restrictions on the selection and use of instructional resources? What are the advantages and disadvantages of having restrictions?
3. What are the different methods of textbook selection and adoption? Should the teacher have complete freedom to select the textbook? Justify your answer.
4. What are the various classifications of audio-visual aids? Which of these are normally constructed by the teacher and the pupils?

[30] *Standards for School Library Programs* (Chicago: American Library Association, Publishing Dept., 1960).
[31] *Ibid.*, p. 17.
[32] National Study of Secondary School Evaluation, Washington, D.C., pp. 257–264.

5. What are the advantages and limitations of instructional television for classroom use? What do the results of research show concerning the effectiveness of instructional television?
6. What are the various types of language laboratories? What is the role of the language laboratory in the teaching of modern foreign languages?
7. What are programed instructional materials? What are the two major types of programing?
8. What precautions should the teacher observe in selecting and utilizing free or inexpensive instructional materials?
9. What are the purposes of an instructional-materials center? How does it contribute to curriculum improvement?

SUPPLEMENTARY MATERIALS

Selected Readings

BROWN, JAMES M., RICHARD B. LEWIS, and FRED F. HARCLEROAD. *A-V Instruction Materials and Methods.* New York: McGraw-Hill Book Co., Inc., 1959. Provides hundreds of examples of the proper utilization of instructional materials in the most appropriate areas of study through the use of both pictures and verbal descriptions.

BURTON, WILLIAM H. *The Guidance of Learning Activities* (3d ed.). New York: Appleton-Century-Crofts, Inc., 1962. Chapter 17, "The Uses of Instructional Resources, Aids, and Materials," provides suggestions for proper utilization of the major types of instructional materials and resources.

CROSS, A. J. FOY, and IRENE F. CYPHER. *Audio-Visual Education.* New York: Thomas Y. Crowell Co., 1961. Discusses the modern developments in audiovisual aids as they relate to the improvement of teaching and learning. Contains many pictures, diagrams, and step-by-step suggestions for the construction of instructional materials.

DEBERNARDIS, AMO. *The Use of Instructional Materials.* New York: Appleton-Century-Crofts, Inc., 1960. A condensed guide for teachers, presenting advantages and principles of using a wide variety of instructional materials and resources.

GWYNN, J. MINOR. *Curriculum Principles and Social Trends* (3d ed.). New York: The Macmillan Co., 1960. Chapter 8, "The Influence of the Textbook," discusses the role of textbooks in American education, both past and present. Chapter 18, "Curricular Aids," devotes attention to the relationship of the library and materials center to the curriculum.

"Instructional Materials: Educational Media and Technology," *Review of Educational Research,* XXXII (April, 1962), pp. 115–221. Summarizes the major research findings pertaining to instructional materials and media since 1955, under five main categories: (1) textbooks and other printed materials, (2) audio-visual materials, (3) learning from instructional television, (4) language laboratories, and (5) self-teaching devices and programed materials.

NORDBERG, H. ORVILLE, JAMES M. BRADFIELD, and WILLIAM C. ODELL. *Secondary School Teaching.* New York: The Macmillan Co., 1962. Chapter 6, "Effective Use of Instructional Materials," discusses principles of selection and use of various types of instructional materials, with emphasis on instructional television.

RIVLIN, HARRY N. *Teaching Adolescents in Secondary Schools* (2d ed.). New York: Appleton-Century-Crofts, Inc., 1961. Chapter 8, "Enriching the Experiential Background for Learning," discusses the proper utilization of various types of instructional materials at the junior and senior high school levels.

STEEVES, FRANK L. *Fundamentals of Teaching in Secondary Schools.* New York: Odyssey Press, Inc., 1962. Written in a forthright and readable style as a guide to preservice or in-service teachers. Chapter 9, "Audio-Visual Learning," discusses the scope and role of audio-visual learning. Chapter 10, "Electronics, Machines, and the Classroom Teacher," is devoted to new developments in educational technology.

AUDIO-VISUAL MATERIALS

Films

Chalkboard Utilization. McGraw-Hill Text-Films. 15 minutes.

Film Tactics. U.S. Navy. 22 minutes.

How To Use a Classroom Film. McGraw-Hill Text-Films. 18 minutes.

The Feltboard in Teaching. College of Education, Wayne University. 10 minutes.

Using the Classroom Film. Encyclopedia Brittanica. 22 minutes.

Using the Classroom Film. Laboratory School, University of Chicago. 22 minutes.

Using Visual Aids in Training. Castle Films. 14 minutes.

Visual Aids to Instruction. United World Films, Inc., U.S. Army. 10 minutes.

11

Criteria for the Selection of Curriculum Materials

One of the major problems confronted in the development of the secondary school curriculum is that of selecting appropriate course-of-study materials and experiences. In many respects, this is the most crucial problem facing secondary schools today. The quality and extent of learning, as well as the attainment of valid educational objectives, depends upon discriminative choice of learning materials and activities.

Many factors have contributed to the need for fundamental criteria for selecting curriculum materials. Of particular significance are the following developments:

1. The great increase in the amount of available curriculum materials makes careful selection imperative.
2. Rapid social changes compel the schools to re-examine their curriculums in the light of the needs of youth and of their own objectives.
3. The increased heterogeneity of the secondary school population necessitates the careful adaptation of the curriculum to the wide diversity of interests, abilities, and needs.

Criteria represent value judgments or generalizations. They should not be confused with the objectives of the school. Objectives serve the purpose of defining the general and specific goals that are envisaged for the school. Criteria aid in the selection of the learning materials most appropriate for the attainment of these goals. Objectives and selection criteria occupy a reciprocal relationship. Changes in the relative emphasis placed upon objectives will often influence the relative stress given to particular criteria. The criteria suggested in subsequent sections of this chapter represent value judgments that are now generally accepted. They are derived from a variety of sources such as the psychology of learning, investigations of the problems and needs of youth, and analyses of the role of the secondary school in modern society.

Inquiries concerning the needs of youth, for example, suggest valuable information as a basis for identifying criteria for selecting curriculum activities and content. Although the term *need* is used in a variety of ways, investigations in curriculum development have been of two major types: first, those that have dealt chiefly with the prerequisites for desirable personality development[1] and, second, those that have focused attention largely upon the types of problems encountered by youths in meeting the demands of society and in finding a satisfactory place within the social framework.[2]

CRITERIA RELATING TO CONTENT OF THE CURRICULUM

Relation of Content to Objectives. It is quite obvious that the nature of the general objectives that are determined for education, as well as those defined for a specific subject or unit of work, will affect materially the nature of the content selected. A study of the curriculum of the secondary school throughout its period of development gives evidence that this criterion has always been operative. As long as the major objective of the high school continued to be preparation for college, the content selected was largely that presumed to prepare students for the pursuit of more advanced studies. When civic, personal, and vocational aims came to be accepted among the objectives of secondary education, the materials of instruction were chosen from more numerous and varied sources. The major purpose of content is to provide effective means for the attainment of educational goals. Therefore, *the content of the curriculum should have a direct relationship to the general and specific objectives of the school.*

The curriculum builder will find many statements both of the purposes of education and of the functions that can be served by the different fields of learning, the separate subjects, and the specific topics of study. Curriculum development at the local level implies the necessity of clarifying purposes and goals. The relative emphasis to be attached to these

[1] Robert J. Havighurst, *Human Development and Education* (New York: Longmans, Green & Co., Inc., 1953). See also "Adolescence," *43d Yearbook,* National Society for the Study of Education, Part I (Chicago: University of Chicago Press, 1944).

[2] *Guides to Curriculum Building, Junior High School Level* (Madison, Wis.: State Department of Public Instruction, 1950).

objectives will be conditioned by the needs of the particular group of pupils to be served and of the community for which the educational program is being planned. There should be a clear and intrinsic relationship between the general and the more particularized objectives. For example, one of the widely accepted functions of the secondary school is to promote health. Lists of objectives in the field of science include such items as these: acquiring scientific knowledge that will tend to free pupils from superstitions and unwise practices in regard to health, understanding the operation of cause-and-effect relationships in disease, valuing the contributions of plants and animals to man's well-being, relating the maintenance of health to the laws of the universe.

Aims for a subject such as biology are stated in terms of the specific contributions of the content of this course to the attainment of the more general objectives. Some of these may be to comprehend the effect of food, oxygen, moisture, light, and temperature upon living organisms; to discover the conditions under which micro-organisms that are inimical to health multiply and operate; and to acquire a knowledge of the structure and processes of the human body. Objectives defined for a particular unit in biology, such as "Infection and the Germ Theory of Disease," may be to gain information concerning the various antitoxins effective in the prevention and cure of communicable diseases; to realize the significance of the investigations of Pasteur, Lister, and other scientists; to become sensitive to the need for personal hygiene and public sanitation; and to develop attitudes of responsibility toward the maintenance of community health. This is but one illustration of the hierarchy of objectives of the modern school. The subject matter selected should contribute toward the attainment of the more general as well as the specific objectives.

Moreover, in selecting learning materials and experiences, consideration should be given to their potential value for attaining *several* of the general objectives of the school. For example, participation in desirable games and sports not only may serve to improve health and physical fitness but may also lead to a wiser use of leisure time and to the achievement of a higher degree of social competence.

Validity and Significance of Content. The term *content* includes not only the actual subject matter that pupils study but also the concepts, understandings, and generalizations to be learned. Traditionally, subject matter was almost entirely drawn from materials prepared by content specialists, whose judgments as to the validity of the facts and concepts presented were generally more dependable than those of an individual teacher. Moreover, the amount and kinds of learning aids available were limited, and the activities in which pupils engaged were often restricted to reading, memorizing, and repeating facts. In current practice, however, materials are drawn from many sources besides textbooks, such as supplementary books, magazines, newspapers, pamphlets, circulars, radio and television programs, phonograph and tape recordings, motion pictures, and, recently, programed materials. At the same time, a great number and variety of learning aids have been introduced into the classroom, such as shop tools, relics, models, pictures, charts, maps, and costumes. Because of the many sources from which learning materials may be derived, it is essential that *the content selected for the curriculum should be valid and significant.*

Validity suggests truthfulness, correctness, verified information, authentic sources, adherence to facts, evidence, and unquestionable authority. We say that a map has validity when it is accurate, complete, drawn from exact data, precise as to scale, and flawless in detail. A motion picture has validity when scenery, dialog, costumes, and action are true to the culture of the time and place they represent. It scarcely needs to be said that, unless curriculum materials are valid, they are inappropriate for use.

Significance implies intrinsic worth. Much of the information in current publications cannot be said to satisfy this criterion. The details given are often trivial and irrelevant, and the subject matter is frequently unwholesome if not pernicious. Likewise, many of the study aids that have recently been produced are not significant enough to occupy the important place they are sometimes given. For example, many workbooks contain items of little consequence and concentrate attention on learning activities that are meaningless and deadening to interest, originality, and effort.

The difficulties that have arisen in evaluating the validity and significance of content have been complicated not only by the quantity and diversity of materials available but also by the growing trend toward encouraging pupils to participate in locating and selecting materials to be used in furthering the learning process. When this is done, a practice that is indeed commendable, the need for judging the validity and significance of content is even more urgent.

CRITERIA RELATING TO THE LEARNING PROCESS

Utilizing the Interests of Students. The significant role of interests in motivating study and learning has long been recognized. For many years, teachers have been impressed by the fact that pupils who are vitally interested in their work not only develop favorable attitudes but also achieve results more commensurate with their abilities. The vast experimental literature of the past several decades strongly affirms the soundness of the principle that, *in selecting curriculum materials and activities, consideration should be given to the interests of students.* However, this criterion should not be interpreted to imply that only content and experiences that have an immediate appeal to children or youths should be included in the curriculum. Blind acceptance of the doctrine of interest can be as dangerous as a rigid adherence to the traditional curriculum, which was too often characterized by mere verbalism, compulsory methods of teaching, and the study of subjects and materials that had little or no meaning for pupils. A clear understanding of the significance of interest is essential.

In the first place, interests must not be confused with the transitory whims and curiosities frequently displayed by individuals. Only those purposes and desires that can contribute to the attainment of educationally sound objectives are of enduring value. The teacher who relies too strongly upon the spontaneous interests of pupils in selecting materials will soon discover the limitations of the approach. Not only is there a danger that learning will be of a fragmentary character, but inadequate attention will be given to the development of higher levels in the organization of experience. Moreover, children and youths are frequently incompetent judges of the worth and satisfiability of their own interests. For example, studies of the vocational aspirations of high school pupils reveal wide divergences between expressed preferences and possibilities of attainment, limited as these possibilities are by occupational opportunities and individual abilities. Furthermore interests, needs, and capacities differ significantly among individuals, as do students' abilities to sense their own needs and interests.

In the second place, through skilful selection of curriculum materials, unsuitable or restricted interests can be redirected and more worthy interests can be engendered. An illustration of a field in which guidance of this type is greatly needed is that of reading. Investigations show that the quality of reading of high school pupils is often poor and the amount very limited—an unfortunate situation since there is little reason to assume that habits will be noticeably different in adulthood. When pupils do read voluntarily, they often turn to printed materials that require minimum effort, such as picture magazines, comic strips, and pulp magazines. It is abundantly clear that the school all too frequently has failed to stimulate pupils to enrich their experiences through wisely chosen reading materials. However, many teachers have already demonstrated that reading abilities, habits, and interests can be developed and improved through skilful guidance and direction.

A knowledge of the immediate interests of pupils is of inestimable value in the motivation of study and learning activities. The teacher, as a curriculum builder, should have some knowledge of the interests of his students. The next step is to determine the relative value of expressed interests for the attainment of subject and unit goals. Subject matter should then be selected that will capitalize upon present interests as well as contribute toward more extensive and profitable learnings.

Continuity and Sequence. Modern psychology maintains that education is a process of continuous and gradual growth, which proceeds most effectively when the learning materials and experiences that are being utilized at any given time bear direct relationships to those previously encountered and lead successively to the understanding of more complex materials and experiences. Various terms have been used in recognition of this principle, for example, "encouraging the use of associations," "assuring relatedness," "providing for correlation," "assuring continuity," "promoting articulation," "arranging for sequentiality," and "planning for integration." The underlying principle, however expressed, is that, unless provisions are made for capitalizing on the previously acquired knowledges, skills, and interests of pupils and for combining the learning elements into a unified pattern, the educational process will be uneconomical and ineffective. Therefore, *the curriculum materials and experiences selected should provide for continuity and sequence.*

For many years, it was assumed that this principle would be fulfilled by presenting a logical arrangement of subject matter. The order of courses in a field was determined on this assumption. For example, the usual sequence in history was ancient, medieval, modern, and American. Topics and units of work were also selected with reference to what were thought to be the demands of the subject rather than in relation to the abilities, interests, and needs of pupils. Remote and abstract facts and knowledges were often introduced before those already within the range of pupils' experiences and concepts. Moreover, overlapping between the various subjects of a field, and even between fields, led to wasteful duplication of effort.

It is now generally recognized that the curriculum as a whole and the materials in each subject should be selected and organized from the standpoint of psychological as well as logical considerations. Learning proceeds from the known to the unknown, from the concrete to the abstract, from the familiar to the alien, from the immediate to the distant. This may or may not be in accordance with a logical organization. The *readiness* of pupils for new learnings in any given area is of paramount importance. Hence, it is essential that the present maturation levels of the students be taken into account and that careful plans be devised that will guide pupils in making uninterrupted progress toward the attainment of higher levels of learning. This is particularly true in directing growth toward the enlargement of concepts and generalizations and in the acquisition of habits of thought. The concept of democracy can scarcely be developed in one learning situation, nor can skill in detecting false assumptions and hypotheses be so acquired. Consequently, the curriculum must provide many opportunities for pupils to engage in learning experiences that will enable them to develop the understandings, insights, and skills essential in the formulation of these more generalized learnings.

The principle involves both horizontal and vertical continuity, that is, relatedness between concurrent and successive learning experiences. Horizontal continuity is achieved by the correlation or unification of materials that pupils are studying concurrently. Vertical continuity is facilitated by presenting at succeeding stages of experience partially mastered concepts and skills at ever increasing levels of difficulty and complexity, in association with the attainment of new or more abstruse objectives.[3] It is dependent upon securing that sequence of the materials and activities that will result in the ability to use the understandings and habits of thought mastered in one experience to clarify and promote those essential in another learning situation.

The Multiple Character of Outcomes. Psychologists, in recent years, have repeatedly emphasized the fact that learning is never single—that, whenever a child is stimulated to make one type of response, several other types of responses extend and deepen the total actual learnings. Such responses are sometimes called concomitant learnings. If the main emphasis is upon learning facts, other types of outcomes such as attitudes and appreciations are inevitably learned also. The pupil who is expected to memorize a poem will, in the process of repetition, learn the words and at the same time find or devise a more economical method of memorizing, but he may also develop an enduring appreciation for the poem or discover a hitherto unsuspected interest in poetry. Unfortunately, the concomitants of learning are not always of a positive and constructive character. Indeed negative and undesirable learnings often develop. The pupil may not only memorize the words of the poem but also develop or accentuate a generalized distaste for poetry. He may also acquire a dislike for the teacher who has made the assignment and for the class of which he is a member. *In selection of learning materials and experiences, it is of utmost importance that recognition be given to the multiple character of outcomes.*

In the past, curriculum materials have been selected primarily from the standpoint of their contributions to one highly significant aspect of

[3] See Jerome S. Bruner, *The Process of Education* (Cambridge, Mass.: Harvard University Press, 1960).

pupils' growth—the intellectual aspect. However, the intellectual aspect has often been narrowly limited to the memorization of facts and the acquisition of skills. Although increased stress has been given recently to the development of concepts, generalizations, and understanding, insufficient attention has been devoted to the attainment of worthy attitudes, appreciations, ideals, and habits of conduct. These latter outcomes, by no means in conflict with the intellectual, should be given appropriate recognition in every area of the modern school, for they are significant determinants of behavior.

It is quite possible to change undesirable or limited habits, attitudes, and appreciations as well as to develop new ones. For example, studies in the field of visual education have shown that a single film may produce important changes in pupils' attitudes. The study of biology can dispel unfounded beliefs and superstitions on such issues as racial superiority, the influence of heredity, and the causes of disease. Mathematics can contribute to the formation of better habits of analysis, problem solving, and critical thinking. The arts can stimulate interests in creative endeavor that will lead to lifelong satisfactions. The study of literature can develop appreciations of the cultural contributions of other races and nationalities. The fact that many types of outcomes may be involved in any learning situation makes imperative the selection of those kinds of subject matter that afford the greatest promise of providing for the well-rounded development of every student.

Adapting to Individual Variations. One of the modern concepts of education is that differences among individuals should be considered desirable. Preparation for democratic living does not proceed from a "leveling down" process. On the contrary, the variations among human beings in ability, creativity, sensitivity, receptivity—in all the complex traits involved in the term *personality*—form one of the greatest assets of a democratic society.

Realization of the need for providing for individual characteristics of individual pupils is extensive; the close relationship between this need and the selection of curriculum content has been widely recognized. Unless a sufficient amount and variety of materials and experiences are supplied, the possibilities of educational growth will be greatly limited. Psychology has given us objective evidence that there are significant differences not only in pupils' capacity to learn but also in the degrees of success they are able to attain through the use of various media. Moreover, pupils profit from coming into contact with diversified content that will guide them into more complete and well-rounded development. Likewise, all pupils need to learn to use the many types of content they will experience outside the classroom.

Many definitions and classifications of individual variation are available for study by curriculum builders. It is sufficient for the purpose of this discussion to point out some of the factors to be considered in choosing content that will provide for these differences. In the first place, the materials and activities chosen should represent varying degrees of difficulty and complexity. For example, the vocabulary level of reading materials may be differentiated, or the problems for study may be of unequal difficulty. Instructional materials should be selected to challenge the abilities of pupils and at the same time permit each one to attain some measure of success. In the second place, a sufficient amount of content should be made available in order that there may be adequate opportunities for the repetition necessary in the development of the various skills, understandings, appreciations, and attitudes. In the third place, curriculum materials should often include several types of learning media such as books, laboratory materials, and audio and visual aids, which will provide for pupils who possess sensory defects or unusual sensory capacities and will provide opportunities for all pupils to participate in both real and vicarious experiences. To summarize: *A sufficient amount and variety of learning materials and experiences should be selected to provide for individual differences among students.*

CRITERIA RELATING TO THE NEEDS OF STUDENTS

Importance of Youth Needs. The difficulties and failures encountered by youth in making satisfactory adjustments in life have challenged educators in their attempts to improve the curriculum. The movement toward designing the curriculum on the basis of the needs of youth has rapidly gained momentum. So significant and promising does this approach appear to be that the following criterion can be stated: *In selecting curriculum materials and experiences, attention should be given to the personal and social needs of students.*

Extensive efforts have been made during the past decade to obtain more precise information concerning the needs of youth. Investigations have been conducted not only by educational agencies such as the American Youth Commission of the American Council on Education but by local communities as well. A variety of techniques have been used in gathering pertinent information, for example, conferences with youth, questionnaires, surveys, community forums, analytical case studies of behavior, and tests and examinations of different types.[4] As a result of

[4] For an excellent discussion of procedures for determining the needs of youth, see "Adapting the Secondary School Program to the Needs of Youth," *52d Yearbook,* National Society for the Study of Education, Part I (Chicago: University of Chicago Press, 1953), Chaps. 2 and 3.

these efforts, there is available today a vast amount of significant information concerning the needs of youth in many areas of experience. It is abundantly clear from investigations that, in many respects, the secondary school has failed to meet the needs of youths in their personal living, in their sociocivic relationships, and in their vocational preparation.[5]

One of the areas of youth needs that is neglected by secondary schools is emphasized in the conclusion reached in the Regents' Inquiry of the State of New York that "irrespective of the schools' judgment of their readiness for citizenship, the leaving pupils as a group are seriously deficient in their knowledge of the problems, the issues, and the present-day facts with which American citizens should be concerned." Furthermore, "once he is out of school, the ordinary boy or girl does practically nothing to add to his readiness for citizenship, nor does he keep alive the knowledge of civic affairs or the interest in social problems which he may have had when he finished his schooling."[6]

The needs of youth in the areas of health and physical fitness have been given renewed significance since World War II by the reports of the Selective Service System.[7] The high incidence of poor health and physical disabilities disclosed by these reports constitutes a serious challenge to the secondary school. Reference was made, for example, to the Hagerstown studies, in which the health and physical fitness defects of individual pupils were recorded over a period of years. It was pointed out that many, if not most, of these same disabilities were responsible for rejections or discharges from military service. Evidence presented shows that one out of six men rejected by the various branches of the service had disqualifying disabilities that could have been easily remedied and that many more had defects that could have been prevented.

This same report records the extremely large percentage of youths who were rejected because of emotional disturbances and personality maladjustments. It seems clear that the school has given inadequate consideration to the problem of providing a school environment and learning experiences that will promote mental and emotional health. It is true that many conditions that may give rise to these deficiencies are not under the control of the school, since personaliy is influenced by the total cultural pattern. Yet it is probable that secondary schools sometimes foster, rather than eliminate, persistent conflicts and worries that lead

[5] See, for example, *Principal Findings of the Follow-up Study,* Illinois Secondary School Program, Bulletin No. 17, 1951.

[6] Francis T. Spaulding, *High School and Life* (New York: McGraw-Hill Book Co., Inc., 1939), pp. 18, 27.

[7] *Wartime Health and Education,* hearing before a subcommittee of the Committee on Education and Labor of the United States Senate (Washington, D.C.: Government Printing Office, 1944).

to personality disintegrations. The highly specialized and compartmentalized program of many schools often prevents pupils from dealing with problems that are significant to them. Such situations may lead to feelings of frustration and discouragement and, consequently, to undesirable compensatory reactions.

Other areas in which secondary schools should give greater attention to the needs of youth are in regard to the wise use of leisure time, training to meet the responsibilities of family life, and provisions for the acquisition of needed information about the world of work, along with relevant work experiences. It is clear that, if secondary schools of the future are to provide realistic programs of education, they must give greater attention to selecting materials and experiences that will aid in satisfying the varied needs of youth.

The Curriculum and Life. The concept that education should be related to life has received almost universal acceptance in theory. However, its implementation in the secondary school curriculum has been blocked and delayed by two attendant dissensions. One is whether the relationship should be made to present or to future life interests, purposes, and activities; and the other is how such a real relationship should be established.

Debate as to the relative importance of immediate and deferred values is not new. Traditionally, the tendency was to select materials and experiences almost entirely on the basis of their supposed efficacy in meeting the anticipated demands of adult life. Education was thus conceived of as a process of preparation. Recently, the trend has been to choose activities that have intrinsic value in meeting and solving the problems of present living, as well as those that may be useful in the future. Much of the content selected should satisfy both of these aspects of need. If life is conceived of as a continuous process of growth, the concept of a cleavage between present and future is untenable. It is rather a matter of emphasis. As Dewey expresses it, "The mistake is not in attaching importance to preparation for future needs, but in making it the main-spring of present effort."[8]

Disagreement as to how to effect greater unity between education and life has arisen in part from a misunderstanding of the learning process. Teachers have anticipated greater results from their efforts to establish closer contacts between school and life because of an unjustified confidence in the theory of transfer of training. Unless the content possesses vital and direct relationships that are perceived by pupils, and unless opportunities for applications to actual situations are provided, the

[8] John Dewey, *Democracy and Education* (New York: The Macmillan Co., 1923), p. 65.

amount of transfer may be small indeed. Another difficulty lies in determining the most efficient and significant methods for achieving unity between education and life. Much time has undoubtedly been wasted by encouraging pupils to engage in home and community activities with a view to acquiring understandings and skills that could have been learned as effectively and more economically in the school. The problem of evaluating the attempts made to establish relationships with reality is far from simple. In many instances, teachers have no means of evaluation except their own opinions or the often unreliable statements of pupils. Despite these confusions and perplexities, it is essential that *learning materials and activities should be selected that provide maximum opportunities for application to real-life situations.*

In the first place, learning takes place more effectively when pupils comprehend the relationships of the curriculum to life and the opportunities it suggests for applications to their daily activities. This is a question of both interest and repetition. Abstract ideas that are meaningless to pupils fail to challenge interest; without proper motivation learning is slow and poor in quality. Likewise, the amount of practice pupils have in using newly acquired skills and knowledge in concrete situations conditions the strength and permanence of their learning.

In the second place, contact with reality is a requisite of desirable personality development. If young people conceive of their school experiences as separate and distinct from life, they may become divided and distorted personalities. The lack of harmony that often exists between the narrow and controlled environment of the classroom and the existing cultural pattern of a community may lead to confusion, antagonism, and frustration. The school should complement and supplement the positive educational influences of society and should arrest and overcome those of a negative character. Moreover, the school should not be so far removed from reality that pupils are unprepared to cope with the experiences they encounter after school hours. They cannot develop complete and unified personalities unless they can meet the exigencies of real life without undue bewilderment and failure. In order that the students may have opportunities for adequate self-development, the content and learning activities of the curriculum should be closely and clearly related to the daily activities of life.

Universality of Need. In recent years, educators have envisioned a secondary school adapted to furthering the development of all normal young people from about twelve to nineteen years of age. Four-fifths of the youth of these ages are enrolled in the secondary schools. It seems probable that, with the greatly increased attention being given to the dropouts, this figure will continue to increase in the immediate future.

Changes in the nature of the secondary school population, from a highly selected and more or less homogeneous minority to an almost completely unselected, heterogeneous majority, have greatly complicated the problems involved in the selection of curriculum materials and experiences. On the other hand, these changes have tended to focus attention on the basic needs of youth. Certain activities and experiences are common in the lives of all individuals, whatever their sex, age, race, ambitions, abilities, or interests. Certain knowledges, skills, and loyalties are required of all. Two of the primary tasks of the curriculum builder are to identify these universal needs and to select learning materials and experiences that will provide for them. It follows, then, that, *in selecting curriculum subject matter, preference should be given to those materials and experiences that have universal application in the present and future lives of all pupils.*

This criterion may be neglected in efforts to provide for the special needs and interests of particular youths, a task that is certainly an important obligation of the school. Pupils with unusual talents in music or art, for example, have, in some instances, concentrated so much of their effort in developing their unique abilities that they have failed to acquire the skills, knowledge, and habits essential to them as citizens of a democracy. Moreover, teachers have sometimes given too little attention to essentials in their efforts to satisfy pupils' interests and to introduce variety into the classroom. Current movements in the direction of defining the purpose and scope of liberal education for all youth are promising and should be studied by teachers and curriculum workers.

Frequency of Occurrence. Some learning materials and activities may have universality of application although an individual pupil will rarely experience the need for them during his lifetime. Other materials and activities will be required by a large percentage of pupils with recurring frequency. If the curriculum is to meet the needs of youth, *stress should be placed on those materials and experiences that have a high frequency of occurrence in daily life.* If these activities also meet the criterion of universality, it is evident that they become "musts" in the curriculum. Basic concepts and understandings in the area of science, social studies, language arts, and mathematics fall in this category.

Many studies that have included frequency counts have recently been made of the activities of children and adults. For example, it is on this basis that vocabulary and spelling lists have often been developed. It is desirable for those who are entrusted with curriculum building in a particular school or community to carry on investigations of the daily-life needs of the pupils for whom the curriculum materials and experiences are being selected.

METHODS AND PROCEDURES IN SELECTING MATERIALS AND ACTIVITIES

Consideration will now be given to the procedures that can be used in selecting curriculum materials. Whether this responsibility falls upon a teacher, a group of teachers, content specialists, or curriculum specialists, the criteria that have been suggested may serve as guiding principles. Several methods of procedure for applying these criteria will be described briefly. Some of the methods are mainly subjective in character; others are more objective and scientific. It is recognized that, since fundamental values relating to the philosophy and objectives of the secondary school are involved, scientific procedures alone cannot solve the problems of selection. However, whenever possible, objective methods should be used. Obviously, no one procedure is equally applicable in all situations. A combination of methods, in most instances, will bring about the selection of the most appropriate materials.

Expert Opinion. This method of selecting the content of the curriculum has been widely used in secondary schools and is one of the most common. Essentially, it consists of examining the recommendations of a specialist or a group of specialists regarding what ought to be taught. Since the turn of the century, the number of yearbooks and special reports of national, state, and local organizations relating to the curriculum has steadily increased.[9] The recent efforts of college and university specialists in such areas as science and mathematics in assisting the schools in the critical selection of instructional materials are also highly commendable.

Although the recommendations of specialists are of great value in suggesting course-of-study materials and activities, it is often difficult, if not impossible, to implement them effectively in local school situations. Moreover, the problem of determining the competence of the specialists who have issued the recommendations is far from simple. It is, for example, not uncommon to find conflicting suggestions offered by different persons or groups. In some instances, specialists have conceived of the curriculum in a narrow sense and have been mainly preoccupied with the perpetuation of subjects and activities that have outlived their usefulness. Encouraging indeed are the recent tendencies of many organizations to focus attention upon the intellectual, personal, and social needs of the

[9] Illustrative are the reports of the Classical Investigation, the Modern Language Study, the Commission on the Social Studies of the American Historical Association, the Commission on the Secondary-School Curriculum of the Progressive Education Association, the National Council of Teachers of Mathematics, the National Council of Teachers of English, the National Society for the Study of Education, and the National Education Association.

pupil and to suggest experiences that will contribute directly to his growth and development.

Job Analysis. This method of selecting the materials and activities of the curriculum was first popularized by Charters and applied chiefly in the field of vocational education.[10] The procedure that is generally followed is to observe and to tabulate the activities of a number of individuals who are regarded as competent in their jobs, in order to discover the kinds and frequency of operations carried on. Such information is then used as a basis for selecting the materials of a course. For example, an analysis could be made of the various types of jobs that must be performed by an automobile mechanic in adult life; each particular job such as grinding valves could be further analyzed in terms of the specialized knowledge and skills the mechanic must possess; the course in auto mechanics would then be organized on the basis of the information obtained. The job-analysis technique can facilitate the selection of materials in many other subjects in the field of industrial arts, the home arts, business education, and agriculture.

Certain limitations of this method should be clearly recognized. In the first place, the activities carried on by adults may not be appropriate for immature youth. In the second place, it is possible that the attainment of the objectives in a specialized course would not necessitate the high degree of skill required in a particular job that is carried on in adult life. This would be especially true of courses designed to serve the purposes of general education.[11] In the third place, there is always the question as to whether the activities carried on by adults are of the most desirable character. The attainment of certain outcomes such as attitudes and ideals has been conspicuously neglected by investigators who have used the job-analysis technique. Finally, courses based upon current jobs may do little to adapt pupils to the types of jobs and conditions of work that they may experience in the future. Despite these limitations, this method can provide the curriculum worker with an abundance of useful information and can enable him to evaluate learning activities from the standpoint of such criteria as validity and significance, frequency of occurrence, and universality of application.

The Survey Method. Periodical literature of the past few decades has included numerous illustrations of the application of the survey method in the selection of curriculum content for nearly every field of instruction. For example, teachers of English have surveyed the most common errors

[10] W. W. Charters, *Curriculum Construction* (New York: The Macmillan Co., 1923).

[11] See "New Insights and the Curriculum," *1963 Yearbook* of the Association for Supervision and Curriculum Development, p. 83.

in language usage, teachers of mathematics have surveyed the types of problems encountered by students in their daily lives, and teachers of the social studies have surveyed pupils' attitudes on various social issues. The method has been used also in analyzing the content of textbooks and published courses of study.

In many instances, surveys have yielded valuable information for instructional purposes. For example, surveys of the reading interests of pupils have disclosed the types of books, newspapers, and magazines that have greatest appeal to young people. Surveys of opinion on various social and civic issues suggest content for courses in the social studies. Surveys of the health habits of youth can be used in choosing relevant and significant content for courses in science and health education.

Many of the limitations of the job-analysis technique apply to the survey method as well. For example, a knowledge of the reading interests and activities of pupils is an inadequate basis upon which to develop an effective reading program. Reading interests are conditioned by a variety of factors such as availability of materials and motivation. A knowledge of what pupils now read must be supplemented by further study of what it is desirable for them to read if continuous progress is to be made. Similarly, the errors pupils make in language usage are of great significance in clarifying objectives and suggesting content, but there are additional tasks of helping pupils to gain ideas to express and of providing rich and abundant opportunities for oral and written expression.

Suggested Techniques for Using Criteria. To facilitate the process of selecting learning materials and experiences, a practicable form is shown in Table 11–1. By means of this check list, the content derived through such methods as have been mentioned can be evaluated in terms of the basic criteria that have been suggested. Subject matter that has the highest rating in terms of the several criteria should normally be given precedence in teaching. Such evaluation, however, should be based upon the criteria taken as a whole and not in terms of single items. For example, it is probable that many learning experiences that do not have a high frequency of occurrence are nevertheless significant and should be included in the course of study. Moreover, it should be clearly recognized that the intelligent selection of content cannot be reduced to a mechanical or mathematical process. The effective use of the check list involves (1) a clear understanding of the philosophy and objectives of the school, (2) an analysis of objectives in terms of behavior to be developed (concepts, meanings, abilities, attitudes), (3) a decision as to the relative importance of each criterion in selecting materials, and (4) selection of materials and activities on the basis of the appraised criteria.

TABLE 11–1

FORM FOR EVALUATING CURRICULUM MATERIALS AND EXPERIENCES

Criteria for Selection	Appraisal of Criteria[a]			Appraisal of Curriculum Materials[b]		
	I	II	III	I	II	III
1. Curriculum materials should have a direct relationship to the objectives of the school.						
2. The materials selected for the curriculum should be valid and significant.						
3. In selecting curriculum materials and activities, consideration should be given to the interests of students.						
4. Curriculum materials and experiences should provide for continuity and sequence.						
5. In selecting learning materials and experiences, recognition should be given to the multiple character of outcomes.						
6. A sufficient amount and variety of learning materials and experiences should be selected to provide for individual differences.						
7. In selecting curriculum materials and experiences, attention should be given to the personal and social needs of youth.						
8. Learning materials and activities should be selected to provide maximum opportunities for applications to real-life situations.						
9. Preference should be given to those materials and experiences that have application in the lives of all pupils.						
10. Stress should be placed on those activities and experiences that have a high frequency of occurrence in daily life.						

[a] Check in Column I if, in your judgment, the criterion is of great importance, in Column II if of some importance, and in Column III if of little or no importance.

[b] Check in Column I if, in your judgment, the proposed content is in accord with the criterion to a large extent; in Column II if in accord with the criterion to some extent, in Column III if only slightly or not at all in accord with the criterion.

QUESTIONS, PROBLEMS, AND ISSUES FOR FURTHER THOUGHT

1. Choose a subject, and indicate the relative importance of the criteria suggested in this chapter for selecting materials of instruction for that subject.
2. Show how variations in the objectives of a secondary school will influence the emphasis to be given to the various criteria suggested.
3. Give illustrations of how knowledge of students' interests may be capitalized on by a teacher of a particular subject in selecting learning materials.
4. Summarize the results of recent investigations relating to the needs of youth. Give illustrations to show how these needs can be met through discriminative selection of curriculum materials and experiences.
5. What is the difference between a psychological and a logical approach to the selection of learning activities? Are the two approaches necessarily antithetical? Explain your answer.
6. To what extent do you think that students at the secondary school level can participate in the effective selection of curriculum materials? Give some specific illustrations.
7. Obtain a recent printed or mimeographed course of study for a subject in your field of interest. Write a brief, critical statement of your own evaluation of this course of study.
8. Using the form for evaluating curriculum materials as a guide, prepare a critical appraisal of two textbooks in a subject of your choice. Summarize the results of your study of each textbook, indicating strengths and weaknesses, grade level and types of students for which the book is best suited, and your recommendations as to the most appropriate use of the textbook.

SUPPLEMENTARY MATERIALS

SELECTED READINGS

ASSOCIATION FOR SUPERVISION AND CURRICULUM DEVELOPMENT. "A Look at Continuity in the School Program," *1958 Yearbook*. An excellent analysis of the role of continuity in curriculum planning.
——. "New Insights and the Curriculum," *1963 Yearbook*. Chapter 4. A broadened conception of knowledge and its sources, with implications for curriculum improvement.
KRUG, EDWARD A. *Curriculum Planning*. New York: Harper & Row, 1950. Chapter 5. Criteria for the development of specific learning aids are established, and illustrations of a practical nature are presented.
McKEAN, ROBERT C. *Principles and Methods in Secondary Education*. Columbus, Ohio: Charles E. Merrill Books, Inc., 1962. Chapter 3, "Practices in Selecting and Organizing Content"; Chapter 6, "Selecting and Using Instructional Materials."
MILLS, HUBERT H., and HARL R. DOUGLASS. *Teaching in High School* (2d ed.). New York: The Ronald Press Co., 1957.
NATIONAL SOCIETY FOR THE STUDY OF EDUCATION. "Adapting the Secondary School Curriculum to the Needs of Youth," *52d Yearbook*, Part I. University of Chicago Press, 1953. Chapters 1–3, 12–13. Teachers and administrators who are engaged in curriculum planning will find in the

chapters cited a careful analysis of the "needs" approach in selecting curriculum materials and experiences.

ROMINE, STEPHEN A. *Building the High School Curriculum*. New York: The Ronald Press Co., 1954. Chapter 13. The selection of curriculum materials including textbooks, the library, audio-visual aids, and community resources; criteria for selection of curriculum materials.

SAYLOR, J. GALEN, and W. M. ALEXANDER. *Curriculum Planning*. New York: Holt, Rinehart & Winston, Inc., 1954. Chapter 12. An analysis of the characteristics of desirable learning experiences and their applications.

SMITH, B. OTHANEL, WILLIAM O. STANLEY, and J. HARLAND SHORES. *Fundamentals of Curriculum Development*. New York: Harcourt, Brace & World, Inc., 1950. Chapters 12, 13. A basis consideration of principles of content selection, together with suggested procedures and applications.

STRATEMEYER, FLORENCE B., H. L. FORKNER, and M. G. McKIM. *Developing a Curriculum for Modern Living*. New York: Teachers College, Bureau of Publications, Columbia University, 1947. Chapters 5–6. Discussion of the "persistent-life-situations" approach in selecting curriculum materials and experiences. Indicates the role pupils can play in curriculum development.

12

Large Units as a Basis for Course Organization

WHAT IS A LARGE UNIT?

Modern psychology holds that a human being reacts as a whole, as one organism, and not by parts. Rapidly growing acceptance of this principle furnished a basic reason for the popular growth of the theory and practice of using large units as a way of organizing school curriculums. From about 1900, the influence of such leaders as the McMurrays, William H. Kilpatrick, H. L. Miller, and H. C. Morrison greatly accelerated the movement in this direction. In more ways than one, these men worked to bring into school practices such concepts as significance, meaningfulness, wholeness, and completeness. Also influential in introducing the unit idea into many schools was its wide and effective application in various vocational subjects.

Definitions of the Large Unit. Most of those who write about large units formulate some sort of definition, usually at the outset of the discussion. All definitions stress such characteristics of the unit as meaning (or "meaningfulness"), significance, wholeness, and completeness. While these definitions have much in common, there are also differences in viewpoints and emphases. As a background for the shorter, more formal definitions, it may be in order here to note Umstattd's "essential elements of the unit idea." They are

1. Arrangement of content in meaningful wholes
2. A five-step mode of attack and study

3. Length of the unit determined by the given situation
4. Interrelation of units[1]

Very similar to these elements are Alberty's principles descriptive of the nature of unit teaching:

1. Unit teaching recognizes that learning takes place most effectively in terms of wholes rather than fragments.
2. Unit teaching recognizes that learning takes place most effectively when there is an understanding and acceptance of goals to be achieved, and when there is full and free participation in planning for the attainment of these goals.
3. Unit teaching recognizes the necessity for providing for individual differences in rates of learning and interests.
4. Unit teaching provides a sound basis for evaluation.[2]

Morrison defined a learning unit as follows:

. . . we may define for our purposes, the external-things-to-be-learned as *learning units,* and further define a serviceable *learning unit* as a comprehensive and significant aspect of the environment, of an organized science, of an art, or of conduct, which being learned results in an adaptation of the personality.[3]

The definition offered by Jones, Grizzell, and Grinstead may be reduced to this:

The unit of learning consists of a group or chain of planned, coordinated activities undertaken by the learner in order to gain control over a type of life situation.[4]

In the current *Dictionary of Education,* two definitions of the unit are:

(1) A major subdivision of a course of study, a textbook, or a subject field, particularly a subdivision in the social studies, practical arts.
(2) An organization of various activities, experiences, and types of learning around a central theme, problem, or purpose, developed cooperatively by a group of pupils under teacher leadership; involves planning, execution of plans, and evaluation of results.[5]

The two concepts of the unit just quoted represent an attempt to discriminate between two major types of units—*subject-matter* and *experience* units.

[1] J. G. Umstattd, *Secondary School Teaching* (3d ed.). Boston: Ginn & Co., 1953), pp. 136–138.
[2] Harold Alberty, *Reorganizing the High-School Curriculum* (Rev. ed.) (New York: The Macmillan Co., 1953), pp. 242–245. See also third edition (1962).
[3] Henry C. Morrison, *The Practice of Teaching in the Secondary School* (Rev. ed.) (Chicago: University of Chicago Press, 1931), pp. 24–25.
[4] A. J. Jones, E. D. Grizzell, and W. J. Grinstead, *Principles of Unit Construction* (New York: McGraw-Hill Book Co., Inc., 1939), p. 19.
[5] Carter V. Good, *Dictionary of Education* (2d ed.) (New York: McGraw-Hill Book Co., Inc., 1959), p. 587.

Types of Units. There are various ways of classifying units by types. Mills and Douglass[6] classify units according to three bases, namely, scope, unifying element or principle, and persons involved in planning. For the sake of simplicity, also practicality, it is proposed to consider here only the subject-matter, experience, and resource units, together with a brief notice of the distinction between *teaching* and *learning* units.

The term *teaching unit* is roughly equivalent to Billett's *unit assignment*[7] and refers to the general plan of teacher-pupil activity, that is, it is the best sequence of such activities that can be formulated in advance. Of course, some parts of every teaching unit must await development until the teaching-learning process is actually going forward. Some authorities would limit the term *teaching unit* to that plan drawn up by an individual teacher. *Learning unit* is generally regarded as the organization of the learning activities and changes in the pupil in the form of concepts, skills, ideals, attitudes, or appreciations. Thus the distinction between teaching and learning units lies in the fact that one is in a sense external to the pupil whereas the other is associated with internal changes in the pupil resulting from learning experiences.

A *subject-matter unit* is usually regarded as "an arrangement of subject-matter materials around a central core found in the subject matter itself, to be studied by the pupil for the purpose of acquiring certain outcomes from mastery of the subject." On the other hand, an *experience unit* may be regarded as "a series of experiences organized around a pupil purpose . . . resulting in the achievement of the purpose and in the acquisition of learning outcomes inherent in the experience."[8]

Because of the inherent differences between the two types of units, preplanning and recording for subject-matter and experience units differ radically. A subject-matter unit can be planned rather definitely in advance, since subject matter is relatively fixed in nature. The record of such a unit might well be the written form of the preplanning, plus such annotations as are needed to indicate the adaptations of the plan as the unit was worked out. On the other hand, as Burton has pointed out, the so-called *log* of a unit of the experience type would more properly be a written account of the learning experience as it actually developed. It should be written up as the unit proceeds.

Contrasts have been drawn between the subject-matter and experience units, almost always unfavorably to the former. For example, it is said that the subject-matter unit begins in the intention of adults to teach

[6] Herbert H. Mills and Harl R. Douglass, *Teaching in High School* (2d ed.). (New York: The Ronald Press Co., 1957), p. 233.

[7] Roy O. Billett, *Fundamentals of Secondary-School Teaching* (Boston: Houghton Mifflin Co., 1940), p. 506.

[8] William H. Burton, *The Guidance of Learning Activities* (3d ed.). (New York: Appleton-Century-Crofts, Inc., 1962), Chap. 13.

approved subject matter, is controlled by the teacher, is centered in the past, has fixed outcomes, and is done with when finished. In sharp contrast, the experience unit begins in the intention of the student to achieve some purpose, is controlled by a cooperating group, is centered in the present, is not confined to outcomes known in advance, and leads to new interests, problems, and purposes. In the face of all this, it requires some courage to remind the reader that the subject-matter unit, in spite of all its apparent shortcomings, still has a legitimate function to perform in large-unit procedures. The illustrations of units that are given in writings about the unit are usually of the experience type. Those from areas where units will necessarily be mostly of the subject-matter type are few and far between. Mathematics is a case in point here.

ADVANTAGES AND DISADVANTAGES OF THE LARGE-UNIT PLAN

Advantages of the Large-Unit Organization. One of the most obvious of the advantages accruing from the use of large units in teaching stems from the fact that it might make possible, and even probable, highly desirable changes in the nature of the class or group activities. Large-unit procedures provide the setting for more natural, functional, and effective types of group activities. For example, at the beginning of a new unit, a visitor might observe such actions as these:

1. The class chairman asks for announcements.
2. The chairman points out that the group completed summaries and evaluations of their previous unit activities at the last session and should today make plans for their next unit.
3. The chairman leads a discussion of possible problems related to the subject (or core theme) that might be attacked; the secretary records on the board the various suggestions made by the class; and the teacher from time to time comments on the appropriateness of the suggestions.
4. The list of possibilities is reduced by group agreement to three; and a committee for each is organized to report back at the next meeting on the possibility of studying the problems.
5. The teacher suggests some sources that the committees and others might consult in investigating the possibilities of each problem, and suggests certain related questions for the committees to consider.
6. Plans are made by the committees as to a time and place for getting together, and for preliminary investigations to be made by each committee member.[9]

This is certainly in sharp contrast to experiences that come by way of a traditional recitation. If teaching by means of large units will help in

[9] G. Saylor and W. M. Alexander, *Curriculum Planning* (New York: Holt, Rinehart & Winston, Inc., 1954), p. 426.

bringing about this one improvement, certainly it will have earned much commendation.

Most of the advantages that can be mentioned specifically are involved, directly or indirectly, in the more comprehenisve changes in the nature of the class activities, as described above. Among these additional advantages, the following may be listed:

1. It is easier to make adaptations to individual differences.
2. The stage is set for more extensive and better teacher-pupil planning.
3. The large-unit plan stimulates the development of pupil initiative.
4. This plan should help to use a variety of educative procedures such as individual research, silent study, and group activity. Also, it should be easier to change from one type of procedure to another as circumstances require.

Disadvantages of the Large-Unit Organization. The disadvantages of the large-unit plan are mostly in the form of difficulties encountered in carrying on schoolwork in this manner. From a practical and realistic viewpoint, the greatest of these difficulties lies in the fact that so many teachers neither have been trained nor have had experience in this type of teaching and learning. There are other difficulties and obstacles in the way of free use of large units. Some of the most important and persistent of these are shown in the following list:

1. The block of time needed for effective work on a unit may not be available. This is a schedule limitation that does not always yield readily to adjustment measures.
2. Inelastic course syllabuses may impede efforts to instal a unit plan.
3. Work on a unit may be affected adversely by demands on the time of students from other sources. A high degree of teamwork and cooperation among staff members is necessary to resolve this difficulty.
4. The teacher may lose the daily check upon achievement and progress of the individual pupil.

Hansen points out the following "pitfalls" in unit-plan teaching:

1. Uncritical adoption of unit planning
2. Failure to utilize other teaching methods
3. Using only one kind of unit organization
4. Teacher domination
5. The unit as a divisive force
6. The inherited unit
7. The stereotyped unit
8. The unnecessary unit[10]

[10] Kenneth H. Hansen, *High School Teaching* (Englewood Cliffs, N.J.: Prentice-Hall, Inc., 1957), pp. 158–162.

CHARACTERISTICS OF A GOOD UNIT

As to the desirable characteristics of large units, two sets of items are presented here. Each set represents the results of composite opinions of groups. In the first instance, writings from seven sources were consulted with a view to ascertaining the consensus as to the valid features of effective units. It seems that the opinions of these writers are typical and, hence, represent a good sample. If this is true, the characteristics identified in this survey of the literature should be of value to those who are responsible for the success of the unit plan in any situation.[11] Those unit characteristics mentioned by the writers, together with the frequencies of mention for each characteristic, are shown in Table 12–1.

TABLE 12–1

FREQUENCY OF MENTION BY SEVEN WRITERS OF CHARACTERISTICS OF A GOOD UNIT

Characteristic	Frequency of Mention
1. The unit is unified	3
2. The unit is organized around purposes of the student	3
3. The unit provides places of beginning and ending	1
4. The learning activities of the unit are significant	6
5. The unit is comprehensive	4
6. The unit is practicable for pupil attack	6
7. The unit provides a variety of activities	7
8. The unit involves full teacher-pupil cooperation	5
9. The unit provides the basis for its evaluation	3
10. A good unit stimulates further action	7

An even more comprehensive list of desirable characteristics of a good unit is quoted below from Mills and Douglass. The items in this list were formulated by a group of junior high school teachers. Specific reference is to a good teaching unit.

1. The teaching unit should have a useful purpose.
2. It should reproduce actual life situations as nearly as possible.
3. It should utilize materials as they occur in life.
4. It should involve a variety of direct sense experiences.
5. It should provide a considerable amount of pupil activities.
6. It should provide for some free, informal associations of the pupils.
7. It should provide a good opportunity for the pupil to originate, plan, and direct an activity.
8. It should make an opportunity for manipulative or physical activity.
9. It should provide opportunity to judge, choose, and evaluate.

[11] Nelson L. Bossing, *Teaching in Secondary Schools* (Boston: Houghton Mifflin Co., 1952), pp. 63–71.

10. It should contain accurate information.
11. It should be possible to complete within the time available for the unit.
12. The exposition should be clear for a new teacher to reproduce the experiences of the unit.
13. It should state exactly where materials may be obtained.
14. When references are given, they should be complete and exact.[12]

PREPLANNING A UNIT

The Scope of Preplanning. There should be just enough preplanning to avoid, on the one hand, loss of time and effort through lack of *direction* and, on the other hand, to steer clear of that crippling condition that comes from placing everything connected with the unit in a predetermined groove from beginning to end. This is a general and not very practical way to describe the scope of preplanning. In other words, as the mathematician would say, this basic and comprehensive statement is *necessary* but it is not *sufficient*.

What is to be included in preplanning parallels roughly the so-called steps by which a unit is developed. First and foremost, the area with which the unit is to deal must be selected. Two or three possible areas may well be submitted to the class for their reactions. In order to do this properly, whoever is doing the selecting must have a clear idea as to the general objectives to be attained in this particular setting. He or she will have to know the place in this setting that has been assigned to the course of which the unit is a part. Also necessary is a thorough knowledge of the individuals for whom the unit is intended. This last prerequisite alone demands much from the teacher; it is a task that is only partially done or is left completely undone in far too many cases.

A tentative statement of objectives is essential. The general objectives of education may need to be recalled; they form the background into which the unit must fit. Goals for the class as a whole and for the individuals that compose it will be needed to round out the "hierarchy of aims," extending from the most general to the most particular. Sometimes it is helpful to state the objectives both from the teacher's viewpoint and from that of the student.

Next in order in the preplanning process comes the list of experiences. As far as possible, this should consist of a series of pupil activities, "things to do," arranged in a sequence that seems to be natural and reasonable. A little later, it will be seen that these activities can be classified into three categories: initiatory, developmental, and culminating. If there is a task in planning a unit that is more important than any other, surely it is this one of choosing the unit activities. They must be challenging to the students; they must be fitted into the students' interests

[12] Mills and Douglass, *op. cit.*, pp. 243–244.

and ability levels; and they must produce learning outcomes that move the students, individually and collectively, from a starting point to the goals formulated and accepted, in the last analysis, by the students themselves.

Aids for those selecting unit activities are available from various sources. Typical of these is the list of types of activities drawn up by a Wisconsin planning group.

1. Research-type activities. (Reading, interviewing, listening to the radio, viewing television, seeing motion pictures, other visual aids)
2. Presentation-type activities. (Reports, panels and round-table discussions, showing of visual aids, making graphs and charts)
3. Creative expression activities. (Handwork, drawing pictures, writing stories, plays and poems, singing and playing music)
4. Drill activities. (Used when students in the group encounter obstacles to further progress. For example, a high school group working on a tax problem might find it needed a review and drill of certain parts of arithmetic)
5. Appreciation activities. (Listening to music, reading for fun, looking at pictures)
6. Observation and listening activities. (Sharpening the senses of the pupils as an aid to learning)
7. Group cooperative activities. (Training in democratic group procedures, division of labor among groups leading to cooperation in carrying out plans)
8. Experimentation. (Learning to try out new ways of doing things, laboratory work, with emphasis on equipment the pupils can make as well as more elaborate types of equipment)
9. Organizing and evaluating activities. (Discriminating among and selecting, ordering, and appraising the types of work done by themselves)[13]

Cooperation in Planning. One prominent feature of work with large units is increased student participation. In no part of the work is this more important than in planning. If a student has had a real part in planning a unit, he is much more likely to be strongly motivated to do his part of the work, and all of the experiences of the unit will be more meaningful and significant for him. Nothing that has been said above should be construed to mean that only the teacher is to plan or preplan. In fact, this phase of the unit, labeled *preplanning* here, is sometimes referred to as a *preparatory* activity. This latter terms probably brings out more clearly the fact that preplanning, or preparatory, activities constitute a definite and integral part of the unit, in the development of which everybody concerned should take a hand. It is in this sense that the term *preplanning* is conceived and used here.

[13] Wisconsin Cooperative Educational Planning Program, *Resource Units in the Curriculum Program,* Bulletin No. 5 (Madison, Wis.: State Department of Public Instruction, 1945), pp. 8–9.

GUIDING UNIT ACTIVITIES

Teacher Responsibility. It was stated above that even the planning of a unit is a complex task, especially if students are allowed to help in the planning and if their changing needs are to be kept in mind. If this is true of planning, it is doubly true of guiding the unit activities once these activities are in full swing. One might even say that, in a moving unit that is developing lustily, the teacher needs to be as active, versatile, and ingenious as a ringmaster in a circus. Especially must he be alert and sensitive to the *timing* of his efforts and attention. He should give help and encouragement at the exact moments they are needed, and he must know when to withhold help and how to do so without giving offense. All of this and much more must be done while the class is busy, as individuals and as small groups, on a variety of subtasks, all of which must be in line with the over-all objectives.

In this connection, Burton stresses the teacher's responsibility for the best use of learning activities, particularly for the maintenance of good order during the work period. In order to accomplish this, he points out that the teacher will:

1. Guide the group during the planning period to develop plans which are so definite and so clear that all know what to do and how to do it.
2. Check with individuals and committees before they disperse for work to see that the more detailed plans are definite and clear.
3. Anticipate difficulties in carrying out plans as made and be ready to call a group conference when the difficulty occurs and before discouragement and work stoppage can result in disorder.
4. Guide during the planning period so that sufficient work is outlined to keep all individuals and groups busy over a reasonably long period of time. Replanning will keep the sequence going so that lack of work does not cause disorder.
5. Call for replanning conferences as work develops unevenly. Workers may be assigned again and activities redistributed.
6. Keep in touch with the varied activities by moving from group to group, by participating, by asking questions, by making suggestions, thus exercising both guidance and control.
7. Foresee certain common opportunities for disorder and will forestall them by developing with the pupils regular routines:
   a. For having materials, tools, and supplies ready before need for them arises.
   b. For distributing materials, tools, and supplies, books, papers quickly and in an orderly manner.
   c. For using reference materials, particularly when many pupils wish to consult an inadequate number of references.
   d. For holding conferences with individual children who need help.
   e. For using as helpers any individuals who may for any reason be unoccupied for a time.

    f. For moving groups, for observing groups, without crowding or
jostling.
8. Introduce new activities to small groups directly concerned so that tryout will be without the confusion which might result from misunderstanding within a large group and from too many persons trying a new
process without sufficient guidance.
9. Give constantly, direct and indirect training in the conventions and
routine of group work: taking turns, not interrupting, turning to some
other aspect of the work instead of standing around waiting for tools
or materials in use elsewhere, signing in and out for tools and materials.
10. Develop with the pupils flexible plans for their own activities: budget-
ting time, scheduling [sic] group conferences, announcing time for
individual conferences, etc.
11. Develop constantly, directly and indirectly, the understanding that
freedom carries responsibility, and that self-control and cooperation are
advantageous to the pupils themselves and not something required by
the school.[14]

The Stages of a Unit. There are various ways of labeling the stages by
which a unit is developed. Umstattd lists as the steps involved introduction and attack, study and work, integration and application, and
appraisal of outcome.[15] Bossing also identifies four steps in the development of the unit: initiation of the unit, planning the unit study, guiding
the work activities, and evaluating unit success.[16] Terminology used by
other writers shows variation as to the vocabulary but very little as to the
basic ideas concerning the essential steps in the development of a unit.

There is much to say for the plan of considering the activities of a unit
as falling into three categories, namely, initiatory, developmental, and
culminating. These three descriptive terms refer to the stages of unit
development in which the various activities play their parts. Let it be
supposed that a civics class is studying the elements of community welfare, *communications* in particular. A much used and effective treatment
of such a topic (unit) is (1) to approach the topic, then (2) to study the
agencies of communication in the community, and, finally, (3) to identify
and illustrate the responsibilities of the citizen in this matter of community communications as a means of promoting the highest type of
community life.

Initiatory Activities. A considerable number of excellent discussions of
initiatory, developmental, and culminating activities for the unit are to
be found in more elaborate treatments of large-unit teaching than is
possible here, and the reader is referred to these for further details. The
initiatory activities may include pretesting and other means of studying

[14] Burton, *op. cit.* (1st ed.), pp. 292–293.
[15] Umstattd, *op. cit.,* Chap. 9.
[16] Bossing, *op. cit.,* pp. 84–91.

the backgrounds of pupils, approaching the unit, motivating the unit, marking out the scope and understanding the significance of the unit, and working out a unit assignment that has the requisite degree of flexibility. Klausmeier considers the following activities in this connection:

Cooperative student-teacher activities
　Focussing attention
　Formulating group objectives
　Developing procedures for engaging in and carrying out activities
　Formulating individual objectives

Teacher-oriented activities
　Learning to know each student as an individual
　Learning the characteristics of the group
　Building a good emotional atmosphere[17]

This is a process, then, of setting the stage for working through the unit, completing the planning, and actually beginning some of the work. In other words, it is "getting started."

Developmental Activities. Activities of the sort usually referred to as *developmental* should serve as the heart and core of the unit. Included here should be as many as time will allow of "things to do" for students, with emphasis on the *doing*. The work at this stage will gain in effectiveness by moving as close as possible to procedures in the original *projects* in vocational agriculture, for instance, wherein purposeful physical activity was given priority. Developmental tasks should be tangible, practical, feasible, and definitely not mere busy work. Entitled to places among the activities should be research of all kinds, committee work in all of its phases, use of teaching and learning aids, reports, excursions, use of guest speakers, and even broader use of community resources. Fortunate is the group or class working on a teaching unit if there is a resource unit available for the same area. In such a case, there will be at hand a rich store of suggested activities, many of which will be adaptable to the special conditions prevailing in the teaching unit. It often happens that time runs out before the possibilities of the developmental activities have been exhausted.

Culminating Activities. In this category are often included at least certain aspects of evaluation. In this, as in other rounding-out activities, the student should be led to play a leading role. Summaries of what has been gained from the unit may be made and presented to the class by individuals or by panels. Conclusions and generalizations are certainly

[17] Herbert J. Klausmeier, *Principles and Practices of Secondary School Teaching* (New York: Harper & Row, 1958), Chap. 7.

in order at this point. Additional and appropriate culminating activities are listed by Mills and Douglass:

1. An exhibit of picture, poster, graph, and pamphlet materials collected for the unit.
2. A "quiz" program as a means of reviewing basic understandings.
3. Presentation by each pupil of a paper revealing his reactions and opinions developed from study of the unit.
4. Committee preparation of an assembly program for presentation by the class to the entire school in the form of a short play, a panel discussion, or a radio program.
5. Review of films used during the developmental period in order to clinch important understandings.
6. Class presentation of a summary of the unit.
7. A final test of basic understandings, attitudes, and interests similar to the test given in the preparatory period.
8. Observation and recording of changes in pupil behavior and improvement in skills and habits in the form of anecdotes set down by the teacher.
9. Pupil evaluation of their own progress in methods of study, initiative, attitudes, profitable use of time, and the like, prepared in the form of check lists.
10. Cooperative appraisal of pupils' diaries and reading records covering the unit period.
11. A final test of basic knowledge and skills.[18]

Unit Evaluation. It should be kept in mind, however, that evaluation is inevitably taking place at all stages of the unit. The choice of the unit in the beginning calls for consideration of the relative merits of several possible units. The unit finally selected in a cooperative manner should be weighed and judged in the light of a list of characteristics that are essential for any good unit. Choice of materials, tools, and aids always brings up the question as to which of these that are available are the *best* under the circumstances. Deciding wisely upon what procedures to follow requires a fine sense of discrimination in order to identify the plan that will be productive of maximum progress in the work of the unit.

Formal tests may be of any type—essay, objective, or some other type. In addition to being assigned these tests, students may be led to do real evaluating by being helped to formulate and consider critically such questions as

1. What can we do about the problems raised in the unit? What further action is indicated?
2. How would we change our procedures if we were to do the unit again?
3. Do we regret the way we spent the time allotted to the unit?

[18] Mills and Douglass, *op. cit.*, p. 251.

Above all, perhaps, it should be kept in mind that evaluation should be done cooperatively rather than by the teacher alone, that evaluation is not merely a post-mortem, that emphasis should be placed on desirable changes brought about in the students, and that the final test of the success of a unit lies in the answer to the question as to whether the accepted goals have been reached.

THE RESOURCE UNIT

What a Resource Unit Is. The preparation and use of resource units probably constitute one of the most effective procedures for advance curriculum planning by a group of teachers. It is a procedure that can definitely be translated into desirable learning experiences.[19] In his intensive "case study" investigations, Klohr[20] found that the use of resource units in secondary schools tends to promote unit teaching and wider teacher-pupil planning, that resource units may be used to enrich and vitalize teaching in one field or in cases where projects cut across several fields, that the development of resource units in a secondary school constitutes a significant step in curriculum reorganization procedure, and that the cooperative development of resource units provides many opportunities for in-service growth of the staff.

The resource unit is well defined by Klohr as follows:

The resource unit may be defined in this study as a carefully planned series of suggestions centered in some problem, topic, or area of experience and organized to serve as a source of ideas, materials, and procedures to help a teacher in planning a learning unit.[21]

This definition serves to distinguish the resource unit from the teaching or learning unit. One is general, the other is specific. Resource units are comprehensive enough to be of benefit to any class or group that might be studying the topic or problem involved. The teaching unit is designed, planned, and carried out for a particular group or class. For the teaching unit, there will be selected from the resource unit's collection those elements that suit the particular group pursuing study of the unit. The relationship between the two types of units is similar to that existing between a very complete, compendium type of textbook and those parts of the textbook used by a teacher in teaching a particular class. The textbook contains more material than any one teacher or class could possibly need or use. It is a collection, a storehouse, of ideas, subject matter, and experiments and other suggested activities. From this collec-

---

[19] Saylor and Alexander, *op. cit.*, p. 402.
[20] Paul R. Klohr, "The Resource Unit in Curriculum Reorganization," *Bulletin of the National Association of Secondary School Principals* (May, 1950), p. 76.
[21] *Ibid.*, p. 74.

tion, each class may select those parts that are usable; another class might make selections that are quite different in many respects.

What a Resource Unit Contains. Speaking generally, Saylor and Alexander indicate that the following are usually included in a resource unit:

1. Explanation of the unit problem
2. Statement of learning outcomes expected
3. Outline of subject matter appropriate to the problems and types being studied (problems, questions, content, etc.)
4. Suggested learning experiences and resources
5. Suggested evaluation procedures[22]

Klohr studied the resource units used in twenty-six junior and senior high schools in five geographical areas and found the following common elements in those units that were judged to be effective:

1. A wealth of suggested learning experiences
2. A survey of possible ways to evaluate the suggested learning experiences
3. A carefully selected bibliography and list of teaching aids
4. A stimulating presentation of the scope of the problem area with which the unit deals
5. A formulation of the philosophy underlying the resource unit and a statement of the specific objectives
6. Suggestions to the teacher for using the resource unit.[23]

Included also was a statement as to the grade level, subject areas involved, and, in general, the situations in which the unit might be most effective. The exhaustive list of teaching-learning aids is usually of maximum help to the teachers who may be looking to the resource unit for ways of locating and actually obtaining the aids needed. Learning outcomes may include attitudes, concepts, skills, and understanding. Learning experiences or activities may be classified in various ways. One classification widely used is that suggested above for the teaching unit, namely, initiatory, developmental, and culminating activities. Suggestions for evaluation should include group and individual evaluations done by pupils, as well as those that can be done by the teacher.

Constructing Resource Units. Making of resource units is strictly preplanning and is a job for adults. For the word "adults" one might substitute "teachers" if the latter word is defined as including teachers at all levels, as well as administrators and supervisors. Resource units may be constructed by the following:

1. Individual teachers
   a. Revamping, expanding, elaborating a unit that has been taught
   b. Anticipating the need for a resource unit for a certain topic or problem

[22] Saylor and Alexander, *op. cit.,* p. 404.
[23] Klohr, *op. cit.,* pp. 76–77.

2. Groups of teachers on the job
   a. In the same school system and in the same subject area
   b. In the same school system and in different subject areas
   c. In neighboring school systems and according to plans arranged by high-level administrators
3. Workshops or work conferences under the auspices of colleges, mostly in summer sessions.

Workshops or work conferences have been responsible for some of the very best resource units. Experienced teachers usually make up the personnel of such groups, and their efforts are well coordinated by members of college staffs. Units coming from such situations are often very complete and useful. For example, one on the subject of insurance for the ninth-grade level can be used in mathematics, social studies, or junior business training, so exhaustive is the coverage of all aspects of the general subject treated.

The National Association of Secondary School Principals and the Council for the Social Studies Program have pioneered a movement to make resource units available for use in classrooms throughout the country. Many school systems and college libraries now have impressive collections of these units; such collections should prove helpful to those interested in better teaching.

QUESTIONS, PROBLEMS, AND ISSUES FOR FURTHER THOUGHT

1. What kinds of records of teaching and learning activities should be kept from day to day? How can one make sure that such records are kept?
2. Discuss in some detail just how you would go about using a resource unit to develop a teaching unit.
3. What part do daily lesson plans play in developing a unit?
4. Describe the activities of any one of several committees that might be set up and activated in carrying out the work of a unit.
5. A panel discussion: "How preplanning may differ for subject-matter and experience units."
6. In what ways do evaluation techniques for traditional teaching differ from those for an experience unit?
7. Outline a plan for training prospective teachers to make fullest use of the unit plan in their teaching in secondary schools.
8. Prepare a check list of fifteen to twenty items for evaluating the adequacy of a unit that has just been developed with a class.
9. What is the value of pupil cooperation in the planning of a unit? Show how you would provide an opportunity for such cooperation.
10. Criticize and evaluate the discussion in this chapter of advantages and disadvantages of the unit plan.
11. Is it possible for pupils' evaluations of a unit to be worthwhile? Make out a form for such evaluation.

12. Can units planned cooperatively by teachers and pupils be prepared for in advance by the teacher? Give reasons for your position on this question.

SUPPLEMENTARY MATERIALS

SELECTED READINGS

ALEXANDER, WILLIAM M., and PAUL M. HALVERSON. *Effective Teaching in Secondary Schools.* New York: Holt, Rinehart & Winston, Inc., 1956. Chapters 14–15. Contrast of long-term with daily planning, involving use of large units.

ALM, RICHARD S. "What Is a Good Unit in English?" *English Journal,* XLIX (September, 1960), 395–99. Assumes desirability of unit teaching. Seven criteria for evaluation of units.

BENNETT, ROBERT A. "Unit Ideas for the New School Year," *English Journal,* XLIX (September, 1960), 400–408. Framework for units in English, grades seven through twelve. Examples of suitable subjects for units.

BOHN, R. C. "Place of the Project in the Industrial Arts," *American Vocational Journal,* XXXIV (December, 1959), 18–24.

BOSSING, NELSON L. *Teaching in Secondary Schools* (3d ed.). Boston: Houghton Mifflin Co., 1952. Chapter 2, "How Develop Units?"

BURTON, WILLIAM H. *The Guidance of Learning Activities* (3d ed.). New York: Appleton-Century-Crofts, Inc., 1962. Chapters 13–14. Principles of using units in organizing the setting of learning.

CLARK, LEONARD H., and IRVING S. STARR. *Secondary School Teaching Methods.* New York: The Macmillan Co., 1959. Chapter 5, "The Unit." Special emphasis on planning objectives, study procedures, and activity guides.

FRIEDMAN, K. C. "Using Curriculum Guides," *Education,* LXXXII (December, 1961), 215–17. Justification for unit organization of the curriculum and some principles to govern choice and development of units.

GRAMBS, JEAN D., W. J. IVERSON, FRANKLIN K. PATTERSON. *Modern Methods in Secondary Education* (rev. ed.). New York: Holt, Rinehart & Winston, Inc., 1958. Chapter 6. Use of the unit in the planning process.

HANSEN, KENNETH H. *High School Teaching.* Englewood Cliffs, N.J.: Prentice-Hall, Inc., 1957. Chapter 6. Organizing learning by wholes.

HENNIS, R. S. "Broad Unit Approach to Literature," *High School Journal,* XLV (February, 1962), 201–7. Presents a good case for grouping study of literature around broad units such as "Propaganda" or "Dictatorships." Also analyzes the basic divisions of such units.

KLAUSMEIER, HERBERT J. *Principles and Practices of Secondary School Teaching.* New York: Harper & Row, 1958. Chapters 6–8 deal with planning the unit and organizing and directing activities.

McKEAN, ROBERT C. *Principles and Methods in Secondary Education.* Columbus, Ohio: Charles E. Merrill Books, Inc., 1962. Chapter 5. Planning classroom experiences; liberal use of units.

MILLS, HUBERT H., and HARL R. DOUGLASS. *Teaching in High School* (2d ed.). New York: The Ronald Press Co., 1957. Chapters 11, 14. Planning and teaching instructional units.

RISK, THOMAS M. *Principles and Practices of Teaching in Secondary Schools* (3d ed.). New York: American Book Co., 1958. Chapter 11. Featuring the introduction, development, and culmination of the unit.

ROMINE, STEPHEN A. *Building the High School Curriculum*. New York: The
    Ronald Press Co., 1954. Chapters 9–11. Stresses values derived from use
    of large units, also actual building of resource and instructional units.
SAYLOR, J. G., and WILLIAM M. ALEXANDER. *Curriculum Planning*. New York:
    Holt, Rinehart & Winston, Inc., 1954. Chapter 12. Analysis and classifica-
    tion of units.
UMSTATTD, J. G. *Secondary School Teaching* (3d ed.). Boston: Ginn & Co.,
    1953. Chapters 6–8. Development of the unit idea, features of eight unit
    plans, cooperatively planned learning process, integration and elaboration
    of unit procedures.
WILLERDING, MARGARET F. "Teaching Unit in Modular Arithmetic," *School
    Science and Mathematics*, LX (October, 1960), 511–18. Adequate content
    and procedures for presenting the modular number system to junior high
    school pupils. Includes assignments for students and a short-answer test to
    evaluate outcomes of the unit.

13

The Evolving Core Curriculum

Since its beginnings in the 1930's, the core curriculum has been lauded, criticized, reviled, and revered. At times it has furnished a convenient scapegoat for the shortcomings of education. It has been without a doubt a highly controversial plan that, on the one hand, has appealed to creative teachers and, on the other, has caused school systems to drop the use of either the plan or the term.

The core grew out of a vigorous period of experimentation in secondary education, sparked by the eight-year experimental study of the Progressive Education Association's Commission on the Relation of School and College, begun in 1932. Continued experimentation with the core and healthy differences of opinion concerning its meaning and implementation have been among its strengths. Attempts to make a core the final answer have slowed down its development, as have other factors discussed in this chapter. Its vigor is in its experimental approach.

What is the core curriculum? To what extent is it found in secondary schools? What evaluation has been made of its effectiveness? How is a core program organized? What are the issues and problems involved? What is its future? How is it related to the most recent lively developments in the secondary school curriculum? These are the questions discussed in this chapter.

CONCEPTS AND CHARACTERISTICS OF THE CORE

Meaning of the Core Curriculum. Some authors have used the term *core* to designate all of the common experiences that pupils ought to have in the curriculum as the required subjects. Some have used it to apply to both the elementary and the secondary school. Common usage, however, refers to the core in connection with the secondary school only. The term *common learnings* more accurately designates those experiences in the high school curriculum that all pupils should have, that is, the general education essential for all, which may include a core program.

The core curriculum is a way of organizing some of the important common learnings in the high school curriculum, using a problem-solving approach as its procedure, having social and personal problems significant to youth and society as its content, and focusing upon the development of behaviors needed in a democratic society as its purpose.

Although one of the core's distinguishing characteristics is a longer block of time than the typical school period, a block of time does not guarantee a core program. Instead, this concept represents a fundamental reorganization of a portion of the general-education phases of the secondary school curriculum, in an attempt to give pupils an experience in democratic living. In its very nature the core exemplifies a revolt against extreme compartmentalization of subject matter. Moreover, it typifies the concern for the total development of the pupil toward acceptable social behavior.

Schools use various labels to designate classes partaking more or less of the nature of "core," such as "common learnings," "general education," "social living," "unified studies," "integrated English-social studies," and "block-time" classes. These classes may have many or few of the characteristics of the core. The same is true of classes labeled as "core." As some authors have pointed out, there is a distinct difference between many of these terms, if they are used in a precise manner.[1]

Characteristics of the Core Program. The core can best be defined by describing its characteristics. The Albertys delineate five types of core programs that possess these characteristics in varying degrees, from one that differs little from the separate-subject-matter organization to the extreme experience-centered type.[2] The type used would vary from teacher to teacher within the same school.

The characteristics discussed below are not peculiar to the core, but, taken together, they essentially distinguish what is known as the core curriculum. Generally, core classes listed in different studies of types or trends would have a number of these characteristics:

1. *The core curriculum utilizes an experience-centered approach to curriculum development.* The emphasis is on the type of experience that

[1] William Van Til, Gordon F. Vars, and John H. Lounsbury, *Modern Education for the Junior High School Years* (Indianapolis: The Bobbs-Merrill Co., Inc., 1961), pp. 92–104.

[2] Harold B. Alberty and Elsie J. Alberty, *Reorganizing the High-School Curriculum* (3d ed.) (New York: The Macmillan Co., 1962), pp. 204–230.

a pupil has in order to change his behavior in socially desirable ways. The subject matter is used as a means to an end, to promote the desired changes in behavior. Both ends and means are flexible; thus, there are no minimum essentials, since learning is considered to have no limits except as determined by the pupil's psychological and mental development. The teacher's focus is on the quality of the experience that the pupil has with subject matter of significance, with books, with people, and with his immediate and larger community. Many of the characteristics of the core are also those of the experience-centered approach.[3]

2. *The change of behavior with which the core is concerned centers on growth necessary to function as an effective citizen in a democracy.* The student has specifically planned experiences that will help him to analyze and clarify the values that he holds. Thus, he deals with his own judgments about social questions, his own and his group's social and personal goals, and his point of view about important issues in his social world. That world is composed of such things as the "Munichs," "Cubas," and "Little Rocks," as well as the decisions made in his own community and school with regard to integration, school bonds, and destruction of school property by vandals.

When the pupil's values are admitted to the classroom for examination, conflicts and positions of sharply controversial nature are bound to be discussed. The classroom is not a "safe" place where teachers and pupils look only at some other nation's or community's concerns. They examine facts that relate to points of view. Modification of beliefs on the basis of analysis and evidence instead of emotion and prejudice is the desired result. The skills necessary for democratic citizenship, including those needed for intelligent communication, are practiced.

3. *The basic class procedure is problem-solving.* When pupils and teacher deal with values and social conflict, they are tackling problems of social and personal concern. Problems center on issues, since there are no convenient answers to social questions. What do others think about the question? What facts are available to arrive at an intelligent solution? What facts and arguments do groups that take a radical position have as a basis for their decision?

These are the kinds of questions that matter as pupils deal with social problems. Techniques of defining a problem, developing possible solutions, gathering data concerning the proposed solutions, examining the issues in light of the facts, and arriving at some conclusion or course of action are used. Thus, the pupil has experience in dealing with social conflict and arriving at reasonable judgments.

[3] See Vernon E. Anderson, *Principles and Procedures of Curriculum Improvement* (New York: The Ronald Press Co., 1956), pp. 74–81, for a discussion of these characteristics.

Effective study of problems can be accomplished with a prestructured plan of problem areas as well as with one lacking such a structure. The important point is that the pupils and teacher have an opportunity to define and select problems within this broader scope.

4. *Content is drawn from social and personal problem areas considered as significant phases of general education.* The kind of problem, of a social and personal nature, also lending itself to learning language-arts skills, is illustrated by these problem areas suggested in different curriculum guides for core programs: Living in the School, Finding Values by Which We Live, Communicating in the Contemporary World, Dealing with Intercultural Relations, Building Better Home and Family Life, Conserving Natural Resources, Understanding Teen-age Youth, Maintaining Health, Understanding Democracy and Communism, Achieving World Peace in an Atomic Age.

Problems developed in core classes as units for study are illustrated by the following: Problems Facing American Education in the State or Community, Orientation to the New School, Problems of Race Conflict, Propaganda and the Media of Mass Communication, The Selection of a Vocation, The Common Market and the World's Goods, Industries and Their Contributions to the Economy of This Area, The Economic and Social Problems of the Region, Formation of Public Opinion in an Election.

Obviously, these problems, as well as any that could be named, could be studied to varying degrees of depth or superficially. They represent significant social and personal problems for the general education of all. However, the teacher can either make them come alive for pupils so that they see how these problems affect their lives or merely skim the surface, never getting into the issues or questions involved.

5. *The subject matter of the core cuts across subject boundaries.* When problems form the basic organization for content, a class can no longer be easily categorized as in the area of social studies, science, or English. The teacher and pupils use content from any area that will help solve the problem. Art and industrial arts skills, mathematics skills, English skills, and science information may all be needed to plan, develop, and solve a problem of a social nature. The literature of the period, or about the topic, may throw further light on it.

English and social studies are the subject areas most frequently drawn upon. In about 90 per cent of the cases, they represent the subjects combined to make up the core. Science and mathematics rank next in frequency. Although arts, crafts, and music activities frequently enter into core units, those subjects are rarely displaced by the core. However, a core program goes further than a combination of two or more subjects, as in indicated by other characteristics discussed here.

6. *Skills are taught as needed.* When pupils develop a problem, they need to know how to organize, outline, make generalizations. In the solving of a problem, books are read, letters written, people interviewed, new vocabulary learned, reports made, sampling techniques used, graphs and charts made, library research done, notes taken, and ideas developed and organized. Each of these represents an important communication skill. Arriving at a solution involves finding facts, weighing factual information against propaganda, discussing, debating issues, evaluating findings, summarizing, and making reports. The alert teacher in a core class sees that these skills are taught in relation to their use.

In addition, drill of any kind need of which is shown by pupils' mistakes in spelling, usage, or sentence structure is a part of the instruction in the core. Such skills are not left to be developed incidentally.

7. *Teacher-pupil planning is used.* While the problem areas may be structured ahead of time, and most frequently are, no external decisions are made for the teacher with regard to the specific content, the activities of the class, the minimum essentials, or the solutions to be arrived at. The teacher plans with the pupils the specific problem to be studied, what data are needed, where they are to be found, and how the students will go about solving the problem. This procedure is a fundamental part of learning the skills of the democratic process.

8. *Provision is made for cooperative planning by teachers.* Schools have come to regard the planning period available for teachers to work together on the core curriculum as an essential feature of the program. Certainly, the cooperative planning by teachers concerned is necessary in an experience-centered approach. Moreover, if the core is the heart of the common experiences, core teachers need to work with teachers of other classes in order to provide for as much unification and common purpose as possible. Such planning gives other teachers an opportunity to contribute to the core from their specialities.

Planning may take the form of grade-level planning of a group of teachers who work with the same pupils. In such cases, the core teacher may be the the chairman of the group. At other times, core teachers of a certain grade level or for the three junior high school grades meet together. In these sessions, there is opportunity for continuous conference and study dealing with the nature of the educational experience, the sequence of the curriculum, and the problems of individual pupils.

9. *The core class is scheduled for a longer block of time than the single period.* This is perhaps the characteristic most common to core programs of various types. The typical time allotment is ten periods a week, but

a substantial proportion of core, or any block-time, classes uses a number of periods a week varying from ten to twenty,[4] depending upon the importance ascribed to the skills and concepts taught in the core or upon the number of subjects replaced by the core. The longer block of time provides opportunities for planning, library research, field trips, and summarizing activities.

10. *The guidance function is an integral part of the core.* The core teacher takes the place of the homeroom teacher; in fact, in a number of schools the homeroom period has been combined with other class periods to form the block of time for the core. For counseling purposes, the pupils in the core class are the special responsibility of the teacher. Since the teacher works with fewer pupils and over a longer period of time, he has the opportunity to get to know them better and to assist them with their personal problems. In some cases, core teachers follow the pupils through the two or three junior high school grades. In a number of instances, the teacher has only two core groups a day, a practice to be recommended, especially if the block-time period is more than 110 minutes.

Group guidance is well adapted for the core, since adolescent needs and problems are among its concerns. "Orientation to My School" and "My Future Vocation" are core units that represent what is ordinarily done in a homeroom. Core teachers carry the responsibility for group and individual guidance in the majority of schools.[5]

11. *The core class includes pupils of various abilities.* One type of experience essential for a democratic society is learning to live in a social situation with others who differ in abilities, social status, race, or vocational objectives.

A common practice in successful core classes is the use of relatively small groups within the class to do research on various aspects of the problems under study. The teacher provides for grouping and for individual work on the basis of interests and abilities, utilizing the potentialities and special abilities of each student. The very nature of this approach (and the time element in the core, which gives the teacher more time to work with individuals and groups) makes the artificial grouping into classes or curriculums unnecessary to teachers who are skilled at taking care of individual differences within a group. The bright, the creative, the less able, and the underachievers all may receive more help and may be enabled to progress at the speed appropriate for the individual.

[4] Grace S. Wright, *Block-Time Classes and the Core Program in the Junior High School,* U.S. Office of Education, Bulletin 1958, No. 6, Washington, D.C.: Government Printing Office, 1958, p. 23; Norman Ward Wilson, *Block-Time Programs in Junior High Schools and Six-Year Secondary Schools of New York State* (Ithaca, N.Y.: Cornell University Junior High School Project, 1962), p. 5.

[5] Wright, *op. cit.,* p. 51.

Trends in Core Development. Any attempt to show the extent of core development is complicated by the many variations in the core and by the loose definition of what constitutes core-type classes. Most of the studies include any block-time type of classes rather than just those that follow the basic concepts of the core.

The most extensive studies were made by Wright, through the U.S. Office of Education. According to her first study, conducted in 1949, 3.5 per cent of all public secondary schools and 9.7 per cent of junior and junior-senior high schools had core classes, reported as those that combined two or more class periods from subjects that would ordinarily be taught separately.[6] A follow-up study in 1956, seven years later, found that 19.3 per cent, or more than twice as many, of the representative sampling of junior and junior-senior high schools had block-time classes. Of schools reporting block-time classes, only 12 per cent had an experience-centered-type core built around problem areas,[7] a considerable percentage decrease from the earlier study, when 42.8 per cent of the schools reported the use of the experience-centered type of core in some of their classes.[8] Thus, according to these studies, it would appear that while the extent of use of block-time classes approximately doubled, the proportion employing the experience-centered approach had materially diminished. A number of schools have discontinued the core.

Surveys of both nationwide samples and individual schools in the period from 1955 to 1960 have indicated that around 40 to 60 per cent of the junior high schools had block-time classes. The figure for California was 87 per cent. Most studies in junior-senior, four-year, and senior high schools show that the core is not employed nearly as often—in a few studies, in only 14 or 15 per cent of the schools included.[9] The core plan is followed principally by the junior high schools.

EVALUATION OF THE CORE

Probably no development in the secondary school curriculum has been subject to more scrutiny than has the core curriculum. Much of the

[6] Grace S. Wright, *Core Curriculum in Public High Schools: An Inquiry into Practices, 1949*, U.S. Office of Education, Bulletin, 1950, No. 5, Washington, D.C.: Government Printing Office, 1950, p. 11.

[7] Grace S. Wright, *Block-Time Classes and the Core Program in the Junior High School*, U.S. Office of Education, Bulletin 1958, No. 6, Washington, D.C.: Government Printing Office, 1958, pp. 2, 64.

[8] Grace S. Wright, *Core Curriculum Development: Problems and Practices*, U.S. Office of Education, Bulletin 1952, No. 5, Washington, D.C.: Government Printing Office, 1952, p. 7.

[9] Van Til, Vars, and Lounsbury, *op. cit.*, pp. 94–95; Gordon F. Vars, "Administrative Leadership—Key to Core Program Development," *Bulletin of the National Association of Secondary School Principals*, Vol. 46 (February, 1962), pp. 92–93.

evaluation has been of the opinion-survey type, but an imposing number of experimental studies were made, including at least eighty unpublished studies made between 1946 and 1955.[10]

Research Studies. The experimental studies have concentrated on measuring growth in language skills and in achievement through use of conventional standardized tests. Few statistically significant differences have been found between core programs and conventional programs when gains were measured by these means, but the results generally show that the core groups did as well or better than the control groups. Although the gains in personal-social development and sociocivic attitudes were not always as great as expected, the evidence indicates that core programs of the experience-centered, problems type were superior to the subject-centered type in gains in attitudes and values.[11]

Other than in the Eight-Year Study of the Progressive Education Association, conducted in the 1930's, little attention has been paid to studying the success of former core students in college. That study gave evidence that graduates of high schools utilizing the core succeeded as well in colleges as graduates of other high schools. Gale's study found no significant differences between college students who had gone through core programs in high school and those who had not.[12]

Teachers and administrators generally have indicated a favorable reaction to the core. Other findings that involve both opinion and collected data indicate that some schools reported greater library-book circulation, better teacher-pupil relationships, improved discipline, improved attendance, and fewer dropouts after inauguration of the core. Some schools indicate that guidance has improved, a greater amount of group- and work-type procedures are used, and there are fewer community complaints against pupils.[13] If these results are valid, the core

[10] Grace S. Wright, *The Core Program: Abstracts of Unpublished Research, 1946–1955*, U.S. Office of Education, Circular No. 485, Washington, D.C.: Government Printing Office, 1956.
[11] Harold Alberty, "Core Programs," *Encyclopedia of Educational Research* (3d ed.) (New York: The Macmillan Co., 1960), pp. 337–341; Vernon E. Anderson and Arthur Goldberg, "Schools for Adolescents: Curriculum Content and Organization," *Review of Educational Research*, Vol. 24 (February, 1954), pp. 32–33; J. Galen Saylor, "Design of the Curriculum," *Review of Educational Research*, Vol. 24 (June, 1954), pp. 208–210; Van Til, Vars, and Lounsbury, *op. cit.*, pp. 294–295 (cites fifteen studies); Grace S. Wright, *The Core Program: Abstracts of Unpublished Research*, U.S. Office of Education, Circular No. 485, Washington, D.C.: Government Printing Office, 1956.
[12] Raymond Gale, "A Comparative Study of College Experiences of Graduates of Core and Conventional Curriculums," *Journal of Experimental Education*, Vol. 27 (June, 1957), pp. 283–296.
[13] Anderson and Goldberg, *op. cit.; How Much Did They Grow?* General Information Bulletin No. 164 (Kalamazoo, Mich.: Kalamazoo Public Schools, 1952) (mimeo.); Gertrude Noar, *The Junior High School: Today and Tomorrow* (2d ed.) (Englewood

goes beyond the conventionally designed curriculum in changing pupils' behavior, as its advocates claim.

What further light can be thrown on the validity of these findings? *The Encyclopedia of Educational Research* contains this summary:

The available research seems to indicate a distinct superiority of the core programs, defined in terms of a large time block devoted to common needs, problems and interests of students, over the conventional program; in providing for more effective guidance of students; for individual differences among students; and for more effective use of community resources in the classroom.[14]

The significance of this statement is that, when the core is defined as the experience-centered, problem-solving type, these results tend to occur.

One of the difficulties in interpreting research on the core is the lack of consistency in definition. If any block-time class is defined as core, there is small wonder that the results are confusing. Fair's research indicates that the potentialities for change of social attitudes and behavior are not fully utilized in core classes. This study tested some of the special objectives of the core: awareness of social conditions, ability to apply facts and generalizations in a social context, willingness to take a democratic position on a social issue, and interest in social affairs. The scores on willingness to take a democratic position were the only ones that showed a significant difference in favor of core programs, but the researchers also observed that the characteristics and techniques of the core classes were not very different from those of classes with which they were compared.[15]

The findings of Toop's investigation further seem to reveal that the reason why experimental studies have not shown greater superiority for the core in development of democratic attitudes and skills may well be the fact that few core programs use the problem-solving, experience-centered approach. This study of core programs found that, in one state, (1) guidance was not being included in the majority of schools (Wilson[16] also found that guidance was included in only 15.8 per cent of the block-time classes); (2) little use was made of teacher-pupil planning, com-

Cliffs, N.J.: Prentice-Hall, Inc., 1961), pp. 165–167; William Reiner and J. Wayne Wrightstone, *A Second Report on the Evaluation of Pupil Growth in Core Programs in Two Academic High Schools, 1952–53* (New York: Bureau of Educational Research, Board of Education, 1954) (mimeo.); L. A. VanDyke, "How Effective Is the Core Curriculum in the Junior High School?" in *Issues in Curriculum Development,* Marvin D. Alcorn and James M. Linley, eds. (New York: Harcourt, Brace & World, Inc., 1959), pp. 247–249.

[14] Alberty, *op. cit.,* p. 340.

[15] Jean Fair, "The Comparative Effectiveness of a Core and a Conventional Curriculum in Developing Social Concern," *School Review,* Vol. 62 (May and September, 1954), pp. 274–282, 346–353.

[16] Wilson, *op. cit.,* p. 10.

munity resources, or the problem-solving method; (3) there was little evidence of inclusion of personal-social problems of pupils; (4) parents and pupils participated little or not at all in the planning and evaluation of core programs; and, most revealing of all, (5) the majority of core teachers had no preparation for teaching the core.[17] All of these are contrary to what are defined either as characteristics of the core or as conditions necessary for successful core programs.

Deliberative Reports. Reports by committees of national importance and by studies by important groups or individuals have always carried considerable weight in affecting practices in American education. In Conant's report of his study of the American high school, his statement on the core was as follows:

> To my mind, there should be a block of time set aside, at least in grade 7, in which one teacher has the same pupils for two or more periods, generally in English and social studies. Otherwise, grades 7, 8, and 9 should be departmentalized; that is to say, pupils should have specialist teachers in each of the subject-matter fields.
>
> .   .   .   .
>
> Though I am not opposed to experimentation with the core approach, I must make it plain that my advocacy of block-time teaching does not presuppose an endorsement of core teaching.[18]

Harl Douglass, who established, in 1917, at the University of Oregon, one of the early three-year junior high schools, has since that time advocated a large block taught by one teacher.

Another statement by an important educational organization, the Association for Supervision and Curriculum Development, takes the following position:

> The good junior high school of today should:
>
> .   .   .   .
>
> 4. Offer block-of-time instruction each year for the three years so that one teacher will have a group of children for a substantial period.
>
> .   .   .   .
>
> Ideally, a block-of-time program also provides a focus on the kinds of general education skills and concepts which the young adolescent needs for a responsible and satisfying life.[19]

[17] Myrtle Dewey Toops, "An Analysis of Core Programs in Selected Junior High Schools of Indiana," *National Association of Secondary School Principals Bulletin,* Vol. 46 (February, 1962), pp. 271–220.

[18] James B. Conant, *Education in the Junior High School Years* (Princeton, N.J.: Educational Testing Service, 1960), pp. 22–23.

[19] Association for Supervision and Curriculum Development, Commission of Secondary School Curriculum, *The Junior High School We Need* (Washington, D.C.: National Education Association of the United States, 1961), p. 15.

While the latter report did not take a strong position for the core, there is no doubt that Conant's reports, with their emphasis on academic subjects and programs, have had the greater impact on practice.

Advantages of the Core. Unless the core had advantages for pupil growth beyond the skills and knowledge connected with English and social studies, it would not be achieving its purposes. Particular advantages cited for the core, as discussed in some of the above research studies, involve development of attitudes, values, cooperative procedures, improved adjustments, skills of planning, expanded interests, and wide reading. However the core has no inherent magic, though it presents opportunity for advantages such as these:

1. *It enables the teacher to know his pupils well.* Usually, the core teacher will have about a third as many pupil contacts a day as other teachers. He may teach two classes of core or two plus one period of a conventional class. He is in a position to counsel pupils, hold parent conferences and meetings, and give more personal attention to each pupil. This, of course, is an advantage of both block-time and core classes.

2. *As defined by its characteristics, it is compatible with what we know about how people learn.* Active student participation is possible. Cooperative planning helps pupils to define their own purposes and makes for unification of learning around real problems.

3. *It can serve as a focus for the student for his whole program, where experiences in and out of school may be related to the problems studied.* The flexibility of the problem-solving approach in the core makes it possible to relate knowledge and skills from other areas of study in the school.

4. *It provides an opportunity for youths to study their own social and personal needs and problems.* Perhaps nowhere else, in some schools, can pupils systematically study in depth these concerns so vital to them.

5. *It facilitates the use of the community as a laboratory, through field trips, individual or group investigation, and resource people brought to the classroom.* The longer block of time and the concern for community development and problems of government and education are conducive to using the resources in the immediate community.

6. *It includes activities and functions often assigned to special periods in the schedule, such as homerooms, social affairs, clubs, and other extra-class activities.* Here, again, the principle of relating different areas of the school, such as guidance and extracurricular activities, to the instructional program is a sound one.

7. *It provides a situation in which more functional learning of the basic as well as the social skills can be planned.* The experience-centered unit, with its provision for interviewing, contacting the community, writ-

ing to people, reporting, using varied materials, and planning activities concerned with learning skills of democracy through practice, is a natural medium for learning functionally.

8. *Cooperative and flexible planning is more easily achieved.* The teacher is expected, not to structure each two-hour period ahead of time, but instead to see that learning opportunities are capitalized on as they arise.

9. *Greater variety of class activities is possible.* Besides the use of the community and cooperative planning, the core facilitates utilizing audio-visual aids, group work, individual and group research, reporting, and individual projects.

Disadvantages and Problems of the Core. To its opponents, the core curriculum seems to have limitations, as compared with the conventionally designed curriculum. They assert, with a great deal of force behind their arguments, that neither teachers, school leaders, nor parents understand enough about it to put the core concepts effectively into practice. The dropping of core programs in a number of communities where they have been used gives further weight to their arguments. The proponents of the core believe these are stumbling blocks, not inherent disadvantages, and recognize the obstacles that exist.

1. *Few teachers are well prepared to teach the core.* This argument is indeed a cogent one. The successful core teacher needs to have a broad understanding of subject matter; a depth of understanding of at least two fields of study; a good understanding of the adolescent, his needs, and his society; and some experience in classes in which he can gain confidence in the use of the core approach. These are not easily achieved in teacher education. Few teachers are experts in more than one subject field. For example, in their teaching, they may neglect social studies if they were prepared as English teachers. There is some evidence to indicate that school systems and colleges can cooperatively achieve the objective of competently prepared teachers more effectively through in-service education or continued education beyond the bachelor's degree. The rapid teacher turnover in some schools contributes to this problem.

2. *It is more difficult and requires more time, especially at first, to teach core classes than the conventional classes with a preplanned sequence.* Any core teacher can attest to this fact. Pupil-teacher planning done effectively requires more work and more planning by the teacher, as well as a *broader* understanding of different areas of knowledge. At the same time, however, the core teachers testify that they are happier in their work than when they used a different approach.

3. *The public can find a convenient point of criticism in an unfamiliar or new type of curriculum organization and approach.* The success of

the core depends a great deal upon the courage and vision of the administration and staff and their skill in working with the public. Irresponsible attacks on the schools can find in the core a likely spot for attack, because it promotes inquiry, looking into socioeconomic questions impartially and critically, and studying local problems. In this day of fear of liberal ideas, many sincere people will believe such attacks. The new and the different are always vulnerable.

4. *More materials are needed in a core class.* This is a disadvantage to schools that have a limited budget for instructional materials. In this sense, a core class may cost more than a conventional class. However, it can also be argued that the teacher in other classes could do a better job with more materials. The difference is that many teachers remain satisfied with the single textbook.

5. *The core program takes more staff time in planning together.* In certain schools, the staff seems committed to achieving as few meetings as possible. Unless a group is genuinely interested in cooperative planning, it would consider the time factor a disadvantage.

6. *Teachers have difficulty in operating at the level of a broad system of values.* The core considers the development of democratic skills and values important. For some teachers, the study of a problem is just another form of factual study of questions or topics. The examination of values in class is even more difficult for them.

7. *There is a lack of relation between core and the subjects taught outside the core.* Frequently, this is augmented by a critical attitude of faculty members who look upon new procedures as a threat to them. But the fact is that not enough core teachers have effectively utilized other faculty members or related the core problems to what pupils were studying in the rest of their program.

8. *The core class can become as routine and mechanical as any other class.* Sometimes it does. Teachers who lack imagination, time, or both, go through the same routine of problem analysis, doling out subproblems to committees to investigate and subjecting the class to interminable hours of dull reports by committees. This represents the crystallization of *a* procedure that stultifies the core.

9. *The administrative mechanics and problems of scheduling, oversized classes, insufficient time for planning, classrooms built for conventional classes, and lack of equipment present serious handicaps.* The administrator of the school holds one of the keys to the success of the program. Unless he can see the benefits of a core program and overcome these handicaps, the core is not likely to succeed and flourish. Lack of administrative leadership is often a major obstacle to the development of a successful core program.

One interesting point to note in weighing advantages and disadvantages of the core is that, in some surveys of schools that have abandoned core-type programs, the lack of qualified teachers ranked far above community dissatisfactions as a reason for dropping the program.[20]

ESTABLISHING A CORE PROGRAM

Considerable evidence has been accumulated concerning the necessary preparation, materials, and faculty and community readiness that a school needs to have to inaugurate a successful core program. The principles apply equally well to any curriculum change that differs considerably from the old pattern. One can rightly look with suspicion on any curriculum innovation that does not follow a sound pattern of analysis, study, and continued evaluation.

In-Service Preparation. It is likely that only a few teachers in a school are able to use successfully an experience-centered approach. Most of those who are new feel more secure in traditional practices they have experienced. Others have taught for years without making much use of problem-solving activities, variety of materials, field trips, or planning with pupils. Yet, sincere, experienced teachers who are successful have made some of the best core teachers. This change did not just happen.

State surveys reveal that often far too little time is spent on planning and orientation, in one case 2 per cent of the schools reporting no time whatsoever spent in preparation.[21] In a nationwide study, principals reported that, in approximately half of the schools with block-time programs, about a year was spent in orientation and study and, in about a fourth of the schools, less than six weeks were spent in preparation.[22] In another study, only 14 per cent of the schools spent a year or more in planning, and 6 per cent did not have in-service programs for block-time teachers.[23] These facts reveal a great deal about the failure of core programs to live up to expectations, especially when one considers that the concept of core teaching is quite radically different from lesson learning.

The principal and director of instruction are key factors in the preparation for a core program. Their leadership, insight into learning and teaching, and understanding of the basic concepts fundamental to core teaching are vital to the success of the program. When principals cite "necessity for constant in-service training of teachers" as an obstacle to

[20] Gordon F. Vars, "Leadership in Core Program Development," *Educational Leadership*, Vol. 19 (May, 1962), p. 521.

[21] *Ibid.*, pp. 518–519.

[22] Wright, *Block-Time Classes and the Core Program in the Junior High School*, U.S. Office of Education, Bulletin 1958, No. 6 (Washington, D.C.: Government Printing Office, 1958), pp. 28–29.

[23] Wilson, *op. cit.*, p. 16.

the core, they show an ignorance of what is demanded. If education is to be experimental, vital, and challenging, it demands constant in-service training. In fact, a criterion of a dynamic, growing school is the existence of continued study on the part of the faculty.

Though the general principles may be described, it is doubtful that anyone can tell a teacher exactly how to use problem-solving procedures. This is a concept learned through actual participation in classes using such procedures and through observation of skilful teaching. The workshop is one of the best devices for the orientation, if it is skilfully conducted; the leader will use the same procedures that a teacher of the experience-centered core will use. Local or campus workshops employ cooperative planning, problem solving, and a large block of time.

Involvement of Teachers and Parents. Schools establishing block-time programs report that in less than a fourth of the cases were either the total faculty or the public involved in the study. Yet, these are essential ingredients for establishing a core program. Teachers of core classes may profit much from the support and the active assistance of other faculty members.

One of the reasons for dropping the core is the fact that parents have not understood it. In most such cases, they were not brought into the study either before or during the operation of the core program. Successful core teachers meet with parents often in individual conferences and invite parents of the pupils to the class for various occasions. The change from the straight subject-matter approach is a considerable one and needs understanding by parents as well as teachers.

Many schools have found it a good principle to allow pupils as well as teachers to decide whether or not they wish to take a core class. Inevitably, of course, the parents enter into the decision as well. Certainly, parents of pupils in core classes should be informed in advance about the nature of the core program.

The Transition Period. A core program should be established by assigning such classes only to teachers ready for this experience. Establishment of the core for all pupils before the necessary number of teachers are prepared intellectually and psychologically is a serious error.

Many schools have combined English and social studies classes with the same group of pupils under one teacher as a first step toward a core program. Under such a plan, some teachers will be able to move faster toward integration than others. In fact, some may always remain in the stage where the subjects combined in the block-time class are correlated but not fused.

Block scheduling will probably be the only step, however, unless the principal works with the teachers to develop ways of using subject matter as a means for the solution of problems. The planning period for teachers is essential. Yet, time for teachers to plan together during the school day was scheduled by only about one-third of the schools surveyed.[24]

A logical beginning step is to use the experience-centered approach in English, social studies, and other classes as much as possible under the recognized limitations of prescribed subject matter. Planning with students can be carried on in any class. Social studies classes can be taught around problems rather than in chronological fashion. English classes can use real situations and current problems of the individual and of society instead of artificially assigned ones as a basis for oral and written experiences. Mills found that although problem-solving behaviors occur to some extent in core classes, few behaviors that occur in problematic situations can be considered problem solving.[25] The need for continued in-service education for use of experience-centered concepts is evidently constant.

Resources and Materials. The familiar rectangular-shaped, bare-walled classroom and screwed-down seats, now not so commonly employed, are certainly no inducement to a teacher to use a problem-solving approach. A classroom needs to be a laboratory rich in pamphlets, books, audio-visual aids, work materials, and work space. With the role of the teacher and the way pupils function changed, the concept of what is needed to make a classroom a learning laboratory has also changed. It is not only the science laboratories that need materials and equipment at hand. The library and curriculum laboratory serve as a central pool to supplement materials in the classroom and furnish places for independent investigation and study.

If a wide variety of materials is to be used, the classroom needs to be a laboratory with space for a classroom library, filing of pamphlet materials collected by the pupils, current materials, maps and globes, and other types of materials. Most of the wall space should be devoted to bulletin boards rather than blackboards. Lack of sufficient space, suitable furniture, equipment, and adequate instructional materials was mentioned as a major problem by a considerable number of the administrators in Wright's study of core practices.[26] Successful teaching of the core requires many kinds of materials including books for different levels of reading ability.

[24] Gordon F. Vars, "Leadership in Core Program Development," *Educational Leadership,* Vol. 19 (May, 1962), p. 518.

[25] Ruth I. Mills, "The Nature of Problem Solving and Its Application to Core Curriculum (1959)," *Bulletin of the National Association of Secondary School Principals,* Vol. 46 (February, 1962), pp. 133–134.

[26] Wright, *Core Curriculum Development: Problems and Practices,* U.S. Office of Education, Bulletin 1952, No. 5, Washington, D.C.: Government Printing Office, 1952, p. 67.

COMPARISON OF TEAM TEACHING AND CORE

The purposes, nature, and types of team teaching are discussed in Chapters 8 and 28. For an understanding of this concept, the reader is referred to those chapters. In this chapter, team teaching is considered only from the standpoint of comparison with the core curriculum organization and approach in terms of principles, assumptions, structure, advantages, etc.

Principles and Assumptions. As was pointed out earlier in this chapter, the core curriculum is a fundamental reorganization of certain aspects of general education in the secondary school in order to bring organization, procedures, and content into closer harmony with adolescent and societal needs and to provide a better learning situation. Does team teaching have the same goals?

First, it must be recognized that either core or team teaching as a curriculum or organizational design can be a hollow shell. No substantive changes in approach or content need occur. That should be unmistakably clear from the data indicating the small proportion of core programs that actually are the experience-centered type. But the significant questions are Can team teaching in some form serve the same purposes as the core? Is it a form of administrative organization incompatible with the core approach?

In order to answer these questions, one has to start with the assumption that neither the core curriculum nor team teaching is a fixed, immutable pattern; rather they are in essence experimental approaches. Otherwise, any answer is likely to be an argument for a never changing idea that has its own built-in vested interests.

One of the most extensive carefully planned and evaluated experiments with team teaching is the Claremont Graduate School Team Teaching Project, in which the college cooperated with several school systems in the area in a five-year experiment begun in 1959–1960. The assumptions stated for that program generally underlie the experimentation with team teaching in secondary schools throughout the United States under the auspices of the Committee on Staff Utilization of the National Association of Secondary School Principals. A number of these are also assumptions of the core, for example,

1. Members of the faculty cannot function effectively in isolation.
2. Teachers should have personal knowledge of their students.
3. Relationships among the fields of knowledge should be developed.
4. Students must learn increasingly to accept responsibility for their own education.
5. Students with difficulties in learning need special assistance when difficulties occur.

6. To operate at peak performance, schools should augment their programs with the talents of citizens.
7. Schools should be flexible with respect to scheduling classes and grouping students.
8. Schools should be flexible enough that students may move ahead in their studies according to their abilities.[27]

Any good core teacher would accept these as his operating principles. In addition there are assumptions, such as that teachers' particular talents should be used, that are more peculiar to team teaching.

Structure. Instead of the basic group of thirty students under one core teacher, the team has two or more teachers with two or more classes or sections combined. Block scheduling is a characteristic of the team, as it is of the core, although the team frequently may use a longer block, often three to five periods. As in the core, group-counseling sessions are held in team situations and field trips take place within this block of time.

One of the "models" for the block-time schedule in the Claremont project includes three seventh-grade teachers in a "core" arrangement, each teacher having a different specialty. It is possible either for each one to teach the total group for the three periods, using the content from the three areas, or for the three groups to be combined into one for English, social studies, or mathematics instruction, each teacher working with part of the group, or all three teachers working with the total group of about 100 students. Frequently, these teachers in a block would constitute a team of different specialists within a subject such as English.

English	Social Studies	Mathematics
social studies	English	English
mathematics	mathematics	social studies[28]

According to the studies under the Committee on Staff Utilization, the most frequent team-teaching subjects are social studies, English, and physical education. This is quite similar to the content included in core, with the exception of physical education. As basic to team teaching as it is to the core is conference or planning time for teams of teachers, provided for in almost all schools.[29] Students have a teacher-counselor

27 Selected from total list in John A. Brownell and Harris A. Taylor, "Theoretical Perspectives for Teaching Teams," *Phi Delta Kappan*, Vol. 43 (January, 1962), p. 150.
28 Brownell and Taylor, *op. cit.*, p. 153.
29 Ira J. Singer, "Survey of Staff Utilization Practices in Six States," *Bulletin of the National Association of Secondary School Principals*, Vol. 46 (January, 1962), p. 5.

from the faculty team who sees them frequently in class and in conferences, serving the same guidance functions as the core teacher.

The teaming of teachers with different specialities, in order to utilize their talents with maximum effectiveness and to develop interrelationships of subject matter, and the use of large and small groups and independent study are some features of team teaching that are not characteristic of the core. The use of teacher aides, interns, clerical workers, and team leaders is another aspect peculiar to team teaching and is discussed elsewhere in this volume.

Advantages. Typical advantages claimed, but not yet definitely proved to exist, for team teaching are found in statements of hypotheses being tested in experimental studies and include

1. Cooperative teacher involvement in planning and developing the curriculum
2. The ability to group and regroup frequently within the total team in large or small groups
3. Improved guidance of students because of knowing them well
4. Improved correlation of subject matter because of team cooperative planning
5. More use of community resources
6. Improved climate because of stress on individual identity
7. Flexibility of schedules providing for adjustment to individual differences
8. More use of a variety of materials
9. Increased opportunity for independent study
10. Better results from a team of teachers each qualified in a different field
11. Facilitation of field trips

The cooperation of teachers in planning, the inclusion of the guidance function, the relating of subject matter, the use of community resources and a variety of materials, and the flexibility of schedule are prominent among advantages usually cited for the core.

Team Teaching as an Extension of Core. This chapter began with the assumption that the core curriculum is a growing, dynamic, flexible concept that is experimental in nature. Thus, it rationally changes as new needs and demands for general education develop. The way subject matter is currently being analyzed by scholars in the disciplines should have a telling impact on the approach to the study of each subject. The trend toward unity in and among subjects, such as in the various sciences and branches of mathematics, as developed by scholars, has profound implications for the curriculum. Consequently, the core curriculum may look considerably different in the next few generations than it did in the

1940's. In fact, its progenitors might not recognize it. But—if the core is a fundamental concept about curriculum and learning that uses problem-solving procedures and the other characteristics of an experience-centered approach rather than merely a form of curriculum organization—these changes should be neither startling nor disturbing. For, within the structure of team teaching, there are many features that are particularly conducive to core practices. The fact that team-teaching situations may be quite traditional in nature, with a subject-centered emphasis, should certainly be no surprise. One can conclude from Wright's and other studies cited in this chapter that the majority of the core classes were of the same nature. The creative, imaginative teacher team can apply core procedures with effectiveness in the block of time within which these teachers work, if they have the vision, desire, and encouragement to do so.

One example of where the use of team teaching has been taking place is a junior high school in a suburban area where teams were formed to teach the core in the eighth and ninth grades. The teams were composed of teachers who were qualified and had experience in the teaching of the core. Teacher members have primary responsibility for certain subject areas in which they have special competence, but all four team members are concerned about those areas that are common.

Something that rarely happened in core is occurring in relation to team teaching. Buildings are being designed specifically to take care of different size groups, teacher planning, and teacher-pupil conferences, and to provide for work centers and laboratories of all types.[30] Many of the newer instructional media are being utilized.

Thus, team teaching in reality can become an extension, a further refinement, and an improvement of the core. The team-teacher plan can be utilized with important areas of general education. Team teachers have good opportunities to use teacher-pupil planning, problem solving, personal and social problems, related subject matter from different fields, and skills in relation to ongoing situations. They have the opportunity to use the experience-centered approach. Moreover, they have the propitious opportunity to use their subject specialties and talents, a lack in the core program.

But this is an opportunity, not an inevitable result. A study of significant social issues is no more guaranteed by team teaching than it is by the core, unless creative, dedicated, intelligent teachers work together under good leadership with a determination to make these things come to pass. The core is an idea that will continue to evolve in fertile minds, even though the fears and vicissitudes that characterize educa-

[30] Evans Clinchy, *Schools for Team Teaching* (New York: Educational Facilities Laboratories, Inc., 1961).

tional ventures representing extreme departures from the normal may cause its name to be changed.

QUESTIONS, PROBLEMS, AND ISSUES FOR FURTHER THOUGHT

1. Here are three specific recommendations for improvement of the core curriculum; analyze each one as to its validity for the current day:
   a. Greater stress should be placed on communication skills of all kinds.
   b. The method used in core classes should be based on scientific, objective study of social problems.
   c. Considerable individual research and study should be done by pupils in addition to group study.
2. Develop a plan for relating one of the courses that you are teaching to the core in a hypothetical school situation.
3. Why do you think there has been such a great stress on group reports in core classes? Have these been fruitful for learning?
4. To what degree and in what way is the core curriculum involved in the controversy about alleged anti-intellectualism in schools?
5. Invite a teacher of core classes to meet with the group and discuss his plan of operation.
6. Interview students in core classes about their experience in the core and their reactions to it.
7. Should a national organization of core teachers be formed? Give reasons why or why not.
8. If you were an administrator in a school with a core curriculum, what would be your principal problem regarding core teachers' relations to other teachers? How would you solve it?
9. Do you think that teach teaching and the core are compatible? Reinforcing? Mutually restrictive?

SUPPLEMENTARY MATERIALS

Selected Readings

ALBERTY, HAROLD B., and ELSIE J. ALBERTY. *Reorganizing the High-School Curriculum* (3d ed.). New York: The Macmillan Co., 1962. Chapter 6 analyzes and evaluates five types of core programs and discusses recent trends.

BROWNELL, JOHN A., and HARRIS A. TAYLOR. "Theoretical Perspectives for Team Teaching," *Phi Delta Kappan*, XLIIII (January, 1962), 150–57. A concise and pertinent statement of the theory of team teaching and the evaluation done in the Claremont Teaching Team Program.

FAUNCE, ROLAND C., and NELSON L. BOSSING. *Developing the Core Curriculum* (2d ed.). Englewood Cliffs, N.J.: Prentice-Hall, Inc., 1958. Chapters 4, 6, 9. In a text devoted to the philosophy, purposes, and methods of the core, these chapters deal especially with purposes, a description of a core class in action, and the role of the teacher of core.

FLANDERS, NED A. "English and Social Studies—or Core? Which for Better Basic Skills?" *School Review*, LXVI (Autumn, 1958), 351–60. Reviews the results of research study on a core program in a junior high school as well as other studies.

"Junior High-School Development, Practices, and Research," *Bulletin of the N.A.S.S.P.*, XLVI (February, 1962), 91–103, 129–34, 205–25. Reports on status studies and practices in core programs.

Leese, Joseph, Kenneth Frasure, and Mauritz Johnson, Jr. *The Teacher in Curriculum Making.* New York: Harper & Row, 1961. Chapter 11 deals with teachers' responsibilities in a core program and its development.

Lurry, Lucile L., and Elsie J. Alberty. *Developing a High School Core Program.* New York: The Macmillan Co., 1957. Chapters 4 and 6 describe a core program and the making of a problem area study; the whole book also deals with developing and designing a core program in a school.

Van Til, William, Gordon Vars, and John H. Lounsbury. *Modern Education in the Junior High School Years,* Indianapolis: The Bobbs-Merrill Co., Inc., 1961. Unit III contains a descriptive account of a core class and an extensive discussion of procedures and present practices including problem-centered teaching and teaching the basic skills, literature, creative writing, and the arts in the core.

Vars, Gordon F. "Leadership in Core Program Development," *Educational Leadership,* XIX (May, 1962), 517–22. Contains much information on the status of core programs as indicated in the surveys in a number of states and nationwide. Centers on leadership in the core and obstacles to core development.

Wright, Grace S. *Block-Time Classes and the Core Program.* U.S. Office of Education, Bulletin 1958, No. 6. Washington, D.C.: Government Printing Office, 1958. This pamphlet is the most recent U.S. Office of Education survey of block-time and core practices in secondary schools of the United States.

———. *The Core Program: Unpublished Research, 1956–62.* U.S. Office of Education, Circular 713. Washington, D.C.: Government Printing Office, 1963. Brief abstracts of doctoral dissertations and state and university research not readily available in printed form.

Zapf, Rosalind M. *Democratic Processes in the Secondary Classroom.* Englewood Cliffs, N.J.: Prentice-Hall, Inc., 1959. Especially Chapters 5–7, 9. Describes methods and procedures in the core, from the author's rich background of experience in teaching core.

14

Construction of
Educational Guides

CHANGING CONCEPTIONS OF COURSE OF STUDY

In recent years, there has been a radical change in the conception, formulation, and construction of courses of study. Although these changes have been under way for over two decades, they have become most rapid and far-reaching in their implications within the past ten years. This over-all change is clearly evident in spite of the apparent stampede, usually temporary, to the old in many places since Sputnik. This regressive movement has been limited in scope and now appears about to have run its course.

Older Concept of Course of Study. The age-old notion of "a course of study" had at least three well-recommended characteristics:

1. *The course of study was inflexible in content and organization.* Some thirty years ago, a president of a then nationally known normal school used to emphasize inflexibility as an essential of a good course of study. At teachers' conventions and institutes in the state served by this normal school, its president never lost an opportunity to insist that, if, for example, on March 10 he could visit a sixth-grade class in arithmetic at 10 o'clock in the morning, at schools as widely separated as at each end of the state, he would expect the pupils to be working the same problems on the same page of the same textbook. In another state,[1] where local

[1] In that state, a system of state-adopted textbooks existed, and only one textbook for each subject was adopted by the state textbook commission.

school systems were allowed to determine their own courses of study within the framework of a rather general state-approved course of study, the superintendent of schools of a sizable city school system proudly boasted to visitors to his school that he knew exactly what was taking place in every classroom of his system.

2. *Often the textbook served as a course of study.* In the past, where textbooks were adopted by state textbook commissions or local school-system-wide committees, the textbook frequently served as the course of study, or the course of study, in fact, slavishly duplicated the textbook, possibly with time allotments for chapters and a few suggestions about methods added. It was assumed that the textbook would be studied from the first to the last page in deadly sequence.

3. *Courses of study were prepared by subject specialists.* Implicit in what has been said is that, where a specific textbook was a *must*, subject specialists determined the content of the course and, in most such situations, determined the logical sequence in which the subject was taught. Even where the older course of study did not rest upon an adopted textbook in an earlier day, usually it was prepared by subject specialists. As time passed, school administrators often undertook to develop the local curriculum and, to some extent, the courses of study. As one superintendent of a medium-sized school said to a visiting educator: "I have just finished working on the teaching of reading in my school; I am now going to give attention to adjustments in the rest of the curriculum."

Particularly since Sputnik, there has been some evidence of a reappearance of the subject specialist in the construction of curriculum and course guides. This has been most apparent in the areas of science and mathematics. The tendency of these groups has been to assume full responsibility for the development of school curriculums and courses of study. Notable among these has been the Physical Science Study Committee, which has prepared a physics course for high schools—replete with textbooks, teaching manuals, and laboratory exercises. The same type of activity is reported of the Biological Science Curriculum Study.[2] This re-entry of the academic specialists into curriculum making is described with enthusiastic approval by Bruner:

Major efforts in curriculum design had been launched by leading physicists, mathematicians, biologists, and chemists, and similar projects were in prospect in other fields of scientific endeavor. . . . A tour of the United States in the summer of 1959 would have revealed a concentration of distinguished mathematicians in Boulder, Colorado, engaged in the writing of new textbooks for primary, junior high, and high school grades. . . . In Cambridge, Massachusetts, work was progressing on an "ideal" physics course for high school students,

[2] *Education U.S.A.,* Washington, D.C., September 27, 1962, p. 1.

engaging the efforts not only of text writers and film producers but also of men who had earned world renown in theoretical and experimental physics.[3]

Newer Concept of Course of Study. The old-time "course of study" has been replaced rapidly in the past decade or two with new titles in keeping with corresponding changes in the concepts of learning and curriculum.

More Flexibility in Title and Form. With increasing rarity is the title "course of study" now used in curriculum parlance. A quick survey of the titles of curriculum aids to the school and teacher in a library curriculum-materials center will find relatively few titles under "Courses of Study." These are rapidly being replaced by titles such as "Curriculum Guides" or "Course Guides." Checking through the curriculum section of a university library, the author found, under the general classification "Curriculum Guides" a few titles such as "Course of Study in Biology," but by far the most frequent titles carried with them the implications of a newer educational point of view.[4]

Implication of the Newer Titles. There is a general recognition in the new approach to the development of curriculum and course guides that education can no longer be static or conform to the deadly curriculum uniformity suggested earlier in this chapter. Slowly but surely, educators have come to recognize that no two communities are similar, no two classes are alike, and no two pupils are identical in background and achievement. Wide differences exist between communities, and even within average communities of any size, in their economic, social, and cultural patterns. This sociological fact is now well documented and understood.[5]

The development of an extensive body of research findings, reflected in many publications, on the subject of individual differences makes it educationally indefensible to offer in the schools stereotyped curriculums.

[3] Jerome S. Bruner, *The Process of Education* (Cambridge, Mass.: Harvard University Press, 1961), pp. vii-viii.

[4] See such varied titles as *Curriculum Guide–Grades 7–8, 1958,* Gary Public Schools, Gary, Ind.; *Science and Health: A Curriculum Guide–Grade Eight,* Office of Curriculum, Louisville Public Schools, Louisville, Ky., September, 1961; *Curriculum Bulletin, General Science, Grade 9,* Cincinnati Public Schools, 1958; *Industrial Arts Instructional Guide–Grades 8–12,* Jefferson County, Colo., School District No. R-1, 1958–1959; *Teachers Guide for Homemaking, Grades Seven and Eight,* Santa Clara Community Schools, Calif., 1959; *Guide for Social Studies, Grades 7–12,* Curriculum Bulletin No. 72, St. Paul Public Schools, 1959; *Source Materials of the Educational Program: A Guidebook of Living and Learning Experiences,* Chicago Public Schools, 1956.

[5] Two recent books that make this abundantly clear as it affects education are that of Patricia Cayo Sexton, *Education and Income: Inequalities in Our Public Schools* (New York: The Viking Press, Inc., Publishers, 1961); and B. J. Chandler *et al., Education in Urban Society* (New York: Dodd, Mead & Co., Inc., 1962).

The varied background experiences and interests of pupils suggest the necessity of individualizing the curriculum, as far as possible, to provide learning situations appropriate and meaningful to each pupil. Also, the fiction that approximately the same maturity levels exist in each grade has long been exploded, although grade classification still persists in our grade-level system of school organization.

Under these circumstances, the present tendency is to make the content of curriculum and course guides flexible. Now major areas are proposed with suggestions for scope and sequence in the large curriculum or narrower course guides broadly suggested. The local school and the classroom teacher are left wide latitude in the development of course content, its organization, and the instructional devices employed.

THE CREATORS OF CURRICULUM AND COURSE GUIDES

Now that *learning* is commonly defined as the change in behavior of the learner that results from all of his experiences, and the *school curriculum* is defined as the conscious determination of the total environmental situation, or situations, that provides the medium for the learning experiences of the pupil, it is obvious that education is very much more than the memorization of vast areas of facts set out to be learned, or the achievement of skills by rote performance. Consequently neither rigidity of the curriculum nor its determination by subject specialists can meet the learning needs of boys and girls. Many interrelated forces contribute to the total learning environment of the pupil. These are now recognized to have an important part in curriculum and course-guide development.

The Community. In years gone by, when education was thought to consist primarily of imparting whatever facts or skills were acquired in the school, it was thought that only subject-matter experts were competent to determine what was taught. With the recognition that the total living environment of the child provides the basis for his total learning experiences, the community has come to be recognized as an important contributor to his education. A wholesome community environment will contribute measurably to the efforts of the school, just as an unwholesome community situation will have much influence in counteracting what the school is attempting to do in the time the pupil is in the school.

For a number of years, educational and community leaders have understood education to be a mutual responsibility. Consequently, service organizations, religious groups, recreational organizations, business, the press, and many other community agencies have contributed money and ideas to provide a better learning environment and opportunity for the youth of the community. For example, in one community, an advisory committee of citizens widely representative of major community interests was set up. With the school staff, this committee made extensive studies of the educational needs of the community's children and youth. As a result significant suggestions frequently were made for the improvement of the school program and community conditions that would create a better educational environment. In another community, the American Association of University Women cooperated with the school in a study of local youth delinquency and what the community and the school might do about this recognized problem. Later, with the cooperation of the American Legion, a recreational center for youth was developed for later afternoon and evening under the joint supervision of public-minded citizens and the school staff.[6]

The importance of lay participation in curriculum development is too often insufficiently appreciated. Repeatedly, the schools have found the communities much ahead of them in their thinking, or much further ahead than the schools had dared to hope. Too often, changes in the curriculum, such as the introduction of driver education, sex education, etc., have been forced upon the school because of hesitancy on the part of the school, engendered by its fear that the citizen was not ready for such a curriculum advance. Sometimes, unfortunate curricular changes have come when leadership has been taken over by the lay citizens by default. On the contrary, the cooperation of laymen should always be advisory; curriculum and course guides are the responsibility of professionally trained educators in the technical aspects of specific phases of curriculum content and structure.

The Parents of Students in Schools. Modern learning theory makes the parent a very important factor in the effectiveness of the school. Desirable behavioral patterns cannot be developed in maximum degree by the school alone nor by the parents alone. Their development is a cooperative task in which parents and teachers work together. On the one hand, the teacher must have the parents' cooperation to see that desirable behavior patterns being developed at school receive the reinforcement of parental support at home, and, on the other hand, for the parent to be able to reinforce the behavioral skills the school is trying to develop,

---

[6] See Chapter 4 of this volume. For a wealth of suggestions on the way the local community can help in the curriculum of the school, see E. G. Olsen *et al.*, *School and Community* (2d ed.) (Englewood Cliffs, N.J.: Prentice-Hall, Inc., 1954); Roland C. Faunce and Nelson L. Bossing, *Developing the Core Curriculum* (2d ed.) (Englewood Cliffs, N.J.: Prentice-Hall, Inc., 1958), Chap. 14; L. C. Wilson *et al.*, *School-Community Improvements* (New York: Harcourt, Brace & World, Inc., 1959); J. Minor Gwynn, *Curriculum Principles and Social Trends* (3d ed.) (New York: The Macmillan Co., 1960), Chap. 20; Vernon E. Anderson, *Principles and Procedures of Curriculum Improvement* (New York: The Ronald Press Co., 1956), Chaps. 7, 9; H. J. McNally and A. H. Passow, *Improving the Quality of Public School Programs* (New York: Teachers College, Bureau of Publications, Columbia University, 1960).

the parent must know what the school is attempting to do and how best to cooperate. Likewise, the teacher should know the desirable attitudes and behavior patterns the home is trying to develop, so that the school can be an intelligent participant. Cooperation is by both the individual and the parental group. There should be far more teacher-parent conferences, teacher visitation of pupils' homes, and parent visitation of the schools, the teachers, and the pupils' classes.

The School's Students. One of the basic principles of modern learning psychology is that the student cannot learn that which he does not understand. The best way to create this understanding is to have the pupil participate in curriculum study and make helpful suggestions for curriculum improvement that reflect his sense of educational need. In one school, pupil representatives of the high school grades participated with the faculty in a serious study of their school curriculum. As extensive reading was done and reports were made by students and faculty of curricular practices in other schools, the students became conscious of the fact that, in many of the schools studied, the student body had a student-government organization as part of its extracurricular activities. This led to further study by the student representatives and all the other students. Finally, the students asked for the privilige of setting up a student-government organization, with the definite purpose of developing better morale in the student body. Under the guidance of the administration and teachers, a successful form of student participation in school government resulted.

The Teachers. The same principle of learning that was given above to justify pupil participation in curriculum making applies with equal force to the teacher. It is a psychological truism that a teacher cannot teach well what he does not understand. In recent years much greater participation of teachers in curriculum making has become quite general practice.

Whereas it was once thought that teachers should accept the curriculum and courses of study handed to them, it is now the practice in the better schools for the teachers to accept a major responsibility for the creation of the curriculum and course guides according to which they teach. Few curriculum and course guides are produced now without teacher help. In fact, many of these curriculum and course guides have been developed largely by groups of teachers working closely with a few trained specialists from the central school office, sometimes assisted by curriculum specialists from the universities. Some teacher committees have worked extra hours during the school year on the curriculum, and in the summer have devoted full time toward the completion of curriculum and course guides. In the development of the curriculum and course-guide content around sample units, the teachers appear to carry major responsibility.

Many schools now look upon curriculum-improvement participation by the teachers as a very important form of in-service education. Nothing, of course, improves the quality of teaching more than a thorough understanding of the curriculum. It is the heart of the educative program. In a recent study of curriculum-development practices, it was found that four-fifths of the curriculum guides studied had been developed by the cooperative efforts of committees of teachers and administrators.[7]

The State Departments of Education. There has geen a general movement away from the old form of state rigid courses of study to suggested curriculum and course guides, presented as examples earlier in this chapter. In many states, the recent efforts of state departments of education have been to formulate suggestive guides that may provide some over-all idea of the purposes and general area to be explored in a given content area. It is recognized that these become more useful in the small school, where the less well-trained teachers may be in need of some guidance.

In an effort to assist local committees responsible for the development of curriculum and course guides and at the same time provide some semblance of an over-all consistent curriculum pattern, some state departments of education, through their own staffs or in cooperation with university and school-system representatives, have produced curriculum bulletins that present rather broad suggested patterns of procedure in developing curriculum and course guides.

The City School Systems. Larger cities have provided help for guide construction similar to that provided by the state departments of education. Usually, large cities have curriculum directors who are leaders in developing curriculum and course guides through administrator-teacher committees, frequently assisted by curriculum specialists from the universities, and selected teachers with good backgrounds, creative impulses, and imaginations, given reduced teaching loads.

In a recent article, a city school-curriculum official attempted to set up a suggested "course of study" statement outline for the guidance of local curriculum-development committees. He set up the following outline of the major parts of a course of study and then indicated the broad steps that should be followed in the "units of work." (No statement

[7] Eleanor Merritt and Henry Harap, *Trends in the Production of Curriculum Guides* (Nashville: George Peabody College for Teachers, 1955), p. 40.

was offered as to what the content should be. This, he assumed, was the responsibility of the local curriculum committee.):

The Guide–Course of Study Statement Outline

1. Forward
2. Table of Contents
3. Introduction
4. Philosophy of Department of Instruction
5. Units of Work
6. Tables and Illustrations
7. Reference Matter (footnotes and reference material)
8. Appendixes
9. Bibliography

Units of Work–Outline Steps

1. Overview
2. Objectives
3. Instructional Development
   a. Content of Instruction
   b. Activities
4. Time Allotments
5. Evaluation
6. Resource Material[8]

EXAMPLES OF CURRICULUM AND COURSE GUIDES

The following examples of contemporary curriculum and course guides have been selected to present typical educational thinking of those responsible for the development of curriculum guides, and to indicate the newer patterns of such guides.

State Guide for Science—Grades 10, 11, and 12.[9] The basic background of curriculum-guide development has been set forth by the State-Wide Secondary Curriculum Committee made up of teachers, administrators, school curriculum directors, and university professors. This committee first set up broadly eight basic assumptions that should govern the total curriculum of the secondary school, such as "The learning experiences for youth in grades seven through twelve should be included in the secondary curriculum" and "the scope of the curriculum should be based on the needs and interests of adolescents, insofar as practical and possible" and then set up general procedures that should govern the formulation and use of these guides.

---

[8] Wayne Alford, "Guide to Developing a Course of Study," *Peabody Journal of Education*, Vol. 29 (March, 1962), pp. 297–300.

[9] *A Guide for Science—Grades 10-11-12* (Jefferson City, Mo.: State Department of Education, 1958), pp. 23–25.

The course guide in Physical Science considers these general approaches to the course as follows:

I. What Are the Basic Reasons for Offering a Course in Physical Science?
II. What are the General Objectives of Physical Science?
III. What Are the Suggested Approaches to Teaching Physical Science?
IV. What Constitutes the Instructional Program? (A list of suggested units follow[s].)

The steps for unit teaching are brief and uniform
(1) Outline of Content
(2) Experiments and Related Activities

City Guides. City wide Curriculum Guide.[10]

I. FORWARD. "Teacher committees from each subject area with a representative of each high school worked with the secondary supervisors to identify and record the major topics to be covered in each of the subject areas."
II. INTRODUCTION. The planning council, the teacher-committee chairman, and the school principals who were responsible for the development of the curriculum guide.
III. JUNIOR HIGH SCHOOL PROGRAM. Lists the required and elective subjects of the junior high school, grades 7–8.
IV. HIGH SCHOOL GRADUATION REQUIREMENTS. The lists of subjects and the minimum of units required or recommended for grades 9–12.
V. MAJORS AND MINORS. The major and minor requirements for high school graduation are given.
VI. CREDIT FOR SUBJECTS. Those subjects for which a full unit of credit [is] given, those subjects for which a half unit of credit is given, and those subjects such as Driver Education for which no credit is offered. The development of uniform procedures in the teaching of each subject in the curriculum
(1) Major Areas
(2) Emphases or Outcomes
(3) Typical Activities
(4) Aids for Instruction and Evaluation

City-Broad-Area Curriculum Guide—Social Studies.[11] The introductory page of this curriculum guide lists the teachers who participated in the development of the guide. Then follows a suggestion of three basic considerations that are pertinent to the curriculum at the junior high school:

I. Some Characteristics and Needs of Young Adolescents.
II. Some Needs and Characteristics that Have Classroom Implications.
III. Suggested Areas of Study and Topics (units).

(This general form is followed in introducing the section of the guide for the senior high school.)

[10] *Curriculum Guide—Grades 7–12*, Gary Public Schools, Gary, Ind., 1958.
[11] *Social Studies for Secondary School Youth—Grades 7–12*, Curriculum Bulletin No. 72, St. Paul Public Schools, 1959.

Following this broad introduction to the curriculum guide, typical steps are suggested for the development of the unit, as follows:

(1) Objectives
(2) Understandings
(3) Attitudes and Habits to Be Developed
(4) Skills to Be Developed
(5) Outline of Content
(6) Initiatory Activities
(7) Developmental Activities
(8) Culminating Activities and Evaluations
(9) Evaluation
(10) Bibliography

City-Grade Course Guide—Homemaking.[12] This course guide is divided into the following major divisions:

I.   Objectives and Philosophy
II.   The Eighth-Grade Girl
III.   Suggested Units and Time-Allotments
IV.   Plan of Unit Development
    (1) Statement of Unit
    (2) Suggested Time-Allotment
    (3) Overview
    (4) Suggestions for Starting the Study
    (5) Problems-Understandings-Skills
    (6) Suggested Activities
    (7) Culmination and Evaluation
    (8) Teaching Aids

With the more inclusive participation of all community and school groups in the approach to curriculum study and change, there has come more frequent resort to segmental curriculum change. Curriculum specialists have long recognized that curriculum change should be evolutionary rather than revolutionary. Even when major over-all changes are planned, it has been assumed that the implementation of these proposed major changes would be gradual and probably of uneven development in the school system. Since it has been recognized that teachers are key persons in curriculum change, and that curriculum study is one of the most profitable means of the professional improvement of the teacher, there has been much more use of teacher study and modification of limited segments of the total curriculum.

Those undertaking the production of curriculum and course guides should be aware of the fact that the better guides usually contain a common body of suggestions and helps for the teacher. The accumulated

[12] *Homemaking—Grade Eight,* Kansas City, Mo., Public Schools, Curriculum Bulletin 104, June, 1958, pp. 5–13.

experience of curriculum workers in the making of these guides should be helpful for those who find themselves with the responsibility for the development of such guides. A searching study of what should be expected in a good curriculum reveals these as desirable items:

1. *Suggested goals or directions for the curriculum, with illustrations of how to translate these general goals into behavioral terms.* Such statements often include the point of view of the faculty concerning the curriculum.

2. *Suggestions on how to plan with pupils, indicating how each teacher can use the ongoing situation in developing with pupils the problems on which the group will work.* Techniques for using the problem-solving approach may be included.

3. *The general framework for the scope and sequence of the curriculum.* Usually this is presented in a chart form showing the areas of experiences, areas of interest, social functions, or some other general category around which the curriculum is planned for the different grade levels.

4. *Suggestions on how to study children, indicating specific kinds of techniques to use and the types of records to keep.*

5. *A statement of characteristics, needs, and developmental tasks of children and youth.*

6. *A list of types of experiences to assist children in their growth toward desired kinds of behavior changes, with suggestions for selecting, organizing, and developing these experiences.*

7. *Identification of resources upon which to draw, such as the community, people, books, films, charts, and maps.* To be helpful, such resources should be annotated and some indication should be given as to the maturity level or the reading level to which the materials are best suited.

8. *Suggested means of evaluation.* Suggestions are included to assist teachers in evaluating growth toward various kinds of behavior outcomes.[13]

It is clear that the development of curriculum and course guides represents an over-all consistent pattern of curriculum procedures. Even when teachers form the major personnel for the development or revision of a course guide, there are generally agreed desirable procedural steps that should be followed, whatever the nomenclature used to designate these steps.[14]

---

[13] See Eleanor Merritt and Henry Harap, *Trends in the Production of Curriculum Guides* (Nashville: George Peabody College for Teachers, Division of Surveys and Field Services, 1955), p. 43 ff. This is a very valuable research study for those wishing to keep abreast of curriculum and course-guide development.

[14] For examples of some outstanding curriculum-revision programs and the procedures employed, plus some discussion of principles governing curriculum making, see Harold J. McNally and A. Harry Passow, *Improving the Quality of Public School Programs: Approaches to Curriculum Development* (New York: Teachers College, Bureau of Publications, Columbia University, 1960). For practices in the development of curriculum and course guides, see Eleanor Merritt and Henry Harap, *Trends in the Production of Curriculum Guides* (Nashville: George Peabody College for Teachers, 1955).

PROCEDURES IN DEVELOPING CURRICULUM
AND COURSE GUIDES

At this point, it may be well to call attention to the separate yet over-lapping phases of curriculum and course-guide construction. In a well-organized, planned, and coordinated curriculum-revision plan, general procedural steps are followed to give the curriculum meaning and an over-all sense of unity. Quite generally, these steps are followed in a somewhat sequential order in that part of the curriculum development known as curriculum and course guides. If, for example, there has not been established a clear statement of social-educational philosophy and principles of learning psychology to serve as a basis for all subsequent curriculum work in the school, then, when a committee undertakes to set up some necessary course guides, it has the obligation to determine what are or what should be the philosophy and psychological concepts that undergird the school and its curriculum, or proceed to develop workable statements to guide subsequent steps in the creation of its proposed guides. The characteristics of a good curriculum and course guide are usually set up in a sequence of procedural steps to give direction and meaning to its development. In general, some approximation to the procedural steps outlined below is followed in good course-guide construction.

Step 1—Statement of a Social and Educational Philosophy. World War II brought us face to face with the necessity for developing a clearly thought-out philosophy of society and government if democracy is to survive. Much confusion in thought about such matters is prevalent in adult circles. There is woeful inability among adults to distinguish between the practical operation of Fascist and democratic principles in ordinary processes of civil life.

Our educational philosophy has been even less clear. Educators have often given voice to conflicting educational ideologies. Frequently, they have given expression to educational ideals which they have negated in the classroom, in staff relations, and in the larger public-education pro-gram. This is partly because our educational system has been but par-tially indigenous to our American culture. In recent years, responsibility for planning curriculum programs forced schools to a realistic and practical consideration of a social-educational philosophy compatible with the democratic ideal we professed.

When a curriculum program has clarified these issues and formulated clear-cut statements of principles, these should be incorporated into the course of study. If this step has not been taken previously, those respon-sible for the construction of the course of study must take the initiative in clarifying these issues and in formulating a statement of principles that may govern the development of that course of study.

Step 2—Statement of the Accepted Basic Principles of Learning. After a statement of principles embodying the best thinking on society, government, and education has been formulated, it is essential to adopt a set of equally clear principles of the psychology of learning. These principles should be in full agreement with the social-educational statements of Step 1.

Too often, teachers, administrators, and the public have shown confusion as to what principles of learning should be accepted and applied. Much is known about economical methods of learning. These should be clearly appraised and presented in the course guide.

The formulation of a statement of the guiding principles of learning is the responsibility of those who develop the curriculum program. Where the statement has been formulated, it may be taken over bodily for the course guide. Where the individual or committee responsible for the course guide must execute this step *de novo*, it would seem desirable to enlist the cooperation of as many of the staff as possible in developing this statement of learning principles.

There has been a great diversity of practice in the extensiveness with which lists of principles have been formulated for this step as well as for Step 1. Many school systems in an earlier period of curriculum making tended to develop very extensive lists of principles, while others tended to confine the lists to a few broad and vague generalizations.[15]

Step 3—A Clearly Defined Conception of the Curriculum. A clear-cut and well-defined conception of the curriculum is fundamental. Without it, no consistent intelligible curriculum or course guide can be produced. The conception of the curriculum determines the direction as well as the general nature of the curriculum or course guide.

If the construction of the curriculum or course guide follows in the local sequence of steps in a program of curriculum development, the definition of the curriculum for the school or school systems in questions has been formulated. It is only necessary to accept it and make its meaning clear. This should be done most carefully and fully.

Unfortunately, even now, all too often individuals or committees are presented with instructions to construct, in a short period of time, curriculum and course guides for which no groundwork has been laid

---

[15] For this earlier tendency to long lists of principles, probably Denver developed the most extensive list and the Fort Worth list is unusually long. See *Preliminary Reports of the Special Appraisal Committees* (Denver Public Schools, 1951), pp. 12–17; and *Language Arts: A Tentative Course of Study for Grade Six,* Curriculum Bulletin No. 146 (Fort Worth Public Schools, 1949), pp. iii–viii. For a shorter-type list, see *Handbook on Curriculum Study* (Salem: State of Oregon, 1937), pp. 75–82.

through a well-considered statement of social-educational philosophy and psychology of learning, much less a carefully developed definition of curriculum. Under these circumstances, the committees must develop these three steps before they can proceed with the construction of curriculum or course guides. The functions of over-all curriculum construction and course-guide construction thus become merged. It is desirable under these circumstances, where there may be some doubt as to the general acceptance of a proposed definition, to enlist the cooperation of the entire school staff so that the definition ultimately agreed upon can be accepted with the assurance that the curriculum or course guide built upon it will not later be rejected.

Step 4—Statement of the Aims of Education. Some considerations may well be offered for those who may not have had the benefit of evolving the statement of aims through participation in the larger curriculum program, and who find it necessary to set up a complete statement of aims.[16] Older courses of study were likely to include lists of "aims and objectives," "general objectives and immediate objectives," or some classification that presumed to distinguish between broad inclusive objectives and those with limited or more immediate significance. The practice in recent years has been to avoid efforts at such distinctions. "Aims" and "objectives" are now used interchangeably.

The course guide, particularly if it is concerned with some limited phase of the total curriculum, may properly distinguish those aims that in their broad social and educational significance are thought to be appreciated by adults but not appropriate to the maturity level of the student. Aims readily understood by the young are more immediately challenging, because they are adjusted to the experience level of the student. Such aims may be included and distinguished from the former by the simple designation of "pupil" aims as against "teacher" or "general" aims.

In the past, it has been customary to think of aims as somewhat discrete and specific in character, very often in terms of mastery of a bit of subject matter. Aims typical of this point of view have been expressed thus:

To learn the correct use of the verb
To develop the habit of seeing one's doctor at least once a year
To distinguish between the transitive and the intransitive verb

[16] For more detailed treatment of this step, see Nelson L. Bossing, *Teaching in Secondary Schools* (3d ed.) (Boston: Houghton Mifflin Co., 1952), pp. 47–50; J. Galen Saylor and William M. Alexander, *Curriculum Planning* (New York: Holt, Rinehart & Winston, Inc., 1954), Chaps. 4–5; William Burton, *The Guidance of the Learning Activities* (3d ed.) (New York: Appleton-Century-Crofts, Inc., 1962), Chap. 6; and J. Minor Gwynn, *Curriculum Principles and Social Trends* (3d ed.) (New York: The Macmillan Co., 1960), Chap. 12.

Thirty years ago, this was the typical form in which statements of aims were cast. This conception of the nature of aims led to the formulation of long lists of minute objectives, or aims, often running into several hundred for a given subject. Basic to this approach were the ideas that education consisted of a series of learnings acquired in additive fashion and that, consequently, aims could be organized in some serial order and learned separately. It was usual to see such lists of aims arranged with a certain number blocked off for achievement at different grade levels.

Today, aims are usually thought of as broad characterizations of desired behavior patterns or outcomes. Where the concept of experience learning is accepted, there is a growing tendency to use the terms *aims, objectives,* and *outcomes* interchangeably when referring to desirable behavior patterns or goals of education.[17] Significantly, these desirable behavior patterns are not assumed to be capable of perfect achievement on any given rung of the educational ladder. They are aims or outcomes toward which education strives, in which the total behavior pattern takes on more and more surely the characteristics of the ideal. Aspects of the total pattern may be given special emphasis in a grade or a given area, but these aspects must be recognized as a part of the whole pattern that continues to emerge as the total educational process develops.

Typical of the newer expression given this concept of the nature of aims or outcomes are the examples of objectives made notable by the Educational Policies Commission more than two decades ago. The uniqueness of this statement is that the Commission accepts the concept of learning as change in behavior and, therefore, has tried to introduce a series of objectives or aims each in the characterization of a behaving person. Under the heading

Reading. The educated person reads the Mother tongue efficiently.
Writing. The educated person writes the Mother tongue effectively.
Friendships. The educated person enjoys the rich, sincere, and varied social life.
Tolerance. The educated person respects honest differences of opinion.

Step 5—Scope and Area of Curriculum and Course Guides. The next major task in the development of a course guide is the determination of some delimiting device by which to ensure inclusiveness and at the same time provide direction for the learning experience. Two major devices are popularly employed. Textbooks for statements of broad fields of information have served to orient and delimit the content of the course guides for the protagonist of subject matter. For those who accept the experience concept of the curriculum,[18] the usual attack upon this problem is to conceive of the range of human activities the normal person

[17] See Chapter 2, for statements and a discussion of aims, objectives, and outcomes.
[18] See Chapter 13.

must engage in to live successfully as the basis of limiting, as well as the basis of orienting, the scope of activities of the course guide.

Step 6—Sequence and Time Allotment. Sequence is a device by which the course guide suggests some orderly arrangement of curriculum content. Since, in the past, scope has been concerned with subject matter, the problem of sequence has been to determine some principle that would govern the order in which subject matter within given areas would appear, or even the order in which areas would appear.

The three most common criteria for the sequential arrangement of subject matter have been (1) from the simple to the complex, best illustrated in language where the traditional arrangement has been word, sentence, paragraph, story; (2) chronological order, so popular in older courses of study in history, where items appeared in order of chronology; (3) the arrangement of materials on the basis of an internal logical-development sequence. For example, in the area of mathematics, it has been customary for schools to begin with arithmetic in the elementary grades and follow with more advanced courses in the secondary school, such as algebra, geometry, and trigonometry. Arithmetical facts and skills are carefully plotted in serial order, usually on the basis of the criteria of difficulty and internal logical development. Partly on the basis of internal developmental consistency and partly on the basis of tradition, advanced courses in mathematics have appeared in most older courses of study in a definite sequential pattern.[19]

The acceptance within recent years of the experience conception of the curriculum has popularized a quite radically different idea of sequence arrangement.[20] This criterion is based upon the evolving maturation levels of the experiences of the student. While essential to the experience approach, it is not exclusively applicable to the experience curriculum. There is an evident tendency to try to combine this approach with the three criteria of arrangement traditionally associated with the subject-matter type of curriculum.

The significance of this plan of sequence arrangement is that, while the three criteria previously mentioned are based upon adult notions of learning, the idea of maturation levels of experience takes into account

---

[19] Even where more traditional conceptions of the curriculum still prevail, there is a noticeable shift on the part of many to attempt to impose newer methods on the old. Language-teaching trends are in the direction of plunging into meaningful expression of ideas both in reading and speaking, the latter becoming more a part of language instruction. Better history-teaching trends are in the direction of grappling with ideas and utilizing historical data to give significance to the ideas.

[20] For a more detailed consideration of the issues and techniques in scope and sequence in the construction of course guides, see the references above to the Virginia, Mississippi, Wells High School, Chicago, Santa Barbara, and Long Beach, California, approaches to this problem.

the psychological factors of the range and wealth of the student's experiences. Consequently, attention is focused primarily upon the levels of understanding at which the student's experiences take place and the kind of environment most conducive to normal and challenging experiences at a given period in his developing life. This plan provides for continuity in learning and enables the student to utilize past experience as a basis for understanding and adjusting to progressively more complex life problems. It has been common practice, where this plan is used, to arrange the sequence by years or grades, with the adoption of some general theme as the basis of orienting the experiences of the student. These themes both provide a unification of learning activities and serve to provide continuity of the learning experiences appropriate to the maturity levels of the student. Characteristic of this approach is the core-curriculum sequence plan developed and widely heralded several years ago by the Santa Barbara, California, Schools. The plan was unique and merits study.

Kindergarten and First Grade: Growth in Effective Living Through Self-Adjustment within the Immediate Environment.

Second Grade: Growth in Effective Living Through Adjusting to Our Community.

Third Grade: Growth in Effective Living by Further Adjusting to the Community Through Developing Insights into the Manner in which the Natural and Controlled Environment Is Contributing to the Life in Our Community.

Fourth Grade: Growth in Effective Living by Further Adjusting to the Community Through Insights into the Manner in which the Present Culture Groups Are Adjusting to Life in Our Community.

Fifth Grade: Growth in Effective Living Through Developing Insights into the Manner in which Present as Compared with Former Culture Groups Carry on the Basic Functions of Human Living in Santa Barbara and California.

Sixth Grade: Growth in Effective Living Through Problem-Centered Experiences Directed Toward Understanding How Modern Technics Are Being Utilized in Carrying Out the Basic Functions of Human Living in the United States.

Seventh Grade: Growth in Effective Living Through Problem-Centered Experiences Directed Toward Understanding and Interdependence of Individuals in Our School, Our Community, the Regions of Our Nation, and in the Countries of Our American Neighbors.

Eighth Grade: Growth in Effective Living Through Problem-Centered Experiences Directed Toward Understanding How Man's Courage, Knowledge, Discoveries, and Inventions Have Effected His Way of Living.

Ninth Grade: Growth in Effective Living Through Problem-Centered Experiences Directed Toward Understanding and Appreciating the Individual's Privileges and Responsibilities as an American Citizen.

Tenth Grade: Growth in Effective Living Through Problem-Centered Experiences Directed Toward Happy and Effective Personal, Spiritual, Social, Recreational, and Vocational Living in the Home, School, and Community.

Eleventh and Twelfth Grade: Growing in Effective Living Through Problem-Centered Experiences Directed Toward Achieving the Highest Possible Quality of Human Experience Through Striving for Social, Political, and Economic Democracy in its Local, State, and National Setting, and for Peace and Cooperation on the International Scene.[21]

The problem of time allotments within a course guide is not completely divorced from scope and sequence. The sequence plan of Santa Barbara roughly allocates certain core themes to a given grade or year. The common practice in sequence arrangement of subject matter often definitely assigns to a given grade a section of the material to be learned,[22] for example, in arithmetic it is customary to indicate certain skills to be attained at various grade levels. The designation of "Spring Semester—Solid Geometry, Trigonometry," for example, places a time limit of one semester on either of those courses. Early practice in course-of-study writing tended to extreme specificity in the allocation of subject matter, so much so that, not infrequently, weekly and even daily apportionment of a semester's or year's work was attempted. The general trend of recent years has been toward greater flexibility consonant with the newer conceptions of the nature of learning and the functions of education.

Step 7—Determination of Content Materials and Activities. The extent to which the selection of the content of the course guide must be carried forward at this point will be determined by the thoroughness of what has been done in Steps 5 and 6 and by the educational point of view held by those responsible for the construction of the course guide. Where skills and certain factual data are to be emphasized, their place in the total curriculum is a matter for designation in appropriate places in the course guide.

The same procedure is necessary where the experience curriculum is planned. In this approach, attention will be given primarily to the indication of the type of experiences or competences it is desirable for the student to have or achieve in the different areas and at various levels in order to ensure the realization of the aims of education. Where certain skills and understandings are anticipated as necessary for successful adjustment at given maturity levels, these should be suggested in addi-

---

21 *Developmental Curriculum*, Bulletin No. 1, rev. ed. (Santa Barbara, Calif.: Santa Barbara Public Schools, 1941); *General Framework of the Social Education Aspects of the Curriculum of the Long Beach Public Schools* (Long Beach, Calif.: Office of Curriculum Development, 1954); reproduced in Vernon E. Anderson, *Principles and Procedures of Curriculum Improvement* (New York: The Ronald Press Co., 1956), pp. 282–283. A recent article pleads for more attention to vertical curriculum and course construction, even for the more traditional type of curriculum approach. See Fred M. King, "A Trend in Curriculum Development," *Education*, Vol. 80 (March, 1960), pp. 433–437.

22 This is characteristic also of the plan of the Long Beach, California, scope and sequence organization, referred to in the previous footnote.

tion to the types of activities called for to contribute to the experiences desired.

Step 8—Suggested Organization of Content Materials and Activities. A multiplicity of problems is faced at this stage of course-guide construction. If the subject-matter approach is being used, the issue of correlation, fusion, broad fields, or some form of integration must be settled, if these problems have not been indirectly anticipated in Steps 5 and 6. If the core-curriculum approach is to be used, the organizational problems will be different. The extent to which unit organization is to be used and the type of unit idea accepted are parts of the organizational problem. How to set up learning situations when the experience curriculum approach is the basis of the organization will require a somewhat different treatment in the course guide from that of the more traditional subject-matter approach. Other problems of organization are involved if an attempt at functionally bridging the gap between the experience and subject-matter approaches is undertaken. It is sufficient here to call attention to the nature of the task. A more detailed discussion of these curriculum issues and organizational problems will be found in Chapters 13 and 28.

Step 9—Suggested Teaching Procedures. In harmony with the past definiteness and inflexibility of course-of-study organization, it was not unusual to find the teaching procedures rigorously prescribed. Modern education frowns on any attempts to shackle the teacher or cramp his freedom to utilize whatever procedures the given learning situation appears to demand. This does not mean the omission of teaching procedures in the modern course guide. A careful analysis of contemporary course guides will reveal the large degree of emphasis given to teaching procedures as related to the objectives and content of the courses.

Instead of prescription of a specific teaching procedure or method for the teaching of a particular phase of the course guide, numerous suggestions may be offered in the form of "Pupil Activities" or "Teaching Suggestions," or both.[23] The teacher is recognized as the one who can choose most wisely what form of attack to make upon a specific learning situation. This flows from the emphasis now placed upon motivation in learning;[24] the necessity of capitalizing upon the time, place, and general circumstances of pupil background to create the most acceptable learning situation possible; and the recognition that individual teachers may vary widely in their effectiveness in the use of teaching method and procedure. "Secondary School Teachers and Principals must be free to try out better methods and materials without threat to their security. Otherwise

[23] See Chapter 10, for a discussion of resource units, which include these items.
[24] See the curriculum and course guides given in Chapters 10 and 12, or similar guides of recent origin, for a wealth of illustrations on this point.

the individual initiative and creativity will be a lost virtue" is the sage advice with which a recent course guide approaches this problem.

Step 10—Suggested Evaluation Procedures. *Measurement* is the term found in the older courses of study. It centered attention upon devices for the determination of the extent of achievement of quantitative learning. *Evaluation,* which has a more inclusive meaning, is the term generally found in contemporary course guides, as well as in the literature of the curriculum.

Evaluation has come to be looked upon as many-sided. In the course guide, the original function of determining the degree of success of the student probably will continue to be of primary importance, although its interpretation has been greatly enlarged. The teacher utilizes evaluation as an important means of determining the significance of the curricular materials and procedures used as aids to learning. Thus, evaluation becomes a means by which teachers and administrators are able to reach some judgments as to the success of the school in achieving its larger objectives of education. Attitudes and the general progress of the youth of the school in the broader achievement of successful citizenship behavior patterns are now important aspects of evaluation, the procedures for which are now used to help the student become intelligently critical of his own learning activities and achievements in areas not readily evaluated by the older, traditional measurement devices.

Consequently, every course guide should provide for a somewhat full consideration of the nature and meaning of modern evaluation. It should also provide extensive suggestions of evaluation procedures for pupil and teacher, and should give practical suggestions of available instruments, or sources of such information, for different phases of evaluation.

Step 11—Pupil-Teacher Reference Materials. No course guide should be considered complete unless it lists an abundance of reference materials. These reference lists or bibliographies should be of two types. There should be rich reference lists of source materials for pupils and teachers in connection with each unit or phase of the subject, however organized. These lists should be supplemented by a general bibliography for the main areas or subjects at each grade level, or group level if grade levels are no longer maintained. This is particularly important where the newer emphasis upon wide latitude in the use of teaching procedures and materials is encouraged. All too often, teachers would like to exercise more freedom and variety in their teaching to meet the needs of individual differences in pupils but are handicapped by lack of a convenient listing of suggested source materials in the course guide. Contemporary course guides also make extensive use of the voluminous listings of films and filmstrips now available, appropriate to each unit suggested in the course guide.

Step 12—Mechanical Makeup of Course Guides. A course guide may have its usefulness enhanced or limited by the way it is put together. Certain aspects of content organization contribute in maximum degree to the usefulness of the course guide. The larger the course guide, the more important it is that it have certain features.

Every course guide should indicate clearly when it was produced. This is particularly important when its format permits of no modification. Many changes take place in educational thinking and procedures, and valuable additions to bibliographical and film materials take place over a period of a few years. Most course guides, in some degree at least, are out of date within a few years of publication. The teacher who is called upon to use a course guide ought to be constantly aware of the possible adjustments necessitated by developments since its construction.

Every course guide should have a Table of Contents and appropriate divisions covering the content of Steps 1–11 discussed above. The larger course guides such as those issued by state agencies should contain an Index.

Whether a course guide should be printed or mimeographed, bound or in loose-leaf form will depend upon a number of considerations. Educational considerations should be paramount for most schools. If the curriculum is conceived to be a somewhat static thing that should be changed only at long intervals, it may be more economical to print and bind the course guide. If, on the other hand, the curriculum is conceived of as a growing, evolving, dynamic thing constantly changing and necessarily subject to modification, the course guide should be set up in such a form as to be capable of easy modification at crucial points without requiring a complete change. For this purpose the mimeographed, loose-leaf form, in general, is best. There are many considerations of volume of usage and the impracticality of constant modifications, for instance, in state guides or very large city school systems where printed and bound course guides may be the most feasible and practicable. In general, mimeographed, loose-leaf course guides are the more practical for the average school that wishes to keep its curriculum or course guides relatively fluid.

QUESTIONS, PROBLEMS, AND ISSUES FOR FURTHER THOUGHT

1. How do you distinguish between the educational terms *curriculum* and *course guides?*
2. Why is a program of curriculum and course guide construction considered by many to be an excellent device for the in-service education of teachers?

3. Distinguish between a general or social philosophy and an educational philosophy. Show concretely the dependence of the one upon the other.
4. In what way is psychology related to curriculum and course-guide construction?
5. How are "principles" related to curriculum and course-guide construction?
6. Have one group in the class attempt to develop a set of principles in harmony with an extended statement of philosophy and psychology. Let another group assume a statement of principles and try to derive these from an implied theory of philosophy and psychology.
7. From one subject field, select an objective and try to state it in behavioral terms.
8. Explain (a) how the idea of "scope" has changed in curriculum and course-guide construction and (b) what the educational theories are back of the traditional and newer meaning of "scope."
9. How do "sequence and time allotment" operate differently in subject-matter and in experience curriculums?
10. Explain why teaching procedures tend to be less rigidily prescribed in recent course-guide construction.
11. Why is the term *guides* quite generally substituted for the older term *courses of study* in modern curriculum-construction projects?

SUPPLEMENTARY MATERIALS

SELECTED READINGS

ANDERSON, VERNON E. *Principles and Procedures of Curriculum Improvement,* New York: The Ronald Press Co., 1956. Chapters 12–14. The entire book is valuable for those developing a school curriculum. The specific chapters listed are most applicable to the considerations of curriculum and course-guide construction.

BLOOM, BENJAMIN S., *et al. Taxonomy of Educational Objectives,* New York: Longmans, Green & Co., Inc., 1956. An excellent analysis of objectives, with a classification of different types. Presents illustrations of ways of evaluating objectives.

BOSSING, NELSON L. *Principles of Secondary Education* (2d ed.). Englewood Cliffs, N.J.: Prentice-Hall, Inc., 1955. Chapters 12–13. In these chapters, the organization of the subject-matter and experience types of curriculum approach are discussed, and the problems involved in setting up courses of study or course guides are considered.

BURTON, WILLIAM H. *The Guidance of the Learning Activities* (3d ed.). New York: Appleton-Century-Crofts, Inc., 1962. Chapters 6, 13–17. A very penetrating discussion of the place and use of objectives in the curriculum and the classroom.

FAUNCE, ROLAND C., and NELSON L. BOSSING. *Developing the Core Curriculum* (2d ed.). Englewood Cliffs, N.J.: Prentice-Hall, Inc., 1958. Chapters 4–5, 13. The philosophical and psychological principles that must guide the development of curriculum and course-of-study construction are considered. The peculiar implications of experience learning for the determination of objectives, scope, areas, and sequence in curriculum making are pointed out, as well as the organization of classroom units.

GWYNN, J. MINOR. *Curriculum Principles and Social Trends* (3d ed.). New York: The Macmillan Co., 1960. Chapters 12–13. A study of changing conceptions of aims in education and the curriculum and of ways of developing the curriculum for classroom purposes.

KRUG, EDWARD A. *Curriculum Planning* (2d ed.). New York: Harper & Row, 1957. Chapters 2–3, 7. Discusses the development of objectives and their psychological, social, and philosophic bases. A full chapter is devoted to the development of curriculum guides.

MCNALLY, HAROLD J., *et al. Improving the Quality of Public School Programs.* New York: Teachers College, Bureau of Publications, Columbia University, 1960. This book presents an excellent discussion of principles of good curriculum making and then summarizes several major types of curriculum reorganizations.

MERRITT, ELEANOR, and HENRY HARAP. *Trends in the Production of Curriculum Guides.* Nashville, Tenn.: George Peabody College for Teachers, Division of Surveys & Field Services, 1955. A very thorough and valuable study of types of curriculum guides being developed and the evident trends thus revealed.

ROMINE, STEPHEN A. *Building the High School Curriculum.* New York: The Ronald Press Co., 1954. Chapters 6, 12, 16. The problems and procedures of curriculum and course-of-study construction associated with the determination of the nature of learning, purposes of education, and the procedures involved in organizing curriculums and courses of study; special attention is given to the development of the core-curriculum instruction and resource units.

SMITH, B. O., W. O. STANLEY, and J. H. SHORES. *Fundamentals of Curriculum Development* (2d ed.). New York: Harcourt, Brace & World, Inc., 1957. Chapters 5–9. A most thorough discussion of the problem of objectives, selection of curriculum content, sequence, and time allotment.

STRATEMEYER, FLORENCE B., *et al. Developing a Curriculum for Modern Living* (2d ed.). New York: Teachers College, Bureau of Publications, Columbia University, 1957. Chapters 4–6. The idea of "persistent life situations" as the basis of curriculum and course-of-study construction; how the organization of instruction can be developed around these "persistent life situations."

15

Education for Work

"The job world of the future obviously calls for people who have a marketable skill. The day of 'I can do anything' apparently is definitely passed. In these days of increasing complexity of jobs and of professional specialization, no one, whether young or old, will be able to offer such versatility in the job market."[1]

Thus, increasingly, young people in high school and college will learn some marketable skill. Frequently the initial job skill will be upgraded by an in-service program on the job. The day of the "little red school-house" and a minimum period of "readin', ritin', and 'rithmetic" is long since gone.

No one can say exactly how many persons are learning marketable skills, for many young people are gaining work experience or job skills in non-vocational classes or by part-time paid or unpaid jobs. But the number enrolled in vocational classes in secondary schools is impressive.

In 1960, the number of persons enrolled in vocational classes was 3,768,149. Of these, 796,237 were in agriculture, 303,784 in distributive occupations, 1,588,109 in home economics, 938,490 in trades and industries, 40,250 in practical nursing, and 101,279 in area programs.[2] Of these, 1,740,776 were enrolled in daytime classes[3] and constituted principally the young adults in school.

[1] *Occupational Outlook Handbook,* U.S. Department of Labor, Bulletin No. 1300, 1961, p. 27.

[2] *Digest of Annual Reports of State Boards for Vocational Education to the Office of Education, Division of Vocational Education,* fiscal year ended June 30, 1960, p. 7.

[3] *Ibid.,* p. 8.

HIGH SCHOOL GROWTH AND THE NEED FOR
WORK EDUCATION

The growth of the American high school has been one of the most striking phenomena of contemporary life. High school enrolment has roughly doubled every decade between 1880 and 1960. Nowhere else in the world has there been so large an increase in secondary school population, although there are beginnings in other countries.

Reasons for Increased Secondary School Enrolments. A major reason why boys and girls attend high school in such large numbers is that the United States has become an urban society. In 1890, less than 40 per cent of Americans lived in urban areas. By 1960, more than 65 per cent were city dwellers. In cities, there are fewer chores and other tasks for children to do about the home, which in themselves have educational value. For this reason, among others, parents have come to accept the idea that their children should go to high school as a matter of course.

Perhaps a more important reason for high school growth is the rapidly increasing productivity of industrial workers in this country. Each year, the amount produced per worker has risen. In the past quarter-century, in many industries, the output per worker per hour has doubled. Thus, production can be carried on successfully without the need for children to enter the labor market at an early age. Consciously or unconsciously, we have kept our young people in school, because our tremendous productivity has allowed us to do so. In fact, there is almost no opportunity open for full-time jobs to boys and girls under sixteen years of age and little opportunity for those under eighteen or for older ones who have not graduated from high school.

A third reason may be found in the legislation in every state requiring school attendance, usually until the age of sixteen, although several states require attendance until high school graduation or the age of eighteen.

Furthermore, the recognition of the value of secondary and higher education has for economic and social reasons become more general. A new tradition has been established of the completion of high school and attendance at college. In many communities, over half of the graduating seniors attend some institution after high school.

Other Possibilities. Young people could be placed in a large military establishment, which is not in keeping with our democratic heritage and which would be more expensive than a system of public high schools. They could be put to work and older people retired, but this does not fit with our democratic traditions either, or with the desires of older workers. Consciously in part, but more frequently without conscious thought, we have kept our young people in school, because the nation's tremendous productivity has allowed us to do so.

Since the American people have decided in favor of increased school attendance, it has been necessary to work out an educational program richer in content and extending over a longer period of years. Guidance programs, work experience, the development of varied programs of extracurricular activities, vocational training, and a vast amount of curriculum reconstruction were due to the growth of schools. All were necessary to provide educational experiences that would be meaningful for a heterogeneous school population that needs and desires preparation for work.

OCCUPATIONAL TRENDS AS GUIDES FOR WORK EDUCATION

Technical Training. The technical skills in the highly trained occupations require relatively long periods of training. An expert stenographer requires a considerable training period. The training of a tool and die maker is a long and arduous process, which a student may begin in secondary school and continue for years as an apprentice in industry. For the highly skilled occupations such as repair of dynamos and of gasoline or diesel engines and for the professions, relatively long periods of preparation, either in secondary schools and higher institutions or in industry supplemented by schools, are imperative.

When we consider occupational categories, in contrast to degrees of skill required, the changes in patterns of American employment are also clear. As Figure 15–1 indicates, the percentage of persons engaged in agriculture and manufacturing has declined rapidly in the past 100 years. Manufacturing and mechanical employment have declined somewhat. Percentages of employment in the trade and transportation fields, in clerical services, and in the professions have increased markedly in recent times.

Today's numerically largest white-collar occupation, the clerical workers (close to ten million) has grown at a faster rate than any other except the professional group. Between 1950 and 1960 the number of clerical workers grew over 30%; in the next ten years a further growth of 26% is expected. The growth has occurred in spite of the introduction of laborsaving office machines and more efficient management methods.

In 1950 almost five million persons were employed in professional and technical occupations. By 1960 their total had reached seven and a half million. By 1970 the number will exceed ten million, which is a rise of 20% from 8% to over 12½% of the total employment.[4]

[4] Occupational Outlook Handbook, U.S. Department of Labor Bulletin No. 1300, 1961, p. 24.

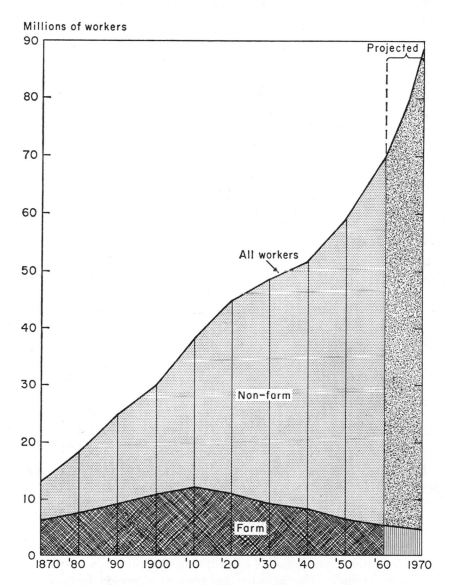

Fig. 15–1. More workers in business and industry; fewer on farms. (*Occupational Outlook Handbook,* U.S. Department of Labor Bulletin No. 1300, 1961, p. 16.)

Professional, clerical, and sales occupations have grown
most rapidly.

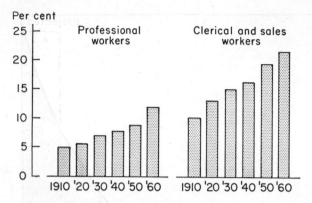

Farm and unskilled occupations have lost ground.

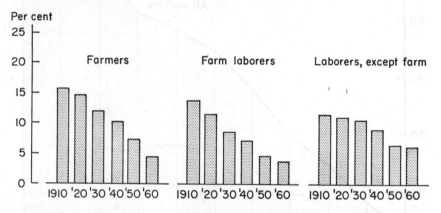

Fig. 15–2. Proportion of experienced labor force in each occupational
group, 1910–1960. (Data for 1910–1950, U.S. Bureau of the Census; data
for 1960 estimated by U.S. Bureau of Labor Statistics. *Occupational Outlook Handbook,* U.S. Department of Labor Bulletin No. 1300, 1961, p.
22.)

The important contribution of education in distribution in the past year
has been recognized by industry, government agencies, business, and
educators as a service that is helping increasingly to improve the nation's
marketing system. "A few states are conducting pilot executive development programs in cooperation with businesses. In the programs, selection
of students is required to obtain the type having potential for management."[5] This will require a whole rethinking of distributive education.

[5] *Digest of Vocational Education Programs,* p. 28.

Millions of workers

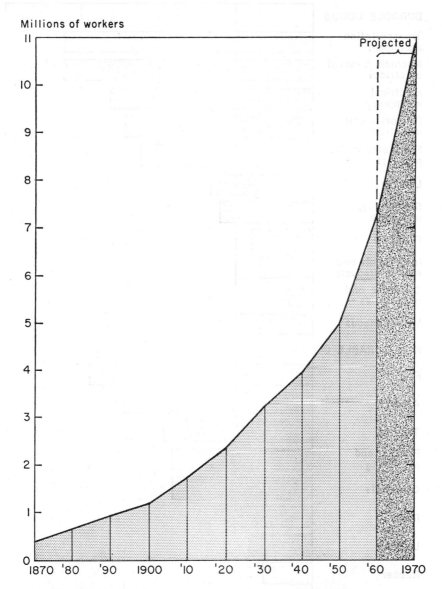

Fig. 15–3. Growth of professional, technical, and kindred occupations. (*Occupational Outlook Handbook*, U.S. Department of Labor Bulletin No. 1300, 1961, p. 31.)

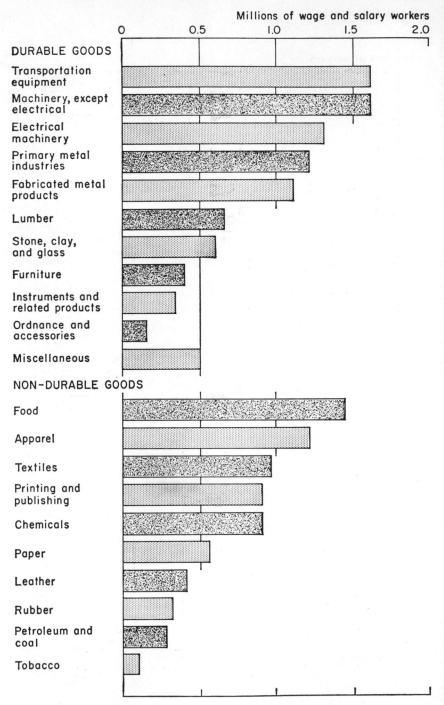

Fig. 15–4. Employment in major branches of manufacturing, 1960. (*Occupational Outlook Handbook*, U. S. Department of Labor Bulletin No. 1300, 1961, p. 18.)

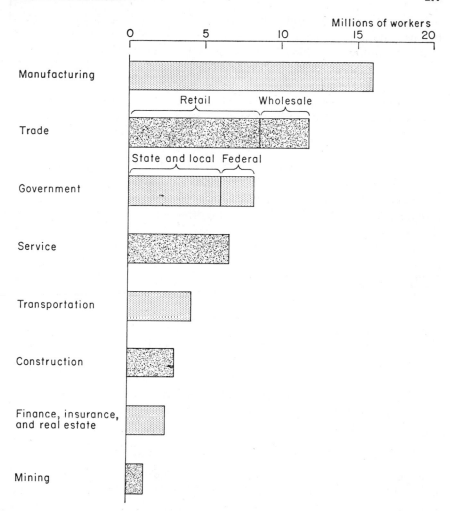

Fig. 15–5. Employment in eight major industry groups, 1960. (*Occupational Outlook Handbook,* U.S. Department of Labor Bulletin No. 1300, 1961, p. 18.)

A growing occupational group called "service workers" offers many job opportunities ranging from some quite unskilled jobs to those requiring specialized education or training. For example, janitors are included here, but also waiters, cooks, barbers, laundry workers, beauticians, policemen, firemen, practical nurses, and FBI agents. By 1970, we can expect a numerical growth to more than 10 million, on a par numerically and proportionately with professional workers.[6]

[6] *Ibid.,* p. 26.

In recent years, more girls and women have been employed as beauticians, who are also called hairdressers or cosmetologists. The estimated number employed in 1960 was approximately 300,000,[7] with more than twice that number licensed. There were 329 public vocational schools offering programs in cosmetology, and 1,922[8] private schools. The enrolment in both kinds of schools totaled 107,000.[9] The employment outlook is excellent, as women are increasingly aware of the part good grooming plays in social and business life. Many married women are part-time beauty operators.

Several states, especially those that are attractive to tourists, are beginning to establish programs to provide training for the rapidly expanding hotel and restaurant industry. In addition to training for the established programs in the industry, such as meat cutting and quantity food preparation, some training is provided for waiters, waitresses, and hostesses.[10]

Mechanics and repairmen of all kinds have increased rapidly. Thus, during the first half-century, the number increased from 300,000 to 2.5 million. Members of some once-pre-eminent skilled occupations, such as blacksmiths and shoemakers, total only 100,000 together among today's 8.5 million skilled workers.[11]

Much of the preparation for work is in classes in vocational agriculture, homemaking trades and industries, and "diversified occupations." The newest programs in practical nursing and area vocational programs are encouraging. The area programs draw young adults, often high school graduates, from an area for training for jobs in the area that would not be feasible in local communities because of small enrolments.

FEDERAL AND STATE PLANS

Expenditures for vocational education in 1960 totaled $238,811,764, of which $45,313,236 were federal and $82,465,770 were state funds. The balance, nearly half of the total, was local funds.[12]

The federal government and the states cooperate in the administration of programs of vocational education of lower than college grade. The principal purpose is to fit persons for useful employment. Under the Smith-Hughes Act of 1917 and the George-Barden Act of 1946, federal funds are available for allotment to the states and territories for the various programs listed above.

[7] *Occupational Outlook,* p. 325.
[8] *Ibid.,* p. 326.
[9] *Ibid.,* p. 326.
[10] *Digest of Annual Reports of State Boards for Vocational Education to the Office of Education, Division of Vocational Education,* fiscal year ended June 30, 1960, p. 44.
[11] *Ibid.,* p. 25.
[12] *Ibid.,* p. 13.

The needs of two distinct groups of people are served by these programs. They are those who have entered upon and those who are preparing to enter upon the work of various occupations in the field of vocational education. Vocational-education programs provide training for young persons in regular day schools and for out-of-school youth and adults, both employed and temporarily unemployed. The federal-state cooperative effort is based on the fundamental ideas that vocational education is in the national interest and is essential for the national welfare and that, therefore, federal funds are necessary to stimulate states in making adequate provision. In general, the federal funds must be matched by local or state funds. The state plans encompass operational activities in the various fields, as well as the training of vocational teachers and counselors.

There can be little doubt that the vocational-education acts have been very important to many young people who are preparing for the specific occupations involved. There has been criticism to the effect that the acts are unduly prescriptive and that, with the lessened emphasis on agriculture in our economy, some changes in the administration of vocational education would be desirable. The most extreme criticisms have suggested that specific aids for vocational education should be eliminated and that federal aid for education should take its place. At this time, such criticisms do not seem likely to be realized.

Blue-Collar vs. White-Collar Workers. We now have more white-collar workers than blue-collar workers, and there is nothing in the offing that will change this major contour of our work force, shown by the following tabulation:

	1910	1959	1970
All workers	100%	100%	100%
White-collar	22	42	45
Professional and technical	5	11	13
Proprietary and managerial	7	11	11
Clerical and sales	10	20	21
Blue-collar	37	37	36
Skilled	12	13	13
Semiskilled	14	18	18
Unskilled	11	6	5
Service	10	12	13
Farm	31	9	6

POPULATION GROUPS AT A DISADVANTAGE IN SECURING JOBS

Youth. For thirteen consecutive quarters, at least one out of every eight teen-age boys has been unemployed. The record for the teen-age girls is just about the same; their unemployment rates are at least double the national average. Somewhat higher unemployment among youth may be expected, since they do move more extensively from one job to another and are at the beginning of their career development. But among them are the school dropouts, whose unemployment experiences are very severe. All of this is made all the more serious, since we have already seen that this decade will bring an unparalleled 26 million new young workers into the job market, and, if current levels prevail, 7.5 million of them will be dropouts, without a high-school diploma and very ill-fitted for the job world ahead.

The problem of the dropout is critical. The job structure, already oriented toward the professional, technical, and skilled trades, leaves a narrower band of employment opportunities for the youngster without adequate preparation. His unemployment rate is triple the national average; when he is employed, it is likely to be at a most menial and low-paying job.

Unskilled Workers. For a long time now, the difference in unemployment experience among the different skill groups in our working population have been very marked. Most severely affected have been the unskilled manual workers—not only under the impact of recessions but also in terms of the long-range substantial decline in the number of unskilled jobs. Today, one in every five of our unskilled workers is unemployed—a rate two-thirds higher than that for semiskilled workers, 100 per cent higher than that for skilled craftsmen. There is nothing in the offing that can serve to alter these differentials, again especially in the light of our current and expected industrial and occupational structure.

Negroes. Negroes tend to have the least amount of educational attainment, are highly concentrated in the unskilled trades, and still, of course, experience a substantial amount of discrimination in employment. As a result, their unemployment rate is double that of their white counterparts; they account for about one out of every ten workers, but two out of every ten unemployed.

Older Workers. Unemployment rates among persons forty-five years of age and over have compared very favorably with those of other age groups during the postwar period, especially under the protection of the seniority systems that prevail in a significant number of industrial sectors. However, the older worker is at a significant disadvantage when he loses his job; he has a much more difficult time getting re-employed. Right now, 40 per cent of men forty-five to sixty-four years of age who are unemployed have been out of work continuously for sixteen weeks or longer.

Workers in Depressed Areas. Cutting across these groups is the changing geography of American industry, which is leaving in its wake areas of substantial unemployment. Our most recent data (for March, 1961) show that fully 101 out of the 150 major labor areas in the United States are now classified as "areas of substantial labor surplus." Another 184 smaller areas are in this category, too. Experiencing an unemployment rate of at least 6 per cent, all of these depressed areas now account for more than 3 million unemployed, or about 55 per cent of all the unemployed in the country.

Pathways to Solutions. These five groups represent some of the more intractable social and economic problems of today and the decade ahead. Leaders in education, as elsewhere, will find, more and more, four major pathways in the forefront of discussion as possible routes to be taken to arrive at solutions:

1. **Education, Training, and Skill Development.** One definition of education contains this dimension: "To help the person withstand the inevitable changes between what he learns and what will be expected of him throughout his life." This argues for viewing education and training as a development process that continues throughout the lifetime of an individual. It calls for the development of guidance and counseling at the elementary school level; for more creative and meaningful curriculums, especially for the manually talented, at the secondary school level, in order to increase the holding power of the schools; for the broadest kind of training to increase the flexibility, the adaptability, of persons vis-à-vis the changing job world; for an organized, systematic program of supported retraining and reskilling of unemployed workers to fit them for new, different employment opportunities. A good beginning toward this last lies in the Area Redevelopment Act now in effect.

2. **End of Discrimination.** Vigorous action, on all fronts, is needed to end discriminatory education and employment practices against Negroes, older workers, and other members of our population. Given the challenge ahead of us, discriminatory practices add a dangerous dimension to our already grave domestic situation as well as to our posture in the international field. The current efforts in the field of government-related employment are indicative.

3. **Mobility.** The 1960 Decennial Census indicates the substantial migration and mobility of our population. Just as much attention should be paid to the changing geography of industrial and business employment opportunities. The geography of our nation's employment has also changed. And mobility, in fact, is the traditional manner in which we have matched the changing location of our population and the changing location of our economic opportunities. Support will be asked for to change the institutional forces that hinder mobility and, on the positive side, to take concrete steps toward increasing mobility wherever neces-

sary—from steps toward vesting pension rights to the possibility of help in relocating unemployed persons to areas of economic opportunity.

4. Automation and Technological Development. Cutting across many, if not most, of our current and expected employment and unemployment problems is the factor of productivity. It is fundamental to our aspirations for higher economic growth. Yet increased productivity can and does have important effects on the displacement of workers. Not only government but labor and management as well have shown increasing concern with this problem. Studies made in the Department of Labor show that, in a number of instances, action has been taken that has mitigated and even prevented the displacement effects of technological improvements. We need to focus, coordinate, and broaden our efforts in this field, as well as in the areas of education, full opportunity for all, and mobility. These are some of the major social and economic issues emerging from our rapid population changes in the 1960's.[13]

Implications of Occupational Trends. With more than 20,000 occupations from which to choose, the young person faces a bewildering decision. If the school is to aid him, it must train him so that he can choose between large fields of occupation rather than concentrate on one specific job. It seems fair to say that vocational education must enable workers to get along with each other and to understand the society in which they live, that information about occupations and mobility within occupations is vital, and that, at the professional and technical levels, specific skills must be learned. Narrow vocational training, except at the professional and technical levels after one has left the secondary school, does not have major usefulness in a society where occupations change as rapidly as they do in ours.

THE NEED FOR EDUCATION TO WORK

Values of Earning Money While in School. When one works for pay, certain other important values are inherent. Paid employment provides training in the value of money and gives experience in the spending or saving of money and in the mathematics involved in these things. Paid work by youth thus develops an early appreciation of thrift—ordinarily acquired only by long experience—which furnishes a concrete basis for understanding what prices are paid, in terms of hours worked, for goods and services bought with earned money.

Work for pay also enables many young people to improve their personal appearance and engage in social and recreational activity beyond

[13] Seymour L. Wolfbein, "Social and Economic Implications of Our Rapidly Changing Population," paper read at the Fourth National School Finance Conference, April 27–28, 1961.

the level possible with the allowances available from their parents. It enables them to pay their way in the school world, which has become one of fees and incidental expenses of extracurricular activities. In the determination of social attitudes and the development of self-confidence, as well as of personality, this consideration is indeed an important one.

Paid work should also help to keep in school the many young people who drop out because they do not have the money for fees and extracurricular activities. Fees, dues, admissions, and costumes cost the individual high school pupil and his family in the "free" American high school in Wisconsin in the school year 1949–1950 an average of $124.02.[14] Hummell found even greater expenses in Oregon high schools in 1959–1960 (Table 15–1). It is recognized that not all secondary school students will incur all expenses; nevertheless, these figures may provide a guide as to approximate financial demands placed on secondary school pupils.

TABLE 15–1

INCIDENTAL COSTS OF STUDENTS ATTENDING OREGON SECONDARY SCHOOLS, 1959–1960[15]

(averages of 197 Oregon secondary schools)

Student-body tickets	$ 4.26
Other ticket costs	6.79
Book rental	6.32
Book purchases	9.13
General supplies for year	7.92
Locker rental	.89
Gym or towel fees	2.16
Gym suit and shoes	7.36
Insurance other than athletic	2.56
Athletic insurance	9.69
Annual	3.27
Class dues	1.14
Club dues	1.73
School paper	.99
Transportation	65.28
Lunch	50.83
Expenses on trips	9.67
Knicknacks	23.96
Novelties, booster caps, etc.	2.85
Special clothing	15.48
Special transportation	6.18
Total	$238.46
Special class jewelry	$ 21.04
Special graduation expense	$ 46.82

[14] Raymond E. Schultz, "Can Parents Afford To Send Their Children to High School?" *The School Review,* Vol. 60 (May, 1952), p. 286.

[15] Errett Hummell, personal communication, September 4, 1962.

Credit for Work Experience. It seems clear that, while work experience is important, the amount of time spent at it is, in most instances, somewhat out of proportion to learning of a type for which school credit is given. It would seem to follow that credit in limited amounts should be granted.

Coordination of Work Experience with Class Study. The federally aided vocational programs have always provided coordination. Schools that are serious about work-experience programs are now providing coordinators.

OBSTACLES TO PROVIDING WORK EXPERIENCE

In developing a satisfactory program, responsible administrators have some difficult problems to solve. There are a number of obstacles to providing real work experience in the schools, even in having young people carry real jobs outside the school. Except in a war period, organized labor looks with disfavor on production by young people still in school, and many manufacturers feel it to be unfair competition, even where labor and management are sympathetic to work for young people. Jobs secured must be of value to the students, and the service rendered by the young people must be of value to industry.

Child-labor laws present an obstacle. Problems of social security legislation will vex the small employer, for an addition of one more worker may change his classification. Workmen's compensation laws in some states are such that employers dare not use young people, even if they are willing to do so. This does not imply that child-labor laws, social security legislation, or compensation regulations are unwise. They are indeed desirable, but, in some cases, they need revision so that young people may work without exploitation. A supervisory program must be provided for the purpose of rendering service to both students and employers, and also to provide a better program of evaluation.

A panel, appointed by Abraham Ribicoff when he was Secretary of Health, Education, and Welfare, to investigate the need for vocational education, consisted of twenty-five citizens representing the general public, education, labor, and business. For more than a year, the committee studied the impact on vocational education of automation, technical advance, population mobility, racial and other discriminations, urbanization, and also the relationships of local-state-federal programs.

The study group was under the chairmanship of Benjamin C. Willis, general superintendent of Chicago public schools. Director of the administrative staff was J. Chester Swanson, a professor of education at the University of California.

To finance and expand the program, the panel recommended to President Kennedy that annual federal funds for vocational education be increased from the current $75 million to $400 million. The group urged state and local governments to increase the more than $500 million they now spend annually for vocational education.

School administrators must recognize the need for vocational education and have knowledge concerning the nature of a program which can adequately serve the people of their community. It cannot be merely a program for second-class citizens, academic or social. It must be geared to realistic employment opportunities, taught by teachers who are acknowledged masters of their occupations, and evaluated constantly in terms of the job placement of those who complete training and their ability to succeed on the job.

Vocational training should be provided in more schools, for more occupations, and extended into post high school programs. The community, management, labor and employment services must take some responsibility and perform some services. Schools alone cannot provide an adequate program.[16]

THE AMERICAN EDUCATION-VOCATION DAYDREAM

If the dignity of work is to be a reality in the life of every individual, certain attitudes of parents and educators must be changed. It is only natural that parents should desire for their children a higher status in society than they themselves enjoy. For many individuals, upward mobility was possible during the rapid expansion of our nation, but it has become increasingly more difficult as the frontier has disappeared. As our productive economy frees all the young children for secondary school attendance, graduation from the high school ceases to be the road to the white-collar job.

Here the educational daydream clashes with reality. Parents and many educators feel that the bare fact of high school graduation in itself will enable young people to "get on in the world." For many students, working while attending school is the only hope of staying in school, for frequently family income and the size of the family are inversely related. Thus, a work-experience program becomes a democratizing factor in the community.

Changes in school organization are demanded by the inclusion of work for all as part of the curriculum. Time schedules must be flexible. Records must include the amount and an evaluation of work experience. Coordinators will be supplied to make the experience educational and to prevent exploitation. A quarter of a century ago, the inclusion of cocurricular activities in the school organization demanded far-reaching

16 J. Chester Swanson, "Here's What the New Demands for Vocational Education Mean for Schoolmen," *Nation's Schools*, February, 1963, p. 61.

changes and made the schools more difficult to operate. Yet activities made the school program fit more closely the needs of the young people enrolled. The inclusion of work experiences will also add to the difficulty of administering a school and will make its organization more complex. But it must be provided, if the schools are to fit even better the needs of the adolescent.

The Golden Opportunity. This chapter is not intended to be an exhaustive description of the means whereby young people can best be fitted into the productive economy of our nation. The main point to be made here is that work experience, a good general education, vocational information, the ability to do some specific task, adequate counseling, placement on the job, following up on the job, and retraining are minimum requisites in a satisfactory plan for vocational adjustment. This chapter has attempted to highlight two aspects of the problem: (1) the importance of securing some marketable skill and (2) the importance of additional training or retraining of many young adults as the job situation changes.

QUESTIONS, PROBLEMS, AND ISSUES FOR FURTHER THOUGHT

1. List a number of occupations that require chiefly (a) vocational *training*, (b) vocational *education.*
2. Trace the development of the service industries as an important element in the occupational pattern.
3. Contrast the percentage engaged in agriculture and manufacturing now and in 1870, and indicate what this implies for vocational education.
4. Indicate why work experience has become recognized as important, and present some illustrations of work experience that have been closely articulated with instruction in secondary schools.
5. Indicate, by using statistical data, how six occupations have changed in relative importance in the total employment in the United States since 1900.
6. Write a brief essay indicating the implications of the availability of positions classed as skilled, semiskilled, and unskilled.
7. What are the relative advantages of the general shop and unit shops?
8. Indicate what citizenship training is necessary for future workers.
9. Should the American high school be free to everyone? Explain.
10. If work experience should be provided for all, what is the responsibility of the secondary school?
11. Should our young people give service to the community? Explain your answer.
12. What are the relative advantages and disadvantages of work during the summer as contrasted with work during the school year?
13. What can and should high school teachers do about the "American education-vocation daydream"?
14. Should all young people be ready to assume some productive job when they terminate full-time school attendance? Explain your position in writing.

SUPPLEMENTARY MATERIALS

SELECTED READINGS

ANDERSON, STUART. "High School Work Experience Programs in Action," *American School Board Journal,* CXXIII (August, 1951), 18–19. A brief study of local practices respecting credit and participation in an organization of work programs.

ARNOLD, W. M. "Area Vocational Education Programs," *School Life,* XLII (January, 1960), 16–21. A summary of area vocational education.

BRYAN, J. G., and F. L. BLUNE. "How Can the School Develop Placement Services and Work Experience Education for Youth?" *Bulletin of the N.A.S.S.P.,* XXXVII (April, 1953), 31–35. A general statement by two administrators in large city systems.

Digest of Annual Reports of State Boards of Vocational Education to the Office of Education, Division of Vocational Education. For the fiscal year ending June 30, 1960. OE-80008-60 Washington, D.C.: Government Printing Office, 1960. An authoritative summary of enrolment, expenditures, and other statistical information.

IVINS, WILSON H. "Providing the Work Experience and Outside Activities," *National Society for the Study of Education Yearbook, 1953.* Part I, pp. 180–95. An excellent review of the issues involved in work experience.

McCLURE, W. P. "Future of Vocational and Technical Education," *Bulletin of the N.A.S.S.P.,* XLV (February, 1961), 7–12. A look into the future.

Occupational Outlook Handbook. U. S. Department of Labor, Bulletin No. 1300, 1961. This book has the most up-to-date information available in jobs.

POUND, J. L. "Total Programs of Industrial Education, Industrial Arts and Industrial Vocational Education," *Teachers College Journal,* XXXI (January, 1960), 74–76. A forward-looking summary.

——— and WILLIAM B. RUNGE. *Work Experience in High School.* New York: The Ronald Press Co., 1951. An excellent review of work experience.

SEYFERT, W. C. "How Much Work Experience in Our Programs for Youth?" *Bulletin of the N.A.S.S.P.,* XXXVI (March, 1952), 184–89. A brief discussion of values and problems of work experience.

SHARTLE, C. L. *Occupational Information: Its Development and Application,* Englewood Cliffs, N.J.: Prentice-Hall, Inc., 1959. An up-to-date book on occupations.

Vocational Technical Education for American Industry. Circular 531, U.S. Office of Education, 1958. An authoritative statement about vocational-technical education for American industry.

WOLFBEIN, S. L. "Outlook for Skilled Workers in the United States: Implications for Guidance and Counseling," *Personnel and Guidance Journal,* XL (December, 1961), 334–39. An article by an authority on vocations.

16

Industrial Arts and Agriculture[1]

VOCATIONAL INDUSTRIAL EDUCATION

Beginnings. Toward the latter part of the nineteenth century, in more and more secondary schools, courses were established in various types of industrial arts and crafts, including courses intended primarily for vocational education. Vocational shop courses were very expensive as compared to academic courses, and the quality of the equipment, instructors, methods, and materials of instruction in industrial arts and vocational courses were at first very inferior.

Various groups of people in the United States, including the National Association of Manufacturers, urged that vocational education in these areas be extended and improved. In 1917, Congress appropriated $1,660,000, since increased to more than $20,000,000, for vocational courses in trades and industries, home economics, business, and agriculture. These funds may not be used for general-education courses in these fields.

Objectives and Place of Industrial Arts. Industrial-arts courses are of two types: (1) vocational and (2) non-vocational, or general. General-education courses are offered in order to provide general industrial experience of common value to high school students, to provide exploratory activities with a view to leading students to discover their aptitudes

[1] Acknowledgment is gratefully made here to the late Professor Walter H. Magill, University of Pennsylvania, and Dr. Lewis V. Newkirk, Director of Industrial Arts Education in the Public Schools of Chicago, for permission to use some of their materials on industrial-arts education that appeared in previous editions of this book.

and to learn about activities in various fields of industrial arts, to develop an appreciation of design and quality in the products of industrial arts, and to offer basic training for students who may elect to follow a vocational curriculum in trades and industries.

In spite of the opposition of those interested only in intellectual education, more and more schools are installing courses in industrial arts and other fields of vocational education, and enrolments are increasing materially each year. As a result of the steady and very material increase in enrolments in the senior high school since 1950, including of course many students of below-average academic ability and interest and many students who would formerly have dropped out at the age of sixteen, enrolments in industrial arts are certain to increase greatly; already the variety of "trades and industry" courses have expanded, particularly in the fields related to electronics. With the development of new occupations, automation, and the spread of secondary education into new fields of vocational preparation, this area of education is becoming increasingly important.

Specific preparation for vocations is no longer found in the junior high schools but is found almost entirely in the upper two years of senior high schools and in junior colleges.

Determining the Occupations. The first step in the organization of a program of instruction in vocational industrial education is that of determining the occupations for which training shall be offered. This should be done through an occupational survey of the region to be served by the school. It is highly important that this occupational survey be conducted with the active assistance of a small advisory committee composed of sympathetic representatives of employers, labor unions, and the taxpaying public. All of these groups have a direct and vital interest in the program of vocational education; they are in a position to give invaluable advice and judgment, and their approval is essential to the effective operation of the resulting program.

The determination of the occupations for which training shall be offered is no simple matter. Production processes and personal-service techniques are in a state of rapid evolution; old occupations are continually being subdivided through the increase in specialization; and new occupations are being developed. With the increasing elaboration of machines and the development of mass production, skills have been transferred to machine operation, and the old trades have been broken up into operations. The field of the building trades is the only important industrial field in which the old hand skills still are dominant. The indications are that this field will also be revolutionized by factory-built construction units.

The bulk of industrial production is now performed by machine operators. Such operators are frequently referred to improperly as unskilled; they are highly skilled in the operation of their particular machines, but their skills are simple and uncomplicated, so they can be learned in a short time on the job. Training for the great majority of such occupations cannot be effectively or economically given under school limitations. The machines involved are usually elaborate, costly, and subject to rapid obsolescence. Machine processes often vary widely among different establishments. The skills are highly specific, and they must be learned substantially as they will be used; they afford little transfer value when a worker is transferred to a new type of machine. The operations are usually steps in a production sequence from which they cannot be separated. The rate of production of the machines is such that the school can neither provide the raw material nor dispose of the product. The school's function for such occupations is largely that of guidance and placement, rather than training, though some training may be given in the fundamentals of machine operation and personal safety.

Coupled with the great mass of machine operators, at the other end of the occupational range, modern mass production has developed an expanding need for new, advanced types of workers with broader, more complex training than that possessed by the old-fashioned skilled worker. These workers are needed for planning, designing, experimenting, constructing, selling, maintaining, and repairing the machines of production; for planning and supervising production processes; for training workers; for research in industrial science and technology. It is in this field that the school finds its principal opportunity for industrial education. These high-level workers need a broad foundation of science and technology coupled with basic skills and trained judgment, which industry is in poor positions, and the school in good position, to furnish.

Occupations selected for school training should meet the following criteria:

1. They should be of such a nature that effective training can be given under school limitations.
2. They should exist in sufficient volume and be sufficiently stable in character to absorb all of the graduates of the school without producing an oversupply of workers in the field.
3. The expenditure upon the training should be demonstrably of the nature of an investment for the school district, returning to it values in increased opportunity for its youth and in improved service to consumers that are sufficient to warrant the expenditure.

Extent and Grade Placement of Training. After the occupations have been selected, the next step is to determine the extent of training to be given in school and the grade placement of the training. Ideally, this determination should be made for each occupation independently, according to the following criteria:

1. Pupils should be admitted to a course only when they are mature enough to profit from instruction on an adult level and after they have had opportunity for an extent of full-time general education appropriate to their talents and their future station in society.
2. The pupils should be immediately employable upon completion of the course.
3. The course should give the pupils a sufficiently broad and thorough foundation to enable them to grow in efficiency after they have entered employment, to enter more advanced occupations, and to adapt themselves to technological changes as they may occur. At the same time, it should consume only the minimum time necessary for this purpose.

Actually, many circumstances interfere with the free application of these criteria: the form of organization of the school system, the compulsory-school-attendance laws of the state, the age requirements of employers, the social habits of school attendance of the locality. It is customary to begin industrial education in the seventh grade, although most pupils are not mature enough for specific vocational education until the eleventh grade.

The training for some occupations is, desirably, based on the maturity and degree of general education represented by high school graduation. Such training courses are appropriately placed in the junior college. At present, federal subsidy is available only for courses that are "of less than college grade," which precludes subsidy for junior-college courses. All of the reasons applicable to the subsidizing of high school industrial-education courses apply with equal cogency to similar courses in junior colleges that are parts of public school systems. It is to be hoped that this will soon be recognized through appropriate changes in the interpretations or regulations that govern federal subsidies.

Industrial education has been badly handicapped in the past by the tendency of pupils to drop out of school before finishing their programs. As long as employment opportunities were open to them, this tendency was hard to curb. In some occupations, for instance, the servicing of household apparatus, a minimum age of twenty-one was fixed by many employers. In this instance, the employers did not wish to be represented by employees who were immature in appearance. In other cases, the restriction arises from occupational hazard or responsibility for the safety of others. Whatever the occasion for such restriction, it should be recognized by the school in the placement of the training. It is essentially undesirable for a graduate of a training program to be unemployable in the line of his training merely because of age.

The length of the industrial-education curriculum, admission usually being restricted to those who are sufficiently mature for adult standards of attainment, is usually two years. Experience seems to indicate that it takes this length of time to meet the criterion of employability for most occupations and that more than this cannot be profitably spent away from the realities of actual employment. A subsequent year on a cooperative part-time basis affords the most effective transition from school to work.

Development of the Program. When the grade placement of the training has been determined, the next step is the development of the program of instruction. Curriculums for pupils in day vocational schools and departments should include an adequate proportion of general education. The objective of the school should be not merely to train workers for industry but also to educate worker citizens for the democracy. All of the types of educational activity that are appropriate for pupils in the general curriculum are correspondingly appropriate for pupils in the vocational curriculum, and should be made available to them. The graduate of the vocational curriculum will be a citizen and a member of a home and will have leisure to be used, to the same extent as the general-education graduate. The attainment of both vocational and general-education objectives is a matter of some difficulty and requires a school day that is longer than the conventional school day. With a seven-period day and students carrying five subjects, experience has demonstrated that both general and vocational objectives can be attained in highly satisfactory degree.

To effect the proper integration of the vocational and general-education objectives and activities, the curriculum content should be developed by committees of both vocational and general-education instructors, working together under the direction of the supervisor of vocational education. This obtains the benefit of group judgment, produces a common understanding of objectives and procedures on the part of all of the participating instructors, and makes possible both the elimination of non-functional units of instruction and the efficient integration of the various courses into a unified program.

Trade Instruction and Related Subjects. The vocational-training section of the vocational curriculum is conventionally divided into two parts: "vocational instruction" and "related subjects instruction." Federal authorities recognize as "related subjects" for purposes of subsidy the fields of mathematics, science, mechanical drawing, industrial hygiene, and social studies. The distinction between the two kinds of instruction has been a matter of much confusion, and, partly as a result of this, the related-subjects field has bene poorly handled. The occasion for a group of courses called "related" arises from the need for certain types of instruction which cannot be efficiently conducted in the vocational shop, which do not require the equipment of the shop, or which can be taught better by a specialist in the field than by the shop instructor. The function of the vocational shop is to develop in the pupil the abilities and understandings that find direct application in the work of the occupation. The function of the related subjects is fourfold:

1. To give the pupil foundational abilities such as those of computation and the reading of drawings, which can be taught in advance of their application in the shop instruction without using shop equipment
2. To give the pupil a broad understanding of the science and technology that underlie practice; the possession of such understanding gives the worker a comprehension of the reasons for procedures, makes him more versatile in meeting unusual situations and difficulties, and aids him to adjust himself to changes in production procedures
3. To give the pupil an understanding of the general plan of production of which his work is a part and of the work of others who precede and follow him in the production process; thus, a machinist would be given an understanding of the general process of metal manufacture, of the smelting of iron, the production of steel, the work of the designing draftsman, the patternmaker, and the molder
4. To give the future worker an understanding of the social organization of industry, of the social problems connected with production, and of the points of view, interests, and rights of the various groups involved

Job Analysis. The determination of the content of vocational shop courses is accomplished by an analysis of the work of the occupation. Two common types of analysis are used for this purpose: job analysis and operation analysis. Job analysis derives from the various jobs that constitute an occupation the items of knowledge, the muscular skills, the powers of judgment, and the motives needed in the performance of the jobs. Job analysis is appropriate to occupations made up of a restricted number of definite jobs, such as plumbing. Operation analysis breaks down the work of the occupation into the various operations employed in it and from them derives the specific objectives of the course of instruction. Operation analysis is particularly appropriate to occupations in which the number of jobs is large and indefinite, such as machine work. In most occupations, the variety of operations employed is much smaller than the variety of jobs performed; hence, operation analysis is usually a simpler procedure than job analysis.

Particular care should be exercised in selecting the objectives to ensure that all of the four basic types of instructional result—items of knowledge or understanding, muscular skills, powers of judgment, and motives— are properly represented. There is a common tendency for shop courses to be restricted too exclusively to the development of muscular skills, and academic classes to the development of knowledge; both are likely to overlook important powers of judgment and motives.

After the objectives for a projected vocational course have been se- lected, they should be checked and approved by the advisory committee referred to above and by representatives of any other groups that may be potential critics of the work. Suggestions and criticisms so received should be used to revise the list of objectives until it meets with general approval.

The content of related subject courses cannot be adequately de- termined by an analysis of the work of the occupation, because many of the understandings that make for a broad-minded, versatile worker do not enter directly into the work of the occupation. Ideally, there is no limit to the extent of understanding of science, technology, industry practice, and labor relations and problems that it would be desirable for workers to have. Because of time and other limitations, a judicious selection must be made of what is of considerable importance from these extremely large and indefinite fields. The only recourse for much of the selection lies in the personal judgment of those who are broadly experi- enced in the given field as to what related understandings have been useful to them. Judgment in the matter is widely variant, but a poll of a sufficient variety of experienced persons can be made to yield a core of content that is supported by representative opinion.

The content of most related subject courses, as these are now taught, is determined in a highly arbitrary manner, often by instructors with little or no experience in the industrial field. It is not surprising, there- fore, that related subject courses are frequently very unpopular with pupils because of obvious lack of functional value and have little to show in the way of results for the time and effort they consume.

The Jury–Check-List Approach. A widely used method for a more ade- quate determination of the related subject fields is the following: A vocational instructor who is broadly experienced in a given occupational field and who has been trained in the techniques of curriculum con- struction prepares a check list of the possible objectives to be attained in related instruction, using his personal judgment as the criterion. This check list is then sent to a sufficient number of other qualified persons to obtain a representative judgment as to the value of the listed objectives. Directions on the questionnaire request a check mark after each item, in one of three columns—"Essential," "Desirable but Not Essential," "Unimportant"—and the addition of other items, not on the list, that should be included. To keep the check lists reasonably short, so that qualified people will give adequate attention to their returns, it is necessary to divide the related subject fields into sections of limited extent.

Essential Features. The outlines of courses of instruction in industrial education, as commonly prepared, consist merely of lists of topics or features of work to be covered. Such lists merely suggest the course, because they leave entirely to the imagination of the reader the nature of the instruction provided by the course. An adequate outline of a course of instruction must contain at least four features:

1. The specific objectives to be attained
2. The nature of the activities through which the pupil is to attain each of the objectives
3. The nature of the instructor's activities in directing the learning of the pupil for each of the objectives
4. The means of evaluating student learning

In organizing such an outline, there is always the problem of determining the degree of detail to incorporate in it. The most effective criterion seems to be that the outline should contain sufficient, and only sufficient, detail to enable a qualified instructor to conduct the course in the absence of the regular instructor. The definiteness of procedure that such an outline represents should be considered to be not restrictive in its influence but merely descriptive. An instructor who follows such an outline should not hesitate to depart from it whenever his judgment dictates. The definiteness of the outline simply ensures carefulness and adequacy of preparation of the instruction on the part of the instructor. The objectives of the course, if they have been validated by the procedures already outlined, should be constant, but the instructor's and pupils' activities, through which the objectives are to be attained, can profitably vary according to the discretion of the individual instructor. There are often many instructional roads to a given objective; which is most efficient depends, to a considerable degree, on the instructor's temperament, and experience and other factors in the instructional situation.

Types of Vocational Industrial-Arts Programs. Industrial-arts programs in the secondary schools may be of different types; indeed, many schools offer more than one type.

In the all-day vocational program, the student devotes approximately three consecutive clock hours to practical work on a useful and productive basis and is given instruction in segregated classes, if necessary, in

technical related subjects. There has been an increasing trend to substitute general-education courses for some of the work in related technical
subjects.

Work Experience as Vocational Education. The "diversified occupations" program and the "distributive education" program are good
examples of cooperative work-experience vocational programs. Both may
be approved for state and federal subsidies.

In the cooperative work-experience programs, usually offered as
courses in "diversified occupations" with state and federal aid, the following types of occupations are commonly included among those in which
students may get training:

1. Occupations in the field of the selling of goods and services
2. Clerical occupations
3. Restaurant and other food-preparation and -handling positions
4. Various building and automobile trades
5. Other trades and occupations in industrial fields
6. Various types of positions as aids to nurses, dentists, embalmers,
   or printers

The "distributive education" program includes training for a variety
of occupations related to the sale and distribution of goods.

Students in "diversified occupations" or "distributive education" courses
usually work between fifteen and twenty hours a week and receive one
full academic unit of credit. They usually carry three courses at school,
are paid for their work at slightly less than the local going rate, and
are visited and inspected by a coordinator from the school several times
a month. There are definite agreements between the employer, the
student, and the school, including

1. Agreement of the student to give honest conscientious service and
   to be regular and prompt in his work hour
2. Agreement of the employer to teach the student about the occupation

The courses are usually open to eleventh- and twelfth-graders only.

Fields of Vocational Industrial-Arts Instruction. Most secondary schools
offer, for at least two or three types of occupations, vocational courses
involving two subjects in each of the eleventh and twelfth grades, which
students carry in addition to their general-education courses and in
which no work experience outside of school is included.

Many smaller schools offer a general industrial-education program in
which a number of related occupations are taught in a single curriculum,
for example, a course might include auto mechanics, auto body painting,

body and fender repair, wheel alignment, and other allied phases of automobile repair.

Continuation or part-time programs are offered in many schools for students who are graduates or dropouts and wish to continue their education along the line of their occupation or to get general education.

Among the fields for which training may be received in at least a few senior high schools are the following:

Air conditioning and refrigeration	Jewelry and watchmaking
Airplane maintenance	Landscape gardening
Appliance repairing	Machine-shop work
Auto-body repairing	Masonry
Automotive maintenance	Meat cutting
Building trades	Needle trades
Cabinetmaking	Optical repairing
Carpentry	Painting and paper hanging
Commercial art	Patternmaking
Diesel repairing	Photography
Drafting	Plastering and lathing
Dry cleaning	Plumbing and pipe fitting
Electrical communication	Printing
Electrical maintenance	Radio and TV repairing
Electrical wiring	Sheet-metal fabrication
Farm-implement repairing	Shoe repairing
Food trades	Structural and ornamental iron
Foundry work	fabrication
Hospital-aide service	Tool and die making
Instrument repairing	Upholstery

INDUSTRIAL ARTS AS GENERAL EDUCATION

Today, more boys, and indeed a great many girls, are enrolled in classes in industrial arts and in related crafts courses that are not essentially vocational in nature but are taken because of contributions to general education, including such things as leisure and hobby activities and skills, understanding of the industrial world, exploration of potential talents and skills, and prevocational work in grades seven through ten with a view to laying the foundation for vocational industrial arts in grades eleven and twelve.

Objectives. It is a major function of industrial-art education to interpret the machine age to the oncoming generation. In colonial times, children could easily observe the cobbler, the tinsmith, the harness maker, the broom maker, and the blacksmith at work in the community. Today, most of the things that we use are made in factories, sometimes hundreds of miles away. Modern children have lost the easy contact with the crafts that was typical of the colonial village. Courses in industrial arts give boys and girls an opportunity to work with tools and materials typical of modern industry and to gain an understanding of the production line and manufactured products. It helps them to choose a vocation and to become more intelligent consumers of the products of the machine age. Experiences in industrial-arts courses result in an increased understanding of the problems of labor and management.

Industrial-arts education contributes to preparation for effective living and competent citizenship in the machine age by providing developmental experiences that deal with the materials, processes, products, occupations, and problems of our modern industrial world. Its development has paralleled the machine age, and its content deals with industry and the use of the products of industry.

Industrial-arts education is apparently of much importance in modern schools where complete preparation for life is the ultimate objective. Industrial-arts education interprets in its own area the philosophy and aims of the general-education program. More than 4 million boys and girls were enrolled in 1963–1964 in some form of industrial arts, and the number increases materially each year. Significant is the trend for girls to elect at least one year of industrial arts.

The objectives of modern programs may be stated as follows:

1. To provide experiences with tools and machines typical of modern industry so that the students can explore and test their interests and abilities in industrial work
2. To develop social understanding and the ability to work with others as a leader or as a cooperative member of the group
3. To develop wholesome personality balance by integrating the child's mental, emotional, and physical training and growth
4. To develop the skill to recognize quality and good design in manufactured products
5. To teach the essential elementary skills and scientific concepts necessary to keep the commonly used products of industry in efficient and safe working order
6. To develop the tool skills and knowledge necessary to plan and construct useful projects with common hand tools, simple machines, and construction materials in a workman-like manner
7. To develop an interest in handicraft as a valuable medium for creative expression in leisure hours
8. To develop skill in reading and making drawings, charts, and graphs
9. To provide an objective medium for learning in mathematics, science, language arts, and the social sciences
10. To develop pride in workmanship
11. To encourage inventiveness and ingenuity in dealing with tools, materials, and simple machines

The modern curriculum in industrial arts is taken from industry and the trades. The instructional content is evaluated in terms of man's needs for an understanding of the machine age and for ability to work with tools and construction materials in meeting the problems of daily living. The industrial-arts area is commonly divided into large units of instruction, such as mechanical drawing, electricity, metal, wood, plastics, graphic arts, ceramics, and leather. The instructional content is frequently analyzed into information, hand-tool skills, and machine skills.

The General Non-vocational Course. Activities taught in no-vocational general shop courses include many of the following and similar activities:

1. *General.* Replacement of broken glass in window or door; splicing of rope and tying of common knots; nailing on half soles and rubber heels; repair of garden hoses; firing of heating plants; framing of pictures; and repair of plastered walls
2. *Electrical Work.* Detection and replacement of blown fuses; assembly or repair of attachment cords; hooking up doorbells and buzzers, wiring of extension cords for lamps; reading of electric meters; giving first aid to one who has received severe electric shock; making of N.E.C. splices; installation of radio sets; simple house wiring, 110 volts, A.C.; construction of antennae for TV reception; and repair of connections on electric stoves, tubes, etc.
3. *Drawing.* Reading of working drawings; making sketches; and simple lettering
4. *Woodworking.* Use of simple tools in squaring stock to dimensions; making of window screens; use of glue for general repair; strengthening of weak joints; selection and use of nails and screws; setting of hinges; use of different types of bits and drills; and study of lumber and the different kinds of woods
5. *Finishing.* Application of paint to new or old surfaces; application of stain, filler, and varnish on new wood; and refinishing of furniture and woodwork
6. *Plumbing.* Repair of leaking compression faucets; repair of fuller-ball faucets; repair of leaking flush tanks; cleaning of drain traps; and cutting and threading of pieces of pipe
7. *Metal Working.* Sharpening of knives; repair of cooking utensils; replacement of springs of mortise locks; whetting of planes or chisels; shaping of points of screwdrivers; cleaning and tinning of soldering coppers; use of taps and dies; filing of keys; adjustment and sharpening of lawn mowers, filing and whetting of ripsaws and crosscut saws; and use of solder in repair work
8. *Auto Mechanics.* Draining of crankcases and filling of crankcases with new oil; removal of carbon from, and grinding of, valves; fitting of new sets of piston rings; overhaul of cooling systems; checking of fuel systems and adjustment of carburetors; wiring of ignition systems and testing of spark plugs; testing of, and care

for, storage batterys; cleaning of commutators on generators and motors; wiring of cars for headlights, dash lights, and taillights; adjustment of steering gear; rebushing of front axles, and testing for caster and camber; cleaning and adjustment of front-wheel bearings; repair of leaks in the inner tubes and assembly of tires; overhaul and lubrication of rear axles; adjustment and cleaning of clutches; adjustment and relining of emergency and service brakes; taking up of connecting-rod bearings; taking up of main bearings; pitching tops and curtains, recovering of tops

9. *Concrete Working.* Casting of small articles from concrete; construction of sidewalks, cement floors, and feeding platforms; reinforcement of concrete work; and drilling of holes in masonry with star drills

Electrical Work in Industrial-Arts Education. We cannot make projects out of electricity, but we can manipulate various metals, plastics, and woods in meaningful ways by means of electricity. Electrical work in industrial arts involves the use of materials and manipulations associated with other units, and thus afford an example of the connected and interrelated nature of the unit arrangement.

The emphasis must be on understanding rather than on skills, for the manipulations necessary to construct and operate simple electric devices are not complex. For example, complicated electronic devices like television and radio receivers are assembled and soldered by unskilled factory workers trained on the job for specific operations.

What is important, and what our industrial-arts objectives point toward, is the understanding of the nature of electricity, of electrical circuits, and of component parts of electric devices. The projects and experiments in the unit are means by which such broad understandings may be attained.

The objectives of training in the electrical area are

1. To interpret to the students the electrical industry and the importance of electricity in the world today
2. To provide opportunity for the students to construct simple projects illustrating various electrical effects
3. To provide opportunity for the students to conduct simple experiments that show electrical effects, for the purpose of learning more about electricity
4. To acquaint the student with some of the occupational opportunities in the electrical fields, for example, generation, construction, wiring, communication, electrochemistry, electric appliances, and electric motors
5. To provide the students with the knowledge and techniques for carrying on electrical work as a worthwhile leisure activity

6. To develop in the students appreciation of good materials, design, and workmanship in electrical goods
7. To assist the students to discover their own interests in, and liking for, electrical work

Among practical projects of educational value are those involving construction of the following: fuse and lamp tester, extension cord, telegraph sounder, buzzer, door chime, electric motor, burning pencil, electric soldering copper, grill or toaster, current detector, arc-welding tool, table, desk or pin-up lamp, step-down transformer, fluorescent light fixture, electric arc lamp, and simple radio receiver.

Typical of educationally valuable experiments and demonstrations are the following: conductor and insulator (non-conductor) test; resistance experiment showing differences in brilliancy of a bulb, with various resistances in series; short-circuit test to show fuse protection; connection of door bell and buzzer circuits on wiring panel; generation of electric current by plugging magnet through coil of several lines of wire connected to galvanometer; making of a simple wet cell and testing it; connection of a charger to the wet cell and later retesting it.

Things the Student Should Learn To Do

1. Read and make simple electrical-circuit diagrams
2. Instal fuses in electrical circuits
3. Make electrical connections to batteries
4. Assemble extension cords
5. Wire lamps
6. Splice wire
7. Solder joints in wire and metal
8. Tape splices and connections
9. Insulate parts from one another
10. Service storage battery
11. Wind simple coils
12. Make electrical connections in series
13. Make electrical connections in parallel
14. Assemble parts of an electrical project
15. Locate trouble in simple electric devices
16. Use precautions in handling electrical apparatus

Things the Student Should Understand

1. The nature of magnetic force, its origins, effects, and applications
2. The nature and characteristics of electricity and its transformation into heat, light, mechanical energy, and chemical energy
3. The transformation of chemical, heat, light, mechanical, magnetic, and sound energy into electricity
4. How electricity is generated by chemical and mechanical means

5. How electricity is distributed from the generating plant into and through our homes; the National Electric Code
6. The kinds and the principles of the electric appliances that furnish heat, light, power, communication, and chemical change
7. The occupational opportunities to be found in the electrical fields of generation, transmission, house wiring, communication, power, and electric-appliance manufacturing and upkeep
8. The safety measures that should be followed whenever electricity is being used; the Underwriters' Laboratory; fuse protection
9. Some of the myriad applications of electronics in radio, television, etc.

Basic Principles. The industrial-arts instructor guides student learning through pupil-interest projects, demonstrations, experiments, class discussion, related reading, student tests, individual instruction, visual aids, and trips to industry. The pupil-interest projects should require the use of the fundamental processes and learning materials and should be considered of value and interest by the pupils; formalized projects or tool exercises are not in keeping with modern teaching of industrial arts. Under the general direction of the instructor, the projects should be well planned by the students, and the teacher should require consistently correct use of tools and construction materials in their development.

The teacher of industrial arts should appraise the pupils' accomplishments by judging finished projects, using objective information tests, and checking to see if pupils can apply the information from the course in industrial arts to help solve life problems. For example, a boy or girl who has had a course in electricity should be able to select a well-made electric toaster, assemble an extension cord correctly, hook up a simple electrical circuit, and understand the vocational opportunities in the electrical field. Progress charts are available to teachers of industrial arts for use in keeping accurate records of students' achievements.

The most common shop arrangement for industrial arts is the general shop. The general shop is very well suited for use in small schools where it is necessary for one teacher to present the entire program.

Trends. Industrial-arts education has developed extensively at the secondary school level, but the future will see further development and a greater educational service to more boys and girls. The following are significant trends in the development of industrial-arts education:

1. More schools will include industrial-arts courses for girls. The courses will be along the lines of home mechanics and crafts for leisure.
2. The general shop will continue to expand rapidly during the next ten years, because it makes possible the presentation of an ade-

quate industrial-arts-education program even though the teaching staff is limited to one or two industrial-arts-education teachers.

3. Industrial-arts instruction in the late afternoon and evening will expand in community centers for leisure-time interests.
4. More and better instructional materials in the form of pupil texts and reference books will be developed.
5. Industrial-arts teachers will more fully comprehend their mission to interpret the machine age to the oncoming generations of boys and girls.

AGRICULTURE

To Produce Farm Commodities Efficiently. Contributory objectives necessary to the attainment of this major objective may include ability to effectively

1. Determine the kind and amount of livestock to produce
2. Select livestock for the farm
3. Procure desirable farm animals
4. Improve livestock on the farm
5. Care for farm animals
6. Feed livestock
7. Determine the kinds and amounts of crops to produce
8. Select and store seed
9. Produce improved seed and crops
10. Prepare the seedbed and seed the crop
11. Fertilize the crop
12. Cultivate and harvest the crop
13. Store the crop
14. Control diseases and parasites
15. Formulate and use production standards
16. Select, procure, and maintain farm equipment
17. Make needed farm appliances
18. Finance specific farm enterprises
19. Manage the different enterprises

To Market Farm Products Advantageously. Contributory objectives necesary to the attainment of this major objective may include ability to effectively

1. Interpret market demands and trends
2. Produce farm commodities to meet market demands
3. Assemble products for marketing
4. Grade and prepare products for market
5. Process certain farm products
6. Package products for marketing

7. Transport products to market
8. Follow sound storage practices
9. Sell farm products
10. Finance marketing programs and practices
11. Advertise farm products
12. Maintain desirable relationships with marketing agencies
13. Expand present markets for farm products
14. Develop new markets
15. Support desirable legislation for marketing

To Conserve Soil and Other Natural Resources. Contributory objectives necessary to the attainment of this major objective may include ability to effectively

1. Make land-use surveys
2. Adjust farming to soil types and topography
3. Rebuild depleted soil
4. Terrace farmland
5. Construct and maintain dams, ponds, and water-spreading systems
6. Irrigate farmlands
7. Grow soil-conserving crops
8. Maintain appropriate cover crops
9. Apply appropriate kinds and amounts of fertilizers
10. Adjust grazing practices
11. Reforest or regrass depleted and submarginal lands
12. Practice selective cutting of farm woodlands
13. Plant and maintain shelter strips
14. Protect grassland and farm forests from fires
15. Analyze causes of wasteful exploitation of resources
16. Practice wildlife conservation
17. Understand the social implications of conservation
18. Analyze and use conservation programs
19. Evaluate the effectiveness of conservation programs
20. Support effective legislation for conservation

To Manage a Farming Business Effectively. Contributory objectives necesary to the attainment of this major objective may include ability to effectively

1. Analyze farm enterprises
2. Determine the type of farming to follow
3. Formulate a long-time farming plan
4. Determine kinds and combination of enterprises for efficient farming
5. Keep and analyze farm records
6. Analyze a farm business

7. Equip a farm adequately and economically
8. Rent certain farm equipment
9. Get maximum efficiency from machinery, equipment, and live-stock
10. Manage farm labor
11. Draw contracts, mortgages, leases, and notes
12. Select, procure, and maintain insurance and social security
13. Finance a farming business
14. Develop satisfactory volume in the farm business
15. Devise a desirable crop-rotation program
16. Buy supplies and equipment advantageously
17. Adjust farm organization plans as needed
18. Produce food for the family
19. Process and store foods for the family
20. Provide facilities for processing food
21. Provide storage on the farm
22. Provide and use community storage and processing facilities
23. Analyze the year's farm business, including problems of taxation

To Maintain a Favorable Environment. Contributory objectives essential to the attainment of this major objective may include ability to effectively

1. Analyze local situations
2. Evaluate economic resources of a community
3. Evaluate human resources of a community
4. Analyze the general objectives of a community program
5. Influence trends in a community
6. Provide and maintain suitable farm homes
7. Provide sanitation and protect health
8. Provide adequate clothing
9. Provide modern home and farm conveniences
10. Provide recreational and social activities
11. Secure good roads and other transportation facilities
12. Secure desirable rural institutions
13. Determine the effects of national and international situations, debts, wars, trade agreements, and tariffs on agriculture
14. Determine the effects of monetary policies on agriculture
15. Determine the effects of shifts in industries on agriculture
16. Evaluate the trends of exports and imports

To Participate in Rural Leadership Activities. Contributory objectives necessary for the attainment of this major objective may include ability to effectively

1. Cooperate for the common good in rural activities
2. Exercise and follow desirable rural leadership

3. Get along with others
4. Organize constructive group activities
5. Finance group activities
6. Maintain desirable relations with urban groups
7. Decide whether or not to participate in agricultural programs

Most of the youngsters interested in agriculture in some form or another, even to a small degree, belong to a 4-H (Heart, Home, Head, and Hand) Club. The objectives and activities of the 4-H Clubs are broader than vocational agriculture, including emphasis upon character education and education for home living.

Vocational agriculture courses are offered only in grades ten, eleven, and twelve, often only in the latter two. Usually four yaer units constitute the student's program, though some students take five.

Related Courses. The education of future farmers should include courses in such other fields as science, general mathematics, economics, and general business. There is a trend toward better general education of the future farmer in the fields of English, history, science, and mathematics. Much of the training needed can be and is acquired on the job. Compared to several decades ago, the average farmer today is much better informed and uses much better methods, and he can pass them on to young people working with him.

General Agriculture. In a small but slowly increasing number of schools a course is offered in general agriculture for the general education of students not intending to be farmers, though it serves somewhat as an exploratory course for those who include agriculture among their vocational possibilities.

QUESTIONS, PROBLEMS, AND ISSUES FOR FURTHER THOUGHT

1. In European secondary schools there are no courses in vocational education. These are given in separate schools. What are the principal arguments pro and con for the practice of having separate vocational schools in the United States?
2. Why do you think that many boys who should be taking vocational courses do not do so but register for courses in the general or college-preparatory curriculum? What do you suggest could be done to improve this situation?
3. What are the principal arguments pro and con on offering in secondary schools curriculums on preparation of foods?
4. Select one so-called academic subject taught in most secondary schools and make a list of the more important things that can be done in that field to prepare young people for successful participation in a vocation.
5. Be prepared to give a five- to ten-minute talk in class on the values of work experience and of the diversified-occupations and distributive-education programs. Why are not more students enrolled in these programs?

6. To what extent do you believe that potential dropouts should be strongly encouraged to take vocational courses? Would it prevent them dropping out? What type of vocational courses would you recommend?

7. Do you believe that there should be set up in most secondary schools a course in which training is given for the operation of small businesses? If so, what would be included in such a course, and what kind of a teacher should be obtained for it?

8. Do you believe that vocation courses should be provided in secondary schools on evenings and Saturdays for students who have graduated or who have dropped out who wish to take such courses? Why or why not?

9. After careful study, make a list of occupations for which vocational training might be given in high schools and for which training is not now given in many schools.

10. Do you believe that agriculture as a regular full curriculum should be dropped from secondary schools or retained? What are the arguments for giving agriculture courses only as short-term courses, let us say, of three or four months each, during the winter to beginning farmers?

11. What part do you think that secondary schools could play in the training of people who are among the unemployed and who have not been trained well enough to obtain employment in a skilled occupation?

SUPPLEMENTARY MATERIALS

SELECTED READINGS

AMERICAN VOCATIONAL ASSOCIATION. *A Guide to Improving Instruction in Industrial Arts*. Washington, D.C.: The Association, 1953. A 120-page paperback booklet worked out by a distinguished committee of leaders in industrial-arts education; gives the philosophy and objectives of industrial arts, the major content of the instructional areas, and extensive professional and instructional references.

CARDOZIER, V. R. "Redesigning Agricultural Education Programs for the Public Schools," *Bulletin of the N.A.S.S.P.*, 272 (March, 1962), 173–83.

GIACHINO, J. W., and R. O. GALLINGTON. *Course Construction in Industrial Arts and Vocational Education*. Chicago: American Technical Society, 1954.

KELLER, F. J. *The Double Purpose High School*. New York: Harper & Row, 1953. A presentation of the cases for and against the comprehensive high school—its advantages and disadvanatges. Outlines of specific schools.

KRUG, EDWARD A. *The Secondary School Curriculum*. New York: Harper & Row, 1960. Chapter 15, "Industrial Arts," pp. 361–84.

MICHAELS, W. J. "The Analysis Technique," *Industrial Arts and Vocational Education Magazine*, XXXIV (November, 1949), 349–50. A brief description, with illustrations, of the analysis technique as applied to curriculum construction.

WILLIS, BENJAMIN C. "The Changing Story of Vocational Education and What's Needed Now." *Nation's Schools*, No. 2 (February, 1963), 57–58.

17

The Curriculum for Home-living Education

THE SCHOOL'S RESPONSIBILITY FOR EDUCATION FOR HOME LIVING

Dramatic changes are taking place in home living and in the pattern of women's lives. American women have always contributed to the economic life of the nation, but until recently this contribution was made largely through skills and services performed in the home. Now, many services used in the home are purchased or performed with modern equipment and new products. This frees the time of women for more extensive participation in civic and political life and in paid employment outside the home. Recent statistics show that almost one-third of all workers are women, more than half of these working women are married, and many of them have young children. With these changes in the lives of women, the effective management of the home is still their central responsibility, particularly during the period when children are growing up. Women are largely responsible for the spiritual, intellectual, and aesthetic tone of the home and for its stature in the community. They guard the mental and physical health of members of the family and are the greatest single influence in all aspects of the early development of children.

For these multiple responsibilities, the women of tomorrow now enrolled in secondary schools need basic education of the highest possible quality. Boys too should have education focused on home living. Families start with the partnership that husbands and wives assume in marriage.

The early responsibilities of working out relationships, choosing realistic goals, and establishing the new home are critical for the future of the new family. In fact, family development should be a shared responsibility throughout the family cycle. It is indispensable, then, that both sexes have substantial opportunity for education that aims to broaden their concepts of the functions of homes and families, to encourage clarification of family values, and to motivate adherence to these values. In addition, education should assist young people to develop and enjoy the basic competences for the practical aspects of family living. This can be accomplished in large part through dealing with the common problems and opportunities for participation in homes and families represented in classes.

BASES FOR THE CURRICULUM

Social Realities. Many curriculum groups are trying to find answers to the question of what young people must know, understand, and be able to do reasonably well if they are to function effectively and happily as family members now and as home-makers and as parents in homes of their own later. Basic in searching for answers are considerations of social realities and ideals, how they influence home living today, and what effect they may have on home living in the future for which these young people are being prepared. Important among the realities of current living that should significantly influence curriculum content in education for home living are early marriage and parenthood; the increase in the number of women working outside the home; the interchanging roles of family members; the mobility of families; the trend toward urbanization, suburbanization, and informality in living; the dramatic rise in living standards and per-capita income; the family's shift from a producing unit to a consuming unit; the ever widening range of choice among consumer goods and services; the greater awareness of the importance of the affectional role of the family; automation as it affects the length of the work week; leisure-time activities, employment possibilities; and the diversity in national and cultural backgrounds among pupils in the public schools.

Bringing of awareness—of the rise in the aspirations and expectations of people on a worldwide basis; of the closeness of diverse cultures, due in part to rapid transportation and communication; and of the humanitarian programs of United Nations specialized agencies—gives opportunities for critical examination of values that should have priority in a society committed to democracy and to leadership in the search for peaceful solutions in world affairs.

The fact that the specifics in these trends change as new knowledge is discovered and used increases the importance of keeping information, attitudes, beliefs, and practices under examination as they relate to the *what* of education. Research findings in the areas of psychological needs of various age groups and on how learning can be motivated and made more functional and more challenging offer leads to the *how* and the *when* of education.

Social Ideals. The social ideals of American democracy presuppose concern for the freedom of the individual to develop his potential as a person and for the protection of human rights. Important among the human rights and of special concern to those planning education for family living are the rights to establish a family, to work with adequate remuneration, to health, to education, to full participation in cultural life, to attain fair standards of living, to own property, to legal protection, and to freedom from discrimination based on race, sex, nationality, religion, or class. These rights should influence the teacher's relationships with students in guiding them toward becoming effective persons at each age level while finding satisfactions in their personal lives and in relationships in homes and communities.

These rights are all included in the Universal Declaration of Human Rights, which sets standards for social achievement. Active concern for securing them will be developed to the extent that education interprets public issues related to them. Among such public issues at community, national, and international levels are movements to deal constructively with child welfare, public health, social security, housing, consumer protection, regulation of the use of credit, and many others that directly affect individual and family welfare.

The Community Situation. Teachers in specific communities should study the situation in the homes represented in their classes and take time to think carefully about the implications for education against the background of the overall social realities. Essential community information includes awareness of the major occupations represented; the housing conditions; the resources for cultural pursuits, recreation, health, education, and buying; and the availability and cost of services generally used in homes. Teachers should know the ethnic and religious groups represented, and they should study adolescents, what they seem to be thinking and doing and what they seem to be striving for. Also, teachers should consider the role of parents in influencing adolescents and enlist the cooperation of parents in planning education. They should be observers, listeners, and active participants in school and community life. Their concern should be to make curriculum decisions in terms of the basic needs of the young people.

Major Concerns in Teaching. The selection of curriculum experiences is a continuous challenge. Major concerns in teaching should be the development of the ability to think—to use the best information available in solving problems and developing skills, to evaluate experience, and to think about and state generalizations that are indicated and will be applicable in new situations. In a rapidly changing society, this ability to find and use new information and to make decisions based on intelligent study using new knowledge and generalizations from past experience will be the best possible safeguard for the future.

THE CONTRIBUTION OF HOME ECONOMICS

Home economics is the only area of education at the present time that has as its major concern the total well-being of the family and of the individual in the family setting. The home-economics curriculum in secondary schools should give substantial evidence that the social realities and ideals have been considered in selecting content for the three major responsibilities of education: general education, vocational education for homemaking, and education to develop special interests and aptitudes.

General Education. Some of the experiences that general education for home living should make available to both boys and girls and for which the home-economics teachers in many schools are well equipped to take leadership include

1. Directed study and discussion by the students of what it means to grow up and to assume the roles expected of them in each of the stages of development from youth to maturity and through the normal stages of the family cycle
2. Study of human development focused on understanding of their own behavior and that of other people and what it means to assume responsibility for one's own behavior in relationships with others
3. Guidance for understanding relationships with parents and for dealing with conflicts that occur in family relationships, and motivation for becoming increasingly supportive in family relationships
4. Guidance for making and keeping friends, for dealing with differences in standards of behavior among friends, and in courtship
5. Guidance for selection of a marriage partner, for assessing their own readiness for marriage, and for looking upon marriage as a way of life that requires adaptability, collaboration, and many skills
6. Guidance for clarifying concepts of a good marriage, of a good parent, and of the variety of ways families can work together to achieve values to which they give priorities

7. Orientation in the practical managerial skills involved in home-making—providing for good nutrition, management of time and money, creating a pleasant home environment, care of possessions, and utilization of community resources

Cooperative Planning of General Education for Home Living. General education for home living can be furthered through experiences that deal directly with the real materials of day-to-day living, under the guidance of teachers whose interest, training, and experience have given them appreciation of the possibilities for practical application of the information and the concepts of the subjects they teach. Teachers of literature, art, economics, sociology, political science, psychology, business education, health and physical education, and biology, chemistry, and other sciences have excellent opportunities to help students use what they learn in more intelligent approaches to health, money management, family and community relationships, and many other aspects of home living. Cooperative planning among teachers, and with teachers whose major concern is for these practical aspects of living, is an important means to ensure maximum functioning of the so-called academic subjects in home living as well as to avoidance of unessential duplication of information and experiences in the limited time allotted to home economics.

The quality of education in any field is determined by depth of scholarship coupled with understanding of, and concern about, maximum development of youth. Courses in the area of personal development, human relationships, marriage, and parenthood should be assigned to teachers with broad experiences, demonstrated skill in human relationships, and scholarship in psychology, human development, sociology, economics, and family life. Teacher education in home economics includes basic courses in these areas of learning as well as specialized courses dealing with application of concepts from them to daily living. Home-economics teachers should be given opportunity to participate and lead in programs of general education for home living. Brief descriptions of cooperative planning in specific communities are on pages 336–337 and 344–348.

Vocational Education in Homemaking. Since the passage of the Smith Hughes Act, in 1917, the contribution of home-economics education for the vocation of homemaking has been recognized as important at the secondary school level. This legislation and later vocational-education acts set standards for broad education for the specific responsibilities of life in the home. Child care and guidance, management of resources, development of the basic skills needed in homemaking through laboratory practice followed by supervised home experiences and projects of increasing complexity were all assumed to be essential. Vocational education emphasizes the importance of using home problems common to class members as class problems and of motivating and supervising of home projects that young people and their parents agree will be assets to education as well as worthwhile as contributions to the life of the family. Home projects vary in complexity with the age and experience of members of classes. They involve varying degrees of responsibility for such home activities as

1. Planning and preparing meals and serving them attractively within the limits of the money, time, and facilities available in homes of class members
2. Arranging work and storage space in homes for greater convenience and for efficiency in work procedures
3. Taking major responsibility for the care of, and some aspects of the guidance of, younger members of the family
4. Purchasing the family food, using as guides nutrition knowledge and principles of consumer buying considered in foods classes
5. Assisting with record keeping to maintain budget standards agreed upon in family councils
6. Adding to the attractiveness of the home, using art principles and skills acquired in class study and practice
7. Keeping the home clean, orderly, and sanitary through planned cooperation of family members in carrying out good housekeeping practices
8. Planning and carrying out home hospitality and/or equipping and arranging for recreational activities in the home

All of these home activities require knowledge, management of resources, and a variety of homemaking skills, in addition to planning with the family. The teacher's role is to guide the application of science principles to health and housekeeping practices, of psychology and sociology principles to child care and family relationships, of economics principles to family finance and buying, and of art principles to creating the home environment and ensembling wardrobes.

Federal legislation dealing with vocational education sets up requirements for time schedules that permit teachers to give personal attention to assisting individual students to plan and evaluate carry-over into home living. These directives have been considered too detailed by some educators, but they have been definite factors in developing the concept of home economics in secondary schools as education for all the basic aspects of family living. A recent national study shows that non-vocational home-economics departments, which traditionally tended to devote major attention to foods and clothing, are increasingly offering comprehensive programs quite comparable in scope though less adequate in the distribution of time among the various aspects of home living and less specific about guided home and community experiences.

For purposes of study, home economics has to be subdivided into areas such as foods and nutrition, child development, consumer education, family relationships, home management, furnishing and equipping homes, clothing and textiles, and money management. Seldom does the homemaker consider one of these areas independently. Most decisions in homemaking involve family relations, family economics, and other aspects of management. Good teaching and home projects help to keep these interrelationships in focus as decisions about the use of resources or changes in family practices or procedures are considered.

The program of the Future Homemakers of America, the secondary school home-economics club program, sponsored by the Vocational Division of the U.S. Office of Education and professional organizations in home economics, supplements class and home experience and gives girls leadership opportunities in the school and the community. The state and national promotion of this program gives home-economics students opportunities to relate themselves constructively to state, national, and international movements in the interest of good family life. For instance, the Future Homemakers of America have united to contribute to the United Nations–sponsored programs for child health and welfare and the education of women and girls in developing countries, through participation in UNICEF and UNESCO projects. This is one of the ways in which home-economics experiences extend into the world citizenship aspects of education.

Education To Develop Special Interests and Aptitudes. Many schools provide opportunities for students who discover special aptitudes in general and vocational home-economics courses to develop these aptitudes further in advanced semester-long courses, in such special areas as child development, which includes laboratory experience in nursery schools and community day-care centers, foods and nutrition, clothing design and construction, home furnishing, home care of illness, family finance, and consumer economics. This type of offering is described in a recent release by the American Home Economics Association as "A dynamic outlook in High School Home Economics."

In Schenectady, New York, senior high school boys and girls study personality development and human behavior side by side with parents in an interrelated program designed for the whole family. Observation of nursery school children and their development, and practice in dealing with the variety of behavior problems that arise among them are the bases for class study and discussion.

In Wilkes County, North Carolina the home-economics department offers a child-care course for boys only! The response is reported to be enthusiastic. In Stockton, California, students in a homemaking class learn how to plan a family's financial security in a family-finance and budgeting unit that covers savings, insurance, and investments. Other schools plan credit courses for special groups, for instance for a group of college-bound students and business-education majors and for seniors who have had no previous opportunities to study home economics. Still others offer short units in special-interest areas that may be fitted into free periods in student schedules. Illustrating these are the following examples: In Belding, Michigan, seniors who are college- or business-bound take a one-year survey course in nutrition, consumer education, child development, housing, money management, and wardrobe care. In Arlington, Virginia, eleventh- and twelfth-grade boys and girls substitute short-term elective courses in home economics for study hours. Using community leaders as resource people, the classes focus on social and family relationships and foods and clothing for young men and women.

Skills for Wage Earning. Increasingly, high schools will be called upon to help students develop skills that may lead to wage earning. Home-economics departments with adequate staff for education beyond general and vocational homemaking purposes can offer courses with the view to wage earning in food service, in child-care centers, in clothing-repair and -construction centers, and in specialized retailing services. Home economics also has much to offer in areas that can further employability of boys and girls in any vocation, such as guidance in standards for, and habits of, personal grooming, health, social usage, poise, and clothing selection and care.

Objectives of the Home-Economics Curriculum. In planning the new curriculum in terms of the larger social needs and the purposes of education, the home-economics teacher thinks of the understandings, skills, appreciations, attitudes, and values desirable for all secondary school boys and girls in their personal and family living and sets up objectives in terms of behavior outcome. A committee of the American Home Economics Association published in 1959 a carefully compiled list of competences that, in the estimation of leaders in the field, will be needed and effective in personal and family living, regardless of the particular circumstances of the individual or family, and that will help the family of today meet the challenges of social change. The report reads as follows:

Fundamental to effective living are the competences to:
Establish values which give meaning to personal, family, and community living; select goals appropriate to these values.
Create a home and community environment conducive to the healthy growth and development of all members of the family at all stages of the family cycle.

Achieve good interpersonal relationships within the home and within the community.

Nurture the young and foster their physical, mental, and social growth and development.

Make and carry out intelligent decisions regarding the use of personal, family, and community resources.

Establish long-range goals for financial security and work toward their achievement.

Plan consumption of goods and services—including food, clothing, and housing—in ways that will promote values and goals established by the family.

Purchase consumer goods and services appropriate to an over-all consumption plan and wise use of economic resources.

Perform the tasks of maintaining a home in such a way that they will contribute effectively to furthering individual and fa[m]ily goals.

Enrich personal and family life through the arts and humanities and through refreshing and creative use of leisure.

Take an intelligent part in legislative and other social action programs which directly affect the welfare of individuals and families.

Develop mutual understanding and appreciation of differing cultures and ways of life, and cooperate with people of other cultures who are striving to raise levels of living.

As home economists we can measure the success of our work by the extent to which we can contribute to the development of these competences.[1]

More specific objectives may be set by teacher and students for each of these competences in terms of the problems individuals and families meet in living together. These have been variously stated:

1. To plan and select food and prepare nutritious meals—breakfasts, lunches, or dinners—with available resources of foods, money, equipment, time, and energy
2. To maintain good health through learning and practicing good food habits
3. To be an attractive, well-groomed, well-dressed, well-mannered person with ability to get along well with others
4. To help conserve present materials of clothing and household textiles through good care or renovation and clothing construction
5. To share in the home activities—meal preparation, child care, or clothing upkeep—for the satisfaction of all members
6. To evaluate the needs for individual and family consumption in terms of desired values and make wise use of available money

Home-economics courses are sometimes organized around student and family problems, each selected to bring realism into class activities in

[1] *Journal of Home Economics,* 52d-annual-meeting issue, Vol. 53, No. 7 (September, 1961), p. 555.

terms of the competences that are essential to good living. Problem organization might include these:

1. In a junior high school child-care unit—How can I be more helpful and add to the enjoyment of caring for my preschool-age sisters? Or—How can I become more patient with, and companionable to, my ten-year-old brother?
2. In a clothing unit—How can I make the best use of the new textile fabrics when selecting or constructing my clothing?
3. In a housing or management unit—How can I rearrange our kitchen to make it more convenient, more attractive, and more easily kept orderly, as well as more of a center for shared activities with family members?
4. In a unit on hospitality or recreation—How can we have fun at home and entertain our friends with the time and money available?
5. In a nutrition unit—How can we be reasonably sure we are providing food for adequate nutrition for all members of the family?
6. In a foods unit—Without increasing our food expenditure, how can we serve more attractive, appetizing, and nutritious meals?
7. In family-relationships or -management unit—Now that mother is working in a paid job, how can we be more cooperative as a family in getting meals and housekeeping jobs done, so that mother and the rest of us can have the free time we want? What time-saving methods used in our home can be shared with others in the class?

As conditions of family living change, the home-economics curriculum content must change accordingly. In the light of increased availability and multiplicity of consumer goods and services, persuasive salesmanship, and changing income and employment situations, it becomes increasingly important that families define clearly what to them are the permanent values in family living and plan to maintain and enhance them through ever better methods of making decisions about the use of time, money, energy and abilities of family members, and resources offered commercially and by the community.

Providing for the health, happiness, and the developmental needs of each family member will always be a central function of family living. Education for family living must, then, give first importance to assisting young people to grow in understanding of developmental needs—their own and those of others—and how these needs can be met most effectively through the use of the arts and the skills of human relationships, through dedication to family living, through effective management of resources, and through housekeeping skills and the application of important new knowledge to make family living productive of health and happiness.

The "doing" aspects of homemaking are essential, but their importance takes on significance only as they are used to nurture individual and family development, to express love and concern for members of the family, and to give the home stature in the eyes of family members and the community.

If we are to expect young people to establish homes that will enrich our culture and be centers in which family members find fulfilment of psychological, spiritual, intellectual, and physical needs, education must give more substantial attention to guiding learning in terms of these important family and social values.

ORGANIZATION OF HOME-ECONOMICS COURSES

In order for desirable educational objectives to be achieved, materials may be organized in several ways: in separate courses, in core curriculums, as short units in connection with other subject-matter courses, or around important school and community enterprises to which several school departments contribute materials.

Materials may be organized in separate courses for the year, for the semester, or for shorter periods of from one to eight weeks. The trend is toward the study of units, problems or projects of varying lengths, in different areas rather than a whole course devoted to the study of one aspect of home economics, because it is desirable that the student have contact with, and see, relationships between the different phases of home economics. The length of a unit will depend upon the objectives set up by the teacher and students, as well as the time and resources available. The emphasis and content in selected units should be determined by the actual social situation and the needs and interests of the students in the particular community.

A year's course in homemaking in the junior high school, for example, might include units in nutrition and health, personal care, making friends, suppers or luncheons, room arrangements, safety in the home, care of younger children, selection, and construction and care of clothing.

In the senior high school, a year's course in homemaking could well include such units as clothing selection and construction, food for the family, child development, home planning and furnishing, home hospitality, family relationships, family finance, and home nursing.

Consumer education and related art or home-management materials may be organized in separate units, but they will also be made an integral part of other units. Making of choices as to whether to buy or not to buy, considering values received from goods in relation to the values desired, and techniques of purchasing might well be emphasized in each unit dealing with food, clothing, housing, and other aspects of home economics. Certainly art principles should be emphasized and applied in relation to clothing and textiles, household surroundings, and food service. Likewise, management is increasingly a requisite of all personal and home-living activities. Planning and decision making are necessary in relation to money, time, energy, and the human resources in the family. This plan provides opportunity for better integration and should be carried on in large measure. However, there is real danger that certain important considerations of consumer education and related art and home management will be lost sight of unless at some time direct concentrated attention is given to these aspects of homemaking.

Within the separate courses, materials may be organized on the basis of problems the individual meets in making satisfactory adjustments—in flexible units in areas of home living or in projects or activities for home and school. But whether the materials are organized as problems, units, or projects, learning experiences should be planned through which the objectives for personal and social development of the student can be achieved.

Current Status of Home Economics in Public Schools. A recent national study made by the Home Economics Education Branch of the Division of Vocational Education, U.S. Office of Education,[2] reports that 95 per cent of all the public secondary schools in the United States in 1959 offered home economics, that 49 per cent of an estimated 2,353,000 girls were enrolled in home-economics courses, and that 1 per cent of an estimated 63,000 boys were also enrolled. Home economics was required in many communities—93 per cent of the schools in smaller communities and 74 per cent in the larger communities required home economics for seventh- and eighth-grade pupils. In a few schools—9 per cent in small communities and 5 per cent in the largest—home economics was required for grades eleven and twelve. Home economics for adults was available in 40 per cent of the public secondary schools studied. Homemaking or Home Economics was the title used for 73 per cent of the courses. Family Living, Foods, and Clothing were frequently used. At the upper levels, seven areas of instruction were usual: Child Development, Clothing, Consumer Education, Family Relations, Foods and Nutrition, Health and Home Nursing, and Housing and Home Management. The time was fairly reasonably divided among these areas, while, in grades below the twelfth, between more than one-half and three-fourths of the time was given to foods and clothing.

The Placement of Home Economics and Time Schedules. The Office of Education 1959 study reports that more home-economics courses are

[2] *Home Economics in the Public Secondary Schools,* U.S. Office of Education Publication 83010.

offered at the ninth- and tenth-grade levels than at other levels, but, when these were divided into vocational and non-vocational courses, it was found that more courses in grades nine to twelve were vocational than were non-vocational and that there were more seventh- and eighth-grade non-vocational courses than in grade nine or ten. About 30 per cent of all home-economics courses offered were required. The seventh- and eighth-grade courses taught for shorter periods of time were the most frequently required. There were distinct regional differences with respect to required courses.

Eighty per cent of the ninth- to twelfth-grade courses were taught for five periods a week; 63 per cent of seventh- and eighth-grade courses followed this time schedule; 22 per cent of the seventh- and eighth-grade courses were taught one or two periods a week; 11 per cent were taught three or four periods a week; less than 1 per cent of the courses were taught for one period a week.

More than half of the schools with vocational programs offered three years of home economics, and 81 per cent offered three or four years.

Home-economics teachers have had to consider carefully the best use of time. Questions they are asking are: What managerial skills are important today? What manual skills? What skills in relationships? At what grade levels can they best be developed?[3] Study of the proportion of time spent on the various aspects of home living led to the following questions: Do courses reflect as clearly as leaders believe they should the significance of child development, of the relations between individuals and between homes and communities, of consumer and management responsibilities, and of health and nutrition? Are the areas and aspects taught in different ways, those most important in the stage of development of most pupils?

TRENDS IN RECENT DEVELOPMENTS IN CONTENT AND ORGANIZATION

Each school and community makes its own plans for education, but state departments of education, the U.S. Office of Education, and professional organizations give leadership and provide resource materials to guide scope and content. Illustrative of the types of leadership provided are the following descriptions of state and national programs. The New York State plan is given first, in considerable detail. It is typical of the kinds of study and action taking place in many states and communities.

---

[3] The questions included in this paragraph were raised by the interpreter of the National Study, Beulah I. Coon, Specialist in Research Home Economics Education in the U.S. Office of Education.

New York. New York State reports the following areas of learning in grade seven: The teen-ager as a person, the teen-ager within the family, the teen-ager in the school and community, food and the teen-ager; in grade eight: The child in the home, understanding children, sharing in the care of children, the teen-ager and her wardrobe. In the ninth grade, two plans are offered, one for those who begin a major sequence in home economics, the other for those who select an elective course for one-half or one unit of credit.

For the senior high school, a sequence of three courses is planned to prepare students to assume responsibilities as homemakers by providing a well-rounded program in all areas of homemaking. The focus in high school courses is on management, family relationships, and human growth and development. Each course is developed around concepts and generalizations that are basic for home economics at the secondary level. The third course in this sequence gives special attention to living in the community, creating a family, and establishing a home. A series of special-interest courses are also offered on a one-semester basis for students who cannot take the three-year sequence. A one-term course that deals with interpersonal relationships, marriage, and family living is a special-interest course offered to seniors and mature juniors only.

Recently issued guides to curriculum development include *Enriching Homemaking Education Through Future Homemakers of America*, and source materials for a senior course to meet the needs of the academically talented, entitled *Family Values for a Democratic Society*. Four units are included: Families in Our Society, Families in Other Cultures, The Individual in the Family, and Marriage. Curriculum guides for two other groups are in process for slightly retarded students and for senior students who wish to develop skills for wage earning.

The series of special-interest courses mentioned above are available to students in grades eleven and twelve. Each course focuses on a particular area of family living, reviews and extends one or more concepts introduced earlier in the students' experience, uses new knowledge and techniques in dealing with significant personal and family situations, and at the same time projects into the future the values and skills that traditionally have centered in the family, with the purpose of expanding and deepening appreciation of those most likely to enrich the lives of class members and their families. Identification of potential employment opportunities in each area studied will be one of the outcomes anticipated. The titles of the special-interest courses are Family Economics, Family and Community Health, Family Clothing and Textiles, Family Nutrition and Meal Management, Child Development, Care and Guidance, and Family Housing and Decoration. Students who plan to enter the labor market directly from high school, or who want salable skills to enable them to earn while continuing their education beyond high school, may select an employment-preparation sequence of courses to include major or special-interest courses in home economics in grades nine through eleven and an employment-preparation course in the senior year. This senior course will concentrate on the development of skills, provide orientation to employment, and include work experience when it can be arranged to the advantage of the students and potential employees. The areas of home economics most likely to lead to wage earning in homes or in institutions are food preparation and service, child care, and housekeeping services. Details of employment-preparation courses for New York State high schools are still under study.

Curriculum revision in New York State is placing emphasis on

1. Basing all learning on the activities and concerns of families
2. Identifying those phases of family education that are of greatest significance to students in grades seven through twelve
3. Selecting methods that will best lead to desired learnings

Ways of increasing depth and breadth of learning are under examination. Methods in effect include elimination of unnecessary duplication, careful identification of essential concepts, and arranging of sequences in learning in terms of developmental levels of students. Committees working in the field of foods and nutrition have recommended the following areas of learning as essential: Sound nutrition for health, management of family meals, scientific and creative aspects of food preparation, social and aesthetic values in the service of meals, and food and nutrition throughout the world. Experiences appropriate for each year of a three-year sequence showing increasing depth and breadth of learning from year to year are being compiled for the guidance of teachers.

Georgia. In Georgia, similar effort is apparently going into planning experiences of increasing difficulty for a three-year sequence in home economics recommended for high schools. Each year deals with seven areas of family living: clothing construction and selection, meal planning and preparation, home care of the sick, housing and home management, child care and development, consumer education, and family relations.

Georgia has specialized semester courses, and eighth-grade homemaking is planned for both boys and girls. A comprehensive course in family living for boys and girls, with focus on establishing and maintaining new families, is in effect. This course emphasizes self-understanding, understanding families, preparation now for marriage in the future, being married and what it means, planning to secure satisfaction from family income, planning livable homes, planning for parenthood, caring for the infant, and living with children.

Michigan. In Michigan, the State Superintendent of Public Instruction invites annually persons throughout the state to serve on twenty-nine different curriculum committees. One of these is the state Committee on Home and Family Living. This committee seeks to stimulate thinking, planning, and action designed to promote programs of home and family living at various levels of education throughout Michigan. On the committee are home economists, sociologists, guidance personnel, administrators, and representatives from the elementary, high school, and university programs. The state committee defined home- and family-life education as follows:

Education for home and family living helps to develop understandings, skills, experiences and to provide knowledge and counseling designed to strengthen family life today and to prepare one for the family responsibilities of tomorrow. Schools, churches, and community agencies may be the instruments for its achievement.

Family life education includes the concept that the whole school program should be permeated with an awareness of the need—pre-school, elementary, junior and senior high schools—and that at certain points in the curriculum there should be specific classes appropriate to the age groups involved. Somewhere in high school, usually in the junior and senior years courses are offered which center on the needs of students to help them better understand themselves and their relationships to their families; and to prepare them for living, successfully in the families of which they are almost certain to be a part. There is evidence from student testimony that a specific course is needed in the early junior high years.

The departments in which family living is offered vary from school to school. In some schools, family-living classes may be included as a part of the program in home economics, biology, physical education, social studies, or guidance. In other schools, several departments cooperate in the teaching of family living.

Home- and family-life education forms a part of a core or is a separate offering in some junior high schools; it is offered to boys and girls as a separate course in the eleventh and twelfth grades in many schools. More schools offer such a course to seniors in high school than at any other level in the public schools. The content recommended includes learning about ourselves, preparing for marriage, moving into marriage, developing interpersonal competences important in living together in marriage, management for personal and family living, housing the family, and planning for parenthood.

Principals were asked to evaluate this course. These answers are typical of replies to this request:

This is a course which should be a part of the curriculum. A course somewhat similar to the 12th grade course is offered in the 9th grade level.

In view of the high percentage of marriage failures and teen-age problems, I believe this is one of the most important courses in the curriculum. The students recognize the importance since, though offered as an elective almost 100% of our seniors elect it. [This reply is from a large city high school.]

[This reply comes from a thickly populated suburban area:] It is most necesary, in view of the fact that many students marry shortly after completing high school. Such a coure recognizes the importance of the home in our social structure and represents an attempt to strengthen it through an educational approach.

Seeing their problems, facing them and learning how to do something about them helps them mature and become responsible adults.

The advisory committee of parents working with students and teachers helps make a better informed community and a better rounded program.

We have done an intensive testing of the value of this course, partly because of the controversial value of the content. We have felt the need for close parent contacts and we each semester give students an opportunity to evaluate the course. We have open meetings for parents and students. The results of these evaluations all point to enthusiastic support of the community and a recognition on the part of the student[s] of the extreme value of the course to them.

Recent State Curriculum Guides. Several states have recently issued curriculum guides that provide guidance for semester-long units in one area for the later high school years in preference to the multiple-unit courses widely used in recent years. These plans were developd to give greater depth in study of each area. Florida outlines six possibilities: child development; personal, family and social relations; clothing and textiles; housing; home furnishing; and home management and family finance. Illinois provides for four areas of study: family relationships and child development; clothing and related areas; foods and nutrition; and housing and home furnishing. Management is incorporated in each area of study rather than in a separate course.

A National Secondary School Home-Economics Curriculum Project. A recent release—October 17, 1962—from Edna Amidon, Director of the Home Economics Branch of the U.S. Office of Education, reports the following steps taken to date in an extensive continuing secondary school home-economics curriculum project:

1. February, 1961—A meeting of state home-economics leaders and representatives of professional organizations was held in Washington, D.C., to consider how a national group might give leadership to a re-examination of home economics in secondary schools in the light of changing social and economic conditions in the world. The committee recommended developing guidelines for this area of education that could serve as criteria for determining what in present programs has continuing

value, what should be dropped, and what added, in order better to serve today's youth—boys as well as girls. This group explored the idea of defining the unifying elements in home economics, that is, identifying the central concepts in the field of home economics. A progress report was ready for review in January, 1962.

2. January, 1962—Five of the February, 1961, group considered a tentative outline of concepts for home economics with some generalizations to support them, and a revised tentative outline of the place of home economics in secondary schools, which had been in preparation as a follow-up of plans made at the earlier meeting of teachers, supervisors, and teacher trainers.

3. March, 1962—Two regional conferences (central and Pacific regions) worked on the use of concepts and generalizations in curriculum development.

4. July, 1962—A workshop at Iowa State University focused on the area of family relations, and a workshop at Pennsylvania State University worked on home management and family economics. At these workshops, specialists and consultants worked with teachers, teacher educators, and supervisors to develop statements of generalizations that are basic for home economics at the high school level. These materials are considered tentative and will be further reviewed and revised before they are ready to be used in four workshops in which the focus will be on other areas of home economics.

Cooperation in the Total School Program. In many schools, teachers concerned with health education and home economics take special responsibility for planning educational programs for the school lunch hour to highlight nutrition information, to encourage social amenities, and to develop social responsibility for cleanliness, order, and respect for the rights of others. Home-economics classes prepare exhibits and sometimes fliers to present criteria for a good lunch; they check and evaluate lunch selection from time to time and use the school paper or assembly spots to call attention to what is good and what needs correction.

Practical experience in lunchroom service is used in schools that develop courses that aim to perfect skills for wage earning in food service. Teachers arrange for laboratory practice in lunchrooms in a variety of ways.

Students in advanced nutrition courses sometimes offer advisory service to students needing assistance for problems of overweight or underweight. They prepare bulletin-board presentations exposing food fads and fallacies and keep current nutrition findings available to interested students. Students in advanced courses in clothing offer advisory service on line, design and color, clothing care, and clothing appropriate for the occasions most high school students attend. Classes in child development in some schools arrange for play groups of children whose mothers are attending a parent-education class or a P.T.A. meeting. Classes in home furnishing often plan and assist in carrying out refurnishing of special rooms in the school—rest rooms, lounges, the lunch room. All of these are means of making practical application of learning and of contributing to the general school program.

Exchange of Classes. In some schools, by agreement, home-economics teachers exchange classes with teachers of economics, agriculture, industrial arts, or art for the teaching of specialized areas of mutual concern—in effect a form of team teaching. Home-economics teachers participate, in many schools, in the planning and teaching of core courses, contributing units on nutrition and health, aspects of consumer education, social and family relations, clothing selection and care, wardrobe planning, etc.

Meeting Needs of Special Groups. More needs to be done to meet the needs of special groups—those with superior ability, those who have not demonstrated ability to enter college, the retarded, and the handicapped. All of them should have full opportunity to develop their abilities in a plan that does not segregate them to their disadvantage. Inconspicuous ability grouping may be arranged subject by subject rather than arbitrarily at the average level of two or three groups. Progress has been made through grouping of the talented and the severely handicapped. Focus is needed on the average students, particularly those that drop out of school now only to find that no employment is available. The home-economics classes planned for seniors are often geared to the needs of the able students. They tend to stress reading in breadth and depth and stimulation of interest in the most significant aspects of family living, seeing the family in the larger social setting and thinking about the meaning family life can have. Experimental programs are under way that bear watching. For the dropouts, flexible schedules to permit supervised part-time work following courses with pre-employment emphasis may have possibilities. Learning to motivate greater effort in basic education areas will be important to their economic future; in addition, opportunities to develop a rising level of skills should be provided.

Throwing of all ability groups into ungraded classes, which has been a practice for classes in the so-called special subjects in some schools, has been detrimental to all concerned, and there now should be enough evidence that better ways of handling the problem of ability must be found.

"School and Community" Programs. The pilot programs under way in many schools are heartening evidence of a deepening sense of responsibility for making appropriate education for home living available to all school groups, and extensive community programs are developing at church, government, and organization levels. Education can play a larger part in assisting individuals and families to adjust to change and to reap the benefits of all the new knowledge that has significance and can play a part in promoting higher ideals and improved standards of living for a greater number of families.

STEPS IN CURRICULUM CONSTRUCTION: A SUMMARY

Curriculum development is thought of as a continuous process. Efforts are being made to have all teachers participate in curriculum planning assisted by professional consultants and lay people. There are many decisions to be made by each curriculum-study group in finding answers to these major questions: What are the basics in home-life education? Where, when, by whom, and how shall they be taught? Essential points of departure will include

1. Reaffirmation of beliefs about the importance of family life and of education's opportunity to contribute to the strengthening of family life
2. Review of cultural, social, and economic settings of families
3. Review of current practices in schools, to discover what is good and what can be omitted because it is obsolete or inappropriate in the light of more critical concerns in family living
4. Tentative decisions about inadequacies that should be eliminated immediately as part of a long-range plan for progressive strengthening of education for home living
5. Statement of objectives to be achieved
6. Statement of the basic learning, concepts, and generalizations to achieve the objectives
7. Organization of learning units to include activities and experiences
8. Plans for evaluation to determine progress in learning

All curriculum-study groups should keep before them as guidelines the social ideals of American democracy, the developmental needs of the young people for whom education is being planned, and the most convincing findings on how people learn. This process carried on in the light of a developing philosophy of family life and education for a changing society should result in a functioning curriculum for home living.

QUESTIONS, PROBLEMS, AND ISSUES FOR FURTHER THOUGHT

1. What, from your point of view, are the important values in family living? How do they compare with those specified by writers on the family, by your parents, and by your friends?

2. List the responsibilities of family living that can be shared by men and women for which they should receive education. At what age or maturity level should these learning experiences be provided?

3. Plan a series of learning experiences for an elective class of eleventh- and twelfth-grade boys and girls that would contribute to their readiness for establishing homes of their own.

4. What differences would there be in the home-economics curriculum content when used for each of the following purposes: general education, vocational education, development of special interests, pre-employment experience?

5. Make plans for a health program in a secondary school. What major responsibilities should be carried by the home-economics department?

6. After studying the latest home-economics course of study in your state, indicate necessary changes in the light of new products available, facts, or research findings. Be specific.

7. Indicate agencies and community activities useful in a school-community program in home economics.

8. If you, the home-economics teacher, were a member of an all-school committee to plan a core curriculum, what content would you suggest from your field to help solve the common problems of ninth-grade adolescents?

9. What contributions could be made through home-economics instruction to the reduction of juvenile delinquency?

10. What competences would you list as essential for success in marriage?

11. What are significant contributions that the family has to make in a democratic society?

12. Write concise statements on the following:

    a. Why you do or do not believe in education for family living.
    b. What you mean by "education for family living."
    c. Why you do or do not think it is important.

SUPPLEMENTARY MATERIALS

Selected Readings

ALBERTY, HAROLD. "Helping Teen-agers Explore Values." Columbus: Ohio State University, 1956. A resource unit for high school teachers prepared by a seminar in secondary education under the direction of Dr. Alberty.

BROWN, MURIEL W. *With Focus on Family Living: The Story of Four Experiments in Commmunity Organization for Family Life Education.* Home Economics Bulletin 249. Washington, D.C.: Government Printing Office, 1953.

COON, BEULAH I. "Home Economics in Public Secondary Schools of the United States." U.S. Office of Education Publication 83010. Washington, D.C.: Government Printing Office, 1962. A study to show the status of home-economics programs in public secondary schools of the nation as a whole. It reports the proportion of pupils reached and the content of offerings. The findings should be useful to supervisors of home economics and teachers, as one basis for evaluation of programs they are sponsoring.

DEPARTMENT OF HOME ECONOMICS, NATIONAL EDUCATION ASSOCIATION OF THE UNITED STATES. *Concepts, Skills and Techniques for Teaching Family Relations.* Washington, D.C.: The Association, 1958

————. *Consumer Education for Family Life.* Washington, D.C.: The Association.

————. *Enriching Homemaking Education Through the Arts and Humanities.* Washington, D.C.: The Association.

————. *Teaching Principles of Science in Homemaking Education.* Washington, D.C.: The Association.

HALL, OLIVE A., and BEATRICE PAOLUCCI. "Teaching Home Economics," New York: John Wiley & Sons, Inc., 1961. A college textbook on methods of teaching.

HOME ECONOMICS COMMITTEE ON RESEARCH, AMERICAN VOCATIONAL ASSOCIATION, *Family Focus in Home Economics Teaching.* Washington, D.C.: The Association. A statement of philosophy and brief descriptions of programs of education with family focus.

KRUG, E. A. *Secondary School Curriculum.* New York: Harper & Row, 1960. Chapter 19, "Home Economics."

OTTO, ARLENE. *New Designs in Homemaking Programs in Junior High Schools.* Teachers College, Bureau of Publications, Columbia University, 1958.

SIMPSON, ELIZABETH, and LOUISE LEMMON. *Teaching Processes of Thinking in Homemaking Education.* Washington, D.C.: National Education Association of the United States, 1959.

UNIVERSITY OF MINNESOTA, DEPARTMENT OF HOME ECONOMICS EDUCATION, IN COOPERATION WITH STATE OF MINNESOTA DEPARTMENT OF EDUCATION, VOCATIONAL SECTION. *Home Learning Experiences in the Home Economics Program,* 1961. Available from University of Minnesota bookstore, St. Paul.

18

Physical Education and Health Education

INTRODUCTORY CONSIDERATIONS

Meaning of Physical Education. Physical education is the area of education that seeks to produce desirable changes in human behavior through the medium of carefully selected and competently conducted physical activities. Physical education has the same broad goals of education as give purpose to the other learning experiences of the school.

Aim of Physical Education. The aim of physical education like that of other subjects is to contribute to the optimum physical, social, emotional, and intellectual growth of pupils. Physical education can provide experiences important in helping each boy and girl to develop and maintain fitness, to acquire useful skills, and to act in socially acceptable ways.

Contributions of Physical Education. The unique contribution of physical education is that of helping each individual acquire such attributes of fitness as sound functioning of the bodily processes, organic vigor, strength, endurance, agility, and coordination. Certain motor skills basic to everyday living as well as to success in sports activities may also be developed through physical education. The most common are walking, running, jumping, hopping, skipping, starting, stopping, dodging, balancing, pushing, pulling, lifting, climbing, throwing, catching, rhythmic movements, and relaxation.

Physical education offers opportunities for the learning of desirable aspects of social behavior involving respect for self and for others.

Probably no other area of the curriculum provides the unique opportunities for leadership development provided by physical education. A class may be divided into squads each having a leader. Leadership may be permanent or rotated at periodic times so that each squad member has the opportunity to assume the role of leader. Physically gifted children may be used as skill demonstrators. In intramural and interscholastic sports, team captains have important leadership opportunities. At the same time, the important role of "followership" is provided.

Physical Education vs. Physical Training. Physical education should not be confused with physical training. *Training* implies exercise primarily for physical values, for instance, to train for combat or a contest. The term connotes authoritarianism: the response to a command. Physical *education,* conversely, suggests self-discipline, considered responses, reflective thinking: the learning of the why as well as the how. An individual or team may train for a contest or event by developing strength and endurance, while the physical-education program is intended, in addition, to teach attitudes, skills, and appreciations involving many sports activities and related experiences.

Forces Opposing Physical Education. The traditional scholastic considers the mind to be in opposition to the body. He asserts that it is only necessary to provide for the strictly mental functions of the school child while disregarding the physical needs. This concept is not new. It dates back to the time when certain sects of monks punished their bodies with the hope that this practice would sharpen their mental functions. Such a philosophy is no more valid now than it was then. Because of automation and the availability of transportation, purposeful physical development seems more important today than it was in the past.

The philosophy of asceticism holds that, in order to acquire excellence of the soul, man must degrade the body. This philosophy was exemplified in the old Puritan code by such phrases as "play is evil" and "pleasure begets the devil." Remains of this philosophy are the Sunday blue laws, which place time limits on Sunday baseball games and the like. This spirit continues in many communities and flares up occasionally when the competition between church and community activities becomes too great.

Theoretically, the scholastic and the ascetic would separate the mind and the body or the soul and the body. However, these approaches are not practical. Man functions as an integrated whole and cannot be separated into a physical and a mental part. When man experiences pain from a sore tooth or an injured limb, his mental capacities are affected, sometimes to such an extent that rational thinking may be impaired if not impossible. Reason dictates that a feeling of physical well-being could increase one's mental output. This has long been recognized in the schools. For instance, at the elementary level, the solid subjects such as reading, arithmetic, and the sciences are taught in the morning, when the children are "fresh." Art, music, and other cultural subjects are taught in the afternoon schedule. The scientist who works long and hard in his laboratory certainly needs a degree of physical endurance in order to produce his best work. The preceding would seem to indicate that man functions as a unified whole and that what he produces is a result of a total rather than a partial effort.

Background of Physical Education. Physical education is not new or unique to our times. It is as old as man. Man has needed to develop physically to survive and sustain himself, to perform his daily work, to maintain his health, and to pursue selected leisure-time pursuits of his culture.

The degree to which a given purpose has been emphasized in sports has varied with the current culture, society, and era. Its form or emphasis has been modified, depending upon the philosophical beliefs of each society or era. The Greek philosophers believed that it was necessary for the physical potential as well as the intellect to be developed, if the individual was to make the optimum contributions to his society. Militant nations have stressed fitness for combat, while others have emphasized the need for a sound body to support an active mind.

Movement. The urge for movement is an inherent characteristic of the nature of man. Basic movements such as running, jumping, climbing, throwing, and striking, involving flight and pursuit, were requisites for survival of primitive man. If a man could not run, climb, or strike, he and his family perished. These movements as now expressed in tag games, ball games, and stunts provide necessary stimulation for the biological, sociological, and organic development of the individual.

The content of the program is the science of skill in movement. The development of this skill and the satisfactions that accompany successes in sports, games, dance, and physical achievement are basic outcomes of the physical-education program. Movement is not confined to physical achievement. Man may express thoughts or emotions as he leaps or dances with joy, trembles with fear, or gestures in emphasis.

The schoolchild's social development encompasses attitudes, habits, and skills. Physical-education laboratories provide a unique opportunity for this phase of education. One of democracy's greatest problems today concerns race and creed. Many athletic coaches have long recognized that team membership should be based upon a participant's ability rather than his religion or the color of his skin. Competition in physical-education classes, as well as in intramural activities, gives each child the opportunity to participate with and against those of his schoolmates who differ in race or creed and to develop a respect for personal worth and ability, thus contributing toward the practical application of the intent of our democracy.

Coeducational activities can help develop good social habits and skills. In rhythms, the boy is taught how to ask a partner for the "pleasure of this dance." The girl is taught how to politely accept or refuse. Conduct during coeducational activities is carefully monitored so that local customs and mores are not violated. It is hoped that lasting habits are developed as a result. Certainly, the learning of the various skills involved in dance contributes a great deal toward the child's social growth. When a child goes to a dance, he can participate and enjoy the companionship of the opposite sex rather than being a "wallflower."

Everyone wishes to be a winner. That is part of our heritage. From the beginning to the end, life is competitive. However, one cannot expect to win all the time, nor should one expect to lose all the time. One should try as hard as one can to win, but, if one loses, one should be able to accept the loss gracefully. One should learn to play by the rules governing the game, just as one should play the game of life according to the laws of the land. In this area of learning, practical experience under good leadership should be provided through the physical-education program.

Physical education provides an education for the spectator. While spectator interest should not replace active participation, it must be recognized that every person is not gifted in certain skills. For instance, the weekend golfer is likely to enjoy observing a professional golf match. In order to appreciate what he sees, the spectator should know some of the fine points involved in the game. The observer of a contest should be able to recognize good play on the floor or field. Girls especially, who have little or no opportunity to play a game such as football, need to be taught how to watch a contest. They should be familiar with the rules and the nomenclature related to the game. This could provide for a higher degree of enjoyment and could improve spectator sportsmanship.

Physical education is a very broad and inclusive area in education. Closely associated with this field are health education, education for leisure, and safety education. The field of physical education itself has several areas of emphasis. The core of the physical-education program is the class-instruction program, the primary purposes of which are to teach skills and to develop physical fitness. Intramural, extramural, and interscholastic sports programs provide opportunities for students to practice and improve skills learned in instruction classes.

Education for Leisure. One of the "Seven Cardinal Principles of Education" is worthy use of leisure time. Our modern society provides an ever increasing amount of leisure time. Whether leisure is an asset or a liability depends on how it is used. The schools have a responsibility to teach skills and develop interests in worthwhile recreational activities that can enrich the present as well as future lives of its students. Recreation programs are not limited to physical activities. However, physical education can make a contribution to the worthy use of leisure time by developing skills and interests in wholesome physical activities to be enjoyed during school days as well as throughout the rest of life.

In many communities, the schools serve as centers for community recreation. Since schools are built with taxes, it seems logical that school facilities should be available to the community for public recreational activities evenings and holidays when they are not being used for school activities.

THE PHYSICAL-EDUCATION INSTRUCTION PROGRAM

Two Basic Questions. Design of the physical-education curriculum involves two basic questions: What activities are to be offered? and How much time is to be devoted to each activity?

Each school community should decide what attitudes, skills, or characteristics it wishes its graduates to possess. These qualities should serve as the objectives of the physical-education programs. After objectives have been decided upon, activities must be selected to be taught in such a manner as to contribute to the desired objectives.

The curriculum may be defined and conducted as a series of planned situations and meaningful guided experiences directed toward the attainment of specific objectives in harmony with the educational aims and philosophy of a given community. Physical-education demonstrations provide an opportunity for the parents to observe class activities and to some degree to determine if the aims and objectives are being met.

The activity program should be designed to meet the needs of growing children, with consideration given to physical, emotional, psychological, and social maturity. The program should articulate from kindergarten through succeeding grades and show progression from grade to grade in each activity.

The Junior High School Program. The junior high school student needs an activity program different from those of either elementary school children or senior high school students. He is undergoing rapid physical changes, as well as less obvious but comparable social and emotional adjustments that must be considered when designing the physical-education program for the junior high school. Junior high school students need a program of physical education that is vigorous in nature and rich in variety of activities and experiences.

This is an exploratory period in which the individual should have opportunities to become acquainted with many sports activities. The school physical-education program should provide experiences for each individual to "try out" many positions in many sports rather than to become a "specialist" at an early age "for the good of the team."

If sound elementary and junior high school programs have provided training in a wide variety of physical-education activities, it may well be that the senior high school student will have sufficient information and experience to select activities for his physical-education classes intelligently. The program would then be an elective one in the sense that each student, with proper advising, can elect the courses or activities he wishes to pursue. All students, kindergarten through twelfth grade, should have a daily physical-education class. The President's Council on Youth Fitness recommends that at least fifteen minutes of each such class should be devoted to vigorous activities.

The Senior High School Program. Dual and individual sports should be emphasized in the senior high school. More attention should be given to recreational skills such as those involved in bowling, golf, and tennis, which have greater carry-over value. Whereas the junior high school was a period of exploration and experimentation, the senior high school pupil may wish to specialize in a favorite sport or activity, because one enjoys doing the things one does well. He may develop proficiency at specific positions in a selected sport in order to be a member of a team and make a contribution to team, school, or community effort.

Girls' Physical Education. Basically, girls run, jump, dodge, throw, catch, kick, and hit as naturally as do boys and, within the limits of their capabilities, need the same fundamental program of activities as boys. At the elementary school age, there is little difference in the needs, interests, and abilities of girls and boys, and classes can be combined. After the fourth-grade level, anatomical sex characteristics become more pronounced and girls are usually handicapped in strength and speed. Beyond this level, boys' and girls' classes are scheduled separately except for rhythms and less vigorous activities. Girls' classes and activities should be conducted by properly trained women instructors.

Modified Programs. Pupils who are well enough to attend school should be considered well enough to attend physical-education classes. Insofar as possible, every school should include special modified remedial or adaptive activities for those who, by reason of handicap, disability, or illness, are unable to participate in the regular program. Handicapped persons should be assigned to modified activities or rest. Assignment of activities should be based on results of medical examinations and in accordance with policies and procedures agreed upon by medical and school personnel.

Time Allotment and Grade Placement. It is recommended that all students have a daily physical-education class comparable in length to the normal school class period. At least, fifteen minutes of this period should be devoted to vigorous conditioning exercises and developmental activities designed to build vigor, strength, flexibility, endurance, coordination, and body control.

Careful organization is essential, if the objectives of the physical-education program are to be attained. Unless students are assigned to classes according to training and experience, continuity and progression in the physical-education program are impossible. Pupils should be homogeneously assigned to classes, on the basis of medical examinations, age, size, maturity, experience, and ability. The simplest method of assignment probably is on the basis of grade level.

In view of the currently crowded curriculum, every effort should be made to prevent duplication in the teaching of the various sports. Too often, time that should be utilized to teach skills in additional sports and activities is misused in repetitious playing of games previously learned.

Physical educators are not in agreement as to the grade levels at which the various activities should be emphasized or the proportional amount of time that should be devoted to each activity. The amount of time allotted to each activity in junior high school should depend upon how comprehensive and extensive the physical-education instruction has been in the elementary grades. The senior high school program, in turn, should be based on the type of program the student has experienced in the elementary and junior high schools.

Activities usually include team sports, individual and dual sports, gymnastics, rhythms, and aquatics. In most programs, considerable attention is devoted to conditioning drills, fitness exercises, and testing. Team sports that receive much emphasis are touch football, soccer, speedball, basketball, volleyball, and softball. Such activities as archery, badminton, bowling, deck tennis, golf, handball, table tennis, track and field, weight training, and wrestling are typical in the individual- and dual-sports category. Gymnastics, rhythms, and aquatics represent activities that may be modified in view of the abilities, previous training, and needs of individuals.

Progress in gymnastics, rhythms, and aquatics is largely dependent upon maturity and past experience, and some time probably should be devoted each year to training in these fields. In gymnastics, emphasis might well be placed on mat work for seventh-grade pupils or those with less maturity. Parallel-bar or apparatus activities might well be delayed until necessary arm strength has been developed through a program of body-building activities such as rope or pole climbing designed to develop arm and shoulder muscles.

Rhythmic activities should be included at each grade level. Progress, however, is determined more by experience, training, and maturity than by grade in school. Activities should be selected according to the skill level of the pupils.

Each pupil should have an opportunity to learn to swim. Water safety might well be the most important phase of the physical-education program. When schools do not have facilities for swimming, community or social-agency pools may sometimes be used.

Suggested Time Schedule. The schedule in Table 18–1 is suggested as a guide for the allocation of activities. Adjustment may be necessary because of limitations of teaching personnel, scheduling, facilities, weather, equipment, and past experiences. It may be necessary to

TABLE 18–1

PHYSICAL-EDUCATION TIME SCHEDULE

Categories	Per Cent of Time	
	Junior High School	Senior High School
Boys		
Aquatics	15	15
Rhythms	10	15
Individual and dual sports	20	30
Gymnastics	10	10
Team sports	35	20
Class organization and fitness testing	10	10
Girls		
Aquatics	15	15
Rhythms	15	20
Individual and dual sports	25	30
Gymnastics	15	10
Team sports	20	15
Class organization and fitness testing	10	10

lengthen the school year or the school day or to provide additional time during the noon hour to include these and many other learning experiences that are worthy of a place in the school program. Reorganization of school districts with bus and transportation schedules to be met will tax the ingenuity of the administration to provide an opportunity for all to participate.

The current interest in such innovations as a three-semester plan to utilize the school facilities better may give more opportunity for pupils to participate in an enriched physical-education activity program. Administrators, in this event, will need to consider types of activities such as swimming or outdoor sports that would lend themselves to summer intramural or interscholastic competition.

Developing and Maintaining Fitness. Physical education is especially concerned with physical fitness as evidenced by strength, vigor, endurance, and muscular and cardiovascular efficiency. Growth and development may be influenced by the type and amount of activity experienced by the individual. The organic systems are developed largely through physical activity.

Physical achievement tests provide a means to measure achievement, diagnose weakness, and evaluate fitness. Standardized tests also provide motivation and an incentive for individual pupils as well as for the school or community. Schools are urged to develop and use their own local tests. Many states and school systems have developed tests to determine the extent to which the objectives of their programs are being achieved.

Physical fitness is only one phase of fitness. While physical fitness is considered the basic objective of physical education, conscious effort should continually be directed toward the improvement of the moral, mental, social, and spiritual fitness of the individual.

COMPETITIVE SPORTS

The daily period of physical instruction can only partially meet pupil fitness needs. Additional opportunities should be provided for participation and competition in fitness-producing activities under competent leadership.

Opportunities should be provided for all pupils to participate in competitive sports at their levels of ability. Some competition may take place during the instruction class in the form of drills and/or self-testing situations. Provision should be made at recess, after school, or on holidays for children to enjoy the skills learned during instruction periods. Intramural, extramural, and interscholastic programs offer opportunities to practice and perfect the skills taught during instruction classes.

Participation on intramural, club, or recreation teams may provide an outlet for those who do not have the ability or time to "make the varsity team." The school or community has an increasing responsibility to make these so called extracurricular experiences possible to youth as larger high school enrolments tend to minimize the opportunity for the individual students to "make the varsity."

Intramural Programs. The intramural program is concerned with competition in sports activities conducted within a school. All children should be given the opportunity to participate in intramural competition. The intramural program should be well planned and carefully organized. Facilities, equipment, time allotment, leadership, and supervision should be comparable to that of other phases of the school program. It should be a truly educational experience that will challenge the interest and ability of participants. If properly administered, intramural participation can be organized to challenge the performance of those who have superior ability as well as those of average ability. Leagues can be formed to provide an opportunity for participation for those of less ability or training without the pressures for winning associated with interscholastic contests, or the frustrations incurred by those of less ability and training competing with more capable athletes.

A well-planned intramural program may well be the most important phase of the physical-education program. It should be skilfully planned; have competent, properly trained leadership and adequate facilities and equipment; and be as attractive and interesting to pupils as the inter-scholastic program. The success of all athletic competition is dependent, to a large degree, upon competent officiating.

The broad intramural program also includes non-competitive recreational activities such as hiking, swimming, skating, boating, scuba diving, hunting, fishing, and camping. Many of the above lend themselves nicely to a coeducational program. School camping as a phase of outdoor education moved into prominence during the last decade. Such states as California, Michigan, and Illinois are the early leaders in this area. In some cases, the school owns the camp, and in some the facilities are leased. Camp experience may be provided as a day situation where the students are transported daily to and from their homes, or as a weekend or week-long experience including both day and night. The advocates of school camping and outdoor education claim that much more can be taught in a shorter time by taking the children to nature rather than by trying to bring the wonders of nature to the classroom. Also, with the great increase in family camping, physical-education leaders believe that basic principles involved in camping should be taught in the regular physical-education program even if a school camping situation is not available. With the move to increase the length of the school year, the summer camp experience deserves important consideration. Summer school camps may be more feasible in that the camp leadership may be more readily available and there would be less need for permanent structures for student housing. Camp leadership at its finest should include all segments of the faculty, including especially the areas of botany, zoology, geology, speech, drama, sociology, art, music, mathematics, business, health, safety, and physical education.

Interscholastic Competition. Interscholastic athletics should be an outgrowth of a broad intramural program that, in turn, has its foundation in instruction provided in the physical-education classes. Interscholastic athletics is broadly defined to include all school-sponsored games or sports in which gifted children are provided with the opportunity to compete with those of similar ability from other schools. These activities should be considered a part of the physical-education program. The interscholastic-athletic phase of the physical-education program is a potential educative factor of great value that is not used as much as it could be and is too often misused.

In order to provide participation for greater numbers, interscholastic competition should be provided in many sports. Golf, tennis, softball, bowling, swimming, volleyball, soccer, wrestling, badminton, handball, and horseshoes, as well as the more common track and field, baseball, basketball, and football offer opportunities for interscholastic competition.

Sports should be included in the interscholastic program on the basis of their values to the participants and their contributions to the educational objectives of the school, and not on the basis of gate receipts or to provide entertainment for the public through the exploitation of pupils. Athletics conducted so that they can be defended by their contribution to the total school program should be supported from general education funds common to all school activities. When athletics are administered as entertainment rather than education, undesirable practices are almost certain to occur. If the interscholastic athletic program depends upon gate receipts for support, the financial pressures will be a source of trouble.

If a school places undue emphasis on a highly organized sport such as football, basketball, or baseball, participants, especially those who show athletic promise, often are exploited into a high degree of specialization demanded for participation and, thus, may be denied the opportunity to learn skills in less highly publicized or locally stressed sports such as swimming, tennis, golf, or bowling, which might have even greater contributions to make to the lives of the participants. Emphasis on developing a school team trained to achieve success in championship play may divert personnel, time, facilities, and leadership that might better serve to teach a broader variety of activities to greater numbers. However, a properly designed physical-education program should teach skills and stress excellence of performance that will prepare the participant for successful competitive varsity experience.

As school districts become organized into larger units, it becomes obvious that more teams must be organized in each school if the educational opportunities inherent in interscholastic competition are to be available to pupils now enrolled in the increasingly larger school systems. Consideration should be given to equalizing competition of participating teams through a sound method of classification. Organization of teams on the basis of age, height, and weight has proven satisfactory in many situations. Competent leadership and adequate facilities and equipment must be provided for all participants. Programs that make athletic participation available to greater numbers require ample resources. It is, of course, more costly to support a program of athletics for all than it is to finance athletics for the few. The same is true, of course, of any phase of the school program. It is desirable to organize as many teams or squads in each sport as student interests and enrolment require and the available funds, coaches, equipment, and facilities permit. Thus, any boy who has reasonable ability and who is willing to practice and train may find an active place on an organized team.

There is nothing inherently wrong with interscholastic athletics. They can be helpful or harmful. Athletics will be what they are made to be by schools and communities. School administrators have the responsibility to direct athletic programs in such a manner that they contribute to the objectives of the total school program.

Pre-High School Competition. Highly organized varsity-type interscholastic competition in elementary and junior high schools represents an increasingly controversial phase of athletic competition. School officials may have unwittingly contributed to this situation by adopting a negative attitude toward competition at these levels. The result has been that well-meaning but often uninformed community agencies have assumed leadership in sponsoring competition for children below the senior high school level. Unsupervised "sand-lot" competition in vigorous sports is extremely dangerous.

It may well be that the schools should assume leadership for sponsoring modified competitive sports activities to satisfy the needs of the elementary and junior high school pupils. Such programs should be based on factual information and scientific study rather than on bias or mere opinions.

Extramural Participation. Extramural athletic competition commonly takes place in the form of play days, sports days, or club activities. They may include informal games between teams from neighboring schools. Extramural athletics are not highly organized and do not involve leagues, championships, or season-long schedules. Skill and ability are of less importance than interest and the satisfaction of participation.

Some small schools may encounter difficulties in conducting intramural programs if enough pupils are not available to form leagues of equal ability. In such schools, where the enrolment is small, sports-day competition or occasional informal games between neighboring schools of similar size, ability, and policies may provide desirable incentives and increase interest in worthwhile activities.

Competition for Girls. There are differences of opinion among educators, parents, and participants regarding the desirability of interscholastic competition for girls. Because of the potentially undesirable pressures often associated with more highly organized participation, most recommend that competition be confined to intramural and sports-day activities. Others believe properly conducted interscholastic competition may provide enriched programs for skilled players.

Coeducational competition at the high school level is usually successful. Interest is rather high among girls at this age, so considerable progress may be made in the area of social relationships if the activity is properly conducted. Golf, tennis, volleyball, and softball are sports that are well adapted to coeducational activities. The values of any participation are dependent upon the quality of leadership and administration.

School-Community Relationship. In some situations, the schools and community recreation departments cooperate in joint school-park development and maintenance of mutually used park and playground facilities.

Just as school facilities should be available for community activities when this is feasible, so may community recreation facilities such as playing fields, tennis courts, golf courses, and possibly commercial bowling lanes and agency swimming pools be available for school usage. It is considered good economy to construct school plants adjacent to recreation-department playing fields so that outdoor facilities may be used cooperatively. When outdoor facilities become crowded during the daylight hours, artificial lighting should be considered.

The programs of schools, youth-serving agencies, and park and recreation departments should complement and supplement, not duplicate or compete with, each other. Cooperative planning is necessary. The school should be represented on the recreation council, just as the recreation department should be consulted by the school's activity council.

TEACHERS AND TEACHING MATERIALS

More than is the case in most other subjects, the "curriculum" in physical-education courses is determined by the teacher. Physical-education teachers should have adequate professional training in physical education and related fields. They should also have general education and cultural training comparable to that expected of all teachers. The teaching competence of the physical-education instructors and the availability or lack of adequate facilities and proper equipment will greatly influence the quality of the physical-education program.

It is the responsibility of the administration to obtain teachers who are qualified to teach the activities that should be included in an educationally sound physical-education program. It is also to be expected that teaching materials and conditions will be provided to the same extent as in other subject areas where good educational results are expected, and will be of comparable quality. The use of audio-visual aids is important in teaching health and physical activities.

Physical-education teachers have found that the use of textbooks greatly improves the learning process. There are a variety of good texts on the market today. Also, the central school library should be well stocked with health, physical-education, and recreation materials including narratives, biographies, rule books, periodicals, and pamphlets containing vocational information. Superior teaching; proper facilities, equipment, and supplies; sufficient time; and a well-planned program of activities are essential if effective learning is to take place.

HEALTH EDUCATION

Primary responsibility for a pupil's health rests with the pupil and his parents. Doctors and various community agencies also are concerned with health. However, the schools have a unique opportunity as well as responsibility to assist in developing and maintaining the optimum level of health in each child by maintaining an effective school health program. The school health program is the sum of activities and learning situations pertaining to health that are associated with the total school program. It includes health environment, health services, and health instruction. Its aim is to improve and maintain the health of the school children. This refers to all aspects of health, including physical, mental, emotional, and social well-being. Health education is concerned more with capacity for activity than with freedom from disease and other infirmities. Effective health instruction associated with vital health services in a healthful environment must prevail if the foregoing objectives of the health program are to be realized.

School Health Environment. A healthful, safe environment is needed to prevent and control communicable diseases and to maintain healthful and sanitary conditions and freedom from safety hazards. Teaching methods and learning situations should motivate and stimulate learning without developing fears, tensions, and frustrations unfavorable to emotional, social, and physical well-being.

A healthful school environment demands premises and facilities that are adequately lighted, well ventilated, and sanitarily maintained. Safe playground equipment should be provided, and play areas should be free from hazards so that they contribute to, rather than detract from, healthful school experiences.

School Health Services. The health-service program should serve to appraise the health status of pupils and school personnel, to help prevent and control disease, to provide emergency treatment for injuries or sudden illness, to assist in the identification and education of atypical children, and to maintain cumulative health records for guidance in determining the school program for the individual schoolchild.

A vital school health-service program requires the active participation of many. Teachers, administrators, physicians, dentists, nurses, psychologists, bus drivers, custodians, food-service employees, and many others can contribute to the health of pupils and school personnel. The pupils themselves, as well as parents and members of the local community, play an active part in developing the health program of the school community.

The school health-service program is concerned with immunization against such diseases as smallpox, and protection from exposure to others such as tuberculosis. Screening techniques should be used to identify vision and hearing defects, dental abnormalities, or nutrition deficiencies.

Medical Examinations. Health examinations are recommended for seventh- and tenth-grade and all other incoming students. Participants in strenuous activities should have a medical examination before each sport season. Students returning to class after prolonged illness or severe injuries should receive medical approval before returning to vigorous activities. Information obtained through periodic medical examinations and from daily teacher observations should be filed in a confidentially maintained cumulative health record. The program of physical education prescribed for each individual should be based on the health appraisal contained in this record. Each teacher should be informed regarding any physical deviations that might affect the activity program of individual pupils.

Health Instruction. A sound basic health and safety instruction program is necessary to provide learning experiences for the purpose of influencing knowledge, attitudes, or conduct relating to individual, school, and community health. The major objectives of health education are not only to impart health information but also to stimulate the development of attitudes and practices that will favor optimum growth and development.

Health instruction may be conducted in a special, regularly scheduled class or through separate units in classes such as physical education, biology, and home economics, or it may be emphasized in all subjects when the proper situation occurs in what is often referred to as "incidental" teaching. In planning of the health curriculum for the secondary school, consideration must be given not only to the integration of content between the junior and senior high schools but also to the health instruction pupils may have received in the elementary schools. Curriculum content at a given level should be based on material covered in previous grades. If a given school system provides a comprehensive health program at the elementary or junior high school levels, less time may need to be allocated to formal health classes in succeeding grades.

In the crowded curriculum, it often is difficult to schedule formal classes in health instruction. Many authorities agree that a one-semester course offered in alternate years is most satisfactory in the secondary school. Thus, a semester course would be taught during the seventh or eighth grade, another during the ninth or tenth grade, and a final pre-graduation course during the final twelfth-grade semester. An alternate plan is to teach a full-year course of health. Another plan is to combine health and physical education whereby physical education and health are taught on alternate days, weeks, or comparable blocks of time. Any plan that does not provide a definite place in the pupils' schedule for health classes is considered undesirable.

The correlation of health instruction with other subjects such as biology, psychology, social or physical sciences, or homemaking is advocated by some administrators. Others believe that most of the health education given in the school can be taught as an incidental by-product of many subjects. Most agree that health instruction can be more meaningful and functional when integrated with other school learning experiences, if teachers are prepared to point out solutions to health problems, which too many of them are not. Too often, in many classes, the health material covered is of little interest to the students. Only when content is meaningful in terms of personal needs and interests will instruction be effective.

Perhaps, well-organized, regularly scheduled classes correlated with strategically integrated units in related subject fields can result in the most effective organization for instruction. In any plan, teachers must be trained to be aware of opportunities for health instruction and to utilize these situations to help pupils form habits and attitudes based on scientific knowledge of health and disease.

Role of the Teacher. The teacher is a key person in the school health program. The classroom teacher who has day-to-day contact with the children while they are in school should be qualified to recognize the characteristics of normal, healthy children and to detect signs of illness or deviations from normal behavior. Through preservice and in-service training, the teacher should be especially aware of vision or hearing difficulties that may interfere with normal learning progress. Obviously, the teacher cannot work alone. The most important service of the non-specialist teacher may well be in referring pupils who exhibit abnormal health or behavior characteristics to appropriately trained persons. Teachers are also in a strategic position to cooperate with parents, school officials, and medical authorities in agreed-upon medical or follow-up programs.

Emotional Health. The emotionally healthy individual understands his own worth and has a sense of responsibility toward others. He possesses a set of values and recognizes his relationship to society. Junior and senior high school boys and girls are in a period of dramatic emotional and social as well as physical transition, and the schools can provide a favorable environment and understanding guidance to assist student progress toward mental maturity.

Some school systems can develop extensive mental-health programs in which trained counselors cooperate with child-guidance centers or mental-health clinics. In all schools, the teacher probably has the major responsibility for the personality and character growth of each pupil.

Approaches to development of a healthy personality are

1. Provide the basic needs of children. Feeling secure and feeling that one is important to one's self and to others are fundamental emotional needs. Children must develop a sense of responsibility toward others. They need kindly direction which does not threaten their growing independence.
2. The emotional climate of the school and the classroom should evoke a feeling of warmth and security. A sensitive person can frequently judge the predominant feeling of a school by walking through the halls. A principal who is a rigid disciplinarian will breed a cowering fear. Some teachers are emotionally unfit for the classroom. A teacher who is ridden by fears or worries, or is suffering pain, or is much disturbed and poorly adjusted himself can produce a class of nervous, tense, fearful children. They are entitled to happy, well-adjusted, understanding adults in their school environment.
3. The physical environment of the school and the classroom should encourage peace of mind and relaxation as well as opportunity for activity. Beauty is necessary in all lives. Well-landscaped yards which stir a child's pride and welcome him to the doors of the school, well-lighted, pleasantly decorated halls and rooms, adequate ventilation and heating, potted plants on the window sills, lively little animals in the elementary classrooms—all of these make a child comfortable in his home away from home.
4. A well-planned mental health program and curriculum which is designed to help the child understand his physical and emotional changes at all ages will give him the knowledge and insight for handling his own personal problems and for living harmoniously with others.[1]

Organization and Administration. School Health Council. An advisory school health council or committee may be formed to coordinate the efforts and interests of the many individuals within the school who have responsibilities in the school health program. Through this organization, many persons including teachers, students, parents, medical specialists,

[1] Alma Nemir, *The School Health Program* (Philadelphia: W. B. Saunders Co., 1959), pp. 224–225.

custodians, and food-service personnel may cooperate in planning and carrying out the school health program and in democratically establishing school health policies and procedures.

Health Coordinator. It is recommended that each school system have a qualified person designated as health coordinator with the responsibility of coordinating the activities of the various personnel concerned with the school health program. This person would be especially concerned with providing information regarding teaching aids and materials in health instruction at the various grade levels and with taking the lead in forming a school health organization.

Physical Education for Mental Health. It has been becoming increasingly evident that the individual who engages in sports and games is most likely, by giving expression to strong inner urges and deep-seated emotions, to enjoy not only better physical health but also better mental and emotional health. Indeed, even brisk walking is now thought to be a valuable expenditure of time along those lines. It has also been observed that young people at both the elementary and secondary school levels are less likely to become disciplinary problems if they are engaged in some kind of regular energetic physical activity.

SAFETY EDUCATION

Safety education is also a part of the total school program. Safety may be included in the school health program or taught in special classes such as driver-education classes or as units in various school subjects. The health, safety, and welfare of all pupils surely should be considered a responsibility of all school personnel. Statistics indicate accidents are one of the foremost causes of death among children of school age. Basically, accidents may be said to be due to environmental hazards or to unsafe behavior.

Inasmuch as a majority of accidents to children occur in connection with the schools, school authorities have a definite responsibility in the area of safety instruction. It would seem the first objective of the school safety program would be to provide a reasonably safe physical environment. While the many conveniences of modern society have contributed to the enjoyment of life, they have also added many potential hazards. Accidents due to unsafe behavior may not, in many cases, be due so much to lack of knowledge of safety rules as to improper attitudes, careless habits, and immature judgments.

While the need for safety education is quite apparent, schools have not been able to agree on the best procedure to formally introduce this relatively recently recognized area of instruction into the crowded curriculum. Safety education is sometimes considered a phase of health education, and the curriculum content may follow the same patterns of organization that is found in school health-instruction programs.

Units of safety instruction may well be integrated into the content of most courses such as physics, chemistry, biology, homemaking, shop, or physical education. These same courses offer many opportunities for the incidental teaching of safety.

Many school systems find it advantageous to organize a school safety council to aid in planning, coordinating, and evaluating the environmental and instructional features of the school safety program. An adequately trained and personally interested member of the faculty should be designated to serve as safety coordinator in each school system. One of his responsibilities should be to secure and make available to appropriate school personnel current materials and teaching aids in safety.

In planning of the safety-education program, content may logically be divided into such areas as pedestrian, bicycle, home, rural, vocational, fire, waterfront, and traffic safety. Subject-matter fields such as physics, chemistry, shop, homemaking, and physical education also are concerned with elements of safety. Driver education is the area that most frequently includes safety as a specific subject.

DRIVER EDUCATION

Instruction in the driving of automobiles is now offered in the very great majority of senior high schools. It is open only to boys and girls who are old enough to obtain a driver's license. The prevailing practice is to give credit toward graduation for successful completion of the course.

There are two phases to a course in driver education. One is a preparatory unit of classroom instruction and the second is controlled practice driving. Both should be taught by specifically trained teachers. Most states have standard certification requirements for teachers in driver education.

Many insurance companies have recognized the value of training in driver education by reducing insurance costs for youths who have successfully completed such courses.

Automobile firms often cooperate with school systems by furnishing dual-control training cars at nominal cost, to be used in accepted training programs conducted by qualified professionally trained instructors.

Driver-education courses are often considered expensive because of the necessarily low pupil-teacher ratio. In some localities, state organizations or insurance or service agencies make funds available to reimburse local school systems conducting traffic-education programs. Some parents are willing to pay a fee because they believe in the value of this type of education. Reduced insurance rates might make this a sound financial investment even if the safety factor were not considered.

Extensive skill and knowledge tests are a part of all driver-training programs. The true measure of a traffic-education program, however, would be the extent to which the pupils become more safety-conscious and less susceptible to traffic accidents.

RECOMMENDED POLICIES

The following recommended policies are considered basic to an adequate and educationally sound health and physical-education program:

1. Basic to the success of any program of education is instruction by competent teachers.

2. Adequate facilities, equipment, and time should be provided. Specific activities are necessary to meet each of the objectives of health and physical education. Special items of equipment may be needed for certain of these activities.

3. Adequate funds for personnel and supplies essential to an effective program for *all* girls and boys at all levels of maturity should be provided by the board of education in the regular school budget.

4. All pupils should be enrolled in daily physical-education classes. Those who, by reason of illness or disability, are unable to take part in the more vigorous forms of activity should be assigned to modified activities. A physician's recommendation should be one of the bases for determining the kind of program each pupil should have.

5. Pupils normally should be assigned to physical-education classes on the basis of year in school. Classes should be of sizes to permit effective instruction. These should be comparable to the sizes of other school classes.

6. The physical-education period should be utilized for instruction directed toward realization of the expressed objectives of the program.

7. Grading or marks in health and physical education should follow the same procedure established for other subject areas in the curriculum. The grade should represent the accomplishment of objectives. Since there are many objectives, the grade should be a composite of the various aspects. An adapted program should be provided for the individuals who are incapable, motorwise, to participate successfully with average pupils. It is recommended that the grades reflect the accomplished obtainable objectives for that individual. To differentiate between the accomplishments of the two, the modified or adapted program could be so labeled.

8. Teachers of health and physical education should be bona fide members of the faculty, duly certificated, and with professional prepara-

tion for the classes they teach. Above all, the teachers should be interested in the welfare of children. In-service training and effective supervision can increase the competence of teachers.

QUESTIONS, PROBLEMS, AND ISSUES FOR FURTHER THOUGHT

1. The President's Council on Youth Fitness has advocated that each pupil have a daily period of physical education that includes fifteen minutes of vigorous activity. To what extent does this meet the objectives of a physical-education program?
2. Present a plan for evaluating the effectiveness of a physical-education program.
3. Indicate the content, scope, and sequence of health subject matter that should be covered in grades seven through twelve. How might this material be covered, organized, and scheduled in the typical school curriculum?
4. How would you satisfy the desire for sports competition in the junior high school?
5. Discuss the role of the schools in preparing citizens to "make worthy use of leisure time."
6. Outline the boys' and girls' physical-education curriculums you would recommend for the junior high school.
7. Describe the physical-activity program you would recommend for a handicapped child.
8. Discuss the effects athletic, social, and academic pressures may have on the mental and emotional health of the schoolchild.
9. Present a plan for organizing a school health council in the senior high school. Who might be members? How would it function? What contributions could it make to the school health program?
10. Should interscholastic competition be considered a part of the physical-education program?
11. Present a plan to improve spectator appreciation and conduct at interscholastic activities.
12. What contributions can the academic-subject teacher make to the school health program?
13. What are the advantages and disadvantages of incidental teaching of health?
14. What are the three areas of the school health program? How can health environment and health services be considered a part of health education?
15. Describe a plan for evaluating the school health program.
16. Outline the content of a report for an administrator to present to a school board in support of the introduction of a course in driver education into the school curriculum.

SUPPLEMENTARY MATERIALS

SELECTED READINGS

AMERICAN ASSOCIATION OF SCHOOL ADMINISTRATORS. *Health in Schools* (rev. ed.). Washington, D.C.: The Association (a department of the National Education Association of the United States), 1951. Pp. 89–141, 165–211.

Discusses a healthful school environment, including a purposeful approach to school mental hygiene.

EDUCATIONAL POLICIES COMMISSION. *School Athletics: A Report Prepared by the Board on Problems and Policies.* Washington, D.C.: National Education Association of the United States, 1954. Includes a complete report concerning the place of athletics in the school program.

Fifth Annual Conference Proceedings of the American Driver Education Association. Washington, D.C.: National Education Association of the United States, 1962.

FLORIO, A. E., and G. T. STAFFORD. *Safety Education* (2d ed.). New York: McGraw-Hill Book Co., Inc., 1962. Pp. 45–75. Basic principles and policies for planning the school safety program. Teaching aids and evaluation of safety education.

FORSYTHE, CHARLES E. *Administration of High School Athletics* (4th ed.). Englewood Cliffs, N.J.: Prentice-Hall, Inc., 1962. Pp. 246–55, 387–425. Provides a brief background concerning the problems of athletic awards for boys and athletic participation for girls.

JENNY, JOHN H. *Introduction to Recreation Education.* Philadelphia: W. B. Saunders Co., 1955. Chapter 4 presents the activity areas that should be considered in school recreation.

NATIONAL ASSOCIATION OF SECONDARY SCHOOL PRINCIPALS. "Administration of the Health, Physical Education and Recreation Program in Secondary Schools," *Bulletin of the N.A.S.S.P.,* XXXVII (May, 1953), 93–136. Treats in some detail the purpose, place, and scope of the intramural program in today's secondary schools.

——. "Health, Physical Education and Recreation in the Secondary Schools," *Bulletin of the N.A.S.S.P.,* XLIV (May, 1960), 20–38, 41–46. Presents rather clearly the responsibilities of the director of health, physical-education, and recreation; also includes the duties of the health coordinator.

——. "Outside Education for American Youth," *Bulletin of the N.A.S.S.P.,* XLI (May, 1957), 23–90. Discusses in detail outdoor education in the high school program.

PRESIDENT'S COUNCIL ON YOUTH FITNESS. *Youth Physical Fitness: Suggested Elements of a School-centered Program.* Washington, D.C.: Government Printing Office, 1961. Parts I and II provide much useful material for inaugurating a school youth-fitness program.

SMOLENSKY, JACK, and FRANKLIN B. HAAR. *Principles of Community Health.* Philadelphia: W. B. Saunders Co., 1961. Chapter 5 suggests methods and materials that may be used in teaching community health.

19

The Social Studies in the Curriculum

The social studies are those subjects whose content is centered in human relationships. These relationships are varied and complex, involving persons with persons, persons with groups, and groups with groups. In addition, they include man's relations to his environment, its effects upon him, and his efforts to modify its influences. The complexity of the relationships and the variety of the concepts with which the social studies field deals underline the need for a curriculum organized and taught so as to be rich and stimulating and the need for teachers whose preparation for their duties is both broad and deep.

The field of the social studies at the secondary school level includes history (local, state, national, and world), civics or government, human or social (as distinguished from purely physical) geography, economics, sociology, and various combinations of elements of these under such headings as problems, social living, current affairs, and the like. Occasionally, one finds in the social studies courses in psychology; still rarer, courses in anthropology. More often, however, psychology and anthropology are utilized to broaden, to enrich, and to sharpen the concepts taught in the more commonly offered social studies subjects. The same is true of science, the arts, and the humanities.

The term *social studies* applies, properly, only to the school subjects in which both content and purpose are focused on human relationships. *Social studies* is an over-all, descriptive term for such subjects, not a specific, definitive label. As the report of the Committee on American History in Schools and Colleges put it, "The social studies constitute a field and not a subject, a federation of subjects and not a unified discipline."

CONTRIBUTIONS TO GROWTH AND DEVELOPMENT
OF ADOLESCENTS

There is no lack of statements of objectives of the social studies. Many of these statements are so voluminous that the task they set is formidable indeed. Some are organized in categories of skills, understandings, and attitudes. Some are posed in terms of behavior. Some are concisely put; others are wordy. Some are stated as absolutes; others, in terms of growth. The following statement is from a curriculum guide prepared in Minneapolis:

Every pupil should have an opportunity to participate in learning experiences which will enable him to achieve maximum development as an individual and as a member of society—so that to the limit of his capacity, *he will be a citizen who*

is well adjusted and lives and works in harmony with others.

strives to achieve worthy values and ideals.

makes satisfactory adjustments to his problems through an understanding of himself, his personality, interests, abilities, and limitations.

maintains democratic relationships with other persons, respects the worth of each individual, and realizes that each individual with his unique background contributes to the common good.

acts as a responsible member of his family and of the community.

thinks critically about social problems and assumes responsibility for contributing to their solution.

appreciates our American heritage and has the attitudes, skills, and understandings required for effective citizenship in our American democracy.

has faith in democracy and acts in accordance with democratic principles.

uses his knowledge of the history and geography of our country for a better understanding of the present day.

understands the processes of American government and accepts the responsibilities of good citizenship.

thinks critically about problems in our community, state, and nation and assumes responsibility for contributing to their solution.

understands the need for and promotes international cooperation to improve the welfare of mankind and to attain world peace.

uses his knowledge of geography and history for a better understanding of the world and its peoples.

appreciates the contributions to world civilization by the many different peoples past and present.

understands the interdependence of the peoples of the world.

thinks critically about world problems and assumes responsibility for contributing to their solution.

functions effectively in his daily economic life and makes valid economic judgments.

maintains a sound personal financial program and purchases and uses goods and services wisely.

makes an intelligent choice of vocation.

understands and appreciates the contributions of the many groups of workers who produce goods and services.

understands how the environment affects the ways in which people live.

interests himself in and understands how our economic system operates.

thinks critically about economic problems and assumes responsibility for contributing to their solution.[1]

TYPES OF ORGANIZATION

There are four principal types of organization of the secondary school social studies curriculum: subjects, correlation, fusion, and the core.[2] Respectively, these represent successive steps away from the generally accepted logical structure of human knowledge, represented by classification by subjects, toward an organization in which the previously accepted structure disappears. The purpose behind all modifications of subjects is to facilitate understanding.

Organization by Subjects. Most widespread by far is organization by subjects, as history, geography, civics, and the like. Organization by subjects has been widely criticized for three or four decades, but there is little evidence that the criticism has resulted in any substantial movement away from subject organization, except in the junior high school, where modifications of the subject pattern have been more sympathetically received. It may be that the trend is now in the opposite direction; scattered evidence indicates that the subject pattern is, for better or worse, more firmly entrenched than ever.

Correlation. In this type of organization, subject lines are maintained, but data from other subjects are brought in at appropriate places. This cross-referencing may be casual or incidental, such as the mention or description of an economic fact or idea in connection with the study of a topic in sociology, or reference to a piece of American literature in connection with the study of some period in American history. Or it may be systematic, in which case the teacher makes definite plans to draw

[1] *Social Studies, Grades 6-12* (Minneapolis Public Schools, 1957), p. 1.

[2] There are, of course, variations and combinations of these four. There is perhaps one other type, called "integration," which is sometimes put in an intermediate position between correlation and fusion. Subject lines are maintained, but materials are taken from any or all of the social studies with reference to each topic studied. It is also employed to refer to a type of organization quite similar to the core. The social studies are organized along with materials from other subjects around problems or centers of interest as found in non-academic life.

on particular materials from other social studies subjects or from else-where. Finally, correlation may take the form of a joint venture by a teacher of the social studies and a teacher of some other subject, most often literature and sometimes oral and written language, so that the learnings in one field will clarify and reinforce the learnings in the other.

Fusion. In this method of organization, the content of several or of all the social studies subjects is brought together into a "broad field" with subject lines disappearing. Materials are selected on the basis of problems or topics. The product may be called, simply, "social studies," though such a title is no guaranty of a fused course. Such a form of organization has been employed mainly in the junior high school and has been com-posed of geography, history, and civics. The senior high school "Problems of a Democracy" course is *sometimes* a fused course, drawing on materials from sociology, civics, and economics.

Core Curriculum. Strictly speaking, the core curriculum perhaps does not constitute a type of organization of the social studies curriculum. The core purports to take care of individual needs and social require-ments important to the development of all students; thus, it cuts across subject lines and may be organized completely without regard to subject boundaries. However, the goals of the core curriculum demand a social studies framework or at least the teaching of a large number of social studies concepts.

The core curriculum is characteristic chiefly of the junior high school. Few senior high schools have core programs. Many so-called cores are such in name only; they are simply a block of two classes, both of which are taught by the same teacher in consecutive periods. Wright reported that only about 30 per cent of the block-time classes she studied in 1958 could be called true core programs.[3]

Though the various types of organization described above may seem fairly discrete, lines are not always so clearly drawn in practice. The teacher of a "subject" program may, and frequently does, draw on the other fields for enrichment and clarification. A "core" program may be simply a poorly correlated program, and a course entitled "Social Living" may be no more than a subject course with a progressive title. In fact, many so-called curriculum-revision programs have resulted in little more than changes in course titles. Furthermore, the investigator must look not only at course titles and course organization but also at instructional method, in order to characterize a program accurately.

[3] Grace S. Wright, *Block-Time Classes and the Core Program in the Junior High School,* Bulletin 1958, No. 6 (Washington, D.C.: U.S. Office of Education, Depart-ment of Health, Education, and Welfare, 1958).

THE CURRENT SOCIAL STUDIES CURRICULUM

Unfortunately, no extensive survey of social studies offerings in secondary schools has been reported in the last decade or so,[4] and such surveys as have been reported are not strictly comparable with those of earlier years. The most informative of those that have been reported is Moreland's, based on a study of responses from 281 schools in 1962. His findings regarding the most frequently required social studies courses are indicated in Table 19–1.

It is evident that there is no nationally accepted sequence in the social studies. There are some modal offerings, however, and there are many schools in which the social studies programs, at least in terms of course titles, follow the modal program throughout. On the other hand, there are at least as many in which they do not. One of the prominent features of social studies curriculums in the United States is their diversity. Literally scores of different courses appear in these curriculums. One can be fairly certain of one thing, however: Because of state law, regulations by state departments of education, or local prescription, each program will contain required courses in United States history and in civics, the former tending to appear in both junior and senior high school grades and to be two semesters or more in length at each level.

Typically, social studies courses offered are required in seventh and eighth grades, and in many schools the ninth grade offering is required as well. Elective courses are rare in junior high schools. Moreland found that, in practically all senior high schools, two years of social studies were required, and that almost half of the schools reporting required a third year.[5] Most senior high schools offer social studies electives in addition to required courses. Moreland's findings regarding the most frequently offered social studies electives are shown in Table 19–2.

Specimen Curriculums. The programs whose main features are sketched in the next few pages are offered only as examples, not as models. Each has its strong points, and each has features that could be construed as weaknesses. The programs do have this in common: They represent serious efforts by groups of teachers to provide what they consider to be solid, appealing, and learnable, taking into consideration the various legal and regulative requirements and other restrictions to which

---

[4] A new U.S. Office of Education Bulletin on offerings and registrations in high school subjects was scheduled to be issued in 1963.

[5] In 1960–1961, thirty-two states required two or more years of social studies for graduation from high school (four-year programs). See *High School Graduation Requirements Established by State Departments of Education*, Office of Education Circular No. 455 (Washington, D.C.: U.S. Office of Education, Department of Health, Education, and Welfare, 1960).

TABLE 19–1

MOST FREQUENTLY REQUIRED SOCIAL STUDIES COURSES
IN GRADES SEVEN THROUGH TWELVE

Subject	No.	Subject	No.
Grade 7		**Grade 11**	
World geography	28	American history	165
American history, geography	28	American history, government	13
American history	27	World history	13
Geography	21	American history, economics	3
State history, geography	21	American government	3
Social studies	14	Problems of democracy	3
State history	13	American history, state history	3
Grade 8		**Grade 12**	
American history	105	Problems of democracy	46
American history, state history	19	American government	36
American history, civics	17	American history	19
American history, geography	16	Problems of democracy, American government	12
World geography	10	American history, American government	4
Grade 9		Problems of democracy, economics	4
Civics	66	American government, economics	3
World geography	24	American history, problems of democracy	3
World history	17	American government, sociology	3
State history, civics	17	Sociology, economics	3
Social studies	15	Social studies	2
Grade 10		American history, economics	2
World history	98	Psychology, economics	2
American history	10		
World history, geography	6		
Social studies	3		
Modern world history	2		
World geography	2		
World history, driver education	2		
Civics	2		
Civics, world history	2		

SOURCE: Willis D. Moreland, "Curriculum Trends in the Social Studies," *Social Education*, Vol. 26, pp. 74–75. Used with permission of the author and of the publisher.

curriculum-revision committees must conform. The California program, the product of a half-dozen years' work by hundreds of teachers, college professors, and others, follows the national norm in part but has some interesting deviations. The suggestions for ninth and tenth grades reflect increasing interest in non-Western cultures. The Minneapolis program also reflects the national pattern, but it emphasizes the citizenship and civics aspect in the ninth grade and, for the tenth and eleventh grades,

TABLE 19–2

MOST FREQUENTLY OFFERED SOCIAL STUDIES ELECTIVES
IN GRADES TEN THROUGH TWELVE

Subject	No.	Subject	No.
Grade 10		**Grade 12**	
World history	63	Problems of democracy	38
World geography	20	Sociology	32
Modern history	6	Economics	31
Economic geography	4	Psychology	18
State history	4	American government	13
World history, geography	4	World history	11
European history	4	International relations	9
Sociology	4	World geography	9
Geography	3	Business law	6
Ancient and/or medieval history	3	State history	5
Economics	2	Latin American history	4
Bible	2	Consumer economics	4
		Current history	4
Grade 11		Family living	3
		Modern history	3
Economics	21	Contemporary Issues	2
Sociology	15	Law	2
World history	14	Civics	2
World geography	12	Bible	2
Problems of democracy	8		
Psychology	7		
Current history	4		
Business law	4		
State history	3		
International relations	3		
Consumer economics	3		
American government	3		
Modern history	3		
Advanced geography	2		
Civics	2		

SOURCE: Willis D. Moreland, "Curriculum Trends in the Social Studies," *Social Education*, Vol. 26, p. 76. Used with permission of the author and of the publisher.

provides an attempt to sketch a widely advocated but rarely practiced integration of world history and the history of the United States.

STATE OF CALIFORNIA
SECONDARY SOCIAL STUDIES CURRICULUM

Grade Seven. Theme: Life in the World Today: The Mediterranean Area and the Middle East; Europe; and the European Backgrounds of the United States.

    A. Interrelations Among Countries of the Mediterranean Area, the Middle East, and Europe

    B. The Mediterranean Area and the Middle East

C. European Nations
D. Studies of Selected Cultures
E. The European Backgrounds of the United States

Grade Eight: Theme: The United States and Our Heritage

A. The People of the United States
B. Contributions of Individuals and Groups to Developments in the United States and to Our American Culture
C. The Emergence and Continued Usefulness of Basic Principles and Ideals
D. Contributions of National Resources, an Expanding Economy, and Scientific Advances to Developments in the United States
E. Services to the People by the Federal, State, and Local Governments; Responsibilities of Citizens
F. The United Nations

Grade Nine: Theme: History of Western European Civilization: Its Social, Economic, and Political Characteristics; Its Present Position in the World

A. Western Europe from the Crusades and the Renaissance to the Founding of Colonial Empires
B. Western Europe's Founding of Worldwide Empires; Widened Horizons
C. Rivalries and Nationalism: Struggle for Power in Europe
D. The Breakdown of Absolute Monarchies: the People of Western Europe and America Strive for Freedom
E. The Congress of Vienna to World War I: Western Influence Spreads Around the World
F. Two Wars of World Proportions Threaten to Destroy Civilization

Grade Ten: Theme: The New Nations and Economically Underdeveloped Countries of Asia, Africa, and Latin America; the Communist Countries; and the Challenge of Totalitarianism to the Free World

A. Areas of Asia, Africa, and Latin America, and the Communist Countries
B. Geographic Factors: Influence of Geography upon the Development of the Societies in These Areas
C. The Cultural Heritage of Each Area: Earliest History to the Present
D. Economic Background and Its Influence on the People and Nations
E. The Philosophical, Religious, and Political Concepts as Influenced by the Experiences of the People
F. Communism: Its Nature and Plans for World Domination
G. The Free World: Its Social, Political, and Economic Philosophy; Its Goals

Grade Eleven: Theme: The United States: Its Development; Its Emergence as a World Power; The Contemporary Scene

A. Shaping of the Federal Union and the Development of Constitutional Government
B. The Early Growth of an Industrial Economy and Its Contributions to an American Way of Life
C. National Expansion, Civil War, and Reunion
D. America Comes of Age: Post Civil War Economic, Political, and Social Issues

E. Emergence of the United States as a World Power
F. World Leadership Thrust Upon Our Nation
G. The Role of American Institutions in Maintaining and Developing the Life of the People [*sic*] in the United States
H. Internal Problems of Democracy; the Nation's External Role as a Bulwark of Freedom

Grade Twelve: Theme: Government in the United States and Problems of Democracy

A. The Constitution, Its Expanding Meaning, and How it Meets the Problems of a Rapidly Changing Civilization
B. The Processes of Governmental Budget-building and Taxation
C. Activities of Government Affecting Our Daily Lives
D. State and Local History and Government
E. Intelligent, Active Participation as Citizens of the United States in Local, State, National, and World Affairs
F. The American Economy: Capitalism and the Free Enterprise System; Wise Use of Human and Natural Resources
G. Influence of Individuals Upon the Stability and Effectiveness of Social, Political, and Economical Institutions
H. United States and International Affairs: Strengthening of the Free World[6]

MINNEAPOLIS PUBLIC SCHOOLS
SECONDARY SOCIAL STUDIES CURRICULUM

Grade Seven: Orientation to the Junior High School
Orientation to Social Studies in the Secondary School
Overview of the Eastern Hemisphere. Sample area studies from each of seven major regions of the Eastern Hemisphere:

Monsoon Asia
The Dry World (Northern Africa and Asia Minor)
U. S. S. R.
Buffer States (between U. S. S. R. and Western Europe)
The Mediterranean Rim
Humid Tropical Africa
Middle Latitude Southern Lands

Major guidelines for the study of the sample area:

Location and extent
What the area and its people are like
Why the area and its people are the way they are
Comparisons with other areas and peoples of the world
Significance of the area to the U. S. A.

Basic Concepts of World Geography

World patterns
Basic processes and problems common to mankind

[6] *Social Studies Framework for the Public Schools of California,* California State Department of Education, Sacramento, 1962.

Grade Eight: Narrative History of the United States of America. The Story of the Great Events, Persons, and Movements in the Development of our Nation up to the Present Day:

> Importance of geographic and economic factors on [in] the history of the U. S. A.
> Discovery and exploration
> Colonial settlement
> Winning of independence
> Establishment of a new nation
> Democracy and the westward movement
> Emergence of sectional differences in national growth
> Preservation of the union
> Emergence of the industrial age
> Rise of the U. S. A. as a world leader
> The U. S. A. and the world since World War II
> Life in a changing world

> During the year, as early teenagers, the pupils will be concerned with problems of personal growth and development. Appropriate occasions should be utilized to guide the development of desirable understandings, attitudes, and skills in such areas of personal concern as

>> Adjustment to school life
>> Effective relationships with other people
>> Personal development

Grade Nine: The Young Citizen and His World

> Areas of Personal and Social Concern

>> Building effective personal relationships in the family
>> Understanding maturity
>> Planning for one's life work
>> Consuming goods and services intelligently
>> Preparing for safe driving

> Minneapolis as a Metropolitan Area

>> Factors of economic geography and human resources in the development of Minneapolis
>> Educational, recreational, and cultural opportunities in Minneapolis
>> Organization of the city government
>> Problems of the city government
>> The responsibilities of teenagers as citizens of the community

> The State of Minnesota

>> Factors of economic geography and human resources in the development of Minnesota
>> Organization of the state government

> Citizenship in our Nation

>> The rights and duties of citizens of the U. S. A.

The Building of World Cooperation
Present day needs requiring international cooperation
Ways in which nations cooperate
Impact of the air age upon world cooperation

Grade Ten and Grade Eleven: History of the United States in a World Setting

Grade Ten: Orientation to the senior high school
Introduction to the study of history
Early man's adaptation to natural environment
Development of the earliest civilizations in the Near East, in Asia, and in the Americas
Our heritage from the Greeks and Romans
Our heritage from the European cultures of the Middle Ages
Civilizations in other areas of the world that may have contributed to the Renaissance in Europe
Expansion of Europe into the New World
Establishment of the government of the U. S. A.
Analysis of the structure of the government of the U. S. A.
Attempts to gain more representation in government in other parts of the world
Strengthening of democratic concepts in the U. S. A.
Conflict between the North and South

Grade Eleven: Preview and review
Impact of science and invention upon man's economic life
Economic effects of the industrial revolution in the U. S. A.
Social, Intellectual, and aesthetic effects of the industrial age in the U. S. A.
Impact of the industrial age on political development in the U. S. A. up to the 1930's
Political and economic developments in various areas of the world and their effects upon the U. S. A., 1865–1914
Rise of the United States as a major world power
World War I and its aftermath; the rise of dictatorships
World War II and its aftermath; events up to the present day
Area studies of specific nations or areas to be made during the year; the intensive study of at least one or two selected from any part of the world:

historical background
significant geographical characteristics
social and economic conditions
the people and their culture
the government
relations with other countries and particularly with U. S. A.

Grade Twelve: Modern Problems. Senior high schools may offer a general course in modern problems, or any of six "equivalent" courses. The equivalent courses are:

Problems of government	Psychology of daily living
Current world problems	Social problems and community
Economics in everyday life	study
	Occupational relations

The equivalent selected determines the emphasis in the course, but regardless of which equivalent is taught, the following problems are to be covered:

Government
  The effective citizen
  Meaning of democracy
  Government in the
    U. S. A.
  Comparative governments
  Political parties and
    elections
  Taxation
  Foreign relations of the
    U. S. A.
  Public education
  Conservation of resources

Current World Problems
  Factors in the unequal
    development among
    countries
  Forces creating inter-
    national tension
  Factors promoting inter-
    national cooperation
  Problems of world trade

Economics
  Comparative economic
    systems
  Labor-management relations
  Economic stability
  Personal economic security
  The role of banking in the
    economy
  The farm problem

Psychology
  Psychology of personality
  Our relations with other
    people
  Career planning
  Orientation for military
    service

Social Problems
  A wide variety of problems is
    offered, together with cri-
    teria for the selection of
    specific problems for study
    and guidelines for their
    study

Occupational Relations
  This equivalent is intended only for those students who are enrolled in the part-time occupational training program.[7]

CURRICULUM TRENDS AND PROPOSALS

The last several decades have brought changes in the social studies curriculum in American secondary schools. In part, these changes have been alterations in the over-all structure of the curriculum, in the general framework of courses. Some courses are growing in popularity; others are, or seem to be, on the wane. In addition to this, and in some ways more important, are changes occurring within the subjects, trends almost impossible to quantify, because they do not lend themselves to statistical treatment. But that they have taken place, and are taking place, is evident in new courses of study, new textbooks, and new units, and well as in the oral and written pronouncements of almost innumerable reporters, advocates, and proponents.

[7] *Social Studies, Grade 6–12,* Minneapolis Public Schools, 1957.

At the same time, and especially in the last decade, it has been charged that the social studies field has not changed nearly fast enough and that, in its general framework, it resembles the kind of curriculum envisaged in the post-World War I days rather than one designed for the 1960's. On the other hand, there are those who apparently feel that it has changed too much, who would have us return to a more restricted diet of history, geography, and civics, or even to some perennialist version of the social studies.

Trends in the Over-All Structure of the Social Studies Curriculum. If one takes a long view of the social studies, since the 1920's, for example, certain trends in the over-all structure of this social studies curriculum are evident. Tables 19–3 and 19–4 indicate the shifts in grades seven through twelve between 1934 and 1947, and, in slightly different form, the shifts in grades nine through twelve from 1922 to 1949. The tables need to be interpreted with care, for the following reasons:

1. Table 19–3 is based on a relatively small sample.
2. The percentages in Table 19–3 are percentages of social studies enrolments, while those in Table 19–4 are percentages of total pupil enrolments in all subjects. For example, Table 19–3 indicates that 33.8 per cent of all pupils enrolled in the social studies in the last four years of high school were enrolled in United States history, while Table 19–4 shows that 22.8 per cent of *all* enrolled pupils were taking United States history.
3. Not all subjects are listed in Table 19–4, for example, ancient, medieval, and modern history have been omitted.
4. Small shifts in percentages are probably not significant.

Even considering the limitations noted above, one can make certain generalizations about the changes that had taken place by 1949.

1. United States history has become practically a "national" offering in grades eight and eleven.
2. World history had largely supplanted the earlier ancient, medieval, and modern European history.
3. The senior high school offering was becoming more diverse, particularly in the senior year.
4. The junior high school offering was becoming somewhat more standard, with United States history, geography, and civics predominating. A marked decline in geography was evident.
5. In part, shifts in the junior high school appear to be changes in terminology rather than changes in subjects.

TABLE 19–3

TRENDS IN REGISTRATIONS IN SOCIAL STUDIES, GRADES 7 AND 8, AND IN THE LAST
FOUR YEARS OF HIGH SCHOOL

Offering	Percentage distribution of pupil-semesters			
	Grades 7 and 8		Last 4 years of high school	
	1933–34[a]	1946–47[b]	1933–34[c]	1946–47[d]
All social studies	100.0	100.0	100.0	100.0
United States history	33.7	53.3	24.8	33.8
World history	2.5[e]	6.3	17.7	19.3
Civics, citizenship	6.8[f]	10.1	12.1[g]	14.1
Government, civics	—	—	6.0[h]	5.4
Problems of democracy	—	—	4.4	4.3
Geography	29.0	15.6	2.5	4.3
Modern history	—	—	2.7	3.6
Social science	21.0	10.1	3.6	3.2
Economics, economic problems ..	—	—	4.4	2.7
Sociology, social problems	—	—	2.2	1.7
State history	.3	3.8	.4	1.5
Ancient and medieval history	—	—	14.8	1.3
Occupations	—	—	3.2	.9[i]
International relations	—	—	.1	.4
Others	5.0[j]	.8	1.2[k]	3.6

[a] The figures for 1933–1934 are derived from data on 1,097,121 pupils. The basic data are on pp. 54–58, *Offerings and Registrations in High School Subjects, 1933–34*, U.S. Office of Education, Bulletin 1938, No. 6.

[b] These figures are derived from data on 34,410 pupils in the sample.

[c] The figures for 1933–1934 are derived from data on 3,534,204 students. The basic data are found on pp. 54–60, *Offerings and Registrations in High School Subjects*, U.S. Office of Education, Bulletin 1938, No. 6.

[d] These figures are derived from 91,159 pupils in the sample.

[e] Includes English history, world history, and ancient history.

[f] Includes community government and civil government.

[g] Includes community government.

[h] Includes civil government.

[i] A decline in occupations courses does not mean that information about occupations is not being taught but rather that such information is incorporated in other social studies, e.g., problems of democracy and civics.

[j] Includes occupations.

[k] Includes English history, industrial history, psychology.

SOURCE: Howard R. Anderson, *Teaching of United States History in Public High Schools*, Bulletin 1949, No. 7 (Washington, D.C.: Federal Security Agency, U.S. Office of Education, 1949), p. 6.

TABLE 19–4

NUMBER AND PERCENTAGE OF PUPILS ENROLLED IN SOCIAL STUDIES SUBJECTS
IN THE LAST FOUR YEARS OF PUBLIC SECONDARY DAY SCHOOLS,
1922, 1934, AND 1949

Subject	1922		1934		1949	
	Number	Per Cent	Number	Per Cent	Number	Per Cent
United States history(1)	329,565	15.3	779,489	17.3	1,231,694	22.8
English history	61,766	2.9	21,913	.5	1,043	(2)
World history			536,178	11.9	876,432	16.2
Civil government	416,329	19.3	192,497	6.6	431,916(3)	8.0
Community government			387,910	13.4	(4)	(4)
Geography			94,071	2.1	301,652	5.6
Problems of democracy			156,707	3.5	282,971	5.2
Economics	103,540	4.8	221,874	4.9	254,770	4.7
Sociology	51,288	2.4	111,718	2.5	185,901	3.4
Psychology	18,786	.9	15,025	.3	46,547	.9
Consumer education					36,024(5)	.7

(1) Data are for U.S. history (advanced) only, grades 10–12.
(2) Less than 0.05 per cent, or fewer than 1 pupil in 2,000.
(3) Data are for American Government or Advanced Civics only, grades 10–12.
(4) Comparable data for 1948–1949 not available.
(5) Includes 5,092 pupils enrolled in Consumer Buying who are also included in home economics.

SOURCE: Adapted from *Offerings and Enrollments in High School Subjects, Biennial Survey of Education in the United States, 1948–1950* (Washington, D.C.: Federal Security Agency, U.S. Office of Education, 1949), pp. 107–8.

For the years since 1949, one must rely on scattered evidence. The Moreland study[8] suggests increasing popularity of geography in both seventh and ninth grades, and in the senior high school, as well as strengthening of the relative position of world history in the tenth grade and of Problems of Democracy, government, and economics in grade twelve. Jones's studies of 1953 and 1962, based on responses from districts of over 100,000 population, regarding social studies requirements in grades nine through twelve, generally confirm the conclusions reached above. Whether these conclusions would hold true in a nationwide survey of all school systems is a matter with regard to which generalizations can be only tentative. Pertinent data from Jones's study are shown in Table 19–5.

Trends Within the Curriculum. In no other period in our history has our country undergone more rapid changes or more shocks and severe dis-

[8] Willis D. Moreland, "Curriculum Trends in the Social Studies," *Social Education,* Vol. 26, pp. 73–76, 102.

TABLE 19–5

SOCIAL STUDIES COURSES REQUIRED IN CITY SCHOOL SYSTEMS

Course	Number of Systems Requiring		Grade Most Frequently Indicated
	1953	1962	
United States history	105	130	11
World history	28	64	10
Civics or government	47	64	12
Problems of democracy	36	34	12
Economics	6	19	12
Geography	8	18	9
Local, state history	3	12	9
Driver education	5	11	10
Intr. to social studies	0	3	9 or 12
Consumer economics	3	2	12
Family living	0	2	10
Latin America	2	1	10
Far East	2	1	10
Human relations	1	1	10
International relations	0	1	12

SOURCE: Emlyn Jones, "Social Studies Requirements in an Age of Science and Mathematics," *Social Education*, Vol. 27 (January, 1963), pp. 17–18. Used with permission of author and publisher.

locations than in the last thirty years. The years of the Great Depression brought to millions of Americans the sobering realization that our economic system, despite its virtues, had some grievous faults which apparently were not self-correcting; if they were, we could not afford to wait to find out. Out of this grew both a demand for economic safeguards and a greater sense of social responsibility, manifested in agricultural price supports, social security, insurance of bank deposits, and the like. World War II thrust the United States into a position it had never occupied before, with new responsibilities and new obligations, and with much greater and more dire consequences attendant on the failure to solve its problems.

The rise of new political and economic ideologies forced upon the schools the need to teach about fascism and communism. In the last decade or so, the need for a rededication to our basic liberties has become apparent. Apathy toward political responsibilities has, in the minds of many, become extremely serious. Our position as a world leader, coupled with a more sensitive social conscience, has turned our attention increasingly to the minority groups in our population and to means for remedying the conditions that have meant second-class citizenship for many of their members. Coupled with all of this (and more) has been a technology that, spurred by war and economics, has steadily increased the cultural lag.

These conditions have brought vast new requirements to citizenship and have caused teachers of the social studies, as individuals and in groups, to call in question parts of the traditional curriculum and to examine their efforts critically. This questioning and examining has produced, and is continuing to produce, some curricular changes in the social studies. Obviously, they have not all taken place in every curriculum, nor even in the majority; the cultural lag applies to the schools as well as to the other social institutions.

Continuing and Increasing Emphasis on Recent History and on the History of Social, Political, and Economic Institutions. For some years, ancient and medieval history have been losing ground in the social studies in curriculum. As was noted above, their appearance as separate courses has become almost a rarity. Even in courses in world history, attention has been focused largely upon the modern period, in some cases on the last several centuries. The various proposals for the improvement of the world-history curriculum almost invariably urge emphasizing recent history; this is the case with the proposal to build the world-history course around areas, and is obviously so in the proposal to build the course around world affairs. In courses in the history of the United States, the trend is perhaps not quite so apparent, partly because the chronological and geographical scope of the subject is only a fraction of that of world history. However, in United States history too, and particularly in the senior high school offering, the more recent receives more attention than formerly.

The tendency to stress the development of institutions is by no means new; it has been going on since historians discovered that there was more to history than wars and political events. Yet the tempo of the change seems to have increased during recent years. World-history courses frequently contain units on religion, on the economic system, on the development of modern political institutions, on education, and the like. Some courses are built mainly around such themes. Similar observations can be made about courses in the history of the United States; discussions of the growth of democracy and our political institutions, schools, culture, industrial machine, and ideas constantly loom larger in the student's study of the history of his country.

Continuing Emphasis on Matters of Personal and Social Adjustment. Whether there is an increasing emphasis on this area in the social studies is debatable. The conservative pressures of recent years have undoubtedly brought about some retrenchment in some districts. On the other hand, there are many school systems in which the legitimacy of such emphases in the social studies field is unquestioned. A factor tending to support more intensive and sounder attention to matters of personal and social adjustment is the surge of interest in better guidance in schools. This may, or may not, affect the social studies curriculum, depending on how much of the guidance responsibility the social studies teacher is asked to assume.

It is principally this last point that disturbs some teachers of the social studies. The legitimacy of dealing with certain personal-social topics in the social studies meets with general agreement. Getting along with others in our highly interdependent society is essential. Reducing the number of vocational misfits by better counseling should pay big dividends. The desirability of preventing emotional maladjustment through learning to know oneself better is apparent. The same kind of generalization can be made about many of the other personal-social topics and units that have found their way into the social studies curriculum. The question is not as to their propriety in the school program, but as to whether the social studies field should carry as large a share of this responsibility as is expected in many schools.

Increasing Emphasis on World Affairs and World Understanding. In order to overcome or to reduce Americans' shortcomings in the field of world understanding, we find much greater attention to geography and to geographical concepts, particularly those of a global character. We find persistent attempts to destroy the inaccurate stereotypes many Americans have of people in other countries, an unintentional product of several generations of teaching, coupled with the efforts of many writers of fiction and those of travel bureaus. The study of contemporary world cultures is getting a larger share of attention. Courses of study about peoples of other lands emphasize better understanding. Units and topics on the United Nations are commonplace. Some schools underline the world setting of the history of the United States. Others teach courses in contemporary world affairs or in international relations. All in all, today's students are getting a far better picture of the world they live in than did students of a generation ago.

In recent years, there have been several promising developments in the field of education for international understanding. One such is the growing interest in courses in world cultures. In some instances, this course is a substitute for, and in others an addition to, the course in world history. Several high school textbooks written on a culture-area basis are available. Another program that has had considerable influence is the North Central Association's Foreign Relations Project, begun in 1955 with a grant from the Ford Foundation; the pamphlets that have been written for, and distributed by, the Project have been widely and profitably used. Of quite a different character, and involving an approach on a number of fronts, is the Glens Falls (New York) program known as "Improving the Teaching of World Affairs" (ITWA). Though centering in the schools, it has reached out into many phases of community life, has stimulated a wide interest in the community in learning about foreign affairs, and has been reported as having had tremendous impact.[9]

Increasing Emphasis on America and on American Ideals and Institutions. Concomitant with our growing awareness of our world responsibilities and of our consequent need for more study about world situations and the world's people has come a heightened interest in the study of our own country. Perhaps it is the former that has brought about the latter; our concern with the dangers abroad has alerted us to the fact that our ideals and institutions must not be taken for granted, that we must constantly be on guard against forces that would destroy what has been so arduously achieved. These forces are both within and without our borders; they are embodied both in the threat from a totalitarian power and in the machinations of those who would capitalize on this threat to undermine our liberties.

All of this has meant more study of America. As was noted above, more students are studying the history of the United States, an increase due in part to increased prescription on both local and state levels. Moreover, there is some evidence that the character of courses in United States history is changing, particularly in the direction of greater differentiation between junior and senior high school offerings.[10] A rededication to basic American principles is being sought through units on democracy, civil liberties,[11] the Bill of Rights, and the Constitution, as well as increased study of American government.

Increasing Emphasis on Better Family Living. The quality of homelife in a nation is important to individuals and to society alike. Wholesome home environments contribute to the making of happy and well-adjusted individuals; and these in turn improve the quality of social life outside the family. Considerable deterioration of family life has been apparent in the United States for years. Its marks are a high divorce rate, lack of unity in family enterprise, maladjustments in children (and in parents), juvenile delinquency,[12] and the popularity of "advice-to-the-lovelorn"

[9] Lewis Paul Todd, "ITWA: the Glens Falls Project," *The Civic Leader*, February 18, 1963, pp. 1, 3.

[10] Along the lines suggested by Edgar B. Wesley in *American History in Schools and Colleges* (New York: The Macmillan Co., 1944).

[11] Two excellent recent books on this subject are *A Program for Improving Bill of Rights Teaching in High Schools* and *A Bibliography of Civil Rights and Civil Liberties,* both published in 1962 by the Civil Liberties Educational Foundation, Inc.

[12] It is not intended to suggest that home factors are the only cause of juvenile delinquency and maladjustment.

columns. Schools have been called upon to do a better job of education in this regard, and, in this effort, the social studies field plays a major part.

A certain kind of teaching about family life has long been a part of the social studies curriculum. In the past, it took place chiefly in courses in sociology and social problems and leaned toward the pathological, with some attention to forms of the family and of marriage and other sociological data. Today's efforts are more positive. The importance of strong families in the structure of the community is emphasized, as is an understanding of the impact a changing society has had on family life. Consumer education has been broadened to include much more than good buying practices. Authoritarianism and democracy (as well as chaos) as patterns of authority in the home and the whole field of interpersonal relationships in home situations are examined. The responsibilities of family members are studied. Throughout, the aim is to teach pupils how to make their homes places where happy, satisfying lives can be lived.

Increasing Emphasis on Improving Intergroup Relationships. Ashley Montagu once wrote that the present-day school should deal first with humanity—that its other functions should be regarded as subsidiary. Perhaps no school would accept such a dictum literally, but it is significant that our increased sensitivity to the position of minority groups in our culture has led to the inclusions of a great deal of study about intercultural and intergroup relations. Such study has not been limited, of course, to groups and cultures within our own country; if "one world" is ever going to be more than a verbalism, our understanding of other peoples and their culture, our acceptance of them as individuals, our grasp of the "fallacy of race," our appreciation of cultural diversity must extend to those beyond our national confines.

In the social studies, this trend has taken many forms. The scientific facts about heredity and race have been studied. Units on the meaning of democracy, on civil rights, and on minorities in our culture are widespread. Pupils are being helped to understand the position of members of minority groups through the use of song, picture, and story. Efforts to reduce and eliminate stereotypes are being expended. The concept of cultural diffusion is being explored. The facts that produce cultural diversity are being identified. History, geography, and sociology are being used to throw light on minority groups and their problems, past and present. Students are being taught to think critically about these as well as other, problems. It is perhaps too early to say how effective this emphasis has been, but many teachers are optimistic, and some are enthusiastic, about what is being done.

Increasing Emphasis on the Relationship of Government to the Society and to the Individual. During the years 1914 to 1963, the expenditures of the federal government increased about one hundredfold. Though one must be chary about drawing conclusions from the blunt statement, it does give some indication of the degree to which government's relation to the society and to individuals has changed. Its importance in the economic life of the society is, of course, tremendous.

There are many spheres of activity into which government has penetrated in these years. It has extended its control over our banking system. It has recognized collective bargaining and has set up rules governing many of the actions of both labor unions and management. It takes one-quarter of our income in taxes. It has set up a mammoth social-insurance plan, which now provides retirement coverage for practically all workers, as well as other benefits. It regulates much of our communications system, and a substantial amount of power and transportation. It provides price supports for farmers and participates in decisions as to how much they will produce. It does many, many other things.

This is not to imply that this penetration is wrong or unwise; it is simply a recital of facts. Many of these activities were controversial when they were inaugurated; some still are. Nevertheless, they exist, and the social studies teacher has had to allow for them in at least two ways: to explain why and how they have come about and to help students understand what they mean—how they affect the society, groups, and individuals. Consequently, we find increased attention being paid to labor-management relations, financial security, agriculture, national income, conservation, what government does for consumers, monopoly, and a host of other topics and ideas.

The lack of economic understanding among Americans has been a matter of much concern since World War II. Several organizations have been prominent in working to correct the situation. Of these, the most active and influential has been the Joint Council on Economic Education, founded in 1949 and supported mainly by grants from individuals and from private firms and organizations. The Council has carried on an extensive publications program, has stimulated the organization of a large number of locally financed workshops in economic education for teachers, and has encouraged and assisted in-service economic education, in addition to a number of other activities. Also of significance in the movement has been the work of the Council for the Advancement of Secondary Education, established in 1952 through the joint effort of the National Association of Secondary School Principals and the National Better Business Bureau. It has made studies and has issued publications for use by high school students. The most recent effort in this direction is the report of the National Task Force in Economic Education, financed by the Committee for Economic Development and prepared by a committee appointed by the American Economic Association.[13]

Increasing Emphasis on Community Study. More and more, social studies teachers are turning to the community as a laboratory. The reasons for this are varied. In part it stems from an awareness that the community is a microcosm of society at large—that in it one finds the social processes at work that function in larger and more distant societies. The student learns to grasp social concepts in a familiar setting and, thus, is better able to understand similar concepts in larger or more distant settings and in more difficult contexts. In part, it is attributable to a desire to help students identify with concepts or problems of social concern so that they can see the degree to which their welfare is tied to the decisions and actions of local governments and other local civic groups and organizations. In part, particularly in the last decade or so, it has grown out of the very energetic and worthwhile work being carried on by the various citizenship-education-promoting projects in which students in hundreds of schools have been enrolled, which call for a great amount of community study and, in some instances, for direct action in community affairs.

Increasing Emphasis on the Study of Communism. In the last three or four years, there has been a surge of interest in the study of communism. Citizens, organizations, and legislatures have insisted that the study of communism be included in the school program. One does not have to look far into history to the time when many teachers were urging this very thing and were being opposed by some of the same individuals and groups who are now so articulate and insistent. At least three kinds of motives seem to be operating: that of the intelligent citizen who recognizes the international threat of communism and believes that "knowing our enemy" is essential to citizenship, that of the fearful citizen who has been influenced by various "crusades" and sees domestic Communists behind every tree, and that of the calculating citizen whose goal is to identify liberal movements and ideas as communistic and to foist upon youth a distorted picture of their country and of its condition and problems. This last kind of person generally is interested in a course that suggests that almost every act of government is a prelude to communism.

A rational person must agree that the study of communism, particularly of the Soviet variety, is essential in the school program; good teachers have been saying so for years. But what kind of study should it be?

[13] Two publications have been issued: *Economic Education in the Schools,* the report of the National Task Force on Economic Education (New York: Committee for Economic Development, 1961) and *Study Materials for Economic Education in the Schools,* the report of the Materials Evaluation Committee (New York: Committee for Economic Development, 1961).

Certainly not the highly emotionalized kind of program, full of inflammatory phrases and passages and superficialities, that has been put into operation in some localities. Certainly not a program that aims only at indoctrination and is concerned more with what we are against than with what we are for. Certainly not a program that serves only as a vehicle through which various narrow concepts of Americanism are foisted on unwary and unsophisticated students.

An effective program must be rational, not emotional; it must help youth build a meaningful dedication to democracy as well as an alertness to, and understanding of, democracy's competitors. Among the more desirable statements about this kind of program is that issued jointly by the National Education Association and the American Legion.[14]

A Look to the Future. What has been said in the preceding pages may suggest a good deal of ferment in the social studies. To some degree, this does exist: much activity has taken place in the last several decades; hundreds of curriculum-revision programs have been inaugurated; and the social studies field has been changed considerably thereby.

But much of this has been patchwork. Gaps in the program have been recognized, and steps have been taken to fill at least some of them. Shifting of subjects has taken place, sometimes from one grade to another; units have been shifted from one grade to another or from one course to another. Some subjects have steadily lost ground in the program; others have gained. Some new subjects have been introduced, as have some new units. But very little has been done along the line of thoroughgoing revision such as what has taken place in the sciences and in mathematics. To some extent, this lag may be attributed to operating on the assumption that the existing subjects and the traditional subject matter consitute the best vehicle for achieving the objectives sought. Curriculum revision, then, takes the form of manipulating the usual subject matter into new arrangements.

That the social studies program is decades behind the times has been said with increasing frequency in the last half-dozen years.[15] Many individuals and groups have pointed to the fact that the present social studies curriculum, in its main elements, is a product of the years immediately following World War I, and to the need to rethink the objectives of the

[14] *Teaching About Communism: Guidelines for Junior and Senior High School Teachers* (Indianapolis: The American Legion, 1962). For an excellent analysis of the subject, see the three articles by Lewis P. Todd in *The Civic Leader* for January 14, March 12, and December 3, 1962. A very good bibliographical reference is *A Selected Annotated Bibliography To Assist Teachers in Teaching About Communism* (Washington: National Council for the Social Studies, 1962).

[15] National Commission on the Social Studies, *Curriculum Planning in American Schools: The Social Studies* (Washington, D.C.: National Council for the Social Studies, 1958).

field and then of the means to reach these objectives. Moreover, it is being recognized that the more "contemporary" social sciences, particularly the behavioral sciences, have too long been on the periphery of school programs.[16]

Fortunately, there are some encouraging signs on the horizon. A number of the scholarly organizations are becoming constructively critical and are expressing, through word and deed, an interest in helping with social studies curriculum revision. The American Historical Association revitalized a long standing interest in the social studies when it established, in 1956, its Service Center for Teachers of History. In the intervening years, it has issued a number of excellent pamphlets on various topics in history and, in addition, has provided other kinds of scholarly help to teachers. The American Economic Association created a Committee on Economic Education a half-dozen years ago; this committee has been active and has participated extensively in the preparation of the Committee on Economic Development's recommendations for schools.[17] Professional geographers, working through the Association of American Geographers and the National Council for Geographic Education, have contributed their knowledge and skill to a High School Geography Project, designed to produce a high school geography course on tape, together with other study materials; pilot programs are now in operation.[18] The American Anthropological Association, through its Anthropology Curriculum Study Project, has identified a number of units through which anthropological concepts may be taught, and is in the process of preparing pamphlets on each.[19]

This involvement of the scholars should be welcomed by teachers. It is true that most of these groups tend to think only of school courses in their respective disciplines; this may at first glance seem discouraging, since what is needed is a fresh look at the whole field of the social sciences. But, with sober thought, one must regard this activity as encouraging; the scholars need to identify the school potential of their separate fields before an over-all program can be discussed intelligently.

[16] An excellent discussion of the current situation and of the problems involved in revision will be found in Lewis P. Todd, "Afterword: Revising the Social Studies," pp. 282–303 in *The Social Studies and the Social Sciences* (New York: Harcourt, Brace & World, Inc., 1962).

[17] See note 13, page 395.

[18] Gilbert F. White, "A Joint Effort To Improve High School Geography," *Journal of Geography,* Vol. 60, pp. 357–360; William D. Pattison, "High School Geography Project Begins Experimental Year," *Journal of Geography,* Vol. 61, pp. 367–369; and the High School Geography Project *Newsletter,* edited by Dr. Pattison, University of California, Los Angeles.

[19] Malcolm Collier, *Activities and Plans for the Anthropology Curriculum Study Project* (mimeo.) (Chicago: Anthropology Curriculum Study Project, n.d.); American Anthropological Association Fellow *Newsletter,* November, 1962.

And it should go without saying that the determination of an over-all program should involve teachers as well as scholars.

Some headway toward a fresh over-all look has already been made. In several state curriculum studies such as that in California[20] one of the first tasks was to try to identify the basic concepts in each of the social science disciplines; these would, it was hoped, help to indicate a framework around which a program might be built. The National Council for the Social Studies, in 1957, issued a report in which somewhat the same effort was made, save that the Council organized its report in integrating themes rather than by disciplines.[21] Finally, in 1958, the Council established a Commission on the Social Studies, intended to bring about a joint effort on the part of the Council and the various scholarly organizations in the social sciences that would eventually lead to major curriculum revision. The Council succeeded in enlisting the support of the American Council of Learned Societies; the fruit of the joint undertaking, to date, has been the preparation and publication of a book entitled *The Social Studies and the Social Sciences*.[22]

Programs for Abler Students. Many school districts have inaugurated special programs for abler students since the middle 1950's, and most of these include the social studies. These programs vary considerably in character, scope, and quality. Some are intended only for gifted youth; others provide for much larger percentages of school populations. They range in scope from those that represent minor modifications of traditional content to interdisciplinary seminars.[23]

Other Trends. It is evident that the effectiveness of a curriculum depends on much more than *what* is set up to be taught. *How* the curriculum is taught is of no less importance. Curriculum may well be thought of, indeed is by many, as including both materials and methods of instruction and learning.

In the social studies field, some promising trends in method can be discerned. Teachers, in general, are becoming more concerned with the quality of discussion that takes place in the classroom; they are learning

---

[20] *Social Studies Framework for the Public Schools of California*, California State Department of Education, Sacramento, 1962.

[21] *A Guide to Content in the Social Studies*, report of the Committee on Concepts and Values (Washington, D.C.: National Council for the Social Studies, 1957).

[22] *The Social Studies and the Social Sciences* (New York: Harcourt, Brace & World, Inc., 1962).

[23] Descriptions of programs will be found in Ruth W. Gavian (ed.), *The Social Education of the Academically Talented* (Washington, D.C.: National Council for the Social Studies, 1958); Milton M. Klein, *Social Studies for the Academically Talented Student in the Secondary School* (Washington, D.C.: National Education Association of the United States, 1960); and *The Changing College Preparatory Curriculum* (Princeton, N.J.: College Entrance Examination Board, 1962).

new techniques for use in both large and small groups, and they are improving their use of techniques of long standing. Recognizing the importance of sharing in the determination of goals and procedures, more and more teachers are experimenting with pupil-teacher planning, some with marked success. Problem solving as a basic method has captured the interest of teachers in every part of the country; through its use, they hope that students not only will learn more about the problems they study but also will become familiar with a basic method of attack. Closely allied with this is increasing emphasis on critical thinking—helping students to resist the temptation to leap to superficial conclusions, to evaluate sources and kinds of data, and to be willing to reserve judgment until the facts are in, or at least until as many as possible can be secured.

To these trends might be added a number of others such as the increasing use of television, exposure of students to a much wider variety of materials (particularly paperbacks and the excellent collections of "little books" on special topics that are coming from both commercial and university presses), and the rapid extension of team teaching, in which social studies teachers are participating in ever increasing numbers.

QUESTIONS, PROBLEMS, AND ISSUES FOR FURTHER THOUGHT

1. If you were to visit a number of secondary schools in the United States, what social studies courses would you be likely to find in the various grades?
2. Do you believe it would be wise to have a single nationwide curriculum in the social studies? Do you believe there should be some national minimum essentials, or a minimum group of concepts? Explain your answers.
3. Examine three or four state courses of study in the social studies. What similarities and diffrences do you find?
4. Compare the United States history portions of the courses of study referred to in question 3 with the proposals in *American History in Schools and Colleges.*
5. Examine some course of study for the secondary social studies program; then try to decide whether it follows logical or psychological principle.
6. If you were going to organize a course in modern problems for high school seniors, what would you include? Justify your answer.
7. Compare a current textbook in United States history for grade eleven with one published in the 1930's. What differences do you find?
8. Examine some current social studies course of study to discover which, if any, of the trends indicated in this chapter are evident.
9. Why is a thoroughgoing revision of the social studies curriculum hard to bring about? Is the problem different from these in other fields?
10. Prepare an analysis of several social studies programs for gifted students.

SUPPLEMENTARY MATERIALS

SELECTED READINGS

Books listed below have been chosen primarily because of their extensive treatment of the social studies curriculum.

CARTWRIGHT, W. H., and R. L. WATSON (eds.). *Interpreting and Teaching American History*. 31st yearbook, National Council for the Social Studies. Washington, D.C.: The Council, 1961. Part I deals with new interpretations in American history, and Part II with the history curriculum in schools and with the teaching of history.

ELLSWORTH, RUTH, and OLE SAND, (eds.). *Improving the Social Studies Curriculum*, 26th yearbook, National Council for the Social Studies. Washington, D.C.: The Council, 1955. A description of the curriculum making and curriculum revising processes.

GROSS, R. E., and L. D. ZELENY. *Educating Citizens for Democracy*. New York: Oxford University Press, 1958. Parts II and III provide considerable detail about the various subjects in the social studies curriculum.

HUNT, ERLING M. *et al. High School Social Studies Perspectives*. New York: Houghton Mifflin Company, 1962. Contributions by distinguished social scientists on the potential contributions of their fields to the social studies.

HUNT, MAURICE P., and LAWRENCE E. METCALF. *Teaching High School Social Studies*. New York: Harper and Brothers, 1955. A stimulating book which calls into question the traditional content of the social studies as well as traditional methods of teaching.

JAMES, PRESTON E., (ed.). *New Viewpoints in Geography*, 29th yearbook, National Council for the Social Studies. Washington, D.C.: The Council, 1959. Contains chapters by professional geographers on new interpretations in their fields of geography.

NATIONAL COUNCIL FOR THE SOCIAL STUDIES. *A Guide to Content in the Social Studies*, Report of the Committee on Concepts and Values. Washington, D.C.: The Council, 1957. Provides a description of fourteen "themes" around which a social studies curriculum might be built.

NATIONAL COUNCIL FOR THE SOCIAL STUDIES AND THE AMERICAN COUNCIL OF LEARNED SOCIETIES. *The Social Studies and the Social Sciences*. New York: Harcourt, Brace and World, Inc., 1962. The report of the joint project on the social studies curriculum.

PATTERSON, FRANKLIN (ed.). *Citizenship and a Free Society: Education for the Future*, 30th yearbook, National Council for the Social Studies. Washington, D.C.: The Council, 1960. A twenty-year look ahead in the fields of government, economics, intergroup relations, mass culture, and world affairs, and implications for the curriculum.

PRICE, ROY A. (ed.). *New Viewpoints in the Social Sciences*, 28th yearbook, National Council for the Social Studies. Washington, D.C.: The Council, 1958. Chapters on new interpretations in the various social sciences, with applications to the school curriculum.

QUILLEN, I. J., and LAVONE, HANNA. *Education for Social Competence* (rev. ed.). Chicago: Scott, Foresman & Co., 1961. The first three parts of this book deal with the curriculum.

WESLEY, E. B., and S. P. WRONSKI. *Teaching Social Studies in High Schools*. (4th ed.). Boston: D. C. Heath & Co., 1958. Extensive description of the curriculum and of the curriculum-making process.

20

The Language Arts and Literature

During the early stages of the child's life, language is learned intuitively and imitatively. But, through the controlled environment of the school situation, language is subject to refinement, change, and growth that does not occur spontaneously.

Earlier in this volume, *curriculum* was defined as the control of segments of the maturing individual's environment so that direction, distance, and breadth of his growth might be conditioned. The present chapter deals with attempts that are being made to control the direction of growth of language skills, on the one hand, and the development of certain value insights, on the other. The responsibility for this two-pronged job is the province of a class called "English."

PROGRESS FROM AN OUTMODED CURRICULUM

English as a separate subject does not have a long history in American schools. During the eighteenth century, numbers of individual tutors offered to help people learn how to write and spell. When Franklin proposed his plan for the Academy in the middle of the eighteenth century, he suggested that it should offer instruction in penmanship, spelling, and, particularly, composition. His dream was of a school that would train people for a new kind of social order. He saw that citizens in a democracy needed communication skills. During the nineteenth century, the academy became increasingly esoteric in its offerings and the new public high school imitated it. Instruction in penmanship, spelling, and grammar were standardly given, but the principal offerings in English were in courses called "rhetoric." These were concerned largely with the study of models to be used in planning formal speaking and writing. It was not until the end of the nineteenth century that Harvard University instituted its famous "English A" course, a course in basic composition for all entering freshmen.

However, the patterns for the program used in the majority of the schools even today were created by the educational reforms that took place in the last decade of the nineteenth century. At that time, the various strands taught in separate subject matters were drawn together into one subject called "English." It was established as a "core subject" required of all students for three out of the four high school years. The content became fixed by the stipulations of college entrance requirements. In literature, students preparing for college entrance had to answer questions on a list of fourteen specific classics of literature. Although changed slightly from year to year, it included such works as *The Lady of the Lake, The Rhyme of the Ancient Mariner, Ivanhoe, Evangeline, Snowbound, Speech on Conciliation with the American Colonies,* and *The Deserted Village.*

Students also had to demonstrate their ability to control language by writing a theme, which was judged solely on the student's proficiency in the mechanics of writing (punctuation, spelling, capitalization, word usage, sentence structure) and not at all on the merit of the ideas or the level of creativity.

These rigid standards led the secondary schools, which at the time were educating only a small, select group of the population, to set up a lock-step program required of all. The fourteen classics were scattered throughout the high school years, each being studied intensively by itself. Language drills designed to improve the mechanics of writing were used in great numbers. Even in the occasional themes students wrote, the emphasis was on the accuracy of the mechanics rather than on creativity demonstrated.

TWENTIETH-CENTURY DEVELOPMENTS

Landmarks in Reform. During the 1920's and 1930's, major policy-making statements attempted to move English teaching away from the rigid lock-step patterns of the early part of the century. Among these were James Hosic's committee report on the teaching of English, a part of the report on *The Reorganization of Secondary Education in 1918;* John Clapp's report on the place of English in American life in the mid-twenties; and the curriculum guide (*An Experience Curriculum in English*) published by the National Council of Teachers of English in the thirties. The writers of these documents viewed the content of English as a series of experiences rather than as a body of factual information. They saw that language is learned as a habit or pattern of action rather than as an intellectual feat. They viewed literature as a form of communication rather than a cultural ornament of the genteel. The curriculum in English, according to these studies, should be designed around a series of activities or experiences rather than around a body of factual information. The student should have frequent experiences in letter writing, reporting, panel discussions, interviewing, response to lyric emotion, projection of themselves into the lives of characters in stories, and reading and evaluation of current magazines and newspapers. It was assumed that all of these experiences would occur in rudimentary form at an early age but that they could be constantly refined through repetition as the individual matured.

Actual implementation of these suggestions would have produced a course of study far different from that used in the schools at that time. For such a program would demand that there be no set works of literature covered at any given grade level, no set body of grammatical rules presented, no set body of factual material memorized. Instead, the information to be given would be left to the discretion of the individual teacher in terms of that teacher's evaluation of the class's needs and the students' readiness for a particular body of information in relation to a particular project.

Only a relatively few schools put the suggested program into effect in its entirety. But the thinking behind these documents did create changes in parts of the English program. Letter writing became a fairly standardized activity of English classes. Units on the use of the library, on how to write research papers, on proper parliamentary procedure slipped into the English curriculum. Permissive browsing in books became a fairly usual procedure. But the complete experience program of study was not substituted for the rigid, standardized, college-bound program of the nineteenth century. Instead, bits and pieces of it were grafted onto the old curriculum with its set body of factual information and literary classics.

The Influence of New Knowledge of Child Growth and Development. In the last two decades, the English curriculum has been somewhat influenced by the tenets of child growth and development. It seems increasingly apparent that there is a developmental order in the way an individual matures and gains control of language and certainly in the growth of his appreciation of literature. In language, people move from the egocentric, personal-experience type of language use to the language of genuine communication where information or ideas are transmitted.

As skill in the use of language progresses, longer sentences are used, and language structures undergo greater and greater modification.

In literature, rather clearly defined stages of growth in interest can be predicted. Yet, in spite of this demonstrable information, large segments of the secondary school English program are completely out of step with the interests and abilities of young people. Great bodies of materials are presented before boys and girls are capable of understanding or mastering them. A sound course of study would be one in which the program parallels the normal growth patterns of the individuals.

The impact of such thinking has been utilized largely in the junior high school. Here, increasingly, the text materials and the teaching units center around such things as animal stories, adventure, and growing up around the world—all of which are normal reading interests of early adolescents. In a good program, students are encouraged to write freely and spontaneously about their own experiences. However, at the senior high school level, the concerns attacked tend to be overly mature, formalistic matters for which the students are not psychologically ready.

Recent Reactions. In recent years, English has not escaped from the general criticisms leveled at all education. Powerful voices advocate stepping up the level of requirements. Curriculum formulators respond by formalizing and intellectualizing the content. In English, this means a weekly theme, the close reading of a few classics, a study of the language structure for its own sake. Such a program has a tremendous advantage for the teacher, because it is precise and definite. It has tremendous appeal for the public, because they can understand both the means and the goals. It has tremendous disadvantages for the nation, because it assumes that creative thinking and maturing ideas can be forced into a mold. In the final analysis, each teacher must decide the extent to which the students before him are vessels to be filled and the extent to which they are lamps to be lighted. Are facts and their repetition enough? Or must there also be creative tending of the bright something that can be blown into a flame in many a student?

Objectives for a Modern Program. Presentation of the literary classics that "all cultured people are supposed to know" and an absolute standard of language usage still maintain a strong grip on the English programs in the country today. But individual schools and certain national organizations of English teachers have proposed a set of objectives designed to meet the needs of today's youth:

1. *Young people should be helped to perform adequately the language activities of daily life.* From studies made of language use, it is apparent

that people listen more than they speak and that they speak far more than they read, writing constituting the least used of the language arts. Logically, then, the oral-aural communication skills should predominate in the curriculum or at least be given equal attention. But this is seldom seen in the actual organization of instruction.

Investigation has shown the situations in which people use each of the language skills. For example, conversation is the most used oral language activity, with telephoning, friendly chats, and the asking of questions and giving of answers next in order of use. Common writing activities of daily life include letter writing, note taking, and list making. In the reading area, newspapers, magazines, and advertisements head the list of media read. Obviously, to undertake to teach boys and girls to perform the activities of daily living implies a very different kind of program from the ones using the objectives of the nineties.

2. *Today's program should help boys and girls understand the role of communication and its methods in the world today.* Young people need to consider the role of the newspaper, the magazine, the motion picture, television, and even the telephone in our scheme of communication. They should study why and how these communication devices developed, who controls them, how they can affect the ideas of people, and their degree of reliability. Furthermore, young people need increasing awareness of elemenetary semantics so that they can judge the relationship between words used and the facts they represent. They must be made aware of the devices of propagandists who commonly use language to achieve their ends.

3. *Today's programs should help boys and girls find deeply satisfying experiences in literature that will help them grow in socially approved directions.* Through literature, young people should have personalized for them the values of our culture, of the democratic way of life. They should grow in their awareness of the quality of life in all parts of the world. They should, step by step, mature in their understanding of the behavior of people, their motivations, their strivings, and the outcome of those strivings. Through their reading, students should be enabled to test various value patterns vicariously for size and perhaps come eventually to understand themselves. Ideally, the literature program should help young people expand their experiential horizons so that they break the bonds of narrow, bigoted provincial thinking.

The impact and content of a literary work would be the bases for selection, not its position on some abstract scale of literary excellence. Because a given understanding may evolve from a number of different works of literature, no one piece of literature is indispensable for all to read.

4. *Through the use of language, as well as through the use of litera-ture, students should have frequent opportunities to explore their ideas, their emotions, and their reactions to other people and to their physical environment.* Many of the projective techniques of modern psychology are similar to practices in English classes. Teachers may use writing assignments to help students explore their ideas or perhaps project their tensions through poetry or a short story. Through writing, students may be helped to straighten out some of their confusions in thinking. For example, writing an autobiography may help a student see how and why he has developed the ideas he holds. Thus, not all the activities of the English class need to be directed toward the purely practical ends of communication. Language can also be used as a medium for stating personal problems and for deepening understanding of values.

PROBLEMS FACING CURRICULUM MAKERS IN THE LANGUAGE ARTS

How Much Time Should Be Given to English? Today, in most schools, English is required of all students for one period a day through the eleventh grade. In the majority of schools, twelfth-grade English is an elective but is usually required of a student planning to attend a college or university. At the junior high school level, usually five periods a week are devoted to English. In a few schools, a second course, called "read-ing," "spelling," or "literature" is presented to all students in addition to the period called English.

In larger senior high schools, electives in English are offered that supplement but do not replace the regular English course. The most commonly given is speech, which is generally open to juniors and seniors. Second in frequency offered is journalism, with dramatics, creative writ-ing, business English, and remedial reading representing other possible courses. Because these areas are taught elsewhere, teachers should not bypass them in basic classes. Speech activities, creative writing, and instruction in reading should be part of every class, reserving elective classes for giving specialized help to students with special interests and needs.

A few senior high schools operate on a double- or multiple-track system, offering a series of alternative courses often designated as college-preparatory, business, or general English. Usually this system brings about an unsought type of ability grouping, for the better students take the college-preparatory English; the more vocationally minded choose busi-ness English; and the rest of the students are relegated to general English.

There is, at present, considerable dissatisfaction with the basic unit-of-time pattern that was established by Carnegie in the early twentieth century. The so-called Rutgers plan has attempted to adapt the Trump plan of large classes, small classes, and individualized work to the English program. In schools using the Rutgers plan, students spend some time every week in large lecture sections for generalized instruction, some time in small discussion-type groups for reactions, and some time in individualized reading assignments. Evidence from schools using this arrangement of time indicates that students learn as much in this type of program as in the conventional type of hour classes, but it is yet to be shown that they learn more. One is tempted to ask whether the manipulation of students is really worth the effort, and yet only through such experimentation can the best methods be found.

What Is To Be Done About Individual Differences? In the 1920's, teachers and schools became acutely aware of individual differences and their impact on the work the schools were attempting. In the various skills that make up the language arts, it was found that students average an eight-year span of achievement differences by the time they arrived at the junior high school level. This span increases each year, so that by senior high school a span of ten to twelve years is not unusual. These differences are the result of good teaching rather than of bad, for if all children are stimulated to learn to the maximum of their capacity, the bright children will learn more rapidly than the slow children and each year the two groups will become more unlike.

Out of this discovery came the proposal to group students by ability for instructional purposes. In most situations, English classes have been grouped according to students' reading ability and general intelligence, on the basis of teachers' recommendations. In some large schools, grouping in English classes was attempted on a ridiculously fine scale with as many as fifteen levels of classes within each grade level. However, for the past decade, the standard practice in most schools has been one of grouping students in three levels in each grade. The top group of students are placed in a special section, the severely retarded in a special section, and the bulk of the students in the middle, or standard, section.

The logic of the idea makes it appealing to teachers and to many parents in the community. In general, teachers seem to prefer teaching grouped sections. Visits to actual classes, however, often reveal that the plan is not completely successful. The top classes are usually exciting. Ideas and information pour out from both students and teachers. The retarded classes are frequently smaller in size than are normal classes and, in the hands of a trained teacher who adapts the level of instruction to practical concerns, the students receive not only real help but also sympathy, understanding, and encouragement that produce some good results. But, frequently, the middle classes, where the majority of students are taught, are deadly. Often there is no real adaptation of the content to the students except in the rapidity with which it is covered.

Actually, young people learn as much from one another as they do from their teachers. Therefore, grouping cuts off whatever impact the superior students might have on their less fortunate peers. Furthermore, because of the diversity of skills involved in English, students who are grouped in reading are not necessarily grouped correctly for their ability in other skills. There is also a tendency for the most able teachers to work with the superior students, relegating the less proficient and less experienced teachers to working with the students who probably have the greatest need of superior teaching. More often than not, courses of study are not geared for the differences in the varying groups. Research studies on the effects of grouping on achievement have not supported each other's findings. Thus there is no clear-cut evidence that grouping produces superior results in learning.

For these reasons, teachers in increasing numbers are looking for new ways of individualizing instruction so that some of the problems of ability grouping can be overcome and some of its advantages maintained.

Team Teaching. In team teaching, three or four teachers work together with a group of approximately 100 students. The group meets together perhaps two days a week, in which a single teacher makes a presentation of material and may lead a limited class discussion. Through this device, students are given a chance to respond to one another and to profit as they can from a careful presentation. The large-group classes are followed by smaller work groups sometimes based on interests, sometimes on needs. Thus, students may receive both the benefits of small-group instruction and a feeling of membership in a larger situation. Because grouping is not for a semester's duration, a student may be in a retarded group for spelling practice one week and in an accelerated group for reading practice the next week.

Programed Learning. Programed instructions, which breaks specific learning tasks down into small sequential steps and provides self-correcting exercises, may be a boon in handling individual differences in English. Frequently, in English, problems are individual ones and not group ones. A given student has trouble with the verb "to come" but not with other verbs; another has trouble with the spelling of words in which a suffix has been added to a root. One child's problem is his reading speed; another child has difficulty comprehending; and a third cannot find central meanings. It seems almost within the reach of present practice to have a class situation in which a part of each week is devoted to individualized work for each student on the particular skills in which he is deficient. Even without the use of highly elaborate machines, programs can be worked out through simple paper-and-pencil devices.

Individualized Reading. The program of free reading developed by some teachers in the 1930's has suddenly been revived today under the label of "individualized reading." In this program, students and a wide variety of reading material are brought together in a relaxed atmosphere. The student is given time to browse, to select material that holds his interest, and to settle down to the actual process of reading. In such a program, students of widely differing abilities and backgrounds may all find books that hold significance for them. Furthermore, the teacher gains time for individual and informal conferences with students as they read. The recommendation made is to give a block of at least six weeks' time to individualized reading in each grade level from seven through twelve.

The Elective System in English. A few schools are experimenting with offering a series of elective courses in place of a single standardized course at each level. In the University High School at the State University of Iowa, junior and senior students are free to design their own programs in English for the last two years by selecting from ten courses each offered for one semester each year. Some of the courses offered are traditional, such as the courses in "The Story of American Literature" and "The Story of English Literature." Others are experimental, such as "Individualized Reading" and "Landmarks of Literature." Three courses stress composition: "Writing Problems," "Writing Laboratory," and "Creative Writing," and three are speech-oriented: "Essentials in Speech," "Readings in Drama," and "Readings in Public Address." These courses are planned with the probable needs of the students in mind, and, through their own choices, students tend to group themselves. Because all courses are elective, it is possible for students especially interested to take additional work in English in place of other electives in their programs. Thus the superior students tend to take five or six semesters of English in their last two years, rather than the expected four.

The Use of Clinical Situations. Many schools have found, particularly in the area of reading, that the clinical situation is best equipped to handle the special needs of students. The clinic operates apart from course requirements or credit. Students are assigned to the clinic according to their own needs—sometimes twice a week, sometimes for one period every day. They may continue in the clinic for a short period or for the whole year. Students may come during the English class period or during their study-hall assignment. The success of the clinical approach in reading suggests that it might work equally well in other language skills, such as spelling, mechanics, or composition.

A Program Combining Common Instruction and Individualized Projects.
It is possible to design a program that picks out certain elements or
situations for common instruction and uses these as a springboard to
individual work projects on the students' part. A single work of literature
read together in a class may lead to a series of individualized projects:
reading other books related to the common reading in either theme or
mood, small research projects, creative writing inspired by something in
the selection.

What Kind of Literature Should Be Taught? It is not unusual to find
a teacher today who says, "Shouldn't we present literature to our students
that they would not ordinarily read by themselves?" Many feel that
exposure to a common body of classics of literature builds a feeling of
commonality or togetherness among people in later life. At least students
will know the names of some of the "great" accomplishments in literature
so that they can turn to them as adults. On the other hand, there is
evidence to support the contention that the student who had been guided
to read selections that get completely "under his skin" because they are
at his interest and ability level is the one who actively seeks for more
and more mature reading throughout his lifetime. Teachers who believe
in the latter point of view realize that the same piece of literature will
never have the same effect on all students. They do not set up a priori
judgments about the general worth of the study of Shakespeare or Milton
or Washington Irving. Rather they experiment with a wide body of selections and attempt to use the pieces best suited for the particular student.

In experimentation, they have found that the body of modern literature
written by serious writers for the adolescent audience usually produces a
greater impact than the literature designated as classic. John Tunis' book
Go Team Go tells of a championship basketball team in an Indiana town.
The members decide they are invincible and indispensable. When one of
the quintet is disqualified from playing because he has been serving as
a "bookie" among the high school students, the other members of the team
resign in protest. They are sure that the school cannot exist without their
teamwork on the basketball court. The story details the psychological
struggle of one boy to evaluate the situation in which he finds himself.
Such a story and its implications lead to a far more penetrating and
valuable discussion for the immature reader than do the problems in
Hamlet, for example, or those in *The Vision of Sir Launfal.*

The most forward-looking programs in the country, therefore, are
selecting literature for the effect a particular selection may have on
students rather than because of its position on an abstract scale of literary
merit. This has meant the use of an increasing amount of contemporary
American material and a greater dependence on the works of writers for

the teen-ager. The objective set up is not knowledge of so-called classics, but increased understanding of oneself, one's culture, and humanity in general.

What Should Be Done About Reading Skills? In the past, it was assumed that a child learned to read in the elementary school and that he would make use of this skill in many areas of the secondary school. When only a limited number of young people could attend secondary schools, this assumption was partially valid. Students who could not read by the time they reached the seventh or eighth grade were failed and forced to leave school. But, with the change in school population, the apparent reading difficulties of students have become more evident. Often the reading skill in a single class will differ by as much as an eight-year range of ability. Yet this does not indicate that in all cases the variation is caused by students' retardation or need of remedial help. Most of them are reading up to their own potentialities; in other words, they are reading at the capacity that their native intellect permits. Only 10 to 15 per cent of the youngsters in a typical school are actually remedial cases in the sense that their difficulties can be remedied. It is possible for all students to improve in their basic reading abilities through a sensibly administered program, but under no circumstances can the group be made homogeneous.

Most of the newer anthologies have contributed to reading-skills programs by the direction of their discussion questions and suggested activities that follow a selection. The danger in such a program is that literature may become a mere tool to point out reading problems, just as at one time in the past it was used to demonstrate grammatical structures. Another approach is the use of reading workbooks or continuations of the basic readers. But the objection to such a program is that it takes reading practice completely out of normal context; student interest flags when a skill is practiced simply by itself, and the program defeats itself.

The program that seems most sensible, not only for students but also for teachers, is one in which the teaching of reading is the concern of all the teachers in the school. Thus, as problems of interpretation come up in science, mathematics, or homemaking classes, teachers of these subjects help the students tackle the special reading problems in those courses. Thus, reading emphasis takes its rightful place as a means to an end—understanding—not an end in itself. The English teacher should help students attack reading problems presented in recreational reading including magazines and newspapers; the teacher of mathematics gives help in the problems in reading mathematics or interpreting equations; and the social studies teacher gives instructions in how to read maps, graphs, and charts. The range of reading situations that occur in a typical secondary school is so great that the concerted efforts of teachers in the various subject areas are needed to make the different skills understandable. Students with differing abilities need materials with differing levels of difficulty if they are to achieve the set objectives.

More and more schools are instituting special classes in remedial reading under the jurisdiction of a full-time expert. Students are usually assigned to such classes on the basis of their scores on a standardized reading test. The school sets a somewhat arbitrary cutting score. The personnel of the classes are usually retarded intellectually as well as in reading. Since in many schools this class supplants the usual English class for these students, it becomes, in effect, a homogeneously grouped section in which the students stay for their whole senior high career. One cannot help questioning the wisdom of having students who will make little use of reading throughout their adult lives give all their attention to developing this skill at the expense of other phases of English.

Developmental reading, improvement of the reading skills of all students, is becoming fairly common in the junior high schools of the country. Frequently, a unit of four to six weeks is devoted to a frontal attack on reading problems in each of the junior high school grades. Often teachers work with prepared kits of material by means of which individual weaknesses and reading levels are diagnosed and then each child works with the section of the kit that helps remedy his weaknesses. In Andrews, Texas, junior high school students and their English teacher move into a reading laboratory for a six-week period each year. This laboratory is under the direction of a reading expert. With two teachers simultaneously working with the group, it is possible to have subgroups of students working on different reading difficulties.

In a very few schools, a true reading clinic or laboratory is set up to which a student may be assigned or to which he may go of his own choice. A teacher may find a student with a specific reading handicap and assign that student to the laboratory for as long as it may take him to improve upon, or conquer, his difficulty. This may be a week, a month, or the whole year. An expert works with the young person on an individual basis to solve his particular problem.

What Is To Be Done About Teaching Language and Grammar? Perhaps the biggest change in the teaching of English in the twentieth century is now in the making through the efforts of the modern linguist. American schools have long held to the belief that the short cut to facility in the use of language was *grammar*. This belief is a carry-over from the eighteenth-century grammarians, interested in regulating the language, who foisted on the public the notion that knowledge of grammar automatically increases an individual's ability to express himself. What teachers have seldom realized is that the grammatical system used by the old grammarians was simply borrowed from the Latin language and imposed upon the English language. But the two languages have only rudimentary points in common, so the results are as strange as attempting to describe a scientific formula in the vocabulary of an artist. Investigations in the early part of the century showed that facility in this Latinate grammar did not materially improve ability to write, to speak, to learn either English or a foreign language, or to develop logical thinking.

Quietly but surely, the linguists of the twentieth century have discovered more and more about the nature of language in general and the English language in particular. From their work have come the first attempts in the history of the English language to write its own grammar. The thinking of modern grammarians is similar in many respects to that of modern mathematicians. Six times nine still produces a product of fifty-four, but the approach to this conclusion is different. Students are taught the processes by which the answer was obtained so that, whenever the memorized fact escapes them, they can follow the logcial processes to the answer. The new grammars still deal with such common concepts as that of the sentence, noun, verb, modifier, and the like, but the approach to them is different. Instead of simply memorizing the definition that a noun is the name of a person, place, or thing, students are shown what positions in a sentence a noun will occupy and how its structure may change. Thus, if the memorized definition fails him, the student can determine whether or not a word is a noun by its position. There are, at present, two new descriptions of the language: one is called "structural grammar," the other is known as "transformational grammar."

It now seems certain that the present Latinate system of grammar will rapidly die, since few major institutions of higher learning still teach it. Obviously one of the newer systems will eventually become the standard of the English language. The impact of this new grammar on the secondary schools is still uncertain. Where the new grammars are being taught, teachers report that the material is both interesting to students and teachable for the staff, neither of which has been true with the Latinate grammar. What the effect will be on the expressional abilities of students is still open to question, but most linguists feel that knowledge of grammar will not automatically increase a student's ability to handle language. Some even advocate the teaching of linguistic material as a humanistic study not only as showing the patterns and changes of language but also as an indicator of human personality, giving youngsters an essential key to self-knowledge.

In present curriculum thinking, there is a strong tendency to use information about language and its operation as an area of content, often beginning in the upper elementary grades and continuing throughout the secondary schools. Units are structured around such things as the history of language, the American dialects, semantics, and the structure of language. The Portland Public Schools are experimenting with a series of such units. This material is not intended to produce changes in the student's use of language, but rather to give him a understanding of the language he uses as information important for its own sake.

How Should Spelling Be Taught? Spelling continues to be a bugaboo in most school systems, not because of its intrinsic importance, but because it is so often used as a measure to judge the outcome of instruction. Spelling programs can be planned in a more definite fashion in the curriculum than any of the other areas in English, providing the department will make use of the pertinent research findings.

Basically, spelling must be taught according to the principle of diminishing returns. Obviously, teachers cannot assume as an objective teaching students how to spell all or even half of the approximately 500,000 words of the language. In selection, the vocabulary most used by the majority of the people is the obvious criterion. Research has determined that a list of about 2,500 words comprises 95 per cent of the average person's written vocabulary. The other 5 per cent is made up of technical or professional words peculiar to a small group. Thus, the schools may set out with relative security to teach students the correct spelling of a basic list of words.

Research indicates that it is most profitable to have regular spelling periods, of fifteen minutes duration two or three times a week throughout the junior high school years, rather than one long period once a week. Throughout the elementary school and the junior high school, a student should have practice on the 2,500 words. In the senior high, each English teacher needs periodically to determine which words on the basic list are still troubling students. Drill in the senior high should be individualized and confined to the words on the basic list that the student has not mastered. Such a systematized program reduces considerably the wasted energy now expended in trying to teach students random lists of words, and it gives the schools definite material to present to parents, boards of education, and businessmen about the spelling program.

Should the Language Arts Be Fused or Separate? It has been traditional in language-arts programs to isolate particular aspects for concentrated and individual study. In three out of four high schools today, composition and grammar are taught one semester of each year and literature in the alternate one. Speech activities are often presented in separate elective courses taken by only a few students. Some school systems require two semesters of speech work, one at the junior high school level and the other in senior high. Reading is taught in a few junior high schools as a separte subject. Many schools that do not follow these semester divisions of the language arts do use a plan of alternating units, for example, grammar for a week, spelling for a week, reading skills for a week, and so on through the semester.

The trend for many years has been steadily away from such practices. The most forward-looking programs recognize that a single language skill is almost never performed in an isolated fashion in life. One moves from one language activity to another in a rapidly changing pattern. For this reason, experts have suggested that the various aspects of language are so interrelated that they are best taught in a unified pattern rather than in isolation.

At its simplest and most traditional, the pattern of fusion might be set up in the teaching of English much as it is almost universally used in foreign-language instruction. Here, the texts begin with a reading assignment, and out of this reading grow assignments in conversation, discussion, vocabulary building, grammatical considerations, and com-position work.

At its best, integration of the language arts involves the unit plan of organization. The curriculum is planned as a series of ideas or undertak-ings that students will explore through the media of the language arts. The unit focus will provide the content about which students will read, write, speak, and listen. In the background, the teacher will help direct the communication activities so that students are constantly refining their skills.

For example, a tenth-grade group of students may decide to study "people under pressure" as a center of interest. They begin by planning what they want to do. Next, they organize themselves into a number of discussion groups, each attacking a different facet of the subject, and each gaining practice in arriving at a decision through the medium of discussion. Sometimes, students may decide to organize their study by having each group read a different type of literature: fiction, drama, poetry, or biography. The purpose of such a division would be to see how authors using different media of writing show people's behavior in situations of pressure. They may be led to draw up a questionnaire to submit to schoolmates about their reactions under the pressure of a sports event, a test, or an irate parent. Here they will be forced to use oral language situations. They may decide to invite a judge or psychologist to give expert opinion on the subject. The issuance of the invitation, the introduction of the speaker, the thank-you note—all provide language experiences.

In such a unit, students are called upon again and again to participate in the language activities of daily life. The teacher uses each opportunity that arises for review of the technique involved or to point out difficulties inherent in its performance. The skill is thus learned, not as an end in itself, but rather as a means to attaining the kinds of goals that one seeks to attain in life.

While there is increasing evidence to show that the language arts are most effectively developed through the patterns of interrelationships created by the unit technique of teaching, there has been a developing suspicion of the whole unit concept of teaching in English. Such suspicion probably arises because many of the early advocates of unit teaching, especially the "core enthusiasts," recognized the validity of only one type of unit. Some advocated entire courses of study built around personal-problem-type units. They wanted to deal with such things as "getting along in a family," "getting along in a group," or "growing up." Others advocated just as enthusiastically, units built only on social needs: "minority groups," "international understanding," "rural-urban contrasts," or "conservation of resources." Parents and students alike were often confused and asked, "Is this English?" In recent years, curriculum workers have tried to find centers for unit construction that are peculiarly related to the subject matter of English. Such centers can be roughly categorized into three types:

1. *Fact-centered Units.* Such units use a body of factual information within the purview of English as the center for reading, writing, speaking, and listening practice. A unit on any one of the mass media of communication is such a fact-centered unit. Increasingly, such units are constructed around the nature, history, and operation of language. Units on the major literary genres—the short story, the novel, drama, poetry, biography—are often fact-centered units. Occasionally units are designed around intensive reading of a single author's works or perhaps the works of a particular school of writers. Depending upon the care the teacher uses in constructing them, these studies may have great significance.

2. *Project-centered Units.* A project undertaken by a whole class or a group within the class may give students a vital educational experience besides giving unity to their practice of the language arts. Traditional projects have been the writing of a research paper, an autobiography, or a short story. Several weeks' time is devoted to a careful consideration of the problems involved, culminating in the production of each individual's particular piece of work. In addition, many teachers with greater imagination have found other projects most exciting and worthwhile. A class may prepare a manual of recreational facilities in their community

for distribution to other students in the school. Some classes have written a history of the school or community as a cooperative venture with other groups. In some cases, a class has been given fifty dollars from the school library budget to use for books they feel will be valuable for the library to add. This means a four- to six-week period of reading and evaluating books before a selection can be made. Junior high school teachers have frequently found that having students build poetry notebooks of their favorite poems is a valuable project.

3. *Idea-centered units.* English as a subject deals with the whole range of human experience, for books are records of how sensitive human beings have evaluated themselves, life, other people, and experiences. It seems highly desirable, therefore, to give a part of the program to the direct presentation and discussion of major human thoughts and feelings. In junior high school, this may eventuate in units organized around such ideas as "the call of adventure," "exploring the supernatural," "man and animals," or "the delight in sensation." In the senior high schools, units might center on such subjects as "men in crises," "the feeling of loneliness," "the right to be different," or "the search for significance."

A good course of study for today's schools would probably be a carefully planned sequence of all three types of units. Each unit, of course, would involve some reading, some writing, and some oral language activity. Each, in turn, would necessitate drill in spelling certain words, presentation of new vocabulary concepts, and discussion of specific problems in the mechanics of language. Thus, throughout the sequence, there can be both progress and repetition, without monotony.

Because the problem is somewhat remote from the immediate goals of adolescents, units organized around a particular skill do not seem educationally productive. Frequently, teachers will attempt a unit on punctuation, letter writing, spelling, or getting the central meaning in reading. No one questions that these skills are important, but they are best developed in relationship to other activities rather than by a frontal attack.

How Are Textbooks Used? From the period of the 1920's to the present, the English course of study has been dictated largely by the textbooks purchased by the school system for the department. These have usually consisted of two kinds of books; an anthology of literature and a composition-and-language book. The structure of the sets of books determined the structure of the courses that were offered. Because the literature and language materials were presented in two separate sets of books, the courses tended to preserve this separation. Recently, there has been a significant trend away from the use of sets of textbooks. Many schools have been supplementing a basic text with paperbound sets of individual works or specialized collections. A wide diversity of material for instruction in reading has supplanted the basic-reader type of book in the junior high school. Schools now are able to plan programs and then find materials suited to their objectives. English teachers, therefore, have far more freedom in setting up sensible programs than they had in the past.

Should Language Instruction Be Confined to English Classes? One of the most promising movements today in the language arts is the assumption by all teachers of responsibility for the language development of boys and girls. In all classes, teachers are beginning to teach the vocabulary and the spelling of words peculiar to their subject area, and some may call to individual students' attention their oral and written language mistakes, occasionally bringing up to the entire class those that seem to be common ones. Many teachers recognize that reading is a series of relatively discrete skills that are often related closely to one particular subject area. Propaganda techniques, reference skills, and judging the authoritativeness of reading material are frequently taught now in social studies classes. Social studies, science, and homemaking teachers increasingly introduce students to imaginative literature that centers on their subject-matter field, in order to give living flesh to the bones of their content. Commercial teachers include units, if not whole courses, on the use of business English, the letter form, and punctuation. Much of the work in distributive-education classes deals with practicing the language one will use on the job. Many English departments set up standards for student work and consistently hold students to acceptable form in written and oral activities in all their various classes.

In many schools, teachers are finding that the cocurricular activities of the school provide the laboratory for meaningful practice of language activities. All clubs utilizing parliamentary procedure offer practice in the democratic means of solving problems through discussion. Student forums sponsored by social-science clubs or by the student council give further practice in discussion techniques. The newspaper, annual, assembly committee, and dramatics club offer valid opportunities for practice in writing and speaking. The FTA, FFA, and FHA clubs, through their local and national organizations, provide students with a place and reason to use language in a controlled situation. In many states, for example, the FFA organization has state contests in the oral presentation of facts pertinent to groups of farmers of the neighborhood. Entrants gain considerable practice in the formal speech situation.

What Is the Status of Combined Courses? In the early years of the elementary schools, there is little separation of the language arts from the other areas of the child's learning experience. The program is a series of undertakings necessitating many different skills and learnings that the teacher brings in casually as the program unfolds. Later in the elementary schools, a period called English may be a regular part of each day's instruction. But, even here, the teacher's firsthand information of the kinds of goals the student is striving to attain throughout his school day helps to serve as a point of reference in directing specific drills or explanations in the use of language. Reports on social studies or science projects are used as the content for class discussion of use of research tools, organization of materials, and giving of oral presentations. Punctuation and usage drills frequently find their content in the language problems students have demonstrated in their actual language use. Even the literature that students read subtly reinforces interests in other subject-matter areas.

Theoreticians have long realized that language and literature are not matters of form alone. Language form is inextricably bound up with ideas, experiences, and emotions. Literature is a patterned structuring of the infinite richness of human life. Discussion of literature almost inevitably leads into discussions of social problems, human relationships, or personal values. When students read, write, and speak, they necessarily must have something to read, write, and speak about.

Out of such thinking has come the experimentation in fusing instruction in English with one or more of the other subjects in the curriculum. The most usual combination has been with the social studies, although the fine arts and the sciences have sometimes been used. There was a growing movement in this direction during the thirties and forties, but interest waned during the fifties, although there has been a slight revival in this direction recently. Such programs are ordinarily best established at the junior high school level, particularly in grades seven and eight. However, senior high schools frequently have honors classes that utilize the basic idea of fused content. In Cedar Rapids, Iowa, the eleventh-grade program is entitled "The American Heritage" and combines American literature with American history. Several senior honors courses are organized as courses in the humanities that combine music, art, and literature.

In an unusually successful program in the laboratory school at Kansas State College, in Emporia, students and teachers examine copies of several different social studies books and several different English books designed for seventh-grade students. Using these as a point of departure to gain insight into what professional writers think should be included at this grade level in the two subject areas, the students drew up a list of the topics they would like to study. This list is sent home for parent additions or changes. Out of this preliminary work comes the definition of a dozen or so major blocks of content for the year's work. The teacher then works with the students on a project outline, to plan the work for each block. Trying to think through the program, they discuss the reading that should be done on the topic, the kind of writing and oral activities that would be feasible, what spelling words might be useful, how vocabulary should be tackled, the language mechanics that might be studied, and how reference study should be set up. This plan for selection of the topics accomplishes several things: It allows for some units that are primarily centered in social studies content, such as "Rivers and How They Were Formed" and others that are primarily centered on English content, such as "The Lure of Adventure." In practice such units give the students a clear-cut picture of the relationship between the content they are studying and the language skills they are trying to master.

Experimental evidence seems to show that students gain as great proficiency in language skills in such areas as spelling, punctuation, and composition when taught in core courses as they do in separate English courses. They seem to gain far more in unmeasurable aspects of the program, such as their ability to define and solve problems, their enthusiasm for the class, their use of reference tools, and their general maturity.

QUESTIONS, PROBLEMS, AND ISSUES FOR FURTHER THOUGHT

1. Discuss the shortcomings of English instruction in the nineteenth and early twentieth centuries with regard to the needs of present-day students of English.
2. Discuss the basic assumptions that underlie the objectives of a modern program in English. What has been the basis for these assumptions, and how do they differ from earlier assumptions regarding the English program?
3. Discuss the relative strengths and weaknesses of the various attempts to provide for individual differences in the English program. Indicate in your discussion which of the methods bodes best for the welfare of both student and teacher, and give the reasons for your selection.
4. Discuss the basic assumption that underlies the literature program outlined under "What Kind of Literature Should Be Taught?" (pp. 410–411). Compare this assumption with nineteenth-century assumptions about the purpose of literature in the secondary school.
5. What seem to be the major advantages of modern linguistics over traditional grammar? Discuss the possible effects of modern linguistics upon the purpose and objectives of the teaching of grammar in the secondary school.
6. Discuss the problems relevant to the teaching of reading skills in the high school. In your discussion, consider how reading skills might be most effectively developed within the framework of the typical English classroom and the problems that may result.
7. Teacher A teaches spelling through the use of a word list, making students responsible for about seventy words a week throughout the school year. Teacher B uses only about twenty-five words per week, drawn largely from spelling errors in the written work of the students. Discuss the relative merits and weaknesses of both approaches and the basic assump-

tions about the teaching of spelling that are characteristic of each approach.

8. Discuss the advantages of integrating the language arts rather than teaching them separately. What considerations with regard to individual students and the class as a whole need to be made before deciding upon the type and topic of the unit, if the unit method of teaching is to be used?

9. Discuss the effect of textbooks upon the English curriculum, and the problems which have occurred as a result of their use. In what ways might textbooks be used so as to eliminate their influence upon curriculum formation?

10. Several problems that continue to face the teaching of English are mentioned in this chapter. Select any one of them, and discuss it, indicating ways in which it might be approached and the issues involved.

SUPPLEMENTARY MATERIALS

Selected Readings

Baughman, M. Dale. "Special Reading Instruction in Junior High Schools," *Clearing House,* XXXV (March, 1961), 394–97.

Evans, William H. "Composition, Reading, and the Conant Report," *The High School Journal,* VIII (May, 1963), 268–78.

Fraser, Dorothy M. *Current Curriculum Studies in Academic Subjects.* Washington, D.C.: National Education Association of the United States, 1962. Chapter 4, "English Language Arts," 43–51.

Haugh, Oscar M. "Developing a Course of Study in English in the Small High School," *University of Kansas Bulletin of Education,* XVII (May, 1963), 127–32.

LaBrant, Lou. "High School English Today: A Brief Overview," *Bulletin of the N.A.S.S.P.,* No. 282 (April, 1963), 52–61.

Morelock, Charles F. "Journalism Teaching in Kansas High Schools," *University of Kansas Bulletin of Education,* XVII (May, 1963), 121–26.

National Society for the Study of Education. *Development in and Through Reading.* Sixtieth Yearbook, Part I. Chicago: University of Chicago Press, 1961. Chapters 17, 18. Reading programs in junior and senior high schools.

Audio-Visual Materials

Film

Teenagers Will Read. McGraw-Hill Text-Films. 26 minutes.

21

The Foreign Languages

RECENT INCREASES IN ENROLMENTS

No branch of the secondary school curriculum has experienced a more dramatic reversal of enrolment trends since 1950 than the foreign languages. At mid-century, only 21.5 per cent of the public high school population were enrolled in foreign-language classes: French, 4.7 per cent; German, 0.8 per cent; Latin, 7.8 per cent; and Spanish, 8.2 per cent. In 1960, the corresponding percentages were 29.3 per cent for the ancient and modern languages combined: 8.6 per cent in French, 1.7 per cent in German, 7.6 per cent in Latin, and 10.8 per cent in Spanish.[1] In addition, over 9,600 pupils in some 500 high schools were studying Russian in 1960, as compared with almost none ten years before.

However, one has to go back to 1910—a full half-century—to find the "golden age" of foreign-language teaching in the United States. In that year, 83.3 per cent of the high school population were enrolled in a second language—the highest figure recorded in the past six decades. The period 1948–1954 represented the low point in foreign-language teaching. During those years, the percentage fell to 21.5—little more than a fourth of the 1910 high.

---

[1] J. Wesley Childers, "Foreign Language Offerings and Enrollments in Public Secondary Schools, Fall 1960," *PMLA*, Vol. 77 (September, 1962), 11–30.

A comprehensive as well as highly detailed summary of enrolment trends in foreign languages in elementary schools, secondary schools, junior colleges, and four-year colleges and universities, both public and private, is contained in *Reports of Surveys and Studies in the Teaching of Modern Foreign Languages* (New York: Modern Languages Association of America, 1961), pp. 1–126. For enrolments in languages studied by less than 1 per cent of the secondary school population (Hebrew, Italian, Russian, Swedish, etc.), see especially pages 28 and 30. For current enrolments, see periodic subsequent reports.

Despite the recent reversal of trends, the foreign languages have far from regained the position in secondary education that they occupied a half-century ago. As William R. Parker has indicated, the enrolment figure of 19.1 per cent recorded by the modern foreign languages in the fall of 1959 "almost restores modern foreign language study to the status it enjoyed about 1934, when language teachers were pronouncing the situation desperate."[2] Fortunately, the figures tell only part of the story. The reversal of enrolment trends since 1950 is actually more dramatic than the gain of only 7.8 per cent between 1948 and 1960 would seem to show.

The fact is that the increase in foreign-language enrolments has exceeded the growth in the total school population at all levels of schooling. For example, within just one year (1958–1959), the foreign-language enrolment in public secondary schools alone increased six times as much as the high school population generally.[3] At the college level, the increase was twice that of the total college population during 1958, 1959, and 1960. At the elementary school level, the gain has been equally pronounced. Well over a million children were learning a second language in kindergarten and the elementary grades in 1962.[4] All told, close to 3 million high school students were taking foreign languages in 1959–1960.

The Growing Demand for Languages. The gain in foreign-language enrolments noted in the preceding paragraphs is commonly attributed to six factors. Since these factors are themselves growing in strength and scope, it is not unreasonable to assume that they will contribute to even greater gains in foreign-language enrolments in the future.

Increasing international travel. Approximately 1.7 million American citizens went overseas in 1960. Counting tourists to Mexico and Canada, the total probably exceeded three million.

Increasing numbers of United States citizens in residence abroad. In recent years, some 1.4 million Americans have been living abroad for extended periods.[5] Owing to the increased need in languages in the armed forces, the Army Language School at the Presidio of Monterey, California, alone has graduated close to 30,000 students in more than twenty languages taught by over 400 instructors. Because of the growing need in languages on the part of private citizens, as well as of representatives of business concerns with interests abroad, the Berlitz Schools of Languages —the best known of the commercial schools in the United States—in-

[2] William R. Parker, *The National Interest and Foreign Languages* (3d ed.) (Washington, D.C.: U.S. Government Printing Office, 1962), p. 25.
[3] Donald D. Walsh, "The MLA FL Program in 1961," *PMLA,* Vol. 77 (May, 1962), 34–38.
[4] Parker, *op. cit.,* p. 18.
[5] *The World Almanac and Book of Facts* (*New York World-Telegram & the Sun,* 1962), p. 251.

creased from eighteen in 1947 to thirty-one in 1962, with an average enrolment of 15,000 annually.

Increasing opportunities for study abroad. The number of Americans participating in foreign study programs now averages 80,000 a year.

Increasing opportunities to make vocational use of foreign languages at home. The growing number of foreign visitors to our shores each year and the expansion of American corporations into foreign markets via subsidiaries abroad have served greatly to increase the occupations in which foreign languages can be put to profitable use at home.[6]

Increasing competition resulting from the Soviet Union's use of foreign languages as instruments of propaganda.[7] In just one year (1959), the Soviet Union published 16,000 book titles in sixty-eight languages. In the same year, the United States published a mere 176 book titles in only seventeen languages—less than one per cent of the Russian effort. It is estimated that 300 million copies of Lenin's works alone have been issued, about six times the number of copies of the Scriptures distributed by the American Bible Society. Some observers find here the reason that more people now visit Lenin's tomb in Moscow each year than journey to Jerusalem, Bethlehem, and Mecca combined.

Increasing support of foreign-language study by educational foundations and the federal government. From 1952 to 1958, the Modern Language Association of America received grants totaling $235,000 from the Rockefeller Foundation, to promote foreign-language teaching. By enlistment of the support of national leaders in many walks of life, the need for foreign-language study was brought to public attention through articles in mass-circulation magazines, editorials in newspapers, and commentaries on radio and television.

An important result of the Association's efforts was the inclusion of the modern foreign languages along with the sciences and mathematics in the National Defense Education Act of 1958. Among other things, this act provides (1) substantial stipends to qualified teachers willing to attend institutes to improve both their command of foreign languages and their skill in teaching them, (2) low-interest loans to college students desiring to master a modern foreign language—especially one not commonly taught in school, and (3) grants covering up to half the cost of language laboratories and audio-visual equipment. Between 1958 and 1961, nearly $30 million were spent under the act to promote foreign-language study.

[6] See the *Wall Street Journal*, New York, June 14, 1962, p. 1.
[7] Nicholas DeWitt, *Education and Professional Employment in the USSR* (Washington, D.C.: National Science Foundation, 1961), 114–116.

OFFERINGS

Scope. Listed in descending order of the percentage of the total high school population enrolled in them, the foregin languages most commonly taught in American public secondary schools are Spanish, French, Latin, and German. Languages studied by less than 1 per cent of the nation's high school youth are growing in number but are still found only in a few communities (for example, Swedish in Rockford, Illinois; Arabic in the Bountiful High School, Bountiful, Utah; and Chinese in the Bonneville High School, Ogden, Utah, and the New Trier Township High School, Illinois—the last-named school offered instruction in eight languages besides English in 1962: Chinese, French, German, Greek, Italian, Latin, Russian, and Spanish).

In the non-public secondary schools, the percentage of the total student population taking foreign languages is close to three times as great as in the public schools—82.5 per cent as compared with 29.3 per cent.[8] In the independent schools, the most widely taught foreign languages are, in descending order of popularity, Latin, French, Spanish, and German. It is interesting to note that Latin outranks all other languages in the private secondary schools, and all but Spanish in the public high schools. In a few states (for example, Indiana and Mississippi), Latin is still the most widely taught foreign language.

Because of changes in the content and methodology of foreign-language teaching in recent years and the widespread introduction of foreign-language classes in elementary schools, tryout courses providing an introduction to several languages (for example, "General Language") are no longer as common in junior high schools as they were before 1950. For the same reasons, "culture courses" taught primarily in English and placing the major stress on the arts, customs, geography, etc., of a foreign country have lost rather than gained popularity.

Although most secondary schools are willing to offer four or more years of a foreign language whenever enrolments justify advanced classes, the study of foreign language is still commonly limited to two years, in grades nine and ten. For this situation, three reasons are commonly advanced: (1) the small size of many of the nation's secondary schools—the majority of which have total enrolments of less than 500; (2) the fact that between 30 and 35 per cent of teen-agers drop out of school when they reach age sixteen, thus further reducing the number of pupils available for advanced courses; and (3) the high rate of discontinuance of

[8] *Reports of Surveys and Studies in the Teaching of Modern Foreign Languages,* p. 37. See note 1, page 422.

language study on the part of students upon completion of the two years of work commonly required for admission to a university. Between 30 and 40 per cent of pupils beginning a foreign language drop it by the end of the first year; at the end of the second year more than 70 per cent have dropped out.[9] This leaves few candidates for advanced courses in small schools or in languages (regardless of size of school) in which first-year enrolments are limited.

James B. Conant's recommendation that third- and fourth-year offerings be provided regardless of class size[10] has led to increases in enrolments in advanced courses, principally in the larger high schools. Further increases await implementation of his suggestion that small schools be combined to make advanced offerings economically feasible through the increased enrolments that consolidation usually ensures.

Grade Placement. As in previous decades, the ninth grade is the level at which the large majority of American young people begin the study of a second language. In the elementary schools, the most frequent starting levels are grades three, four, and five. However, less than 4 per cent of the nation's elementary school children are as yet enrolled in foreign-language classes.

Although few junior high schools offered classes in French, German, Latin, or Spanish below the ninth grade during the 1940's and 1950's, the reintroduction of offerings in grades seven and eight has been widespread in recent years. During the year between September, 1959, and Sptember, 1960, the enrolment in these grades increased 49.9 per cent to a total of 173,171 pupils. The reintroduction of foreign languages in the first two years of the junior high school has been motivated in many cases by the desirability of accommodating pupils who wish to continue study of the languages they have taken in the lower elementary grades.

THE PLACE AND OBJECTIVES OF THE STUDY OF FOREIGN LANGUAGES

Common Questions Regarding Foreign-Language Study. In discussions of the place of foreign languages in the curriculum, four questions are raised more frequently than others: Who should study foreign languages? Which language should be studied? What benefit may be derived from foreign-language study? When should one begin to study a foreign language? After extensive consultation, the Modern Language Association

[9] *Reports of Surveys and Studies in the Teaching of Modern Foreign Languages,* pp. 22–23. See note 1, page 422.

[10] James B. Conant, *The American High School Today* (New York: McGraw-Hill Book Co., Inc., 1958), p. 69.

of Southern California issued a bulletin containing the following concise answers to these queries:

Who should study foreign languages?

Everyone who is interested in a first-hand knowledge of other peoples.

Everyone who plans to travel in a foreign country.

Everyone of foreign ancestry who wishes to understand his parent's traditions more completely.

Everyone who is likely to associate with foreign people.

Everyone who is interested in the root meanings of English words and idioms.

Everyone who wants to understand the sources of American culture.

Everyone who expects to continue academic studies beyond the Bachelor's degree.

Everyone who aspires to a career in foreign trade or government foreign service.

Everyone who plans to enter a learned profession.

Which language should be studied?

For community advantage: The languages of large sections of the local population: Spanish, German, Italian and others.

For awareness of foreign contribution to English language and culture: Latin, Greek, French, German, Italian, Spanish, Portuguese.

For proficiency in many major fields, in the new area curricula, in advanced study and research: Western European, Slavic, and Oriental languages.

For higher degrees and professional schools: Languages specified in official bulletins of colleges and universities.

What benefit may be derived from foreign language study?

The pleasure of being able to speak and read the foreign language.

Understanding the foreign elements in our speech and culture.

Improving relations with people of foreign ancestry.

Appreciating the ideas and traditions of other countries.

Enjoying personal contacts while traveling abroad.

Qualifying for positions overseas.

Delight in first-hand acquaintance with literary treasures of the world.

Satisfaction in attaining a traditional requisite of a liberal education.

Preparation for advanced study of research.

When should one begin to study a foreign language?

Before one's imitative faculty begins to decline.

Before youthful self-consciousness begins to hamper expression.

Before actual need arises; several years are required for mastery.

Before reaching the college level where many departments recommend a reading knowledge of a foreign language.

Before selecting a major, because a second foreign language is frequently recommended or required.

At the earliest opportunity offered in the school curriculum.[11]

[11] *Bulletin, Spring 1952, of the Modern Language Association of Southern California, Inc.*

Contribution of Foreign-Language Study to the Needs of Youth. In 1947, the National Association of Secondary School Principals of the National Education Association listed ten essential needs that all youths in a democratic society have in common.[12] Excellent statements of the potential contributions, either direct or indirect, of foreign-language study to the satisfaction of these needs are available in numerous courses of study published during the past decade. One of the best statements is contained in the course of study for Russian developed by the Modern Language Department of the University High School, University of Minnesota, under the direction of Professor Emma M. Birkmaier. Here the "imperative needs of youth" and the potential contribution of foreign-language study to their satisfaction are presented concisely in parallel columns.

OBJECTIVES   The Foreign Language department bases its program upon objectives with which the secondary school must concern itself in the development of a sound program for all youth. It examines these objectives to see how the learning of a foreign language implements these objectives.

NEEDS OF YOUTH	IMPLEMENTATION THROUGH THE FOREIGN LANGUAGE PROGRAM
1. All youth need education in the skills and knowledge of their occupations.	The student makes the study of a foreign language, area and civilization his career, or he increases his vocational efficiency by extending the use of his services in his particular vocation through the knowledge of another language and culture.
2. All youth need to develop and maintain good health and physical fitness.	The student acquires knowledge about the health and physical fitness programs in other countries and, if possible, participates in them. He appreciates the wholesome traits of a foreign people, which have a bearing on emotional and physical health and deserve emphasis in our own daily life.
3. All youth need to understand the rights and duties of the citizen, and to be diligent and competent in the performance of their obligations as members of the community and citizens of the state and nation.	The student increases his effectiveness as a citizen of the world. The acquisition of another language as a tool permits the student a kind and quality of relationship which does not exist without such communication [sic]. He participates in the culture of a foreign people *directly* through use of their communication skills, he lives in their houses, eats their foods, joins in their festivals, their work and their play. He wipes out the distinction between "foreigners" and "us."

[12] *The Imperative Needs of Youth,* Bulletin 31 of the National Association of Secondary School Principals of the National Education Association of the United States, March, 1947, p. 2.

NEEDS OF YOUTH	IMPLEMENTATION THROUGH THE FOREIGN LANGUAGE PROGRAM
4. All youth need to understand the significance of the family for the individual and society and the conditions conducive to successful family life.	The student learns about the role the family plays in another culture, the social relationships which exist, the effect these have upon the individual, his particular society and the world.
5. All youth need to know how to purchase and use goods and services intelligently, understanding both the values received by the consumer and the economic consequences of their acts.	The student sees the causal relationships between the physical and social environment [, for example,] the effects of climate and environment on customs, diet, consumption of goods and services, architecture, recreation, etc., and their effect upon the social and economic life of the country.
6. All youth need to understand the method of science, the influence of science on human life.	The student extends the resources at his command for gaining information and solving problems in other areas of learning.

He becomes conscious of the universality of scientific endeavor in discovering facts concerning the nature of the world and of man and of all mankind's strivings for the good life. |
7. All youth need opportunities to develop their capacities to appreciate beauty in literature, art, music, and nature.	The student breaks his culture-bound attitude toward beauty in literature, art, architecture, music and the dance, handicrafts and nature by sharing vicariously and directly in the creative activities of the foreign people. He understands their forms of artistic expression.
8. All youth need to be able to use their leisure time well.	The student extends the scope of his leisure time activities which yield satisfaction and are socially useful. He develops the learning of a foreign language as a hobby or avocational pursuit by such ways as participating in goodwill international organizations, foreign language study groups, travel. He can participate with greater insight in activities and programs of his community, in the theatre, the opera, ballet, radio and television. He enjoys a greater variety of books, folk-songs, art-songs, magazines and local foreign culture activities.
9. All youth need to develop respect for other persons, to grow in their insight into ethical values and principles, and to work and live cooperatively with others.	The student increases his effectiveness as a citizen of his own country and as a representative abroad. He learns to respect the values and customs of other countries as being as valid as his own. He builds an attitude of open-mindedness.

NEEDS OF YOUTH	IMPLEMENTATION THROUGH THE FOREIGN LANGUAGE PROGRAM
	The student builds a more creative and enlightened way of life by integrating the cultural heritage of another country with his own, by helping the members of his society appreciate the extent to which American culture is indebted to that of other peoples, and the contributions American culture has made to other countries. As a result he appreciates the worth of and treats more fairly his fellow citizens of foreign birth.
10. All youth need to grow in their ability to think rationally, to express their thoughts clearly, and to read and listen with understanding.	The student develops an understanding of the role of language as culture, the functions language performs and cannot perform. He gets direct experience in manipulating the language and becomes skillful in contrasting various language structures.[13]

Objectives in the Teaching of Latin. In Latin, the aural-oral abilities are not stressed to the same degree as in the modern languages. Instead, the time and effort commonly devoted to learning to speak the foreign tongue is devoted in Latin courses to studying the classical backgrounds of Western civilization, to increasing the pupils' English vocabulary through work with Latin prefixes, suffixes, and roots, and to reading in the original the works of Latin authors who have left an indelible impression on the history and culture of the West.

Although modern Latin teaching has been influenced greatly by new resources in the way of audio-visual aids and by recent developments in the field of linguistics (as will be noted in a later paragraph), its objectives differ little, except perhaps in emphasis, from the aims proposed in 1924 by the American Classical League. Adapted in abbreviated form these objectives were:

1. *Primary and Immediate*
   Increased ability to read and understand Latin

2. *Instrumental*
   Increased understanding of those elements in English that are related to Latin
   Increased ability to read, speak, and write English
   Increased ability to learn other foreign languages

3. *Cultural*
   Development of a historical and cultural background
   Development of right attitudes toward social institutions

---

[13] Emma M. Birkmaier, *Russian Language and Civilization: A Four Year Course,* Bulletin No. 1, Modern Language Department, University High School, University of Minnesota, 1958, pp. 1–3. Quoted by permission.

Development of literary appreciation

Elementary knowledge of the simpler principles of language structure

Improvement in the literary quality of the pupil's written English

4. *Disciplinary*

Development of correct mental habits[14]

TRENDS IN FOREIGN-LANGUAGE TEACHING

Recent Developments. Although the aims of foreign-language teaching have remained relatively constant over the years,[15] the degree of emphasis placed on certain objectives as compared with others, and the means for attaining them, have changed noticeably. Among the recent trends in foreign-language teaching, the six described below deserve mention.

Shifts from Reading to Speaking as the Immediate Primary Objective of Modern-Foreign-Language Study in Elementary and Intermediate Classes. Increasing personal contacts with the nationals of other lands (facilitated by marked improvements in the means of transportation and communication) have lead to widespread demands for stress upon the spoken language.[16]

Increasing Use of Audio-visual Aids as Basic Media of Instruction Rather than as Means for Merely Supplementing or Enriching Courses. Thanks mainly to subsidies available under the National Defense Education Act, over 2,500 high schools had installed by 1962 some kind of equipment for recording and reproducing the human voice. Some junior and senior high schools now boast of fully equipped language laboratories.

---

[14] Classical Investigation League, *General Report* (Princeton, N.J.: Princeton University Press, 1924), pp. 78–79.

[15] Compare the statements of values and objectives in this chapter with the statements of earlier years in Algernon Coleman's *An Analytical Bibliography of Modern Language Teaching: 1927–1932* (University of Chicago Press, 1943), pp. 69–73. See also W. V. Kaulfers, *Modern Languages for Modern Schools* (New York: McGraw-Hill Book Co., Inc., 1942), pp. 349–372.

[16] Reading, as was recommended by the famous Modern Foreign Language Study, 1924 to 1927, remained the immediate *primary* (but by no means *exclusive*) objective of modern-foreign-language teaching until World War II. The recommendation was based on returns from a nationwide poll of expert opinion. The majority of the consultants felt that learning to read the literature and published research of other lands would be the most valid general objective for most United States schools and colleges for three reasons: (1) most students were not taking languages long enough to learn to speak them. (2) A few students would go abroad or have occasion to speak to foreign nationals. (3) Mastery of the spoken language is the most difficult of all objectives to attain in large classes, especially if the teacher has more than one or two such classes daily. See Algernon Coleman, *The Teaching of Modern Foreign Languages in the United States* (New York: The Macmillan Co., 1929), p. 107 and *passim*.

In Latin the use of audio-visual aids is almost as extensive as in the modern languages. Following the claims of some linguistic scientists that ability in reading and writing is best achieved via the oral approach, some teachers of Latin are experimenting with oral methods in first-year classes.

Although television has been widely used as a means of teaching foreign languages in the elementary grades, its use to date has been very limited at the high school level.

Increasing Use of Methods Favored by Linguistic Scientists.[17] To date, the linguistic scientists have served greatly to strengthen the arguments of methodologists and textbook writers who have long favored an oral approach in language teaching. They have also greatly strengthened the influence of teachers who, long before the advent of modern linguistics, advocated approaching the learning of a second language through precept and example primarily, that is, through abundant guided practice in close imitation of models or examples, now often called "patterns." In Latin, the influence of modern linguistic science is reflected in the experimental materials developed by Waldo Sweet at the University of Michigan.

Increasing Stress on Area Study Through Audio-visual Aids and Student Travel. Whereas supplementary reading in English once served as the chief medium for such study, learning about the foreign country and its people through the foreign language itself is becoming increasingly possible in the newer "audio-visually aided" language courses.

Excursions, state and regional conventions of foreign-language students, and conducted study-travel tours under school auspices have also increased during the past decade. The annual state conventions of Pan American League Clubs in Illinois have an average attendance of 400 delegates from forty communities. In 1960, the Junior Classical League numbered close to 75,000 students of Latin. In that year, its annual convention in Albuquerque, New Mexico, drew 1,129 teen-agers from forty-six states. Beginning in 1962, the Classical Travellers Guild of Canada even organized private yacht cruises to places famous in Greek and Roman history.

Increasing Cooperation Among Teachers of Foreign Languages. Since 1950, foundation grants and subsidies available under the National Defense Education Act have served to promote conferences on foreign-language instruction, to provide institutes for the in-service training of teachers, and to stimulate publication of the reports of regional and national study groups. Many state associations (as well as some state universities) now issue foreign-language bulletins to facilitate communication among

[17] Parker, op. cit., pp. 74–75.

teachers. Among the newer publications is *The DFL Bulletin* of the Department of Foreign Languages created within the National Education Association in 1961. Between 1958 and 1960, the number of state consultants and supervisors of foreign languages rose from six to fifty. The increase in opportunities for professional consultation, communication, and cooperation has served greatly to stimulate professional growth and morale.

Restoration of College Entrance Requirements in Foreign Languages. Owing to declining high school enrolments in foreign languages between 1915 and 1950, many liberal-arts colleges dropped their entrance requirements in this field. Although more than 85 per cent of the accredited four-year colleges and universities required a foreign language for the bachelor of arts degree in 1962, hardly a third actually required a language other than English for admission. Since 1962, however, at least twenty-six institutions have restored the entrance requirement, and as many more are contemplating such action.

MAJOR CURRENT PROBLEMS

Five unresolved problems still confront the secondary schools, apart from the problem of securing qualified teachers in sufficient numbers to accommodate growing enrolments in foreign-language courses.

Reducing the Rate of Dropout in Foreign-Language Courses. As was indicated earlier, between 30 and 40 per cent of high school beginners in a foreign language discontinue it after one year, and more than 70 per cent by the end of the second year. Many students of the problem believe that this "mortality rate" (while no worse than it typically has been over the past forty years) could be reduced substantially through appropriate curriculum adjustments and more effective guidance and counseling of students.

Providing for Effective Articulation of Curriculums Throughout the Educational System. Pupils who have had a year or more of a foreign language in the elementary grades are now entering secondary schools in growing numbers. Accommodating them in high school classes requires special attention to prevent maladjustments of serious proportions. Placement of transfers on the basis of their previous records and scores on achievement tests has been advanced as a possible solution. In any case, standing coordinating committees for each language, with rotating representatives from each level at which the language is being taught, are a necessity if complications are not to arise.

This problem will require increasing attention as more and more school systems attempt to provide an unbroken sequence of offerings in a foreign language from kindergarten through grade twelve. Although, in 1961, only one public school system in the United States—that of El Paso, Texas—offered a full foreign-language program from the first grade through high school, the number of such systems is expected to increase. According to a bill passed by the California legislature, beginning in 1965 all public school systems of the state must offer at least one foreign language, starting no later than grade six and continuing through high school.

Resolving the Question of Diversification. It has been estimated that over 90 per cent of our foreign-language teaching has nothing to do with 70 per cent of the world's people. For example, Chinese, the most widely spoken of the world's languages, is being taught in no more than forty-eight high schools. Many more of the globe's inhabitants speak Hindustani than speak Spanish, but the former language is absent from the secondary school curriculum. Since approximately 3,000 languages are spoken in the world today, the problem of selection is one of considerable complexity. In the absence of more specific guidelines, the criteria listed below have often been suggested as bases for choosing the languages to be taught. The language that meets the majority of these criteria would normally be given preference over a language that satisfies only one or two.

1. Will knowledge of the language help promote understanding and cooperation among the free nations of the Western community?
2. Will knowledge of the language serve the national interest by meeting the language needs of our Armed Forces, of our expanding international commerce, of our consular and diplomatic service, and of such agencies as the Peace Corps?
3. Will learning the language afford the children of foreign-born parents the opportunity to perfect themselves in the tongue they may have understood and spoken, at least to a limited extent, at home?
4. Will the language attract enough students to make at least a four-year program feasible?
5. Will the language meet the entrance and degree requirements of the colleges to which most of the school's graduates go?
6. Are competent teachers of the language available?

The foregoing criteria obviously assume that highly specialized language needs (for example, knowledge of Yoruba for members of a Peace Corps mission to Nigeria) will be met through intensive language instruction supplied by the employing agency as part of its own training program.

Accommodating Individual Differences. In schools large enough to provide classes sectioned according to abilities, interests, and aptitudes, grouping of students into fast- and slow-moving sections on the basis of intelligence quotients, previous achievement in academic subjects (especially English), or scores on foreign-language-aptitude tests has been tried with varying degrees of success. Because of the limited reliability and validity of these criteria as predictive measures, however, provision for a regrouping of students after a tryout of fifteen weeks to a semester is imperative.

In languages enrolling too few students to permit ability grouping, gifted students have been accommodated in one or more of the following ways:

Through special assignments to enable the academically gifted to progress at their own speed, or to develop such special competence in the language as may be needed to pass college entrance examinations or to satisfy personal ambitions and interests. Programed materials now appearing on the market should facilitate the differentiation of assignments in the years ahead.

Through extra-credit work in the way of special reports, supplementary reading, or projects relating to the life and culture of the people whose language is being studied.

Through appointment as editorial assistants to help in the evaluation of written work, or as consultants to assist members of the class who need special help with pronunciation, oral reading, or specific aspects of grammar.

Through appointment to committees to prepare special programs for the class or foreign language club.

Through promotion to more advanced sections on the basis of periodic guidance-placement tests and personal counseling. In recent years more than 1350 of the nation's secondary schools have been offering one or more college-level courses to selected students of foreign languages and other subjects.[18]

Although retarded pupils can often compete with other students as long as the language is absorbed directly from guided participation in activities involving its use, their handicap becomes increasingly apparent the more the classwork shifts to the conceptual level—that is, to reading, writing, or grammar. For this reason, major emphasis in dealing with the retarded student has usually been placed upon the following:

1. Learning of very short, useful dialog or conversations from scripts suitable for dramatization in class
2. Composition of semioriginal dialogues by recombination of phrases from previously learned conversations
3. Participation in simple competitive games that afford practice in the use of numbers, previously learned vocabulary, or verbs in specific persons or tenses

[18] Walter V. Kaulfers (ed.), *Foreign Language Teaching in Illinois* (Carbondale: Southern Illinois University Press, 1957), pp. 48–51.

4. Dramatization of short stories, anecdotes, or playlets for which appropriate scripts are provided
5. Group singing in the foreign language, using songs that not only have special appeal as music but also present opportunities for dramatization or vocabulary enrichment
6. Avoidance of highly technical work such as formal exercises in translation from English into the foreign language, where such work depends upon mastery of rules phrased in grammatical terms
7. Extensive use of filmstrips, sound films, recordings, and visiting speakers, either to dramatize work in the language itself or to motivate it through the development of interests in the people and country
8. Enlistment of special individual interests and talents in the service of foreign-language study

Because of previous failure in schoolwork, retarded students are likely to be easily discouraged. For this reason, provision of opportunities to win personal recognition and appreciation is one of the surest ways of encouraging individual effort and of maintaining morale favorable to continued learning.[19]

Translating Research in Foreign-Language Teaching into Action. Although no branch of the secondary school curriculum can boast of a greater backlog of competent research into almost every aspect of the learning process than the foreign languages, rarely is this research drawn upon in devising courses of study, textbooks, manuals of methods, or means of evaluating outcomes. Progress in foreign-language teaching is difficult in these circumstances, if progress implies profiting from past experience instead of merely duplicating the errors of former days.

Inasmuch as all the important research of the past forty years is readily available in conveniently summarized form[20] in almost every college library, this neglect need not be inevitable. Expansion of methods courses to allow time for study of the research and its implications would partially remedy present shortcomings. Advanced graduate offerings drawing upon the research could profitably form an integral part of the professional training of specialists in foreign-language teaching from department heads to supervisors or coordinators of instruction.[21]

[19] Walter V. Kaulfers, "Foreign Languages for the Exceptional Child," *Modern Language Form,* Vol. 41 (December, 1956), 112–116.
[20] For example, see the *Analytical Bibliographies* of Algernon Coleman for the years 1927–1942 (Volumes I and II are published by the University of Chicago Press; Volume III is published by the King's Crown Press of Columbia University). See also Chester W. Harris (ed.), *Encyclopedia of Educational Research* (3d ed.) (New York: The Macmillan Co., 1960) and the two preceding editions, by Walter S. Monroe.
[21] See Walter V. Kaulfers, "Retooling the Profession in the Light of Modern Research" *Modern Language Journal,* Vol. 35 (November, 1951), pp. 501–522.

QUESTIONS, PROBLEMS, AND ISSUES FOR FURTHER THOUGHT

1. The chapter discusses five problems requiring solution. Choose one and, through questionnaires or interviews with teachers, find out to what extent and how the problem is being solved in your high school district.
2. Many students who have taken two years of a foreign language as freshmen and sophomores in high school prefer to start over in a new language in college, because they feel their preparation has become too "rusty" for successful work in advanced classes. How is this problem being handled in the colleges most graduates from your community attend?
3. What seem to be the current preoccupations of foreign-language teachers, or the contemporary developments and trends in foreign-language teaching, revealed by the content of the latest six or eight issues of the *Modern Language Journal* or the *DFL Bulletin* of the NEA Department of Foreign Languages?
4. What appear to be the current preoccupations of high school teachers of Latin as revealed by the content of the latest six or eight issues of the *Classical Journal's* department called "The Forum"?
5. Choose a foreign language taught in your high school district, and draw up an annotated requisition of highly recommended basic textbooks, supplementary readers and workbooks, films, recordings, and other teaching aids for use in first (or second or third)-year classes. The *Selective List of Materials* of the Modern Language Association of America will be of help here.
6. What objective published tests are available for use in high school foreign-language courses? Select a language, and draw up an annotated list of the tests that have been reviewed favorably by two or more evaluators in Oscar K. Buros' *Mental Measurements Yearbooks* (New Brunswick, N.J.: Rutgers University Press).
7. How would you evaluate a high school's foreign-language program? Chapter 13 in Kaulfers' *Modern Languages for Modern Schools* (New York: McGraw-Hill Book Co., Inc.) will be of help in formulating criteria.
8. What practices in foreign-language teaching does research show to be the most effective? Using the Index of the *Encyclopedia of Educational Research* (New York: The Macmillan Co., 1960), try to select the most promising practices for developing ability in a specific aspect of a foreign language, such as reading, grammar, vocabulary, or the like.
9. In 1961, a committee of five teachers selected by the Modern Language Association visited 1,011 classes in six foreign languages taught by 747 teachers in 136 school districts of thirty-four states. The "best practices" they witnessed are described in detail in Survey XV of the Association's *Reports of Surveys and Studies in the Teaching of Modern Foreign Languages*. Through questionnaires, classroom visits, or interviews with students and teachers, determine to what extent these "best practices" prevail in the schools of your area.

SUPPLEMENTARY MATERIALS

Selected Readings

Brooks, Nelson. *Language and Language Learning.* New York: Harcourt, Brace & World, Inc., 1960. An excellent discussion of theoretical as well as practical problems involved in modern-foreign-language teaching. Recommended: Chapter 7, "Language and Literature."

Huebner, Theodore. *How To Teach Foreign Languages Effectively.* New York: New York University Press, 1950. A valuable manual of practical suggestions for the novice teacher, especially Chapters 6 ("Grammar") and 7 ("The Lesson").

Kaulfers, Walter V. *Modern Languages for Modern Schools.* New York: McGraw-Hill Book Co., Inc., 1942. Contains substantial chapters on the place and role of the foreign languages in American education, as well as on objectives, measurement and evaluation, and extracurricular activities, in terms of specific, practical illustrations. Recommended: Chapter 16, "Rooting the Foreign Language Curriculum in American Life and Culture."

Méras, Edmond A. *A Language Teacher's Guide.* New York: Harper & Row, 1954. A very useful manual of methods and devices in teaching modern languages, especially French. Chapter 18, "The Language Teacher and the Community."

Modern Language Association of America. *Reports of Surveys and Studies in the Teaching of Modern Foreign Languages.* New York: The Association, 1961. An invaluable reference for data concerning enrolments, teaching practices, etc., in foreign-language teaching from the kindergarten through the university, in both public and independent schools. Recommended for special study: Survey XV, on "best practices" in modern-foreign-language teaching.

———. *Selective List of Materials.* New York: The Association, 1962. Evaluations of nearly 2,000 items (textbooks, reference books, films, dictionaries, tapes, discs, etc.), by 180 consultants representing ten languages.

Parker, William R. *The National Interest and Foreign Languages.* Washington, D.C.: Government Printing Office, 1962. Discusses the current situation in foreign-language teaching and the nation's future needs in this field. Recommended: pages 3–6, on problems and issues for discussion.

Stack, Edward M. *The Language Laboratory and Modern Language Teaching.* Fair Lawn, N.J.: Oxford University Press, 1960. Includes both teaching technique and administrative and mechanical techniques relating to the operation of a language laboratory. See especially Chapter 7, "Classroom Procedures."

Audio-Visual Materials

Films

Language Teaching in Context. Audio-Visual Production Center, Wayne State University, Detroit. 16 mm. 28 minutes. Color.

Principles and Methods of Teaching a Second Language. Teaching Film Custodians, Inc., New York. 16 mm. 15 reels. Black and white. A series of five half-hour sound films on different aspects of foreign-language teaching.

22

Mathematics

THE PLACE OF MATHEMATICS IN THE SECONDARY SCHOOL CURRICULUM

There are two foremost considerations for the selection and organization of the curriculum: (1) purposes of secondary education and the requirements of the pupils in the light of these purposes and (2) the nature of the field and its potential contributions to the culture. Here, the considerations must be broad enough to take into account the needs of various groups with differing capacities and vocational plans, as well as the needs of the society for specially trained individuals. In any case, the term *needs* is to be interpreted broadly to include what is desirable as well as necessary. The curriculum should, for example, meet the utilitarian requirements of the informed person, competent to deal with his personal, family, and community problems and to render to society the services required for the national welfare. It should provide the depth of insight into the nature of the field that is required to maintain growth after formal study is ended and to justify career aspirations in science and technology. Beyond this are the understandings and appreciations essential to the cultured individual in our society. What specific contributions does the field of mathematics have for this variety of goals?

Mathematics is the mode of thinking, planning, and communicating that man has developed in attempting to master his physical, economic, and social environment. Frequently, it is referred to as a part of our language. In the twenty-fifth yearbook of the National Council of Teachers of Mathematics, for example, mathematics is said to be the language of quantity and the language of size.[1] While such categorization

[1] Everett T. Welmers, "Arithmetic in Today's Culture," National Council of Teachers of Mathematics twenty-fifth yearbook, *Instruction in Mathematics* (Washington, D.C.: National Education Association of the United States, 1960), pp. 10–12.

is too narrow to incorporate all aspects of mathematics, it is useful in helping to focus on the true nature of the field.

It would be a mistake, however, to suppose that mathematics was developed purely in response to utilitarian demands. Some fields of mathematics were developed in the process of solving problems arising from games of chance. Other abstract areas have been systematically explored and developed incidentally to what might well be called leisure-time pursuits, while still others are prized by mathematicians as having no utilitarian applications at all.

All of us are aware, on the other hand, of the practical effects of what amounts to a technical revolution on our everyday lives. Since these have given rise to extensive popular concern for the field and to widespread curricular activities, they are worth examining in some detail. As merely one example, consider how technology has influenced the ways in which we may make a living. Human effort has become too valuable to be used except at an intellectual level. Per-capita production rises to the extent that people are used to design and operate machines, rather than to do hand labor. Consequently, we witness a displacement of common labor, then of skilled labor, and then of craftsmen, with an increasing demand for those who can build, operate, and maintain complex and often automatic machinery. While the avenues of employment are closing for the high school dropout, new and exciting careers await those with mathematical competence. This traumatic explosion has brought home to everyone the critical significance of mathematics and its relationship to our national survival. Some of the outstanding consequences of this explosion include

1. The industries and other activities that have grown up around the exploration of space and the development of space transportation

2. Automation of industry, with its effect not only on productivity but also on the displacement of craftsmen and the increased demand for technologically trained employees, which outruns the supply

3. The rapid growth of the electronics industry, supplying products that were unknown a decade ago and creating new vocations in the same brief space of time

4. Explosive developments in the field of digital computers and the science of cybernetics, responsible for their development, which have broken a barrier in the process of mathematical analysis, making it possible to do in a few minutes calculations that a few years ago would have required months

5. The introduction of mathematical operations into the basic problems of national defence, including the whole array of nuclear

weapons, the various warning systems for continental defense, and the system of satellites designed to keep us aware of what is going on

Naturally, an individual who lives in a society where these things are taking place needs to have mathematical understanding simply to understand what is going on. It is not surprising that the significance of mathematics has become dramatically evident to almost everyone. The relationship of technical progress to public welfare and even to our continued existence becomes increasingly a concern for the American people. The danger to the public welfare of the mathematical illiteracy of the adult population is at last being recognized.

From the point of view of mathematics curriculum development, the basic situation is excellent. Expansion is encouraged, and experimentation is supported by federal funds. The danger in the situation lies in the possibility that, with widespread moral and material support, there may be an uncritical acceptance of the idea that the more mathematics the pupil studies, regardless of its nature, the better. Notwithstanding the importance of mathematics in general, there is a need to be selective in building the curriculum. There are always choices to be made from among the rich possibilities available at any level. A guiding philosophy is needed to answer the question: What mathematics should be studied in any given grade, or at any given level? Or, to put it concisely, what is the pupil to study it for? From this practical standpoint, the potential contributions of mathematics to the objectives of the secondary-education curriculum—mental and physical health, citizenship, home living, worthy use of leisure, and vocational efficiency—become evident. It is worthwhile to analyze briefly the manner in which these contributions are made.

Mental and Physical Health. The abilities of the individual to adjust, to adapt, and to maintain control over his environment have always depended to some extent on his mathematical literacy. Today, this dependence is increasingly evident. While the momentum of technical change is still increasing, it is important that the individual should not be overwhelmed and insecure, but rather should be able to profit from our technical resources through his mastery of mathematics.

Citizenship. The time has passed when the responsibilities of mathematics relating to government were encompassed in a few kinds of taxes. The national, state, and local government have imposed on the individual and necessity for decisions in a variety of economic areas. Yet, hardly one person in twenty has the sketchiest idea of how our economy functions. While our country is locked in an economic showdown with world communism and exposed to intense competition from the galloping economies of Western Europe and Japan, this ignorance is intolerable. The voter is compelled at every turn to make decisions that are not only difficult but also critical. We are nagged by such questions as these: What should we do about tariffs, trade, and aid to developing countries? How can we assure jobs for millions of young Americans who will reach the voting age in this decade? Should we vote more money for schools? Should taxes be increased or decreased?

These are the bases for political issues that are making our public increasingly aware that to foster stable economic growth and to avoid peaks and troughs, booms and depressions, are among the voter's personal problems. He is expected to know how we measure economic growth in terms of national production and income, and what constitutes a reasonable rate of growth. And everyone is expected to be familiar with a few statistics and know how to tell at a particular moment whether our economy is doing well or poorly. These are questions that challenge the citizen's mathematical literacy.

Home Living. It is increasingly important that education for home living should be sufficiently broad to include education for consumer responsibility. The individual should understand how a basically private-enterprise system fixes its priorities and uses its resources. He should be aware that it is largely the consumer's desires that determine what is produced and in what quantity and quality.

The problems of the home are complicated by rising incomes and rising tax rates, with a more plentiful supply of intriguing consumer goods. The business affairs of the home extend into several areas. One of these relates to sources of income—the number of jobs and careers in various fields, how opportunities are increasing and decreasing in each field, and the kinds of preparation required for each. Another area is business administration of the home. This includes the expenses of running a home and allocating the income so that it brings in the most satisfaction while at the same time providing protection for present and future income. Another related area that is becoming increasingly important, both to the individual and to society, is that of investment. With rising income levels and greater personal savings, the number of families owning stocks and bonds is steadily increasing. This has become a matter of considerable interest to the Securities and Exchange Commission, since most of the individuals now moving into the stock market are completely uninformed about the procedures and risks they are encountering, and the lack of wisdom they display in handling their affairs presents a serious risk to all other investors.

Vocational Values. Here we may differentiate between the indirect and the direct vocational values of mathematics. The former are the propaedeutic values of secondary mathematics that provide the essential foundation for college work in preparation for scientific and technological careers. Among the direct values is the preparation required for several vocations, some of which are not primarily considered as mathematical. Among these, business is a good example. Mathematical illiteracy caused more than 16,000 business failures in the United States in a recent active business year. The economic ignorance of proprietors of small businesses, contractors, and auto mechanics with the happy intention of being their own bosses had led them to plunge into ventures with little knowledge of cost and credit accounting and business management. Calculations arising from the simplest business transaction can be staggering. It is not surprising that the digital computer is becoming a widely used business machine.

Besides these detailed computations, however, are the broader understandings that are essential to business success and that call for mathematical thinking. The successful businessman needs to know how supply, demand, and prices operate, why competition is essential to the market, and how government activities influence competition and the use of resources. He needs to recognize such basic concepts as labor productivity, the law of diminishing returns, savings, investment, capital formation, and the profit incentive. All of these understandings are mathematical in their nature.

Worthy Use of Leisure. Besides the utilitarian aspects of mathematics with which we have been concerned, there are purely personal values of a recreational or cultural nature. The young child who, enchanted by the rhythm and systematic characteristics of the number system, loves to count and work with numbers already experiences this aspect of mathematics. Among adults, these same qualities have led to systematic investigation of fields of mathematics that have no utilitarian values.

Cultural Values. The cultural values of mathematics have been widely discussed but remain relatively ill defined. One way to view them is in relation to some of the basic truths of human existence that the pupil can come to realize through mathematics, such as the following:

We may all be proud of our heritage from the past; perhaps the finest of the things to which the individual is an heir is the field of mathematics. Its origins are lost in the early shadows of history. The early Sumerians already had a sophisticated body of mathematics before they had a written historical record. Each succeeding culture made its contribution to the field, which has been largely a contribution to the art of living.

Human beings work most effectively as members of a team; the goals and achievements of group effort make individual activities seem trivial. The structure of mathematics incorporates the achievements of many races and nationalities. Some of the individuals we can name, others left no record. Yet all of them contributed to a field that is as international in its scope as were their thought and activities.

The human mind is capable of clear and rational thinking and of brilliant intellectual achievement. Mathematics offers two advantages for exploring and appreciating postulational thinking: It is semantically perfect for expressing relationships, and its findings are objectively verifiable. Whether in abstract relationships or in the hard facts of life, its inevitable logic reveals the potentialities of the human intellect.

Appreciation of beauty is an experience that makes life worthwhile. Mathematics opens the way to appreciation both in the field itself and in its applications. With maturity, the pupil may come to appreciate beauty in the elegance, simplicity, and power of the field itself, in the symmetry, proportion, and conformation of the world around us, and in the clarity and penetration typical of the mathematical mode of thinking.

There is nothing automatic in the achievement of the cultural or other objectives through study of mathematics. They come, if at all, through planned experiences in many situations and in various settings, but they never come without clear direction and guidance.

THE JUNIOR HIGH SCHOOL PROGRAM

Special Functions. Outcomes in each of the general areas just outlined are important at all school levels. In addition, the pupils at any specific level have certain special characteristics and needs that place on the mathematics program a responsibility to provide for certain unique functions. At the junior high school level (grades seven and eight in particular) these characteristics are

1. *Acquisition of New and Broader Interests, Especially in the Organization and Activities of Society.* Together with the fact that he will soon be called on to select a mathematical curriculum that is in line with his general vocational plans, this creates a need for exploration both of the environment and of his mathematical interests and aptitudes.

2. *A Wide Range of Individual Differences in Any Class, with Respect to All the Factors That Influence Achievement in Mathematics.*

3. *A Need for Guidance in the Emergence of the Pupil from the Dependent Status of the Elementary School Student to the Relatively Independent Status of the Secondary School Pupil Who Is Expected To Stand on His Own Feet and Seek Help When He Needs It.* The facts that there is a wide variation in the latter status within any group and that some pupils will manifest a desire for independence before they

are ready for it, while others will be slow to exercise the independence of which they are capable, contribute to the significance of this characteristic.

Corresponding to these characteristics are the three unique functions of junior high school mathematics:

1. *The Functions of Exploration and Guidance.* The rapidly broadening interests, actual and potential, at the junior high school level provide an opportunity for exploration of the various fields of mathematics and also of the organization and activities of our social and economic institutions. These explorations have several important objectives. In the first place, they should provide the pupil and the counseling staff with reliable information on his interests and attitudes in various branches of mathematics. In the second place, they should give the pupil a chance to acquire information about various fields of human activity, and also about the interesting careers in these various fields.

It is important that these explorations should not be limited to technical fields. Mathematics, when properly used, affords a most effective approach to an understanding of our economic and business environment. For many pupils, this will be the last opportunity for such explorations.

The exploration of interests and aptitudes in the secondary field commonly takes the form of tryout units in algebra, geometry, and trigonometry. These are designed as vigorous learning experiences, adequate to challenge the pupil's ability and to test his real interests. The achievement record on such a unit should provide valid information on the pupil's aptitudes as required by the counselor who will advise on his choice of courses in the senior high school.

2. *The Transitional Function.* In the elementary grades, the pupil has been studying arithmetic under careful guidance and close supervision of the teacher. In the senior high school, he will study the more advanced fields of secondary mathematics, and considerable initiative and self-direction will be expected of him. It is a function of the junior high school to see that this transition is made smoothly and effectively.

Development of pupil initiative and self-direction is a function of methodology that is, in general, typical of the junior high school. The transition to the secondary fields of mathematics, however, requires careful curricular design. A familiar example is in the study of intuitive geometry in the junior high school, where the development of vocabulary, concepts, and visualization of space relationships makes an important contribution when the pupil studies demonstrative geometry in grade ten. The same transition is now being sought in the development of vocabulary and concepts in modern topics in algebra. In fact, the potential importance of this function is tending, in many instances, to overshadow other, equally important functions to the junior high school mathematics program.

3. *Adaptability to Individual Differences.* Every teacher in the junior high school recognizes the need for provision for variations among the pupils in his class with respect to factors affecting mathematical achievement. These are evident in such things as interests, adequacy of mathematical preparation, personality, study habits, abilities, plans, and probable future needs.

In the junior high school, these differences reach their peak. They have been increasing throughout the grades, and in the senior high school the differentiated curriculums will reduce somewhat the range in any one class. The responsibility of the junior high school requires that, while exploration and guidance needed to make this transition effective are being carried on, these individual differences should still be provided for. Hence, the widest range of pupil differences is found during these years.

A variety of provisions in both content and methods are important in adjusting to these differences. The following are typical:

1. Making the work real, interesting, and important to the pupils, taking into account the diversity of experiences, background, and future plans
2. Adjusting to the slower pupils by
   a. Careful regulation of the rate of progress
   b. Continued help with fundamentals and problem solving
   c. Keeping problem situations concrete and familiar
   d. Careful attention to vocabulary and concepts
   e. Variety in the fields of mathematics used: arithmetic, algebra, geometry, trigonometry
3. Providing for rapid pupils by
   a. Offering problem situations that provide a challenge to insight, ingenuity, and ability to organize and attack
   b. Progressing further into mathematical abstractions
   c. Presenting problem requiring original and imaginative solutions

Extended experimentation is now going on to find the best means of conserving the social resources represented in the gifted pupils. Largely, the adjustment is in the direction of acceleration and the study of abstract mathematics. The criterion for success of the experimentation is usually the ability of the pupil to achieve. It is important that this criterion should be broadened to take into account the kinds of services that will be required of the gifted pupils when they become members of adult society. Not all of them will go into technical fields. No specialized training is justifiable. As an alternative to acceleration, experimentation should include the applications of mathematics to the social, economic, and financial environment.

Obviously a mathematical program designed to serve these functions cannot be specialized or otherwise limited in scope. It will be characterized by a variety of interests. Ideally, it should be an introductory, basic, exploratory program at the secondary level in which the simpler and significant principles of arithmetic, algebra, geometry, statistics, and numerical trigonometry are used as needed to explore the social, economic, and technical aspects of the environment and the potentialities of the individual pupils. This ideal has been approached with varying degrees of success by programs in the past. At the present time, the situation is confused.

Current Studies and Recommendations. Current texts and syllabuses indicate radical changes in content at the junior high school level, with no clear orientation. Several of the groups working intensively on the senior high school mathematics program have recommended courses for grades seven and eight, designed primarily to provide the foundations needed for the modern program. The four groups whose recommendations have received most attention are

1. The University of Maryland Mathematics Project
2. The National Council of Teachers of Mathematics Secondary School Curriculum Committee
3. The National Association of Secondary School Principals
4. The School Mathematics Study Group

In general, the recommendations are directed toward the merging of the study of algebra and arithmetic in examining the properties of numbers; emphasis on development of the mathematical structure; linguistic precision; emphasis on experimentation and discovery; and consistent attention to development of the "unifying concepts" in mathematics, especially sets and inequalities. The topics listed by each group are mathematical, with little reference to contemporary applications.

The studies and recommendations perform a useful service in calling attention to the fact that junior high school pupils can work at higher levels of abstraction than is ordinarily supposed. An overall appraisal, however, must take into account the functions of junior high school mathematics, and the degree to which they are provided for in the recommended programs.

Perhaps it is only natural, in view of our national preoccupations, that the recommendations should be oriented mathematically rather than socially. Emphasis is placed on the structure of the number system and operations, and the use of algebra to explore and understand them, and on the nature and use of proof, precision in vocabulary, and adequacy of definitions. Many new symbols are utilized to facilitate generalization. Some are standard and generally accepted, as with sets. Others are devised for the occasion, as with "frames" for place holding in study of mathematical sentences. Examples of these are

$$5 - \triangle = 2 \text{ and } \qquad 3\square 8 = 24$$

On the other hand, there is little interest in the use of mathematics to explore the institutions of society—government, business, or the home. Attention to problem-solving procedures is largely concerned with those dealing with purely mathematical ideas, scientific applications, and new inventions and technical activities. It is true that social problems have frequently been presented in the past with a singular lack of imagination, which in some instances has properly earned the epithet "dime-store mathematics." On the other hand, as the Joint Committee observed,

> Regardless of how the pupil will some day earn his living, he will always be a citizen and consumer of goods and services. Hence there should be an earnest effort to include in the instruction in arithmetic many problems based on activities and interests of the ordinary citizen. The mathematics teacher should use such topics not merely as material for computations, but because an understanding of them involves quantitative relationships. He should be fitted to discuss many of them. The information that the pupil receives may be more important than the benefit he derived from the computation.[2]

The need that was evident two decades ago is still more urgent today.

The mathematical orientation is notable also in the provision for accelerating the brighter pupils, as commonly recommended, and practiced in many schools. The arithmetic program is condensed to one year, in the seventh grade, and algebra is studied in grade eight. This program has the advantage of occupying the time of the pupil with facilities already available. It also has the disadvantage of deferring the real problem to grade twelve, when the accelerated group will have completed the regular program and must either be provided with a course appropriate to their abilities and needs or study some subject other than mathematics.

Further experimental study with a broader point of view is needed as the basis for designing a program that will adequately capitalize on the resources represented in the gifted pupils. The proper criterion is not what the pupils *can* master, but rather what mathematics they *should* master to prepare for the services society will require from them.

[2] National Council of Teachers of Mathematics, fifteenth yearbook, *The Place of Mathematics in Secondary Education* (New York: Teachers College Bureau of Publications, Columbia University, 1940), pp. 102–103.

The program should take into account also the peculiar advantages offered by the expanding interests of this age group, and their need for exploration and guidance. Grade eight is too early for specialization. Certainly, a plan that is limited to completion of a standard program a year in advance of the regular rate is capitalizing on neither the opportunity nor the resources offered by this group.

THE SENIOR HIGH SCHOOL PROGRAM

The differentiated curriculums found in the senior high school mathematics programs are adaptations to the needs of various vocationally oriented groups. The fact that vocational plans at this level are tentative requires that the curriculums be sufficiently flexible so that the pupil may shift from one to the other as late as the junior year without penalty.

In general, the multiple tracks are designed for the needs of the three groups of pupils that were identified by the Post-war Commission of the National Council of Teachers of Mathematics fifteen years ago. These include (1) those pupils that need mathematics for home, community, and business pursuits primarily, (2) future leaders in fields other than technical, and (3) future technical specialists. Obviously, the distinction between the first group and the other two is not clear-cut, since all pupils have the same personal, family, and community needs.

While the secondary school mathematics curriculum has been subjected to intensive study for several years, this traditional college-preparatory courses—algebra, plane geometry, advanced algebra, solid geometry, and trigonometry—still constitute the core of the program. General mathematics is available for the non-college-preparatory pupils in the ninth grade, and several courses are being tried experimentally in the senior year. The general pattern from which adaptations are made for larger or smaller groups is indicated in the diagram on page 450.

The arrows in the diagram indicate the points at which pupils who discover interests and aptitudes for more mathematics may transfer to a more highly specialized track. Within this structure also are the typical curricular adaptations for various specialized groups of pupils. For example, in the larger high schools, this program for very bright pupils may be found: grade nine—algebra, an extended course; grade ten—plane and solid geometry; grade eleven—trigonometry and algebra; grade twelve—analytic geometry and calculus.

Curricular Modifications. Except in the twelfth grade, where a variety of one-semester courses are being explored, current trends in curricular revision are more clearly evident in the treatment of topics than in the modification of course titles. The major modification in content is the

	Non-college	General College Preparation	Technical
Ninth grade	General mathematics	Algebra	Algebra
Tenth grade	None or special vocational mathematics	Plane geometry	Plane geometry
Eleventh grade	None or special vocational mathematics		Intermediate Algebra (one semester) Trigonometry (one semester)
Twelfth grade	None or advanced general mathematics		Various one-semester courses: solid geometry, statistics, analytical geometry, elementary functions

introduction of "unifying ideas," notably sets and inequalities. These unifying ideas afford new approaches, with emphasis on understanding of the structure of mathematics, utilizing more extensive symbolism. The new emphasis is well summarized by the Commission of the College Entrance Examination Board:

1. Strong preparation both in concepts and skills for mathematics at the level of calculus and analytic geometry.
2. Understanding of the nature and role of deductive reasoning in algebra as well as geometry.
3. Appreciation of mathematical structure as, for example, properties of natural, rational, real, and complex numbers.
4. Judicious use of unifying ideas—sets, variables, functions, and relations.
5. Treatment of inequalities along with equations.
6. Cooperation of plane geometry of some coordinate geometry and essentials of solid geometry and space perception.[3]

The inadequacy of the secondary school mathematics program in view of the rapid growth of mathematical knowledge, the increasing demand for mathematical competence, the critical shortage of qualified teachers,

[3] College Entrance Examination Board, *Report of the Commission on Mathematics Program for College Preparatory Mathematics* (New York: College Entrance Examination Board, 1959), pp. 33–34.

and an awareness of competition from abroad, as evidenced by the Soviet Union's technical advances, have led to formally organized study and revision of the mathematics program on a scale more extensive than in any other period of our history. The National Council of Teachers of Mathematics has, of course, been closely concerned with the problem and with efforts to deal with it. It has published several relevant year-books and encouraged the airing of contrary points of view at conventions, and its periodical, *The Mathematics Teacher,* has publicized important conflicting points of view. In addition it has established several active curriculum committees.

The federal government has sponsored the National Science Foundation, supporting summer and academic-year institutes designed to improve the subject-matter competence of the teachers in service. The National Defence Education Act was also directed in part to improvement of science and mathematics teaching.

Several foundation-sponsored studies are actively engaged in efforts to improve the secondary school mathematics curriculum and its teaching. With ample financial backing, they are able to secure competent mathematicians and educators for preparation of syllabuses, to enlist the co-operation of secondary schools, and to ensure publication and wide distribution of their recommendations. The three most active are The College Entrance Examination Board, The University of Illinois Committee on School Mathematics, and the School Mathematics Study Group (SMSG), the last now with headquarters at Stanford University. Several common trends are evident in their proposals for work in each year of the secondary school program:

Mathematics in Grade Nine. Most, if not all, of the topics found in earlier years are still present. The principal difference is in the approach to the concepts of algebra. Currently, more emphasis is placed on language, number, numeral, pronumeral, sets, sentences, and statements; emphasis is also placed on structure (the real number system and its laws of operation) and on deductive approaches. Most prominent among the recommended changes for content is the introduction of the unifying concepts.

None of the projects have devoted their attention to the problem of those students who cannot benefit from the standard sequence, with the exception of SMSG, which has taken the dubious position that the non-college-bound student can profit from the same sequence, if the concepts are introduced at a slower pace and in a more concrete manner.

Geometry in Grade Ten. The various proposals for tenth-grade mathematics are in agreement that Euclidian geometry should be retained as a central theme but that it should be reduced to a minimum and supplemented by solid and coordinate geometry. The unifying concepts are retained to provide modern approaches to the study of various topics, and precision in language is emphasized to strengthen the logical development and to clarify understandings of basic concepts.

Mathematics in Grade Eleven. Mathematics in grade eleven, in the current proposals, consists of intermediate algebra and some trigonometry. The emphasis is on real and complex numbers, utilizing a deductive approach and incorporating the unifying ideas. Structure is emphasized at all times. "Careful attention has been taken to give the student some insight into the nature of mathematical thought as well as to prepare him to perform certain manipulations with facility."[4]

Mathematics in Grade Twelve. The various proposals for grade twelve are, broadly speaking, in general agreement. Since no textbooks have appeared from the commercial publishers, schools are dependent on materials produced by the projects, and practices vary extensively.

The first proposal for curriculum in grade twelve was by the Commission of the College Entrance Examination Board. It included two one-semester courses—the first entitled "Elementary Functions" and the second, "Introductor Probability with Statistical Applications." An alternative for the second semester is a course entitled "Introduction to Modern Algebra," which deals with fields and groups.

The SMSG also recommends two one-semester courses. The first is "Elementary Functions," which is intended to furnish the student with a good intuitive background for a later course in calculus. The second course is an "Introduction to Matrix Algebra," in which attention is paid to algebraic structure intended to put the student close to the frontiers of mathematics and to provide examples of patterns that arise in the most varied circumstances.

An Evaluation of Project Proposals. The current projects devoted to the secondary school mathematics curriculum, with the collaboration of schools in many experimental centers, have made enormous contributions to our understanding of that curriculum. Notable is the attention to unifying concepts, which in the past has been only partially successful. Other highly desirable areas of emphasis in the modern curriculum are on precision in language, the value of discovery and generalization in learning, and the organization of learning in a structural concept of the field of mathematics.

On the other hand, all the major projects share to a greater or lesser degree several common weaknesses: disregard of the over-all purposes

[4] School Mathematics Study Group, *Letter No. 4* (New Haven: Yale University Press, 1960), p. 21.

of secondary education, preoccupation with the structure of mathematics to the neglect of certain other desirable outcomes, and disregard of individual differences among pupils and groups of pupils whom the schools are intended to serve. These shortcomings are of sufficient importance to deserve illustration.

Disregard of the Purposes of Secondary Education. This is well illustrated in the criterion for grade placement of topics and for introduction of new topics typically used in the several projects, namely, the ability of pupils to master the topic at any given level. No consideration is given to future needs of the pupil, or what contributions society will require from him. Over the years, a series of experiments has clearly revealed that what a pupil can master at a given time, provided he has the prerequisite fundamentals, depends on the capacity and interest of the teacher. At any given grade level, this criterion presents such a wide range of possibilities as to render it inadequate for guidance. Data on what *can* be taught need to be supplemented by information on what *should* be taught, in the light of the purposes of the secondary schools, before the program of curriculum development can be completed.

Neglect of Important Concomitant Outcomes. Perhaps because of the preoccupation with the structure of mathematics, a variety of concomitant outcomes whose importance has been recognized over the years have been overlooked. One of these is development of skill in the techniques of problem solving in a real rather than an abstract problem situation. While we do not know what problems a given pupil will encounter, or even in what area he will encounter them, we know that he should learn the techniques of finding and testing the solution to his problem. Mathematics does not carry the sole responsibility for developing this ability, but the nature of the field is such that it offers the most effective opportunity for learning the techniques of problem solving.

Emphasis on the structure of mathematics, however, has led to deemphasis on applications. Such applications as occur are largely from the physical sciences and are primarily designed as occasions for introducing mathematical concepts or computations. Thus, while discovery and generalization in the area of abstract mathematics are encouraged, the development of systematically applied techniques of problem solving, in the sense advocated, for example, by Polya,[5] is neglected.

While it is probably true that the most interesting thing in the study of mathematics is mathematics itself, it does not follow that the aim in studying mathematics is merely to learn more mathematics. The various fields of mathematics evolved largely as a result of man's efforts to under-

---

[5] G. Polya, *How To Solve It* (Princeton, N.J.: Princeton University Press, 1946).

stand and control his environment. They still have potential values for the same purpose. Mathematics is to be considered a means or mode of thinking by which such an understanding can be brought about. This use of mathematics to increase the understanding of our social, economic, and physical environment has been largely neglected, together with the development of appreciation of the contribution of mathematics to our culture.

Neglect of Differential Needs of Various Pupil Groups. The purposes for teaching mathematics must take into account the abilities, interests, and vocational needs of various groups of pupils, not only as a service to the pupils, but also for the benefit of society, which needs the fully developed resources of each group. Development of these resources cannot be achieved by focusing attention on the technically oriented group and assuming that the study of mathematics for its own sake will meet the needs of the rest.

The questionable assumptions on which experimentation with gifted groups is based has been previously mentioned. Provision for the slower pupils, on the other hand, is based on the premise that, given more time and a less formal approach, slower pupils can cover the same materials as the more rapid pupils. This is in contradiction to research findings as well as to the experience of classroom teachers.

In summary, it may be stated that the weakness of current curricular projects lies in a failure to establish clearly defined aims and defensible criteria for selecting what should be taught at any given level. What one writer says in criticism of SMSG is generally applicable to all projects: "The most disturbing thing about the huge pile of materials published by SMSG is that almost no indication is given to what SMSG is trying to accomplish. No analysis is given about what is wrong about our present curriculum and pedagogy and what ideas SMSG is recommending to improve the situation."[6]

LOCAL RESPONSIBILITY FOR CURRICULUM DEVELOPMENT

Projects of the magnitude of those being undertaken in the field of mathematics are bound to have limitations such as those listed above. It is important that these limitations be taken into account by those who plan to use the materials in any local school system. The selection of materials must be in accord with stated local aims for mathematics instruction. These aims, to be valid, must be based on careful study of the specific purposes of secondary education in the local community, and

[6] Morris Kline, "New Curriculum or New Pedogogy," *New York State Mathematic Teachers Journal,* Vol. 10 (April, 1960), p. 62.

the needs of the groups of pupils who will be studying mathematics.

It is especially important in mathematics that the curriculum be designed in the light of the specific needs of the pupil groups to be served. In some communities, a high proportion of the pupils are college-bound. In others, the percentage of students who will attend college is relatively low. There is variation in the proportion of gifted pupils and in the types of careers available locally to high school graduates. These local differences define basic questions that must be answered by those responsible for the mathematics program: "What are the common mathematical needs of secondary school pupils?" and "What important groups of pupils that have common mathematical needs can be identified?" Teachers and administrators who intend to base curriculum revision on materials from any of the current projects should consider them as important resource material from which a program can be developed. It would be a mistake to accept them as a the finished program.

QUESTIONS, PROBLEMS, AND ISSUES FOR FURTHER THOUGHT

1. Most of the problems listed in this chapter that relate to citizenship responsibilities and to worthy home membership are in the general field of economics. The viewpoint taken is that they are most effectively studied in the mathematics class. In support of this viewpoint, take the topic of stock-market investments and show how it might be developed in grade eight.
2. Assume the opposite viewpoint, and present an outline for the same topic in a course in economics, in a specified grade, that would deal with the same topic. Compare the interest and effectiveness of the two topics you have developed.
3. The content treated in any mathematics course at any level can be analyzed into several major areas, as follows:

> Science of number and operation
> Measurement
> Science of shape and position
> Expression of quantitative ideas
> Systematic problem-solving techniques

Examine a seventh–eighth-grade series published in the early fifties, and record the approximate percentage of content devoted to each area. Do the same for a series published in the sixties. Is there evidence of a change in emphasis? If so, in what direction?
4. Compare the content of an algebra text published in the early fifties with that of one published in the early sixties. You need not use the category areas listed in question 3 unless you wish to. What are the important changes in emphasis? Are they consistent with those described in this chapter as outlined by the College Entrance Examination Board?
5. Examine materials of one or more of the major projects mentioned in the chapter. You will find a citation in the bibliography providing sources of information. Prepare a statement showing which of the criticisms listed in this chapter you think are justified and which ones you think are not.

6. Obtain information on the mathematics curriculums in a large high school and also in a small high school in your vicinity, if they are available. State

    a. How many tracks are provided
    b. What group or groups are provided for in each track
    c. In what school year each track begins
    d. Who decides what track a given pupil shall follow
    e. If adequate data are available for making this decision
    f. When, how, and by whom these data are collected

SUPPLEMENTARY MATERIALS

SELECTED READINGS

BEBERMAN, MAX. *An Emerging Program of Secondary School Mathematics.* The Inglis Lecture. Cambridge, Mass.: Harvard University Press, 1958. A presentation of the point of view and some illustrative practices in the experimental program at Illinois. This is one of the earlier experimental projects, undertaking to introduce new and more rigorous ideas into the secondary school program.

BRUNE, IRVIN H. "Language in Mathematics," *Twenty-first Yearbook, National Council of Teachers of Mathematics,* pp. 156–91, 1953. An exposition of the importance of precision in vocabulary in the learning of mathematics, with illustrations from a variety of fields.

CLARK, JOHN R. "Guiding the Learner To Discover and Generalize," *Twenty-fifth Yearbook, National Council of Teachers of Mathematics,* pp. 62–93, 1957. A presentation of the importance of discovery and generalization in the learning of mathematics, with abundant illustrations from practices in various levels and fields.

COLLEGE ENTRANCE EXAMINATION BOARD. *Program of College Preparatory Mathematics.* New York: The Board, 1959. The recommendations of the committee appointed by the College Entrance Examination Board to study the prerequisites for college science and mathematics.

FRASER, DOROTHY M. *Current Curriculum Studies in Academic Subjects.* Washington, D.C.: National Education Association of the United States, 1962. Chapter 3, "Mathematics," pp. 27–42.

KLINE, MORRIS. "The Ancients Versus the Moderns: The Battle of the Books," *The Mathematics Teacher,* LI (October, 1958), 418–27. A comprehensive and searching critique of aims, procedures, and recommendations of the various major curriculum projects.

"Mathematics in the Secondary School," *The Education Digest,* XXVII (December, 1961), 43–47.

MAYOR, JOHN R., and JOHN A. BROWN. "New Mathematics in the Junior High Schools," *Educational Leadership,* XVIII (December, 1960), 165–69.

MOISE, EDWIN. "The New Mathematics Programs," *The Education Digest,* XXVIII (September, 1962), 28–32.

NATIONAL ASSOCIATION OF SECONDARY SCHOOL PRINCIPALS. *New Developments in Secondary School Mathematics.* Washington, D.C.: National Education Association of the United States, 1959. An excellent summary of current curricular activities in mathematics, from the point of view of those responsible for the over-all secondary school curriculum.

NATIONAL COUNCIL OF TEACHERS OF MATHEMATICS. "The First Report of the Commission on Post-war Plans," *The Mathematics Teacher,* XXXVII (May, 1944), 226–32.

———. "The Second Report of the Commission on Post-war Plans," *The Mathematics Teacher,* XXXVIII (May, 1945), 195–221. This and the preceding are two historically important reports, undertaking to orient the development of the mathematics curriculum in the light of the accepted purposes of the elementary and secondary schools.

SNIDER, DANIEL W. "Secondary School Mathematics in Transition," *School Life,* XLII (March, 1960), 9–13.

THE SCHOOL MATHEMATICS STUDY GROUP. *Junior High School Mathematics.* New Haven: Yale University Press, 1959. Vols. 1–3. The recommendations of SMSG for a program in junior high school mathematics that will be adequate preparation for the study of the Group's recommended secondary school program.

———. *Studies in Mathematics.* New Haven: Yale University Press, 1959. The program recommended by SMSG for the secondary school curriculum.

WARE, HERBERT W. "About That New Mathematics Program . . . ," *Bulletin of the N.A.S.S.P.,* No. 278 (December, 1962), 83–89.

WILMERS, E. T. "Arithmetic in Today's Culture," *Twenty-fifth Yearbook, National Council of Teachers of Mathematics,* pp. 10–32, 1957. A detailed exploration of the development of arithmetic as a means for solving problems in man's environment, its significance in various cultures in the past, and the broad ramifications of its current significance.

23

Business Subjects

Business education is simply one phase of the total educational program. Like other phases or parts of the total program, business education serves both individual and group interests. In the individual sense, business education makes possible and activates successful individual participation in the business society in which a person finds himself. Individual efficiency is increased from the standpoint of buying and consuming business goods and services, as well as in other aspects of personal financial management. Occupationally speaking, business education serves also in identifying and developing aptitudes and abilities for job participation in a great variety of business institutions and offices. From the standpoint of group interests, business education not only helps in providing trained or partially trained workers, it helps also in providing a higher level of business and economic understanding, which, in turn, means increased efficiency in buying, better consumption patterns through better decisions and choices, and greater appreciation of business institutions, goods, and services. Business education, it may reasonably be assumed, is in a position to make a significant contribution in long-range development of community and group interests, simply because business itself is such an important and essential part of the way we live.

BUSINESS EDUCATION AT DIFFERENT GRADE LEVELS

At the high school level, business education is usually thought of in terms of clerical courses such as "bookkeeping," "shorthand," "typewriting." This common threesome does not suffice as a description of business education as it actually operates at the high school level. Neither is the clerical reference entirely satisfactory. Yet, being reasonable and practical about it, one has to admit that there is some truth in these ways of thinking about, or describing, business education—as enrolment trends and descriptions of practice clearly indicate. Increasingly, in more recent years, however, any complete and correct reference to business education in the high school includes as one of the constants a basic course that typically is called "General Business." Sometimes it is called "Everyday Business," "Business Principles," or "Introduction to Business." Typically, too, current references to business education include "Selling," "Business Law," "Business Correspondence," and other courses. In the junior high school, insofar as separately organized courses are concerned, the offering usually and typically is limited to "Typewriting" and "General Business." The grade placement varies somewhat for typewriting, but ninth-grade placement is rather consistently followed for General Business.

This type of preliminary thinking, designed to provide what might be called a quick look or an overview, leads one to the realistic conclusion that good secondary-level business education probably should be thought of in terms of a set of objectives and as a function of the progressive secondary school, and not in terms relevant to certain traditionally listed subjects.

OBJECTIVES OF BUSINESS EDUCATION

Business education in the secondary schools may be described in terms of two sets of objectives: (1) basic, or general, business education and (2) technical, or specific, business education. The terms *non-vocational business education* and *vocational business education* might be used; on the other hand, if they are not intelligently applied, they are not appropriate. For example, in certain training situations, basic instruction of a general type is absolutely essential in vocational training. In the case of a given high school student who has a specific vocational objective, it might well be argued that there are no exact lines between his general education, his basic business education, and his technical business training. Each complements and overlaps the others. The instructional content of secondary business education may be classified and briefly described as including business *skills and techniques*, business *knowledge and facts*, business *understandings*, business *attitudes*, business *appreciations*, and business *ideals*.

Skills and Techniques. The typical office worker of today is employed because he has the ability to perform certain skills, because he has mastered certain techniques, because he knows the general patterns of certain procedures, and because he can fit into certain routines that in general characterize his work. It must be recognized that skill instruction is basic and absolutely necessary in both organized and unorganized education. There need not, and should not, be embarrassment or apology for offering skill instruction at any appropriate grade level or in any type of educational institution. Society needs such skills as business-machine skills, musical-instrument skills, and research-technique skills, and the schools are society's device for getting what it needs.

Certain skills, procedures, techniques, and routines are essential in the training of office workers. Some of these are requisites for all clerical office workers; others are particularly or peculiarly essential for, or appropriate to, each of the many types of clerical office work. Examples include typewriting skills, other machine skills, filing procedures, desk systems and routines, stenographic skill, telephone technique, budgeting and scheduling of time and work, statistical techniques, and, of course, fundamental and basic skills related to reading, use of language, writing, and calculation.

The modern high school must provide this skill instruction, if it is to profess to train clerical office workers. Some of it is technical and specific training, some of it may be said to be basic training, and some of it is general education plain and simple. But it must be provided. How this skill training is organized into related units and into subject areas, along with the other correlated types of instruction, is another part of the larger problem of curriculum development, of course; but the point emphasized here is that the skills and techniques must be identified and recognized as necessary aspects of the instructional content.

Knowledge and Facts. Certain business fundamentals that are almost indispensable in modern life are factual; they are of such a nature that precise use of words will not permit their classification as business understandings or business skills. In other words, elementary business information is knowledge acquired or to be acquired, for, in many business relationships, one actually decides or acts in terms of knowing or not knowing.

To know that, when a letter is heaver than usual, it may require ten or even fifteen cents for postage; to know that, when a piece of paper money is accidentally torn into pieces, these pieces may be exchanged for a new bill; to know sources of business facts; to know whether it would be cheaper to send a given package by parcel post or by express; to know that a canceled check is generally accepted as a receipt—these and innumerable other examples of simple business knowledge are parts of the basic business education that should be included in the training of every prospective office worker.

A typist or stenographer who has failed to acquire in his training in typewriting the factual information that elite typewriter type runs twelve characters to the inch while pica runs ten, and that vertically there are six typewritten lines to the inch, actually lacks facts that every office worker who uses the typewriter to any extent should know. There are specific facts and knowledge that are incidentally related to skill instruction and, of course, others that are incidentally related to instruction having to do with understanding, attitudes, appreciations, and ideals. In other words, such facts and knowledge of them are, to some extent at least, a part of every business course of study, whether basically skill or informational.

Understandings. Business understandings are direct outgrowths of exposure to, and, to some extent at least, acquisition of, business facts and knowledge. Here is the real contribution of general, or basic, business education. Basic business education, of course, is not the function of any single course. It begins in the early elementary grades in arithmetic and related courses. It finds a small place in some elementary social-science classes. Our junior-level general business course, usually called "General Business," has basic business education as its major objective or function. Our secondary social-business subjects serve this end.

Many business understandings are part of general education and, as such, are needed by all. But there are many business understandings, incidental to every type of business employment, that may be singled out for separate attention and that unquestionably are directly related to employability and employment efficiency. Because we are increasingly aware of the need for developing these basic business understandings, we are putting into our business curriculums more instruction related to business organization and management, applied economics, marketing, business communication, and so on. It is not intended, for instance, for students studying certain aspects of business organization and management to do so with the "university attitude" or with the intention of becoming business organizers and managers; rather, it is intended that students should get some feeling of how principles and techniques of business management are likely to affect them as employees and workers within organizations and under management.

Lack of business understanding and judgment—what some businessmen call "plain horse sense"—is probably one of the most common criticisms of our young beginning business workers. Because they lack business experience, they lack business knowledge and understanding; because they lack business understanding, they lack dependable business judgment; because they lack business judgment and trustworthy power of decision, they cannot fit into, and serve efficiently in, certain types of business relationships and situations. Business understandings, then, should be given important consideration in planning for the content and approach of business courses.

Attitudes. Proper business attitudes are not necessarily the results of rich and varied business experience. In fact, appropriate business attitudes are probably just as likely to be the indirect or direct results of appropriate instruction and training as they are to be the results of practical experience.

A clerical worker's attitude toward his work is really quite important. One typist works on "the hardest, meanest thing I've ever typed," while a second works on "a complex and important financial report." One statistical clerk works with "the worst and messiest set of figures I've ever seen," while a second gets out "an important 'rush job' for my boss." So the story of the work attitudes of the two day laborers—one of whom was "moving dirt," while the other was "helping to build a great cathedral"—applies to clerical workers with parallel significance.

Any consideration of current labor problems brings to attention the very important need for attitudes instruction related to employee-employer relations. Of course, in this respect, knowledge and understanding are of basic importance; yet, it is in the realm of attitudes that both employers and employees undoubtedly have their worst troubles.

Appreciations. It is logical to say that certain business appreciations are desirable content for business training. From the standpoint of educational psychology, it probably is not possible to "teach" these appreciations as such. Yet, some business workers obviously possess appreciative tendencies, while others quite obviously do not, and certainly no one will argue that they are inherited. Actually, they are acquired. Surely, any patterns of behavior that can be acquired can be intentionally developed. The mere fact that most classroom teachers have not as yet found efficient instructional techniques for developing attitudes and appreciations is no defensible reason for omitting the effort.

Businessmen often tell us that young office employees do not always appreciate their business employment, that they do not always appreciate the values of business services, and that they do not always appreciate their opportunity to live and work in a free, democratic society. There are general and specific business appreciations to be developed. And appreciations have a very real place in the hierarchy of educational objectives that serve to determine and control the actual instructional content of business courses.

BASIC BUSINESS EDUCATION

Much of the instructional content of good secondary business education is general in nature. The general-education program in the high school of tomorrow will wisely include certain business-education content that really serves general-education purposes. Some of this instruction should be provided in such subject areas as home economics and social studies, for it lends itself easily to effective integration with the basic material of these courses and because, through these courses, the important learnings will reach exactly those students who need the instruction most, if the planning is so directed. As the "core curriculum" idea develops and finds a larger place in the planning of modern high school offerings, the responsibility is greatly increased for determining just what business education should be included as core-curriculum material. Along this line, however, there is evidence of accomplishment and success.

General Business. Two different general business courses have evolved during recent years. Both have been serving general-education purposes with reasonable success. Over a period of years, the first one has been assigned such titles as "General Business," "Everyday Business," "Junior Business," "Introduction to Business," and "Business Principles," but, by this time, the title to be used seems to be pretty well a settled matter. It is "General Business." The grade placement is the ninth grade when the junior high school is involved, and either the ninth or the tenth grade in the typical four-year high school. Enrolments have been increasing sharply in the last few years, both in numbers and in proportion to other subjects. The most important change, perhaps, has to do with the nature of the subject matter: a shift toward more basic business and economic content. New textbooks, textbooks in prospect, and other related published professional literature show this trend clearly. The content is moving toward basic business and economic principles that everyone should know, and there is evidence of an emerging acceptance of the kind of planning and thinking that fits in with usually stated and accepted principles of general education.

The second general business course is an outgrowth of the first. It has been identified by similar course titles such as "Business Principles Everyone Should Know" and "Personal Business and Economic Problems" that tend to imply the philosophy giving direction to the instruction. Students taking this subject usually are in the twelfth grade, which carries a further implication of purpose. Enrolments are not yet significant. Nevertheless, it is believed by many persons interested in critically evaluating secondary business education that this second, more advanced course is and should be more successful than the first. If it develops that this point of view is accepted or established, it may be because teachers better qualified from the standpoint of business knowledge and understanding have been assigned to teach the course.

Unfortunately, many seniors do not have time or room in their program to take all the courses they might like to take or that others might like to have them take. However, it is entirely possible, looking ahead, that this course, combined with a new or revised approach to economics, will be the answer or part of the answer to the questions being raised persistently by those who would exert pressure for more substantial and more defensible economic education. Business education is in a position to do something about economic education, and many curriculum planners sense the implied possibilities. Also, in another frame of reference, an additional idea ought to be mentioned: General business is one business subject that lends itself, almost ideally, to present-day experimental work in team teaching.

Certain other basic business subjects, for example, business law, economic geography, business letter writing, and personal salesmanship, are typically offered in city high schools. Most large high schools offer a number of them. These subjects are properly offered as basic business education for students who are or who will be taking technical business subjects. Some of these basic courses are more or less necessary as fundamental background for vocational business students.

While these subjects have been serving quite effectively as "electives" for students pursuing other curriculum objectives, their primary reason for being included as separate subject offerings should not be overlooked or forgotten. If these subjects serve only general-education purposes in the elective sense, it is difficult to defend all of them as separate subjects, and undoubtedly they should be up for critical review. It is reasonable to assume that the logical result of such a review would be revision and reorganization. Undoubtedly, there would be a shakedown and a sifting and, then, in turn, an integration of the selected content in one or two newly conceived general business courses to be offered as general-education electives.

Typewriting. Typewriting may well be regarded as part of the general-education program as basic business training and, at the same time, as technical vocational training. This fact need not be confusing to those in charge of planning and administering the total high school offering. Beginning typewriting, from the standpoint of skill instruction at least, is fundamentally the same whether the student objective is personal use or vocational. High school principals, then, need not be very much concerned about the personal-use or vocational arguments, as long as their attention is focused on elementary typewriting.

Advanced typewriting, on the other hand, is clearly specialized training. It might well be called "applied" typewriting. It should be directed toward putting typing ability (along with other abilities) to use in arranging and typing certain kinds of finished work such as in filling in blank forms, developing business-letter styles, typing legal contracts, and typing financial statements. It is the character of this "applied" aspect of advanced typewriting that makes it vocational. Of course, in advanced typewriting classes, considerable effort is and should be given to further development and refinement of the fundamental manipulative skills, as well as more practice with general formats and layouts such as manuscripts, letters, outlines, and straight copy work. But this additional drive for a higher level of skill performance does not make the subject non-vocational; it simply emphasizes the point of view that there is in most technical, or vocational, courses some content that serves the development of personal-use, or non-vocational, objectives. It still does not justify permitting aggressive teachers of technical vocational subjects to continue urging that their courses be openly presented to all students on a free elective basis simply because there is opportunity in these courses for general education as well as for strictly vocational accomplishment.

Consumer Education. Consumer education is usually thought of as having basic economic and business procedural implications and, therefore, as being one of the so-called business subjects. In fact, surveys show that consumer-education courses are taught in connection with the business or commercial offering more often than in connection with any of the other departments. If consumer education is to be offered as a separate subject in small high schools where only one teacher can be involved and if the business teacher is the one who can efficiently be assigned to consumer-education classes, he probably has the best chance of developing and teaching an excellent course by reason of the nature of his background of training in economics and basic business education.

TECHNICAL, OR VOCATIONAL, BUSINESS EDUCATION

Some technical, or vocational, business education is offered in the great majority of four-year and senior high schools. How much and just what really should be offered in comprehensive high schools depend on a number of factors, or criteria, some of which are local in effect and differ somewhat from school to school. Among these may be mentioned the probable student clientele, the type of institution in which the training is to be given, the general character of the school community, the philosophy of the administrator and his associates, the social and economic status of the community, the quality and size of the school faculty, the quality and amount of instructional equipment, the local opportunities for cooperative and part-time on-the-job training, and the attitudes and demands of prospective employers.

Probable Clientele. The nature and needs of the people to be provided with educational and training opportunities represent, of course, a fundamental curriculum factor. Age, sex, economic status, aptitudes—all these characteristics are related. The history of secondary business education shows, without serious doubt, that, in many public high schools, it has been administrative policy to use the business subjects as a sort of dumping ground for low-ability students. Nearly all groups of teachers involved in giving technical instruction have argued that their particular type of vocational education does not lend itself to the training of below-average students. All these teachers are inclined, it seems, to ask that poor students be steered "into something else."

Business education, particularly vocational business education, should be considered broad enough to have room for almost all levels of student ability. Business has room for, and does need and use, people of different levels of ability. Business-education leaders and classroom teachers must be willing to recognize that every individual has some capacity for development and that one of the urgent needs of our democratic society is to find effective ways of helping each and every member to develop to his maximum and of helping him find an individually and socially rewarding source of employment in the workaday world.

The Local Community and the Curriculum. The general character of the school community should be considered carefully when a decision is made about what kind of, and how much, technical training should be offered in a given high school. Whether the school serves a rural or an urban community is important. Whether the community work atmosphere is basically industrial or basically agricultural makes a difference. Even among large cities, there are important differences to be considered. The manufacturing atmosphere in Detroit, the financial and "home office" atmosphere in New York, and the government-office atmosphere in Washington are obvious examples. The consideration suggested here is more inclusive and more fundamental than the practical point of available jobs.

Lower-Level Occupations. At the high school level, business-education courses with specific vocational and occupational implications are for the most part focused on what sometimes has been called the "lower-level" clerical positions. Only in training for the distributive occupations is there much of an exception. To a great extent, the situation is to be similarly described in the typical so-called private business school and, as well, in the typical junior college where terminal-type skill-training courses have been established.

Reference to this type of training as being for lower-level clerical positions may be misleading and conducive to misunderstanding. The reference is intended to suggest the assisting and supporting types of business and office work: the typing of the report, rather than the writing of it; the recording and transcribing of the letter, rather than its dictation; the classification and filing of the letter or communication item, rather than the preparation or review of it; the recording of the transactions established in routine or pattern, rather than the creative design of the accounting records or their interpretation; the posting from original entries in established form and pattern, rather than the basic decision related to understanding a complex transaction or adjustment; and the determination of totals, subtotals, and distributions in records of a mathematical character, rather than either the decision related to the nature of the problem or the creative job of deciding exactly what types of figures and totals might be needed. Dozens—maybe, in some instances, even hundreds—of these assisting and supporting workers are needed for every creative, productive, or managerial person. Creative and basically productive business activities are assisted, supported, and even made possible by such workers as typists, stenographers, transcribing-machine operators, file clerks, calculating-machine operators, and many others that might be listed in special categories.

Upper-Level Occupations. Only in cities where it is possible to work with relatively large educational units and in rather sharply specialized institutions is it possible to provide what might be called "finished" skill training in all or many of these clerical categories. On the other hand, businessmen (representing future employers) and pupils (representing future employees) do have a supportable case when they continue to expect of the secondary school educational program in America basic and substantial training opportunities of the type implied. It should be possible for the high school graduate who has received appropriate training to feel the security of knowing that he is ready for an initial position in business or industry. The employer should be in a position to expect reasonable performance and efficiency, even though he knows that all new employees in this beginning category will have in their first jobs only their first chance to adapt to the specialized character of individual assignments, to increase in proficiency and skill, and to advance to higher-level positions by means of the in-service training and supervisory program of the individual business itself. Of course, employees coming out of either specialized training institutions or junior colleges with terminal-type training programs should require less in-service training and supervision and should be ready for advancement quicker. Nevertheless, it is perfectly clear that there is in the area implied in this discussion a business-education and -training responsibility and obligation that falls in line with the accepted purposes of the American high school.

Types of Vocational Business Education. Technical, or vocational, business education at the high school level may be considered in terms of four general areas: stenographic, bookkeeping, general clerical, and distributive education. In some large city high schools such as John Hay High School, in Cleveland, and the High School of Commerce, in New York City, these four areas are pretty well established as separate specialized vocational curriculums. This would also be the case in secondary-level vocational schools, but such vocational schools are not numerous. On the other hand, in most small high schools, at least in practice, the program tends to be confined to a single business emphasis or major, which essentially is stenography supported by a little bookkeeping and general clerical work. Nevertheless, the four areas of emphasis do serve reasonably well as an approach for describing further the nature of vocational business education. If one grants the reasonableness and the typical general acceptance of this four-area approach, a fifth possibility in the area of small business enterprise deserves some consideration.

The Stenographic or Secretarial Curriculum. Almost without exception, high schools, if they claim to give any kind of vocational business and office training, can be found to be giving the traditional courses that at least imply stenographic or secretarial emphasis. Right or wrong, wise or unwise, more high school students are enrolled for these courses than for the courses in the other areas of business specialization.

Successful practice, easily identified in this case at the center of a wide range and variety of practices, makes it possible to make fairly definite suggestions with respect to the stenographic offering in the typical high school. Assuming that all students spend the first two years pursuing general-education objectives, assuming that they will have completed appropriate basic work in English, mathematics, and social studies such as may rightfully be expected of the core curriculum, and assuming that they will have had elementary typewriting, it should be possible to develop acceptable stenographic proficiency in not more than half of the student's program of studies during his junior and senior years. That is, if two of his subjects in each semester of his junior and seniors years are set aside for development of his technical stenographic and related skill objectives, that should be sufficient. Many capable business classroom teachers have demonstrated that it can be done.

There is no implication here that large city high schools and special vocational schools at the secondary level should not develop and provide more extensive programs. They have the advantage of being able to organize their offerings—general education and core curriculum, basic business education and related electives, as well as technical and strictly vocational courses—for homogeneous groups of students.

When one considers the fact that nearly 2.5 million women and girls can be said to be operating typewriters for a living, it is possible that more girls should be permitted to take at least one semester of advanced, or applied, typewriting in order to further develop this particular skill, without any implication of complete stenographic training.

In curriculum and guidance consideration, it should be remembered that business and industry need male secretaries. Not only is there a great demand for qualified men, but it is generally acknowledged that these young men have a first-class opportunity to get started in the business world.

Perhaps at this point it would not be out of order to assure secondary school administrators that shorthand continues to hold a solid place in the training of stenographers and secretaries. Excellent items of mechanical equipment and dictating and transcribing machines of various types have been developed and refined during recent years, but such equipment supplements, complements, and extends, rather than replaces the stenographic field. The broad field of communication actually has been enlarged and extended in a great many ways. The machine aspect of it is simply one phase of a much larger and greatly significant development. The basic communication functions and related operational practices in American business and industrial society undoubtedly should receive more attention than they have in the past—both in general education and in technical education. Communication can easily be identified as one aspect of management operation wherever it is found—in business, industry, education, or government.

Also, since some reference has been made to machines involved in this particular area of consideration, one is led to think about teaching machines and about audio-visual techniques of special significance. It could very well be that teaching machines, as already conceived, will meet some reasonable part of the need for compact and efficient teaching and learning in the development of stenographic skills. For those who know the field, it is obvious that it would not be difficult to identify some of the desired learning outcomes that could be programed for use with available equipment. Then too, as one moves into this kind of thinking about all kinds of opportunities for use of new media of instruction, such equipment as record players, recording machines, tape recorders, and tapes and records in great variety enter the picture. New types of sound-recording and -reproducing equipment have greatly enhanced both current and potential use. Shorthand teachers who have been able to arrange for part-time or available-time use of new modern-language-laboratory facilities have been reporting thrilling experiences. Already there is evidence that a fairly significant number of schools—public and private, high schools and colleges—have found it advantageous to experiment with individual playback stations for students learning how to transcribe recorded dictation. If by this type of experimentation and by further development of these ideas instructional time can be saved and desired learning outcomes achieved, it follows that courses of study will be revised accordingly and other curriculum-development possibilities will come into sight.

The Bookkeeping Curriculum. Bookkeeping has been provided as a high school subject offering for more than 100 years. It was mentioned at least 125 years ago in school laws governing secondary school programs in the states of Massachusetts and New York. Today, bookkeeping can be identified easily as a relatively stable subject offering that is in favorable status in 90 per cent of the public secondary schools of America.

Bookkeeping is typically offered as a one-year course. However, between 10 and 15 per cent of the pupils who take regular or first-year bookkeeping, as it is typically offered, do continue in a second-year course, even though relatively few schools offer a second year. The number of high schools providing a third year is negligible. Bookkeeping is typically offered as an elective course available to pupils in the eleventh or twelfth grade. In a few high schools, it is available to pupils in the tenth grade, but this limited practice in grade placement seems to be giving way to placement at higher grade levels. Bookkeeping is not to be identified as a required subject, although it is true that in a good many high schools all business students are expected to take it.

While more than a half million high school pupils are enrolled in classes in bookkeeping, there is no implication—and there are no research findings to support the possible conclusion—that so large a number are taking *vocational* bookkeeping. In fact, it undoubtedly is fair to say that at least half if not two-thirds or three-fourths of these pupils are enrolled in a single-year course that is frankly defined both by the high school principals and the teachers involved as a *general elective*. This type of offering is what professional business-education writers have called basic business education offered for general-education purposes and not to produce vocational bookkeepers. It should be noted that it is not even basic business education offered as background for technical, or vocational, training to be taken later. It is true that it might serve this purpose, but that has not been its function in the practice described. It may be that the nearest that this more or less typical single-year bookkeeping course has come to assuming basically technical, or vocational, implications is in our typical small high schools, where pupils in the secretarial curriculum are taking the course in bookkeeping on the assumption that stenographers and clerical workers ought to have a little bookkeeping.

Some large high schools and special or technical high schools do provide what may be properly called a "bookkeeping curriculum." Usually the technical training is confined to the last two years and includes, besides the typical bookkeeping textbook courses, special procedural and machine skills. In a few schools, an attempt is made to train specialized workers such as ledger clerks and billing clerks. But it all adds up to what might be called "clerical bookkeeping and accounting." More basic business education is included to back up this type of program, with emphasis on organization and management, business law, and similar subject matter covering some of the principles of business operation.

Current enrolments in high school bookkeeping, and present practice, cannot be justified in terms of vocational preparation alone. Undoubtedly, bookkeeping should be taught so as to combine occupational and personal values, rather than to stress either one separately. Meaningful objectives for the high school bookkeeping course—at least as it is offered in the typical small high school—will grow out of the type of thinking that acknowledges that (1) some of the pupils who enrol in, and want to take, the course will become farmers, professional men, and owners of small businesses while others may find a need for practical record keeping in connection with clubs, lodges, churches, and the management of home and family affairs and (2) the interests of these individual pupils, as well as the interests of those who may possibly someday become book-keepers, deserve thoughtful consideration.

The General Clerical Curriculum. Technical training for general clerical work, specifically and independently organized, may be described as a fairly recent development. In fact, generally speaking, except for a short transitional period at the time of World War I, the development of general clerical training has been largely a product of the last twenty years. Originally, it gained status as an offering to take care of pupils lacking the ability to succeed in other business programs. However, the clerical-employment situation in business and industry, as well as in government offices, has pretty well taken care of that trend. According to the report of a recent Biennial Survey of Education in the United States, more than 100,000 high school pupils were enrolled in office-practice courses, which represented an increase of nearly 50 per cent in fifteen years. There should be little doubt that this trend will continue.

It is not difficult to identify and describe appropriate content for general clerical instruction. Some of it will be included in the clerical-type courses already organized and included in the offering. The remaining part of it can be organized in appropriate course sequence allowing for the necessary flexibility inherent in the idea. It has been determined that more than 85 per cent of the work of beginning general clerical employees in large business organizations involves typewriting, filing, simple adding-machine operation, use of the telephone, and non-specialized clerical work such as classifying and sorting, checking names and numbers for accuracy, filling in forms by hand, collating and stapling, and the like.

Clerical routines that have become more or less standardized in connection with electronic data processing should not be overlooked. On the assumption that these activities represent a type of work done by a group of typical office workers, they, in turn, should be representative and suggestive of the technical needs of the training program.

When one recognizes the rather generally accepted observations that the majority of general clerical workers are relatively young people and that all kinds of opportunities for initial employment are to be associated either directly or indirectly with clerical-type work routines, it becomes even more clear that intelligent curriculum development in the interest of proper and appropriate training of general clerical workers is in order at the high school level.

In some parts of the country, particularly in some of our cities, educational planning must be done to meet the challenge of the dropout problem. A well-organized, well-managed general clerical training program is one answer to part of this problem. Here is one type of technical training that allows for wide variations in levels of achievement, that permits satisfying learning experience, and that has some reasonable chance of leading into beginning-level employment.

Some recognized business-education leaders have argued that general clerical emphasis is a great deal more promising in a technical, or vocational, offering in the small high school than is the traditional stenographic emphasis. They have a point. At the present time, however, the general clerical curriculum has been best organized and most successfully offered in larger cities where a very large number of high school graduates are immediately employed as mail clerks, file clerks, switchboard operators, reception clerks, shipping clerks, multigraph operators, record clerks, verification clerks, transcribing machine operators, typists, etc.

The Distributive-Education Curriculum. That there is a significant latent demand for vocational training in sales or distributive occupations is quite generally recognized. At least one out of every eight persons gainfully employed in this country is working in some type of distributive occupation. The number of new people entering these occupations each year is typically large. Undoubtedly, the explanation is associated with the large turnover of relatively young, inexperienced, untrained, and, more often than not, poorly paid workers. Also related is the disturbing fact that less than half of those who start in distributive business enterprise are in the long run successful. As far as retail stores are concerned, students of business failure report that those who start in this type of business enterprise have only two chances out of three to remain in business one year, an even chance of remaining in business two years, and only two chances out of five of lasting three years. Economists report that the present-day cost of distribution is disproportionately high. Modern science and industrial efficiency have greatly reduced costs of production, but there have not been corresponding reductions in the cost of distributing goods and services.

Such findings and conclusions argue strongly for the position that there is great need for training of workers in the distributive occupations. Yet, even though the passage of the George-Deen and George-Barden acts tended to serve as a stimulus, relatively little technical training of this type has been provided in typical public secondary schools. In recent years, however, there has been some progress.

Most of the leading business educators agree that it is entirely possible to develop practical and genuinely worthwhile retail-selling courses at the high school level. And, in many school communities, this offering would be most desirable. Of course, first of all, a local community survey should be made to determine the feasibility and desirability of organizing a program of training. When it has been determined that enough of the merchants, school people concerned, parents, and pupils are interested in activating the offering, it might well be planned by a committee composed of both school and store representatives. Such procedure would help to control the practical aspects of the instruction as well as to ensure that the program will meet local-business and individual-student needs.

The retail-selling curriculum should be designed to provide broad training related to retailing, including other retail-store practices as well as retail salesmanship. It should include some study of selected merchandise fields. The selected subject matter of principles and practices should be carefully organized for a planned sequence. The possibility of providing practical training for selling work through the use of a cooperative part-time employment plan, worked out in cooperation with local merchants, should be investigated.

Some large city high schools are in a position to organize and offer extensive and more technical programs of training for retail selling. The High School of Commerce, in New York City, has its own laboratory stores, show windows, and other elaborate facilities. However, the opportunity—and perhaps, it may well be said, the responsibility—of providing appropriate instruction in the retail-selling field does not belong only to cities and very large high schools. It belongs as well to many smaller high schools. And it is reasonable to predict that, in the future, some of the best instruction in the field of distributive education will be provided in the smaller and typical public high schools.

Small Business Enterprise. In some high schools, in some parts of the country, especially where the more or less typical comprehensive high school has been organized, it might be a good idea to design a package-type course in small business enterprise that would be available in the senior year to students not going on to college or into any other type of post-high school educational program. In order to include enough substance to be successful, it should be two semesters in length. It should be simply one of the four or five basic subjects taken in the senior year. It should be occupational in approach and in content. Included would be certain basic information about how business is organized and operated; some coverage of partnerships and corporations and how they are established; some minimum essentials of business law, especially certain aspects of contracts; some understanding of government regulations about which one has to know in operating a business; some of the accepted selling techniques; a little advertising, dealing with various media and their typical use in typical small-business operation; some aspects of taxes involved; some record keeping and preparation of simple financial statements; and some generally accepted principles of good management. No attempt is made here to define precisely what the subject matter should be; but the areas listed can be considered suggestive.

The idea of developing and offering a small-business-enterprise course is based on the assumptions that, at least in certain communities, a reasonable number of students go to work in typical small businesses as they leave high school and that, even today, a fairly significant percentage of typical small business enterprise in typical small towns, as well as in some cities, is owned and operated by men or by family units having no education beyond the high school level. If these assumptions hold, the idea does have some merit, and experimentation with such a course should be encouraged. As in vocational agriculture and other specific training programs, enrolment should be limited to those students for whom the special course has been designed. It could very well be that this type of course would add some meaning and focus to a high school program for a limited group of students, some of whom now wind up in the so-called dropout category. Anyway, the idea is worth consideration.

QUESTIONS, PROBLEMS, AND ISSUES FOR FURTHER THOUGHT

1. What are the instructional objectives of business education at the high school level? Show how and to what extent you would modify your general statement of objectives when the size, location, and character of an individual high school is considered.
2. Discuss business education from the standpoint of its relationship to core-curriculum planning.
3. List specific concrete suggestions for the development of business attitudes and appreciations as discussed in this chapter.
4. Who should take shorthand in high school? Defend your position.

5. If you were asked to consider the possible introduction of a single one-semester course in General Business that would be appropriate for all eleventh-grade students, what would your position be? Defend it.
6. What arguments can be presented in favor of the general clerical curriculum?
7. Explain and defend your position with respect to the inherent relationship between business and economic education. List ten ways that you think business educators can contribute to improving economic education in American high schools.
8. What types of distributive education are appropriate for senior high school instruction? In the typical small high school with one business teacher, should the offering include a course in retail selling? Defend your position.
9. Propose and describe a program of business subject offerings for the high school from which you were graduated or for the high school in which you are now employed. Defend your proposed program.
10. What is the future of business education in the secondary school?

SUPPLEMENTARY MATERIALS

Selected Readings

Alberty, Harold. *The Core Program in the High School: Its Implications for Business Education.* Delta Pi Epsilon Lecture, Cincinnati: South-Western Publishing Co., Inc., 1956.

Bahr, Gladys. "The Contribution of Secondary School Basic Business Education to General Education," *National Business Education Quarterly,* XXX (December, 1961), 62–77.

"Business Education: An Administrative Study," *Nation's Schools,* LXIV (September, 1959), 49–92.

Crank, Doris H., and Floyd L. Crank (eds.). *New Perspectives in Education for Business.* National business education yearbook, 1963. Washington, D.C.: National Business Education Association, 1963.

Forkner, Hamden L. "Educating for the Daily *Business* of Living," *NEA Journal,* XLII (December, 1953), 565–66.

Gratz, Jerre E. *Major Issues in Business Education.* Monograph 106. Cincinnati: South-Western Publishing Co., Inc., 1962.

Higginbotham, Louis. "Curriculum Revision in Business Education at the Secondary School Level," *National Business Education Quarterly,* XXVIII (May, 1960), 18–23.

Let's Educate Youth for Effective Business Life. Monograph 98. Cincinnati: South-Western Publishing Co., Inc., 1958. Pp. iv, 26.

Maxwell, Gerald W. "Are You Up to Date in Basic Business Content?" *Business Education Forum,* XVI (October, 1961), 32, 35.

Musselman, Vernon A. "The Business Curriculum," *National Business Education Quarterly,* XXVI (May, 1958), 29–34.

Olson, Milton C. and Eugene L. Swearingen. *Business and Economic Education for the Academically Talented Student.* Washington, D.C.: National Business Education Association, 1961.

Policies Commission for Business and Economic Education. *This We Believe About Business Education in the High School.* Washington, D.C.:

National Business Education Association, 1961. Also in *Business Education Forum*, XV (May, 1961), 19–30. See also, "A Proposal for Business and Economic Education for American Secondary Schools," *Business Education Forum*, XV (February, 1961), 45–52.

ROMAN, JOHN C. *The Business Curriculum*. Monograph 100. Cincinnati: South-Western Publishing Co., Inc., 1960.

ROWE, JOHN L. "Economic and Social Forces Changing the Business Curriculum," *Catholic Business Education Review*, X (November, 1958), 29–39.

The Business Education Program in the Expanding Secondary School. Washington, D.C.: National Business Education Association, 1957. Also published as *Bulletin of the N.A.S.S.P.*, XLI (January, 1957), 5–160.

"The High School Business Program," *American Business Education*, XVII (May, 1961), 195–272. A special issue of the periodical.

24

The Natural Sciences

SCIENCE STUDY CONTRIBUTES TO THE OBJECTIVES OF EDUCATION

Living during an age when science has achieved such a series of brilliant successes that each additional achievement is accepted calmly and complacently by the general public, the current generation has difficulty conceiving the fact that the early American high schools offered no science except a little rudimentary astronomy and natural philosophy (physics). Only during the last half of the nineteenth century were high school science courses accepted as suitable preparation to enter college. Now, in an age of space exploration, attempted weather control, rocketry, synthetic drugs and fabrics, molecular biology, and similar concerns, no school system would seriously consider failing to offer science as a major segment of the curriculum.

Yet, although our generation is ready to accept science education as essential, few people have really thought out the basic values of studying the subject. As students of the curriculum of our schools, we must carefully consider what each discipline has to offer at a time when so much more is available for study than fits within the limitations of school time.

Since World War I, especially since World War II, the United States has become one of the great world powers. Much of this rise in position and prestige can be traced to the technological advances that have come about as results of scientific discoveries. Representing an ideology wherein each man is entitled to dignity, freedom, and opportunity, our nation is feared and vigorously opposed by the ideologies that would subjugate the individual to the state. In order to preserve our ideas in the face of this opposition, we must maintain a scientific superiority over the other powers. Such a superiority can be achieved only by instituting the serious study of science and mathematics early in the school experiences of the child and maintaining interest and study throughout the individual's lifetime.

If our society is to survive as a democracy, its citizens must be worthy and responsible. Each citizen has rights and responsibilities that, if exercised, directly or indirectly influence our national decisions. The wisdom and strength of these decisions depend on a conscientious and well-informed citizenry. Because science constitutes an important factor in many of these issues, citizens need a basic understanding of science. The great need of the average citizen is for a general knowledge upon which insights and judgments can be based, rather than the welter of technical information largely useful to the specialist. Our citizens need to develop their curiosity and to train themselves to analyze problems and reason to logical answers. Inasmuch as one of the basic objectives of science education is to develop critical thought, well-directed and well-planned teaching in science should lead to critical inquiry, examination of evidence, and understanding of the cause-effect relationship.

As our mode of living changed from an agrarian to an industrial economy, the vocational requirements of our society changed. Present demands appear to be for skilled technicians, idea producers, and research and managerial personnel. While predicting future occupational needs certainly is hazardous, the present outlook is for a continued demand for scientifically trained personnel.

Aside from the societal needs, science can greatly enrich the life of the individual. His health and vigor are certainly affected by his application of physiology and hygiene to his personal living. An understanding of ecology can enhance his appreciation of our parks and wilderness areas or facilitate his gardening. The frequently discussed fuller, richer life can certainly be achieved in part through avocational pursuits in the realm of science.

OFFERINGS AND ENROLMENTS

As a relatively new competitor in the struggle for time and space allotments in the curriculum, science does not occupy a standard niche. The most prevalent pattern of grade placement is general science in grade nine, biology in grade ten, and chemistry or physics in grade eleven and the other in grade twelve. Historical research shows that no standard pattern has existed. A number of factors are likely to keep the pattern of offerings, as well as course content, flexible.

Factual information of science is increasing at an astounding rate. The problems of selection of the most appropriate subject matter, the diversity of the organizational patterns of schools, the findings of research about how boys and girls learn science, and the competition for time from other fields of study keep the science offerings from becoming fixed and rigid. In the last survey of science offerings and enrolments,[1] 37.8 per cent of the sample reported their science curriculum as being in the process of revision.

The present pattern and variety of offerings can be estimated by examining the data presented in Table 24–1, adapted from a survey report of the U.S. Office of Education. While the report is subject to the usual limitations of a sample survey, geographical representation by percentages of schools and pupils appears to justify the sample as representative on the basis of these criteria.

In Table 24–1, data are grouped by size of school. Caution must be used in drawing conclusions from the data for small schools, because such schools often alternate courses, perhaps offering general science and chemistry one year and biology and physics the next. The data indicate that some small schools do not offer all the science courses and that some pupils are deprived of the opportunity to study all the sciences. Biology appears to have surpassed general science as the most widely offered subject in grades nine through twelve. Several hypotheses may be suggested to account for the drop in general science. In the first place, much of the exploratory function of science in the junior high schools may have been taken over by elementary science. Schools may have condensed the junior high school science into the seventh and eighth grades, using the ninth grade for biology or other sciences or utilizing the time for other subjects.

Note that an appreciable number of schools offer advanced courses and that about 10 per cent offer other courses in science. In practice, most schools limit enrolment in advanced courses to accelerated and interested students. The term *other sciences* may cover a variety of courses. In a study of science offerings in the schools of Colorado, Potter[2] found thirty-six different course titles.

In reporting percentages of students enrolled in courses, the customary practice is to report percentages of grades nine through twelve rather than individual grades. This practice is necessary, because a particular course may be offered in different grades in different schools or may have pupils from several different grades within a single school. Enrolment

---

[1] *Offerings and Enrollments in Science and Mathematics in Public High Schools, 1958* (Washington, D.C.: Office of Education, U.S. Department of Health, Education, and Welfare, 1961), p. 19.

[2] Donald G. Potter, *Extra-class Science Activities in Accredited Colorado High Schools and Their Relationship to Certain Measures of Student Interest in Science,* unpublished doctor's thesis, University of Colorado, 1960.

TABLE 24-1

NUMBER AND PERCENTAGE[a] OF PUBLIC HIGH SCHOOLS OFFERING CERTAIN SCIENCE COURSES, BY SIZE OF SCHOOL—FALL 1958

| | Size of School (enrolment) | | | | | | | | | Total | |
| | 1–99 | | 100–199 | | 200–499 | | 500 or More | | | | |
Course	Number	Per Cent	Number	Per Cent	Number	Per Cent	Number	Per Cent	Number	Per Cent	
General science	869	81.9	896	87.9	1,133	91.8	631	89.1	3,529	87.7	
Biology	749	78.0	845	95.1	990	98.3	800	97.3	3,384	92.0	
Chemistry	392	42.5	545	61.6	873	87.8	808	98.1	2,618	72.3	
Physics	306	33.4	442	50.4	761	76.8	794	96.9	2,303	63.9	
Advanced general science	49	5.3	58	6.6	128	12.9	196	23.9	431	11.8	
Advanced biology	13	1.4	6	0.6	18	1.8	110	13.4	147	4.0	
Advanced chemistry	7	0.7	4	0.4	8	0.8	63	7.6	82	2.2	
Advanced physics	4	0.4	4	0.4	9	0.9	41	5.0	58	1.6	
Science research seminar	4	0.4	4	0.4	14	1.4	31	3.7	53	1.4	
All other sciences	40	3.7	46	4.5	99	7.8	268	31.3	453	10.7	

[a] In computation of the percentage, only those schools are included that have pupils in the grade where the course is usually offered. For example, if a school did not have pupils in the tenth grade, that school was not included in the data on biology, regardless of whether or not it offered biology. The data are based on information received in 1958 from a randomly selected sample of public secondary schools. The 4,228 usable returns represented about 20 per cent of the total number of public secondary schools in the United States. Although the sample is fairly representative of the United States, the data are subject to sampling variability, which may be large when the number in a particular category is small. In these cases, therefore, generalizations in a national level should be made with caution.

Source: *Offerings and Enrollments in Science and Mathematics in Public High Schools, 1958* (Washington, D.C.: Office of Education, U.S. Department of Health, Education, and Welfare, 1961), p. 8.

trends in sciences over the period 1890–1958 are shown in Fig. 24–1, obtained from the U.S. Office of Education.

Graphs based on percentages can be misleading. In the graph of Fig. 24–1, while only 5 per cent studied physics in 1960 and 19 per cent in 1900, over 375,000 pupils studied the subject in 1960 while less than 100,000 did so in 1900. Biology has had a meteoric rise since its inception in 1908. Unfortunately its predecessors, botany and zoology, are not shown. The drop in their enrolments would be more dramatic than that of physics.

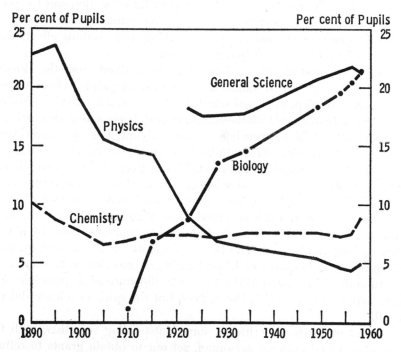

Fig. 24–1. Percentage of pupils in last four grades of public high schools enrolled in certain science courses—1890–1958. *Offerings and Enrollments in Science and Mathematics in Public High Schools, 1958,* Office of Education, U.S. Department of Health, Education, and Welfare, Washington, D.C., 1961.

The 1958 data indicate that, of the 10,635,000 youths in the age bracket fourteen through seventeen only 7,841,000 were enrolled in grades nine through twelve. Of these, 4,670,000 were enrolled in sciences. This number is 59.5 per cent of the group in school and 44 per cent of the age group. Of the 59.5 per cent, one in five were enrolled in general science;

one in five in biology; one in ten in chemistry; one in twenty in physics, and one in thirty in other science courses.

EXTERNAL FORCES CAUSING CURRICULAR CHANGE

When the U.S.S.R. blasted Sputnik I into orbit in October, 1957, smug Americans suffered a severe jolt. Aside from the hysterical attacks by irresponsible persons seeking to blame our schools for the Russian success, the event had a rather salutary effect for American science education. The citizenry became more attentive to the needs of schools. As the adults have demonstrated greater support for education and the press has emphasized its importance, students have gained more respect for academic achievement, and many are making more serious efforts than their counterparts of one or two generations ago.

Perhaps the most significant benefit to be derived from the Russian successes has been the stimulation of interest in public school science on the part of some professional scientists. In fairness, it must be admitted that a few scientists and mathematicians had been active in curricular improvement, but their efforts had not been accepted as meritorious work for the scholar. As scientists scrutinized the curricular offerings in science, they objected strenuously to some conditions. Factual description choked out the investigatory nature of science. The textbooks were quite standardized, bulky, and not very interesting. A workbook accompanied many texts, and pupils were often occupied in copying material from the book to the workbook. Laboratories had limited equipment, some of it very expensive and rarely used. The time allotments for the laboratory were inadequate. The purposes of laboratory work and demonstrations alike were to verify facts stated in the text or to illustrate some principle. Not all the activities were bad in themselves, but the spirit of science did not prevail.

Not content to simply criticize, some outstanding scientists, with the cooperation of educational personnel, set out to obtain grants to reform science teaching. At no time in educational history has as much time, talent, and money been invested in improving the science curriculum as in the last decade. Committees of scientists, secondary school teachers, science supervisors, and representatives of schools of education have collaborated to produce, evaluate in classrooms, revise, re-evaluate, and produce in new form courses in biology, chemistry, and physics. Some aids in teaching earth sciences have also been developed. Studies are under way in elementary school science and second-year biology and may develop in geology.

The renaissance of interest in science education among scientists has been manifested by their willingness, as individuals or groups, to aid teachers, local schools, and regional districts as advisors on projects, guest speakers, sponsors of activities, and judges for science fairs, and in a host of similar activities. An outstanding example is described in this statement by the Joint Board on Science Education of the Washington Academy of Science and the District of Columbia Council of Engineering and Architectural Societies:

The Joint Board on Science Education was established in 1955 by the Washington Academy of Sciences and the District of Columbia Council of Engineering and Architectural Societies. It has the function of coordinating the educational activities of the various technical societies comprising the parent organizations and may initiate and sponsor programs that are not feasible for a less representative group. It is incorporated under the laws of the District of Columbia as a non-profit scientific and educational association.

The Joint Board is comprised of 12 members, six being appointed by each organization. Its activities include the school contacts program, career counseling, sponsoring science fairs, and a program in which scientists and engineers visit schools to lecture on their fields of interest and to replace teachers, permitting them to attend technical meetings or similar activities.

With respect to the science fairs, the Joint Board joins with other groups in financially sponsoring participation in the National Science Fair and defrays many of the expenses of the local fairs, including printing and awards. The Science Fair Committee coordinates such functions as safety, judging, counseling, and various operational details to promote uniformity in the fairs held in the several areas.[3]

Another outside force that has affected science education has been the attempt to improve teachers and their teaching. The National Science Foundation has provided funds for many in-service, summer and academic year institutes for science teachers and supervisors. These institutes have served three major purposes: (1) to improve subject-matter backgrounds of teachers, (2) to disseminate information about the new curriculums, and (3) to direct teachers' philosophies and methodologies toward more emphasis on investigation, critical thought, and scientific reasoning. Other institutions, such as the Science Teaching Improvement Program of the American Association for the Advancement of Science, the conferences and conventions of the National Science Teachers Association, the Regional Counselor Program in Physics of the American Association of Physics Teachers, the American Institute of Physics, and the Science Teaching Exploring for Excellence Program of the Office of Education, Department of Health, Education, and Welfare are making strong efforts to improve teaching through various plans and devices. Teacher-education institutions have generally strengthened their teacher-

[3] *Directory of the Joint Board on Science Education of the Washington Academy of Sciences and the District of Columbia Council of Engineering and Architectural Societies,* September, 1962, p. 1.

preparation programs and continued their programs of summer courses, institutes, and workshops.

Teaching facilities have been improved a great deal, because funds have been available, usually on a matching basis, for remodeling rooms, purchasing laboratory equipment, and securing teaching aids. Provisions have been made for such things as guidance, cooperative research programs, and the like, which will affect science education indirectly.

The present decade has seen the availability of large funds for research leading to the improvement of teaching. Most of these funds have been made available through the National Science Foundation and the Office of Education, but the substantial contributions from foundations and industry should not be overlooked. While the funds do not meet the needs in the area, they have made possible a number of innovations and experiments. The benefits are only beginning to be apparent, but future returns may be considerable.

Many other forces are having an effect on science education. New developments in audio-visual aids, various forms of television, and experiments in class size, team teaching, teacher aids, flexible scheduling, advanced placement, new teacher-certification requirements, improved guidance services, and similar movements have an impact on schools and their science programs. In this interesting age, we can be sure that change will occur.

TRENDS IN JUNIOR HIGH SCHOOL SCIENCE EDUCATION

The Downward Movement. A few decades ago, nature study was the only semblance of science in the elementary school curriculum. Since the 1930's, an ever increasing number of elementary schools have been introducing science into their schedules. Thus, more and more material formerly taught in junior or senior high school has migrated into the elementary program. While many well-meaning persons have questioned the advisability of early teaching of science, research studies rather conclusively demonstrate that pupils can master science earlier than was supposed. Mallinson[4] describes a study where 8,000 pupils in grade six in eighteen schools were given science tests that ninth-grade pupils had taken in 1940. In every school, the present-day sixth-graders had a higher mean than the 1940 ninth-graders. If sixth-graders of today, having learned a great deal of post-1940 materials, can outperform the ninth-graders of a generation ago, it appears that a significant amount of science is being learned in the elementary grades.

[4] Condensed from a report of the Western New York School Board Institute, *The School Board Considers New Trends in the Teaching of Science.* Sponsored by University of Buffalo School of Education and the New York State School Board Association.

The Junior High School Dilemma. As a consequence of the downward migration of subject matter, junior high school science is faced with curricular problems. Shall topics of the lower grades be repeated with more depth and rigor? Shall new topics be brought into the curriculum? Shall courses normally taught in high school be taught in junior high?

Some schools have taught biology in the ninth grade; others, geology; still others, a modified physical science. In general, pupils appear to do about as well when biology is studied in ninth grade as in tenth. The two major problems (neither insurmountable) are

1. A teacher with strong preparation in biology is needed, whereas the usual general-science teacher is expected to be broadly prepared in science.
2. Junior high schools traditionally do not possess appropriate laboratory space, greenhouses, specialized equipment, and similar facilities.

Spiral Curriculum or Fixed Grade Placement. Associated with the problem is the matter of policy as to whether (1) each subject-matter topic should have a definite level at which it should be taught or (2) each topic should be repeated at subsequent levels with variations in treatment and complexity. The first policy is frequently called "fixed grade placement" and the second, "spiral curriculum."

Arguments advanced for the first are (1) logical organization, (2) definite responsibility for pupil and teacher, (3) avoidance of repetition, and (4) definite placement and time for each experience. On the other hand, it is extremely difficult to allot a specific topic or experience to a given grade level and be certain of its appropriateness. The rates of learning and development and the background experiences of children differ; consequently, achievement within any one grade varies greatly. Is not the development of each child to the limit of his capacity our goal, rather than exposure to all experiences once?

The spiral approach for repeated exposure to the same topic or experience increases the likelihood of exposure at a time when the child is ready to profit. Indeed there may be added advantage in repetition to reinforce learning, to overcome forgetting, and to augment understanding. The interests of young people develop and change from grade to grade. Their ability to understand abstraction also increases, as does their vocabulary, reading rate, and knowledge of life activities. However, too frequent exposure leads to boredom, lack of interest, and criticism on the part of pupils. The possible discipline problems and the matter of teaching efficiency raise the question of whether the spiral approach should be accepted completely.

Some school systems have attempted to solve the problem by offering material on a modified three-year spiral. Thus, a junior high school may offer life science in grade seven, earth and space science in grade eight, and physical science in grade nine. The approach is promising.

Ability Sectioning. Because pupils do vary considerably in ability, experience, and maturity, many of the larger junior high schools have multiple sections of general science with considerable variation in the level of subject-matter complexity and expected standards of achievement. With the guidance services basing judgments on pertinent data, pupils are counseled into sections in keeping with their aspirations and abilities. Some flexibility is desirable, so that pupils may transfer during the term, if the teacher agrees, to the section most consonant with their performance.

There are critics who maintain that this operation leads to developing an intellectual caste system. Furthermore, there will be distinct differences in the attainment of the youngsters who finish the ninth grade. The contrary view is that these differences will exist under any type of school system and that youngsters can develop insufferable superiority complexes in the most heterogeneous of groups.

Laboratories, Demonstrations, and Projects. Traditionally the junior high school has not had a laboratory for students. The classroom has generally been adapted for demonstration purposes. Shelves, desks, and some equipment have been available for projects. A few schools have established laboratories, but these tend to be the exception.

Teachers, to some extent at least, have overcome the phobia that an experiment "won't work" (that is, will not fulfil the results expected). Teacher and pupils are more ready to seek explanations for whatever results are observed. The junior high school science curriculum provides many opportunities for class projects that stress observation and participation by students. Many science-education specialists believe that, if a spirit of inquiry and interest can be developed during these crucial, formative years, junior high school science will have achieved its major objective.

Many of the junior high schools have been requiring or urging pupils to prepare projects for presentation in science fairs. Theoretically, such activity should develop the scientific talents of the pupil and give him an opportunity for carrying on personal investigation. Too often, the projects have been forced on the pupils in the nature of a chore. In other cases, the projects have been opportunities for fathers and doting uncles to demonstrate their prowess. In too many cases, praise and prizes have been awarded for aesthetic or mechanical talent rather than investigative skill. Despite these abuses, projects and fairs may be very desirable.

Projects can teach many scientific skills. If this is to be accomplished, the teacher must contribute time and personal assistance while supervising the project. Resource personnel in the community can and should be used, but their contributions should be controlled to protect the interests of the pupils.

TRENDS IN SENIOR HIGH SCHOOL SCIENCE EDUCATION

New Courses Affect High School Curriculums. New courses have been developed in biology, chemistry, and physics. A later section of this chapter will discuss these further. Because the indications are that these new courses will be widely accepted and that the courses or modifications of them are likely to be the most popular offerings, many of the trends reported here are based on their content.

As revisions of the established textbooks come out, many of them are modified to incorporate ideas from the new curriculums. As a rule, when materials are being published by commercial companies, competition will serve to increase similarities in the offerings and, at the same time, stimulate improvements in teaching aids, activities, and content. Revisions in films, teacher guides, and other teaching aids are inevitable.

Increased Emphasis on Laboratory Work. The senior high school traditionally has been expected to provide laboratory space and equipment for all the sciences. In the past, most of the "experiments" were really attempts at verification. For example, if the problem assigned was to find the specific heat of lead, the results obtained were compared with the figures provided in tables and the percentage of difference was calculated. Such exercises in substantiating published constants encouraged dishonesty, especially if grades were assigned on the basis of "accuracy." The frequent practice of "dry labbing" in chemistry is another result when pupils know precisely what is expected in the experiment.

All the new curriculums include experiments that are intended to encourage investigation rather than illustration or verification. If a quantity or quality is found to differ from reported results, the discussion centers on why the disparity occurred. Thus, concepts of reasonable error, sampling fluctuation, and refinement of research techniques and design naturally follow. But, most important, pupils are encouraged to think, not to cheat.

Open-ended experiments, wherein directions tell the students what to do but not what he may expect to observe, have not been confined to new curriculums; witness the experiments published by the Manufacturing Chemists Association.[5] On the basis of research performed to date,

[5] *Scientific Experiments in Chemistry: Student Book* (New York: Holt, Rinehart & Winston, Inc., and the Manufacturing Chemists Association, Inc., 1959).

it appears that pupils learn as much chemistry and express a more favorable attitude toward the subject if they have had open-ended experiments rather than the traditional kind.[6] The creative and industrious teacher can revise almost any experiment to the open-ended form. As a matter of safety, pupils should never be permitted to do work without directions or teacher approval of all activities.

Course-Content Changes. Another objective of the new curriculums' organizers is to reduce the quantity of descriptive material and increase problem solving and investigation. Utilizing an organizational procedure known as the "block and gap," wherein some topics are studied intensively and others omitted, the new studies seek to use the subject matter as the vehicle for the teaching of science. Certain phenomena are produced and observed. Following the observation, a theoretical scheme for explaining the phenomena is presented or developed. In some cases, predictions are made on the basis of the theory. Further experimentation either supports the theory or demands a modification. Destroying the common misconception that science is a body of immutable truths, this approach pictures science as a logical system by which to explain natural phenomena and as a basis for direction in searching for new information.

In the past, fairly large segments of textbooks, especially in chemistry and physics, were devoted to technological and engineering application. These sections have been sacrificed in order to provide more time for study of scientific principles, which are much more likely to endure than technological processes that are revised and improved periodically. Less time has been devoted to applications of principles than to the principles themselves. It is generally accepted that the person who understands the principle will have little difficulty with applications.

The content of the courses differs radically from that of the traditional courses. In fact, even the parallel versions of biology differ greatly. Some topics have been eliminated. Many ideas never included before are now a major portion of some courses. The new materials tie the secondary school science offerings to the interesting science of today. To learn more about this, the student should carefully examine the summaries of the new courses in biology, chemistry, and physics, for example, those given in a small brochure by Paul Brandwein.[7]

New Instructional Media. In additions to the changes in texts and curricular guides, many changes have occurred in the technological fields

---

[6] See George Charen, "A Study of Open-ended Experiments in Chemistry on the Achievement of Certain Recognized Objectives of Science Teaching," unpublished doctor's thesis, University of Colorado, 1962.

[7] Paul Brandwein, *The Revolution in Science Education: An Examination of the New Secondary Science Curriculums,* Teachers Notebook in Science (New York: Harcourt, Brace & World, Inc., 1962), Appendix.

—in audio-visual aids, instructional television, and automated instructional devices. For teaching to be effective, the subject matter should be presented by means that will facilitate learning by children. It is well known that some children learn efficiently by reading while others assimilate learning more rapidly through other means. The new media may also make it possible for teachers to use their own time more efficiently. Certainly, it is to be hoped that the new media will teach routine matters, freeing teachers to work on individual learning problems, to develop higher processes, to prepare laboratory exercises and material, and to follow new developments in their fields. Research is needed to ascertain the best methods for using the new media most effectively.

Educational films offer many opportunities to enrich the instructional activities in science. In some extreme cases, where teachers were not available, entire courses in physics and chemistry have been taught by means of films. While children do have the opportunity to watch a master teacher perform and do receive fine instruction through such films, it appears that they find an entire course on film tedious.

Some newly developed films are intended to present a single concept. Others are intended to teach a single technique. The latter type, some as short as one minute, may be used to give a class instruction in performing a particular activity. Every pupil can see details of the operation. If necessary, the film can be used a second time by youngsters who need additional instruction. One company has prepared series of twelve half-hour film sequences to teach specific aspects of biology (for example, ecology or genetics). Experiments that are not feasible in schools because of costs of equipment or the need for special skills have been recorded on film for presentation to high school classes. These and many other developments in audio-visual education afford excellent opportunities for improving science instruction, especially if they are made available at the appropriate time.

Some school systems have experimented with television as a means of teaching science. This medium has been found especially beneficial for demonstrations that are difficult for pupils to see. In some instances, entire courses are presented by television. According to a recent report,[8] twelve series of telecourses totaling 259 hours of instruction are now available.

In science, as in several other fields, a number of programed learning devices have appeared. Advocates point out that pupils can proceed at their own pace with immediate reinforcement provided by the device. Furthermore, the learning time is at the convenience of the student.

[8] From a quotation in *Science Education News*, October, 1962. Original information from "A Guide to Films, Kinescopes and Video Tapes Available for Televised Use," Instructional Television Library Project, New York, Spring, 1962.

Much of the value of these devices as a method of teaching is that the pupil is not forced to cover material he already knows. Preliminary research has indicated that the devices do save time. Inasmuch as many of the advantages claimed for programed learning can be suggested for textbooks, future research in this area should be studied for further direction.

Traditionally, the major source of content was found in the textbook. Today, a great deal of supplementary reading material is available. The cost of some library materials has been reduced by the appearance of several series of science books in paperback editions. Encyclopedias have been prepared especially for children and adolescents. Periodicals utilizing attractive and well-planned illustrations have devoted large sections to science for the benefit of laymen. Some of these sections have been published as reference sources.

With the increased stress on library skills in elementary and secondary schools, pupils now are capable of individual study in areas of personal interest. It appears that secondary school science teachers might increase the opportunity for, and expectation of, more individual research and project work involving both library and laboratory investigation. Such improvements in instruction will require increased appropriations for library materials and skilled librarians to manage them.

SOME MAJOR PROBLEMS

Need for Continuity and Communication. To achieve maximum benefit, the pupil should have an integrated series of science experiences that enables him to appreciate the unity of science and the complexity of its many divisions. This assumption has been the basis for a demand that there be an articulated K-12 (kindergarten through twelfth grade) science curriculum. Since we do not have a national curriculum, the responsibility for establishing and maintaining an articulated program of science has rested with the state or local school system. A number of these systems have established guidelines and K-12 curriculums, but the degree of continuity varies greatly in the different schools.

A large number of groups are working on this problem. An examination of the literature will provide some limited insight into the scope of the work being done. Because science makes rapid and continuous progress on many fronts, the problem of curriculum organization never ends.

Teacher Recruitment and Training. The science curriculum is effective only to the extent that qualified and energetic teachers are available to direct classroom activities. In all the sciences, especially physics and chemistry, there has been, and continues to be, an acute shortage of prepared teachers. High school physics may cease to be offered, simply because no qualified teachers are available. Science, as taught by those without science experience and preparation, is not the investigative activity needed if science is to fulfil its function in the modern curriculum. The major problem today may well be recruitment of quality teachers.

Guidance for Science Students. Since the modern secondary school offers a number of alternative courses for youth, it is imperative that each pupil choose the one best suited for his needs, abilities, and aspirations. Thus, it is necessary that our youth be informed about the offerings, requirements in science for vocations, career opportunities, and myriad other external factors relevant to a wise decision. In addition, the student must be informed realistically with regard to his potential and the efforts expected from him.

New Facilities and Organization. With the many technological and methodological innovations in teaching and the increased emphasis on laboratory and individual study, modernization and revamping of science facilities in the school become necessary. Science, as investigation and inquiry, requires space, especially space that is adaptable to many types of activity.

Many other problems exist. The problems discussed in the foregoing paragraphs are only the most urgent. In a text such as this, space cannot be devoted to evaluation, research, advanced placement of able students, and many other problems that disturb the entire school curriculum. This chapter has attempted to describe some of the more unique trends and problems that beset science education, but science is a part of the total curriculum and shares the burdens and responsibilties appertaining thereto.

QUESTIONS, PROBLEMS, AND ISSUES FOR FURTHER THOUGHT

1. Examine one of the series of science textbooks for grades one through eight. Note the content and science experiences offered pupils. Tabulate the general areas of content, and determine whether or not elementary science uses a cyclical organization. If it does, how frequently do the topics recur?
2. Contrast the content of any of the traditional high school science books with that of any new science curriculum. Since all these books are now published by commercial companies, you should have little trouble securing copies in your curriculum library or from a public school official.
3. Secure a laboratory manual for any of the sciences, and compare it with the directions for the experiments or investigations of the corresponding new curriculum. In your own words, describe the essential differences in the nature of the laboratory work.

4. Examine the three versions of the Biological Sciences Curriculum Study biology. In view of the differences you find in the content, how can you justify the practice of accepting each of these as a high school biology course?

5. Interview a high school counselor or principal to secure information about the number of science tracks available in his school. Ask how students are selected for, or guided into, each track. What conditions are imposed on the pupil who wishes to migrate from one level to another? What provisions, if any, are made for the difficulty level of the various courses in estimating the class rank of seniors?

6. Secure copies of magazines such as *Current Science and Aviation, Science World, Science Digest,* and *Scientific American.* Compare the content of these with the material you read while in high school.

7. Visit a high school science laboratory, and note the different kinds of equipment and projects. If possible, visit the rooms of several teachers and note differences in activities and materials.

8. Interview a science teacher, asking him about the specialized problems a science teacher faces in the care of equipment and materials. Does he have special problems in laboratory safety?

9. Examine the science curriculum of the local junior high school, noting the amount of time and space devoted to the study of conservation in the science courses. If possible, have friends in the social studies area make a similar study. Do the two fields complement each other? Could conservation be used as an integrating theme in correlating social studies and science in the junior high school?

10. Secure a copy of a physics text of the period 1940 to 1950, and examine the technological material. How much of it is obsolete today? Does this have implications for curriculum?

11. In the Bibliography are listed two articles about teaching biology in the ninth grade. Examine the two studies, and report the conclusions you draw.

SUPPLEMENTARY MATERIALS

SELECTED READINGS

ABOURN, ELLSWORTH, *et al.* "Education in Science," *School Life,* XLV (October, 1962), 2–36.

BINGHAM, N. ELDRED. "Science: Its Significance in the Secondary-School Program," *Bulletin of the N.A.S.S.P.,* No. 272 (March, 1962), 190–97.

FISCHLER, ABRAHAM S. "Modern Junior High School Science: A Recommended Sequence of Courses," *Bulletin of the N.A.S.S.P.,* No. 271 (February, 1962), 226–27.

FRASER, DOROTHY M. *Current Curriculum Studies in Academic Subjects.* Washington, D.C.: National Education Association of the United States, 1962. Chapter 2, "Science," pp. 6–26.

HALE, HELEN E. "Quality Science for the Junior High School," *Bulletin of the N.A.S.S.P.,* No. 260 (December, 1960), 36.

HEIDGERD, LLOYD H. "More on Ninth Grade Biology," *The Science Teacher,* XXVII (March, 1960), 27–30.

JOHNSON, PHILIP G. "Changing Directions in Science," *School Life*, LV (October, 1962), 27–30. Summarized in *The Education Digest*, XXVIII (February, 1963), 48–50.

MCKIBBEN, MARGARET J. "New Developments in Secondary School Science," *The Education Digest*, XXVI (March, 1961), 34–38.

MATHES, GEORGE E., and SAM BLANC. "Biology Achievement in Grades 9 and 10," *The Science Teacher*, XXVII (March, 1960), 23–26.

MORHOLT, EVELYN, P. BRANDWEIN, and A. JOSEPH. *Teaching High School Science: A Sourcebook for the Biological Sciences*. New York: Harcourt, Brace & World, Inc., 1958. An excellent source of biological demonstrations, experiments, and class projects.

NATIONAL SCIENCE FOUNDATION. "Science Course Improvement Projects." *N.S.F.*, LXII (October, 1962), 64. Lists courses, written materials, films, and studies supported by the National Science Foundation.

NATIONAL SOCIETY FOR THE STUDY OF EDUCATION. "Rethinking Science Education," *59th Yearbook*. University of Chicago Press, 1960. Part I. The latest of three yearbooks devoted to study of science education in the United States. The others were the forty-sixth and thirty-first yearbooks.

New Developments in High School Science Teaching. Washington, D.C.: National Science Teachers Association, 1960.

Planning for Excellence in High School Science. Washington, D.C.: National Science Teachers Association, 1961.

Quality Science for Secondary Schools. Washington, D.C.: National Science Teachers Association, 1960.

SCHULZ, RICHARD W. "Quality Science for the Senior High School," *Bulletin of the N.A.S.S.P.*, No. 260 (December, 1960), 71–73.

SCHWAB, J. J. "Enquiry, the Science Teacher and the Educator." *The School Review*, LXVIII, 176–95.

The Geology and Earth Sciences: Sourcebook for Elementary and Secondary School Science Courses. New York: Holt, Rinehart & Winston, Inc., 1962.

"The Place of Science and Mathematics in the Comprehensive Secondary School Program," reprinted from *Bulletin of the N.A.S.S.P.*, September, 1958.

25

Music and Art

MUSIC IN THE CURRICULUM

Why Music? Each world crisis or scientific advancement makes us aware of the growing necessity to make as complete as possible the education of our boys and girls. Music is regarded as a fundamental part of the curriculum, and it is so recognized for its many contributions to the child's educational growth. Every student has a need to explore fine arts in order to determine his creative potential, to enrich his aesthetic life, and to improve his powers of observation for personal use. He needs a balanced curriculum if he is to develop fully his potential abilities. The following six statements of "The Child's Bill of Rights in Music," published by the Music Educators National Conference, a department of the National Education Association of the United States, express this basic philosophy:

I

Every child has the right to full and free opportunity to explore and develop his capacities in the field of music in such ways as may bring him happiness and a sense of well-being; stimulate his imagination and stir his creative activities; and make him so responsive that he will cherish and seek to renew the fine feelings induced by music.

II

As his right, every child should have the opportunity to experience music with other people so that his own enjoyment shall be heightened and he shall be led into greater appreciation of the feelings and aspirations of others.

III

As his right, every child shall have the opportunity to make music through being guided and instructed in singing, in playing at least one instrument both alone and with others, and, so far as his powers and interests permit, in composing music.

IV

As his right, every child shall have opportunity to grow in musical appreciation, knowledge, and skill, through instruction equal to that given in any other subject in all the free public educational programs that may be offered to children and youths.

V

As his right, every child should be given the opportunity to have his interest and power in music explored and developed to the end that unusual talent may be utilized for the enrichment of the individual and society.

VI

Every child has the right to such teaching as will sensitize, refine, elevate and enlarge not only his appreciation of music, but also his whole affective nature, to the end that the high part such developed feeling may play in raising the stature of mankind may be revealed to him.[1]

Through well-planned musical experiences, children can develop their native love for, and interest in, music. The quality of the music program in a school reflects both the musical and educational ideas of its administrators, its music teachers, and local citizens. It is only when these ideas are clearly identified and understood that the music program can make its full contribution to the development of the participants and to the school and community.

There are three main points of view concerning any program of education. First is the teacher's view: Each teacher sees his roles as a specialist and as a part of the entire faculty in a balanced relationship, so that a well-rounded education for each child is assured. Second is the community's view: The community expects a continued cultural growth, which is revealed through the type of music it promotes, maintains, and appreciates. Third is the student's view: Through the development of his musical skills, the student may expect social, mental, and emotional satisfaction that is to continue throughout his life.

There is an over-all view, that of the administrator, which is a fusion of all views. He must maintain a perspective for the other three. The administrator must provide leadership, which, while fusing the above views, must also incorporate his deepest educational convictions.

It is the legal and professional responsibility of the administrator, as the executive officer of the board of education, to control, direct, and manage the entire school program. The music teacher, realizing the broad responsibilities in music education, recognizes this leadership and cooperates with the administrator in developing a music program.

[1] Reprinted with the permission of the Music Educators National Conference, Washington, D.C.

Aims and Purposes of Music Education. The *primary purpose* of music education is to make it possible for each student to develop musically to his fullest potential. If a balanced curriculum is provided, those individuals who will become the consumers of music will have opportunities to explore and test their abilities in making, hearing, and studying music, and to develop criteria by which to build their own record libraries and increase their enjoyment of concerts. The balanced curriculum also provides for the musically talented students, so that they may go beyond the consumer stage and develop into fine performers and/or arrangers and composers of music. Creativeness is encouraged. Not only is it a purpose of music education to make available opportunities for the musically talented, but the music educator has an obligation to society to seek out, discover, and develop such students.

A *second purpose* of music education is to provide musical activities in which the child learns cooperation and develops an awareness of his own individual worth. Music has great socializing power. Every student needs the experience of playing in an instrumental group or singing in a chorus. For the benefit of the group, he learns to submerge his individual personality, and at the same time he discovers his own individual worth as a contributing member. It is not necessary that students become accomplished musicians before they participate in musical groups. Even those who are not particularly talented can gain much from such worthwhile recreational activities.

A *third purpose* of music education is for a wider and deeper appreciation of music, not only for pleasure, but as a medium through which students learn of our cultural heritage. It is also a means of studying and appreciating the culture of other people. James L. Mursell, a leading authority on music education, characterized this transmission role as follows:

First of all, we shall point out, as a matter of historical and sociological fact, that music is a very important element in our common culture. It is a pursuit to which a considerable number of men of the highest genius, and multitudes of others less supremely endowed, have devoted their most serious efforts. From the earliest time it has played a notable and imposing part in the common life of western civilization. Now clearly this is a very strong argument for its inclusion, to some degree at any rate, in a school curriculum which undertakes to reflect our common cultural heritage.[2]

In human relations, music commands a great portion of our lives. To understand the musical impulses that beat upon us from all sides, it is imperative that we give some attention to the science that makes possible

[2] James L. Mursell, *Human Values in Music Education* (Morristown, N.J.: Silver Burdett Co., 1934), p. 255.

this medium of expression. This may vary from the basic emotional expression to the loftiest aspiration. Intelligent listening requires some knowledge of the essences of musical rhythm, melody, harmony, and form, if one is to gain any intellectual satisfaction in the recognition of techniques, devices, and uses of tones, and feel pride in putting one's general learnings to the test of a particular piece and following the composer in his organization of material. Music has power to lift us spiritually above a material world and give us moments of transcendent beauty.

Courses in the School Music Program. To assure the child's continuous musical educational development in the secondary school, attention must be given to vertical articulation of the courses in music, including the elementary music program. This can be done by planning music education on a basis of four three-year sequences, rather than in terms of twelve separate grade levels. Such programing can be developed on through the junior college.

The elementary music program consists of five basic activities.[3] *First is singing.* Children learn to sing songs first by imitation and then by note reading, then to do part singing, and then to participate in large and small ensembles. Each level is presented and taught as the child develops and is ready. Progress is based upon the child's ability to learn and make use of his new knowledge. *Second is rhythm.* Through directed folk and square dances, the child develops and strengthens his sense of rhythm, which is basic to all music. Other rhythmic activities included in elementary music education are responding in various ways to note groups heard and playing rhythmic accompaniments to familiar songs. *Third is listening.* Music must be heard to be appreciated, and one must learn to distinguish the simple elements in music. *Fourth is playing.* If all music were produced only by the human voice, it would be very limited in tonal range and quality. However, through the use of instruments, there are unlimited possibilities in the study of music. Rhythm instruments and easy-to-play melody instruments provide activities for extended study. A more refined accomplishment may be obtained through the study of piano and instruction in orchestral and band instruments. In the upper elementary grades, participation in large and small ensembles adds to the child's musical experiences. *Fifth is creating.* The child's creativeness is encouraged and developed through continued opportunities for original responses in rhythms, songs, playing, and listening. Other elements of music are fostered and encouraged. If the minimum time, twenty-five to thirty minutes daily, as recommended by the Music Educators National

[3] These basic activties are described in an *Outline of a Program for Music Education,* published by the Music Educators National Conference, a department of the National Education Association of the United States, Washington, D.C.

Conference, is allotted to, and used in, providing and teaching the above activities, an adequate musical education is possible for all children. Such a program provides a solid basis for the secondary school music education program.

Secondary school music must be regarded as a continuation and an enrichment of the basic musical education developed in the elementary years. However, it is important that joint planning in terms of basic aims of music education be done by teachers of elementary and secondary school music to ensure a continued and balanced program. A secondary school music curriculum that provides only for the musical activities cannot meet the needs of all students. Such an offering would deny a great many students any further musical education.

Instrumental music in many secondary schools is limited to a band program, which will provide instruction on two or three levels—beginning, intermediate, and advanced. When this is the case, the first, or best, band is called on to perform at many school and community events, which are considered extraclass activities. In connection with the band, the stage band, which has become very popular, provides for specialized training. Some secondary schools have orchestras, but these are not found in so great a number as bands. Small ensembles provide opportunities for further training and study of musical literature. These, too, are often called on to perform in school and community programs. Students are usually taught to play the various instruments in small classes. Some times this is done by homogeneous grouping, for example, by reed instruments, brass instruments, string instruments, or percussion instruments. Each of these groups is at times separated into smaller classes of still more like instruments, for example, clarinets, saxophones, double reeds, small brass instruments, large brass instruments, etc. In other schools, where class time is at a premium, instrumental music classes are taught in heterogeneous groups, that is, by putting all band-instrument students together. This is not the most desirable method, but many teachers do get results. Whenever it is possible, students are taught individually. In some communities, there are professional musicians who, through their private teaching, make possible some highly specialized study for some of the school musicians.

A vocal-music program is provided in a number of secondary schools. This usually consists of a girls' glee club, boys' glee club (sometimes called choruses instead of glee clubs), mixed chorus, and/or *a cappella* choir. Not all of these groups are found in all schools. In some of the small schools, only one or two of the organizations are provided. Some of the large schools also teach voice to classes and/or individually and provide students with opportunities to participate in small ensembles such as trios, quartets, sextets, and madrigal groups.

Music appreciation and/or general music are offered in many schools today. It is through these courses that all students can increase their understanding and appreciation of music. Music history, literature, and theory courses are available in some schools to those who have a special interest. Assembly musical programs, recitals, and concerts by student or professional performers, as well as musical programs in the community, contribute to the students' musical education, be they performers or consumers of music.

The Junior High School Program. The junior high school is a transition school for the pupils during their early adolescent years. As has been pointed out by various writers on the junior high school, its primary purpose is to meet the needs, interests, and abilities of the pupils. Gruhn and Douglass state it this way: "In an effective junior high school program, there is an awareness of every pupil as an individual personality; there is a curriculum which recognizes all levels of pupil ability and interests; and there is a broad offering of extraclass activities which gives every child an opportunity to have satisfying and worth-while educational experiences."[4] This clearly indicates that a balanced and an enriched curriculum, which provides for general education, continued instruction in the basic skills and knowledge, and electives to meet individual needs and interests, must be implemented. As a segment of such a curriculum, let us consider the music-education program in the junior high school. It must be recognized that not all of the following program will be found in every junior high school.

General Music. The concept of a music course designed to provide a better understanding of music in general has been accepted most favorably. Such a course, for which credit is given, is now required in some junior high schools and is found in many others but meets as seldom as once or twice a week for one semester. The general-music class is usually taught by a music specialist. It is open to all students, and the course offers a variety of musical activities. The purpose is to help all students develop their musical maturity. Singing is emphasized and is considered by many teachers as the basic activity. This is natural, since many of the students will not have learned to play an instrument. However, a number of students will be found who do play non-band instruments, for example, banjo, guitar, or piano. The easy-to-play melody instruments are used to teach music reading and to stimulate interest. Audio-visual aids are used to great advantage. America is now a nation of listening and viewing people, and every child needs to develop criteria and principles by which he can make wise selections for his listening and viewing pleasure.

[4] William T. Gruhn and Harl R. Douglass, *The Modern Junior High School* (2d ed.) (New York: The Ronald Press Co., 1956), p. 28.

The course offers additional instruction in understanding music through rhythmic, creative, and listening activities. The general-music class is not a substitute for chorus or choir. It involves those activities and knowledges learned in the elementary school, but on a more mature level to meet the needs and interests of adolescents.

Vocal Music. In the junior high school, membership in glee clubs, choruses or choirs, and small vocal ensembles will be predominantly girls. This is true because boy's voices undergo a change during the early adolescent years. Boys enter junior high school in grade seven as sopranos (there are a few exceptions, however) and leave grade nine as tenors, baritones, or even basses. Their voices drop in pitch and develop new qualities. During the period of change, they will not have complete control of their voices and will no doubt be embarrassed on numerous occasions. However, the *cambiata*,[5] when his problems are understood and music is selected to fit his range, can continue to sing and make a fine contribution to the chorus or choir.

Boys' glee clubs are organized in schools that have a sufficient number of students who are interested and a special music teacher to direct the work. Usually the small schools can not support a boys' glee club and a mixed chorus too.

Being a little more mature, the junior high school girls are able to continue their vocal-music instruction without serious voice-change problems. They are usually more interested in glee clubs and choirs than the boys and are able to accomplish a great deal in these activities. Small vocal ensembles are particularly suitable for girls and are part of the vocal program as an extraclass activity in some schools.

The purpose of the program of vocal music is to provide opportunities for the students who want to acquire skills that are necessary for high-quality group singing. The social and democratic values learned through chorus participation, as well as the capabilities of junior high school students to do part singing of fine quality, excellent blending of tones, and colorful harmonic effects, should not be overlooked. Some schools have organized choirs that do such outstanding work that it is considered a great honor to be a member. When this is so, it is usually the result of fine leadership, excellent teaching, and community support. Time allotted to a choral group is usually two or three periods, with some schools scheduling it as often as five periods per week.

Instrumental Music. Most instrumental-music programs in the junior high schools are patterned after those of the senior high schools, which con-

[5] Dr. Irvin Cooper, of Florida State University, is accredited with naming the "changing voice" *cambiata*. A detailed discussion of the problems of the cambiata is is given in Joseph A. Leeder and William S. Hayne, *Music Education in the High School* (Englewood Cliffs, N.J.: Prentice-Hall, Inc., 1958), pp. 28–31.

sist of instruction and experiences in class lessons, private study, bands, orchestras, ensembles, and other extraclass activities.

The aims of the instrumental offerings are (1) to further the students' musical growth through instruction and active participation in music and at the same time provide a means of recreation, pleasure, and worthy use of leisure time; (2) to acquaint the students with worthwhile music; (3) to help the students develop poise, dependability, cooperation, and leadership; and (4) to build morale, a spirit of responsibility, and a sense of belonging to something worthwhile.

Time allotment for instrumental music varies from school to school, but two, three, or five periods per week are scheduled. Many of the beginning and advanced classes for instrument study are taught homogeneously and/or heterogeneously during the school day. Nevertheless, there is usually more to be done than can be placed in the scheduled day, and many music activities are carried on at other times.

Orchestras in the junior high schools are not plentiful in number, mainly because of the shortage of string teachers, emphasis on bands, and lack of community interest and support. To make orchestras possible in the secondary schools, a string program must be started in the elementary years and continued through the senior high school. Some of the great music literature was created for the symphony orchestra. A string and orchestra program, properly developed and supported, would provide opportunities for students to become acquainted firsthand with works of artistic beauty and design. Students need to develop their artistic appreciations and expressions. The school has a responsibility to help pupils rise above the mundane trivialities.

In those schools that have an orchestra, the strings are taught in classes and/or individually. Private string teachers in the community are a big help in sharing the burden of instruction. Small string ensembles are often employed to develop and strengthen string players. Whenever possible, the orchestra should meet daily.

Bands have become very popular. Because of their versatility and relation to athletic contests they have a strong appeal to most young people. School and public events make it possible for the participating band member to be in a most favorable position. He is "out front" performing for approval and receiving his reward. The adolescent is able to become quite proficient in playing his band instrument in a relatively short period of time. Students are grouped homogeneously and/or heterogeneously, that is, by like instruments or all together, for instruction. Some of the classes meet daily and some less often. Many of the pupils will study with private teachers where they are available.

What has been said about the values gained through participation in other groups is true also for the band. More and more serious composers are writing worthwhile music for the band, which affords much musical satisfaction to both the performer and the listener. The instrumentation of the band will vary according to its size, its purpose (for marching and show or the concert stage), and the director's concept of balance.

Ensembles provide a means for a few instrumental pupils to study in small groups—in trios, quartets, sextets, etc. These may consist of various combinations of instruments (same kind of instruments—three clarinets or four French horns—or a mixed grouping—two trumpets, one French horn, one baritone horn, one trombone, and one bass horn). There is much good music to be studied and performed in small groups. Much self-esteem is realized by the ensemble member. In participating in small groups, the individual develops the music skills, techniques, expression, and interpretation that make him a better performer in large organizations.

Activities outside the school play a major role in the music-education program. Formal and informal concerts are played by both bands and orchestras during the school year. Usually some soloists and/or ensembles share the concert time. The bands are invited to participate in many parades. Clinics, contests, and festivals all enrich the music-education program.

In the typical junior high school, special classes in music appreciation and music theory are offered in grade nine. The content of the appreciation class is more advanced than that of the general-music class. Music theory is taught to those students who look forward to college and a career in music.

The Senior High School Program. The music curriculum in the senior high school provides for a continuation of what was accomplished in the junior high school. At the senior high school level, the music curriculum must be based on the realization that some students will become primarily consumers of music, others will become performers, and still others, a few talented individuals, will become composers. To enable all students to increase their knowledge, skills, technique, appreciation, and creativeness, to the degree of their interest and ability, will require a broad and varied offering. In many schools, there will be need for instruction at the beginning and intermediate levels to provide for the needs of students who were denied musical opportunities during their previous school years.

General Music. Though the senior high school course in general music is similar to the junior high school course, the content of the former is adjusted to the maturity and interest of the senior high school students. Such a course is open to all students and will provide opportunities for them to sing, play instruments, and increase their understanding and appreciation of music. It should be noted, however, that it is not intended to be a substitute for participation in vocal and instrumental organizations. It must be designed for those who will be consumers of music and for those who will be also amateur producers of music. It is usually scheduled two or more periods per week for one semester. However, in some schools it is a full year course.

Elective Course Offerings. Many large schools offer instruction in music theory, music history, and music appreciation. It is possible for students in some schools to study each or all of these courses throughout their senior high school years. A discussion of these courses, which space in this chapter does not permit, may be found in Chapter 5 of *Music Education in the High School* by Leeder and Hayne.[6]

Vocal Music. The senior high school vocal program consists of a variety of offerings: boy's glee clubs, girls' glee clubs, choruses and/or choirs, small ensembles, voice classes, applied voice classes, extracurricular activities. Of course, not many schools have instructors to offer all of the above-named courses, particularly ensembles, applied voice, and extracurricular activities, which must be taught outside the school day. In the larger schools, where it is possible to schedule more than one glee club, instruction and choral training are taught on the beginning and advanced levels.

The boys' glee club is important to many students whose voices have settled and have taken on a more mature quality. The organization provides enjoyment as well as instruction in singing well some of the glee-club literature for the many events during the high school years. Some schools have developed glee clubs of such excellent quality that their musicianship and interpretation equal professional standards. Not all schools can do this, because of insufficient number of quality voices to balance each section of the glee club. The activity is usually scheduled two or three periods per week.

The girls' glee club occupies an important place in the vocal program. Since girls are more interested in singing than boys are, most schools are able to have at least one such group. What has been stated earlier in this chapter about instruction, staff, and objectives applies equally well to the girls' glee club. Membership is usually selected from interested students who have the necessary talent, voice, and musicianship. Time allotted to the girls' glee club is usually two or more periods per week, depending upon the school.

Choruses and choirs are found in those schools large enough to have a special music teacher who is interested in such organizations. In some small schools, one special music teacher instructs both the vocal and

6 *Ibid.,* pp. 149–182.

instrumental groups, and, in other schools, only band or vocal organizations exist. Much that has been said about the glee club is true of the chorus. In some schools, a general chorus is offered to all students who are interested and is used to discover new talent and at the same time give those students of moderate ability an opportunity to get some choral experience. The choir is sometimes the select group and requires the best possible performance from each of its members. Music of the highest quality is studied and performed. Time allotted to the choir or chorus is likely to be two or more periods per week.

Vocal ensembles consisting of boys, girls, or mixed groupings are found in many schools. Such groups appear on school and community programs and participate in contests and festivals. Membership is selected on the basis of ability to perform the part. Rehearsal time is usually arranged for various periods or after school hours.

The voice class, which makes possible the teaching of proper vocal production and good song literature, is included in the music program of some schools. Its chief concern is the performance of the individual and the development of his voice. It should be open to all interested students and scheduled at least two periods per week.

Applied voice, private voice study, is usually taught by private teachers outside the school day. However, some large schools provide for applied voice during the school day, taught by the regular vocal teacher. Such lessons are usually arranged for once or twice per week.

Instrumental Music. In the senior high school, orchestra, band, small ensembles, stage band, and instrumental instruction on various levels make up the instrumental-music program. Only the large schools seem to be able to have or take an interest in a balanced instrumental curriculum.

Instruction is offered on two or three levels in most schools. Many students will not have had the opportunity to learn to play an instrument before entering senior high school. Therefore, in many schools, instruction in the various instruments is started either in classes or privately. The size of the staff and the amount of available time will determine the organization of the instruction program. Where possible, classes are offered in wind instruments, percussion instruments, stringed instruments (usually including violin, viola, cello, and string bass), and keyboard instruments (usually piano). Sometimes the schedule will permit instruction on a homogeneous basis such as by putting all brass instruments in one class and all reed instruments in another. Occasionally, the various instruments are taught privately, but many administrators consider this two expensive and prefer the class method. A similar program is offered on the intermediate and advanced levels in a number of schools.

Orchestras are not found in a large number of senior high schools. More string teachers and school and community support are needed to increase such organizations. To have a successful orchestra program, it is necessary to start string players in the elementary school and not later than the junior high school. However, a very few enthusiastic teachers have succeeded in starting strings in the senior high school and have maintained an orchestra. It seems that the orchestra program has suffered because many educators have lost sight of some fundamental objectives and have been prone to follow the glamorous or what seemed popular. Because of the great contribution that the orchestra can make, it would appear that more schools would be interested in this phase of the music curriculum. What has been said about the orchestra at the junior high school level also applies here.

Bands have dominated the music curriculum for years. Not many senior high schools today are without a band. It is the one school organization that probably appears before more people during the school year than any other group. Its extraclass activities put it before the public at athletic events, parades, concerts, trips, contests, and festivals. Because of such activities, it is popular with young and old alike and also makes for good public relations. Nevertheless, it is considered by many educators to overbalance the music curriculum to the exclusion of other groups.

During a rehearsal period in either orchestra or band, instruction is given in the development and execution of techniques. Attention is given to tone quality, intonation, phrasing, blending of tones, harmonic balance, and interpretation. Many values may be derived from participation in orchestra or band. These organizations are usually scheduled five periods per week. However, some schools schedule them fewer periods per week, and, in some cases, the groups must meet before or after school.

The stage band is becoming ever increasingly popular and is being recognized as a legitimate part of the music curriculum. Many music teachers realize that jazz music is a part of our cultural heritage, that it is here to stay, and that some band members will, on their own initiative, form "combos" for pleasure and hire. Probably it is best that these groups be under the guidance of the schools so that they may receive instruction in the art.

Ensembles of other combinations of instruments form an important part of the instrumental program. These usually are on a non-credit basis and meet at arranged times. Such ensembles at trios, quartets, sextets, and the like are in demand at churches, community affairs, and other public events. Many schools require orchestra and band members to play in an ensemble and to study solo literature as a means of supplementing and increasing their instruction in the techniques of musicianship.

ART IN THE CURRICULUM

Vision shares with speech the distinction of being the most important of the means by which we apprehend reality.—S. I. HAYAKAWA[7]

Recent Progress of Art Education in Secondary Schools. **Three Directions of Secondary School Art.** Although art education has progressed greatly in the elementary school and to a considerable extent in the junior high school, progress has been slow at the senior high school level. Present-day secondary school programs in art tend to operate in three directions:

The first involves a tendency to carry on with the same type of program that has worked successfully in the elementary school. This means that the same type of creative problems are used, and the same approach. The idea of continuing with the expressive freedom that was so effective and that had such fine results in the grade school is quite logical. However, according to Lowenfeld, this creates an embarrassment for the adolescent who has reached a period of "critical awareness" with regard to his own work, which makes such problems unsatisfactory to the adolescent, who does not wish to continue work in a childish manner.

The second direction involves the study of techniques with emphasis on perfection of performance. High standards of performance, almost impossible to attain, are expected not only by the teacher but also by the child who has become very critical of his own work as well as the work of others. This leads to frustration and discouragement, for the student particularly, and gives rise to the comment "I have no talent."

The third and ideal program is geared to the adolescent at his own stage of development and capabilities. A perceptive awareness is necessary for the teacher of art, if he is to accommodate the program to the needs of the adolescent.

There were, at first, few students in the secondary schools, and few of these were interested in the arts. In the elementary school, art was usually a required subject through the seventh grade. The high school was geared to academic proficiency as preparation for college or to preparation for a vocation. As a consequence, art was a "watered down, art-school" type of material presented with the emphasis on skills, "beauty," "good taste," and "art appreciation" of the masterpieces of

[7] S. I. Hayakawa, introductory essay in Gyorgy Kepes, *The Language of Vision* (Chicago: Paul Theobald & Co., 1944).

European art, which few had ever seen, except in the sepia reproductions of paintings that traveled through the communities. Emphasis was on drawing from casts or skilfully reproducing "shades and shadows." Only in an exceptional school was there real concern with art, or creative activity that would be significant to a growing, dynamic student living in a world of new invention, expansion, and new directions.

The "beauty" of our age is often in direct contradiction to what was taught in the first high schools. "Good taste" has changed in concept, and, while the principles remain, such as keeping things in balance, the rules have had to be reconsidered; our homes, ways of living, ideas of clothing, and color sense have changed. Consider for a moment the quiet black or deep blue of the first cars in contrast to the colorful road travelers of the present age. Which is in better "taste"? We are now applying the words "art appreciation" to our cities, to the new architecture, to the handsome engineering feats of relatively new constructions such as the Golden Gate Bridge in San Francisco, to new city plans, and to painters such as Jackson Pollack, in contrast to those of the Hudson River School. We can look at the real thing rather than a reprint of a print of a painting that we would not now consider a masterpiece. We have a rather complex person to work with in the present high school situation, as well a more complex future for our students to consider.

The Junior High School Art Student. The junior high school student, partly child and partly adult, in struggling to break with the patterns of childhood so that he can penetrate the adult world, in desiring to be a part of his peer group yet to retain his own individuality, appears to be facing an almost impossible task for himself. It is at this time that we are prone to try to open too many avenues of art experience without fully considering many of the problems of the student. The person in this chrysalis stage, who is emerging from the child into the adult, cannot yet be ready for a bewildering array of adult problems. The child, uncertain in his direction, reacts either objectively or subjectively, according to his nature. The child who "unfolds" in a "visual" or objective manner is one who reacts as a spectator—who observes and works from the point of view of the observer. The child who "unfolds" in a subjective manner responds individually and emotionally to detail and becomes involved with his production in a most personal manner.

Both reactions may be quite creative. This places a responsibility upon the teacher to be aware and to create problems that will accommodate and encourage responses from both the extreme types of children as well as those who are in between. The questions of whether or not this is the time to present many diverse experiences in skills and techniques and of whether it is a period that should be geared to problem-solving experiences through material available to the student require consideration. Since art opportunities in the junior high school are often of a terminal nature, it is more important than ever that the child receive a rich and rewarding creative experience at this state of his development.

The Senior High School Art Student. High school art is usually given in elective courses. Rarely does the high school include art among the basic subjects, which is an unfortunate thing, as art is a basic human expression that has been used since caveman times. The whole subject of archeology is based on findings of the art of the men of past ages. It tells much of his society, of his economic status, and of his development. Remains that are left on walls, remnants of clothing, utensils for food and storage, and weapons, tell much about the period and the people of the time. Margaret Mead has, in her studies of Samoa and of other areas in the South Seas, been most interested in the cultural expressions of the people with whom she made contact. The art area is perhaps too broad, too-all enveloping for us to be very specific in reacting to it. We are too closely involved with many art problems to be objective about them. We choose our clothing, our homes, our utensils for food preparation, and our furnishings; we even decorate ourselves.

It has been observed by most teachers and students of art education that young children have considerable desire for spontaneous creativity, which leads them into various fields of art and related construction crafts. There is, however, a very apparent and regrettable decline in interest in, and desire for, this creative expression through media other than words as children get older. Of course, this is true with respect to the child's more definitely intellectual interests, but to a lesser extent. With the improvement of the opportunities for self-expression in the elementary school and in the first year or two of the junior high school, there has been less loss of interest, and a desire for creativity and expression through art may be developed in the adolescent years with appropriate materials and instruction, as is now the case in some secondary schools.

One of the serious impediments to maintaining interest in art and self-expression through the arts and crafts has been the limited area of fields of offerings, which has forced students into merely a few of the types of arts and crafts. This situation has, in recent years, been remedied in many schools, and the trend is continuing apace.

The report of the Progressive Education Association's committee of their Eight Year Study referred to six types of students who must be recognized as being somewhat different in their interest, talents, and potentialities and, therefore, in their educational needs:

1. The bright children who are somewhat talented in one or more phrases of art
2. A group of students with ability in the classical arts but little or no interest in two-dimensional expression
3. Students with primarily technical interests, more often boys than girls
4. Students whose real aptitude is for art, with imagination and originality, but with poor motor coordination
6. Students who are noticeably slow in intellectual work but who use their hands well and respond readily to art materials when these can be used in practical situations
6. Students who are excellent or average in academic work but are definitely retarded in the arts (They have been accustomed to using their minds only, in intellectualization and verbalization, but have been without experience, and are lacking in confidence, in working out their own ideas with their hands. In addition, many of these have little consciousness of the patterns of their own emotional lives and have no definite ideas as to how they might express their desires and emotions. Usually they feel inferior in art classrooms and studios and wish to avoid embarrassment.)

Courses and Contributions. There are many well-thought-out courses of study for these age levels, but it is impossible to do more than suggest that they be considered in relation to their problem-solving opportunities for the age-level interest. An involved problem in perspective might be too intricate for a junior high school student but not for a high school senior. However, the problem of distance exhibited through space may be one that either age level could handle successfully. Many courses of study overemphasize skill, others overemphasize two-dimensional training, but rarely do they overemphasize working in the third dimension. Results of studies in creative thinking reveal new ways of evaluating and judging creative responses to material and can be used to challenge and evaluate the present offerings in a course of study.

Americans have traditionally regarded education as a means of improving themselves and their society. They wish to foster the individual capacities that will enable each person to become the best person that he can be. One way of accomplishing this is through "freedom of the mind," a condition each individual must develop for himself. He should have freedom to think, to be aware, and to have the capacity to perceive, and to achieve aesthetic sensitivity, even though different persons achieve this in a wide diversity of patterns of thinking. Each person perceives events through the screen of his own personality and must take account of his personality in evaluating his perceptions. Each person's ability to think about his choices for a home and home living—his choices of color, of the form of his furnishings, of the line direction of his rugs, of the treatment of his walls, and of space arrangements. It is important to solve this kind of problem to the one's satisfaction. Some will surround themselves with antiques; others will appreciate the clean, straightforward lines of the furniture of today.

The problem of more leisure time in the future and of what can be done to make this time valuable to the individual requires thinking. Worthy use of leisure ensures happy, active people; however, creative work with materials must be meaningful rather than "busy" work, as there is little satisfaction in doing something in the art area if it involves too many stereotyped activities. Thinking should be involved in the activity.

Objectives of Art Education. There has been much disagreement with respect to the objectives of art education, not only among teachers of art and general educators but also between different groups of teachers of art themselves. Important in various points of view are beliefs that art should be taught so as to

1. Serve primarily the purpose of appreciation in general
2. Develop taste for the things that have been recognized as outstanding in art, particularly paintings and sculpture
3. Lay the groundwork for the development of fine and commercial artists
4. Explore possible interests and talents in various fields of art
5. Develop interest in skills in one or more media of artistic expression that would carry over to leisure and hobby aspects of life
6. Develop an intellectual understanding of the place of art in civilization—its history and contributions, including the types of art in the various cultures in the world today

Differing in opinion, groups may be characterized by one or several of the above beliefs, and there are those, particularly among the general educators and more modern and thorough students of art education, who think that the objectives of art education include all of these. It has been exceedingly unfortunate that art teachers in junior and senior high schools have been limited to the fields of art they have felt qualified to teach and are interested in teaching and have differed greatly with respect to the importance they attach to the objectives above. This is perhaps the principal reason why, unlike in music, enrolments in art after the eighth grade have not increased materially until the past several years.

Increased recognition of the necessity for offering a wide repertoire of types of expression, and the tendency to recognize the place of art in the practical affairs of everyday life, as well as on canvas, in sculpture, and on religious and historical subjects, has permitted perception of the art in architecture, the interior decoration of homes, human apparel, landscape gardening, packaging of goods, advertising, and many other phases of life and has lead, in an increasing number of schools, to a greatly increased interest in art among adolescents and to correspondingly increased enrolments. Also of this nature and contributing to the these trends has been the increased interest of adults in art in various civic enterprises such as highways, public auditoriums, school buildings, and places of worship.

Media and Materials. Many media and many materials are available for art teaching. Certain art elements—*line, form, color,* and *space* (some people include *texture*)—are involved in use of the available materials. There are principles of organization that can be of help to those working with the elements and materials. There are available for study masterpieces that have made use of these principles, materials, and elements.

Line as an Element. Some teachers have written about the problems in drawing—in line and its use in the depiction of objects. Many teachers concern themselves with problems of using lines in differing media—of developing a sensitivity to the variations of line in crayon in contrast to pen and ink. (The former will be a rather thick and grainy line, while a line in pen and ink could be a flowing line, a hard line, or a sharply focused line.)

Lines may be heavy, light, wandering, wiggly, saw-toothed, straight, crooked, strong, dancing, or wavering. A line may enclose an area; it may be the distance between two points; it might be a dot "walking," it might "push," or it could "pull." It might be expressed in pencil, crayon, pen and ink, brush, watercolor, chalk, string, wire, yarn, etching, block printing, rope, pipe, or thread.

Form as an Element. A form may be solid, light, heavy, hollow, a glob, large, small, oval, square, or triangular. It may be built up or carved into. It may express vigor, weight, activity, or an inert mass. Materials that could be used to express form could be such things as paper, clay, stone, marble, feathers, metal, wood, plastic, wire, wax, soap, or even Silly Putty. Paper sculpture is exciting inasmuch as it is a challenge to find out just what possibilities paper, a flat piece of paper, can have. It can be crumpled, pleated, curled, cut into cone shapes, folded (the Japanese have some very interesting ways of folding paper), rounded, or creased in innumerable ways for most exciting results. Problems of standing, of hanging, and of interrelationship of shapes can be handled with scissors, string, staples, pins, or paste in addition to the paper.

Clay can be built up in a solid manner, or it can be coiled, or slabs of it can be organized into anything from patio lamps or pots to large sculptures. Throwing on the wheel is a skill that can be developed, providing there are enough wheels for such an experience to prove of value. Kilns can bring the element of fire to these clay products, and glazing can enhance and enrich the final product. Carving into material, for example, whittling in wood or working in stone, is especially appealing to some children.

Color as an Element. The color of man himself has caused him to think of color. He has attributed colors to the elements of wind and weather and to the directions north, south, east, and west. He attributes colors to the times of the year; he uses it in his religion and in his culture symbols. Every coat of arms has its color significance; the flag has color meanings. Industrial uses of color are many; advertisers use it not only on bill-boards but also on grocery shelves. Factories use it as a safety device. Telephone and electricity companies use varicolored wires. Color is used in science in many ways, for instance, it can determine factors in a test tube as well as measure light rays and distances from the earth to points in outer space.

Colors are light, dark, warm, cool, deep, heavy, vibrant, wild, opaque, stormy, transparent, weak, or strong. Color has three qualities: *hue,* the color itself such as yellow, red, blue, green, and the various intermediaries; *value,* the lightness or darkness of the color; and *intensity,* or *chroma,* the brilliance or dulness of the color. Materials used in working with color are watercolors, either opaque or transparent; tempera; egg tempera; *gouache;* oil paint; dye; wax crayons; chalk, or pastel; light; and textured materials.

Color in light can be seen through colored gelatin or colored glass, and interesting color effects have been achieved with polaroid lenses. The Denver Public Schools are in the process of working on a film that will illustrate the use of polaroid lenses in a classroom situation. There are new color films. In fact, the alert teacher will find that a study of color through the eyes of his students will open up questions and answers that are prophetic of things to come. This does not seem to have happened as a result of the thinking that has been produced through use of the color chart as an end in itself.

Space as an Element. Space can be investigated in like manner. What is *space?* How is it used to enhance other art elements such as line, color, and form? What is meant by *negative space?* There are art critics who consider the space relationship of work before subject matter or skill in painting. The new emphasis on outer space, the space capsules, and the interpenetration of space bring new thinking and ideas to the classroom. Exercises involving interaction of background and foreground create problems in perception for people of any age from that of the junior high school student to adulthood.

A well-balanced art program will include experiences in two-dimensional as well as three-dimensional media. Drawing and painting should be balanced with work in clay and carving in one of the media that lends themselves to carving. The area of color should be opened to the student, as well as an awareness of the importance of the interaction of line, form, space, and color. Creative, imaginative thinking should be encouraged, and opportunities for experimentation should be expanded.

Offerings and Requirements in the Schools. Recent Expansion of Offerings. With increased enrolments in junior and senior high schools and the necessary planning of new housing, as well as expansion of the teaching staff, developments have been taking place that have contributed to materially increased enrolments in art classes and to the broadening of the scope of instruction and its contribution to the general aims of education and society for human happiness. Instead of a single art classroom or studio, it is most common now to have at least two rooms, often very large rooms, in which are furniture and equipment of various kinds that make it possible to offer instruction in a considerable field of art including such things as modeling, ceramics, print making, cartoons, illustrated posters, various basic art elements, art appreciation, painting, drawing, comparative art, history of art, and related crafts.

Along with this have grown the necessity and the consequent phenomenon of employing a team of several teachers who are competent to teach in at least six various fields of art. In other words, art instruction in larger secondary schools today has become not a single course in art but a group of various departments of arts and crafts.

Requirement of Courses in Art. Art has been a requirement in grades seven and eight in the majority of junior high schools for at least three periods a week and usually four or five. It is almost uniformly required in grade seven. Beyond grade eight, very few schools have required a course in art, although in recent years there has been a trend to require either art or music so that this area of general education will not be neglected and be a blind spot for young people.

With the increased variety of offerings within the art course and the more broadly prepared teachers, enrolments will continue to increase, and it is very likely that in many schools art will be a strongly preferred course, if it is not actually required. It is very likely that an extremely large number of secondary schools will begin to require of those students who have not had at least one year in the junior high school at least a semester, if not a year, of work in art in the senior high school, and, in some senior high schools, students who have not had two years of work in the junior high school will be required to receive credit toward graduation with a course in art.

Certain trends in student enrolment and in scheduling will contribute to increased enrolments in art courses and make it simpler for a required course in art to be fitted into the program. Throughout the country, the number of subjects carried each year and offered toward graduation has steadily increased until a typical student program in a large and increasing number of secondary schools in the United States is equivalent to five and a half units of work; consequently, a large and increasing number of students are graduating with more than twenty units of credit, some with as many as twenty-five, and requirements for graduation have been stepped up from fifteen or sixteen credits to seventeen and eighteen in many schools and, indeed, to nineteen or twenty in a few.

An additional trend that may well contribute to increased enrolments in art is that of scheduling most of the courses previously meeting five times a week in four meetings of not less than fifty-five minutes net a week, including mathematics, science, history, social studies, foreign languages, art, music, physical education, etc.

The abilities to perceive and communicate effectively are necessary for effective citizenship. Sensitivity to materials often helps an individual to respond to others who are also working with materials. A person can often communicate effectively with another in a medium other than verbal. "One picture is worth a thousand words" is an adage of worth. The picture might be created in a medium other than paint; it might be a mosaic, or even a pot. It may say "thank you"; it may say "I am willing to contribute"; or it may say "you have done a good job." Because he has worked in one medium of expression, a person can appreciate and be more sympathetic to the efforts of others; this is one way he can enrich his own life and the lives of those with whom he comes in contact.

Healthy participation in an activity that requires creative thought contributes much to the person. This kind of participation requires activity that develops skills of hand and mind. The thought required in developing a skill or in working with a material preserves an equilibrium within the individual. It gives him an opportunity to produce, to react, to give of himself, and to be successful in a production. Too many people are concerned with passive activities such as looking at TV or at movies without being involved in producing or in actively developing a skill. The center of one's interest becomes expanded through art opportunities resulting in healthful activity of mind and hand.

Creative thinking and planning are essential to the earning of a living at higher levels. The person who has ideas is usually the person with a creative turn to his thinking, who often proves invaluable to his employers or to himself if he is self-employed. Imagination, flexibility, and originality are invaluable assets in the daily working and living of people, and in their relationships with each other and with their surroundings, as well as in reaching their goals in life.

Many changes are occurring in the world. Old answers will not fit new situations, and new answers need to be thought out very carefully. Man has to bring to these changes the best thinking and understanding that he is capable of achieving. His mind needs to be flexible to accommodate new ideas and to deal with new problems. He must bring imagination and originality of thought to these new situations of world and space problems.

The central purpose of the schools is to train the individual to accommodate his thinking to changing happenings—to help him to understand himself and his problems of form, space, and time and to meet these problems in a thoughtful, objective manner, so that he can solve them with some measure of perception and sensitivity. One of the most valuable ways of teaching these things is to emphasize creative thought and work with materials and elements peculiar to an art program that is vital, alive, and based on awareness of the importance of solving problems through materials.

QUESTIONS, PROBLEMS, AND ISSUES FOR FURTHER THOUGHT

1. Give reasons to justify the presence of music education in the secondary school curriculum.
2. Evaluate the music-education program in your school, on the basis of the aims and purposes of music education.
3. If your school could provide only a partial music program, list your music offerings, and defend your selection.
4. Discuss and defend the various methods of raising funds for the music program.
5. Take a copy of your school's daily schedule, and introduce a balanced music offering. Show how it might differ from the school's present music program.
6. Discuss the advantages and disadvantages of the private and class methods of teaching music.
7. Prepare a paper on the contribution of vocal music to the secondary school student's general education.
8. Survey the music-education literature, and determine which musical offerings should receive credit and which should be considered extraclass activities.
9. How important do you think that art is in the secondary school curriculum? Should it be a required subject in one or more years? If you believe that it should be, what years do you have in mind?
10. To what do you attribute the very material increase in enrolment in art in some senior high schools in recent years?
11. What do you think are some of the fields in which secondary school students should be afforded the opportunity to explore their interests and

potential talents? In what fields do you think the advanced specialized training might well be offered in a large secondary school?

12. Do you think that some aspects of art should be worked into the courses of study in other subject fields? What fields do you have in mind, and what kind of art?

13. General music has been given for many years in a great many secondary schools. Do you think that there should be a corresponding course in general art that would go into the basic processes of art, its relation to various aspects of life, and appreciation in art—a course in which little if any actual training in production is given?

14. Do you believe that opportunity should be given for some training in art in such applied fields as the making of posters, cartoon drawing, personal dress and cosmetics, interior decoration, and advertising? Can you think of any other fields in which some training in art might well be given?

15. Discuss the value of creative organization of materials, requiring a sensitive relationship of volume, color, line, and space, as a problem for a high school class.

SUPPLEMENTARY MATERIALS

Selected Readings

BERGAMINI, DAVID. *Mathematics*. New York: Time, Inc., Book Division, 1963. Chapter 4, "A Happy Marriage of Curves and Quantities." An excellent discussion on organization of natural creations and an artistic use of this organization.

D'ANDREA, FRANK. "A New Basis for Music in the Secondary Schools," *Music Educators Journal*, XLIX (February-March, 1963), 33–36. The author shows why music should be a part of the general education of all youth, and suggests some developments and changes in attitudes and practices in many segments of music education.

FAULKNER, ZIEGFELD, and HILL. *Art Today*. New York: Holt, Rinehart & Winston, Inc., 1960. Part I, "The Problem of Human Needs."

LALLY, ANN M. "Art Education in the Secondary School," *Bulletin of the N.A.S.S.P.*, March, 1961. Chapter 2, "The Curriculum," and Chapter 3, "Scheduling Art in the Classroom," are concise, informative chapters.

LEEDER, JOSEPH A., and WILLIAM S. HAYNIE. *Music Education in the High School*. Englewood Cliffs, N.J.: Prentice-Hall, Inc., 1958. Chapter 2, "Music for All: The General Music Class."

MCFEE, JUNE. *Preparation for Art*. San Francisco: Wadsworth Publishing Co., Inc., 1961. Chapter 6, "The Creative Process."

MURSELL, JAMES L. *Education for Musical Growth*. Boston: Ginn & Co., 1948. Chapter 12, "The Developmental Program: Its Content."

———. *Music in American Schools*. Morristown, N.J.: Silver Burdett Co., 1953. Chapter 5, "The Sequence of Music Education."

NATIONAL SOCIETY FOR THE STUDY OF EDUCATION. *Basic Concepts in Music Education*. 57th yearbook. University of Chicago Press, 1958. Chapter 10, "Curriculum Construction in Music Education."

REED, CARL. *Early Adolescent Art Education*. Peoria, Ill.: Chas. A. Bennett Co., Inc., 1957. Chapter 2, "Aims and Objectives."

WILSON, HARRY ROBERT. *Music in the High School*. Morristown, N.J.: Silver Burdett Co. Chapter 2, "Music and the Adolescent."

26

The Subject and the Extrasubject Curriculum

INTERRELATIONSHIPS

The subject[1] curriculum, the extrasubject curriculum, and guidance are inseparable components of secondary education. While each of these elements has its own unique function, no one of them can be dissociated from the others in achieving the objectives of education.

Under the narrow concept of the function of secondary education, as preparation for college, the curriculum was largely restricted to the list of subjects required for graduation from a school. The extrasubject program was limited to such activities as debating, dramatics, spelling bees, and ciphering matches, which were regarded merely as means of reinforcing learning in the regular subjects.

The introduction of other extrasubject activities, which were not clearly related to the regular subjects, was accompanied by the strong conviction among teachers that these activities were *separate* and *distinct* from the regular program and, as such, should be conducted outside of the regular school day. Many of the learning activities that were originally extrasubject have been incorporated into the subject curriculum in the sense that credit toward graduation is granted in many schools. Music, speech, and journalism are examples of former extrasubject activities that have become regular subjects in recent years. In many junior and senior

[1] Throughout this chapter, *subject curriculum* will be used to designate that part of the curriculum that is organized into subjects for which credit is given toward high school graduation.

517

high schools, the functions of the homeroom have been incorporated into the core curriculum as a required academic course.

A further step in the fusion of the two programs is revealed in the inclusion of an "activity period" in the daily schedule of an increasing number of schools. Of even greater significance in the merger of the subject and extrasubject programs is the influence the procedures of the latter has exercised upon formal regular classroom instruction, resulting in the greater utilization of informal pupil-teacher planning based upon pupil interests and needs.

At present, the two programs blend and merge at so many points in the mainstream of educative experiences that it is difficult to distinguish between them at all times. The emerging concept of the curriculum as encompassing all the child's school experiences serves to obliterate the artificial lines of demarcation among subject, extrasubject, and guidance activities. In the organization of a total program of learning experiences, the proper balance of the various elements, based not only upon their uniqueness but also on their relative values, should be established. This balance is difficult to achieve and maintain. The current emphasis placed upon academic excellence in the schools by many members of our society may overshadow some of the other basic functions of the high school. Today the high school must make a value judgment between the expectations of some adults in our society and the needs of adolescents within the society.

Among the basic needs of youth that have far-reaching implications for the coordination of subject, extrasubject, and guidance activities are the needs for security, social acceptance, for a satisfactory form of self-expression, success, and developmental experiences. Since the individual is a unitary organism, his basic needs can be served only by his total environment. The school is one aspect of that environment. Only by a unified program within, and by concerted action with other agencies that influence the personality of the child can the school achieve its youth-serving function.

MEANING AND SIGNIFICANCE OF EXTRASUBJECT ACTIVITIES

The term *extrasubject activities* includes a great variety of *learning experiences, carrying no credit toward graduation, in which students voluntarily engage under the auspices of the school.* Extrasubject activities are specially designed to give students the opportunity to develop capabilities for leading and intelligent following of leadership, to have their interest stimulated, to acquire certain skills, and to build desirable attitudes toward school and life. The essence of the extrasubject program is the provision for student initiative, responsibility, and self-direction through direct involvement and freedom in making decisions, formulating plans, and directing and evaluating their own enterprises.

The recognition afforded extrasubject activities is a unique feature of secondary schools in the United States. The program has no parallel in the secondary schools of any other country. The differences can be readily understood when one compares the objectives of secondary education and the ever increasing high school population with those of other countries. The acceptance of the broader responsibilities of the secondary school in the United States as stated by the Committee on the Reorganization of Secondary Education and the Educational Policies Commission has brought with it an awareness on the part of teachers that the attainment of the numerous objectives of the secondary school requires an educational program broad in scope and variety. The assumption underlying the inclusion of each subject in the high school curriculum is that it makes a distinctive contribution toward attainment of desirable educational goals. Each extrasubject activity, likewise, must be justified upon the basis of its unique function in the total educational program. The various elements of the subject and extrasubject programs, however, have much greater significance when coordinated into an integral design of educational resources.

DISTINCTIVE VALUES OF EXTRASUBJECT ACTIVITIES

Many of the potential values of a program of extrasubject activities also are prseent in regular classroom activities. Some writers have insisted that the majority of the activities should be incorporated in classroom teaching procedures, thus reducing or eliminating the separate extrasubject program. If this could be achieved, there is no doubt that the regular classroom procedures would be greatly vitalized. A properly organized and conducted program of extrasubject activities, free of some of the restrictions of time and the formality of the classroom, serves to reinforce and extend classroom learning. Some of the major distinctive values of these activities are described in the paragraphs following.

Fostering Creativity. Creativity can only be evoked in an atmosphere of freedom for individual endeavors. The freedom of choice of activities and the informality of the procedures in conducting individual and group activities, in contrast to the more formal activities of the classroom, provide many opportunities for the student to develop his latent creative powers.

Contributing to Personal and Social Development. In student-directed group activities, the individual learns to respect the opinions and rights of others. In acquiring an insight into the orderly process of human relations, he obtains an understanding of his personal responsibility to others and a deeper concern for their welfare. The student's self-respect is enhanced by his satisfactory participation in individual and group endeavors.

Enriching and Extending Classroom Learning. The opportunities for using academic knowledge and skills in normal out-of-class situations tend to add meaning and significance to those learnings. The opportunities for using and testing various applications of scientific and civic-social precepts provide a keener appreciation of their value. The student also has the opportunity and time to pursue the study of a problem on his own initiative beyond the point prescribed in the classroom. Many subject-related school clubs are specially designed to enable the members to supplement their classroom activities.

Exploring Vocational Possibilities. The student's involvement in a vocationally oriented club such as a future teachers' club may lead him to consider that vocation as a career, or the members of a junior achievement club can gain insight into a business enterprise by organizing and conducting a business of their own.

Contributing to Physical and Mental Fitness. The spontaneous participation in various games and sports is an aid to physical well-being. The skills acquired as a result of engaging in these activities help in developing feelings of self-confidence. Thus, feelings of inferiority because of an inability to compete successfully in activities with one's age peers tend to decrease. This frequently results in a more wholesome outlook on other aspects of school life.

Developing Worthy Leisure-Time and Recreational Interests. Many of the problems of adolescents have their origins in undesirable leisure-time activities. The secondary school is dedicated to assisting students in acquiring wholesome leisure-time activities not only while they are in school but also in later life. Perhaps no part of the school's program is as instrumental in achieving this objective as a vital program of student activities.

CHARACTERISTICS OF AN EFFECTIVE EXTRASUBJECT PROGRAM

A program of extrasubject activities designed to meet the basic present concerns and future life needs of adolescent youth does not differ in any essential detail from any other program based upon sound educational principles. Among the general characteristics of a superior program are the following:

1. A person who is not an athletic director or coach should be designated as director of student extrasubject activities and should be respon-

sible for coordinating the program and relating it to the subject program. He should have the assistance of an advisory committee consisting of teachers and students. In small high schools that are unable to employ a director, an extrasubject-learning committee composed of teachers and students, with the principal as ex officio member, may assume responsibility for the general direction of the program.

2. A central organization of students under faculty leadership, such as a student council, should serve as a clearing house for student ideas and action.

3. The total program should be planned in terms of the resources of the particular school, including the interests and abilities of the teachers.

4. Teacher leaders who understand the educational significance of the activity and who enjoy working with adolescent boys and girls should serve as guides for each activity.

5. All responsible faculty leaders should have an abiding faith in democratic group participation and be skilled in its operation.

6. Student initiative and responsibility should be promoted in organizing, planning, and conducting their own activities.

7. The activities should be of sufficient variety to provide for the interests of each individual student.

8. The program should be sufficiently flexible to provide for the changing interests of pupils.

9. The activities should be organized to make it possible for pupils to find satisfaction in individual, small group, and all-school activities.

10. The activities should be conducted to promote the spontaneous, joyous participation of students in a worthy enterprise.

11. The program of extrasubject activities should be planned to meet educational needs not provided for students in their other school experiences.

12. Extrasubject activities should be organized to complement and reinforce the other educative experiences of pupils.

13. The high school should provide time in its daily schedule for extrasubject student activities such as assemblies, homerooms, club meetings, and intramural sports.

14. The activities should allow for more student freedom than is usually exhibited in the classroom; no grades should be assigned, credit given, or points awarded.

15. Participation in extrasubject activities except the homeroom should be voluntary. By counseling rather than by point systems or other administrative devices, students should be encouraged but not forced to participate.

16. Adequate records of participation in extrasubject activities should be made a part of each student's permanent records.

17. The program should be subject to constant reappraisal as a basis for improving its services to youth.

18. No student organization that is unwilling to accept the supervision of the school in matters pertaining to membership and activities should be permitted to function.

THE HOMEROOM AND THE CURRICULUM

The growth in the size of enrolments in high schools brought with it a recognition of the need for each school to organize the large numbers of students into small groups, each under the supervision of a teacher, to maintain the personal relationship that had existed between the teacher and the students in small schools. The homeroom is a basic unit of representation of the central organization. A teacher serves as adviser for each homeroom group.

The chief objectives ascribed to the homeroom are to handle routine administrative matters, establish and maintain friendly personal relationships between teachers and students, afford students guidance, supplement the curriculum, provide a "home base" in the school for each student, and supply a forum for all students to discuss school issues and many of their personal and social concerns.

In many schools, the same teacher serves as homeroom adviser to a group during their entire stay in high school. Thus, the teacher is able to get to know each pupil quite well, which provides a sound basis for guidance and individual counseling. However, in the group discussion of many topics, there is opportunity to supplement the curriculum and instruction of the classroom. For example, an important concomitant outcome for many students is the opportunity to express in a small friendly group situation the ideas they may be reluctant to express in a large group until they develop feelings of self-confidence acquired in the small-group discussions.

The nature, procedure, and spirit of the homeroom are essentially different from those of the classroom. In the homeroom, discussion is the principal activity. There is no "ground to be covered" prod or hurry, and there are no recitations, tests, or teacher's marks.

In addition, many things touched upon in the classroom may well be discussed at length and with considerable freedom in the homeroom, involving applications to a degree not possible in the atmosphere of dispatch so common in the classroom.

A list of topics that might supplement those studied in the regular school subjects was suggested by a committee of teachers in the Niles, Illinois, Township Community High School, as follows:

ACADEMIC ACHIEVEMENT

Test scores and grades
Planning a high school program
What to get out of high school
Homework
Study habits
Wise use of time
Excessive use of the phone
Study conditions and techniques
The quality of learning
Taking tests

PLANNING FOR THE FUTURE

Life goals
Discovering your interests
Choosing your career
Vocations in a rapidly changing world
College plans
What do colleges require
Tests for college
Scholarships and aid
Military service
Part-time work
Seeking a job

ATTITUDE TOWARD ONE'S SELF

1. The physical self:
    Dating habits
    Drinking & smoking
    Appearance, dress & grooming
    Posture
    Rest and sleep

2. The emotional self:
    Self understanding
    Self confidence
    Self improvement
    Maturity (self realization, self decision, self determination)
    Defeat and disappointment
    Activities and interests
    The growing need for independence

3. The moral self (values & attitudes)
    Honesty and cheating
    Habits, good and bad
    Money and its management
    Curfew and late hours
    Use of time
    Driving

ATTITUDE TOWARD OTHERS

1. Schoolmates:
    Behavior at school functions
    Social standards and skills
    Interpersonal relations
    Getting along with others
    Leadership and cooperation
    Cliques and their meaning
    Tolerance
    Gossip

2. Boy-girl relationships:
    Understanding sex
    Dating and courtship
    Marriage and planning

3. Home and family

4. Authority figures and others:
    Attitude toward teachers and administrators
    Worth and dignity of others
    Minority views
    Respect for property

ATTITUDE TOWARD THE SCHOOL

Rules and regulations
School policies
School spirit
Orientation to the school and its facilities
Service to the school
Year-end review
Follow-up study
Improving the school

THE STUDENT COUNCIL AS CURRICULUM

The student council is the central coordinating agency of the extrasubject program. This organization is a schoolwide body representative of, and responsible to, the whole student body. In practically all high schools, the chairman, vice-chairman, secretary, and treasurer of the council are nominated and elected in all-school elections. In addition to these officers representing the general student groups, students representing various school organizations comprise the membership of the council. The unit of representation is usually the homeroom, school club, class, or special-interest group such as the athletic pep club.

In a considerable number of large senior high schools, the sophomores, juniors, and seniors each have a student council organized to deal with matters that pertain particularly to each group. These councils are in addition to the all-school student council. In a few large cities with several high schools, a city-wide student council, composed of student representatives of each high school, is organized to consider matters of common concern to all the high schools in the city. A *director of student activities* employed in the city school system usually serves as sponsor of this type of organization. This official may act as coordinator of other extrasubject activities in the school system.

The student council in secondary schools in the United States usually has authority in problems of administering extracurricular activities, particularly in the following areas: chartering clubs and administering the intramural program, traffic and conduct in the lunchrooms and in the halls, matters of school attendance, and the parking of cars. They also participate in developing policies and fundamental principles relative to discipline. Also, they are beginning to have some part in managing the public-relations activities of the school. It is obvious that the participation of the student council in these fields has excellent educational potentialities not only for those participating as members of the student council but also for the student body of the school as a whole.

The student council should be employed to advise the faculty in a considerable number of areas and sit in upon discussions of such problems and give conclusions and observations, as do the teachers. These educational experiences should be very valuable. In addition, a discussion by the members of the council of school issues and problems constitutes a rich educational experience. Properly organized and conducted, the activities of the student council provide an example of representative democracy in action, thus giving added meaning and significance to the students' study of democratic processes in various subjects in the curriculum. Through their involvement in activities, students gain insights into the problems in the application of the principles of self-government and representative democracy in actual situations. The development of a sensitivity to some of the problems encountered in human relations in a free society, as well as the experience in dealing with these matters, provides valuable training in good citizenship.

SCHOOL ASSEMBLY AS CURRICULUM

The school assembly serves as the focus in integrating many aspects of extrasubject and subject programs. The mass involvement of students and teachers as participants presents an opportunity for the presentation of programs that tend to counteract the divisive results of departmental organization and specialization of the high school.

Types of Assembly Programs. The school assembly had its origin as a chapel period with a strong religious emphasis. In the second stage of its development, it was an adult-dominated exercise in which the school principal or a teacher expressed his views on various school matters. In recent years, there has been a trend to make the assembly a true student activity period with students, under the leadership of a teacher, assuming responsibility in planning and conducting the program. Assemblies now are planned to include, during the course of a school year, a great variety of topics. In the presentation of these topics, many types of programs are employed, including

1. Musical programs presented by students, faculty members, and others in person and via the radio, and group singing.
2. The presentation of plays, debates, and other forms of public speech
3. Group and panel discussions of questions and topics in various fields by students and teachers
4. Presentation of radio programs, direct or replayed from tape or other recordings, and television programs
5. Formal ceremonies of various types for various purposes—patriotic, civic, student recognition, etc.
6. Elections and discussions of student candidates and platforms
7. Discussion of school policies and current community problems
8. Demonstrations of science classes and clubs, and exhibition of home economics, art, and shop classes
9. Guest performances by artists, musicians, or speakers
10. Exchange assembly programs with other schools

Contributions to Student Development. The wide range of topics, with the opportunity afforded students to play a great variety of roles in assembly programs, makes the assembly one of the most significant educational activities of the school. Of particular value is the opportunity to acquire self-assurance by participating in programs before one's age peers. This participation should be as widespread as possible.

In many schools, small-group assemblies in addition to the all-school assemblies are held to provide the experience many students need in taking part in programs before small audiences in order to acquire feelings of self-confidence. The students who encounter difficulty in making social adjustments in large group situations often can find their place in small groups. Assembly programs also can be arranged to involve large numbers of participants with different types of talent. By participating in the assembly program, students acquire poise, skill in correct speech, and ability to cooperate with others. The acquisition of socially approved audience habits is one of the most important outcomes of school-assembly experience.

The presentation by students of their interests or hobbies may be utilized for the purpose of arousing new interests among other students. Demonstrations and discussions of different types of vocations may serve to create interest and provide information in regard to various vocational pursuits. Topics pertaining to personal and community health may be presented in such a manner as to contribute to the health objective. Subjects of general school concern may be presented in the assembly to enhance student morale.

Students learn the importance and accepted ways of assuming responsibility for planning, presiding, making announcements, and otherwise taking part in the assembly programs. The students' intellectual and cultural interests may be reinforced and expanded by programs on art; current local, national, and international social and economic issues; music; and science.

A very popular assembly program is the music-appreciation type in which demonstrations of different musical instruments are given by members of the school orchestra, the range of tonal qualities of the human voice is demonstrated by members of the school chorus, or the identification of classical and popular songs is attempted by the student audience.

Many programs are designed to reveal our cultural heritage through the observance of the birthdays of notable persons and the anniversaries of historic events. The student's motivation is strengthened when he is given the opportunity to demonstrate the work he has done in other school activities such as in regular classes, clubs, dramatics groups, and orchestras. The recognition of superior achievement in subject and other extrasubject activities (such as athletics) in assembly programs is an additional incentive to greater student efforts in those areas. The emphasis upon serious educational topics does not preclude the possibility of making them interesting and enjoyable for students. Some programs can be justified for mere entertainment value.

The interschool-exchange assembly is one in which students of one school give an assembly program for a neighboring school, which is reciprocated in a similar manner by the other school. This type of assembly tends to foster good will and cooperation between the two schools and to provide prestige-giving experiences for the students who participate.

The extent to which the school assembly serves the developmental needs of adolescents is largely dependent upon the nature of their participation in them. An assembly committee, comprised of students and teachers, should be given responsibility for planning the all-school assembly programs. The student members are usually appointed by the student council. The committee should invite suggestions for assembly programs from the students of the school. In the making of decisions in regard to the programs, the ideas submitted by the students should be evaluated in terms of the accepted functions of the assembly. Another method of obtaining wide participation in assemblies is to give students the opportunity, near the close of the school year, to evaluate the previous programs and make suggestions for the assemblies to be given the following year.

SCHOOL ATHLETICS AS CURRICULUM

Contributions to Student Development. No part of the high school program has attracted more attention or provoked more controversy than have athletic activities. There has been little disagreement, however, in regard to the necessity for a program of indoor and outdoor sports to satisfy the urge to engage in physical activity that is characteristic of adolescents. There is a widespread acceptance of the idea that a properly conducted program of sports contributes to the physical welfare of youth. There is growing recognition that the physical development of an adolescent not only is the basis of good physical health but is also essential to his mental health. Feelings of inferiority and social insecurity are often associated with an adolescent's recognition of his physical limitations in comparison with the physical condition of his age peers.

Intramural Sports. A program of intramural sports is designed to provide opportunities for participation by students of varying degrees of physical abilities. If sufficiently broad in scope, the program provides physical exercise, social experience, and leisure-time pursuits for all students. Provision can be made for a great variety of student interests by organizing teams representing classes, homerooms, or clubs. These small-group activities may include badminton, basketball, bowling, golf, handball, swimming, track, and volleyball. Opportunities for individual student participation in archery, hiking, and skiing should be included. Facilities should be provided in the student game room for table tennis, bridge, chess, and checkers. While interscholastic competition for girls has been deemed undesirable in most schools, the intramural activities can be adjusted readily to serve their needs.

A survey of pupil interests by the student council may reveal many for which provision can be made. In fact, the intramural program can be varied as teacher leadership and the other resources of the school will permit. Students can benefit by being given general supervision of the program through their student council. Such student control of the activities also tends to ensure a program more attuned to the interests of all the students. Students can acquire a keen sense of relative values by making decisions in regard to the regulations that should govern the organization and procedure of an intramural program.

Interscholastic Competitive Sports. Many educators hold the opinion that competitive activities make an important contribution to the objectives of secondary education. Preceding and during interscholastic contests, cooperation of members of the team, coaches, and other students of the school is essential. The drive for recognition as a worthy member of the school team provides a strong motive for self-discipline. Some students who encounter difficulty in gaining emotional satisfaction in other school activities may find in athletic competition the degree of success that their mental health requires. There is no more effective means of developing school spirit and unity in the student body than through loyalty to the school teams. Likewise, no greater opportunity exists in the school for developing the ideals of good sportsmanship, fair play, and consideration of the rights of others than in situations involving interscholastic competition. These ideals, however, are not achieved automatically. Understanding of their significance and suggestions for their attainment can best be acquired by student-teacher discussions of them in school assemblies, homeroom meetings, club meetings, and regular classes, as well as through the personal example of the teachers. The school also has the responsibility of contributing to the feeling of security of the student participants in the contests by providing periodic medical examinations, adequate equipment, and accident-insurance protection.

Objections to Athletic Programs. The adverse criticisms directed against the athletic program of the high school have been largely centered upon interscholastic contests, especially where

1. Only a comparatively small number of students, who already possess a considerable amount of physical prowess, participate, and these are frequently exploited to the neglect of those students who could derive benefits in the form of physical development by participating themselves
2. The type of competition engendered by interscholastic contests tends to develop attitudes on the part of both the participants and non-participants that undermine the educative values of the activity

3. Excessive local community pride and "old school" loyalty exaggerate the desire to win games to the extent that school authorities are not free to plan and direct a well-balanced program of physical activities for all students

SCHOOL CLUBS AS CURRICULUM

The school club is an association of students with similar intellectual, social, or recreational interests. Through the club activities, each student member is enabled to share with others and to pursue further his own interests. A high school that attempts to serve all its students in this manner will be required to sponsor a great diversity of clubs. The objectives is usually formulated by school clubs generally include the following:

1. To satisfy the urge of students to engage in creative endeavors
2. To assist students in acquiring social skills through association with other students
3. To promote the development of desirable personal qualities such as initiative and self-confidence
4. To enable students to explore and extend worthy vocational pursuits
5. To encourage students to acquire hobbies and other recreational interests

Organization and Procedures. Club membership should be on a voluntary basis. However, if every student is not a member of one or more clubs, the school should re-examine the adequacy of its club program and the effectiveness of its guidance services. The number and types of clubs should be sufficiently flexible to meet the constantly changing concerns of adolescents. The student council should make provision in its procedures for chartering new clubs when sufficient student interest is manifested for their establishment. The council, likewise, should abolish existing clubs when they cease to serve the needs of students.

Student interest in school clubs may be aroused by explanations of their programs in the school orientation activities and through discussions and demonstrations in homerooms and assemblies. The members and officers of a school club gain valuable experience by giving these explanations.

Subject-related Clubs. Some clubs are closely related to the regular high school courses, such as biology, Spanish, and mathematics clubs. Clubs of this type are designed to reinforce and extend the students' interests in the different fields of knowledge. To ensure the attainment of this goal, it is necessary to avoid making the procedures of the club meetings parallel too closely the classroom sessions. The members of each club should elect their own officers. In planning the club's programs, the officers should utilize the suggestions and services of all the members. The activities should include a great variety of individual student projects, as well as small-group and general club enterprises. The club sponsor should be a teacher who possesess a keen interest in, and is thoroughly informed in, the field of knowledge related to the club, as well as the ability to see its possibilities of providing satisfying student experiences. An even more essential qualification of the club sponsor, however, is that he should genuinely enjoy his associations with high school boys and girls on an informal, friendly basis.

Special-Interest Clubs. Many of the clubs should be of the hobby type, leading to the establishment of strong interests and the necessary skills in elevating leisure-time amusements. The importance of planning one's recreational activities should be the topic for discussion in some of the meetings of the club. An analysis of leisure-time activities should include a consideration of the personal satisfactions to be derived by engaging in the activities, as well as their effects upon the physical and economic welfare of the individual. The social implications of recreation should also be emphasized. With an increasing amount of time for recreation, large numbers of persons are rushing nervously about engaging in this or that pastime for no reason except that they have nothing else to do. A fruitful undertaking for the members of a school club would be to examine their reasons for engaging in certain recreational activities.

Recreational Clubs. Opportunities also should be provided for students to acquire skills in creative recreational activities, thus enabling them to derive pleasure and personal satisfaction from their participation in this important type of recreation both in and outside of school. Every high school should sponsor arts-and-crafts clubs in which students can discover for themselves the fun to be derived from manipulating tools and materials in processes such as clay modeling, leatherworking, and woodworking. Significant avocational and vocational skills frequently result from experiences in clubs of this type. Other special interests can be provided for in airplane, camera, glee, social-dancing, public-speaking, and popular-science clubs.

Emphasis should be placed upon out-of-school recreation in which persons in various income groups can engage, since all high school students will not be in the high income brackets. Through music-appreciation, motion-picture, and radio clubs, students may gain powers of discrimination by their audience participation in activities to which practically all our population have easy access. In the area of leisure-time reading, book clubs may be organized for the purpose of studying biography, drama, poetry, or adventure stories; their programs might include book reviews, short-story reading, and discussion of current books and book design. Physical health of students may be promoted by clubs devoted to outdoor activities such as hiking, forestry, gardening, and lifesaving.

OTHER TYPES OF EXTRASUBJECT ACTIVITIES

Speech Activities and School Publications. Speech activities including debate, student-forum discussions, and school plays are and should be closely related to the instruction in the regular English classes. This is likewise true of the school newspaper, which is usually published by a journalism or English class. Intramural or interscholastic competition in debating and forum discussions may be of value in motivating students. The opportunity to present a play before an all-school audience also may "point up" the classroom work in drama.

Commencement Programs. Senior students in many high schools plan and conduct their own graduation exercises. Instead of having the traditional commencement speaker, the students under the leadership of the teachers plan, prepare, and give the program. A topic of local community or general interest is selected and presented in the form of a pageant, musical program, or student discussion. The cooperative effort involved and the experience gained by students from participating in a program of this type, which has so much significance for themselves and their parents, are of great value in personality development. Other results of this procedure are a program of superior quality and a greater public interest.

Social Dances and Parties. The failure of adolescents to develop social skills and experience in worthy recreational activities is the source of many of their problems. Feelings of boredom are easily acquired by high school students and may drive them to seek undesirable amusements and pastimes. A portion of lunch time and some activity periods are set aside in many high schools for social dancing. An effort is made to obtain wide participation in the activity, under the supervision of teachers. Instruction in dancing and a discussion of good manners in homerooms serve to encourage participation by larger numbers of students.

School Camping as Curriculum. The school camp is one of the most recent additions to the list of organizations of the high school. Camping was formerly restricted to the children whose parents were financially able to send them to a camp under private auspices. There is a rapidly growing recognition among educators that outdoor camp experience should be an integral part of *every* child's education. In many school systems, school funds are being used to maintain school camps during the school term. Different groups of students under the supervision of their teachers may rotate two-week camping periods throughout the school term. In other schools, the camps are conducted in the summer.

While one of the chief values of the outdoor camp program is the contribution it makes to the health and physical development of students, it is by no means the only benefit derived. The social maturity of the individual is enhanced by the experience of living with his age peers in the informal, democratic atmosphere of a school camp in which camp responsibilities are shared.

A significant educative experience for students may be achieved by having them make careful, detailed plans before their camping trip. The plans should include a tentative program of general and individual activities, articles needed by campers, and an estimate of camp expenses. After the students return from the camp, they should evaluate their experiences and explore possibilities of relating them to their classroom work.

GUIDANCE AS CURRICULUM

Coordination of Curriculum Guidance. In the implementation of the unitary concept of the school program, teachers relate their work as homeroom sponsors, school-club advisers, and classroom teachers to that of the guidance counselor. The inherent unity of the curriculum and guidance has yet to be fully recognized. The traditionally narrow subject-matter concept of the curriculum and the failure to recognize that guidance permeates every aspect of the school program have served to delay the union. The emerging concept of the curriculum as encompassing all the child's school experiences has made evident the necessity of considering guidance as an integral part of the curriculum.

Essential both to curriculum construction and the formulation of the guidance program is a philosophy of education that gives due recognition to social values and to the abilities and needs of the pupils involved. Since the objectives of education have their counterparts in those of guidance, they should be drawn from the same sources.

Among the basic needs of youth that have far-reaching implications for the coordination of the curriculum and guidance are a sense of personal worth, a feeling of security, a satisfactory form of self-expression, developmental experiences, understanding of oneself and the world of work and its interrelationships to one's personal life and the life of the community, and an insight into the ways of democracy. In meeting these needs, the acquisition of skills in reading, listening, conversation, writing, and arithmetic in meaningful situations is essential. Of paramount importance is the need for a set of values by which the pupil can evaluate his actions, feelings, and thinking.

Out of pupil needs come urges to action. Because of the individual's lack of knowledge of his own abilities and the requirements and possibilities of various vocations, these urges to many adolescents, however impelling, may often be vague. To avoid feelings of frustration and futility on the part of the pupils, the school has the responsibility of assisting them in clarifying and defining their purposes. The school likewise has the obligation of providing services designed to give pupils the knowledge and skills necessary to the achievement of their purposes. Curricular content, properly selected and organized, along with the regular counseling, can be of great assistance to the pupil in this respect.

The affinity of guidance and the curriculum is clearly revealed in the core course, in which subject matter and guidance activities are interwoven into an integrated pattern of learning. The emphasis upon guidance also has affected the curriculum to the extent that a separate course in guidance has been established recently in several high schools.

Counselors can render an essential service in curriculum-reconstruction programs. One of the bases for decisions concerning the substance and organization of the curriculum is the characteristics of the students to be educated. An important source of information about students is that assembled by the guidance counselors. A necessary first step in a general curriculum-revision program is an evaluation of the existing curriculum in terms of the extent to which it enables students to realize their full potentials as citizens in a democratic society. In the process of reconstructing the curriculum, each proposal for revision should be judged in terms of its potential value in meeting the needs of the students enrolled in the school.

Assisting Students with Special Problems. Problems of the curriculum and those of guidance must be approached against the background of the home and the previous experiences of the child. Data relating to these matters are pertinent in ascertaining the fitness of a pupil for a given course of study, in adjusting the curriculum to his needs, and in guiding him toward the attainment of desirable educational and vocational goals. In diagnosing pupil performance and predicting his future behavior, a teacher or counselor must be proficient in the use and interpretation of a wide range of tools and techniques that are significant in studying individual behavior. Among the most useful are sociometric tests; autobiographies; observational techniques; interest inventories; projective personality techniques; psychological tests; cumulative records containing information on family background, health, school marks, and work experiences; and out-of-school activities. These data should be supplemented by a knowledge of the more persistent problems common to all youth in our society.

The large numbers of students who withdraw from high school before graduation present one of the school's most difficult problems. There is an increasing awareness among teachers that the early identification of potential dropouts is possible and necessary if the problem is to be alleviated. The guidance specialist possesses the instruments and techniques to identify individual students who possess the characteristics that predispose a student to withdraw from school before graduation.

Counseling vs. Guidance. Most of the guidance services provided in regular courses and homerooms may be designated as group guidance. Since there is little time in these activities and many teachers have limited preparation to engage in individual counseling, the services of well-qualified counselors are essential in an adequate guidance program. The minimum number of counselors suggested by guidance authorities is one counselor for each 250 to 300 students in the secondary school.

Many guidance specialists regard the guidance activities in group situations as merely supplementary to their counseling. They assert that group counseling is limited to obtaining information about the students and giving them educational and vocational information. What use the individual student makes of this information depends upon his attitude, outlook, and other personality traits that come within the scope of individual counseling by a highly trained counselor.

This point of view, as stated by Stiller, is as follows:

. . . the counseling psychologist views counseling as a process designed to promote an individual's understanding of himself and of his environment. It differs from guidance in the personal nature of the process and in the depth of penetration into the individual's perceptions. To the educator, counseling is one of the guidance services; to the counseling psychologist, it is the guidance function.[2]

Individual counseling by an expert counselor is an essential part of the guidance services in a school; however, if students are to be assisted in meeting problems that stem from physical, mental, emotional, and social needs, the whole school personnel including teachers, principals, deans, nurses, speech therapists, and psychologists must be involved directly or as resource persons. The student's perception of self is formed as a result of experiences with others in group situations as well as in individual conferences. The counselor's success in assisting students in acquiring an understanding themselves is greatly influenced by the man-

---

[2] Alfred Stiller, "The High School Guidance Counselor," *Bulletin of the N.A.S.S.P.*, Vol. 45, No. 265 (May, 1961), p. 152.

ner in which the curriculum is implemented in terms of meaningful learning in the classroom.

While the guidance point of view should permeate the entire school, only those teachers who possess the following characteristics should be given guidance responsibilities:

1. An appreciation of the naturalness of individual differences
2. A concept that all behavior has a cause
3. An appreciation of pupils' problems and a willingness to *help* them solve the problems but not to solve them for them. (Personal and social growth comes about only as pupils are given opportunity to solve their own problems.)
4. Willingness to modify a situation as well as expectation that a pupil will modify his behavior in the situation
5. Willingness to expend effort to give each pupil a fair share of time, rather allowing oneself to become absorbed by the complex problems of a few
6. A sensitivity to early manifestations of problems so that they may be detected immediately and remedied, if possible, thus obviating the need for extensive treatment later
7. A realization that feelings are facts to be considered in any learning situation
8. An appreciation of the learning value in adjusting to controls and limitations, as well as the need for development of self-direction, independent thinking, and initiative

QUESTIONS, PROBLEMS, AND ISSUES FOR FURTHER THOUGHT

1. Present arguments for and against minimum scholastic achievement as a requirement for participation in extrasubject activities by high school students.
2. What relationship exists between participation in extrasubject activities and scholastic success? Vocational success?
3. What are the chief difficulties encountered by high schools in developing a satisfactory intramural program of athletics? Suggest methods of overcoming these difficulties.
4. How may an extrasubject activity be evaluated in terms of its contribution to the objectives of secondary education?
5. Obtain a list of the activities offered in some high school, and determine to what extent they form a well-balanced program.
6. How may group guidance serve to orient the pupil to individual counseling?
7. It has been said that adolescents are absorbed by concerns for the immediate present. How may this preoccupation with new social experiences be translated into learning experiences that serve as a basis for future life activities?
8. Describe procedures for making a case study of a high school student.

SUPPLEMENTARY MATERIALS

SELECTED READINGS

ASSOCIATION FOR SUPERVISION AND CURRICULUM DEVELOPMENT. *Guidance in the Curriculum.* 1955 yearbook. Washington, D.C.: The Association, 1955. Develops the concept that guidance is inseparable from the curriculum.
——. *New Insights and the Curriculum.* 1963 yearbook. Washington, D.C.: The Association, 1963. Reports various new insights, and considers their implications for the curriculum.

FREDERICK, ROBERT W. *The Third Curriculum.* New York: Appleton-Century-Crofts, Inc., 1959. Emphasizes that student activities constitute the third curriculum, paralleling the required first curriculum and the second, the elective or special curriculum.

JOHNSON, WALTER E., BUFORD, STEFFRE, and ROY A. ADELFELT. *Personnel and Guidance Services.* New York: McGraw-Hill Book Co., Inc. 1963. An excellent treatment of pupil services.

MCKEAN, ROBERT C. *Principles and Methods in Secondary Education.* Columbus, Ohio: Charles E. Merrill Books, Inc., 1962. Chapter 10, "Extra-class Activities," and Chapter 11, "The Classroom Teacher and Guidance." Emphasis is on the role of the teachers in these areas.

MAYBEE, G. D., and O. MCCRACKEN, JR. "Do Interscholastic Athletics in the Junior High School Aid or Retard a Desirable Educational Program?" *Bulletin of the N.A.S.S.P.,* XLIV (April, 1960), 96–100. An objective analysis of the pros and cons of interscholastic athletics in the junior high school.

NATIONAL ASSOCIATION OF SECONDARY SCHOOL PRINCIPALS. "Vitalizing Student Activities in the Secondary School." *Bulletin of the N.A.S.S.P.,* XXXVI (February, 1952). The entire volume is directed to discussions of the various extraclass activities by theorists and practitioners in secondary education.

AUDIO-VISUAL MATERIALS

Recording

Improving the Services of Extra Class Activities, #235. J. Lloyd Trump. Educational Growth Series. Los Angeles. 36-44-minute discussion. 33⅓ rpm.

27

Individualization and the Curriculum

Students in the secondary school vary significantly in many ways. Generally, however, the school takes into account only differences that (1) are stable and enduring (for example, sex), (2) can be accurately assessed (for example, age), (3) have a major influence on educational progress (for example, mental age), and (4) are acceptable to society (for example, public schools do not discriminate on the basis of religion). Each characteristic of the student that meets one or more of these specifications presents opportunities for adjusting the curriculum including its organization, objectives, and learning experiences. Should the school make adjustments to individual characteristics? If so, what adjustments, and how should they be made? The search for answers to these questions brings one face to face with the most important issues and trends in secondary school curriculum.

TYPES OF VARIABILITY AMONG STUDENTS

Four areas of student variability have been considered especially salient in influencing the curriculum. The first of these is in the area of intellectual and academic achievement. It is usual for schools and teachers to plan curriculum in the light of the distribution of mental ages and scores earned by pupils on standardized achievement tests. Students in most secondary schools range from those with high mental age and achievement, capable of passing graduate record examinations in major universities, to those with mental ages of ten or less, many of whom cannot read beyond the fourth-grade level. A mental age of ten refers to the level of mental ability possessed by the average ten-year-old. It is not always recognized that individual differences are greater in the secondary school than in the elementary school. Small differences in mental ability and achievement become extended as children proceed in education. Those who have not learned prerequisite skills fall farther behind their classmates in academic achievement, and those more advanced mentally progress in their mental growth at a more rapid rate.

Just as there are differences between students, so there are differences within an individual. For example, one who appears to be incompetent in an aspect of, say, composition may excel in literature. It is not practical simply to label a child as bright or stupid, advanced or retarded. Neither should he be called average. The concept of the all-around person is misleading. He or she does not exist. Given sixty independent measurements, the chance that any individual will be in the median 50 per cent of all of them is about one in a quintillion. The individual student may be highly creative yet fail in his performance of a routine task. So, too, the student is likely to differ in his abilities to use the various intellectual tools required for problems in diverse fields like humanities, sciences, mathematics, practical arts, and human relations.

Differences in personality and character have been a second reason for modifying the curriculum. Schools are often asked to do something about students who do not possess desirable traits of personality or of character. In a limited sense, *personality* refers to the typical ways in which a person reacts to himself and to others, and *character* is that part of personality that has moral implications, such as respect for persons and property. Characteristic dichotomies frequently used to differentiate the personalities of students in schools are active—passive, socially responsive —self-centered, aggressive—submissive, independent—dependent, and anxious—secure.

A third area of differentiation with implications for curriculum has been found in types of personal problems and interests. The adolescent with particular problems of health, academic status, social adjustment, or choice of career directs our attention to what should be taught and how.

The fourth area of human-variability figuring in curriculum is that found in physical characteristics. Age and sex differences are the most obvious physical features in terms of which curriculum has been differentiated. The results of individual growth patterns (in size, weight, sexual maturation, and motor coordination) are sometimes considered in individualizing the curriculum. Although students differ in vision, hearing, speech, and physical vigor, schools generally make adaptations for these differences only when the differences are very great. Currently, an educational strategy is being proposed that holds that, by focusing on "exceptionality," attending to extremes, schools may begin to note that "normals" too are exceptional in these areas and should, therefore, receive differential treatment. Acute defects in the vision of a few, for instance, may lead to more readable printing for all. If instruction is adapted to the deaf child, the advantages of tactile cues may become available to others.

HOW SHOULD WE REGARD VARIABILITY?

There are several alternative responses to the problems created by the fact of individual differences. There are people who want to use knowledge of these differences in controlling and shaping the behavior of students to common ends. One holding this position is somewhat like the congressman who polls his constituents regarding their opinions on a politically controversial matter, not in order to be guided on the issue itself but to find out to what extent he must take steps to change the opinion in his district. A teacher who, for instance, wants all his students to conjugate verbs at a given level of proficiency should, in planning the strategy for ordering instruction, study the characteristics of students. Information about their personal interests and deficiencies in their backgrounds, and identification of influential peers, may be important in getting control over the students to change their behavior in accordance with the prescribed outcome.

Contrary to studying the characteristics of students for purposes of gaining control over them is the practice of identifying talents, deficiencies, interests, and personal needs for purposes of determining the instructional outcomes themselves. The possibility of such a practice is shown in a familiar dialog:

Q: "What will you teach next semester?"
A: "I do not know, I haven't seen my students yet."

This point of view is related to a Copernican step in secondary education taken at the turn of the century. Prior to 1900, the secondary school curriculum was constructed on the premise that the school, its curriculum, was the constant in the equation of school and student. Any student entering the school was to "get with it." If he would not, he would be punished or discharged for lack of effort (deficient moral character). There was little thought of the necessity for adapting either instructional outcomes or procedures to the individual. Rather, it was commonly supposed that any student could learn what was taught as well as any other child, if he would only apply himself with equal industry.

During the twentieth century, the scientific movement in education focused public attention on new notions of individual differences. The development of intelligence tests and controversies over the parts played by nurture and nature made educators conscious that efficiency in teaching might be conditioned by the capacity of the student. Also, for a variety of social reasons, the secondary school changed from a selective institution serving only a few to a common school attended by all. With this change came a new premise, the Copernican step, which made the student the constant and the school the variable. The school was expected to make its content profitable for all students, increasing holding power by adjusting curriculum to the wide range of mental, physical, social, and emotional levels found among the total population of youth.

There is conflict between the responses of those who want the schools to increase the range of variability among students and those who believe that the school should reduce variability. The problem has been to develop a curriculum that will at times divide student from student according to their desired activities in life and at the same time to unite student with student in common humanity and citizenship.

Underlying all arguments about individualization of educational outcomes, materials, and methods are two educational goals: One goal is the extension of ability among those with special talents, "giving to those who have"; the other is the guarding of equity, "giving to those who have not." These goals are, in fact, complementary; they can be sought simultaneously. Students who have the interest and ability to go beyond the content allocated to a grade level by a published course of study or textbook should be given the opportunity to do so. Such acceleration is consistent with their natural pace, and there is little reason for wasting their productive capacity. On the other hand, to place culturally deprived students in custodial classes, which can lead only to a perpetuation of the kind of life these students and their parents are presently experiencing, is a travesty in a school within a democratic society. The nature of our society precludes the encouragement of an intellectual aristocracy and promises opportunity for knowledge in those subjects from which all students go on to relatively certain futures.

Important national consequences follow responses to individual variability. Currently, for example, British educators are concerned that there has been a loss of talent to their nation because of a traditional practice of "streaming," or the assignment of students to particular schools and course offerings (curriculum) on the basis of examinations taken at an early age. On the surface, the scores earned on "leaving" examinations are thought to have much predictive validity, that is, those who make high marks are indeed more likely than those with low ones to succeed in higher education. However, the test scores may be spurious as predictors. The scores predict chiefly because those who make low marks are not given the opportunity to acquire subsequently the prerequisites to higher education. Streaming restricts the population from which potential talent can be drawn.

Contrarily, Soviet leaders prohibited segregation of children on the basis of tests and ordered that "exemplary" and "experimental" schools for gifted children be restored to standard pedagogical practices and that the academic criteria in ordinary schools be raised to the level at which these "exemplary" schools operated. As a consequence, a greater number of academically talented youths were found. It is likely that the Soviet's officially stated assumption that all pupils have the capacity for successful academic performance gives more students opportunities for such performance, although there may be other less desirable consequences accompanying the denial of the theory of innate differences. The educational system may be threatened when students fail, inasmuch as responsibility for failure rests on the instructor not on the student. Since, according to the Soviet doctrine, all students have the capacity for success, failure must be attributable to negligence or incompetence of the teacher and those responsible for planning the curriculum. The early American idea that failure was to be explained by a weakness of character is not available to the Soviet teachers as an excuse either, since they hold character to be also a product of nurture.

In development of curriculum in the United States, administrators, supervisors, and teachers take into account the fundamental values of (1) individual development including the pursuit of excellence for both those with special abilities and those with deficiencies and (2) the shaping of an individual's behavior so that it corresponds with society's intellectual and social norms.

ISSUES AND PRINCIPLES OF INDIVIDUALIZATION OF CURRICULUM IN THE SECONDARY SCHOOL

Individualism vs. Individuality. American secondary schools are opposed to self-indulgence. Our schools make a distinction between *individualism* and *individuality*. *Individualism* is regarded as that which borders on self-centeredness. Under individualism, one is like a spoiled child, acting independently of others and one's effects on them, as if one were the "king or queen of the universe." *Individuality* is more a product of association than of isolation. It involves consideration and responsibility toward others. Often individuality is thought to be the quality or combination of qualities that marks an individual as unique—having special competences and novel ways of doing novel things. But the essence of individuality is shown in behavior that enriches the lives of others. Individuality is valued partly because it gives spirit to life, a safeguard against monotony and the tyranny of uniformity. It is valued chiefly because the talents it fosters are used in fulfilling the wants and needs of the larger society. Accordingly, the curriculum that develops the special talents of individuals also provides the chance to use these talents in representative situations where their social worth is demonstrable.

Schools recognize too that the cultivation of individuality requires a submission to that content or subject matter in which individuality is to be expressed. The student in an art course, for instance, is not expected to imitate models drawn from an artistic heritage. Neither is he urged to "pour out his soul on canvas as spontaneously as possible." Rather, he is equipped with standards for judging excellence in art and with the skills and concepts that enable him to enter into, and make his way about, the realm of art, mixing its substance with his own so that it issues in new and personal forms.

The Individual vs. the Group. Whether the school should minister to the individual or to the group need not become an either-or argument. Both the individual and the group are important and their interests must not always conflict. Under an alert teacher seeking to develop both the group and the individual, the student who plays the piano, has advanced knowledge of the chemistry of color, or has any other special competence may find his individual strength extended in an enterprise of importance to the group. In addition, his fundamental developmental tasks are likely to be met as he is encouraged to apply personal talents to problems faced by the total group. In helping the group advance toward its goal, the individual finds the practical significance of his special ability and meets his fundamental need for recognition.

Usually, the curriculum is planned for groups, but this does not mean that it is not beneficial for the individual. A student can find his best interests served when he is given instruction appropriate to him, even though others receive the same instruction. Much of the current interest in self-instruction materials (tutor texts and teaching machines) rests upon a promise to "individualize" instruction. Actually these individualizing materials are not developed with a unique student in mind. Rather, they are planned for use with individuals who have a common speed of learning and who share the same understandings or misunderstandings.

Sheviakov and Redl[1] have provided a sound principle for guiding a teacher's choice when facing individual versus group interests in the area of classroom management. Their basic principle for guiding curriculum decisions regarding disciplinary practice is the *law of marginal antisepsis*. This law means that a technique that is right in terms of a student's problem must at least be harmless in its effect upon the total group.

[1] George V. Sheviakov and Fritz Redl, *Discipline for Today's Children and Youth* (Washington, D.C.: Association for Supervision and Curriculum Development, 1956).

A technique that is rightly chosen in terms of group effect must at least be harmless to the individuals involved. Cited as examples are the cases of Johnny and Anne:

When Johnny arrives at the stage where he tries to gain group prestige by clowning, but overdoes it so that it disturbs every serious teaching situation in class, it is not sufficient to know that Johnny's behavior is normal and understandable, even desirable from the angle of his own development. The teacher must limit John's clowning, or the whole teaching situation disintegrates. How can the teacher change Johnny's behavior so that it is at least harmless to him? Just punishing him each time he clowns, shaming him before the others, or ejecting him from the school might solve the group problem, but what would it do to Johnny, who, without social approval, would be more confused than before? Cooperation of other students in the classroom in helping Johnny understand the limits to which he can go might reduce his clowning without making his own adjustment problem more difficult.

Anne, a youngster with considerable inferiority feelings, needs much encouragement to regain confidence in herself. As a result, the teacher goes out of her way to give Anne praise—more than she deserves. Anne begins to blossom, is happy and proud in class, and self-confident. However, after a few days, other students misinterpret the special attention given Anne and begin to distrust their teacher and to show what they feel. They become sloppy in their tasks and grouchy about assignments. This is a case where the technique the teacher used was right in terms of Anne's case history but not "harmless" in its group effect. This does not mean that a teacher should not do anything at all for Anne, just so as not to hurt the feelings of others. It does mean that the teacher would have to modify what she did, get others to understand, or work through the group from the start.

Key Concepts and Principles vs. Topics and Activities. There is much protest against "homogeneous" grouping of students on the basis of ability, interest, or some other factor. This protest stems from the fact that, too often, students so grouped are divorced from key ideas, methods, and values possession of which helps one enter aspects of life that are crucial for well-being and adjustment to changing conditions. Exclusive preoccupation with activities in any field of knowledge, apart from the underlying concepts, principles, and methods of that field, is miseducative. When the activities are no longer appropriate, the student is left helpless, without the principles for developing new responses to the changed environment. Courses of instruction for slow learners must be authentic vehicles to the ideas that make life of value.

No secondary school fulfils its functions by resigning certain pupils to preparation of meals, welding, the keeping of records, or memorization of the physical and chemical properties of the cell. The secondary school program should not give undue emphasis to matters of use and application apart from the ideas—intellectual abstractions—that are associated with practical activities. Neither should the school foster the acquisition of verbal principles without making it possible to apply these principles in practical situations. Both slow and rapid learners should have chances to practice language, science, quantitative reasoning, fine and practical arts, and physical coordination. In addition to being helped in performance, students of all ranges of ability should be helped to acquire the meanings (theories, concepts, principles) necessary for the explanation and understanding of these practices. To be sure, not all students will acquire the same level of mastery of the theory or meaning of their actions. A few will grasp little of the abstractions, even though they may learn to value them and to sense the importance of supporting others in the extension of theory.

By way of illustration, it is not enough that students be asked to observe examples of physical phenomena, but they should be helped to acquire and use principles for dealing with other instances of such phenomena. Also, examination of newly developed technical inventions is not as important as understanding of the principles that make these inventions possible. The selection of learning experiences or courses in industrial arts (such as auto mechanics) or in formal science (such as physics) depends upon the characteristics of the students; the selection of the ideas to be taught does not. Ability to apply key ideas of time, space, motion, mass, matter, and measurement in new situations is an important outcome from instruction in both the industrial arts and formal science courses. Although it is important for all students to acquire and use ideas that are central to an aspect of life, all need not come by such outcomes in the same way and apply them in the same situations. To be effective, teachers must link key ideas directly to what appeals to the senses of their slow students, employing more concrete illustrations (models, films, stories, direct activities) than might be necessary in teaching those with a greater ability to work with abstractions. The student who has abstracted, say, the term or concept of *growth* is ready to use the concept in explaining and describing new events in biology, physiology, psychology, and philosophy. The one who does not know the term must have his attention directed to many concrete instances of growth before he can be expected to use the concept as an intellectual tool.

Disagreement over the kinds of experiences offered in school—French vs. Spanish, art services vs. ceramics, *A Tale of Two Cities* vs. *War and*

Peace, a public survey vs. a film on civil rights—must be resolved empiri-cally, by actual trial and observation, that is, we must collect evidence that the chosen experience best helps particular students acquire and use the central ideas of the field.

Not	French or Spanish?	*But*	Has the student acquired the prin-ciples and methods common to learning a language?
Not	Art service or ceramics?	*But*	Does the student understand art as an invitation to create new ways of embodying the forms of art ex-perience?
Not	*A Tale of Two Cities* or *War and Peace?*	*But*	Does the student reflect on what it means to be a human being, or does he raise crucial questions about the meaning of war, death, and friendship?
Not	A public survey or a film on civil rights?	*But*	Does the opportunity result in pupils able both to define, explain, and illustrate the real nature of power and to use the skills neces-sary for effecting social change?

In brief, it seems clear that there should be equality of educational opportunities for all to acquire the most powerful and fundamental intellectual values and tools for thought and action. But acquisition and use of intellectual content are not dependent on identical learning experiences.

ADAPTATION OF THE CURRICULUM TO THE INDIVIDUAL STUDENT

Adaptation of curriculum to the individual student occurs at two important levels—an institutional level and a classroom level. At the institutional level, school authorities (boards of education, superintend-ents, and directors of instruction) wrestle with questions of individualiza-tion related to the functions of the school and the administrative framework for fulfilment of these functions. Their decisions regarding graduation requirements, course offerings, class scheduling, and assign-ment of teachers belong in this category. At the classroom level, the teacher assumes major responsibility for adapting instructional proce-dures (materials and methods), avoiding the extremes of talking down to students and confusing them with abstractions.

Adaptation by Function at the Institutional Level. Administratively, schools have attempted to answer the problems identified in the foregoing pages by means of the comprehensive high school. A comprehensive high school discharges four functions in order that all students may profit from schooling:

The first function is the integrative one of *general education,* the part of education that deals with the common knowledge required of a responsible human being and citizen. The school discharges this function when all students acquire and apply (1) the central ideas, values, and methods for continued learning or for finding meaning in the major fields of knowledge and (2) the ground rules of a free society, including the premises that support variability and that equip each one to share in the management of the community. Required courses in the humanities, social studies, mathematics, physical education, and sciences are established to fulfil this function.

A second function is *supplementation,* or the offering of courses to meet the special needs of students with unusual talents or deficiencies. These talents or deficiencies can be moral, physical, or intellectual. Power reading for the advanced reader and remedial reading for the retarded are examples of supplementation, as is corrective physical education for the handicapped.

A third function of the secondary school is *exploration.* Exploratory courses in all fields are offered with the idea of helping the student develop an interest and find out if they have any potential in the field. Introductory courses in the practical arts, languages, and sciences are often established for exploratory purposes.

A fourth function is *specialization,* which prepares an individual to be an expert in some particular vocation, practice, or area of study. Advanced courses in auto mechanics and advanced-placement courses in college physics are examples of specialized offerings.

All students are required to complete work fulfilling integrative and exploratory functions. Opportunities for supplementation are available, for those desiring it, in both the formal curriculum and informal cocurricular activities. Specialization is provided through the individual's own selection of a particular field and his completion of a major sequence of courses in that field.

Other Administrative Adaptations. Most administrative adaptations can be seen as instances within one of the functional categories above. Some claim that specialistic ends are best served by placing gifted pupils in a special class in which they are challenged by the course work and encouraged to develop their special interests. But the evidence regarding the effectiveness of assigning pupils to classes on the basis of the single factor of ability is inconclusive. Even when, as is common today, grouping is done on a clinical basis involving several criteria such as interest, intelligence, friendships, and achievement, there still remains the necessity of further adaptation to the individual.

A valuable degree of individualization is present when students in the secondary school take college courses in mathematics, English, or history or when students engage in work experience while in the secondary school. The general educational need for developing this latter kind of experience so that it illuminates intellectual principles and has applicability to other aspects of life has not always been met. Work-experience programs should not neglect general education and overemphasize training for a specific job. Such training should be deferred to the post-high school years. Practical work experience is very valuable for those with high academic ability, as well as for others, because all are in need of both kinship with labor and training of the senses.

Scheduling of courses is conducive to individualization. Students needing the acquisition of certain facts can be scheduled in five thirty-minute classes per week, while those needing understanding and implications of these facts should meet in classes for one hour three times a week, because the first objective calls for spaced practice and the second for massed practice.

The assignment of pupils to teachers with appropriate characteristics may be another administrative approach to individualization of the curriculum. Experimentation, for instance, is under way to test the assumption that better results may be obtained by matching students characterized by personality patterns labeled conforming, opposing, wavering, or striving with teachers categorized as self-controlling, fearful, or turbulent. For some purposes, a shy student may need a non-threatening teacher, while an aggressive student may gain most from one who challenges.

The assignment of teachers to instructional teams holds additional implications for individualization. The combined special talents of a team can be utilized in working with either the total class, small groups, or individuals. To the extent that a large class limits student participation, team teaching and its provision for small groups can be a great improvement, if appropriate planning is done. This innovation, as well as that of teaching machines, reveals the peculiar strengths and weaknesses of individual students inasmuch as there is a greater amount of overt student responses. Hence, the teacher is likely to give more pertinent prompting and correction than would be the case in classrooms where only a few express themselves daily.

ADAPTATION TO INDIVIDUAL DIFFERENCES WITHIN THE CLASSROOM

Individualization by Objectives. Instructional decisions regarding functions of courses determine to a large extent the variation in objectives permitted within the classroom. The teacher of a supplementary-type course such as corrective physical education can determine objectives largely in terms of the personal needs or problems of the individual students. But, on the other hand, the teacher of a specialized course must see that all students meet the requirements of the field of specialization regardless of their personal interests. In a specialized course in short-hand, the backgrounds of the students do not determine the objectives, because the standards and skills required of good stenographers are the predetermined outcomes.

Individualization Through Choice of Classroom Learning Experiences. There are two common ways of approaching the problem of individual-ization through the selection of learning experiences: One way is to focus on the specific factors that can be varied in dealing with the character-istics of students. The second is to state and apply fundamental principles for the selection of learning experiences. The following are the specific factors manipulated by teachers in response to the students' character-istics:

1. Frequency of giving praise and special privileges
2. Amount of review given
3. Degree of precision in specifying the task and ways of fulfilling and judging the task
4. Frequency of testing
5. Promptness in giving knowledge of results
6. Amount of extra assistance available from teacher
7. Situations for the student to work alone, with peers, and with total class
8. Extent of self-initiated work permitted
9. Differentiation in basis for grades to be given
10. Amount of time allowed for completion of assignments
11. Distractions permitted in the room environment (use of color and bulletin-board displays that compete with the teacher for atten-tion is detrimental to the learning of some students)
12. The concreteness of the illustrations and activities used in teach-ing an idea or skill

Individualization through the judicious selection and use of instruc-tional materials follows the principles that the experience should (1) be within the student's capability, (2) be rewarding to the student, and (3) give him opportunity to use and practice what is sought by instruc-tion (that is, it should be consistent with the objectives of the course).

In addition to these general principles, there are others that are useful in meeting special objectives. For students who need development of problem-solving skills, there must be problematic situations; for those who desire to be creative, there should be time for speculation and per-haps an environmental inconsistency; for those whose attitudes would be shaped, there must be an influential teacher or model, emotional content, and cooperation from those persons who mean the most to them, as well as specifications of behavior appropriate for the attitude. The teacher who follows these principles must try to discover what has been rewarding or unrewarding to each student in the past and then select the experience (activity, textbook, film, etc.) that will link a prior rewarding task to the new task being taught. The linking of past success to a new aspiration requires that the teacher provide the necessary means for attaining the instructional objective for the individual student. An analysis of the specifications (prerequisites) for reaching the objective is an important element in individualization of instruction. To this end, the teacher asks what the student must know and be able to do in order to attain the competence desired. If the student has not met these specifications, the teacher must either make the learning of the specification a subobjective for the instruction or modify the objective itself.

Before a teacher could expect students to show proficiency in reading a new meter—a hypothetical example of an immediate instructional objective—it would be necessary to make explicit how finely the meter is to be read, that is, the accuracy of the smallest measurements required. Next, the teacher would analyze the task into prerequisite subtasks such as learning the number system used, learning about ratios and the relevance of ratios to the meter, learning the direction in which the numbers are to be read, and learning about contrasting features such as the significance of the pointers on the dials. Those students who do not have the ability to comprehend or manipulate numbers as required or who have had a conflicting set of instructions or experiences with other unlike meters will require special help.

Briefly, the teacher most effective in adapting instruction to individual differences will (1) perform an adequate analysis of the learning task, (2) collect evidence of the student's ability to follow directions, to use illustrations, and to handle all the other small details involved in performing the task, and (3) teach the pupil to succeed on the basis of these prerequisites.

Dropouts. Those who do not remain to graduate from high school may be fairly well identified. They may be characterized in a general way as follows:

1. Their I.Q.'s are below 90.
2. Their grades made in most academic subjects are principally C, D, or F, and their grades in other subjects are not high.
3. They do not belong to clubs or participate in extrasubject activities.

4. They are not wholeheartedly accepted by their peers and have a tendency to feel that they do not belong.
5. They have difficulty in paying for the extra costs and in dressing as well as students from more well-to-do families.
6. They have records of more absenteeism than the average student.
7. They have a tendency to believe that school is hardly worthwhile, particularly since they have developed a dislike for it, growing out of their lack of acceptance by peers and their inability to do well in their subjects.
8. They have a growing desire to leave what they consider the "unreal" world of school life and to become employed, make money, be freed from the parental dole, and be married soon.
9. They have objected more strenuously than the average student to parental control and teacher direction.

There has been, in recent years, a much greater concern for students who have prematurely left school—the "dropouts." A very large proportion of them are unable to obtain steady employment, and those who do generally find themselves in low-paid drudgery-type "blind alley" jobs. While the school cannot take great responsibility for mitigating the tragedies these young people may have to face in life, educators must do what they can to retain in the schools those who will learn a reasonable amount in proportion to the time spent in school, and must develop some sort of program to suit their interests, needs, and abilities.

In an increasing number of schools, the potential dropouts are being identified rather accurately, given special counseling, and enrolled in appropriate courses and sections of various courses including English, social studies, science, and others developed especially for them. They are being grouped into sections for these classes, to which are assigned as teachers individuals who have demonstrated a special skill in dealing with young people possessing the qualities of personality and character typical of the slow and dropout students, and who have had some special training for that type of work.

Developing in the 1940's and reaching a peak in the late 1950's, there has been a material increase in the number of young people being married while still in school. But this number has not increased in recent years. Various actions have been taken by school boards relative to the place of married students, some boards of education going so far as to exclude them. More commonly, boards of education, upon the recommendation of the superintendent of schools, approve legislation barring married students from the usual extracurricular activities. Even this restriction has met with serious criticism, and there has been a slight trend away from it.

In the 1960's, there has been a decline in the percentage of young people becoming married while teen-agers. The glamor built up in the minds of adolescent boys and girls and stimulated and exaggerated unduly by conversations with the young married students has given way sharply before the realization of the disadvantages. Even though both boys and girls obtain positions enabling them to make a living, they have often found it exceedingly difficult to get permanent positions; youngsters may begin to arrive forcing the mother to give up work and become heavily burdened with household duties. These students have been more or less forced to withdraw to a large extent from social life and many of them have been able to manage financially only with the assistance of parents, which leads to misunderstandings and alienations of the normal interpersonal attitudes; many have actually gone on relief and consequently, felt disgraced. Statistics show definitely that the proportion of divorces is higher among those who marry as teen-agers.

Dropouts are usually subnormal mentally. As a result of the investigation of the characteristics needed for employability, it seems clear that a high school program for the mentally subnormal should have the following qualities:

1. It should be a program which uses academics, work evaluation, and work experience to teach vocational, personal, and social skills.
2. It should be programmed to keep the mentally subnormal students in school until they are approximately 19 or 20 years of age.
3. It should aim at the restoration or amelioration of auxiliary handicapping conditions such as poor speech, visual problems, orthopedic problems, or hearing problems.
4. It should provide a concerted program of physical restoration including physical fitness training, cleanliness training, and grooming.
5. It should contain specific curriculum provisions to teach the following:

   a. Self-confidence
   b. Cooperation
   c. Cheerfulness
   d. Ability to accept criticism
   e. Ability to mix socially
   f. Ability to mind one's own business
   g. Initiative
   h. Respect for supervisors

6. It should provide on-the-job training in the high school building (at least one hour of work per day) during the second year of the program.
7. It should provide on-the-job training off the high school campus and be supervised by a high school faculty member (four to eight hours per day) during the third and fourth years of the program.[2]

[2] Oliver P. Kolstoe and Roger M. Frey, "Changing Philosophies of Special Education," *Newsletter*, The College of Education, Southern Illinois University, Carbondale, Vol. 2, No. 4 (January, 1963), p. 2.

QUESTIONS, PROBLEMS, AND ISSUES FOR FURTHER THOUGHT

1. What is the danger in not educating all intellects for control of democracy?
2. If you had a child of your own who was a slow learner, what educational provisions would you want for him? How are these provisions like and unlike those considered desirable for rapid learners?
3. If given the opportunity, would you group students for instruction on the basis of chronological age? Give the reasons for your answer and the principal arguments against it.
4. Contrast the basis for grading student performance in a course fulfilling a specialistic function with the basis for grading in a course designed for meeting the supplemental needs of students.
5. Indicate how specialistic functions can be met without segregation, that is, describe how, within a course of general education, those with special ability and interest can be stimulated even though the class is composed of pupils at all levels of intellectual equipment and understanding of the common learnings sought.
6. How can the new curricular innovations in team teaching and self-instructional materials be used to further the two educational goals of (1) the maximum growth among those with special talents and (2) the guarding of equity?
7. Under which of the following assumptions would education best serve both the individual student and society?
   a. Any student can learn anything, if he applies himself; no individualization is necessary.
   b. Any student can learn anything, if the teacher properly applies the principles for selection of learning experiences.
   c. The student can learn only in keeping with his potential, or native ability.
8. List a key concept or principle in a field with which you are familiar. Indicate how you might teach this concept to (1) slow learners and (2) rapid learners.
9. Visit several different types of courses. Examine the tests given in these courses—tests that indicate the objectives sought. Examine too the socio-economic backgrounds of the pupils in the courses. Is there evidence that the pupils are not segregated by the work status of their fathers or by economic class? Do the tests indicate that all students are given significant materials? To what extent do the tests (including variation in acceptable levels of performance) show that the teacher individualizes objectives in accordance with the characteristics of the pupils? Name the characteristics used in individualizing the objectives.
10. What do you think is the responsibility of the school for attempting to reduce the tragedy of dropouts being unable to find employment and becoming frustrated and delinquent? What do you think is the responsibility of the community outside the school?

SUPPLEMENTARY MATERIALS

SELECTED READINGS

ASSOCIATION FOR SUPERVISION AND CURRICULUM DEVELOPMENT. *What Shall the High School Teach?* 1956 yearbook. Washington, D.C.: National Education Association of the United States, 1956. An excellent description and explanation of basic issues and problems surrounding the question of what the high school should teach to students in the light of the qualitative and quantitative nature of individual differences.

————. *Human Variability and Learning*. Washington, D.C.: National Education Association of the United States, 1961. Shows how certain variables in learning relate to individual differences among pupils.

Educational Leadership, XVIII (April, 1961). The theme for this issue of *Educational Leadership* is "Grouping: Promising Approaches." The articles contained give guidance with respect to grouping for effective learning.

HARVARD COMMITTEE. *General Education in a Free Society: Report of the Harvard Committee*. Cambridge, Mass.: Harvard University Press, 1945. A classic report that sets forth arguments for the schools to foster conformity without sacrificing diversity. Also presents stimulating guidelines for pursuit of this twofold goal.

NATIONAL SOCIETY FOR THE STUDY OF EDUCATION. *1962 Yearbook*. University of Chicago Press, 1962. A summary of many of the concepts, theories, and practices in the individualization of instruction.

SECHREST, LEE, and R. WRAY STROWIG. "Teaching Machines and the Individual Learner," *Educational Theory*, XII, (July, 1962). An article that indicates how education will become more individualized as a result of programed instruction.

SYMONDS, PERCIVAL M. "Individual Differences," *What Education Has To Learn from Psychology*. New York: Teachers College, Bureau of Publications, Columbia University, 1960. One of a series of articles that summarize the experimental findings of psychologists that bear on education and their application to teaching. Emphasizes the extent of individual differences, and discusses the teacher's responsibility with respect to them.

AUDIO-VISUAL MATERIALS

Films

Challenge of the Gifted. McGraw-Hill Text-Films. 11 minutes.

Grouping Students for Effective Learning. Bel-Mort Films, Inc. Portland, Ore. 44 frames. Color. Captions.

Individual Differences. McGraw-Hill Text-Films. 23 minutes.

Learning To Understand Children, Part II—A Remedial Program. McGraw-Hill Text-Films. 23 minutes.

Learning To Understand Children—A Diagnostic Approach. McGraw-Hill. 21 minutes.

Problems of Pupil Adjustment: Part I—The Dropout. McGraw-Hill. 20 minutes.

Problem of Pupil Adjustment: Part II—The Stay-in. McGraw-Hill. 19 minutes.

The Gifted Ones. International Film Bureau. Chicago. 20 minutes.

Recording

Providing for Individual Differences in the Classroom, #213. William C. Trow. Educational Growth Series. Educational Recording Services. Los Angeles. 36-44-minute discussion. 33⅓ rpm.

28

Organization and Administration of the Curriculum

The real test of a curriculum's value is the quality of learning gained by students under the direction of teachers. But departmental programs need to be coordinated, teachers need to be utilized so as to capitalize on their talents, books and supplies must be on hand, teachers and pupils must be brought together at appropriate times and places, and the progression of pupils from one school unit to another must be effected with as little waste motion as possible. These things are the special functions of administration, and the business of learning in schools depends upon their successful performance as well as upon good teaching. Administration and teaching are closely related in the operation of the curriculum, and there seems to be little profit in arguing about their relative importance.

The central purpose of curriculum administration is to facilitate the achievement of educational goals. Therefore, administrative policies and procedures should be consistent with, and designed to accomplish, those goals. For example, if it is an important objective of the curriculum to provide for the needs and abilities of all students, it is the business of administration to develop a program design, a breadth of offerings, and a type of schedule that will provide as many opportunities as possible for students to gain appropriate educational experiences.

The role of administration with respect to the curriculum is chiefly one of organization and service. It is not possible, of course, to describe the

administration of the curriculum in terms of neatly defined job operations. Planning, organization, and servicing of the curriculum proceed
concurrently and continuously. One phase blends with another, and, at
times, each becomes indistinguishable in the complete process. There
are, however, certain special tasks that facilitate the operation of the
curriculum, that may be described as administrative, and that serve,
therefore, as the subject of this chapter. These involve the following:

1. Planning the design of the curriculum to serve the common and
   special needs of students
2. Assisting students in planning school experiences so as to meet
   their educational needs
3. Organizing and administering the schedule and school year to
   facilitate the implementation of the curriculum
4. Articulating curriculum areas to secure continuity in the educational experiences of students
5. Developing special types of programs to solve special instructional
   problems

THE DESIGN OF THE CURRICULUM

The design of a curriculum determines in large measure its appropriateness for a school. It provides a structural framework shaped to the
basic plans or purposes drafted by the patrons and staff of a school. The
scope, or breadth, and the *sequence,* or order, of learning experiences in
which students participate in the school are defined in broad terms by
means of curriculum design.

If the curriculum is defined as all of the learning experiences in which
students participate under the supervision of the school, the scope of the
curriculum includes not only organized knowledge and classroom instruction but also extraclass activities, guidance, and certain community-
related experiences. However, each of these is a broad and important
aspect of education and has been made the subject of complete volumes.
In this book, separate chapters are devoted to community resources,
extrasubject activities, and guidance programs. Consequently, this chapter
will be directed to the nature and organization of the pattern of offerings,
and to ways of administering the program so as to facilitate instruction.

The Program of Studies. *Program of studies* is the term used to refer to
the courses offered by a school and their arrangement into sequences
and patterns so as to serve the needs and interests of students. For
secondary schools, planning of the program of studies involves (1) the
selection of courses or fields of learning to implement the aims of the
school, (2) the arrangement of courses or learning areas in sequences to
serve the characteristics of students and to provide continuity in learn-

ing, (3) the selection of learning experiences that serve the *common* needs of students and the needs of society, (4) the provision of offerings to serve the *special needs, interests,* and *capacities* of students, and (5) provisions for articulation between grade levels and fields of instruction. These will be discussed in the following pages of this chapter.

Criteria for Organizing the Program of Studies. In order to adapt organization to instructional needs, certain empirical guides for planning of the program of studies have been developed by educators during the past three or four decades. One instrument used extensively by regional accrediting associations in evaluating member schools is that of the Cooperative Study of Secondary School Standards. This set of criteria, based on more than thirty years of research and experience, follows:

General Principles

The program of studies:
1. Is based on an analysis of the educational needs of youth.
2. Provides a wide variety of experiences to meet both the common and individual educational needs of youth.
3. Is planned to help meet both present and probable future needs of pupils.
4. Provides opportunities for pupils as well as staff members to participate in the planning and development of curriculum activities.
5. Provides for relating subject-matter fields to life problems of pupils.
6. Emphasizes critical and thoughtful approaches to present-day problems.
7. Provides opportunities for experiences especially adapted to the superior or advanced pupils.
8. Provides opportunities for experiences especially adapted to slow-learning pupils.
9. Provides organized sequences of courses carrying on through several grades.
10. Provides for coordination of educational experiences within each grade.
11. Places emphasis on broad concepts taught for transfer value.
12. Is flexible in time allotments to meet individual pupil requirements (e.g., variation in number of periods for elective subjects, periods allotted to special-help and remedial work, or time devoted to pupil-initiated course work).
13. Provides for the evaluation of pupil achievement in the program in terms of each individual's aptitudes and abilities.
14. Recognizes the contributions made by the pupil activity program.
15. Encourages enlargement and enrichment of the pupil's scope of interests.[1]

[1] Cooperative Study of Secondary School Standards, *Evaluative Criteria* (Washington, D.C.: Cooperative Study of Secondary School Standards, 1950), pp. 49–52.

Types of Programs of Studies:

Four basic types of organization for the program of studies have evolved during the more than three centuries of secondary education in America:

1. *Single curriculum.* This is the common European pattern employed in such schools as the German gymnasium and French lycee. All students take the same courses. No electives are offered and students with different interests select different schools. Only a small percentage of high schools in the United States have employed a single curriculum since the Civil War.

2. *Multiple curricula.* In this type of program, a school offers two or more parallel curricula organized to serve the special interests of different groups of students, such as general, college preparatory, commercial and industrial. Students within a special curriculum are not permitted to elect courses from another. The Committee of Ten proposed this type of organization for the program of studies and it was used extensively from the 1890's until shortly before the 1920's. This plan now is limited largely to specialized vocational programs in a few large high schools.

3. *Constants-with-variables.* Some courses are prescribed as requirements for graduation for all students and other courses are designated as free electives under this plan. The constants-with-variables organization gained steadily in use from around 1920 to the 1960's. A National Education Association survey published in 1959 reported that almost 80 per cent of the 866 schools reporting used a constants-with-variables pattern.[2]

4. *Advisory or combination.* This is a combination of the multiple and constants-with-variables plans. Certain courses are prescribed for all students as in the constants-with-variables plan and advisory curricula for special interest groups are outlined for guidance purposes. However, students choosing a curriculum such as the college preparatory or commercial, are not restricted to that program and may elect courses in other sequences.

GENERAL PROGRAM FOR COMMON YOUTH NEEDS

Because of the widely differing and confused views on the nature of basic education for all youth, the school administrator needs a definition of a program of general education for his school in terms of courses or some other plan for organizing subject matter and activities. To some extent, general education may be defined by state law or regulations. The school statutes and state-department regulations in several states require certain subjects such as American history, government, and health education to be completed for graduation. The local school administrator must first include such state requirements in planning the design of the program of general education for his school.

[2] National Education Association of the United States, Research Division, "High School Graduation Requirements," *Research Bulletin,* Vol. 37, No. 4 (December, 1959), p. 121.

Organization of Programs for General Education. In the majority of secondary schools, faculties have attempted to achieve the objectives of general education by means of a pattern of conventional courses. In other schools, a different type of organization, characterized by a reorganization of content and activities into a "core-type" program, which departs from traditional subject lines, has been developed. In the latter plan, the common experiences of general education are organized around thematic units dealing with social and youth problems. Core-type curriculums often are labeled "unified studies," "common learnings," or "block of time" programs. Core programs most frequently are found in grades seven and eight of junior high schools. A study conducted in 1956–1957 reports that approximately 19.3 per cent of the public junior and junior-senior high schools in the United States offered some type of block-time classes.[3] On the other hand, a study made by a committee of the National Association of Secondary School Principals in 1955–1957 shows that 57.3 per cent of 1,200 junior high schools employed some block-time classes. In large schools of 1,000 or over, 72.5 per cent offered these classes.[4]

From these studies, it appears that about 80 per cent of the junior and senior high schools in the United States employ a conventional subject organization for the design of the curriculum and that programs of general education are composed of specific courses to be completed by all students. Moreover, about 68 per cent of the schools with block-time courses employ conventional subjects within the block of time.

Provisions in Four-Year and Senior High Schools. National data on graduation requirements are reported in a study conducted by the National Education Association during the 1958–1959 school year. Table 28–1 reports the findings of that study, which included replies from 866 high school principals.[5]

It may be seen from the table that almost 80 per cent of the high schools employed a constants-with-variables organization. The average total units required for graduation was 16.5 in grades nine through twelve, of which 9.7 were constants, or specified, and 6.8 were variables, or electives.

Fifty-three per cent had increased their graduation requirements during the five years prior to the study. Almost 12 per cent had increased requirements in mathematics, 10 per cent had increased them in science,

[3] Grace S. Wright, *Block-Time Classes and the Core Program in Junior High Schools,* Bulletin, 1958, No. 6 (Washington, D.C.: Government Printing Office, 1958), pp. 5–6.

[4] Ellsworth Tompkins, "The Daily Schedule in the Junior High School," *Bulletin of the N.A.S.S.P.,* Vol. 40 (May, 1956), p. 177.

[5] National Education Association of the United States, Research Division, *Research Bulletin,* Vol. 37, No. 4 (December, 1959), p. 125.

TABLE 28–1

PERCENTAGE OF SCHOOLS REQUIRING UNITS IN EACH SUBJECT FIELD AND AVERAGE NUMBER OF UNITS, IF REQUIRED, BY COURSES OF STUDY

| Requirement | Schools with Constants with Variables Course of Study (79.8 per cent)[a] | | Schools with Multiple Courses of Study | | | | | | | |
| | | | General Courses (19.3 per cent)[a] | | Academic Courses (20.1 per cent)[a] | | Commercial Courses (13.7 per cent)[a] | | Vocational Courses (11.4 per cent)[a] | |
	Per cent Required	Average Number of Units Required[b]	Per Cent Required	Average Number of Units Required[b]	Per Cent Required	Average Number of Units Required[b]	Per Cent Required	Average Number of Units Required[b]	Per Cent Required	Average Number of Units Required[b]
English	100.0	3.6	100.0	3.7	100.0	3.8	100.0	3.7	100.0	3.4
Social studies	99.0	2.3	100.0	2.5	99.0	2.6	100.0	2.4	100.0	2.2
Mathematics	94.5	1.4	95.5	1.4	100.0	2.4	98.7	1.4	97.4	1.4
Science	94.1	1.5	93.7	1.5	97.1	2.2	89.9	1.4	89.5	1.4
Foreign languages	0.8	2.0	1.8	*	61.5	2.1	3.8	*	–	–
Health and physical education	62.5	1.1	68.5	1.1	62.5	1.1	62.0	1.1	68.4	1.0
Home economics	11.8	1.2	10.8	1.2	8.7	0.9	5.1	*	23.7	3.3
Business education	4.6	1.2	5.4	1.2	5.8	1.3	100.0	4.5	10.5	*
Industrial arts	6.3	1.0	9.0	1.5	4.8	0.9	1.3	*	18.4	2.4
Vocational education	6.3	1.4	2.7	*	3.8	*	3.8	*	86.8	4.3
Music	3.0	0.6	4.5	0.5	1.9	*	1.3	*	–	–
Art	2.1	0.6	3.6	*	1.0	*	1.3	*	2.6	*
Driver education	1.9	0.5	6.3	0.5	3.8	*	5.1	*	10.5	*
Elective units	100.0	6.8	100.0	6.4	100.0	3.4	100.0	2.4	100.0	2.8
Units in specified fields	100.0	9.7	100.0	10.1	100.0	13.2	100.0	14.2	100.0	13.6
Total units[c]		16.5		16.5		16.6		16.6		16.4

* No average computed on fewer than five cases.

[a] Schools offering these courses as a percentage of the total number of schools.

[b] Average for the schools requiring courses in these fields.

[c] Average for all schools offering the course of study indicated.

and about 9.5 per cent had made increases in both English and social studies. Small percentages of schools had added physical education, driver education, and foreign languages as requirements.

The following trends in provisions and characteristics of the program of general education in four-year and senior high schools are evident from surveys of current practices:

1. There has been an increase in the total number of units required on the average for graduation, from about 16 to almost 18.

2. There has been an increase in the number of required courses on the average, from 8 to more than 9. The most common subject requirements are English, 3.5 units; social studies, 2.5 units; mathematics, 1 unit; science, 1.5 units; and physical education, 1 unit.

3. Provisions for options within required subject areas are becoming common in large schools. For example, in the eleventh and twelfth grades, students may be required to take social studies but may choose basal American history; standard American history, or honors readings in history in the eleventh grade; and basal modern problems, or two of several one-semester courses such as economics, sociology, government, or psychology in grade twelve.

4. Some large schools require major and minor sequences. In these schools, students must complete majors of three or four units in two subjects and two minor sequences of two units each.

Junior High School Programs. Most junior high schools offer few electives in grades seven and eight and permit students to elect only one course in the ninth grade. Table 28–2 presents data on course offerings in the seventh and eighth grades in fifty junior high schools in the San Francisco Bay area, for the 1960–1961 school year.[6]

Of these course offerings, most were offered five days per week in all but a small percentage of the schools. However, music was offered less than five days weekly in 50 per cent, science in 30 per cent, art in 28 per cent, and home economics in 24 per cent. Thirty-six per cent allowed no electives and 40 per cent allowed one elective in the seventh grade. On the other hand, 34 per cent permitted no electives in grade eight, and 28 per cent allowed one elective at this level. Thirty-five, or 70 per cent, of these schools reported a block-time program, with social studies and language arts being the most common subjects in the block program.

[6] G. W. Ford, Marshall Miller, and William Spring, "Administrative Arrangements for Seventh and Eighth Grade School Subjects," *Bulletin of the N.A.S.S.P.*, October, 1962, p. 82.

TABLE 28–2

SUBJECTS OFFERED IN SEVENTH AND EIGHTH GRADES

	Number of Schools		Percentage of Schools	
Courses	Grade 7	Grade 8	Grade 7	Grade 8
Mathematics	46	48	92	96
Social studies	44	45	88	90
Science	43	44	86	88
Physical education	42	44	84	88
Music	35	22	70	44
Reading	32	33	64	66
Art	28	21	56	42
Language arts	27	26	54	52
Industrial arts or mechanical drawing	27	43	54	86
Home economics	24	36	48	72
English	19	23	38	46
Study or Homeroom	11	11	22	22
Health	8	8	16	16
Spelling	7	5	14	10
Library	6	3	12	6
Spanish	4	4	8	8
Writing	3	1	6	2
History and/or Constitution	2	2	4	4
Geography	2	0	4	0
Literature	1	3	2	6
Civics	1	3	2	6

The following program for a junior high school of 850 students, with a block-time program in language arts and social studies, is representative of many schools of that size:

SCHOOL "I" (Subject Offerings)

(Enrollment 850; Experimental large classes; Block of time in Language Arts and Social Studies)

R (Required)   E (Elective)

Grade 7
R Arts and Crafts 1 Sem.
R Homemaking 1 Sem.
R Industrial Arts 1 Sem.
a R Language Arts 2 Sem.
R Mathematics 2 Sem.
* b R Music 2½ per/wk 2 Sem.
* a R Physical Education 2½ per/wk 2 Sem.
* R Science & Health 2½ per/wk 2 Sem.
a R Social Studies 2 Sem.

Elective Activities
Assemblies
c Athletics
Clubs
Music—Instrumental & Vocal
School Paper
Sports—Intramural
Student Council

Grade 8
a R Language Arts 2 Sem.
R Mathematics 2 Sem.

a R Physical Education 2½ per/wk 2 Sem.

* R Science 2½ per/wk 2 Sem.

a R Social Studies 2 Sem.

* d E Health 2½ per/wk 2 Sem.

* d E Music–Band or Orchestra 2½ per/wk 2 Sem.

* d E Music–Vocal 2½ per/wk 2 Sem.

* d E Typewriting–Personal 2½ per/wk 2 Sem.

e E Arts and Crafts 1 Sem.

e E Health 1 Sem.

e E Homemaking 1 Sem.

e E Industrial Arts 1 Sem.

e E Service Club–School Helper 1 or 2 Sem.

e E Typewriting–Personal 1 Sem.

Elective Activities
Assemblies
c Athletics
Clubs
Music–Instrumental & Vocal
School Paper
Sports–Intramural
Student Council

Grade 9

f R Language Arts 2 Sem.

* g R Mathematics 2½ per/wk 2 Sem. (Algebra or General Mathematics)

* R Physical Education 2½ per/wk 2 Sem.

R Science 2 Sem.

f R Social Studies 2 Sem.

* h E General Business 2½ per/wk 2 Sem.

* h E Music–Band or Orchestra 2½ per/wk 2 Sem.

h E Music–Vocal 2 Sem.

h E Typewriting–Personal 1 Sem.

i E Arts and Crafts 1 Sem.

i E Latin 2 Sem.

i E Spanish (four-year program) 2 Sem.

i E General Business 1 Sem.

i E Homemaking 2 Sem.

i E Industrial Arts 2 Sem.

i E Service Club–School Helper 1 or 2 Sem.

i E Typewriting–Personal 1 Sem.

Elective Activities
Assemblies
c Athletics
Clubs
Dramatics
Music–Instrumental & Vocal
School Paper
Sports–Intramural
Student Council

* Two-and-one-half periods means two periods per week one semester and three periods per week the other semester.

a In grades 7 and 8, language arts, physical education, and social studies are taught as a three-period core program, which also includes emphasis on group guidance. Core teachers work closely together on a cooperative basis.

b In grade 7 the pupils elect either vocal music, band or orchestra.

c The program in interscholastic athletics is limited. Limited schedules are carried on as follows: track in grades 7, 8 and 9; basketball, football, and wrestling in grades 8 and 9.

d Elect either one or three of these subjects, not two or four.

e Elect none or two of these subjects.

f One group of sixty pupils in grade 9 is being taught on an experimental basis employing more intensified use of audio-visual aids and materials as: motion pictures, overhead projectors, tapes, records, filmstrips, etc. One teacher has the social studies, and the other teacher has the language arts. While the two teachers teach separately they plan jointly to coordinate instruction on a team basis.

g Registrations in algebra and general mathematics are determined by teachers' recommendations, past achievement, standardized test results, and conferences.

h Elect either one or three of these subjects.

i Elect none or two semesters from this group of subjects.

In grades 7 and 8, language arts comprise dramatics, grammar, listening skills, literature, reading, speech, spelling, and writing. In grade 9, language arts includes journalism in addition to the areas treated in grades 7 and 8.

An organized guidance and counseling program is functioning in grades 7, 8 and 9 under qualified personnel.

A planned testing program is in operation.

Ability grouping is practiced in eighth-grade mathematics and ninth-grade science.

Homerooms are organized primarily to serve administrative purposes.

There are no study halls; the one-hour periods provide for supervised study.

Health service is provided with a registered nurse in charge.

A strong in-service education program for teachers, using consultants, is underwritten by the board of education.[7]

PATTERNS FOR SPECIAL NEEDS

The three types of secondary school curriculum patterns designed to serve the special abilities and future plans of students are commonly called (1) the *multiple curriculum,* (2) the *constants-with-variables curriculum,* and (3) the *combination curriculum.* More descriptive labels might be desirable, especially for the so-called combination plan, but these have become fairly well standardized over a period of twenty-five years.

The disappearing multiple-curriculum pattern consists of outlines of two or more parallel series of course offerings and sequences to serve students with special interests in a broad educational field such as business, vocational agriculture, or college preparatory. Students are required to elect one of these series of offerings or curriculums and are not permitted to elect courses outside of the curriculum selected. This type of organization is inflexible and entirely unsuited to an educational program for all youth.

The constants-with-variables type of program provides for the classification of all of the courses offered by a school under two general categories: (1) *constants,* or courses required for graduation and (2) *variables,* or courses that students are free to elect at each grade level. Its essential feature is that it permits a high degree of flexibility in a student's

---

[7] *Junior High Schools for Iowa Youth,* (Des Moines, Iowa: State Department of Public Instruction, 1960), p. 39.

program. It is used in about 80 per cent of the senior high schools and four-year high schools, as is shown in Table 28–1.

The combination type, as its title suggests, is a combination of the constants-with-variables program and the multiple program. Possibly a more appropriate title would be "advisory curriculums," since the distinctive feature of this type is the organization, for guidance purposes, of two or more special-interest curriculums that are non-restrictive and permit students to substitute free electives for recommended courses as their needs justify. Under the combination type, certain courses are designated as constants to serve the common needs of all students, regardless of which special curriculum they elect. The degree of flexibility and the provision for special curriculum outlines, for advisory or guidance purposes, make this type of organization suitable for large four-year and senior high schools. The NEA study (Table 28–1) reports that about 20 per cent of the schools studied used this type of organization.

One of the important trends in curriculum organization has been the increased number of special-interest curriculums offered for the guidance of students in four-year and senior high schools. Many schools now provide a college-preparatory curriculum and a general curriculum as formerly but also have curriculums in trades and industries, business, homemaking, fine arts, and agriculture.

Illustrative Programs in Senior High Schools. The examples below illustrate the two most common patterns of organization for the program of studies now being employed in secondary schools. The first is a combination type used in a large three-year high school in California, and the second is a constants-with-variables type used by a small four-year high school in Iowa. These are not presented as ideal programs, but they do embody several representative features.

Combination, or Advisory-Curriculums, Program for a Large Four-Year High School.[8] This school offers six special curriculums to serve groups of students with similar special preparatory or occupational interests. All students are expected to meet certain requirements for graduation, regardless of which special curriculum they elect. Flexibility is provided by allowing each student to elect at least one subject each year from any of the free electives in which he is interested. The special curriculums are outlined for guidance purposes and are not prescriptive. Space does not permit the reproduction of each special curriculum in detail, but the four curriculums shown below illustrate the general pat-

[8] *The Pathfinder,* William S. Hart, Union High School, Newhall, Calif., 1961–1962.

tern of organization employed. The six advisory curriculums are as follows:

1. Home Economics
2. Secretarial
3. Bookkeeping and clerical
4. College Preparatory
5. Fine arts
6. Trades

FINE ARTS

This curriculum leads to future work as a painter, singer, writer, musician, designer, actor, decorator, etc. It is not college preparatory. Students who expect to attend college should be sure to include the course required for college entrance as their electives.

First Year	Semester Periods	Second Year	Semester Periods
Physical Education, Health and First Aid	10	Physical Education, Health and First Aid	10
English	10	English	10
General Science	10	Biology	10
Basic Math	5	World History and Driver Edu.	10
Music or Art I	10	Music or Art II	10
Elective	15	Elective	10

Third Year	Semester Periods	Fourth Year	Semester Periods
Physical Education, Health and First Aid	10	Physical Education, Health and First Aid	10
English	10	Civics and American Problems	10
U.S. History	10	Consumer Education	10
Music, Art	10	Music, Art	10
*Basic Math	5	Electives	20
Electives	15		

* Required if student fails to pass Comprehensive Math test given at end of the 10th year.

HOME ECONOMICS

This curriculum is designed to meet the needs of the student who is interested in the various problems of homemaking. It is not college preparatory unless the student includes college entrance subjects as electives. This course leads to future work as dressmaker, homemaker, catering, hostess, cafeteria, or household services.

First Year	Semester Periods	Second Year	Semester Periods
Physical Education, Health and First Aid	10	Physical Education, Health and First Aid	10
English	10	English	10
Basic Math	5	Biology	10
General Science	10	World History and Driver Educ.	10
Homemaking I	10	Homemaking II	10
Elective	15	Elective	10

Third Year	Semester Periods	Fourth Year	Semester Periods
Physical Education, Health and First Aid	10	Physical Education, Health and First Aid	10
English	10	Civics and American Problems	10
U.S. History	10	Consumer Education	10
Homemaking III	10	*Homemaking III	10
**Basic Math	5	Electives	20
Electives	15		

  * Either year.

  ** Required if student fails to pass Comprehensive Math test given at end of the 10th year.

COLLEGE PREPARATORY

This curriculum is designed for those who are going to college. It leads to future work as a lawyer, teacher, doctor, social worker, clergyman, etc. While this meets the University of California entrance requirements, special requirements are necessary for [some] colleges. Consult again the college entrance bulletin. Your program should then be checked with your guidance consultant.

First Year	Semester Periods	Second Year	Semester Periods
Physical Education, Health and First Aid	10	Physical Education, Health and First Aid	10
English	10	English	10
Algebra I—Academic Math	10	World History and Driver Educ.	10
General Science	10	Spanish I	10
Elective (Typing I)	10	Plane Geometry	10
Elective	10	Elective	10

Third Year	Semester Periods	Fourth Year	Semester Periods
Physical Education, Health and First Aid	10	Physical Education, Health and First Aid	10
U.S. History	10	Civics and American Problems	10
English	10	English	10
Chemistry, Physics or Applied Biology	10	Advanced Science, Solid, Analytical Geometry and Trigonometry, Advanced Algebra, or Spanish III	10
Spanish II	10		
Elective	10	Electives	20

TRADES

The following curriculum leads to future work as electrician, welder, machinist, woodworker, or draftsman. It is not college preparatory. It is arranged for those boys who expect to enter the trades immediately upon graduation or who plan to study further at a trade school like Los Angeles Trade Technical Junior College.

First Year	Semester Periods	Second Year	Semester Periods
Physical Education, Health		Physical Education, Health	
and First Aid	10	and First Aid	10
General Science	10	Biology	10
English	10	English	10
Basic Math	5	World History and	
Wood Shop I or		Driver Educ.	10
Metal Shop I	10	Wood Shop II or	
Mechanical Drawing	5	Metal Shop II	10
Elective	10	Elective (Mechanical	
		Drawing)	10

Third Year	Semester Periods	Fourth Year	Semester Periods
Physical Education, Health		Physical Education, Health	
and First Aid	10	and First Aid	10
U.S. History	10	Civics and American Problems	10
English	10	Consumer Education	10
Wood Shop III or		Individual Projects	10
Metal Shop III	10	Electives	20
*Basic Math	5		
Electives	15		

* Required if student fails to pass Comprehensive Math test given at end of the 10th year.

Constants-with-Variables Program in a Small Four-Year High School.[9]

The Columbus Community High School, Columbus Junction, Iowa, organizes its program of studies on a constants-with-variables basis. In the ninth grade, most of each student's program is made up of required subjects, but only one-third to one-half of the upper-grade program is required.

Curriculum Offerings

Subjects [italicized] are required for graduation.

FRESHMEN	SOPHOMORES
Physical Education	*Physical Education*
English	*English II & Basic Eng. II*
Algebra or Gen. Math	*World History*
Soc. Studies–U.S. Hist.	Geometry
(after 1865)	Vocational Home Ec II
Industrial Arts I	Vocational Ag II
Vocational Agr. I	Industrial Arts II
Vocational Home Ec I	Drivers [sic] Education
General Science or Biology	Biology
Personal Typing	Spanish I
Band and/or Vocal	Typing
	Band and/or Vocal

[9] *Student-Parent Handbook,* Columbus Community High School, Columbus Junction, Iowa, 1962–1963.

JUNIORS

Physical Education
English
English II or Basic Eng
U.S. History
Vocational Ag III
Vocational Home Ec III
Industrial Arts III
World Geography
Bookkeeping
Spanish II
Shorthand
Alg II & Trigonometry
Chemistry
Band and/or Vocal

SENIORS

English IV
World Problems
Physical Education
Vocational Ag IV
Algebra III–IV
Physics
Office Practice
Bookkeeping
Band and/or Vocal

Aids for Students in Planning Their Programs. It may be unrealistic to expect high school students to make more than tentative plans for their future, but it is also unrealistic to expect a boy who reads at the fourth-grade level to succeed in a course in English literature or a girl who has talent and interest in dramatics, but little background in mathematics, to succeed in high school physics. Certainly those students who plan to go to college should be made familiar with the entrance requirements of the institutions that are their possible choices. Within the limits of their facilities, high schools should do as much as possible to assist students in the selection of courses and activities that are appropriate for their abilities, consistent with their future educational plans, and adapted to their needs for personal and social growth.

Program Guides. One means of assisting a student and his parents in planning the student's high school program is a guidebook that describes all of the class and extraclass offerings of the school. In addition to containing a brief description of courses and activities, the bulletin should include graduation requirements, suggested special-interest curriculums, entrance requirements for nearby colleges, and similar information. Such a publication may serve not only as a valuable guide for faculty, parents, and students but also as an effective public-relations instrument. The bulletin need not be elaborate, but it should be well organized, readable, and attractive. There does not appear to be any high degree of uniformity in the organization and content of such bulletins, but the following outline of content from the bulletin of the Ames Senior High School, Ames, Iowa, is representative of some of the more comprehensive ones:

YOUR EDUCATIONAL PROGRAM

Table of Contents

Program Counseling. A bulletin is a useful device in counseling students with respect to their programs, but the counseling itself is the all-important service. As far as the administrative aspects are concerned, provision for counseling time, arrangements for conferences with parents, a counselor who knows each of his advisees, and adequate records are the chief requirements for a successful program.

The most important provision for advising students about their high school plans is a competent counselor. Space does not permit a discussion of counselor qualifications other than to emphasize that counselors should be interested in students and their problems, trained for the responsibility, and acquainted with each student assigned to them as an advisee. In large schools, homeroom teachers and block-time teachers are more likely to be qualified to advise students about their programs than other teachers. In small schools, without a homeroom or block organization, class sponsors may serve as program counselors. It is important that such counselors be as well trained as possible in advisory procedures and that they have access to the special information needed to confer intelligently with students and parents. A workshop for the in-service training of teacher counselors has served some schools as an effective means of developing good advisory procedures.

Effective program counseling requires provision for adequate time. It is not something that can be handled neatly in an afternoon or two. If it is done well, the counselor must have time to confer with each advisee without being rushed.

Many schools hold preregistration in the spring of the year and schedule planning conferences over a period of approximately two weeks. If they have a block-time program, the conferences are scheduled during the block period; otherwise the homeroom or a regular class period may be used. The following schedule for pre-registration is employed in a large junior high school in Iowa:

April 15—Scheduled group conference hour, 8:45–9:45. All teacher-counselors distribute program guides and registration materials, explain procedure, and have students fill out conference appointment blanks.

April 16–19—Principal and guidance counselors meet with sixth grade students in elementary school and organize a cooperative counseling program with the elementary school faculty.

April 16–21—Teacher-counselors confer with each advisee during home room period or a free period and agree on a tentative program to submit to parents. Students discuss tentative programs with parents, and secure parents' approval.

April 24—Evening conference for parents. Interested parents visit school for a general discussion meeting on the curriculum program and for conferences with teacher-counselors. Parents of sixth grade students in the elementary school are invited.

April 25–30—Teacher-counselors hold individual conferences with each advisee for final review of the student's program for the following year. Programs approved and forwarded to principal's office.

May 4—All sixth grade students visit the high school for an orientation program. These incoming students attend an assembly program, visit some classes, and participate in an informal social hour. Members of student council serve as hosts and guides.

There are, of course, many possible variations of this schedule. Its advantages are that it provides definite time for counselor-advisee conferences and for conferences with parents.

Orientation and Career Days. Some schools conduct orientation days to assist new students in planning their high school programs. Many also hold career days to familiarize students with college and occupational opportunities and requirements. Frequently, local service clubs cooperate with the schools in the latter type of program. Career days may be a "shot in the arm" guidance technique, but they focus attention on the importance of planning and stimulate students to think about their high school program in relation to a career. If conducted as a part of a continuing guidance program, they may be helpful.

ORGANIZING AND ADMINISTERING THE SCHEDULE
TO IMPLEMENT THE CURRICULUM

Daily and Weekly Schedules. The schedule, or time organization, of
the school determines to a large extent the time available to students for
various class and out-of-class activities, who their instructors will be, and
where and when the students will engage in specific types of learning
activities. The nature of the schedule reflects the educational philosophy
of the staff. If the principal end of education is considered to be the
mastery of certain packaged facts and skills, a uniform daily and weekly
timetable providing that certain groups of students shall meet with
certain instructors at regular times on designated days is the logical type
of schedule. The principal of a school so organized may take pride in the
fact that he can refer to his files and tell exactly where each student is
each hour of the day and each day of the week. There may be some merit
in that, from the viewpoint of the peace of mind of the principal, but
it has some serious limitations when viewed in terms of desirable conditions for the educational development of students.

If, however, the philosophy prevailing in a school embraces the viewpoints that education is concerned with the all-around development of
students—social and physical as well as intellectual—and that students
learn through a variety of experiences, a different type of schedule is
needed. It should have flexibility and versatility in terms of the nature
of learning activities that are supposed to take place in the school. It
need not lack system—there is no virtue in chaos—but, somewhere between rigidity and improvisation, a flexible but systematic schedule is
possible, as has been demonstrated by the growing number of schools
employing such schedules.

Types of Schedules. High school schedules may be classified under two
general categories: *fixed* and *variable*. The fixed type provides for uniform length of periods, classes scheduled at the same hour each day,
assigned study halls, and similar uniform provisions. The variable type
includes those schedules in which an attempt is made to introduce a
degree of flexibility by means of functional variations in length of
periods, hours and days of class meetings, activity periods, and similar
modifications. Although the percentage of schools employing some form
of variable schedule is relatively small, the number of such schools is
increasing steadily. The types of variable schedules include such versions
as the *block-time* for core-type classes, the "floating period," or *rotating-
period*, in which classes meet at different times each day of the week,
and the *modular* type (short modules of twenty to thirty minutes), with
classes scheduled for different lengths of time during the week. The

last-named kind includes the type of schedule employed in some team-teaching programs.

Characteristics of Conventional Schedules. Fixed schedules are characterized by uniform provisions within a particular school and possess many common characteristics from one school to another. However, several different types are employed. The most common types are the eight-period, seven-period, and six-period schedules.

Several studies report that from 90 to 95 per cent of the four-year and three-year senior high schools in the United States employ some type of fixed schedule. Sturges reports that, in 1958–1959, 92 per cent of 938 North Central Association high schools in five midwestern states used a fixed schedule, and that 41 per cent of these schools employed a six-period schedule, 29.5 per cent used a seven-period schedule, and 21.7 per cent used an eight-period schedule.[10]

Evidence concerning the influence of the length of class periods on achievement is limited and inconclusive. McElhinney studied the influence of length of class periods on growth in academic achievement during the 1959–1960 school year.[11] His study was conducted in eleven schools that used both long and short periods for the same courses in English, science, mathematics, and social studies. He compared growth in educational achievement in sixty-six pairs of classes. Each pair included one section of a course that met for a short period of forty-five minutes or less and one section of the same course that met for a long period of fifty-five minutes or more. Each section was taught by the same teacher, and the same text and other instructional materials were used.

Achievement was measured by use of the Iowa Tests of Educational Development, administered to the students in September, 1959, and in September, 1960. The study included eighteen pairs of ninth-grade classes, twenty-three for the tenth grade, and twenty-five classes in the eleventh grade.

McElhinney found that, although the test results favored the long period in a majority of comparisons, none of the differences were statistically significant at the 5 per cent level of confidence. He found this to be true for each of the four subject fields; for ninth, tenth, and eleventh grade classes; and for pupils of low, average, and high ability.

Mowrer also found no significant differences in achievement in English among graduates of schools with periods of fifty minutes or more, as compared to graduates of schools using periods of less than fifty

[10] Allen W. Sturges, *Techniques and Practices in Scheduling in Midwestern Secondary Schools,* unpublished doctor's dissertation, State University of Iowa, 1959, pp. 41–60.

[11] James H. McElhinney, *The Length of the High School Class Period and Pupil Achievement,* unpublished doctor's dissertation, State University of Iowa, 1961, pp. 136–145.

minutes.[12] The students in Mowrer's study were matched by scores on the Ohio State Psychological Examination, Form 23. Achievement was measured by grades made by students in first-semester English courses at the University of Missouri and scores on the *Cooperative English Test A: Mechanics of Expression, Form 1* and the *Cooperative English Test B2: Effectiveness of Expression, Form S.*

Conant states a preference for a seven- or eight-period day with forty-five minute periods and double laboratory periods.[13] His principal argument is that the short-period schedule permits academically talented students to enrol in more electives. Conant reports, however, that he found considerable difference in the views of administrators concerning the length of class periods in the schools that he visited.

Characteristics of Variable Schedules. Variable types of schedules are designed to provide flexibility through functional modifications in time provisions. The most common types of variable schedules are (1) block-time, (2) rotating-periods, and (3) modular schedules.

Block-Time Schedules. The block-time schedule grew out of the core-curriculum movement. It involves scheduling one group of pupils for two or three consecutive periods under one teacher or a team of teachers. Often two courses that may be correlated, such as English and social studies, are scheduled during the long time block.

Flexibility to permit a variety of learning activities is provided through the extended blocks. Time for planning is scheduled for each of the block-time teachers. The degree of correlation effected between language arts and social studies will depend, of course, upon the organization and the learning activities that take place under the guidance of block teachers. The block-time schedule may facilitate, but provides no assurance of, correlation. Teachers in schools with a block-time schedule tend to agree that it promotes better transition from the self-contained classroom of the elementary school to the departmentalized junior high school and that it provides a better situation for guidance than a conventional schedule. In some junior high schools, twelve instead of ten periods a week are given to the large block, and there is much to be said in favor of this expanded time allotment.

Rotating-Periods Schedules. This type of schedule provides for one or more courses to meet at different times on successive days. The activity period is scheduled so that it meets at a different time each day or week.

[12] George E. Mowrer, A *Study of the Effect of the Length of the High School English Class Period on Achievement in English,* unpublished doctor's dissertation, University of Missouri, 1956.

[13] James B. Conant, *The American High School Today,* (New York: McGraw-Hill Book Co., Inc., 1959), p. 65.

PROGRAM SCHEDULE—School "G" (Enrollment 650)
THIS SCHEDULE REPRESENTS THE BLOCK-OF-TIME AND DEPARTMENTAL-
IZED PROGRAM IN GRADE 7 AND THE WHOLLY DEPARTMENTAL-
IZED PROGRAM IN GRADES 8 AND 9

Teacher	8:15-9:09	9:12-10:06	10:09-11:03	11:06-12:00	Home Room 1:00-1:10	1:13-2:07	2:10-3:04
Lang. Arts Soc. Stu.	Lang. Arts & Soc. Stu. 7-7	Lang. Arts & Soc. Stu. Rm. 4	Lang. Arts & Soc. Stu. 7-1	Lang. Arts & Soc. Stu. Rm. 4	7-7 Rm. 4	Planning Period	X Soc. Stu. 7-3 Rm. 6
Orch.	Lessons TTh	Lessons TTh	Orch. TTh	Lessons TTh		Lessons TTh	Lessons TTh
Vocal Music	7-2 B&G F	7-1,3 B MF / 7-1,3 G TTh / 7-2 B&G W	9th Boys M / 9th Girls T / 9th B&G ThF	7-4,5B MW / 7-4,5G TTh	8-6 Rm. 9	8th Boys MW / 8th Girls TTh / 8th B&G F	7-6, 7B MW / 7-6, 7G TTh
Science	Planning Period	9th Science Rm. 2	9th Science Rm. 2	9th Science Rm. 2	9-3 Rm. 2	9th Science Rm. 2	9th Science Rm. 2
Lang. Arts	8th Lang. Arts Rm. 7	Planning Period	8th Lang. Arts Rm. 7	8th Lang. Arts Rm. 7	8-1 Rm. 7	8th Lang. Arts Rm. 7	8th Lang. Arts Rm. 7
Lang. Arts Soc. Stu.	Planning Period	Planning Period	Lang. Arts & Soc. Stu. 7-2	Lang. Arts & Soc. Stu. Rm. 1	7-5 Sewing Rm.	Lang. Arts & Soc. Stu. 7-5	Rm. 4
Library	Library S.H.	Library S.H.	Library S.H.	Library S.H.	9-6 S.H.	Library S.H.	Library S.H.
Band	1st Band MWF / 2nd Band TTh	Band Lessons MTWThF	Band Lessons MTWThF	Band Lessons MTWThF	8-7 Aud.	Lessons MTWThF	Lessons MTWThF
Algebra	9th Algebra Rm. 15	9th Algebra Rm. 15	Planning Period	9th Algebra Rm. 15	9-4 Rm. 15	9th Algebra Rm. 15	9th Algebra Rm. 15
Lang. Arts Soc. Stu.	Lang. Arts & Soc. Stu. 7-6	Lang. Arts & Soc. Stu. Rm. 1	Planning Period	X Lang. Arts 7-3 Rm. 6	7-4 Rm. 1	Lang. Arts & Soc. Stu. 7-4	Lang. Arts & Soc. Stu. Rm. 1
Social Studies	8th Soc. Stu. Rm. 12	Planning Period	8th Soc. Stu. Rm. 12	8th Soc. Stu. Rm. 12	8-1 Rm. 12	8th Soc. Stu. Rm. 12	8th Soc. Stu. Rm. 12
Soc. Stu. Math.	8th Soc. Stu. Rm. 6	8th Soc. Stu. Rm. 6	8th Math. Rm. 6	Planning Period	8-2 Rm. 6	8th Soc. Stu.	
Girls' Phys. Ed.	8 & 9 Girls MWF	7-2,3G M / 7-1G W / 7-1,2,3G F	8 & 9G MWF	7-4,5G MW	8-5 Gym MW	8 & 9G MW	7-6, 7G MW
Art and Crafts	7-2 Art MW / 7-1 Art TTh / 7-3 Art F	8th Art MTThF / 7-3 Art W	7-4 Art MW / 7-5 Art TTh	8th Art MTThF	7-6 Rm. 10	7-6 Art TTh / 7-7 Art WF	9th Art MWF / 8th Crafts TTh

X The 7-3 section is the only seventh-grade section not scheduled for the language arts-social studies block-of-time.

Fig. 28–1. This block-time schedule is an example of one for the seventh grade in a junior-senior high school. (*Junior High Schools for Iowa Youth,* Iowa State Department of Public Instruction, Des Moines, 1960, p. 33.)

Several versions of this type of schedule are now employed in secondary schools in different sections of the country, but the following example illustrates its basic features.[14]

Rotating Schedule
Claremont Junior High School
Schedule for week beginning Monday, December 7, 1959

From	To	Period	Monday	Tuesday	Wednesday	Thursday	Friday
8:05	8:20	HR	HR	HR	HR	HR	HR
8:25	9:10	1	A	G	F	E	D
9:25	10:10	2	B	A	G	F	E
10:15	11:00	3	C	B	A	G	F
11:05	11:50	4 or					
(11:00)	(11:35)	Lunch	D	C	B	A	G
11:50	12:25	Lunch					
(11:40)	(12:25)	or 4					
12:30	1:15	5	E	D	C	B	A
1:20	2:05	6	F	E	D	C	B
2:10	2:55	7	G	F	E	D	C

Schedule for week beginning Monday, December 14, 1959

Period	Monday	Tuesday	Wednesday	Thursday	Friday
1	C	B	A	G	F
2	D	C	B	A	G
3	E	D	C	B	A
4	F	E	D	C	B
5	G	F	E	D	C
6	A	G	F	E	D
7	B	A	G	F	E

Clemmer comments, "To date teachers, students, and parents have concurred in thinking that this system of daily class rotation is of real benefit to the instructional program. No longer do teachers or students complain about 'that last period algebra class,' which invariably and eternally falls during late afternoon." It is also claimed that assemblies do not take time from one class more than others and that every teacher has an opportunity to work with every pupil at a time when both are most efficient.

Modular Schedules. Some secondary schools have developed a schedule that employs short time modules of from twenty to thirty minutes. Bush and Allen describe the basic design for this type of schedule as follows:

The curriculum, conceived as an area to be scheduled, is made up of sub-parts called modular units which are derived from units of time and numbers

[14] Elwin F. Clemmer, "The Rotating Schedule at Claremont Junior High School," *Bulletin of the N.A.S.S.P.*, Vol. 44 (March, 1960), pp. 56–59.

of student schedules. The modular unit chosen for time should be cast according to the smallest amount of time that is desired for any instructional purpose.
If 40-minute, 60-minute, or 120-minute classes are desired a 20-minute module
would be appropriate. The number of students selected should also be stated
in terms of desired class sizes. A ten-student module would accommodate
classes of 10, 20, 30, 40, etc. Though any modular unit can be selected for
either period length or class size, it is desirable to select as large a modular unit
as appropriate to reduce the complexity of scheduling.

One possible modular unit is that of 15 students meeting for a single half-
hour period:

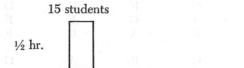

½ hr.   Scale: 15 students = ¼" width
                                                           ½ hour = ½" length

Thus a "class" of 30 students meeting for an hour (a conventional class unit)
would appear as a multiple of the modular unit:

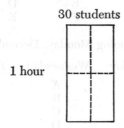

1 hour

A wide variety of structures is possible, all multiples of the basic modular unit.[15]

This schedule is commonly employed in schools with team-teaching
programs, and the day is organized into time modules of twenty to thirty
minutes, which may be shifted from class to class. Table 28–3 suggests
the high degree of flexibility possible in this type of schedule. Trump
suggests that about 40 per cent of the student's time be scheduled in
large-group instruction, 20 per cent in small-group discussion, and 40
per cent in individual study.[16]

CURRICULUM ARTICULATION

Good curriculum articulation enables students to move easily from one
level of the school system to another without being handicapped because
parts of the educational program do not fit together. It also serves to

    [15] R. N. Bush and D. W. Allen, "A Visual Model For Flexible Curriculum Plan-
ning," Stanford University, Secondary Education Project, Paper presented at meeting
of National Association of Secondary School Principals, February 24, 1962.

    [16] J. Lyold Trump, *Images of the Future* (an adapted draft) (Urbana, Ill.: The
Commission on Experimental Study of the Utilization of the Staff in the Secondary
School, 1959), p. 12.

TABLE 28-3

HOW A STUDENT MIGHT SPEND HIS TIME IN THE SECONDARY SCHOOL
OF THE FUTURE

	Monday	Tuesday	Wednesday	Thursday	Friday	Saturday
8:30 9:00 9:30	Large- Group Instruction	Indi- vidual Study	Large Group	Large Group	Large Group	Indi- vidual
10:00 10:30 11:00	Small-Group Discussion		Small Group	Indi- vidual Study	Small Group	
11:30	Large-Group Instruction	Large-Group Instruction	Large Group		Indi- vidual Study	
12:00	Lunch and Activities					
1:00 1:30	Indi- vidual Study	Small Group	Small Group	Small Group	Large Group	Indi- vidual
2:00 2:30 3:00		Large Group	Indi- vidual Study	Indi- vidual Study		
3:30	Small Group	Individual Study			Small Group	

relate learning areas at a given educational level so that they strengthen each other.

The need for good articulation within the curriculum program is emphasized in the published reports of many surveys of public school systems. Although the traditional gap between the eighth and ninth grades has been partially closed with the growth of the junior high school, new breaks have appeared between the sixth and seventh and between the ninth and tenth years. One symptom of the seriousness of the problem is the high percentage of dropouts between the eighth and tenth grades, at the point when compulsory-attendance laws in most states become no longer in effect.

Vertical Articulation. The central problem of vertical articulation is to secure a working interrelationship between successive levels of the curriculum program in order to facilitate the continuous educational progress of students. Procedures that may be employed to secure effective articulation between successive school divisions—elementary school, junior high school, and senior high school—and between grade levels include the following:

1. Development of a common philosophy and common objectives through participation of all teachers in a joint study and discussion program

2. Organization of a curriculum division serving the entire system, with committees set up on a vertical basis so that teachers from each level serve on special area committees dealing with such things as communication, health, moral and spiritual values, or social living
3. Joint elementary and secondary school conferences and workshops
4. Intervisitation by teachers of different grade levels
5. Transmission of comprehensive cumulative records from each level of the school system to the next higher level
6. Development of comprehensive programs for the orientation of students as they progress to a higher division of the school system
7. Coordination of guidance and personnel services at the junior and senior high school levels
8. Coordination of supervisory services for all levels of the school systems
9. Adoption of consistent policies for the promotion of students

All of these procedures are essential in securing good articulation in the curriculum program. Inasmuch as several of them including the development of a common philosophy, the transmission of cumulative student records, student orientation, and provisions for guidance have been discussed in previous chapters, the present discussion will be limited to special problems related to the articulation of curriculum sequences and materials.

In several large systems, the organization of a central curriculum-planning committee composed of teachers, administrators, and supervisors from each level of the school system has served to improve articulation. Other procedures that have been employed in large systems include the organization of curriculum-planning committees for various subject fields so that membership is drawn from each vertical division of the system and the assignment of members of the supervisory staff for a given subject to all grade levels.

In small systems with limited personnel, curriculum committees organized on a vertical basis in each subject and frequent conferences on problems of articulation between elementary and secondary school teachers appear to be the most feasible means of attacking this problem.

In many school systems, there are gaps and overlappings between the elementary school and the junior high school and between the junior and senior high schools in major areas such as social studies, language arts, and science. For example, in one midwestern city of about 35,000, a survey of the curriculum in social studies showed that, over a period of many years, there had been little effective consultation between curriculum committees or teachers from the three levels of the school system. The study indicated that there was little continuity between the programs of the elementary school, the junior high school, and the senior high school in the social studies. The problem was carefully studied by a central planning committee, and its recommendations were

1. The appointment of a social studies curriculum committee made up of teachers from the elementary school, junior high school, and senior high school, with the following special functions:

    a. To develop objectives for the social studies as a broad area of learning extending through all grade levels
    b. To make recommendations for the revision of course offerings and content in terms of grade sequences
    c. To review text and supplementary instructional materials in the social studies area in the light of the problem of articulation
    d. To arrange for a series of workshop conferences to study the problem of articulation for all teachers responsible for instruction in the social studies

2. The organization of study conferences with parents to discuss the goals of the social studies program and to secure their suggestions for improvement

3. The development of a continuing and comprehensive curriculum improvement program in the social studies, providing for joint elementary-secondary school conferences, summer workshops for the planning of course guides, tryout of materials, and evaluation

One of the effective procedures for securing articulation in this area was the conduct of a five-week summer workshop in which teachers from all grades participated. During the workshop, goals for the social studies were revised, course sequences and materials were reorganized to provide for better continuity, instructional materials at each grade level were selected so as to secure better articulation, and course guides were reworked.

A problem in vertical articulation that has developed in recent years and is causing considerable difficulty in some school systems is the moving of certain courses formerly offered only in the senior high school into the junior high school. Involved are modern languages, biology, plane geometry, and the like. In some systems, a problem has developed because of the lack of provisions for credit and advanced placement of students who have completed these courses when they move from the junior to the senior high school. It is essential that a joint junior and senior high school committee be appointed to deal specifically with this problem in systems in which it exists. Probably some modifications need to be made at both levels, but certainly the senior high should adapt its program to these changes and recognize the credit earned in the junior high.

Horizontal Articulation. The development of relationships among the various areas of the curriculum at a given level that further unity and coherence is the central problem of horizontal articulation. Some of the specific problems that plague many secondary schools with respect to this aspect of articulation include

1. The lack of relationships among courses at a given level, with resulting compartmentalization of learning
2. The failure of all teachers to assume responsibility for developing common learnings that cut across departmental lines, such as communication skills, citizenship, human relations, character education, and study skills
3. The lack of coordination in assignments given to students, with resulting "piling up" or inactive periods in the students' study schedules
4. The uneconomical duplication of materials and learning activities among departments in certain curriculum areas such as conservation, planning for a career, educational planning, space-age education, and the like

Much attention has been given to problems of interrelating instructional materials and activities on the theoretical front, but there has been little productive effort on the operational front. The development of block-time and unified-studies programs and such plans as "integration," "correlation," and "fusion" have commanded much space in educational literature during the past two or three decades. Most of these plans for curriculum organization have been described in preceding chapters of this volume. In the relatively few schools that have made a serious effort to do something about them, substantial results in securing effective horizontal articulation have been reported.

An excellent example of what can be done in securing horizontal articulation is shown in the Baltimore program for correlating English with other school subjects. A plan was developed between the English teachers and teachers of other subjects on the same grade levels whereby English teachers used assignments made in other classes to teach English skills and the other teachers checked and taught English skills in their classes. Teachers in other classes studied the standards of attainment established for English classes and cooperated in holding students responsible for what was taught in English. Teachers of other subjects also reported serious weaknesses observed among individual students in English usage and provided opportunities for written work in their classes. Standards of appraisal for all types of communication were mimeographed and given to both teachers and students for evaluation.

ADMINISTRATIVE PROVISIONS FOR SPECIAL INSTRUCTIONAL AND STAFF PROBLEMS

The central theme of this chapter has been that, although administrative arrangements do not ensure good education, they may provide conditions that make possible better teaching. Some of the contributions of special administrative provisions have been described in other chapters, especially in Chapter 27. Therefore, the discussion in this section will be directed largely to descriptions of organizational features.

Among the commoner special administrative arrangements designed to increase the effectiveness of the curriculum are the following: (1) acceleration, (2) ability grouping and ungraded programs, (3) advanced-placement courses, (4) the extended school year, and (5) team teaching.

Acceleration. The principal argument in support of acceleration is that it enables a student to advance as rapidly as his ability will permit. The bright student does better work because he is not held to the pace of his less gifted peers. The slow student is not hurried beyond his capacity and, therefore, does not become discouraged. Acceleration permits the gifted student to complete his general program in less time and to get on with work in the fields in which he has special talent. Its opponents claim that this plan soon results in students being thrown into groups that are not congenial from the standpoint of physical and social maturity.

At the present time, however, some interesting experiments are being conducted which provide for the early admission to college of gifted high school students. Although it is too soon to generalize from these experiments, the evidence to date indicates that superior students who enter college before completing four years of high school get along well both academically and socially.

The early-admissions experiment being conducted under the Ford Foundation Fund for the Advancement of Education has provided some valuable evidence on this question. Coombs reports that, "Academically, the first two classes of Early Admission Students have far out-performed their classmates generally. Interestingly enough they have also tended to out-perform their matching students in the comparison groups. The colleges rated both the scholars and their comparison students quite satisfactory on mental and physical health."[17]

Ability Grouping and Ungraded Programs. Since these plans are described rather fully in Chapter 27, they are referred to here simply to

[17] Philip H. Coombs, "Lessons from Recent Experiments in Articulation and Acceleration," *Current Issues in Higher Education* (Washington, D.C.: Association for Higher Education, National Education Association of the United States, 1954), p. 274.

point out some of their special administrative features. Ability grouping involves the sectioning of students for certain courses according to criteria that experience and research have shown to be related to their ability to succeed in these courses. In practice, such grouping is usually based on several measures of ability and usually is done independently for each course. Most frequently, the measures employed for the grouping are special subject aptitude tests, intelligence tests, previous school marks, and teacher and counselor recommendations.

Studies of the extent of use of ability grouping show that almost 70 per cent of the larger school systems now use it in some form. Van Dyke and Sparks found that 68 per cent of the North Central Association member schools in four states used some type of ability grouping in 1959–1960.[18]

Reported research on the relative advantages and disadvantages of ability grouping tend to support Ekstrom's conclusion that "In experiments that specifically provided for differentiation of teaching methods and materials for groups at each ability level and made an effort to push bright homogeneous classes, results tended to favor the homogeneous groups."[19]

Ungraded programs are adaptations of ability grouping, but students are sectioned, regardless of grade level, according to their ability and achievement in a certain subject field. They proceed from one phase or cycle of a subject to the next as rapidly as they can master the materials and demonstrate their competence on examinations. The following is the schedule of a typical student in the ungraded program of the Melbourne (Florida) High School:

> English Phase 1 (Remedial Program)
> Math Phase 3 (Intermediate Math)
> Art Phase 4 (Depth Study)
> Biology Phase 2 (Basic Skills)
> Amer. Hist. Phase 2 (Basic Skills)
> P.E. Unphased[20]

Advanced-Placement Courses. Between 1952 and 1955, a program developed by the School and College Study of Admission with Advanced Placement resulted in extensive interest in this method of providing for gifted high school students. As a consequence, there has been a steady increase in the number of secondary schools participating in it. The

[18] L. A. Van Dyke and J. N. Sparks, "Four-State Survey of Secondary School Marking Practices," (Iowa City: Research Digest, The Iowa Center for Research in School Administration, 1960), p. 1.

[19] Ruth Ekstrom, "Experimental Studies of Ability Grouping," *School Review*, Vol. 69 (Summer, 1961), pp. 216–226.

[20] Priscilla Kauth and B. Frank Brown, "The Non-Graded High School in Melbourne, Florida," *Bulletin of the N.A.S.S.P.*, January, 1962, pp. 127–134.

central feature of the plan is the provision of college courses for gifted high school students, which they complete under the direction of a high school teacher. Committees of college and high school teachers have constructed examinations that are administered to students upon their completion of the courses. Upon graduation from high school, students who make a satisfactory score on the examinations covering the courses completed may be admitted to a cooperating college with advanced standing in those subjects.

The College Entrance Examination Board has administered this program since 1955, and the number of participating colleges and high schools has increased in large amount. In 1960, about fifteen advanced courses in science, history, mathematics, literature, and languages were available for gifted students through this program. Derthick reported that more than 12,000 students in 650 high schools took advanced-placement courses in 1959.[21]

Extended School Year. Surveys indicate a rapid gain since 1955 in schools offering summer sessions. The Research Division of the National Education Association made a study in 1959 and found that, of 302 schools sampled, 84.7 per cent conducted summer schools that year. The range in length of terms was from four to ten weeks, with a median of 7.3 weeks for secondary schools.[22] The percentage of schools conducting summer sessions in North Central Association high schools increased from 15.1 per cent in 1955–1956 to 52.1 per cent in 1961–1962.[23] The NEA study reports that the dominant purpose of summer sessions in 1959 was enrichment.

Extension of the school year is of significant value in the following areas:

1. *Academic enrichment.* Students with academic interest and talent should be given an opportunity to take courses they were unable to work in during the regular year, such as a second modern language, biological or geological field study, economics, and writers' workshop.
2. *Vocational training and work experience.* Since more jobs are available for students during the summer than during the regular year, a number of schools are offering a combined school and

[21] Lawrence G. Derthick, "Review of the American Educational System," U.S. House of Representatives, Hearing of Committee on Appropriations (Washington, D.C.: Government Printing Office, 1960), p. 20.

[22] Research Division, National Education Association of the United States, "Summer Schools = Opportunity," *Research Bulletin,* Vol. 38 (February, 1960), pp. 23–24.

[23] From the summary statistical reports on file in the office of Gordon Caweiti, Executive Secretary, Commission on Secondary Schools, North Central Association of Colleges and Secondary Schools, Chicago, Ill.

on-the-job training program in the summer. This also relieves the crowded program during the academic year.

3. *Driver training.* Shifting the driver-education program to the summer session also relieves some of the overload during the academic year and permits a much more thorough and less hurried program of driver education.

4. *Art and music.* With the growing emphasis on academic work for superior students, many of them have not been able to take art and music courses in the senior high school. Summer work in these areas serves an important need for college-preparatory students as well as for others.

5. *Recreational activities.* Many schools now conduct some type of summer recreation program, frequently in cooperation with the city recreation department. These programs include a wide range of activities, from athletics, playground games, and swimming to little theater and camping.

6. *Personal-use courses.* Many students in the senior high school find it difficult to schedule such personal-use courses as typewriting, home economics, and home mechanics during the regular year. The summer session provides an excellent opportunity for students to secure this type of enrichment.

Team Teaching. Stimulated in large measure by the National Association of Secondary School Principals' studies and projects on staff utilization, team teaching has been widely discussed and initiated in secondary schools since the late 1950's. The central purpose of the Association's efforts was to develop means for better utilization of the talents of teachers and to enhance student achievement. Financed by grants from the Fund for the Advancement of Education, the N.A.S.S.P. Commission on Staff Utilization in Secondary Schools undertook several experimental projects including the use of technical aids, teacher aids, flexible scheduling, teacher recruitment, and team teaching.

It was a basic assumption of the project that American secondary schools would be faced with a continuing shortage of teachers for the next ten to fifteen years and that ways must be found to make better use of the special talents of teachers and to hold superior teachers in the profession. One of the principal experimental approaches in seeking a solution to better staff utilization has been team teaching.

Team-teaching projects involve the organization of a group of professional teachers, (specialists and general), instruction assistants, clerks, and general aides (non-professionals) into instructional teams. The *professional specialists*, or master teachers, serve as team leaders and are responsible for planning materials and activities, for conducting large-group instruction, and for coordinating the work of the team.

The *instruction assistants* perform specific tasks of teaching below the professional level such as reading themes, reading reports, constructing tests, assisting with student activities, and directing small-group discussions. The *clerks* type and duplicate instructional materials, prepare reports, take attendance, and perform other similar services. The *general aides* (mostly part-time laymen) supervise students in out-of-class activities and perform a variety of routine services.

Theoretically, the professional specialists were to be freed from many routine tasks so as to permit them to spend much more than the usual amount of time in planning materials and instructional procedures and in working with individual students. By conducting large-group instruction, they would not be required to spend time going over the same materials with several small sections but could combine three or four small groups into one large section for a single presentation.

A diagrammatic sketch of how a teacher might spend his time in a school in which team teaching is employed is shown in Fig. 28–2. As was noted earlier and as is shown in Fig. 28–2, a student would spend about 40 per cent of his time in large-group instruction, 20 per cent in small-group discussion, and 40 per cent in independent study. His schedule would be flexible and could be shifted from week to week as the need developed.

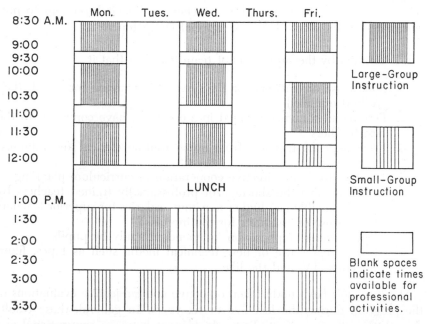

Fig. 28–2. How a teacher might spend his time in the secondary school of the future. (J. Lloyd Trump, *Images of the Future*, Commission on the Experimental Study of the Utilization of Staff in the Secondary School, National Association of Secondary School Principals, Washington, D.C., 1959, p. 24.)

Since 1956, when the Commission on Staff Utilization first organized to sponsor cooperative experimental programs in some 100 secondary schools over the country, team teaching in one form or another has been undertaken in a steadily growing number of junior and senior high schools. Four types of organization have emerged:

Plan I consist of one master teacher, or team leader, with two to five assistant teachers, one or two paraprofessionals or student teachers, and one clerk.

Plan II is organized around two or more associate master teachers, each with special-interest areas within the course, and with two or more paraprofessionals plus a clerk. The master teachers have coordinate status under this plan.

Plan III provides for one master teacher and lecturer who is the coordinator of the program. He is assisted by one or more beginning teachers, who work with small groups and are responsible for much of the routine such as reading papers, preparing tests, and setting up equipment.

Plan IV is simply a team of two or more teachers with coordinate status who do some joint planning and occasionally combine sections of courses for large-group instruction when it appears that such instruction would be appropriate. Occasionally, these teachers may switch sections to present materials in which they have special competence.

It is claimed by the supporters of team teaching that it

1. Makes use of teachers for the type of instruction for which they are best qualified
2. Permits all students enrolled in a course to have contact with the best teachers
3. Frees superior teachers from much routine clerical and administrative work
4. Provides for more effective cooperation in curriculum planning
5. Helps to solve the shortage of professionally trained teachers by making possible (a) higher maximum salaries for superior teachers and (b) use of assistants for routine tasks
6. Places greater emphasis on independent study by pupils
7. Makes greater use of new technical media such as tapes, films, projectors, TV, and the like

Many schools have undertaken objective and subjective evaluations of the program during the last five or six years. In general, these results show little difference in student achievement between conventional and team classes, as measured by standardized achievement tests; a large majority of participating teachers have expressed enthusiasm and the opinion that students profit and make a greater effort; costs have been about the same as for conventional classes, except where inadequate teacher assistance was provided in order to save money; student morale and discipline have been as good as, or better than, in conventional classes; parents have been favorably impressed and have generally supported the program; and the program has stimulated a greatly increased amount of curriculum planning.

Critics, among them some teachers who have had experience with the plan, most frequently have expressed the following objections:

1. In many schools, the large groups are not sectioned by ability and the instruction is directed to the students of average or superior ability.
2. Professional teachers have not been given a reduced class load, nor have they been paid higher salaries.
3. The small-group instruction is ineffective, because there are not enough teachers and assistants to work at it.
4. The large-group instruction casts the student in a passive role; he is occupied mostly with taking lecture notes.
5. Provisions are not made for individual differences, especially for low-ability students.
6. Large-group instruction is inappropriate for such courses as basic English and mathematics, where teachers need to know and to work closely with individual students.
7. Costly space for large-group instruction has been designed so that it is difficult to use for other purposes.

At the present time, many questions seem to be unanswered as to the effectiveness of team teaching in serving the purposes proposed by the Commission on Staff Utilization. Nevertheless, more and more schools are becoming interested, and enthusiasm among students and participating teachers appears to be high. The next few years should yield answers to the many questions now being asked.

QUESTIONS, PROBLEMS, AND ISSUES FOR FURTHER THOUGHT

1. Define the term *program of studies*. What are the distinguishing characteristics of each of the four major types of programs of studies?
2. Examine the program of studies for a high school with which you are familiar. Prepare a brief criticism of this program, judged in terms of the principles formulated by the Cooperative Study of Secondary School Standards.
3. Outline the subjects most frequently required for graduation by high schools in your area. How well do these requirements appear to meet the "Imperative Needs of Youth" as propoosed by the National Association of Secondary School Principals?

4. Select a typical constants-with-variables program for a high school in your area. Describe the changes that you would recommend in this program to serve the needs of youth in the community more effectively.
5. What trends in emphasis in the high school curriculum are reflected in the types of special-interest curriculums introduced in secondary schools during the past twenty to thirty years?
6. What are some of the specific provisions being made in the program of studies in modern high schools to provide greater flexibility in the "constants" or "common" division of the curriculum?
7. What changes need to be made in the conventional schedule of recitations in high schools with which you are familiar, in order to provide for effective implementation of curriculum objectives?
8. Review the research on period length in relation to pupil achievement. Does the research support the claim that the objectives of the curriculum can be served just as well in short as in long periods?
9. What are some of the most frequently employed administrative provisions for individual differences in the secondary school program? Which of these do you believe is most effective?
10. What are some of the weaknesses in the secondary school curriculum that reflect a need for better articulation?
11. Describe the different types of organization most frequently employed by schools with team-teaching programs. What do evaluations show concerning the advantages of team teaching over conventional class instruction?

SUPPLEMENTARY MATERIALS

SELECTED READINGS

BYRNE, DAVID F., and WADE A. STEEL. "Leyden High School 'Early Bird Period,'" *Bulletin of the N.A.S.S.P.*, No. 272 (March, 1962), 79–82.

DOUGLASS, HARL R. *Modern Administration of Secondary Schools* (2d ed.). Boston: Ginn & Co., 1963. Chapters 7, 16.

ELLIS, U. BERKLEY, and STANLEY B. DICK. "Scheduling the Practical and the Fine Arts in the Large High School," *Bulletin of the N.A.S.S.P.*, No. 273 (April, 1962), 36–41.

HAGGERSON, NELSON L., and HASKEL B. SMITH. "The Seventy-Minute Period Schedule Contributes to More Effective Staff Utilization," *Bulletin of the N.A.S.S.P.*, No. 273 (April, 1962), 51–58.

JOHNSON, R. H., *et al.* "Extensive Study of Team Teaching and Schedule Modification in Jefferson County, Colorado, School District R-1," *Bulletin of the N.A.S.S.P.*, XLIV (January, 1960), 78–93.

———— and M. D. LOBB. "Transformation of the Sacred Secondary-School Schedule," *California Journal of Secondary Education*, XXXV (February, 1960), 96–105.

McDOWELL, ARCHIE. "The Santa Cruz Schedule," *Bulletin of the N.A.S.S.P.*, XLII (March, 1958), 72–76.

O'BRIEN, JAMES F. "A New Look in Schedule Building," *Bulletin of the N.A.S.S.P.*, No. 240 (October, 1958), 102–6.

PURNELL, DALE, *et al.* "The Daily Schedule: Shorter Periods, Longer Periods, Variable Periods, or What?" *Bulletin of the N.A.S.S.P.*, No. 264 (April, 1961), 12–17, 110–15.

STURGES, A. W. "The Midwestern High-School Schedule," *Bulletin of the N.A.S.S.P.*, No. 262 (February, 1961), 91–95. A survey of practices in 938 secondary schools.

TOMPKINS, ELLSWORTH. "The Daily Schedule in Junior High Schools," *Bulletin of the N.A.S.S.P.*, No. 220 (May, 1956), 176–221. A study of the committee on junior high school education.

WHERRY, JOSEPH E. "Staggered Schedule in Penn Hills," *Bulletin of the N.A.S.S.P.*, No. 275 (September, 1962), 51–53.

WRIGHT, GRACE S. *High School Graduation Requirements Established by State Departments of Education.* U.S. Office of Education, Circular No. 455, revised January, 1958. Washington, D.C.: U.S. Department of Health, Education, and Welfare, 1958. Report of a survey of state requirements for high school graduation.

29

Special Problems of the Junior High School

SOURCES OF IMPORTANT PROBLEMS

Status as an Intermediate School. Special curriculum problems at this level stem from two factors: (1) the junior high school's position as an intermediate institution in the K-12 (kindergarten through twelfth grade) educational ladder and (2) the nature of its clientele. With elementary schools subscribing by and large to a child-centered philosophy, and with high schools giving subject-matter mastery higher priority, junior high school educators are caught in a philosophical cross-fire between the two. Post-Sputnik demands for higher academic standards have increased the pressure for moving high school courses and curriculum patterns down into the junior high school grades. Foreign languages are being introduced in grade seven, if not earlier; algebra is moving into the eighth grade; and biology into the ninth. The downward extension of high school practices also is reflected in the full departmentalization so common in junior high schools, as well as in multiple-track curriculums, ability grouping, promotion by subject, and the elective system.

In the meantime, certain junior high school practices represent an upward extension of elementary education. The partially self-contained classroom shows up as block-time and core programs, often embodying integration of subject fields and organization of instruction around large units or problems. Emphasis upon general education, attention to basic skill development, and concern for the non-academic aspects of student lives also reflect the influence of a philosophy commonly associated with elementary schools. In many states, either an elementary or a secondary certificate entitles a person to teach in the junior high school grades; this further increases the diversity of viewpoints likely to be present in any one school staff. An attempt to reconcile or blend the two philosophical positions is a necessary first step in curriculum development at the junior high school level.

Also because it is an "in-between," the junior high school lacks a clearly perceived status in the educational community. The boundaries that set off junior high school education are neither clearly defined nor uniform throughout the nation. A great variety of grade combinations may be found in a school labeled "junior high"—7-8-9, 7-8, 6-7-8, 5-6-7-8-9, 8-9, and so forth. Although the 8-4 pattern of grade organization is becoming increasingly rare, some textbook publishers still consider grades one through eight as elementary and begin their secondary series with grade nine. Others label grades one through six as elementary and label seven through twelve as secondary. Colleges of education vary in their definitions; a seventh-grade teacher seeking admission to a National Science Foundation summer seminar may be admitted to the secondary program at one institution, the elementary program at another. Teachers have difficulty profiting from one another's experience, because circumstances in one junior high may be markedly different from those in any other. The general public too is apt to have only a hazy notion of the junior high as an institution. In short, junior high school education means different things to different people.

Lacking precise definition, and confused as to philosophical orientation, it is little wonder that the junior high school often lacks the prestige of other levels. Junior high schools too often inherit hand-me-down school buildings, and the shortage of personnel at this level results in overcrowded classrooms and an excessive number of uncertified teachers. The notoriety attained by some junior high schools of the "blackboard jungle" variety is yet another deterrent to recruitment of teachers. Teaching at the junior high level too frequently is viewed as a "promotion" from elementary school teaching or as a way to fill time while awaiting a position in senior high. Rapid teacher turnover, in turn, makes curriculum planning difficult and continuity of program almost impossible.

The Young Adolescent. A second category of curriculum problems stems from the nature of the junior high school pupil. Like the institution in which he studies, the young adolescent lacks a clearly defined position in society. He no longer finds status and satisfaction in the world of the child, but he is not yet accepted into the world of the adult. American society is notoriously ambivalent in its definition of "adulthood." A youngster may be required to start paying "adult" prices at the movies when he is twelve, but he must be sixteen before he is considered "adult" enough to drive an automobile, and he cannot buy whisky (a presumed adult privilege) until he is twenty-one. In some states, a girl may marry and assume the responsibilities of motherhood at the age of fourteen but must wait seven more years before she is considered mature enough to vote. Two salient characteristics of adolescent behavior—an almost slavish conformity to standards set by the peer group, and the ambivalence reflected in adult-like behavior one minute and childlike actions the next—grow in large measure out of society's failure to give the adolescent a clearly defined role and status.

Further compounding the problem are the rapid physiological and psychological changes that are virtually remaking the young adolescent. Moreover, these changes do not all occur at the same time or proceed at the same rate. Since ours is an age-graded educational system, the result is extreme diversity among students during the junior high school years. The same classroom may contain a preadolescent child and a near-mature adult. As Mauritz Johnson, Jr., points out, "there are greater differences among pupils *within* seventh grade than there are *between* an average seventh grader and an average senior."[1] Student diversity is further increased by compulsory-attendance laws and by the social promotion prevalent in the elementary grades. The result is that slow learners, reluctant learners, and predelinquent youngsters pile up in the junior high school grades, where they too often merely mark time until they are old enough to leave school. Planning of learning experiences for this age group is indeed a challenging endeavor.

As a consequence of these factors, the primary tasks facing the junior high school are (1) clarifying goals and purposes, (2) articulating its program and policies with those of units above and below, and (3) providing learning experiences adapted to a wide range of individual differences.

APPROACHES TO THE PROBLEMS

Clarifying Goals. Curriculum planning must be based upon clearly defined goals and purposes. The philosophical dilemma in which the junior high school finds itself may be solved by examining the over-all purposes of the entire school system. Confusion as to goals has been all too characteristic of American education, but it is becoming increasingly clear that intellectual development must be given highest priority.[2] Intel-

[1] Mauritz Johnson, Jr., "School in the Middle: Junior High—Education's Problem Child," *The Saturday Review*, Vol. 45, No. 28 (July 21, 1962), p. 57.

[2] Educational Policies Commission, *The Central Purpose of American Education*. (Washington, D.C.: National Education Association of the United States, 1961).

lectual development may be defined in a number of ways, but its basic elements are (1) the ability to think and (2) accurate knowledge upon which to base thinking.

Subject-matter mastery, so highly prized in high school, thus represents only one aspect of the desired intellectual development. As important as organized knowledge are the questions and problems dealt with by the discipline, and the methods used to examine them. Furthermore, content comes alive to the student only as these problems are shown to have meaning for him in his daily life. His thinking must be directed toward those of man's most universal and significant problems that are within his level of comprehension at that time. He must be helped to see his personal problems in the context of the larger ones, enlarging his present understanding and extending his area of concern so that he applies his thinking ability to increasingly more complex and significant problems.

For example, the typical adolescent's concern for getting along with his peers should become the springboard for a study of interpersonal relations on a broad scale, including current desegregation problems and the roots of international tensions. To deal only with peer relations is to expose the school to justified accusations of triviality; to deal with world problems without relating them to genuine student concerns is to ignore the role of motivation in learning and to reduce the likelihood that knowledge will make any real difference in student behavior.

It is true, however, that man does not live by knowledge alone. For both democratic citizenship and personal self-realization, development along physical, emotional, social, aesthetic, and moral lines may be as important as intellectual development. Nor can intellectual development be isolated from these other lines of development. Thinking and knowing are effective only within a context of feeling and doing. The human organism grows, learns, and functions as an integrated entity.

It does not follow, however, that the school must give equal attention to all aspects. The principal objection to the attention elementary schools have given to the "whole child" is not so much the scope of the concern as the totality of commitment. Clearly, if the "whole man" is to be served, the "whole child" must be developed. But this does not mean that the school must do the whole job; this must be the task of the whole society. Other functions commonly attributed to the junior high school, such as socialization, exploration, guidance,[3] and even health services, must assume their proper role as subordinate but contributory to intellectual development, lest the school be accused of trying to remake the child's entire life. The statement that intellectual development is the *primary* obligation of the school should not be misconstrued as suggesting that

[3] William T. Gruhn and Harl R. Douglass, *The Modern Junior High School* (2d ed.) (The Ronald Press Co., 1956), pp. 30–37.

it is the *only* consideration. On the other hand, the assertion that the intellectual sphere is *not* the only concern must not be interpreted as an indication of anti-intellectualism or as warrant for the neglect of intellectual development.[4]

Curriculum Coordination and Articulation. One of the early arguments for a junior high school was that it would smooth the transition from elementary school to high school. Articulation with units above and below continues to be a high-priority task of the junior high school, else what was once a single gap becomes two equally drastic ones. The junior high school's role is not mere accommodation, however; providing an educational program of significance to young adolescents here and now is a task of sufficient import in itself, with no need to justify it in terms of what programs are like at other levels. The junior high school curriculum should *articulate with*, not just *prepare for*, the senior high school program, for instance. Needed is a coordinated, developmental program from kindergarten through grade twelve, with scope and sequence broadly defined so as to allow ample variation to meet individual differences.

Central-office personnel usually bear the responsibility for curriculum articulation. Supervisor, coordinator, helping teacher—by whatever name —these staff members provide the leadership necessary to keep a team of highly individualistic teachers working toward common goals. Curriculum planning involves, or should involve, representatives of all levels. Certainly a committee working on the junior high school social studies program should include both elementary and senior high school teachers. The school system that provides time for such professional activity within the work load of its teachers reaps the benefits of more effective curriculum planning and better articulation.

Curriculum coordinators usually are assigned to specific subject-matter areas such as language arts, social studies, or science. This may provide well for articulation of content scope and sequence, but another important facet—the cumulative impact of curricular experiences upon the student—may be slighted. Sitting with every curriculum-planning committee should be representatives of the guidance department, who view the total sequence in terms of human growth and development and assist teachers to relate content to students. A good working relationship between guidance specialists and content specialists, both at the system level and the local school level, can increase the likelihood that intellectual development will be realized in actual changes in behavior.

[4] For further amplification of this point of view, see *The Intellectual Responsibility of the Junior High School: A Statement of Position by Members of the Staff of the Junior High School Project* (Ithaca, N.Y.: Junior High School Project, School of Education, Cornell University, 1962).

Providing for Individual Differences. Attempts to provide for individual differences take many forms, all of which have their advantages and disadvantages. Guidance, homogeneous grouping, acceleration, subgrouping within a class, differentiated assignments and instructional materials, and cocurricular activities all have been applied to this task with varying degrees of success.[5]

Guidance. Many ramifications of junior high school guidance lie beyond the scope of this chapter.[6] As an aspect of curriculum, however, guidance is central to the task of providing for individual differences and stimulating the optimum intellectual development of each child. Guidance is concerned with helping individual students with their personal, social, and vocational problems. It is of tremendous importance during the junior high school years, when problems of growing up tend to reach their peak, and many decisions of lifelong import must be made. One of the chief arguments for a block-time program is the opportunities it provides for guidance. Problem areas that deal directly with common concerns of adolescents are ideal vehicles for group guidance and set the stage for individual counseling by both the block-time teacher and guidance specialists.

But guidance through curriculum is not limited to core. By individualizing instruction and stressing the relevance of subject matter to the daily lives and problems of students, any subject can serve as a vehicle for promoting guidance. For example, in an English class, readings can be selected both for their literary merit and for the insight into life they provide for the young adolescent. Mathematics may be taught so as to demonstrate the qualities of thought essential for scholarship and productive endeavor in technical fields; thus, the student can determine whether or not his abilities and interests fall in this direction. A good homeroom program is another means of providing guidance, especially if the homeroom teacher also has the same students for a regular class at some time during the day. When the school's total program is designed with the needs and characteristics of young adolescents in mind, guidance and curriculum blend into a generalized process of mobilizing subject matter, methods, and special services to promote the optimum development of each child consistent with the school's primary goal of intellectual development.

[5] See Leslee J. Bishop, "Methods of Individualization in Junior High School," *Educational Leadership,* Vol. 17, No. 2 (November, 1959), pp. 80–83, 118; and *Individualizing Instruction,* 61st Yearbook of the National Society for the Study of Education, Part I (University of Chicago Press, 1962).

[6] For a thorough exploration of the subject, see Mauritz Johnson, Jr., William E. Busacker, and Fred Q. Bowman, Jr., *Junior High School Guidance* (New York: Harper & Row, 1961).

Grouping and Acceleration. With such a diverse student body, it is to be expected that junior high schools would also apply various administrative procedures to reduce the range of variability in any one class or group. Although research has yet to prove that students achieve more in classes sectioned by ability, the practice is popular with teachers and found in most junior high schools. Acceleration or retardation also may be used to break the age-grade lockstep, enabling students to study with their peers in academic ability, regardless of their chronological age. The many pros and cons of these administrative arrangements may be compromised by grouping students homogeneously for parts of the program, such as mathematics and foreign-language classes, carefully preserving hetero-geneity in others such as block-time classes and student activities, and permitting occasional grade skipping or retardation according to the merits of each individual case.

Acceleration and ability grouping create problems in curriculum design. If students are divided into fast, average, and slow groups, how should curriculum content be differentiated for each group? (Unless the curriculum *is* differentiated, sectioning by ability cannot be justified.) Should the differentiation be in terms of speed with which required subject matter is covered, as is suggested by the designations "fast," "average," and "slow," or should the quantity of content be varied?

Further complications arise if the school attempts to adopt an "un-graded" or "multigraded" plan, in which each individual student moves through the program at his own rate. One junior high school operating on this plan, for instance, combines seventh- and eighth-graders when assigning students to ability groups. Advanced sections are composed almost entirely of eighth-graders, with a sprinkling of unusually capable seventh-graders; low sections contain mostly seventh-graders, with a few less capable eighth-graders. Social studies, which normally consists of state and local history in seventh grade and United States history in eighth grade, is taught in alternate years. Which course the student takes first depends upon the calendar year in which he moves up from the sixth grade. Every five weeks, a student's group assignment is reviewed and subject to change. Thus, an accelerated student may hop, skip, and jump through the total program in one year, while a slow student may revolve in the cycle for three years. If it is desirable for all students to be exposed to the same basic content, it would appear that this highly indi-vidualized approach might have as many drawbacks as oft-maligned grade skipping. In skill development, however, this approach has more merit, hence its increasing acceptance in the primary grades.

When amount of content to be covered is the variable, curriculum designers must identify minimum essentials for the low groups, basic requirements for the average, and enriched content for the more capable.

Some curriculum guides outline content for the advanced students, with asterisks or other symbols designating topics required of the average and below average. Sometimes parallel columns are used, as in Table 29–1, showing a portion of a curriculum guide prepared by the Cincinnati Public Schools.

TABLE 29–1

TOOLS OF EXPRESSION

GRAMMAR

T—Teach A—Academic M—Maintain G—General S—Special	Grade 7			Grade 8			Grade 9		
	A	G	S	A	G	S	A	G	S
Sentence Recognition									
Simple	M	M	M	M	M	M	M	M	M
Compound	M	M		M	M	T	M	M	M
Complex				T			M	T	
Subject and Predicate	T	T	T	M	M	M	M	M	M
Phrases	T			M	T		M	M	T
Clauses				T	T		M	M	
Verbals				T			M	T	

SOURCE: Cincinnati Public Schools, "English, Grades 7-8-9," Curriculum Bulletin 243 (Cincinnati Public Schools, 1958), p. 28.

More ambitious are the school systems that prepare separate curriculum guides for each ability level or track. These may provide for differentiation in both content and speed, as is illustrated by the following quotation from a language-arts curriculum guide for gifted junior and senior high school students:

How does English for the gifted differ from a regular English program?
We feel that the following course of study provides for three types of differences:

1. *Difference in pace.* Much of the work usually included in the regular English program appears also in the program for the gifted, but the work has been accelerated since the gifted student can master it in a lower grade level. In technical grammar, for example, the regular program provides for a six-year sequence; the program for the gifted accelerates this so that the content is covered in four years; thus the last two years are available for an enriched and advanced program.
2. *Difference in scope.* The program for the gifted is broader in scope than the regular English program; more advanced phases of language

and literature are included than ordinarily would appear in the regular program. For example, the program for the gifted includes such topics as semantics, linguistics, and critical thinking.

3. *Difference in depth.* The program for the gifted provides for a deeper study of material ordinarily covered in regular sections at the same grade level. For example, while a regular eleventh grade college preparatory section would read only an excerpt from Thoreau's *Walden*, the gifted class would read the entire book and spend much time in a discussion of the philosophical position of the rebel in society.[7]

If marked differences exist between levels or tracks, difficulties will be encountered by the occasional student who transfers from one to the other. Moreover, if acceleration is encouraged, articulation with higher grades is crucial. It is stultifying for a student to complete three years of junior high school mathematics in two, for example, only to have him repeat familiar materials when he enters the next grade, or omit study of mathematics for a year to allow the average to "catch up." A coordinated twelve-grade educational program is essential for all students, regardless of track, ability level, or expected pace. Furthermore, care must be taken to ensure that teachers do not assume that there is more homogeneity within a section than is actually the case. *The teacher should individualize his instruction, regardless of the degree of homogeneity achieved by administrative means.*

Exploratory and Cocurricular Experiences. As a young person goes through the transformation known as "adolescence," he continually asks himself, "Who am I? What am I really like? What kind of person shall I become?" Exploratory experiences, coupled with effective guidance, are especially important for these youngsters, helping each to assess his strengths and weaknesses, discover and expand his interests, and chart his future development.

Courses such as music, art, industrial arts, business, homemaking, and foreign languages sometimes are thought of as "exploratory" courses. The assumption is that, in such studies, the student will find out whether or not he has talent or interest in any of the fields. However, exploration, like guidance, can take place in any course or activity, if it is conducted with this object in mind.

Student activities are another admirable vehicle for providing guidance and exploratory experiences. No longer merely extracurricular, student activities have in many schools become truly cocurricular. Clubs, student government, school publications, and musical and dramatic organizations provide excellent opportunities for a student to try himself in a variety

[7] School District of Abington Township, *Teaching the Gifted in English Language Arts: Junior and Senior High School* (Abington, Pa.: School District of Abington Township, 1960), p. 1.

of ways. Subject-matter clubs promote intellectual development by enabling the student to go deeper into a field than is ordinarily possible in a formal course; music and dramatics give opportunities to perfect skills and polish performance; student government and publications provide leadership opportunities, along with many allied skills.

To meet the needs of a diverse student body, a rich program of activities is required. In the list below, note the variety offered in this small junior high school, enrolling approximately 500 students in grades seven and eight. The list was supplied by William J. Craigie, principal of the school.

STUDENT'S ACTIVITY SELECTION LIST
FAYETTEVILLE-MANLIUS JUNIOR HIGH SCHOOL
MANLIUS, NEW YORK
1961–1962

Monday
Seventh Grade Chorus
Sports Appreciation Club
  (Section One)

Tuesday
Eighth Grade Chorus
Future Homemakers of America
Dramatics and Choral Speaking
Seventh Grade Boys' Leaders
School Newspaper
Stamp Club
Eighth Grade Girls' Leathercraft

Wednesday
Eighth Grade Chorus
Student Council
Yorkers (Section One) (New York
  State History Club)
Seventh Grade Girls' Officiating
Civil War
Eighth Grade Girls' Jewelry Craft
Art Club

Thursday
Seventh Grade Chorus
Eighth Grade Ensemble
Yorkers (Section Two)
Junior Red Cross
Mathematics
Eighth Grade Boys' Leaders
Science Club (Section One)
Library Club
Sports Appreciation Club
  (Section Two)

Friday
Activity Band
Dramatics and Choral Speaking
Yorkers (Section Three)
Camera Club
School Service and Radio Programing
Eighth Grade Girls' Officiating
Science Club (Section Two)
Flintlock to M-1
Public Speaking and Debate
Chess Club

Mounting such an extensive activity program requires heavy investment of time and energy by the school staff. Only those activities that truly contribute to the educational objectives of the school should be sponsored, and the program should be carefully scrutinized from time to time in order to keep it in tune with student needs and interests and to weed out "activity for activity's sake."

It is unfortunate that few schools give as much conscious attention to the cocurriculum as they do to more formal course planning. Classroom teachers, accustomed to presenting subject matter, need help in adjusting to the different role they must perform as sponsor or adviser of a student activity. While "courses of study" are inappropriate here, the staff should prepare handbooks or guides that list objectives for each activity group, elaborate possible worthwhile learning experiences, and establish criteria for evaluation. Handbooks that guide but do not unduly limit student initiative would bring out more of the potential educational values of the student-activity program.

BLOCK-TIME, UNIFIED-STUDIES, AND CORE PROGRAMS

The prevalence of block-time programs in junior high schools reflects the degree to which a well-conceived program solves some of the curriculum problems peculiar to this level. Emphasis upon problem solving, both as a method and as a means for organizing content, gives learning to think the necessary priority of concern. Students coming from self-contained elementary school classrooms are introduced gradually to the departmentalized pattern prevalent in high school, easing the transition from one level to the other. Individual and small-group study, basic to the core approach, is well designed to provide for individual differences, especially since it is carried out in a large block of time that enables the teacher to know and understand his pupils as individuals. This intimate relationship also provides some of the finest opportunities for personal counseling, making the block-time teacher an important member of the school's guidance team. The more nearly a block-time program approaches core, the more fully will it reap the advantages summarized below.

Advantages of Core as a Vehicle for Guidance

I. The teacher comes to know each individual student better because:
   A. Teacher and student are together during a longer block of school time.
   B. The teacher sees the student in a greater variety of situations.
   C. The teacher deals with fewer different students per day.
   D. The kind of teaching common in the core tends to reveal more personal information about each student, his needs, interests, problems, and values.

II. Problems growing out of interpersonal relations can be worked out through:
   A. Studying units of work built around real problems of adolescents.
   B. Participation in group work of various kinds.
   C. The catharsis which comes from learning that one's peers have similar problems.
   D. Actually working on problems of this type in a group of friends, both adults and peers.
   E. Sharing beliefs and values in an atmosphere which encourages respect for other people.

III. Counseling is more effective because:
  A. Student and teacher know each other better.
  B. Counseling is more natural, growing out of group problem-solving situations.
  C. The longer time block and more flexible scheduling tend to make it easier to find time for conferences.
  D. Shifting some of the responsibility for discipline to the group frees the teacher to some extent from his punitive role, thereby improving rapport.
IV. Core-centered guidance is more sound administratively because:
  A. Major responsibility for guidance is spread among several teachers, not concentrated in the hands of one specialist. Yet guidance is not so diffuse as to be nonexistent. Core teachers accept guidance as an important part of their job.
  B. Guidance and curriculum are combined in the same person.
  C. Guidance is made possible in the school where resources are too limited to provide for the services of specialists.[8]

Content in core is broadly structured in terms of problem areas, not prescribed in detail; no rigid sequence must be followed. With this built-in flexibility, learning experiences can be adapted to the changing needs and characteristics of students, both as individuals and as groups. Procedures for establishing scope and sequence in a core program have been elaborated elsewhere.[9] Here it will be sufficient to examine the scope and sequence of an existing program, to illustrate how it provides for guidance and exploratory experiences.

Junior high schools in the Shawnee-Mission High School District, Merriam, Kansas, have a unified-studies program that embraces language arts, social studies, and science at the seventh- and eighth-grade level and language arts and social studies in grade nine.[10] Resource units, prepared over a period of years by groups of teachers, are available for the required and optional units listed in Table 29–2. Each unit contains a statement of the significance of the unit, specific objectives, outline of content, activities (introductory, developmental, and culminating), sources of information, and suggestions for evaluation. Also helpful are such bulletins as "Subject Matter Guide for Unified Studies," "Filmstrip Recommendations," "16 Mm. Film Supplement for Unified Studies," "Study Skills: A Suggested Outline," and "Suggested Science Projects for the Early Autumn, Grades 7 and 8."

Guidance and exploration would appear to be primary considerations in such units as "We Are the Junior High School," "Looking Ahead,"

---

[8] William Van Til, Gordon F. Vars, and John H. Lounsbury, *Modern Education for the Junior High School Years* (Indianapolis: The Bobbs-Merrill Co., Inc., 1961), pp. 393–394.
[9] *Ibid.*, Chapter 10.
[10] Ralph E. Chalender, "A Unified Studies Approach," *Educational Leadership*, Vol. 18, No. 3 (December, 1960), pp. 161–164.

TABLE 29–2

UNIFIED-STUDIES SCOPE AND SEQUENCE, SHAWNEE-MISSION DISTRICT, KANSAS

Seventh Grade	Eighth Grade	Ninth Grade
Required	Required	Required
We Are the Junior High School	Looking Ahead	Looking Ahead
Let's Improve Our Communication with Others	Let's Improve Our Communication with Others	Let's Improve Our Communication with Others
How Do We Find Our Way Around the World?	How Did the United States Become a Nation?	Careers
We Live in Many Communities	Westward Expansion and Civil War	Interdependence in a Shrinking World
Living in Harmony with Myself and Others	How Do We Govern Ourselves in a Democracy?	The United Nations
What Is Science?	How Did the United States Become the Greatest Producer of Goods in the World?	One or more of the following: Africa, China, Russia, South America, Western Europe
How Do Plants and Animals Grow?	Conservation of Natural Resources	
Optional	Optional	Optional
How Can I Use My Spare Time?	How Can I Use My Spare Time?	How Can I Use My Spare Time?
Citizens Elect Their Officials	Citizens Elect Their Officials	What Can I Do To Promote a Better Life for All of Us?
How Does Weather Affect Us?	America—A Melting Pot of Nations	Money and Banking
Rocks and Minerals	Insects	Forming Public Opinion
	Birds	My Part in the World of Books

SOURCE: Dr. Ralph E. Chalender, Principal, Milburn Junior High School, Shawnee Mission, Kan., personal communication, March, 1962.

"Careers," and "Living in Harmony with Myself and Others." Other units, dealing with science, language arts, and social problems, promote guidance and exploration less directly. Such a block-time program, taught with a heavy emphasis upon problem solving, teacher-student planning, and small-group work, and with adequate time for personal counseling by teachers, goes far toward solving the special problems of curriculum at the junior high school level.

Clearly such a program demands careful curriculum design, specially selected teachers, and, above all, constant help and encouragement from principals and other administrative leaders.[11] Time and effort are required

11 State and national surveys support the last-mentioned contention. See Gordon F. Vars, "Administrative Leadership: Key to Core Program Development," *Bulletin of the N.A.S.S.P.*, Vol. 46, No. 271 (February, 1962), pp. 91–103.

to move from a conventional, narrowly subject-centered curriculum to one that provides greater integration of knowledge, adaptation to individual differences, flexibility of approach, and intellectual challenge. In the long run, however, staff involvement in such an endeavor may prove to be the best way to stimulate improvement of instruction.

RECENT DEVELOPMENTS IN JUNIOR HIGH SCHOOL CURRICULUM

The importance of articulation with other levels is underscored by some recent developments in junior high school curriculum. Rapid expansion of foreign-language programs at both the elementary and junior high school levels is a case in point. Consider the plight of a ninth-grade French teacher who, in one classroom, has some students with no previous language experience, several with one semester of study, a number with two semesters of study distributed over two years, some with four years of instruction in elementary school and junior high school, and a few with three years of elementary experience and two full years of prior study in junior high school.

National Curriculum Studies. Curriculum studies carried out by national groups create further complications. Sparked by the Physical Sciences Study Committee, numerous groups of scholars, psychologists, and educators are at work revising the curriculum in science, mathematics, English, and the social studies. Programs in modern mathematics, developed and field-tested by such groups as the School Mathematics Study Group (SMSG) and the University of Maryland Mathematics Project, are already finding their way into standard textbooks. Many ninth-graders are studying new biology courses prepared by the Biological Sciences Curriculum Study, and, under Project English and Project Social Studies, the humanities have joined with the sciences in engaging in fundamental curriculum reform.

Such studies provide a much needed face-lifting for many subject areas, bringing in newer content previously available only to students of unusually capable teachers. Before adapting any of these exciting new programs, however, a junior high school staff must take a hard look at how it fits into the total twelve-grade program. Are we justified in introducing SMSG mathematics into junior high school, for instance, if the student must revert to conventional ways of thinking to succeed in senior high school mathematics courses? If structural linguistics is to be used in the junior high school grades, it should be introduced in the lower grades so that students will not have to unlearn one system before learning the new one.

Fortunately, some steps are being taken to bring curriculum-revision programs into line. The curriculum study of the American Association for the Advancement of Science, for instance, covers both elementary and junior high school levels, and both Project English and Project Social Studies are concerned with the total sequence. Even when national curriculum proposals are welded into a coherent design, however, each local school still must modify it to fit local conditions and adapt it to the needs and abilities of individual students. In other words, nationally developed programs, like the ubiquitous textbook, provide only a basic curricular framework, which means nothing until it is brought to life by a skilful teacher working creatively with youngsters.

Programed Instruction. One of the major arguments for programed instruction is the ease with which individual differences may be provided for by its use. Each student may proceed at his own rate, and, in the case of branching programs, all students need not cover the same material in order to master basic content. Although hyperbole characterizes some of the statements made by advocates of programed learning, it does appear that such devices, properly used, represent yet another valuable tool for providing for individual differences among students.

Like textbooks and the curriculum designs of national study groups, however, programed devices may pose the threat of a "national curriculum," a deadly standardization of scope and sequence throughout the nation. Fortunately, the trend is away from the programing of an entire course and moving in the direction of smaller units of instruction. For example, programs recently published by Coronet include "Our Solar System," "Number Bases and Binary Arithmetic," and "Your Study Skills."[12] Programs of this type can be utilized with less likelihood of distorting the total fabric of a particular school's curriculum. As with all instructional resources, the materials must be fitted to the curriculum, not the curriculum to the materials.

Team Teaching and Staff-Utilization Studies. No examination of current developments would be complete without discussing the proposals of the Staff Utilization Study, commonly referred to as the "Trump plan."[13] It is not yet clear to what extent these staff-organization proposals will affect the curriculum. A number of junior high schools have used variations on the team-teaching idea, but, thus far, emphasis has been on better or more efficient teaching of conventional content. Too often, what is called adoption of the large-group–small-group approach

[12] Coronet Learning Programs, Chicago, 1962.
[13] See, for example, J. Lloyd Trump and Dorsey Baynham, *Focus on Change: Guide to Better Schools* (Chicago: Rand McNally & Co., 1961).

goes only as far as having masses of youngsters herded into lecture halls, without opportunities for the small seminars and independent study so vital to full implementation of the plan. Under these circumstances, content may be selected, almost unconsciously, in terms of what can best be presented through mass instruction.

A skilful lecturer, whether in the lecture hall or appearing via television, can provide information. However, interaction between students and a perceptive teacher is essential to adapt instruction to individual differences and to stimulate optimum thinking with, and about, the information provided. Young adolescents, with all their diversity, are least likely to profit from mass instruction and most in need of opportunities to interact in small groups. Schools unwilling or unable to provide the full range of large-group, small-group, and individual-study opportunities should approach team teaching with caution.

SUMMARY

Curriculum problems peculiar to the junior high school level are created by the characteristics of the age group being served and by the junior high school's intermediary position between the elementary school and the senior high school. These call for clarification of goals, careful articulation between levels, and adequate provision for individual differences. The philosophical dilemma may be resolved by establishing a priority of goals, with intellectual development, functionally defined, at the top of the list. Maintaining coordination and articulation among the various levels of a school system requires strong leadership, adequate provision for staff planning by all who are involved, and cooperation between subject-matter specialists and those responsible for guidance. The total educational program also must be kept in mind when adapting programed materials and curriculums developed by national study groups.

Ministering to individual differences requires an effective guidance program, wise use of grouping and acceleration, and a rich selection of exploratory and cocurricular experiences. A carefully planned and staffed core program provides an excellent vehicle for solving some of the curricular problems peculiar to the junior high school. It is not yet clear what effects the concept of the non-graded program or the newer staff-organization schemes will have upon the junior high school curriculum. While the characteristics of junior high school youngsters impose some special conditions upon curriculum planning at this level, proper perspective requires that the junior high school be viewed as but one unit in a total system devoted to the development of fully functioning citizens.

QUESTIONS, PROBLEMS, AND ISSUES FOR FURTHER THOUGHT

1. Educators disagree on whether the ninth grade is best placed in junior or senior high school. What are the arguments for each position? What are the implications for curriculum of each position?
2. In many states, either an elementary or a secondary certificate is acceptable for junior high school teaching. Since, in the final analysis, the curriculum consists of the learning experiences each individual teacher selects for his particular class, which type of preparation would be most suitable for junior high school teaching?
3. In what ways would the junior high school curriculum be different if it were designed to *articulate with,* rather than *prepare for,* the senior high school program?
4. Which of the advantages of core as a vehicle for guidance apply equally to other block-time programs such as the subject-area block or unified studies? What are the disadvantages of providing guidance through core and other block-time programs?
5. When guidance and curriculum are as interrelated as it is suggested in this chapter that they should be, what precisely is the role of the guidance director? Of the curriculum coordinator?
6. An ungraded or multigraded junior high school program is sometimes advocated as a means of providing for individual differences. What problems of curriculum scope and sequence are created by this approach? What are its advantages and disadvantages?
7. Some educators recommend that the entire student-activities program be under the direction of the guidance department. How does this square with the viewpoint that these activities should be cocurricular in nature?
8. Debate the pros and cons of homogeneous grouping as it applies particularly to curriculum problems of the junior high school.
9. Examine the ways in which the newer programs in mathematics and science for the junior high school grades differ from the conventional curriculums.
10. Compare the usual block-time approach, in which one instructor teaches two or more subjects to a single class, with a team-teaching setup in which specialists from several disciplines work with a large group for an extended period of time. Examine each approach with respect to both curriculum and guidance.

SUPPLEMENTARY MATERIALS

Selected Readings

Periodical literature on the junior high school is voluminous and rapidly becomes out-of-date. The reader is urged to consult the bibliographies entitled *Selected References to the Junior High School,* published and revised periodically by the National Association of Secondary School Principals, Washington, D.C.

Brimm, R. P. *The Junior High School.* Washington, D.C.: The Center for Applied Research in Education, Inc., 1963. Chapter 3, "The Instructional Program," 15–38.

COMMISSION ON SECONDARY CURRICULUM OF THE ASSOCIATION FOR SUPERVISION AND CURRICULUM DEVELOPMENT. *The Junior High School We Need.* Washington, D.C.: The Association, 1961. This is the most forward-looking of the recent statements on junior high school education.

CONANT, JAMES B. "Conant Looks at the Junior High School," *Nation's Schools,* LXV (April, 1960), 82.

———. "Recomendaitons for the Junior High School," *The Education Digest,* XXVI (December, 1960), 5–9.

FAUNCE, ROLAND C., and MORREL J. CLUTE. *Teaching and Learning in the Junior High School.* San Francisco: Wadsworth Publishing Co., Inc., 1961. See especially Chapter 6, on the program of student activities, and Chapter 12, on community-service projects; also pp. 71–103.

GRAMBS, JEAN, CLARENCE G. NOYCE, and JOHN ROBERTSON. "The Junior High School of the Future: The Junior High School We Need," *The Education Digest,* XXVII (September, 1961), 15–19.

GRUHN, WILLIAM T. "What Is New in Junior High School Education?" *Bulletin of the N.A.S.S.P.,* No. 253 (February, 1960), 6–11.

———. "Developments in the Junior High School," *Bulletin of the N.A.S.S.P.,* No. 271 (February, 1962), Part 1: Chapter 1.

———. "Major Issues in Junior High School Education," *Bulletin of the N.A.S.S.P.,* No. 266 (September, 1961), 19–25.

——— and HARL R. DOUGLASS. *The Modern Junior High School* (2d ed.). New York: The Ronald Press Co., 1956. Chapters 5–9.

GWYNN, J. MINOR. *Curriculum Principles and Social Trends.* New York: The Macmillan Co., 1960. Chapter 14, "The Junior High School Curriculum."

MOTT, KENNETH. "Language Arts–Social Studies Fusion in the Junior High School Block Period," *Bulletin of the N.A.S.S.P.,* No. 254 (March, 1960), 124–31.

NOAR, GERTRUDE. *The Junior High School Today and Tomorrow* (2d ed.). Englewood Cliffs, N.J.: Prentice-Hall, Inc., 1961. Stresses the school's role in meeting the needs of youth, with considerable attention to core and language arts.

SOUTHERN ASSOCIATION OF COLLEGES AND SECONDARY SCHOOLS. *The Junior High School Program.* Atlanta: The Association, 1958. Chapters 5–7 deal with administrative matters such as organization, staffing, and facilities.

THAYER, LLOYD Y., and JOHN V. MAIER. "What Educational Program Is Needed in the Junior High School?" *Bulletin of the N.A.S.S.P.,* No. 208 (April, 1957), 94–98.

"The Instructional Program in the Junior High School," in *The Junior High,* Southern Association of Colleges and Secondary Schools, 1960. Pp. 36–71.

VAN TIL, WILLIAM, GORDON F. VARS, and JOHN H. LOUNSBURY. *Modern Education for the Junior High School Years.* Indianapolis: The Bobbs-Merrill Co., Inc., 1961. Chapter 5, "Organizing the Curriculum for Instruction"; Chapter 6, "Social Realities Influence the Junior High Program"; Chapter 15, "Exploration Through Industrial Arts, Homemaking, Arts and Crafts, and Music"; Chapter 22, "A Junior High School Program for the 1960's."

WRIGHT, GRACE S., *Block-of-Time Classes and the Core Program in the Junior High School.* U.S. Office of Education, Bulletin No. 6. Washington, D.C.: Government Printing Office, 1958.

30

Methodology and the Curriculum

NEEDED CURRICULUM DEFINITIONS

In attempting to determine the relationship between problems of curriculum and problems of method, it is necessary to clarify certain semantic difficulties. This may be done by setting up a few operational definitions, which may be used as guides in the discussion that follows. At least three such definitions seem to be needed for the purposes of this chapter.

Curriculum Problems. First, *curricular problems* will be characterized as those that involve any question concerning *what to teach* in the schools. Obviously, this may be expressed also in terms of problems having to do with *what is to be learned* in school. If pursued further, this implies the determination of *what is worth learning,* which may become the determination of relative values among all things that may be proposed as worthy of school learning.

A very concise limitation may be placed upon the above definition. Many things are learned by young people through agencies other than the school. Curricular problems are concerned with things to be learned in school as distinguished from things that may be left to other educational agencies in our society.

Problems of Method. Second, *problems of method* are those concerned with *how to teach* the things that have been determined to have sufficient value to be included in a school curriculum. Again, it may be preferable to express this in terms of *how* pupils *can learn best* that which is worth learning.

It would seem from the foregoing that method is concerned mainly with *how* learning takes place or with *how* the teacher can direct learning processes, and not primarily with the determination of *what* to teach or *what* to learn. It is, then, obvious that, in the sequence of school operations, it becomes necessary first to determine what is to be learned before it is possible to devise a suitable methodology for getting the learning accomplished. First it must be agreed that the training of automobile drivers is a school obligation. Then it becomes necessary to determine what components of good driving are to be taught. Only after these two steps have been completed is it possible to come to grips with problems of how would-be drivers can best learn rules of the road or avoidance of traffic jams.

Problems of Administration. Third, *problems of administration* are those concerned with *how to provide an optimum environment* for learning. More specifically, administrative, as related to curricular, problems are those that deal with provision of building and floor space, staffing, equipment, library facilities, textbooks, appropriate furniture, lighting, costs, and sources of financial support.

Interrelationships of Problems of Curriculum, Method, and Administration. It can be admitted at once that these three types of problems are so interrelated in practice as to make them almost inseparable. No matter how important a particular curricular item may be, if the item cannot be learned by the pupils for whom it is proposed at present maturity levels, little or no learning takes place. The curriculum making is stalled by the seeming impossibility of devising a method that will implement the learning of the proposed curricular item. As an illustration, examine the curriculum proposals found in the Science Manpower Project monographs on *Modern High School Biology*.[1] If the proposed content of the course outlined is to be taught to tenth-grade pupils, there seems to be serious doubt as to whether biology teachers can devise any methods for getting the subject matter learned by the pupils. If this doubt should turn out to be justified, it would be possible to say that methodology is inadequate for the curricular materials proposed. In such a case, the curricular planning would be defeated by difficulties in learning and by a methodology that is unable to cope with the learning difficulties implied in the selected content. The proposal of *what to teach* breaks down before an inadequate knowledge of *how to teach*.

[1] Dorothy F. Stone, *Modern High School Biology*, Science Manpower Project Monographs (New York: Teachers College, Bureau of Publications, Columbia University, 1959).

In a like manner, both curricular choice and methodology may break down because the administrative forces are unable to provide the means for implementing a desirable school venture. If it is proposed to introduce courses in Russian in a secondary school, there are no inherent curricular difficulties in determining suitable content. The methodology of current foreign-language teaching in better schools should prove adequate for the learning tasks implied. However, if a competent teacher of Russian cannot be found or cannot be employed at the budgeted salary, the course cannot be established.

Likewise, if it is proposed to offer a course in business machines within the secretarial curriculum, there would seem to be no great difficulties in determining content or in devising suitable methods of instruction. The success of the course hangs upon the provision of the machines that must be available for building up necessary skills. The machines must be purchased or leased, or cooperative arrangements must be made with business establishments owning suitable machines. The availability of funds may be an issue here too. The rapid obsolescence of the machines also becomes a problem. Such matters fall within the scope of school administration. The curricular problem was solved at the point where it was determined that a course in business machines was needed or desirable and with the determination of the kinds of machines to be used in the training program.

Other Operational Definitions. It is possible to include other categories in our operational definitions, to separate the problem of establishing goals for education from the problems of content and to assign agreement upon goals or purposes to a philosophy of education, or to make some distinction between the psychology of learning and method, which would suggest that the determination of laws or principles of learning constitutes a psychological problem and that the application of such laws or principles in the hands of the teacher in a classroom situation involves methodology. This chapter is concerned primarily with the first proposed distinction—that between curricular problems, determining what to learn, and the problems of methodology, determining how to accomplish learning. It assumes that it is first necessary to establish goals before defining specific curricular problems or trying to select a suitable methodology; it admits the practical limitations set by administrative operations; and it tends to ignore hair-splitting distinctions between the psychology of learning and teaching method, suggesting that any method is sterile if it is not founded upon an awareness of sound principles of learning.

CURRENT CONFUSIONS BETWEEN CURRICULUM AND METHOD

In attempts to trace relationships between curriculum and method, a number of current confusions tend to spread a cloud over school operations and to bring down upon the schools a host of criticisms from patrons and "axe grinders."

Confusion of Activities and Subject Matter. The first of these confusions has to do with the failure to make a distinction between *activities* and *subject matter*. Such a term as *activity school* illustrates the point. In a literal sense, all schools are activity schools in that all school pupils are active, dynamic beings and that no learning takes place without some form of activity. In reverse, all schools tend to be subject-matter-centered institutions in that there must always be something that is worth learning, about which activities can be centered. It is impossible, and indeed undesirable, to abolish subject matter in favor of activities of the moment. Even if we choose to engage in a series of activities in school, apparently for the sake of the immediate sensations enjoyed, there will arise the question of a choice of the sensations that young people should appreciate. These could be characterized as a form of subject matter, and the decisions involved would imply curricular choices.

The issue here is that, educationally, activities are not ends in themselves. In schools, activities are set in motion to teach something toward the learning of which the activities lead. This is true whether the activities are selected in terms of a predetermined curricular pattern, selected by the teacher in terms of the immediacy of the present class situation, or selected by the pupils in some "democratic" class procedure.

Activities in themselves tend to be evanescent. When a given activity ceases or is carried to completion, what remains is the effect that participating in the activity has had upon the pupils. It is this remainder effect that is of greatest concern in education.

Consider the following as an illustration: Many art teachers speak of the planning of an art course in terms of "art activities," which include poster making, cutting of linoleum blocks, silk-screen printing, painting of autumn landscapes, drawing of still lifes, clay modeling, wood carving, metal etching, toy making, and many others. The list of potential art activities is almost endless. How does the teacher determine which of these activities are preferable, other then by leaving the choice to the whims of the pupils in deciding what for the moment seems to be the most fun?

Somewhere in carrying out such activities there must be some *art* to be learned. This consists of the principles of design, facts and principles of color combination, rules of composition, knowledge of various styles of lettering, some basic manipulative skills needed in art craftsmanship, and possibly some ideas or ideals of aesthetics. It is to be hoped that, when the activities of an art course have been completed, the drawings have faded, and the objects have been stored in the attic, some residues of art will remain with the pupils. Such art skills, ideas, knowledge, attitudes, ideals, principles, and rules make up the subject matter of art. Some of these elements are the things the pupils are to retain and carry away from the art class. The activities are relatively incidental.

No one can object to the selection of an activity that a pupil will enjoy while it is going on or to the selection of an activity that will produce an object that pleases the maker and is one in which he can take pride when he carries it home to exhibit. At the same time, it is important that the student become aware of the art subject matter involved and that he be able to transfer the uses of such subject matter to other activities and to other art objects, in or out of school.

From the foregoing illustration, it can be seen that the primary curriculum problems are these of identification and selection of the subject matter to be learned. In effect, the selection of the activities that implement the learning of the subject matter becomes a matter of teaching methodology. Those activities are to be selected that are richest from the point of view of giving more effective experiences with the subject matter. Other factors of methodology are important. Activities must relate not only to important items of subject matter but also to the maturity levels of the pupils concerned. The activities the pupils prefer are most important clues to their basic motivations. There are also seasonal factors and those of the customs of the society in which the pupils live. There is a reason for doing Christmas art in season, but Christmas need not be divorced from the subject matter to be learned, which may be used in other seasons and at other times.

Basically the curricular approach to a high school course is to be found in the subject matter that pupils are to learn to control. The determination of the activities through which the pupils gain control of subject matter is largely a matter of methodology. It may be that, for many of the pupils, the obvious format of the course seems to be centered around major activities. Undoubtedly, this concern with activities may enhance the motivation of a majority of the pupils in the course. However, the teacher cannot lose sight of the subject-matter items that pupils are to control when the work is completed. To the society that supports the school enterprise, the control of subject matter developed by the pupils is of ultimate value.

This confusion between activities and primary subject matter has permeated the teaching of courses in practically all those subjects found in the secondary school program in which pupils have evidenced a high degree of interest in either the activities of the moment or the products of these activities. In addition to applying to art, which was used as an illustration earlier, this applies to music, physical education, industrial arts, junior high school science, home economics, speech, and citizenship. The confusion has reached a stage where many teachers in these subjects have great difficulty in identifying the items of subject matter for which they are responsible. This may help to explain the present wave of popularity of machine teaching and programed learning, which do, in general, identify the subject matter. In many situations where a curriculum-improvement program is being set in motion, the attempt to involve the teachers in the program might well take the form of identifying the subject matter to be taught in the courses now assigned to them.

Confusion of Pupil Experiences and Subject Matter. A second confusion, quite similar to that between activities and subject matter, is a confusion between experiences and subject matter. This second confusion is even more subtle, since all subject matter must begin with the experiences of some people in a given time and place. In this sense, every individual builds his own subject matter out of his own continuing experiences.[2] However, in the education of the young, an attempt is made to utilize the accumulated and organized experiences of others, either living or dead, to avoid having each individual attempt to relearn in his own lifetime all that has been accumulated in the culture in which he lives. This accumulation of useful experiences of our own and preceding generations, organized and expressed as skills, operations, established facts, rules, laws, principles, and theories, constitutes what we have been calling "subject matter."

In the increasing complexities of a culture such as that of the United States, the schools are charged with the responsibility for aiding young people in learning to use at least some parts of the cultural accumulation.

It is possible to imagine that, somewhere in the dim past, there was an individual who devised or discovered a number system of his own and that he learned to do some simple calculations with it, at least simple additions. Many children learn some things about numbers and simple numerical calculations before coming to school. However, it is almost inconceivable that a particular youngster will ever develop a system of algebra or discover the possibilities of the calculus on his own and without recourse to the contributions of various mathematicians over the ages. The understanding and uses of mathematics must be taught.

[2] Cf. John Dewey, *Experience and Education* (New York: The Macmillan Co., 1938).

The development of subject matter in its various classifications has progressed to the point that it becomes extremely unlikely that any student below the level of a research student at the graduate level will discover anything new in a given field. Most of an individual's experiencing will take the form of interpreting and making use of elements of accumulated cultural experiences, although it must be granted immediately that many experiences of the young seem to them to be new and unique.

What has been said implies that the school experiences of secondary school pupils are largely means of learning existing subject matter considered to be of value by the society that operates the schools. Schools are not to be concerned with random or unorganized experiences engaged in by young people merely for the sake of experiencing. The choosing of the subject matter to be dealt with in school is the curricular problem. The selection of experiences through which pupils may learn the subject matter is primarily a problem of method.

An illustration of the need for the distinctions made above can be found in the physical-education classes of secondary schools. Some schools have adopted a laissez faire policy in physical education. Pupils engage in sports during the physical-education period for the sake of the enjoyment of the experiences of the day. The same games are played by the same pupils for weeks. The same youngsters tend to win all the games. Often, at the end of a season of play, little learning has taken place. Few pupils, even the most skilful, have made any real progress in game skills or game strategies. It is entirely possible that, in many instances, awkward performance and poor play have become fixed by continuous use from day to day. Pupils have had relatively wholesome experiences. They have had some physical exercise. They have played a popular game. Some of them have had a good time. But what learning has taken place? Where is the subject matter? Could a controlled selection of pupil experiences result in better methods of instruction and so lead to some conscious improvement of game skills and strategy? More experience with a popular game does not seem to be enough. After all, these experiences are taking place in a school that has provided extremely expensive floor space and equipment in order that they may go on. A *teacher* is paid a salary to see that learning does take place.

In the first place, the teacher in charge in such a situation must identify the subject matter of the sport involved. This consists of some knowledge of the game and its rules, the primary skills needed to perform the plays well, and the strategies needed for a winning game. It then becomes necessary to select and to attempt to control the pupil experiences that will contribute to the learning of the subject matter.

For example, more learning may take place if squads of differing levels of performance are organized. An awkward player may profit more from his playing experiences if these are with those more nearly his game peers. The better performers are more likely to develop improved strategy in competition with other players with well-developed skills. It may be profitable to have experiences in watching the performances of unusual players. Experiences with analysis of performance from motion pictures of games may be desirable. Some individual practice may be needed. Certainly, in order to develop learning, both teacher and pupils must become aware of the outcomes that are to develop from the experiences.

No coach of a high school football team can expect to develop a winning team with a series of laissez faire practices. The boys on the team would be likely to have a very good time at first, but, in the long run, everyone concerned would be unhappy. From this point of view, the coach is often a better teacher than the physical-education teacher who is inclined to allow pupils just to have enjoyable experiences with games.

It should be added that there is increased satisfaction and, in the long run, greater enjoyment in performance if experiences produce greater knowledge, improved skills, and better strategy. No amateur enjoys many games of bridge with a card shark unless he can improve enough to win occasionally. In reverse, a skilful player gets little satisfaction in continuing to win from a dub who shows no improvement.

Confusion of Applications and Primary Subject Matter. A third confusion involving subject matter and method, similar to the first two but differing in specific connotations, lies in the interpretation of the notion of *application* of generalized skills, attitudes, principles, laws, and rules of operation. Again, in the movement toward improved motivation and the selection of content of more immediate value for secondary school pupils, school courses have emphasized application. This emphasis can be seen in textbooks for such courses as English composition, general mathematics, junior high school science, general biology, and chemistry, and in the syllabuses for courses in art, music, industrial arts, and physical education.

One great difficulty found in the use of applications as the center of curricular organization for school courses lies in the fact that the array of possible applications becomes practically endless. Books and course outlines continually increase in length. There seems to be no place to stop. There are advantages in the potential adaptation of content to individual needs through the selection of applications of most concern to particular people. However, this does not remedy the bewilderment of a teacher facing the increasing volume of possible applications in his own field.

A second difficulty with curriculum organization, in terms of application, occurs when the applications seem to obscure the primary subject matter they may serve to illustrate. This leads to failure to identify important skills or essential principles on the part of both teachers and pupils. This failure to identify primary subject-matter elements becomes a major stumbling block to desirable transfers in the learning process. The pupil is likely to be able to use outside the classroom only those applications actually taught. He will have no means of relating the need for a new application in a unique situation to a given skill or principle, because he has never identified the basic skill or principle involved or gone through the processes of reapplication in the classroom. With such lack of identification, teaching becomes training in an almost endless array of applications. If the applications chosen are not those that occur to pupils out of school, the pupils are helpless in attempting to work out solutions to new problems. Two examples follow:

Citrus fruits are to be eaten as a desirable source of vitamin C; so we all buy citrus fruits and orange and grapefruit juices. We may be unaware that vitamin C occurs in a variety of fruits and vegetables and that often there are more economical sources than the citrus fruits, for example, cabbage, tomatoes, tomato juice, green peppers, and apples.

Tennis players try to get shots into the corners of the court. This doesn't always work. The opponent may turn out to be left-handed or to have an unusually strong backhand return. It might be better to operate on the principle of playing to the opponent's weakness and then, by diagnosis, to determine the application needed in a given game situation.

Years ago, an attempt was made by a group interested in science teaching[3] to cut through the welter of expanding applications of science by attempting to determine the major generalizations underlying the sciences to be taught. At least, this kind of curricular approach does fix limits to subject matter to be taught. In turn, it produces the danger that students may memorize abstract generalizations, as such, without an understanding that can lead to intelligent application. To be learned and adequately understood, generalizations must be taught in a setting of significant applications. At the same time, students must become aware of the generalizations and their relationships to the applications. To be sure of pupil interpretations and to offer some guaranty of future transfer

[3] National Society for the Study of Education, *A Program for Teaching Science,* 31st Yearbook, Part I (Bloomington, Ill.: Public School Publishing Co., 1932).

of learning, one must have students go through a stage of reapplication of the generalizations in new situations which differ from those experienced in the original learning.

The attempt to improve curricular organization by identifying the generalizations and then grouping the applications around them is an approach that can be used in the various natural sciences and the applied sciences. It is obviously operable in mathematics and English composition. It can be used in subjects where much of the learning has to do with the development of fundamental skills. Cases in point are to be found in industrial arts, applied music, and physical education. Insofar as there are established and agreed-upon principles in the social sciences of government, economics, and sociology, the same approach seems valid there.

There are apparent difficulties in applying this attack to history courses. However, if it is possible to isolate a relatively few major trends or issues in the development of human society, these might be used as the primary threads for history courses, and the historical events might be treated as applications in tracing the main threads. Some such analysis is desperately needed for a course in world history. World history is growing at an amazing pace. If the high school course is to be taught in terms of historical events taking place through time, it will soon be necessary to have ten courses rather than the one now allocated to world history in the traditional secondary school program. Perhaps establishment of twelve to fifteen continuing themes for the course and organization of the events around these as illustrative applications is a way out of the difficulty.

From the foregoing, it can be seen that something can be done in the organization of curricular detail through the identification of what may be characterized as primary subject-matter elements. These are important basic skills, controlling attitudes and ideals, assumptions, definitions, rules, laws, principles, theories, trends, issues, or major generalizations. The applications can be thought of as the materials of a methodology for establishing and making understandable the generalizations. If the teacher can identify the primary curricular elements, a significant part of his method of teaching will be concerned with the selection of the more pertinent applications of the curricular elements with which the students can have meaningful experiences.

THE FUNCTIONS OF METHOD

What has been said concerning the confusions between elements of subject matter and methodology is not to be interpreted as minimizing the importance of teaching method. In curriculum construction, school people are concerned with the determination of what is worth learning and with the attempt to sort out the obligations of the school for teaching from what may be taught adequately by other agencies. In selecting appropriate methods, teachers are concerned with the finding of experiences that may contribute to the learning of the desirable curricular elements. Method becomes concerned with the motivations of pupils, their maturity with respect to particular curricular items, and with their comparative abilities to learn, inasmuch as the selection of the experiences and the extent of learning are limited by the inherent capacities of different pupils. It can be imagined readily that it may seem highly desirable to learn some things for which no appropriate method can be devised for the pupils concerned.

In the period when Latin was emphasized in the secondary school program, there were always some pupils who were so unwilling to work at Latin that no apparently clever method succeeded in getting those who "dragged their feet" to learn any significant amount of Latin. The Roman banquet, building Caesar's bridge, costuming in togas, making models of Roman artifacts, even interlinear translations, were all ineffective for recalcitrant students.

Method and the "Pushing Down" of Subject Matter. Method cannot always solve the problems presented by the "pushing down" of subject matter from higher to lower grade levels, which has been so prevalent in secondary schools in recent times. This is particularly acute when the methodology of the upper grades is "pushed down" along with the subject matter into the lower levels. However, if the maturity of pupils is such that they are not ready to learn a proposed body of subject matter, manipulation of methodology is unlikely to solve the problems presented by the immaturity of the pupils. Some questions of this kind may be raised in the present attempts at reorganization of secondary school mathematics.[4] It is possible that some of the mathematical concepts proposed for ninth-graders are too difficult for the majority of pupils at this level of maturity. If this turns out to be true, changing of problems of application, introduction of new illustrative materials, even mathematical programing, may be found to be quite ineffective.

Conversely, the willingness of a teacher to consider the adaptation of illustration, assignment, application, and use to the nature of the subject matter at hand and to the differing abilities and experiential backgrounds of pupils may seem to work wonders in situations where motivation has been at a low level or subject matter apparently quite difficult. An

---

[4] See School Mathematics Study Group, *Study Guide in Modern Algebra* (New Haven: School Mathematics Study Group, 1959); or University of Illinois Committee on School Mathematics, *The Arithmetic of Real Numbers* (Urbana: University of Illinois Committee on Mathematics, 1959).

imaginative teacher skilled in the application of a variety of methods can work wonders with what has seemed to be dull and difficult subject matter. There have been teachers who have been able to get high school pupils to read and discuss *Silas Marner* or *Lady of the Lake* with enthusiasm and apparent profit, and there have been teachers who have succeeded in getting tenth-grade girls to work willingly on the theorems of Euclidian geometry.

Methods Must Fit the Learning Situation at Hand. Enough has been said to indicate that there is no such thing as a magic method that will solve all the problems of learning with all kinds of pupils and with any and all subject matter. There is no such thing as a methodological panacea that can be applied to all the ills inherent in poor learning. A method must be selected and fitted to the particular learning situation at hand, which will change from day to day and from hour to hour with the subject matter to be learned and with the characteristics of the students. What will work with one group of pupils at nine o'clock may not work with the next group at ten o'clock. Methods applicable to an English class are not likely to succeed with a mathematics or biology class. Most often, methods suitable for superior pupils will not work with slow learners. Sometimes, methods applicable to socially privileged pupils will not work with the less privileged. There may be some useful general principles of method, but the applications in practice are almost infinite.

Methods Must Fit the Nature of the Subject Matter To Be Learned. Methods must be adapted to the nature of the curricular items to be learned. Although there are certain well-established principles of drill developed through knowledge of the psychology of learning, the methods applicable to the development of skills in typewriting are not appropriate to learning to block in football. Methods suitable for analysis of the merit of a work of literature are not particularly useful in learning to proofread and correct one's own manuscript, although both may be carried out within the scope of a high school English class. The methodology appropriate to learning of a foreign language may not be readily adaptable to learning of the native language. What may work quite well in teaching foods may not apply in teaching clothing. In other words, the inherent nature of the subject matter to be taught is a major determinant of what may be a suitable method of teaching.

Programed Learning as Method. The foregoing finds application in the development of programed learning and machine teaching. In programing, the exact nature of what is to be taught must be known in considerable detail. Much of the programing is concerned with the inherent relationships of the elements of subject matter, which are to be arranged in an assumed sequence of learning order or progression. The identification of the subject-matter items and, to a certain extent, of their relationships represents a curricular problem as it was earlier defined. The arrangement of these items in order to produce effective learning represents a problem of method. Basically the programing, as such, is methodological.

To date, the strength in programed learning and machine teaching has been on the curricular side in the exact identification of what is to be learned and in unraveling the logical relationships of the subject matter items, while the weakness has been on the programing side, in relationship to maturity of pupils, motivation of school-age pupils, and the bringing about of potential out-of-class transfers, through the manipulation of many meaningful applications of the subject-matter elements. In spite of the contributions of the psychologists to programed learning, the emphasis has been upon subject-matter relationships rather than upon the learning process from the point of view of a total psychology of learning and much that has become known about useful teaching methods. Perhaps, at the same time, it should be admitted that we do not yet know enough about either details of the learning process or teaching methods to do distinctly superior programing of learning. Much that goes on is *memoriter*, relatively dull after the newness of the machine wears off, unrelated to the realities of life outside the classroom, and often abstract and unrelated to meaningful pupil experiences. Pupils are readied for passing of school-type tests rather than for interpretation and use of what is learned.

THE PLACE OF CURRICULUM AND METHOD
IN A TEACHING CYCLE

It is possible to summarize much that has been presented in this chapter in the form of a cycle or sequence of operations that go on in teaching. In this cycle, it is first necessary to decide upon the purposes or goals of school experiences in terms of desired effects upon the pupils. With these goals in view, it then becomes necessary to select the subject matter that can contribute most to the attainment of the goals, the changes to be produced in the pupils. There follows as a third stage in the cycle the finding of those methods of treatment of the subject matter that can contribute most to efficient learning within the limits of the defined goals and the selected subject matter. It is at this point that a knowledge of the psychology of learning is needed. Finally, as learning develops, there must be worked out some means of evaluation of the whole process. It will be seen that the evaluation can be manifold. First, it may be possible to determine whether or not pupils have achieved the goals set up. Secondly, it is possible to determine how much of the subject matter has been learned and is retained. Thirdly, it may be possible to determine the effectiveness of the methods used. Note that evaluative devices and procedures may need to vary in terms of the emphasis upon each of the above.

THE POSSIBILITY OF METHOD BECOMING CURRICULAR

There remains one further consideration with regard to the relationship of curricular items and methods of teaching: this relationship may involve a situation where the method of learning is in itself of greatest importance, where the method itself becomes the curricular content. In this case, the teacher is confronted with the problem of devising a method for teaching a method. A condition develops in which the "how to learn" is emphasized. Science teachers have long said that the importance of laboratory work in high school is found in what pupils may learn about scientific methods of attacking problems. If this is true, the learning of how to attack a problem and the selection of an appropriate laboratory procedure become important. These then become the subject matter, or the curricular items. The particular factual items or principles are of less significance. The teacher's methods involve finding the science that best furnishes the experiences for learning the important method. It would seem not too important whether or not the method of attack and the laboratory procedures are learned in physics or in chemistry, in working with plants or in working with animals. However, a word of caution is to be inserted here. It should be remembered that the point was made earlier that method is quite intimately associated with the nature of the subject matter to be learned. Therefore, methods used in teaching scientific methods may also be tied intimately to the nature of the science subject matter to which the investigative methods apply.

Another illustration of the condition where a method of instruction turns into the subject matter to be taught is found in *group dynamics*. There have been advocates of the utilization of processes of group dynamics as a generalized teaching method. It can be doubted that many kinds of important learnings can be approached through group dynamics. It would seem to be extremely doubtful if many of the facts of physics or mathematics can be learned effectively through group-dynamics procedures. This doubt may extend to facts and interpretations of history as well. On the other hand, if what is to be learned consists of democratic group processes, it may well be that the best method of learning involves participation in the processes themselves, in which case group dynamics becomes both the subject matter and the method.

SUMMARY

The distinctions between method and content made in this chapter and the relationships between curricular problems and those of method would seem to be important to teachers and curriculum planners in clarifying work to be done and in sweeping away much of the fuzzy thinking that seems to permeate some of the literature in the fields of both curriculum and method. What has been presented is not in itself new, but it has been an attempt to sharpen the attack upon curricular selection and the application of methods to improved learning. If the reader is helped by such treatment, the purpose of the chapter will be accomplished.

QUESTIONS, PROBLEMS, AND ISSUES FOR FURTHER THOUGHT

1. How are curricular problems to be distinguished from problems of methodology?
2. Gather and document some of the current criticisms of public secondary education. Can you demonstrate that many of these criticisms are rooted in the confusions between curriculum and method elaborated in this chapter?
3. What is the fundamental difference between resource units and instructional units for secondary school courses, in terms of the operational definitions given at the beginning of this chapter?
4. Find in the literature of secondary education a report on pupil participation in planning of an instructional unit. Is the pupil participation primarily concerned with curriculum determination or with methods of learning? How can you justify your position?
5. Examine the material presented through a teaching machine. To what extent is the programing concerned with the selection of curriculum items, and to what extent is it concerned with method?
6. Prepare a list of ten or twelve continuing themes of human development to be used as a center of organization for a course in world history. Select the historical events to be used in illustrating one of these proposed themes. Set up the experiences recommended for the pupils in the class to be used as assignments for learning. Then indicate which of these operations have been curricular and which have been concerned with method. Are there overlappings?
7. Suppose that you are a school administrator planning a workshop for curricular improvement for teachers in a selected secondary school. Indicate what uses can be made of ideas presented in this chapter in working with these teachers.

SUPPLEMENTARY MATERIALS

Selected Readings

ANDERSON, VERNON E. *Principles and Procedures of Curriculum Improvement.* New York: The Ronald Press Co., 1956. See especially Chapter 6, "The Nature of the Learning Process and the Learner."

BILLETT, ROY O. *Fundamentals of Secondary School Teaching.* Boston: Houghton Mifflin Co., 1940. Read especially Chapters 5 and 6, on the organization of learning, and Chapter 7, on selection and organization of subject matter.

BURTON, WILLIAM H. *The Guidance of Learning Activities* (3d ed.). New York: Appleton-Century-Crofts, Inc., 1962. Read especially Part I—"The Principles of Learning," Chapters 1–6.

CANTOR, NATHANIEL. *The Teaching-Learning Process.* New York: Holt, Rinehart & Winston, Inc., 1953. Examine from the point of view of methodology that may become subject matter.

CHARTERS, W. W. *Methods of Teaching.* Evanston, Ill.: Row, Peterson & Co., 1912. Out of print but available in libraries. Contains essential interpretation of the nature of subject matter. See Chapter 2, "Subjectmatter," Chapter 3, "Distinctions in the Meaning of Function," and Chapter 4, Section 1, "Subjectmatter of the Race and of the Pupil."

DEWEY, JOHN. *Experience and Education.* New York: The Macmillan Co., 1938. Title indicates pertinence to the chapter at hand.

LUMSDAINE, A. A., and ROBERT GLASER. *Teaching Machines and Programmed Learning.* Washington, D.C.: National Education Association of the United States, Department of Audio-Visual Instruction, 1960. A useful summary of developments in programed learning and teaching machines, with extensive bibliography of additional literature.

STILES, LINDLEY J., LLOYD E. MCCLEARY, and ROY C. TURNBAUGH. *American Secondary Education in the United States.* New York: Harcourt, Brace & World, Inc., 1962. Part III—"Organization and Program," Chapter 10, on curriculum, and Chapter 11, on instruction.

TROW, WILLIAM CLARK. *Educational Psychology* (2d ed.). Boston: Houghton Mifflin Co., 1950. Part IV—"Learning Process."

WATKINS, RALPH K. *Techniques of Secondary School Teaching.* New York: The Ronald Press Co., 1958. Chapters 3–12 contain further elaboration of points developed in this chapter.

WILDS, ELMER HARRISON. *The Foundations of Modern Education* (rev. ed.). New York: Holt, Rinehart & Winston, Inc., 1950. For historical development of educational theories, see especially Chapters 15–17.

WILES, KIMBALL. *Teaching for Better Schools.* Englewood Cliffs, N.J.: Prentice-Hall, Inc., 1959. See Chapter 2, on the basis of method.

WOODRUFF, ASAHEL D. *The Psychology of Teaching* (3d ed.). New York: Longmans, Green & Co., Inc., 1951. Part III—"The Development of Human Behavior."

31

Size of School and the Curriculum

CAN SCHOOLS BE TOO BIG OR TOO SMALL?

An examination of the literature about the effectiveness of secondary schools will reveal a considerable number of references to the relationship of school size and the educational program. In terms of benefit to the individual student, the question arises as to whether or not a school can be too large or too small. There is a trend in our political and social life to emphasize bigness. The concentration of population in urban areas has affected education to the extent that secondary schools are often found housing 2,000 to 4,000 students. The principal is exceptional if he knows all his teachers, to say nothing about getting acquainted with individual students. If education is a personal matter, if the guidance-concept is fundamental in the curriculum, is there not danger that the student in a large high school will be "lost in the shuffle"? By the same token, will not a very small high school be so limited in program, staff, and facilities that the student, although well known by all as an individual, will receive a low-quality education? One well-known recommendation from James B. Conant's *The American High School Today* is that a comprehensive high school should have a graduating class of at least 100 students to ensure a quality education. In 1962, there were over 15,000 secondary schools below this "minimum"; so, whether or not small schools are desirable, they apparently are very much with us.

A further study of the literature reveals that those working with the small schools are concerned but not entirely discouraged. Consider, for example, the challenge in the following titles:

"Curriculum Problems in a Small High School: Imagination May Be the Answer"

"How Can Better Staff Utilization Help To Improve Small High Schools?"

"The Picture Brightens for the Small High School"

"Are Small High Schools Worth Saving?"

"Enrichment for Talented Rural Youth"

"How Can the Program in the Small High School Be Improved?"

This chapter will attempt to given an affirmative answer to some of these questions by presenting some curriculum practices especially suited for secondary schools with enrolments of less than 200 pupils. To some extent "smallness" is a relative matter. That is, a school of 200 would seem tiny in New York City but large in Poland Springs, Maine. The statistician can cite figures to show that

1. Two-thirds of our high schools are located in rural areas.
2. Of the regular four-year high schools, 42 per cent enrol fewer than 200 pupils.
3. Twenty per cent of all youths attending high schools are dependent on small schools for their secondary education.

Of course, one's conclusion as to whether or not students get a "better" education in large high schools will depend on one's own philosophy and objectives concerning quality education and the criteria by which its results are judged. Since many factors affect success in life, and since there are many kinds of success, a common procedure is to look at something more immediate and somewhat more tangible—college grades. While such an index may fail to take into account factors such as personal motivation, levels of aspiration, and capacity to study and learn, reports of studies such as those at Lafayette College cited below should give the educators in small schools additional challenges. There is an indication that students who graduate from larger high schools perform considerably better academically in their first year of college.

The studies consisted of an examination of the freshman grade point averages for each student entering the college in the fall of 1955 and in the fall of 1958. Included in this study are 417 students who entered in the fall of 1955 and completed the first year of college and 354 who entered in the fall of 1958 and completed the freshman year. The correlation coefficients between the size of high school class and grade point average for the freshman year in college as computed by the Product Moment Technique were +.17 for the class entering in 1955 and +.19 for the class entering in 1958. These correlations are low but positive and significantly different from zero.

The data are shown in Table 31–1, from the same source as the above quotation.[1]

[1] J. Marshall Brown, "Large High Schools Are Bad?" *PSEA Education Bulletin,* Vol. 29 (June 5, 1961), p. 113.

TABLE 31–1

SIZE OF HIGH SCHOOL GRADUATING CLASS AND FRESHMAN-GRADE POINT AVERAGE FOR
STUDENTS OF TWO ENTERING COLLEGE CLASSES

Size of H. S. Grad. Class	Class Entering 1955		Class Entering 1958	
	1st Yr. Col. Average Grade	No. of Students	1st yr. Col. Average Grade	No. of Students
Less than 100........	70.9	114	71.9	94
100–199	73.9	147	75.3	87
200–299	73.4	78	75.1	62
300–399	75.8	37	75.6	45
400–499	72.2	13	75.1	22
500–599	75.2	7	74.1	21
600 or more..........	77.6	21	79.5	23
Total Class	73.3	417	74.6	354

Thus, some, seeing value in bigness, cry out, "Consolidate," "Eliminate," while others, believing in the virtue of small, near-the-home units,
urge, "Perpetuate." Many schoolmen frankly admit shortcomings in both
smallness and largeness and wish hopefully for a school of the "optimum
size" as determined by a selected group of educators.[2] Wishful thinking,
theorizing, and even organizational trends should not cause one to overlook the fact that the small high school will be here for a long time to
come. Some call them the "necessarily existent" small schools.

There will be a minimum of discussion of the problems—those who
work in a school with a limited student body are strongly aware of the
difficulties. However, problem identification will be followed by some
guidelines that may help reduce the curriculum-making frustration.

SOME PERENNIAL PROBLEMS

Basic Problem: A Well-rounded Program. We need to reorganize the
major factors that most persistently block curriculum improvement. A
state supervisor working in an area where rural high schools were frequent asked what seemed to be the basic question: "How on earth,"
she queried, "do you organize a program broad enough to meet pupil
needs and yet allow teachers to work in the fields of their qualifications?"

[2] 2-year junior high school—300 to 500 students
     3-year junior high school—500 to 800 students
            senior high school—600 to 1000 students
     4-year   high school—800 to 1200 students

This consensus was reported by Harl R. Douglass in *Trend and Issues in Secondary Education* (Washington, D.C.: The Library of Education, 1962), p. 70.

Two ideas important in this connection also add disproportionately to the problems of the curriculum maker in the small high school: general education, on the one hand, and vocational training, on the other. The young person who will finish his formal schooling either in high school or junior college needs to know both how to earn a living and how to live. Ideally, the school will not only equip him with a trade but also stir his imagination and fling open before him the great horizons of man's achievement, to make him a richer personality and a better citizen of his nation and the world. This is a large order for the curriculum planner in the small high school.

In 1948, the U.S. Office of Education polled leaders in secondary education in the various states on "What, in your opinion, are the major factors in your State limiting the services of the small high schools?" The majority of answers indicated restricted curriculum offerings. Thus, the pupils do not get enough of some kinds of experiences. The following reply indicated several aspects of this limitation, which still exists too commonly in the 1960's:

Perhaps the greatest need of our small high schools is the bringing about of the recognition of the importance of building the curriculum in terms that would make use of the problems and difficulties as well as the opportunities which are found in the immediate environment. This would have to do not only with economic and social matters, but could be made to include cultural, political, health, and other phases of a well-rounded program of school activities. While our typical small high school at present has a definite trend toward doing these things, it is still bound to the traditional pattern.[3]

In the framework of limited offerings, the courses of study are built around the traditional college-preparatory pattern. Although the majority of the pupils will never go to college, it is important that those few who do will succeed. To the extent that the limitations of smallness *seem* to dictate one program, the result is an academic plan, since this offers purpose for the pupil, has prestige in the eyes of parents, and represents the preparation background of the teachers.

A teacher in a school serving a mining community related his efforts:

I was assigned a class in algebra in our school where almost no one goes to college. A study of my group of 30 pupils indicated that only one had any intention of entering college—and his expectation was based on his half-back ability rather than a foundation of sequential mathematics. I decided to give the class applied experiences along the general mathematical line.

Within a very short time I was visited by the principal and a school board member who informed me, "Here *we* prepare for college. You were hired to teach college preparatory algebra. Stop fooling around with that watered-down general course!"

[3] Walter H. Gaumnitz and Grace Wright, *Bulletin* 1948, No. 9 (Washington, D.C.: Office of Education, 1948), p. 3.

As long as one thinks of planning for diversified interests through courses, the small high school faces the improbable solution of many small classes and the imposition upon teachers of responsibilities not in line with their best preparation.

These limited-program tendencies have been reflected in some national studies. Edith Greer and Richard Harbeck conducted a national survey of high school pupil programs in 1957–1958. They found that most of the students in the larger public secondary schools were given a choice of several curriculums instead of being confined to a single curriculum and that the breadth was not so great in the small high schools (enrolment of less than 200). One conclusion was that students in the latter schools tended to complete fewer credits than did their counterparts in high-enrolment schools.

What might be the nature of the differences in the program offerings? Since Sputnik and with the encouragement of the National Defense Education Act, attention has been focused on mathematics, science, and foreign languages. Greer and Harbeck noted,

Perhaps because the lowest enrollment schools had a comparatively narrow range of subjects, the greatest proportion of these schools increased their offerings in mathematics, science, and foreign language. In fact, over 50 per cent of these schools increased their offerings in these areas in 1957–58 and almost 90 per cent had scheduled such expansion for 1959–60.[4]

This certainly looked hopeful and indicated that smallness might not in itself restrict key offerings. However, in 1961, the NEA Research Division conducted a survey[5] of the nation's small schools (those with enrolments under 300) as to the availability, in grades nine through twelve, of certain mathematics, science, and foreign-language courses. While most of these schools offered some courses in these fields, not all did so every year. The following situation is most limiting:

Foreign Languages, Mathematics, and Science in Small High Schools in 1961

(per cent of schools *not* offering certain courses at any time)

Foreign languages	28.9
Chemistry	10.2
Physics	19.6
Trigonometry	40.2
Solid geometry	56.8

[4] Edith S. Greer and Richard M. Harbeck, *What High School Pupils Study* (Washington, D.C.: U.S. Office of Education, 1962), p. 24.
[5] "Subjects in Small High Schools," *NEA Research Bulletin*, Vol. 40 (May, 1962), pp. 56–58.

The summary of this NEA survey highlights the program limitations along with the educational implications:

A large percent of the small high schools do not offer any course in foreign languages or advanced courses in science and mathematics. When these courses are offered, they are usually limited in the number of semesters of study available or in the frequency of availability. The problems facing small high schools in offering a broad and comprehensive program are not hard to find. Small high schools lack students—the average school enrollment was 145. They lack teachers—the average number of teachers per school was nine. They lack a broad tax base—71 percent of all the small high schools are located in communities of fewer than 2,500 persons. They lack accreditation—only a little over one-fourth of all the small high schools are accredited by a regional accrediting association.

Guidance and Other Services. A well-rounded educational program provides special services: guidance of many types, health facilities, varied instructional aids, suitable offerings for the exceptional (the gifted as well as the mentally retarded, physically handicapped, etc.), library services, facilities, and resources. Can a secondary school with sixty-five pupils and four teachers (including the principal, who teaches five or six classes) offer such services? Time to do, training to handle adequately, finances, school boards reluctant to provide funds for such services (the per-pupil cost already *seems* to be excessive)—all tend to furnish a negative answer.

Mobility of Population. This involves several factors that produce headaches for the curriculum maker. Various sociological studies show that rural youths *do* go to the city. Also, since farm and village people have large families in the sections least able to support population increases, the Educational Policies Commission[6] pointed out that many youths *must* move to urban areas to preserve rural stability. If the curriculum is to prepare for future living, how can the teachers focus sights on both rural and urban living, especially when they may be unable to predict which ones will move and which will stay? Furthermore, if one learns best from the familiar and the near-at-hand, how can local rural-community resources serve as preparatory experiences for effective existence in some indeterminate, distant city? Will rural youths be handicapped in seeking and succeeding in employment in competition with their "city cousins"? Has the guidance program prepared them for a possible dulling of the glow of city lights? Will they have "guilt feelings" bordering on a sense of "desertion" of the farm life?

[6] Educational Policies Commission, *Education for All American Youth: A Further Look* (Washington, D.C.: National Education Association of the United States, 1952), p. 41.

A related problem is faced in those communities where migrant workers come and go. How can these children be given continuity of education? As one migrant boy reported. "I went to the ninth grade, but I didn't go often." Later on in this chapter, reference will be made to courses given in alternate years. Can these alternations be synchronized so that a migrant child can go from school to school within a state—or even between distant states—and find offered this year the alternate that he needs?

In a special sense, mobility, as applied to transportation, is offering some solution by bringing youth from scattered areas to a central school that is able to provide more staff, more facilities, and, presumably, an expanded curriculum. Some resist that organizational tendency on the grounds that it replaces a home community school with a distant, somewhat unnatural, and impersonal environment. "In trying to serve the many, you lose the few" is their plea. There is also the fact that some will have to spend two to three hours daily just going to and from school (perhaps early training for the life of the suburban commuter). Furthermore, the distances involved may prohibit many from attending evening and late-afternoon activities. The youth who lives forty miles away cannot readily go to school dances, parties, and athletic events.

Limitations Related to Staff. Regardless of the nature and extent of the program on paper, there must be competent personnel to put it into operation. There obviously are not as many human resources in a faculty of 2 to 10 as in one with 20 to 100. Indeed, opportunities for professional participation are rare, so the rural teacher is not often found involved in school matters such as legislation, curriculum building, and attendance at professional conventions.

Going beyond the paucity of numbers, one notes the tendency to find inadequately prepared teachers in small high schools. This stems from several sources: lack of understanding of rural culture, inexperience in teaching (teachers too tend to "get started" in small schools and move to larger), teachers not well prepared by teacher-training institutions to cope with problems of smallness, and impracticability of gaining enough diversified background to qualify for the many demands that would go with a diversified program handled by few people.

From a curriculum leader's standpoint, the turnover tendency creates a slowing-down process. This year's staff may make a fine start on exploring purposes and proposing programs. Next year, the key three or four (and that may well be 50 to 75 per cent of the faculty) have moved to other schools. So he wearily starts over again reorienting another group. Of course, he too may not be there next year, since this is but his stepping stone to bigger jobs.

Most states are trying to help the teacher in the small town by asking for a single salary scale for all schools, regardless of size and location. In these states, teachers also receive benefits from the same legislation on retirement; yet rural salaries tend to run lower and, hence, mean smaller retirement checks. Too many teachers have to put up with poor living conditions. Then there are also those who prefer to be nearer the "cultural opportunities" of large population centers and will thus prefer an urban or suburban position even if the rural school will pay more.

How does one help these teachers improve instruction? The customary city-wide in-service opportunities are non-existent. The superintendent often has several scattered schools under his jurisdiction, so visits and personal confrences are rare. The principal, usually inexperienced in cooperative supervision, has little time available. Some counties such as Bucks County in Pennsylvania are providing excellent specialists in reading development, preparation and use of instructional aids, testing, guidance, etc. These services, however, are in great demand by the newer county schools, so they are not always readily available for the individual teacher when he needs them. Greater continuity of competent leadership at the local level must be sought, in order to improve supervisory practices.

One could go on enumerating curriculum-improvement obstacles; yet, it would seem these are perplexing questions more than impossible problems. In our debating days, we used to declare hopefully, "Yes, there are difficulties here, but they *are not inherent.*" In the paragraphs that follow, there is the underlying thesis that good curriculum planning can remove many of the "ifs" previously implied as well as provide possible solutions to the "ifs" that remain.

EXPLORING POTENTIALS

First of all, why not "accentuate the positive"? Is smallness synonymous with shortcomings? Does largeness mean solutions? Let us see where curriculum workers in a small high school may focus on potential merits and develop them into educational assets.

The findings at Lafayette College, as reported in the first part of this chapter, may be a bit discouraging, but another investigation, at North Carolina College,[7] suggests that small schools can produce good results. The North Carolina study was organized with respect to 412 students who had entered during the 1958–1959 school year. The hypothesis tested was that "the measured language, reading, and mathematical achieve-

[7] Paul M. Smith, Jr., "The Large or Small High School?" *Journal of Secondary Education,* Vol. 36 (November, 1961), pp. 389–392.

ment of students from relatively large high schools would be considerably better than for those students who graduated from comparatively small high schools" (having two to ten teachers). Grade-point average after one year in college was used to indicate college success, while the California Achievement Test Complete Battery was used for the specific areas of language, reading, and mathematical comprehension. The findings failed to support the hypothesis and indicated that there are numerous examples of both large and small schools doing excellent work. The challenge comes in one of Smith's conclusions that "talent may be discovered and developed just as well in one kind of situation as the other if Americans will make up their minds that education is not a money saving enterprise."[8] How can this potential be realized?

School and Community Communications. A sound statement of the importance of school and communications was made by Gaumnitz:

> One of the most promising aspects of good school administration in a small community is a well-planned program of school public relations. The best public relations will, in the last analysis, depend upon a sound program of educational services which is understood by the people of the community, endorsed by them, and supported with enthusiasm. Understanding, endorsement, and support will, however, not come about spontaneously; they must be cooperatively achieved; there must be wide discussion; there must not only be consultation but positive selling of the school and its services. These will require a continuous program of school news, of meaningful reports to parents, of active participation by parent-teacher associations, of public exhibits and demonstrations, and many other activities concerned basically with helping the people understand what the schools are trying to do and how they are succeeding in it.[9]

One advantage of the small high school is that the teacher has opportunity to become thoroughly familiar with the home, the background, and the personality of each pupil. It is in the classroom that each teacher, knowing his pupils as individuals, can provide real enrichment. Teaching by units, utilizing a variety of instructional aids, and creating a classroom setting that will turn it from a mere four-walled room to a learning laboratory—all will help strengthen the curriculum. In fact, smallness has another asset—that of permitting correlation among classes. For example, the English teacher can readily discover what his pupils are discussing in other classes and can thus make reading recommendations along those lines. Also there is the possibility of developing class projects involving cooperation on the part of several teachers.

---

[8] *Ibid.*, p. 392.
[9] Walter H. Gaumnitz, "Overcoming Administrative Problems in Small High Schools," *1951 Schoolmen's Week Proceedings* (University of Pennsylvania), p. 244.

A teacher who lives in a small community comes to find that everyone knows everyone else. While this can be annoying, it does suggest—unlike in the large city school, where the pupil "disappears" after school hours and in school is sometimes encountered only fifty minutes a day for one out of three years—that the teacher can readily become acquainted with his relatively few pupils, their brothers and sisters, and their fathers and mothers. Thus, he has the opportunity to understand the capabilities and the problems of each pupil.

Working Together. With small groups, as the whole staff will be, informality and integration are readily possible. Through small round-table discussion of pupils, programs, and problems comes a chance to work shoulder to shoulder in developing a curriculum that will serve the pupils and benefit the community. Light refreshments, absence of long red-tape announcements, a rolling up of the sleeves—all provide a setting for a study of pupils. Role playing has been used to advantage here, with a teacher becoming the belligerent one, the daydreamer, the show-off, or the overconscientious one. This not only presents object lessons with challenges on what to do but also leads to a teacher's growth by expressing his feelings relative to certain details of pupil behavior.[10]

Whenever a faculty continues the process of looking carefully at pupil needs, desirable change takes place in the teachers' attitudes toward pupils and toward the curriculum. Again and again teachers have been heard to say, "This pupil doesn't seem to be a problem any longer," after they have studied him in a faculty meeting. One school faculty began the study of student councils in an effort to provide pupils with more of the responsibility they had come to realize adolescents need. Even curriculum change does not seem so forbidding when faculties carefully examine and accept the needs of boys and girls.

In short, the many chances for personal contacts between pupils and teachers are an asset that counts much in curriculum development.

Pupil Participation. Large schools "segregate" in that they have selected teams or individuals to represent them on the playing field, on the stage, or in "show" activities. The small school affords—indeed, almost requires—100 per cent participation in the health and athletic program, as well as general contributions to dramatics. Tommy may hit some sour notes on the tuba, but he joins, and he shares. Participation takes precedence over performance.

Boys and girls have good ideas. Good curriculum development calls for the use of these. When pupils and teachers know each other, these ideas are more readily transmitted.

[10] An actual illustration of this point, as well as the quotation that follows, is presented by Glyn Morris in "The Faculty Meeting as a Guidance Resource in Small Rural Schools," *Education*, Vol. 74 (April, 1954), pp. 501–506.

Flexibility. In a small school, the faculty can readily change the schedule for special events. The unexpected appearance of a special guest, who may have a message of interest to youth, occasions no flurry of changing bell schedules, no whipping out of Plan X (and changing to Plan Y, if assembly goes beyond the allotted forty-two minutes). If a group is to be on a field trip, there are only a few teachers to contact to consult with them (not announce to them) about certain ones being away from other classes.

Schools of all sizes must seek to arrange their resources of time, staff, students, space, and equipment to get the most from the curriculum. The daily schedule *can* provide a great variety of opportunities to make arrangements. A willingness to experiment and a little imagination—two major ingredients in curriculum change—are necessary. The unique assets of the small school—relatively small classes, opportunity for all faculty members to know all students, less highly structured school and community life—make flexibility a potential that can be realized.

The traditional pattern of subjects meeting every day for the same length of time and at the same time of day has a certain stiffness as well as a lack of relationship to the nature of various learning situations. The optimum time for practice in a foreign language is less than that needed for laboratory sciences. Courses based chiefly on a film series, such as the Harvey White filmed course in physics, require more time than the conventional forty-five to fifty minutes. Teachers handling multiple course sections (as will be explained later) can utilize longer blocks of time. West Grand High School in Colorado worked out a flexible schedule to show what some small high schools can do:

		Mon.	Tues.	Wed.	Thurs.	Fri.
8:37–9:46	[69] min.	6	1	1	1	1
9:51–11:01	70 min.	2	6	2	2	2
11:05–12:00	55 min.	3	3	3	3	3
12:00–1:00	60 min.			Noon Hour		
1:00–1:32	32 min.		Music-Activity Period			
1:36–2:46	70 min.	4	4	4	6	4
2:50–4:00	70 min.	5	5	5	5	6

All students are registered for six subjects.

Class meetings of 70 minutes will be devoted to about one third of the time for supervised study.

Students not enrolled in music will be assigned to a study hall.

GUIDES TO AN EFFECTIVE EDUCATIONAL PROGRAM

An analysis of these and other potentials would indicate that the "patient" is not sick so much as he is suffering from an inferiority complex. The treatment calls for diligent use of some good curriculum practices.

Rethinking Purposes. Any school, large or small, needs to start with an examination of its purposes. It might be expected that even small high schools have studied their goals and have developed a statement expressing their beliefs; yet, a nationwide sampling made by the writer of this chapter indicated that only 40 per cent of the small secondary schools in this country had written philosophies. While nearly two-thirds of the schools reporting philosophies indicate that these statements were formulated by their faculties, it is apparent that most small schools are neglecting to use the curriculum principle that all who are affected should have a part in curriculum development. Here, in the development of guiding philosophy and objectives, is an excellent opportunity to share participation by utilizing pupils and laymen, as well as the entire faculty. The basic principle in modern curriculum development is *cooperation*. The pooling of ideas is essential to deciding what, for this community and for these students, are the goals of greatest worth.

However, what a philosophy includes as it functions is more important than the mere existence of a written statement. Let us assume for the moment that, generally speaking, all rural high schools should strive toward the attainment of all the objectives of secondary education. Such was the conclusion of the late Emery N. Ferriss, who, in his time, was a guiding force and thinker in improvement of small schools. It would not be surprising to find most committees on philosophy and objectives agreeing to include such ideas as education for social efficiency; orientation to the world of work; growth in democratic living; self-discovery; provision for the needs, interests, and abilities of the individual; recognition of peculiar problems and potentialities of the local environment, and concern for the total growth of the student.

The underlying curriculum principle is that even small schools should provide both general and special education—general education for training in democratic living, special education for the orientation and preliminary preparation of the individual for his life's work.

However we may organize our school, we must sell ourselves, our teachers, our pupils, and our townspeople on the idea that our business is to provide for each student the curriculum best suited for him. Ideally, that will mean 100 curriculums for 100 students; practically, that seems like an administrative and an instructional impossibility, especially if one defines "curriculum" as "courses." When "curriculum" is viewed as what the individual obtains from the total school experience, the challenge to the teacher is to individualize his work. The hope lies in a flexible educational program that gives priority to a program of common learnings.

A start for deciding what small schools should try to emphasize most may be obtained by considering the "Big Twelve"[11]—the dozen items from a total list of fifty-eight that received the highest rating. These are, in order of emphasis,

1. Citizenship training
2. Maintenance of health
3. How to study
4. Reading for comprehension
5. Development of self-reliance
6. Oral expression
7. Conservation
8. The dignity of labor
9. Reading critically
10. Intellectual initiative
11. Safety education
12. International relations

In short, the small school should seek to develop a good citizen who is healthy, who can read understandingly and discerningly, and who can express himself effectively and with assurance on the problems of his society and the greater world society. All this is to be experienced later on in the framework of a family unit; hence, there is a common need for education in personal and family relationships.

When the faculty of a small high school considers the special-education phases of its program, it becomes quickly aware of what it means when we say that a good curriculum is built upon the needs of its learners and their community. For example, college preparation usually comes to mind as a special need. To accomplish this in the traditional pattern, however, calls for a disproportionate amount of teacher energy and courses. A consideration of the conclusions of the Eight-Year Study, of the current Michigan Agreement, and of the investigations of Yates, Boardman, Douglass, and others is leading educators to the conclusion that general success in high school is as good as, if not slightly better than, a special arrangement of academic subjects, as an indicator of probable success in college. College preparation can be fostered by training in expression, vocabulary, good work habits, investigational methods, and social activities, which need not be restricted to special courses. Even in geometry, long regarded as a prerequisite for college success, there is increasing realization that critical thinking as presented by mathematics as a way of thinking is of far more value than the traditional list of theorems. It is *how* we think that is ultimately of the greatest importance.

A philosophy committee, then, must consider and clarify the beliefs of the school. In the small school especially, this committee on philosophy of the school is the faculty plus advisory representation from the student body and from the community. They will have to formulate for them-

[11] Reference is made ot the doctoral study of Albert I. Oliver on *The Small High School Curriculum*, for which a jury of experts was asked to rate the importance of fifty-eight items. The twelve receiving the highest ratings are listed below. See the *School Review*, Vol. 57 (November, 1950), pp. 458–467, for a discussion of details.

selves some searching questions and then seek tentative answers. These questions might well include

In the merging of rural and urban life,

1. What distinctly rural values should be preserved?
2. Whom shall we serve?
3. Are we interested in growth of the individual or in attainment of some arbitrarily determined, obsolete standards?
4. Shall we explore our cultural birthright primarily to find answers to such matters as
   a. How did our ways of life develop?
   b. What are the foundations of our economy and our government?
   c. How has science shaped civilization through knowledge and as a way of thinking?
   d. Shall we help pupils discover in the arts and in literature an enlargement of experience, an enrichment of living, an avenue of expression that may lead to either avocational or vocational pursuits?
5. To what extent should and can pupils share in planning educational experiences?
6. Do we see adolescence as a period of value conflicts so that we should help adolescents to learn how to live with themselves as well as with others?
7. Do we believe that there are competences that are basic and hence should be developed as a common-learnings program?

Enlightened Leadership. Although the principal may be reluctant to assume the curriculum-development leadership for which he has had little training, most of the promising small-school programs can be traced to this key person. It is more an attitude of encouragement, of reassuring support, of "let's work this out together," rather than "the man with the answers." When committees are set up, it is easy to have rotating leadership.

Cooperation is the key to the improvement of the small school's curriculum. The principal should be the social engineer and bring together interested participation by all groups concerned—school board, laymen, pupils, teachers, and nearby resource people and agencies.

Identification of their own problems is a basic group technique. The administration may help by using sections or examples from such reports as:

Rural Renaissance: Revitalizing Small High Schools (1961)
Catskill Area Project in Small School Design (1959)
Forward with the Texas Small Schools Project (1962)
Colorado Accepts the Challenge (1961)[12]

[12] See chapter bibliography for details on these reports.

PROJECTS ON THE SMALL HIGH SCHOOL

A fundamental approach to the solution of curriculum problems is to experiment, to make systematic studies. A small school by itself lacks staff, time, funds, and know-how. However, there are currently several area projects that are organized attempts to eliminate the obstacles, to capitalize upon the strengths of smallness, and to try out different ideas. Included among such endeavors are

1. The Catskill Area (New York) Project in Small School Design
2. The Rocky Mountain Area (Colorado) Project
3. The Texas Small Schools Project
4. The Western States Small Schools Project

The value in such endeavors is that they bring leadership through staff and experts along with organized efforts to study ways and means whereby the quality of the "necessarily existent" small schools will be improved. Much attention is given to fostering cooperative efforts, especially in the nature of shared services. Self-study is important, with each school analyzing its student body, its community, and its educational program. Experiments are carried on to find out how technology—particularly through TV, films, tapes, and other instructional aids—can enrich and extend learning opportunities. Emphasis is put upon planning by the teachers themselves. In the Rocky Mountain Project, each participating teacher puts in a month in the summer (with pay) to develop units and learning materials and to study instructional media and methods.

Already the participating schools are demonstrating ingenuity in utilizing time and materials. They are experimenting with instructional procedures. Fundamentally, they are discovering what the characteristics of a good small school are.

At present the above-mentioned projects affect directly only a few participating schools, but their progress reports mentioned in the section above can be used as inspiration for small-school units anywhere in the United States. Furthermore, another coordinating agency is now available in the Committee on the Smaller Secondary School. This Committee of the National Association of Secondary School Principals was organized in 1961 to concentrate on the problems of the "necessarily small school." The Committee Chairman notes,

> There are many communities in which consolidation is either a physical or a fiscal impossibility, unless boarding schools are to be constructed. There are other areas in which the community cultural atmosphere is so closely knit with the school that consolidation would prove unsuccessful. It is in these areas that such schools are necessarily existing and need help.[13]

[13] Morris C. Jones, "Summary of the Meeting on the Smaller Secondary School," *Bulletin of the National Association of Secondary School Principles,* No. 274 (May, 1962), p. 333.

Meetings of this Committee at the annual convention of the N.A.S.S.P.; their publication, *Exchange;* their drawing of attention to the need for group action and study as well as individual leadership—all serve to provide a pool of ideas and actual experiences from which the interested curriculum worker can draw as he seeks to instil quality education in his school, be it large, medium, or small in size.

STATE LEADERSHIP

While the crux of curriculum development eventually lodges in the local school, and while reports on the above-mentioned projects may provide stimulation in any area of the country, each state is in a position to provide rather direct help. The projects in New York, Colorado, and Texas have definite ties with their respective state departments of education. Most states have an individual or a bureau charged with rural education or specifically with small schools. Several principals' associations at the state level are using their bulletins to aid in the improvement of the educational programs. These should aid at the administrative level.

Some states such as Vermont set up workshops expressly to help teachers working in rural environments. Such sessions go far to reorient young teachers to a somewhat different culture that will be the setting for the new curriculum. Thus, the young lady fresh from a select Eastern woman's college will be less likely to complain that her country pupils "have no experiential background."

These various projects and agencies should help define just what curriculum adaptations are important in the nature of the offerings, in the organization of the school, and in the materials and methods used. Some clues to the important differences between small and large schools are provided by an analysis from the first *Newsletter* (October, 1958) of the Catskill Area Project. Generally, these are

Small School	*Large School*
Serves small groups*	Serves large groups
Informal relationships*	Impersonal relationships
Mobility of operation*	Consistency of operation
Integrated organization	Segmented organization
Generalized personnel	Specialized personnel
Multipurpose facilities*	Specialized facilities
Pupils participants*	Pupils recipients
Interpersonal relationships basic*	Organization basic
Dependent for services	Self-contained services
Integrated with community*	Self-sufficient operation
Individual identity*	Group identity

The above items that are starred (*) were not so designated in the *Newsletter,* but they should be looked upon as strengths to be capitalized upon when studying the small school's curriculum improvement. How, then, can a curriculum relatively limited in quantity be enriched to increase its quality?

ENRICHING THE PROGRAM IN THE SMALL HIGH SCHOOL

The ultimate goal of curriculum activity is to provide better learning. Those working with small schools have been seeking to increase the variety as well as the quality of educational experiences. Following are some notations on avenues for improvement.

The Program of Extraclass Activities. To provide broad general education, special education, and personalized guidance requires an enriched curriculum. How can this be accomplished in the small school? A carefully planned extraclass program that becomes an integral part of the educational program affords many opportunities for profitable exploratory and enriching experiences.

When the program of activities is considered by the faculty, the students, and the community to be an integral part of the curriculum, it can produce many rewarding experiences, regardless of the size of the study body. In fact, in the small school, there is greater chance for participation by all than in the larger student populations where only the more talented and aggressive get recognition. To be sure, the variety may not be so great if there are only six to ten teachers to furnish sponsorship, but careful planning can help realize the optimum use.

What is the nature of the offerings experts feel are best adapted to the small secondary school? When a well-qualified jury was asked to check those items that seemed to have greatest value, their responses suggest a selection in order of importance as arranged in Table 31–2.

In practice, the small schools tend to emphasize interscholastic sports more than the intramural type. In spite of the fact that football requires expensive equipment and a fairly large number of boys, a majority of schools have football teams. It is true that some sections of the country are emphasizing modifications much more adapted to the school with limited finances and few students—six-man football and touch football. A more popular competitive sport is basketball, which is found in 85 per cent of the small schools. An analysis of the other sports played showed that softball, archery, and field hockey are the chief other sports for girls but that they affect only a small percentage of the small high schools.

A long-range goal of the activity program is to develop "carry-over" sports, ones the participants will use after they complete their formal education. While a few students do eventually go into professional sports, football, baseball, and basketball are spectator sports for the majority. Group games are well adapted to the small high school program, and

TABLE 31–2

PER CENT OF EXPERTS BELIEVING CERTAIN ACTIVITIES TO BE WELL ADAPTED FOR
SMALL HIGH SCHOOLS

Activity	Per Cent of Jury* Preferring
Intramural sports	90.2
Glee clubs	87.8
Student government	82.9
Group games	79.3
Dramatics	79.3
Hobby clubs	78.0
Social dancing	76.8
Community singing	72.0
Arts and crafts	67.1
School newspaper	62.2
Band	62.2
Orchestra	58.5
Service clubs	57.3
Boys' interscholastic sports	53.7
Debating forums	45.1
Individual sports	42.7
Vocational clubs	37.8
School yearbook	32.9
Student handbook	28.0
Girls' interscholastic sports	23.2
Subject-matter clubs	19.5

*The "jury" consisted of 86 educators whose contact with small schools and their curriculum insight suggested they were "experts" in this area. See note 11, page 636.

many of these have definite carry-over value in the community life so often found in the small villages and towns.

Most adolescents today dance or would like to dance; yet, only about a third of the schools sponsor and teach social dancing. Folk dancing has recently been "revived," and here some small schools outdo their "big-city brothers."

Some of the schools are using planned activities during the noon hour. One of the possible important outcomes of a good lunch hour is to carry out good health procedures in terms of diet and a relaxed environment. Following the meal itself, there is opportunity to plan for both informal and organized social relationships.

The program of activities, then, should be utilized to develop more effective use of leisure, and provide the community with opportunities for social enjoyment, as well as supplement the skills and knowledge of the program of studies.

Alternation of Subjects. A small high school with only four or five teachers can offer but a limited program of experiences to its pupils, unless planning and ingenuity are employed to utilize various instructional and administrative devices that will broaden the curriculum. Local facilities, needs, and staffs will determine the particular combination of the devices available, but the important task is to select and to plan so that as much advantage as is possible will accrue to the individual child.

It is a common practice to alternate courses (such as physics-chemistry, English 11-English 12, French 9-French 10) so that, over a period of two years, twice as many courses will be given as in one year. Those who have tried alternation find merit in the cautions of Soper, who suggested five principles for alternating courses:

1. The program of alternation should involve a large unit, preferably a state, and must be practical for every school within the unit.
2. It must work equally well for one-year, two-year, three-year, or four-year high schools.
3. It must be adaptable to changing needs within any given school and, when once adopted, continue over a period of years.
4. No combination of classes should be made in which one course is alternated with another to which it is a prerequisite.
5. Only students classified in the same or adjacent years should be combined into the same group.[14]

The fourth point is occasionally violated in schools that alternate English 9 and 10, so half of the group is handicapped by not having had the necessary sequential background. For that reason, it is more common to offer as alternates such subjects as chemistry and physics. Difficulties may be further eliminated by organizing the curriculum on a basis other than the usual subject-matter approach. Alternation will be of greater value in the special elective areas not included in the common-learning program.

Multiple Classes. One of the organizational devices currently receiving much emphasis in the various small-school projects is known as the "multiple class" technique. This, basically, is an arrangement by which two or more subjects are taught by the same teacher in the same room at the same time. The key lies in effective use of small groups. The mathematics teacher may be working with an algebra class while another small group studies general mathematics. One or two capable students may be doing independent study with an advanced mathematics course such as trigonometry. While the technique is not new, the operation has become more effective through increased know-how in handling small-group instruction, in supplementing the teacher's efforts through tape

[14] Wayne W. Soper, *The Small High School,* University of the State of New York Bulletin 1071 (Albany: State Education Department, 1935), p. 31.

recordings and other devices, and in recognizing the value of self-instruc-tion in place of the traditional lecture-listen-recite situation where the teacher felt that he had to be "in the act" all the time.

Some schools have recognized this possibility by building for the busi-ness classes rooms with glassed partitions. Thus, a group may practice typing while those on the other side of the partition may study book-keeping, general business, or shorthand. A small language laboratory at the rear of the room may permit some to work on advanced language courses while the teacher gives attention part of the period to a beginning class, and then the groups may change places.

In any event, this multiple-class approach calls for considerable plan-ning by the teacher, or, as in the case of the projects, groups of teachers. Dittoed work sheets need to be prepared so that the individuals will have a guide for proceeding at their own rates. These guides must indi-cate the purposes, suggest activities, and contain references to varied resource materials. Fundamentally, then, the teacher becomes a guide and a resource person rather than a director. The process of getting teachers to accept this role and to develop the necessary skills is an impor-tant part of curriculum development.

Supervised Correspondence Courses. The multiple-class idea can be enhanced on an individual basis if some are taking courses via the corre-spondence method. One boy may be taking solid geometry (not offered in the regular program) by correspondence as he sits in the room where the mathematics teacher conducts multiple groups as was mentioned above. Indeed, one of the best opportunities for individualization of the curriculum lies in supervised correspondence study. A superintendent in Iowa declared, "I have found correspondence courses for high schools sponsored by some of the state universities very helpful in supplementing the meager offering we have." In one New England school, pupils have used this method to study such subjects as radio, advanced auto me-chanics, driver training, animal husbandry, advanced chemistry, advanced biology, commercial law, etiquette, agriculture, Latin III and IV, Span-ish, German, anatomy, meteorology, differential calculus, meat cutting, and music. The tremendous variety of courses listed (about forty differ-ent universities and colleges offer a total of 230 different courses at the high school level) in the *Guide to Correspondence Study* of the National University Extension Association indicates that there are ample oppor-tunities to challenge the superior student to earn a limited number of high school credits in partial fulfilment of the requirements for a diploma and to provide personal enrichment and exploration whether credit is sought or not.

The Bureau of Business and Distributive Education of the State Education Department of the State of New York suggests that correspondence materials might be used in several ways including the following:

1. As a supervised correspondence course—with the teacher in the room to aid pupils when necessary
2. As supplemental material for the better pupils
3. As drill and remedial work (depending on course) for slower pupils
4. As an aid to the teacher in making lesson plans
5. As a means of keeping the teaching load within reasonable bounds.[15]

To realize these possibilities, it is important to deal with a correspondence school that is reliable. Suggestions for courses and materials can be obtained from the National University Extension Association at the University of Minnesota and from the National Home Study Council in Washington, D.C.

Although there are attendant problems that have to be anticipated—materials not arriving on time, students losing interest in the course, students already overburdened with academic subjects and extraclass activities taking on a course because it looks easy—much can be forestalled by careful planning and by competent guidance for students in selecting courses suitable to their needs and to their ability level. The Catskill Area Project has received student evaluations such as "You get a feeling of achievement when you finish an assignment because you have figured out things for yourself and in discussion with other students" and "You learn to make decisions and to budget your time." Such concomitant outcomes make correspondence courses worthy of careful consideration.

Instructional Aids. Technological developments are coming to the aid of efforts to effect curriculum enrichment. The Midwest Project on Airborne Television makes available lessons to schools, regardless of size, in a six-state area. All a school needs is the desire, the necessary receiving sets, and planning to bring a variety of subjects taught by competent teachers into the classroom. Many schools use films directly in their own buildings (1) as a course of study that a teacher supplements, (2) as a supplement to the course prepared and presented by a teacher, or (3) as a complete course with little or no teacher contribution. Schools cooperating on a regional basis, with county offices, or with a university-affiliated study council can draw upon a film and filmstrip library more extensive than they could themselves operate, underscoring again the cooperative feature.

Tape recorders enable a teacher to prepare in advance a lesson that can be used at different times by different individuals or small groups. Able students may make a resource tape for later use by other classes.

[15] New York State Education Department, *Multiple-Class Teaching Procedures Used in Small Group Business Education Classes* (Albany: State Education Department, 1962), pp. 24–25.

Tape recorders, recordings, and language-laboratory equipment can in many ways enrich the foreign-language offerings.

The communication systems set up by telephone companies for the homebound have been modified in the Catskill Project as an open circuit telephone. Through this adaptation, one French teacher might serve seven schools simultaneously in a two-way communication. A famous actor or government authority might, from his home or office, enrich the English or the social studies in several cooperating schools at once.

From the curriculum development point of view, all of the above devices have in-service possibilities that have not as yet been fully utilized. Teachers scattered in several small schools can thus be "brought together" in a learning and sharing situation without having to take their busy time to travel long distances under unfavorable travel conditions.

Any consideration of devices and materials to enrich individual curriculums should include the burgeoning field of programed instruction. Predicated upon the ability of the individual to profit from self-instruction and opportunity to proceed at his own rate, a careful selection of teaching machines and/or programed texts can do much to individualize the curriculum—the ultimate goal of many curriculum planners.

School Aides. People as well as devices can expand and strengthen the educational program. Schools of all sizes are studying ways to relieve teachers of non-professional duties so that they may have more time and energy for instruction, supervision, and guidance. The need is especially critical in the small high school where the teacher has a heavy load of several preparations and is expected to serve the school and the community in many other ways than just in the classroom.

School aides are usually resourceful adults who, on a paid basis, relieve teachers of many time-consuming responsibilities. Many of the aide jobs are clerical—checking rolls; handling film and materials orders; checking and scoring objective tests; general secretarial work; supervision of playground activities, study halls, and cafeteria; proctoring examinations; and operating projectors. Some aides may contribute to the health program by assisting dentists, doctors, and nurses. Their work in library service may provide an enrichment that might not otherwise be available.

While not usually considered in the concept of school aides, nevertheless, the use of lay readers accomplishes the same basic purpose—that of assisting teachers so that the curriculum can function more fully. A fundamental question to ask is "Are the teachers thus gaining time to utilize more fully their professional skills?"

Shared Services. While not limited to enriching the program of studies, the principle of shared services is valuable in situations where small schools are located in the same region. A highly competent language teacher might not be available for each of three or four small schools.

Music specialists, driver-training experts, agriculture teachers, counselors —all can be hired on a cooperative basis by school boards and then shared on a visiting circuit basis with the schools involved. The number of handicapped children in any school is usually small, but, in a school's democratic philosophy, each one is important. Thus, under a comprehensive concept of curriculum, shared services provide enrichment through the persons of audiometer technicians, speech correctionists, psychologists, remedial-reading experts, and the like. Physical-education teachers and librarians, although not in every school every day, can bring added dimensions to the program.

Programed Instruction. Among the more recent developments in instructional materials are "teaching machines" and programed texts. Both use the same teaching-learning principles; the chief difference lies in the physical way in which the written information is presented—one by a mechanical device, the other in a variation of the usual textbook form. Many experiments have shown that students can learn with programed material. Usually the learning is at a faster rate and the retention higher than under the conventional classroom procedure. The point usually overlooked in all the literature, however, is that this approach to instruction can be a boon to the small school.

In the programed-instruction format, the student is presented with a bit of information (a "frame") about which he is asked a question. He responds, finds out immediately whether or not he is right, and then moves on to correctional or additional material. In accomplishing all this, he does not have to wait for a teacher to explain, someone to recite, or a teacher to correct. The student can move ahead at his own rate. The teacher is freed to do other tasks.

For the small-school situation, these "other tasks" mean that a greatly expanded curriculum can be offered. The multiple-class practice can be extended even further. The ideal of individualized instruction can come closer to reality. Several students might be using the same program, for example, Algebra I, but each could be at a different stage according to his own rate of learning. Others could be independently studying trigonometry, geometry, spelling, English grammar, electricity, or psychology. The teacher, meanwhile, acts as a general supervisor or can be conducting a group discussion session with others, for instance, on the social implications of current political events.

The cost of the simpler types of "machines" or of the programed text materials would be far less than hiring the number of teachers necessary to give attention to even a few students for widely diversified courses. At present, the number of carefully developed and tested programs is relatively small, but new offerings are appearing on the market all the time. Faculties in small schools should study these possibilities, match them against student needs, and establish criteria for making final selections.

The Small School as a Community Center. In one sense, the small high school tends to be isolated. Those "necessarily small" are geographically situated so that they serve a limited population and cannot readily join with another community. This does not mean, however, that the school must be isolated from the community it serves. In program planning, deliberate efforts must be made to have the teaching become community-related. A town, however small, has a government. There are a variety of vocations. Education commands much time and thought. Above all, there are people, with their hopes, aspirations, and problems.

All of these aspects—and many more—suggest that the curriculum need not be isolated. Problem-centered instruction can draw upon problems from the local environment. Townspeople can be called upon as resource individuals to enliven the words of the printed page. A science teacher can find the fields and streams abounding in live specimens. While the local drugstore, gas station, grocery store, and beauty parlor offer but limited opportunities for a possible work-experience program, these, plus community projects and even home chores, can be organized to provide valuable job-learning opportunities. In one community, some boys grew vegetables at home for the school lunch program. In another, a typing class, as a community service, addressed envelopes for a Red Cross drive.

If the curriculum is to be more than a limited set of textbooks, the community must be a part of the learning situation. Furthermore, additional reading resources are necessary. Trained personnel are necessary for the best use of these materials; so there is the problem of hiring a librarian. The *NEA Research Bulletin* of February, 1963, reports that 59.4 per cent of the small high schools (enrolment under 300) had a part-time librarian. In some cases, this part-time person also served as a librarian for the community. Merely by having its library open certain evenings and Saturdays, the school serves as a cultural center. Thus, "shared services" can be used in school-community relationships.

The availability and the uses of school facilities vary considerably throughout the nation. In some of the very large cities, buildings are not open to the public, except for occasional events. This stems from janitorial problems and from security measures in a large, crowded urban area. The small school, on the other hand, serves as a rallying point for many community activities. Where these are viewed as a kind of adult education and the planners of the education program expand their concept to include a community curriculum, there, truly, the school is taking the initiative.

There is some discussion as to whether or not the school should lead or follow the community. In the case of the small school, the chance to exercise leadership should be listed as one of the potentials. Having the building open evenings for library service, group meetings, and social events is fine. Making the plant available Saturdays for various types of recreation is moving toward optimum utilization of public property. However, all this should have some direction and not just be an indiscriminately beckoning open door. Schoolmen and adult leaders should get together and plan programs for the school as a community center as well as a center for the formal education of its children and youths.

In the long run, this planning for, and with, the community will strengthen the "regular" curriculum, on the principle that mutual involvement and sharing will bring understanding of what the school is trying to do as it studies and revises its offerings. McClusky believes that a community-centered school is a demonstration of the "law of increasing returns,"[16] that is, a little increase in effort to use the leadership and the facilities of the small school will yield a large additional return.

QUESTIONS, PROBLEMS, AND ISSUES FOR FURTHER THOUGHT

1. Outline a plan for pupil participation in curriculum development in your small high school. How can you ready both teachers and pupils to do effective teacher-pupil planning in the classroom?
2. What distinctly rural values should be utilized as the basis for curriculum study?
3. How can your high school help pupils become oriented to the world of work?
4. Make a follow-up study of past students—graduates as well as dropouts. What school experiences (do not limit to subjects) do they find of greatest value? Of least value? What suggestions do they have for an improved program?
5. Prepare a report to be presented to your school board outlining the possibilities of supervised correspondence studies for your school.
6. How can you enlist the interest of your community in a curriculum study? Show how you would organize community resources for curriculum betterment.
7. Take some basic objective such as "economic competence," define its meaning, and then make a survey of your educational program to see in what ways and to what extent you are already working toward that objective. After the survey, what proposals do you have for curriculum change?
8. Look for articles in the various subject fields, such as Torrance's "Small High Schools and the Improvement of Mathematics and Science" (*Educational Administration and Supervision*, Vol. 45 [May, 1959], pp. 127–134), and draw up a blueprint for enrichment in the department of your interest.
9. Draw up a research design to be used in studying the effectiveness of any one of the organizational approaches suggested in this chapter.

---

16 H. Y. McClusky, "Some Propositions in Support of the Community School," *Journal of Educational Sociology*, Vol. 33 (December, 1959), pp. 179–183.

10. Develop a proposal for a program for the gifted (or slow) learner in the small high school.
11. Explain how the team-teaching concept can be adapted to fit the small-school situation.

SUPPLEMENTARY MATERIALS

SELECTED READINGS

BUTTERWORTH, JULIAN, and HOWARD DAWSON. *The Modern Rural School.* New York: McGraw-Hill Book Co., Inc., 1952. An analysis of educational leadership necessary to take cognizance of the unique socioeconomic backgrounds of rural education. The authors have (1) reorganized the significant changes in rural America, (2) documented the socioeconomic background, (3) described in considerable detail the educational program needed for rural America, and (4) presented ways and means of implementing the program.

CATSKILL AREA PROJECT IN SMALL SCHOOL DESIGN. Oneonta, N.Y.: State University College of Education. Printed reports from this project, established in 1957 to search for theory and techniques that will improve the variety and quality of education in rural secondary schools, include *Small School Design* (1959), *School Aides at Work* (1959), and *Sharing Educational Services* (1960).

DEGOOD, K. C. "Profile of the Small High School," *Educational Leadership* Vol. XVIII (December, 1960), pp. 170–72. A study of 103 school districts in Ohio, in an effort to identify differences that may exist owing to the size of high schools. Considers salaries, teacher experience, master's degrees held, financial support, and guidance.

EVERETT, SAMUEL, (ed.). *Programs for the Gifted.* 15th yearbook, John Dewey Society. New York: Harper & Row, 1961. Chapter 7, "Enrichment for Talented Rural Youth," by HOWARD G. SACKETT and GLYN MORRIS, is the story of an experiment with gifted rural youth in Lewis County, New York, who met once a week from scattered schools to hold a seminar for a stimulating intellectual experience. Chapter 8, "An Enrichment Program in a Small High School" by HENRY SCATTERGOOD, shows how the Germantown Friends School (Pa.) faculty has sought to rethink, to reassess, and to re-model the curriculum in order to challenge students more deeply. A description is given of the various courses of study, the student activities, and guidance.

FORD, EDMUND A. *Rural Renaissance: Revitalizing Small High Schools.* Washington, D.C.: U.S. Office of Education, 1961. A summary of promising attempts to break the bonds sometimes associated with smallness. The various approaches and the belief that learning should be placed upon an individual basis (which can be done in a small school better than in a large one) call for versatile teachers. Are teacher-training institutions ready?

FROELICH, CLIFFORD P. *Guidance Services in Schools* (2d ed.). New York: McGraw-Hill Book Co., Inc., 1958. Froelich believes that, since the first edition (entitled *Guidance Services in Smaller Schools*), it is no longer necessary to protest the lack of guidance services in smaller schools as a group. "The size barrier has been broken!"

MORRIS, GLYN. *Practical Guidance Methods for Principals and Teachers.* New York: Harper & Row, 1952. This is a helpful book of suggestions, based on the experience of a principal of a small high school. It shows how an administrator and his teachers can develop a good guidance program without the benefit of a specialized staff or a special budget. In-service education provides the basic approach.

NIMMICK, GLENDON P., and ARTHUR PARTRIDGE. *Designs for a Small High School.* Greeley: Colorado State College, 1962. A report on a study supported by a grant from the Educational Facilities Laboratory of the Ford Foundation. Summarizes the latest thinking and experience on the strengths and weaknesses of small schools.

ROCKY MOUNTAIN AREA PROJECT FOR SMALL HIGH SCHOOLS. *Second Annual Workshop Report.* Denver: Colorado State Department of Education, 1959. A presentation of the discussions by consultants and the findings of work groups and committees on teaching methods and devices.

———. *Colorado Accepts the Challenge.* Denver: Colorado State Department of Education, 1961. Written especially for persons not directly involved in professional education, this summary of the activities of the Project, nevertheless, has a message for teachers and administrators. It substantiates the thesis that factors other than size affect the quality of the curriculum.

TEXAS EDUCATION AGENCY. *Forward with the Texas Small Schools Project.* Austin: The Agency, 1962. Although a proceedings of their second annual workshop on small schools, this report includes a backward glance at the origins and first steps of the venture. Evaluation of the present situation plus projection of next steps are included, along with reports from various high school subject-matter groups.

UNIVERSITY OF THE STATE OF NEW YORK. *Multiple-Class Teaching Procedures Used in Small Group Experimental Business Education Classes.* Albany: State Department of Education, Bureau of Business and Distributive Education, 1962. A report, in cooperation with the Catskill Area Project, of some experiments conducted in schools with less than two full-time business teachers. Presents hints for teachers interested in experimenting with multiple classes.

32

The Curriculum in Religious Secondary Schools

RELIGIOUS SECONDARY SCHOOLS IN THE UNITED STATES

Since the early days of American public education, strong and vocal minority groups have felt the need to set up school systems in which secular religious instruction could be given. The legality of these schools was not seriously challenged until shortly after World War I, when a law was passed in Oregon requiring all children to attend public schools. The U.S. Supreme Court, in a momentous decision, declared this statute to violate the Fourteenth Amendment of the Constitution. The opinion of the Court held that "The fundamental theory of liberty upon which all governments in this Union repose excludes any general power of the state to standardize its children by forcing them to accept instruction from public teachers only. The child is not the mere creature of the state. ...."[1] This decision has been considered the "Magna Charta" of private education in America.

Secondary schools operated by religious groups increase in number and influence throughout this nation with each passing year. Figures for both elementary and secondary school enrolment show that, while nonpublic schools accounted for 8.02 per cent of all students in 1899–1900, the figure rose to 13.08 per cent in 1953–1954, and it is predicted by the U.S. Office of Education that it will stand at 14.60 per cent in 1965.[2] The

[1] *Pierce* v. *Society of Sisters*, 268 U.S. 510 (1925).
[2] Fred F. Beach and Robert F. Will, *The State and Nonpublic Schools* (Washington, D.C.: Government Printing Office, 1958), p. 1.

vast majority of non-public schools are religious, since religious schools enrol 96.03 per cent of all pupils attending non-public institutions.[3]

Educational Positions of Religious Groups. Since it is clear that religious schools have a legal right to exist, an examination into the motivation for their establishment will shed light on their purpose and contribution.

The Roman Catholic church operates the largest private system of elementary and secondary schools in this country, with Lutheran groups far behind in second place.[4] Statements of purpose from these two religious bodies can be taken as representative of others that operate their own systems of education.

The official Roman Catholic position on education is found in canon law and in papal pronouncements:

Canon 1372 states, "From childhood all the faithful must be so educated that not only are they taught nothing contrary to faith and morals but that religious and moral training takes chief place."

Canon 1374 states, "Catholic children must not attend nonCatholic, neutral, or mixed schools."

Canon 1375 states, "The Church has the right to establish schools of every grade, not only elementary schools but also high schools and colleges."

In 1929, Pope Pius XI issued an encyclical letter on "The Christian Education of Youth," which set forth the Catholic position.[5] Essentially, it maintains that every person is born into three societies: the family, the state, and the Roman Catholic church. The duty of the family is to generate and care for offspring; the duty of the state is to look after the temporal welfare of the community; and the duty of the church is to care for the eternal salvation of men's souls. The Catholic church, inasmuch as it deals with supernatural affairs, has priority over both the family and the state, which deal only with natural affairs. Thus, the Catholic church claims the right of the education of its children.

The Lutheran Church—Missouri Synod holds a somewhat similar position:

According to the Lutheran philosophy of education, it is pedagogically unsound and inadmissable to exclude religious instruction from the child's schooling and religate [sic] it to the after school hours or to Sunday morning. . . . From the Christian viewpoint, complete education is impossible apart from religion.

[3] *Ibid.*, p. 2.
[4] *Ibid.*
[5] *Five Great Encyclicals* (New York: Paulist Press, 1949), pp. 39–55.

. . . Since our children cannot receive a Christian education in the public school we have no other course but expand our parish school system.[6]

Other denominational groups supporting their own schools have comparable philosophies. The common element in each declares that complete education requires religion as a part of all instruction and, therefore, makes it necessary to set up private religious schools.

Extent of Religious High School Systems. Several church bodies have felt it necessary to operate secondary schools because of their stand on religion in education. Table 32–1 presents information on the extent of some of the larger secondary school systems sponsored by religious groups.

TABLE 32–1

EXTENT OF THE FOUR LARGEST DENOMINATIONAL SECONDARY SCHOOL SYSTEMS

Sponsoring Church	Year	No. of Schools	Enrolment
Roman Catholic[a]	1961	2,433	886,295
Protestant Episcopal[b]	1961	104 (including 83 boarding academies)	22,184 (including 17,984 boarding-school students)
Seventh Day Adventist[c]	1959	290 (including elem. schools with a grade 9 or above in the school)	13,380
Lutheran Church– Missouri Synod[d]	1962	32 (including 11 boarding schools)	11,495 (including 1,556 boarding-school students)

[a] Felician A. Foy (ed.), *The National Catholic Almanac* (Paterson, N.J.: St. Anthony Guild Press, 1962).

[b] Protestant Episcopal Church—Unit of Parish and Preparatory Schools, New York. Many of these Episcopalian schools do not compare to other institutions noted here in the amount of religion in their curriculums. Other than requiring attendance at chapel services, they probably differ very little from non-religious private secondary schools. Some question may, therefore, be raised as to whether or not they should be classified as religious high schools.

[c] Seventh-Day Adventist General Conference, Department of Education, Washington, D.C.

[d] The Lutheran Church–Missouri Synod, Board of Parish Education, St. Louis.

The Roman Catholic church dominates religious secondary schooling. In 1959, it accounted for more than 89 per cent of the enrolment and more than 79 per cent of the number of schools.[7] Because of this denomination's paramount position in the field, the discussion hereafter will center upon Catholic education.

[6] *Report of the Board of Parish Education,* The Lutheran Church–Missouri Synod, 1950 Convention (Mimeo.) (St. Louis, 1950), p. 370.

[7] Bureau of Research and Survey, National Council of the Churches of Christ in the USA, *Information Service* (New York: National Council of the Churches of Christ in the USA, 1959), pp. 3–4.

Not only does Catholic secondary education stand pre-eminent in the area of religious schools, its growth in recent years has been more rapid than that of public high schools, as is revealed by Table 32–2.

TABLE 32–2
PUBLIC AND CATHOLIC HIGH SCHOOL ENROLMENTS—1950–1960

1950	Public	5,725,000	100%
	Catholic	505,572	100%
1954	Public	6,290,000	110%
	Catholic	623,751	123%
1958	Public	7,860,000	137%
	Catholic	796,741	158%
1960	Public	8,484,869	148%
	Catholic	880,369	174%

SOURCE: Winifred R. Long, "Enrollment Growth in a Decade—Public and Catholic Schools," *National Catholic Education Association Journal,* Vol. 58, No. 4 (May, 1962), pp. 30–31. These figures were taken from the U.S. Office of Education, *Biennial Survey of Education,* and National Catholic Welfare Conference, *Survey of Catholic Education.*

Control of Religious Education. Roman Catholic secondary schools fall into three general categories:

1. Parish high schools
2. Diocesan high schools
3. Private high schools

Parish high schools are maintained by large parishes for the young people within the limits of the parish itself. The control and cost of operation are assumed by the local church authorities.

When the parish is not large enough to support its own high school, the diocese may organize one that is open to students from several parishes. These diocesan schools are responsible to the diocesan superintendent of schools and ultimately to the bishop.

Religious orders within the Catholic church, for many years, have operated private high schools open only to selected students. These institutions are controlled by the board of education of the particular order maintaining the school. The proportion of schools in each category can be seen below.

Control of Catholic Secondary Schools, 1958–1959[8]

1. High schools under parish control... 1,166
2. Private high schools under control of religious orders............ 783
3. Central high schools under diocesan control........................... 400

[8] Neil G. McCluskey, *Catholic Viewpoint on Education* (New York: Doubleday & Co., Inc., 1959), p. 100.

SPECIAL FACTORS AFFECTING THE CURRICULUMS OF RELIGIOUS SECONDARY SCHOOLS

Many of the elements that influence the curriculums of public high schools are similar to those shaping the programs of studies in parochial high schools. However, certain influences peculiar to religious institutions produce curriculums somewhat different in pattern and emphasis from those of public schools. A number of these forces will now be discussed.

Aims and Objectives. Underlying and infusing the activities of sectarian schools is the desire to further the religious development of students. This "spiritual atmosphere" is exemplified by the following quotation from a mimeographed statement of the *Philosophy* for St. Thomas Academy, a diocesan boys' school in St. Paul, Minnesota:

St. Thomas Academy works toward the end of Christian education: "To cooperate with divine grace in forming the true and perfect Christian." In this work the school believes that its specific task is to guide the young student to the knowledge and love of truth in religion, the sciences, the humanities and thus to form him intelligently in order that he may be enabled to make, in accordance with right reason, the choices which lead to wisdom and virtue. This training takes place in an environment regulated by the Christian spirit. It is informed by a profound respect for the dignity of each individual student; events in its course are memorialized by sacred liturgies which establish and enoble their significance; and the whole enterprise is oriented to man's final purpose, the knowledge and love of God.

To implement such an aim, courses in religion are always given and the religious implications of secular subjects are stressed. Doctrinal approaches are used in teaching, with varying degrees of dogmatism, depending on the school and the teacher.

Size of the Schools. The profound effect of enrolment on the curricular offerings of a school is evident to everyone. A wide variety of courses is not economically feasible where only a few students are available for each class. Conant has suggested that no school be so small that less than 100 students are graduated each year.[9] Small enrolments have plagued parochial high schools for many years, forcing them to limit their curriculum to the essential subjects. In 1959, one-third of the Catholic secondary schools in the United States had enrolments of less than 100, and one-half had fewer than 200 students.[10] With this handicap upon them, Catholic educators are laboring to expand course offerings and provide variety in curricular patterns.

[9] James B. Conant, *The American High School Today* (New York: McGraw-Hill Book Co., Inc., 1959), p. 80.
[10] "Secondary Education Notes," *Catholic Educational Review*, Vol. 57, No. 9 (December, 1959), p. 625.

Government Regulation. Religious schools on both the elementary and the secondary level are often required to meet certain requirements by state educational authorities. While sectarian groups are free to set up schools in which children may satisfy the compulsory-attendance requirements, such institutions must meet certain basic curricular standards. Often these regulations are more stringent upon the elementary than the secondary school. An example of how explicit and detailed these criteria may be is provided by Pennsylvania law.

Public School Code of 1949 (title 24 Chapter 1)

Article XV Section 15

In every elementary public and private school established and maintained in this Commonwealth, the following subjects shall be taught in the English language and from English texts:

English—including spelling, reading and writing
Arithmetic
Geography
History—of the United States and of Pennsylvania
Civics—including loyalty to the State and National Governments
Safety Education
Humane Treatment of Animals
Health—including physical education and physiology
Music and Art

In secondary education, curricular requirements imposed by the state on parochial schools are less inclusive and specific. Table 32–3 shows state regulations that apply to religious high schools.

The degree of standardization varies greatly among the states, so, where in one state the parochial high schools must meet all the requirements for public institutions, in another they are not bound by any rules on curriculum.

Accrediting Agencies. A significant influence is exerted on the program of any high school by accrediting groups by which the institution wishes to be recognized. Whether the agency be a regional organization (such as the North Central Association of Colleges and Secondary Schools), the state university, or the state department of education, pressure is brought to bear to conform to certain basic criteria. Catholic high school curriculums must be rather similar to those of public institutions, since 91.2 per cent of the Catholic secondary schools are accredited by some non-religious standardizing agency.[11]

[11] Walter S. Monroe (ed.), *Encyclopedia of Educational Research* (New York: The Macmillan Co., 1952), p. 205.

TABLE 32–3

STATE REQUIREMENTS FOR RELIGIOUS SECONDARY SCHOOL CURRICULUMS

	Instruction in American History	Instruc. in U.S. Govt. & Const.	Instruc. in State Govt. & Const.	Instruc. in Health & Phys. Ed.	Inst. in Safety	Inst. in Moral Values	Instruction in Special Areas
Alabama		X		X			
Arizona							
Arkansas	X						
California	X	X					
Colorado		X					
Connecticut		X					
Delaware		X	X				
Florida							
Georgia							
Idaho		X					Use of flag & patriotic songs
Illinois							
Indiana		X	X	X	X	X	
Iowa	X	X	X				
Kansas		X					
Kentucky	Identical to state requirements for public schools.						
Louisiana							
Maine						X	
Maryland				X			Alcohol & Narcotics
Massachusetts							
Michigan		X					
Minnesota		X					
Mississippi							
Missouri	X	X					
Montana					X		
Nebraska	X	X				X	Exercises on patriotic holidays
Nevada		X	X				
New Hampshire		X	X				
New Jersey		X			X		
New Mexico	No requirements.						
New York		X	X	X	X		
North Carolina							
North Dakota		X					
Ohio							
Oklahoma							
Oregon			X				
Pennsylvania		X	X		X		Use & display of flag
Rhode Island		X	X	X			
South Carolina							
South Dakota		X				X	Alcohol & Narcotics
Tennessee	X	X					
Texas							
Utah			X				
Vermont							
Virginia							
Washington	X	X	X				
West Virginia	X	X	X		X		
Wisconsin		X					Worth of dairy products
Wyoming							

SOURCE: Fred F. Beach and Robert F. Will, *The State and Nonpublic Schools* (Washington, D.C.: Government Printing Office, 1958), pp. 31–151.

Special Instructional Materials. A practical definition of the curriculum of any school might be "what goes on in the classroom." Since reading constitutes an important part of learning in the high school, the nature of basic textbook material forms a vital aspect of the curriculum. In religious schools, it is natural to find textbooks that present subject matter in the light of sectarian doctrine. Publishers frequently print editions of standard textbooks specially modified for parochial schools. It is not uncommon to find single texts and even complete series of books written particularly for use in religious schools. This does not imply that secular textbooks are never adopted, since, in many cases, such volumes are used. The basic approach, however, necessitates the teaching of religion in all subjects, secular textbook or not.

The Roman Catholic position on this point was made clear in Pope Pius XI's encyclical on "The Christian Education of Youth": "For the mere fact that a school gives some religious instruction . . . does not . . . make it a fit place for Catholic students. To be this it is necessary that all the teaching and the whole organization of the school, and its teachers, syllabus and textbooks in every branch, be regulated by the Christian spirit."[12]

A recent study of more than 100 textbooks, in the areas of science, mathematics, and languages, used in religious schools revealed that sectarian doctrine is integrated into the subject matter wherever possible.[13] There would be little point in such special editions if this were not the case. The author of this investigation concluded that there were several ways in which religion was incorporated into textual material:

1. Religious symbols and subjects used in examples for arithmetic and grammar drills.
2. Specific sectarian doctrines taught where controversial matter appears in the text.
3. A general theistic Christian approach to all matters.
4. Appeals to church authority for proof of a point.
5. Defense of church social ideas and regulations.[14]

This special instructional material must be classified as a curricular influence of the first magnitude. It is a natural outgrowth of the desire to achieve the aims of religious education, but it forms a significant difference between public and parochial schooling.

Cost of Maintenance. Education is an expensive commodity, and those who undertake to provide it must shoulder heavy financial burdens. In

---

12 *Five Great Encyclicals, loc. cit.*
13 George R. LaNove, "The National Defense Education Act and 'Secular' Subjects," *Phi Delta Kappan*, Vol. 43, No. 9 (June, 1962), pp. 380–387.
14 *Ibid.*, pp. 384–386.

secondary education, efforts to offer a wide variety of courses involve additional expenditures not present in a curriculum with limited offerings. Certain subject areas require a greater outlay of money than others, and, when funds are limited, variety is curtailed and high-cost subjects are eliminated.

The cost of Catholic education has been held to a minimum because of the large number of teachers from religious orders who receive little in terms of monetary payment for their work. This situation is rapidly changing so that, whereas in 1959 there was only one lay teacher for every three religious teachers, it is predicted that in the 1970's there will be two lay teachers for each religious teacher. The price of parochial education will, therefore, be raised, and course offerings may be restricted as a result.

CURRICULUM SUBJECTS AND PATTERNS

Offerings. The actual course offerings and curricular patterns of religious secondary schools are results of general and special factors to which they are subjected. General factors common to all secondary education, such as the nature of American society, the need for training in citizenship, college entrance requirements, and knowledge of fundamental processes play a significant role in developing parochial high school education. The special factors have been covered in the preceding section.

An examination of studies on the programs of religious secondary schools shows that a considerable similarity exists between their offerings and those of public institutions. A study by the National Catholic Educational Association points up the conclusion that "Our schools [curriculums] tend to mirror the public schools with the notable exception of technical training."[15]

Secular Subjects in Religious Education. The most recent information on the types of courses available in Catholic secondary schools reveals a fairly standard but somewhat limited group of offerings. Three hundred schools of all sizes, types, and locations were polled regarding their curriculums, with the following results:

Social Studies (5 most popular subjects)

American History	281 schools
Civics	184 schools
World History	167 schools
Modern History	108 schools
Ancient History	106 schools

[15] C. Albert Koob, O. Praem, Associate Secretary, Secondary School Department, National Catholic Educational Association, Washington, D.C., personal communication, April 4, 1963.

English (3 most popular courses)
Composition .... 300 schools
Literature .... 300 schools
Speech .... 94 schools

Foreign Language (3 most popular courses)
Latin .... 273 schools
Spanish .... 195 schools
French .... 164 schools

Science (4 most popular courses)
Chemistry .... 235 schools
Biology .... 202 schools
Physics .... 192 schools
General Science .... 180 schools

Physical Education
Physical Education .... 274 schools

Mathematics (3 most popular courses)
Algebra .... 278 schools
Geometry .... 272 schools
Trigonometry .... 178 schools

Business Education (3 most popular courses)
Typing .... 238 schools
Shorthand .... 191 schools
Bookkeeping .... 173 schools

Home Economics (2 most popular courses)
Sewing .... 89 schools
Cooking .... 66 schools

Industrial Arts (2 most popular courses)
Mechanical drawing .... 77 schools
Shop .... 26 schools[16]

Fine Arts

Today's Catholic high schools, though listing music and art among their offerings either state explicitly or show by the amount of time devoted to them that they are extracurricular and that a comparatively small number of students engage in them.[17]

From these figures it is clear that nearly all schools offered the following courses:

1. American history
2. English (composition and literature)
3. Latin
4. Physical education
5. Algebra
6. Geometry

Comparatively few schools offered much coursework in industrial arts, home economics, or fine arts.

[16] Mary Janet, *Catholic Secondary Education: A National Survey* (Washington, D.C.: Department of Education, National Catholic Welfare Conference, 1949), pp. 68–87.
[17] *Ibid.*, p. 84.

Religion in the Curriculum. The amounts of time and emphasis devoted to the religious aspects of any subject-matter area are difficult to estimate. Fichter analyzed the practice of one school, at the eighth-grade level, for the percentage of time spent on religion, with the following results:

English	37.3%
Social Studies	16.0%
Arithmetic	15.0%
Religion	10.0%
Music	6.7%
Science and Health	5.3%
Art	4.0%
Recess & Misc.	5.7%
	100.0%[18]

A distinctive feature of religious secondary education is the class in religion taught from a sectarian and doctrinal viewpoint. Typical of such courses are those listed below. It was found that, in the study of 300 Catholic high schools previously cited, nearly two-thirds of the schools questioned devoted 200–300 minutes weekly to some or all of these classes.

1. Morals and Dogma
2. The Creed
3. The Sacraments
4. The Commandments
5. The Beatitudes
6. Church History
7. Apologetics
8. The Life of Christ
9. The Liturgy[19]

Time Devoted to Religion. Assuming the average amount of time available in a school week to be about 1,500 minutes and the median number of minutes spent in religion classes to be near 250 minutes weekly, it can be seen that 16.6 per cent of the total time is devoted to religion classes as such. Add to this the average of the time spent in secular classes given to religious instruction, as mentioned in Fichter's study[20] (11.2 per cent of the school week, or 168 minutes), and the following figures can be seen:

Average percentage of total class time per week spent in teaching religion—27.8 per cent

Average number of minutes per week spent in teaching religion—418 minutes

[18] Joseph H. Fichter, *Parochial School: A Sociological Study* (Notre Dame, Ind.: University of Notre Dame Press, 1958), p. 106. A school week of 1,500 minutes of class time was studied.

[19] Mary Janet, *op. cit.*, p. 68.

[20] Joseph H. Fichter, *op. cit.* This does not include the 10 per cent for religion classes.

Such a large proportion of time spent in religious instruction must result from at least one of three conditions: First, the school day must be proportionately longer in parochial schools than in public schools; second, the instruction must be much more effective in religious schools; or, third, the number of subjects offered must be smaller to make room for the religious instruction. The last possibility seems to be the most likely, although, in some cases, the other two may also contribute to a certain extent.

Comparison of Sample Public and Parochial Secondary School Curriculums. An examination of actual curricular patterns will illustrate the type of course work available in parochial high schools. No claim is made that these are typical curriculums, but they constitute examples of current practice.

The first curriculum is that of Derham Hall, a college-preparatory girls' high school in St. Paul, Minnesota, enrolling approximately 171 students in 1960–1961.

Freshman	*Sophomore*
Religion I	Religion II
Algebra	Geometry
Latin I	Latin II
Phys. Ed.	Phys. Ed.
English I	English II
World History	Biology
French I	French II

Junior	*Senior*
Religion III	Religion IV
Higher Algebra	Trig. & Solid
Latin III	Latin IV
Chemistry	Physics
Art	Art
English III	English IV
Am. History	Social Problems
French III	French IV
Homemaking	Homemaking
Choral	Choral

Number of courses in subject areas offered:

(34 courses in 10 areas)

Religion	4 courses	Science	3 courses
Mathematics	4 courses	Phys. Ed.	2 courses
Foreign Language	8 courses	Art	2 courses
English	4 courses	Homemaking	2 courses
Social Studies	3 courses	Choral	2 courses

The second school is St. Bernard's High School, a parish secondary school in St. Paul, Minnesota, with 477 pupils in 1960–1961.

Freshman

Religion I & Phys. Ed.
English I
Chorus (1 day a wk.)
Latin I
Spanish I
German I
World History
Algebra
General Science
Civics
General Algebra
Band (3 days a wk.)

Sophomore

Relig. II & Phys. Ed.
English II
Biology
Latin II
Spanish II
German II
Geometry
World History
Record Keeping
Typing I
Art I
Chorus (3 days)
Band (3 days)

Junior

Religion III
Fine Arts Apprec.
English III
Am. History
Latin III
Plane & Solid Geom.
Higher Algebra
Geometry
Chemistry
General Chemistry
Physical Science
Typing I
Clerical Typing II
Shorthand I
Bookkeeping
Record Keeping
Art I
Art II
Chorus (3 days)
Band (3 days)

Senior

Religion IV
English IV
Social Problems
Latin IV
Trigonometry
Higher Algebra
Physics
Chemistry
General Chemistry
Physical Science
Typing I
Clerical Typing II
Shorthand I
Transcription
Bookkeeping
Record Keeping
Office Practice
Clerical Practice
Art I
Art II
Chorus (3 days)
Band (3 days)

Number of courses in subject areas offered:

(49 courses in 10 areas)

Religion	4 courses	Music (including band & chorus)	2 courses
English	4 courses	Art	3 courses
Foreign Language	8 courses	Business Education	8 courses
Mathematics	7 courses	Physical Education	2 courses
Social Studies	5 courses		
Science	6 courses		

It is possible to take industrial arts and homemaking through arrangements with a nearby public high school.

Derham Hall, in keeping with its stated objective of college preparation, offers an academic, traditional, and rather narrow curriculum. St. Bernard's, a more comprehensive school with a larger enrolment and less select clientele, teaches a wider variety of courses, with stress on the vocational business-education subjects.

Individual differences exist among schools as they do among the students in them, and, therefore, comparisons are often difficult. Each institution must be judged not only on the basis of the facilities available but with proper attention given to the aims of the school, the effectiveness of the instruction, and the products it turns out. Since course offerings can be compared more easily than some of the other criteria, a brief analysis of a public high school curriculum will serve as a rough index of relationship.

The New London–Spicer, Minnesota, Junior Senior High School enrolled 427 students in 1961–1962. A listing of the course offerings in the various subject areas for grades nine through twelve shows the following:

(48 courses in 12 areas)

English	4 courses	Industrial Arts	4 courses
Social Studies	5 courses	Agriculture	4 courses
Science	6 courses	Physical Education and	
Mathematics	6 courses	Health	2 courses
Foreign Language	4 courses	Art	2 courses
Business Education	6 courses	Speech	1 course
Home Economics	4 courses		

When St. Bernard's is compared to New London–Spicer High School, the difference in community background must be considered. New London–Spicer is in a rural area, and this is reflected in the agriculture courses. St. Bernard's is located in a metropolitan district, which shows up in the emphasis on business-education course work. Except for foreign-language and religion courses, the two curriculums are remarkably similar. The vocal and instrumental music work at New London–Spicer is offered on a no-credit basis. Inferences cannot be drawn from this comparison, except that, in two secondary schools selected by chance, the similarity of course offerings and emphasis is rather striking.

CURRICULUM PROBLEMS AND ISSUES

In the sixth decade of the twentieth century, what are the more important problems and issues facing religious high schools with regard to matters of curriculum? It is difficult, if not impossible, to separate out this one aspect of education and treat it as if it were not closely bound to all other facets of school operation. Despite this, some conclusions especially related to the curriculum may be mentioned:

1. There is much more similarity than difference between parochial and public secondary schools. The general controls of government regulation, the standards of accrediting agencies, the same local and national communities, and the demands of college entrance requirements, together with many other forces, shape the two types of curriculums in very similar molds.

2. Catholic educators feel a general need for more technical vocational subjects in the curriculums of most parochial high schools. While the more academic, college-preparatory type of school is not greatly concerned about this lack, the majority of Catholic secondary high schools are of the comprehensive type[21] and feel keenly that more technical vocational training should be given. The roadblocks are the expense of installing equipment and the upkeep and cost of materials and operation. In this connection, many parochial high schools have, for some years, operated with public schools a "shared time" program in the area of industrial arts.

3. The problem of school size affecting directly the curriculum has been troublesome to religious secondary schools. Some of them are solving this difficulty in the same way public schools handle it—by consolidating districts until a sizable group of students has been gathered together. When this is done, however, the cost of education rises, since buses are needed to transport the pupils to and from school. In many communities, public funds are used to provide this service.[22] More diocesan, community-type schools will probably be established, with larger student bodies and, consequently, more variety in course offerings.

4. Expansion of academic subjects is tied together with enrolment. Many parochial schools have a sound "meat and potatoes diet" of the essential subjects but would like to include more in the areas of fine arts, speech, economics, sociology, and other such "dessert" items. The time factor also is important here, since, in a six-period day, one class hour must be given to religious instruction. This restriction alone cuts down heavily on the variety of courses available.

5. A lack of academic freedom can always be a problem when teaching is done within the atmosphere of a strong bias. In areas where church bodies have taken a stand, as the Lutheran Church—Missouri Synod has done on evolution, a totally unprejudiced approach simply is not tolerated. Catholic textbooks were found by LaNove's study to give "Selective emphasis on Catholic institutions and contributions to the culture

[21] Mary Janet, op. cit., p. 39. In 1947, the latest date for which figures are available, 64.4 per cent were comprehensive high schools, and they have been growing proportionately faster than other types of parochial high schools.

[22] R. B. Dierenfield, Religion in American Public Schools (Washington, D.C.: Public Affairs Press, 1962), p. 84. Nineteen per cent of public school districts do this.

and on facts favorable to the Church and omissions of institutions and contributions to the culture by nonCatholics and of facts unfavorable to the Church."[23]

6. The homogeneous grouping of students is made difficult when small numbers are involved. Sectioning in terms of vocational aim, college plans, or ability into various "tracks" is impossible, if only enough students are available for one basic curriculum. Remedial sections and "fast classes" must also be sacrificed when adequate enrolment is not available.

7. The "shared time" approach to expansion of non-public high school curriculums is undergoing some study and experimentation. Under this plan, students from parochial schools would go to nearby public high schools for certain classes such as industrial arts, homemaking, and science courses. Since the equipment is expensive and costs of operation are high, the private institutions would save by this plan. A basic assumption here involves the principle that such subjects are not closely bound to religion and, therefore, a secular approach would be acceptable. Catholic educators are not in complete agreement with this arrangement, mainly because many feel that all subjects should be taught in a religious atmosphere. Some public school educators have had doubts about the feasibility of "shared time," owing to the scheduling problems involved and the additional facilities and instructors that would be needed.[24] It is certain that more experimentation and study will be necessary before "shared time" will become widely popular.

8. The cost factor in providing curriculums that are both wide and deep is of most pressing concern to religious educators. The added burden of providing a secondary school education system in addition to paying for the regular public schools has prompted requests for financial aid from both state and federal governments. Although there is no universal agreement within the Catholic church, spokesmen for the National Catholic Welfare Conference contend it is a matter of "distributive justice" to allow federal aid to education to go to both public and religious institutions. Groups who are not in favor of this action base their opposition on the contention that such grants would violate the "establishment of religion" clause of the First Amendment. If federal aid is given to parochial schools, it will enable them to expand their curriculum and establish new schools at a much more accelerated pace than has been possible to date.

Quo Vadis Parochial Education? Religious high schools form an important part of American secondary education. Their continuing growth in size and influence points to an even more important position in future

---

[23] George R. LaNove, *op. cit.*, p. 386.
[24] William L. Shunk, "Shared Time: New Light on an Old Problem," *Phi Delta Kappan*, Vol. 43, No. 9 (June, 1962), pp. 377–379.

years. The curricular problems facing these institutions are similar in many respects to those of any small high school with a lack of funds. What the future will hold depends upon a number of the factors mentioned in this chapter. One thing appears certain: After the struggle put forth by religious groups to establish, maintain, and improve parochial high schools, these institutions will continue to play a significant role in educating American young people.

QUESTIONS, PROBLEMS, AND ISSUES FOR FURTHER THOUGHT

1. Select one academic subject, and describe a manner in which it might be taught differently in a church-affiliated school.
2. Do you believe that all young people should attend a public school for a period of at least five or six years? At which ages would this be best?
3. What is your opinion of the plan of shared time in which a student spends half a day in a public school and half a day in a church-affiliated school?
4. What is your opinion with respect to the use of public funds by church-affiliated schools for (a) transportation, (b) textbooks, (c) library materials and laboratory equipment, (d) salaries of teachers who work under the supervision of the city or county superintendent of schools?
5. What do you think about a plan of having students of all denominations attend a religion-oriented, non-public school?
6. What do you believe should be the type of instruction about religion offered in a church-affiliated school?
7. Dr. Conant recommends that all secondary schools should be enlarged to have at least 100 students in the graduating class. The majority of church-affiliated secondary schools are not that large. Be ready to comment on this situation. How large should a church-affiliated school be to warrant its continuance and support?
8. Teachers for public secondary schools are required to obtain state certificates, while this is not true of non-public schools. Do you believe that a certificate should be required of teachers in church-affiliated schools? Should teachers in church-affiliated schools have at least some courses in education? If so, what courses would you suggest as a minimum?
9. To what extent do you believe that church-affiliated schools should be under the supervision of a city or county superintendent of schools or a state department of education in order to have attendance at the church-affiliated school meet the compulsory-education requirements?

SUPPLEMENTARY MATERIALS

Selected Readings

Blair, Bertha. "Church-related Elementary and Secondary Schools in Continental United States," *Information Service*, National Council of the Churches of Christ in the USA (January 3, 1959), pp. 1–8.

D'Amour, O'Neil C. "Status of Catholic Education, 1960," *Catholic School Journal*, LX (September, 1960), 69–72.

DIERENFIELD, R. B. *Religion in American Public Schools.* Washington, D.C.: Public Affairs Press, 1962.

JANET, MARY. *Catholic Secondary Education: A National Survey.* Washington, D.C.: Department of Education, National Catholic Welfare Conference, 1949.

LONG, WINIFRED. "Foreign Languages in Catholic High Schools," *National Catholic Education Association Bulletin,* LVIII (May, 1962), 25–28.

McDOWELL, JOHN B. "Challenges to Catholic Education," *National Catholic Education Association Journal,* LVII (August, 1961), 223–31.

MALONE, JAMES W. "Adaption of the Catholic Secondary School Curriculum to Contemporary Society," *National Catholic Education Association Journal,* LVIII (August, 1961), 228–39.

MEYER, C. S., (ed.). *Lutheran Secondary and Higher Education.* 6th yearbook, Lutheran Education Association, River Forest, Ill., 1949.

MULROY, RICHARD. "The Associate Secretary Reports on Catholic Secondary Education," *National Catholic Education Association Journal,* LVIII (August, 1961), 240–45.

33

The Curriculum in Independent Schools

It is an oddly satisfying entertainment for many people to think of "the independent school" as a single, recognizably shaped, solid thing with one set of qualities. The people who do this often have quite different images of "the independent school," of course. Yet the picture is definite, and they are naturally quite disturbed if told of differences in philosophy and practice among independent schools, or even if they hear that there are over 1,000 independent schools associated, directly or through affiliates, with the National Association of Independent Schools. Actually, "the independent school" is at least as general and widely embracing a phrase as "the public school."

Life in the rural areas, villages, towns, and cities of the United States makes it obvious that there is a huge variety of experiences and practices within public schools. Thus "the public school" as a phrase is almost meaningless until it is joined with a description of where a school is, what students it is for, and what concerns its community has. "The independent school" continues to stand as a phrase that is supposed to have relatively narrow meanings. Its meanings actually extend widely. The variety among independent schools is not just in philosophy, size, teaching aims, and kinds of persons who teach or study in them. It exists also in the curriculum. The unifying fact in most independent schools is that most of their students are college-bound. This still involves great diversity.

College is an enormously inclusive term. There are over 1,100 of them, and their number is growing rapidly in the United States. An independent-school graduate who is called "college-bound" may be headed for a private liberal arts college, a state university, or an engineering, art, or business school, among other destinations. And, *within and among* each of these, there exist major differences that the independent-school curriculum needs to take into account. Probably the largest group of an independent school's graduates each year go on to private liberal arts colleges. Yet, the day when the most traditional, prestige-laden independent schools sent most of their graduates to one favored college, with the rest scattering out to two or three other almost equally favored colleges is long since gone. That day never existed for more than a tiny percentage of independent schools.

Today a long-established, traditional boarding school with a graduating class as large as 250 students might send up to 60 per cent of its graduates to five or six "favored" colleges. The remaining 40 per cent scatter among thirty or forty other colleges and universities, many of them highly demanding in their academic challenge, some of them not. Among these there will exist a wide range of emphasis and offerings in the curriculum. A handful of the independent schools graduate that many students in a year. Those graduating a class of 50 or 60 are more usual. Most of these will be unlikely to send more than four students to any one college, and, again, a senior class of 60 will scatter to perhaps thirty or forty different places for future study. This scattering is only partly a result of the current crush for admission to fifteen or so colleges of traditional prestige. A college-bound student in public and independent schools today seems more and more to choose a college or a type of college experience on the basis of much careful thought about "what is right for *me*," an attitude college-guidance officers have worked hard to develop.

Thus, it is clear that "college-bound" has many meanings in independent schools as well as in public schools. The chances are that more independent-school students are likely to be heading for some kind of further generalized study in liberal arts colleges and universities than is the case with public school students around the country.

RANGE OF THE CURRICULUM

Most independent schools have as the basis for their curriculums the major academic fields—English, history, science, mathematics, and foreign language—with a wide range among independent schools in curricular emphasis on the arts. The size of the school, its financial resources, and the post-high school aims of its students point away from complex vocational programs, many of them requiring expensive and elaborate equipment. Few, if any, independent schools could offer the range of equipment and training in shopwork, for example, that would be available to large groups of students in a major comprehensive public high school. This is partly because of the great expense involved and partly because so few of an independent school's students, nearly all bound for further study, would elect such specific vocational training during the elementary school or junior or senior high school years. Perhaps unfortunately, shopwork as general education is offered for independent schools.

A leading independent-school head has described the curriculum in this way:

> A good curriculum is an organism rather than a mechanism and so no blueprint suitable for all schools is possible. In an organism, the curriculum is responsive to its environment—to society at large, to the needs of the times, to the particular individuals whom it serves, and to the local community (especially in day schools). Its capacity for growth and development should be reassuring to planners in new schools, indeed in all schools.[1]

This statement implies a good deal of flexibility and individual challenge in a school. The flexibility is shown in *what* is offered and explored within the basic liberal arts areas and *how* it is offered and explored. The expectations of many colleges ensure that most high schools will have their college-bound students take four years of English; two, three, or often four years of history; and at least two years of foreign language, with the assumption that most academically minded students will have four years of one language and possibly some experience in a second language; three and possibly four years of mathematics; at least one laboratory science, possibly three: biology, chemistry, and physics.

The "arts" are an important part of the curriculum in many independent schools, an "extra" in some. More and more, as the challenge and opportunity of good programs in choral and instrumental music, studio art, and drama have become known among school people, schools have seen these experiences not as "frills" but as significant disciplines in themselves. Outstanding work in these can be found in schools that would never think of their music, art, or drama program as "extracurricular." Programs in physical education are offered generally, with the idea of an experience for *all* students, whether or not they may be competing on teams in major sports.

VALUES

Since many independent schools are related to a special religious organization or tradition, many varying programs in religion, values, ethics, Bible history, or history of a particular religious sect are to be

[1] Jean Fair Mitchell, headmistress of The Brearley School, from her chapter on "Curriculum" in *Independent School Operation*, edited by William Johnson (Princeton, N.J.: D. Van Nostrand Co., Inc., 1961).

found in such schools. Some of these are full-time academic courses; some are part-time or ungraded courses; some are simply required, scheduled meetings with the school head, a chaplain, a teacher, or a series of speakers and discussion leaders. Those involved in running religion-oriented schools would, of course, stress that the religious values that are central to the school should be pervasive in the life of the school, rather than simply embodied in a series of required classroom meetings.

Religious and ethical values are central to the philosophy and practice of many schools, whether or not they are related to a church. One crucial aspect of a school's "independence" is its freedom to teach explicitly and implicitly in the area of values, and a good many schools are demonstrating this well beyond lip service and testimonials in catalogs.

Perhaps the best evidence of a stress on religious and ethical values in independent schools is the importance given to developing responsibility in students. This responsibility goes beyond simply keeping out of trouble and getting the homework done, in a great many of the schools. It is a matter of active participation in the school community's life, dealing with the school's morale and its day-to-day running. It reaches out into relations with the community beyond the school in many ways: community work camps and social-service activities; local, state, and national meetings and seminars on matters of government, religion, student responsibility, and the relating of students to a world beyond school. All this is no longer considered "extracurricular."

ADVANCED PLACEMENT

Independent schools have been greatly influenced by the advanced-placement programs developed by pilot schools, public and independent, in the early 1950's. A crucial push in the direction of what became a major venture in "advanced placement" and great enrichment of high school and college courses came from an experimental project in advanced placement involving three independent schools (Phillips Exeter Academy, Phillips Academy at Andover, and Lawrenceville School) and three universities (Yale, Harvard, and Princeton). This effort, and the resulting report, focused attention on the whole question of the quality of high school courses and of freshman and sophomore college courses, and had a part in bringing considerably more challenge into the school and college sides of the curriculum picture.

Now, more than ten years later, many schools have special sections for outstanding students to explore more widely and penetrate more deeply in a subject. Other schools stress flexibility and variety in assignments and grouping, within a single course, so students in the same section of a course may be doing quite different work and studying a quite different range of material. Some schools stress the idea of actual advanced placement in one or more college courses, once a student has done the advanced work in school and has taken the required college advanced-placement examinations. Other schools stress more the idea of enrichment of the regular required fare, with or without the later skipping of relatively elementary courses in college.

There is no question that the whole advanced-placement program has had an enormous effect on the high school curriculum of public and independent schools around the nation. Courses that began as extra work for the most ambitious students caused teachers and curriculum planners to look again at the standard, "regular" courses, and the "regular" courses have come more and more to be enriched and extended as a result. Flexibility in assignments and in material studied, within a course, may have been designed for the most able students, but it now has become more and more a matter of policy for all the students in the actual teaching of a course.

Naturally, the added depth and range of the high school experiences in the major academic fields, not only for advanced-placement students but also for regular academic students, have caused colleges to look again at their own curricular offerings and requirements and have brought to colleges a good deal of flexibility in the way they place incoming students in courses and sections.

EXPERIMENTS IN CURRICULUM

The freedom to experiment has been a major banner for independent schools to carry. Some have done the experimenting; some have not. This freedom does not automatically *cause* the experimentation, nor do the schools expect to agree on what kinds of experimentation, in what areas of the curriculum, are appropriate to a given school and to education itself. It is fair to say that within many independent schools there is available to teachers an opportunity for creativity and initiative in planning their own courses and in working with other teachers an administrators to design the total school program in curriculum. Thus, an extraordinarily gifted English teacher might develop a course in the ninth grade that some colleagues might consider outstanding and others eccentric. Let us say the administration of the school and the teachers responsible with it or to it for curriculum planning found the course a significant contribution to the students. They would then be likely to plan the school's English program around it. When this teacher retired, the new arrival would not, however, be presented with the same materials and approaches as "what we do in ninth grade."

Experiment within traditional fields can be found side by side with special courses outside these fields in certain independent schools. The talents and interests of a whole school, a teacher, or a community have resulted in significant experiments including experimental courses in anthropology in some schools and historical geology in others, surveys of the humanities, establishment of relationships between school science courses and local science laboratories, study of paleontology, study of linguistics, and specialized area studies in international relations in still others. Sometimes this work goes on as an aspect of a regular required course. Sometimes it becomes the course in a certain field offered during a certain year.

Often the school has to make arrangements with college admissions officers with respect to experimental courses. But schools themselves can develop a respectable reputation for certain experimental courses or emphases, or they may simply carry on their experiments irrespective of college admissions officers and let the students' records in what are classified as the major subjects stand for themselves. There is clear evidence, in any case, that a good many independent schools are using their independence in ways that may be useful to their students and enriching to the educational community at large, and these uses of independence include experimentation *within and beyond* the conventional academic liberal arts subjects, both in the kind of materials and techniques studied and in the way these are approached by teachers and students.[2]

FOCUS ON THE INDIVIDUAL STUDENT

The constant attention to the individual student in an independent school may seem rather automatic, simply because the independent

[2] See David Mallery, *New Approaches in Education: A Study of Experimental Programs in Independent Schools* (Boston: National Association of Independent Schools, 1961). See also the series of booklets issued several times a year by this association that describe outstanding practices in the schools. The most recent series, beginning in 1962, includes these:

No. 1: William Hull, *An Introduction to the Cuisenaire Rods: An Approach to the Teaching of Elementary Mathematics*

No. 2: David Mallery, *Developing Student Responsibility: A Study of Practices in Five Schools and an Urban Project*

No. 3: David Mallery, *The New Dimension in Foreign Language Teaching: A Message to the School Head About the Language Laboratory*

No. 4: David Mallery, *Asia and Africa in the Study of History: Examples of School Programs Seeking To Teach Students To Think Historically about Non-Western Civilizations*

No. 5: David Mallery, *Imaginative Teaching in Elementary Schools: A Description of Programs Dealing with Gifted Children*

No. 6: David Mallery, *Teaching About Communism: A Definition of the Problem and a Description of Some Practices*

No. 7: David Mallery, *A Community-School Venture: Top Professionals Work with School Students* school may be smaller than the public school in the same community. This is far too easy an assumption. It is possible for the planning for individual attention to be better and more effective in a public or independent school with a graduating class of 300 than in one with a graduating class of 30. Since so many of the independent schools tend to be relatively small, there is at least the opportunity for closer attention to the individual student's own education. There can be a longer and more personal *association* of students and teachers, in many independent schools, in which the student grows up over a period of twelve years. In a relatively small school community, a student can feel himself a part of the total community, and teachers can be aware of the student's relationship to the total school community, not just of his performance in one subject or activity. But there is nothing automatic about this, just because a school is independent, or because a public school may be relatively small. It comes back to the philosophy of the school, to how important the teachers (and students) believe the individual's experience in school is, and to how imaginatively and perceptively the school's administrators and teachers carry out their philosophy. Many independent schools stress the idea of curriculum planning for each student, according to his own needs, abilities, and interests, and carry out this emphasis in their planning and teaching. Others may publicize education of the individual but actually may offer relatively rigid programs and requirements in which all the "individuals" are supposed to participate (presumably in their own individual way).

A LOOK AT THE PROGRAMS OF FOUR GRADUATING SENIORS

It would be perfectly possible for a graduating class of an independent school to have side by side in the commencement procession students who had been in the school twelve years and had had in their final four years these experiences in the school's curriculum:

Mary did advanced-placement work, in special courses, in English and chemistry, took three years of French, four years of history, the three basic science courses, and four years of mathematics.

Joe took the school's required four years of English and history, its minimum mathematics requirement of three years, four years of French, five years of Latin, and one of laboratory science.

Martin took the required English and history courses plus all the history electives possible, no foreign language after the first year's basic course (mainly an exploratory course in the nature of language in the eighth grade, let us say), four years of mathematics, and a full major in studio art each year.

John took the required four years of English, three years of history, a major in shop each year, a special restricted mathematics program of two years, and no foreign language beyond the first year's introductory course, and built the rest of his program out of half-time electives of substance and of interest to him.

Obviously, each of these four would be headed for quite a different experience after graduation from school. Mary's ability was outstanding enough to put her in advanced-placement programs in two subjects, to get her all the science she wanted; yet she had to have a relatively thin foreign-language diet (three years) for one headed for a "high-powered" academic college. Joe's special interest and ability in languages were balanced by the standard requirements, even though he might have had something of a struggle to keep his head above water in the three years of mathematics and in the one experience he had in laboratory science. Martin had a special interest in the social sciences, though he was not able to manipulate words with any sophistication. He was very able in handling numbers and had strong interest and talent in art, hence the full mathematics program and full-time elective major courses in studio art. John was a so-called general student whose program was planned so that he could participate as fully as he could in the school's required curricular offerings, but he was directed away from courses that were clearly beyond his ability to handle. Yet other courses were planned for him that he *could* handle and that challenged him.

Naturally, it had to be made clear to each of these four students what the implications of his own personal curriculum were. Mary might well head for advanced work in two fields right away in college. She might even start in college with sophomore standing, though she would have to pass a foreign-language requirement, in certain colleges. Joe's college planning would take into account his interest and ability in languages and his struggle—though successful to the point of a C—, say—with mathematics. The school had to work hard to convince Martin's parents, who found it difficult to accept their child's limitations in language, but it persuaded them that it was futile for him to struggle hopelessly with foreign language and that his gifts in two non-verbal areas, art and mathematics, were major assets offering him a wide range of choices, outside of conventional liberal arts programs, for college study. John and his parents understood that his program was not college preparatory. Yet they agreed that the decision four years before to keep him in the school on a modified schedule was more than justified by his contribution to the life of the school and by what he had seemed to be gaining from the experience he had been having in, and out of, his program of courses.

Some people's stereotypes of independent schools would be rudely shattered by the idea of John's being present at all, and perhaps even by the presence of Martin. Some independent schools, especially those offering only the final four or five years, would, in fact, not have accepted John, or even Martin. Other schools, having had John from the kindergarten on, might have felt before the beginning of high school that John would be lost among the school's challenges of the last four years. However, many schools *emphasizing college-preparatory work of real challenge* have the flexibility and individual interest of the reasonably typical independent school described here, which graduated Mary, Joe, Martin, and John, with whatever adjustments in requirements, special advanced challenges, transcript descriptions, and awarding of diplomas or certificates that the school worked out. Such a school would manage to arrange suitable intellectual and personal challenges for each of these four, Mary, Joe, Martin, and John, and to bring each of them into his or her own kind of contributing relationship with the life of the school.

USE OF INDEPENDENCE

Finally, the major challenge to an independent school, and its major strength, can be imaginatively used of its "independence." Aside from meeting state requirements and college-preparation standards of many kinds, it can introduce into its curriculum courses, activities, experiments, and programs *that it considers good education,* whether a course in the history of Africa, a special required music course, a plan of student-faculty school government, or a program of community service. Such a school can go far beyond the specific requirements of its state and of the various colleges to which its students may go. This freedom from a system or a set of syllabuses handed down from above contributes a basic strength to this kind of school, and the people connected with such a school would speak up strongly for the fact that this freedom, used well, also strengthens our society.

QUESTIONS, PROBLEMS, AND ISSUES FOR FURTHER THOUGHT

1. List as many different types of non-public and non-church-affiliated secondary schools as you can, and, for such type, suggest something about the kind of student you would expect to be enrolled in such a school.
2. In what ways do you think a curriculum program aimed at ensuring success in college would differ from one designed for a good, general, all-around education?
3. To what extent do you believe that preparation for passing College Board Examinations provides a program of good preparation for success in college?

4. What are some of the important types of experiments being conducted in the independent secondary schools today? Be able to describe each fairly well.

SUPPLEMENTARY MATERIALS

SELECTED READINGS

A Community-School Venture: Top Professionals Work with School Students. Boston: National Association of Independent Schools, 1963.

Advanced Placement Programs in Independent Secondary Schools. Boston: National Association of Independent Schools, 1959.

Choral Music in the Life of a School. Boston: National Association of Independent Schools, in press.

General Education in Schools and College. Committee report by members of the faculties of Andover, Exeter, Lawrenceville, and Harvard. Cambridge, Mass.: Harvard University Press, 1952.

GUMMERE, J. F., E. T. HALL, and M. A. NEVILLE. "Schools of Independence," Teachers College Record, LII (March, 1961), 1–67.

MALLERY, DAVID. Negro Students in Independent Schools: A Statement for School Heads and Trustees, Describing Experiences and Practices. Boston: National Association of Independent Schools, 1963.

New Approaches in Education: A Study of Experimental Programs in Independent Schools. Boston: National Association of Independent Schools, 1961.

Syllabus for a Music Major Course (High School). Boston: National Association of Independent Schools, 1958.

Syllabus for Music in the Junior High School. Boston: National Association of Independent Schools, 1961.

The New Dimension in Foreign Language Teaching: A Message to the School Head About the Language Laboratory. Boston: National Association of Independent Schools, 1962.

Index